THE WRITINGS OF
JOHN BRADFORD

The Writings of JOHN BRADFORD

Volume Two

THE BANNER OF TRUTH TRUST

THE BANNER OF TRUTH TRUST
3 Murrayfield Road, Edinburgh EH12 6EL
P.O. Box 621, Carlisle, Pennsylvania 17013, U.S.A.

*

The Writings of John Bradford
This edition first published volume 1 1848
volume 2 1853. Both volumes reprinted
by the Banner of Truth Trust 1979
ISBN 0 85151 284 4

*

Printed in Great Britain
by W & J Mackay Limited, Chatham

THE WRITINGS OF JOHN BRADFORD, M.A.,

FELLOW OF PEMBROKE HALL, CAMBRIDGE,
AND PREBENDARY OF ST PAUL'S,

MARTYR, 1555.

CONTAINING

LETTERS, TREATISES, REMAINS.

EDITED FOR

The Parker Society,

BY

AUBREY TOWNSEND, B.D.,
OF TRINITY COLLEGE, DUBLIN, CURATE OF ST MICHAEL'S, BATH.

CAMBRIDGE:
PRINTED AT
THE UNIVERSITY PRESS.

M.DCCC.LIII.

CONTENTS.

* The articles marked thus are now, it is believed, printed for the first time.

† Parts of the articles thus marked, are now, it is believed, printed for the first time.

PREFACE OF THE EDITOR.

The former volume of Bradford's writings, issued by the Parker Society, 1848, comprised sermons, meditations and prayers, treatises, public addresses, examinations and prison-conferences. The present volume contains all the remaining writings of this remarkable man, which are known to exist. These remains are derived from a variety of sources, written and printed, and are full of interest. They may be classed as letters, miscellaneous pieces, treatises.

Bradford's letters have ever been most highly valued. Seven of these, chiefly from his own autograph, are now for the first time published. A similar statement applies to four short pieces, and considerable portions of other remains. Some of his writings are now reprinted for the first time since the Reformation. Bishop Ridley's Reply to bishop Hooper on the vestment controversy, A.D. 1550, three letters of Ridley, two of Hooper, five of other individuals, together with portions of Ridley's other letters, never before published, are included in this volume. It has not been found practicable to give the translations from Chrysostom, Melancthon, and Artopœus[1]. To the present volume is prefixed a brief memoir of Bradford, compiled by the editor. An index to both volumes is appended, prepared with very great care.

In addition to the fifty-two MSS. of Bradford's pieces, belonging to the former volume, sixty-two belong to the present, forming a total of a hundred and twenty-one MSS. of his writings, which have been carefully copied or collated for this edition. Twenty-two of these are in his autograph, and others were transcribed by friends within a few years after his death. They vary in length from one to fifty-two printed pages. It

[1] The title-pages of the two publications, which contained those translations, together with Bradford's three prefaces, have appeared in Volume I. pp. 2—24.

may be well to add, that the five autograph MSS., referred to in Volume I., pp. 306, 351, and in the present volume, pp. 169, 194, with autograph MSS. of Ridley and others, formerly belonging to D. Turner, Esq., are now the property of this nation, and may be examined in the British Museum, Additional MSS., No. 19,400.

Further particulars may be obtained from the editorial prefaces of the former volume; and of the present, pp. xlvii, 267, 297, 359, 363; and from the biographical notice which follows this preface.

It is the editor's pleasing duty again to return his best thanks, in behalf of the Parker Society, to the Reverend the Master, the Librarian, and the Fellows of Emmanuel College, Cambridge, for the privilege of access to their very valuable collection of manuscript remains of Bradford, bishop Ridley, and other English Reformers. The Society is much indebted to G. Offor, Esq., the Rev. T. Corser, F.S.A., and the Chetham Society, Manchester, as well as to S. Christy, Esq., M.P., for free access to early editions of Bradford's writings, of extreme rarity.

The editor has very great pleasure in recording his obligation to Henry Gough, Esq., of the Middle Temple, for valuable assistance; to the Rev. J. Piccope, the Rev. W. R. Keeling, the Rev. Josiah Pratt, and the Rev. W. Goode; to R. Lemon, Esq., of Her Majesty's State Paper Office, and the Rev. J. Romilly, Registrar of the University of Cambridge; and very especially to the Rev. A. J. Macleane, Master of King Edward's Grammar School, Bath, and the Rev. J. Evans; as also to other friends, whose exceeding courtesy and kindness it is a real satisfaction to him thus cordially to acknowledge.

He desires to express, in conclusion, his earnest prayer that the Divine favour may rest upon this and every other effort to make known the great principles of the English Reformation.

A. T.

BIOGRAPHICAL NOTICE

OF

JOHN BRADFORD.

THE martyr John Bradford, whose entire writings are now for the first time given to the public, occupied a prominent position among the Reformers of the English church. He was a learned and eloquent man, zealous to maintain Christian truth, and to eradicate papal error. He possessed qualities of a yet higher order. Deep spirituality and heavenly-mindedness, a humble and self-denying walk before God, evinced in him an unwonted measure of "the wisdom that is from above, which is first pure, then peaceable, gentle, and easy to be entreated." In these respects he was enabled, his enemies themselves being judges, to reflect, in no slight degree, his Divine Master's likeness. His gentleness, combined with firmness, outstripped the age in which his lot was cast.

The year of his birth has not been exactly ascertained. The conjecture of one of his biographers, that he "was born about 1510," appears not unlikely. A local tradition, which claims Bradford as a native of Blackley, an ancient chapelry of the parish and deanery of Manchester, yet survives at that place. Almost the earliest memoir of him known to exist, written in 1559[1], informs us that he, being "born in Lancastershire, in Manchester, a notable town of that country, was of his gentle parents brought up in virtue and

[1] The account which is given in the early Latin edition of Foxe's Acts and Monuments, the *Rerum in ecclesia gestarum commentarii, Basil.* 1559. "The original of his life," prefixed to that very rare volume, his Examinations and prison-conferences, printed for the first time in full, in English, by Griffith, 1561, was translated from the Latin of Foxe; and the quotation that follows is taken from that brief memoir, as printed in 1561. The earliest notice of Bradford's life, known to exist, is that contained in Bp Bale's Scriptorum Britanniæ Catalogus, cent. VIII. 87. pp. 680, 1, Basil 1557. The short sketch published 1561 was enlarged in Foxe's

good learning even from his very childhood; and, among other praises of his good education, he obtained as a chief gift the cunning and readiness of writing, which knowledge was not only an ornament unto him, but also an help to the necessary sustentation of his living." Baines, the historian of the county of Lancaster, also observes that Bradford, having received a liberal education at the free grammar-school in Manchester, founded by bishop Oldham who died in 1519, attained there a considerable proficiency in Latin and arithmetic[1].

To this early period of his life Bradford, writing from prison in the days of Mary, feelingly adverts:

"I cannot but say that I have most cause to thank thee for my parents, schoolmasters, and others, under whose tuition thou hast put me. No pen is able to write the particular benefits, which I have already received in my infancy, childhood, youth, middle age, and always hitherto. . . . I could reckon innumerable behind me, and but few before me, so much made of and cared for as I have been hitherto[2]."

Foxe records that Bradford, at a later period, "became servant to Sir John Harrington, knight, [of Exton in Rutlandshire,] who, in the great affairs of king Henry the eighth, and king Edward the sixth, which he had in hand when he was treasurer of the king's camps and buildings, at divers times, in Boulogne, had such experience of Bradford's activity in writing, of [his] expertness in the art of auditors, and also of his faithful trustiness, that, not only in those affairs, but in many other of his private business, he trusted Bradford in

Acts and Monuments, 1563, and 1570, and after editions. Sampson's account of Bradford was prefixed to the Two Sermons, 1574. These, with Bradford's own letters, examinations, and conferences, are the original sources of information respecting his life.

Brief notices afterward appeared in Holland's Herωologia, Lond. 1620; in Lupton's Modern Protest. Divines, Lond. 1637; in Fuller's Abel redivivus, 1651; in Clarke's Marrow of eccl. hist., 1654; in Bp Tanner's Biblioth. Britann. Hibern. 1748; and a memoir of some length and research in the Biographia Britannica, Vol. II. 1748; short notices also in Middleton's Biogr. Evang. 1779, and in Chalmers's Biogr. Dict. 1812. Recent accounts have appeared, by Stokes, "British Reformers," Rel. Tract Soc., 1827; by Stevens, including letters, examinations and conferences, London, 1832; and a memoir of much interest, by archdeacon Hone, Lives of Bradford, Grindal and Hale, Soc. for prom. Christian Knowl., 1843.

[1] History of the county Palatine and duchy of Lancaster, by E. Baines, Esq., M.P., 4 vols. 4to, Vol. II. p. 243, Lond. 1836.

[2] Vol. I. Meditation on commandments, pp. 162, 3.

such sort, that above all others he used his faithful service[3]." At the siege of Montreuil in particular, conducted by the English army under the duke of Norfolk in the year 1544, Bradford discharged, under Sir John Harrington, the office of paymaster[4].

Three years later, not long after the accession of Edward VI., on the 8th April, 1547, Bradford entered the Inner Temple as a student of common law[5]. His character then underwent a complete change. Twenty-seven years later Sampson, his friend and fellow-student at the Temple, and who, it has been said[6], was the human means, under a higher power, of that great transformation, writes: "I did know when, and partly how, it pleased God by effectual calling, to turn his heart unto the true knowledge and obedience of the most holy gospel of Christ our Saviour; of which God did give him such an heavenly hold and lively feeling, that, as he did then know that many sins were forgiven him, so surely he declared by deeds that he 'loved much.' For, where he had both gifts and calling to have employed himself in civil and worldly affairs profitably, such was his love of Christ and zeal to the promoting of his glorious gospel, that he changed not only the course of his former life, as the woman did (Luke vii.), but even his former study, as Paul did change his former profession and study.

"Touching the first, after that God touched his heart with that holy and effectual calling, he sold his chains, rings, brooches and jewels of gold, which before he used to wear, and did bestow the price of this his former vanity in the necessary relief of Christ's poor members, which he could hear of or find lying sick or pining in poverty. Touching the second, he so declared his great zeal and love to promote the glory of the Lord Jesus, whose goodness and saving health he had tasted, that[7]," "with marvellous favour to further the

[3] Foxe, Acts, &c., ed. 1583, p. 1603, or ed. 1843-9, Vol. VII. p. 143.

[4] Vol. I. p. 593. See Boter's curious account of the army at Boulogne, in Turner's History of reign of Henry VIII. Vol. II. p. 525, note 36, Lond. 1828.

[5] "Johannes Bradford de Exton in comitatu Rotelandiæ, octavo die Aprilis, plegii, Richard Chamber, Thomas Sampson." (Anno primo Ed. VI.)—MS. Admission Book, Inner Temple, London.

[6] See Vol. I. p. 30, note 1, extract from Wood's Athenæ Oxonienses.

[7] Vol. I. Preface by Sampson, A.D. 1574, pp. 31, 2.

kingdom of God by the ministry of his holy word, he gave himself wholly to the study of the holy Scriptures. The which his purpose to accomplish the better, he departed from the Temple at London, where the temporal law is studied, and went to the university of Cambridge, to learn, by God's law, how to further the building of the Lord's temple[1]."

An incident occurred, while he was in London, which occasioned him deep anxiety. He "heard a sermon which that notable preacher, Master Latimer, made before king Edward the sixth, in which he did earnestly speak of restitution to be made of things falsely gotten[2]." This "did so strike him to the heart," on account of a fraud, committed by his master, Sir John Harrington, which "was to the deceiving of the king," and which it would seem Bradford had concealed, "that he could never be quiet till by the advice of the same Master Latimer a restitution was made[3]." That he had not been an interested party to this fraud would appear from his words to bishop Gardiner, January 30, 1555: "My lord, I set my foot to his foot, whosoever he be, that can come forth, and justly vouch to my face that ever I deceived my master: and, as you are chief justicer by office in England, I desire justice upon them that so slander me, because they cannot prove it[4]." A challenge, which he could scarcely have ventured to make, if he had himself defrauded the government. It was through his firmness, in fact, that Sir John Harrington was compelled to make restitution to the king of the sums falsely obtained, in the two successive years, 1549 and 1550.

[1] Foxe, Acts, &c., ed. 1583, p. 1603, or ed. 1843-9, Vol. VII. p. 143.

[2] It is conjectured in the Biographia Britannica, Vol. II. 1748, that the sermon preached by Bp Latimer, at Stamford, October 1550, on "rendering unto Cæsar the things that are Cæsar's," (Works of Bp L. Vol. I. pp. 282—308, Park. Soc.) may have been the sermon he had preached at court in 1548, while Bradford was at the Temple. The subjects however of the sermons only in part coincide.

[3] Sampson adds, that for this object Bradford "did willingly forbear and forego all the private and certain patrimony which he had in earth:" Vol. I. Preface, pp. 32, 3. This however may seem doubtful, as Bradford, on going to Cambridge, writes: "I trust, as I said, for three years' study I have sufficient:" "I have for this life more than enough, thanks be to God."—Letters VI., VII., pp. 18, 21.

[4] Vol. I. Last exam., p. 487. These words seem to disprove the statement of Sampson, Vol. I. p. 32, that Bradford had made "one dash with a pen without the knowledge of his master," which "was to the deceiving of the king."

The first letter in this volume, from Traves to Bradford, written probably about February 1548, is entirely occupied with this subject, and conveys to him bishop Latimer's advice. The next letter, addressed by Bradford to Traves, from the Temple, 1548, perhaps early in March, states:

"Sithens my coming to London I was with Master Latimer, whose counsel is as you shall hear: which I purpose by God's grace to obey. .... He willed me, as I have done, to write to my master, ... and to shew him that if within a certain time, which I appointed, fourteen days, he do not go about to make restitution, that I will submit myself to my lord protector and the king's majesty's council, to confess the fault and ask pardon[5]."

Another letter from Bradford, written at the Temple, March 22, 1548, chiefly treats upon the same topic, and mentions the desire of Harrington to evade the payment, if possible, and the measures taken by himself to compel restitution[6]. A few weeks later, May 12, he states: "Concerning the great matter you know of, it hath pleased God to bring it to this end, that I have a bill of my master's hand, wherein he is bound to pay the sum afore Candlemas next coming," that is, February 2, 1549. "This thinks Master Latimer to be sufficient[7]." Subsequently Bradford writes, it would seem, November, 1549: "You know how that God hath exonerated the loaden conscience of the great weighty burden (for so I did write to you): yea, the Lord hath in manner unburthened me of the lesser burden also; for I have an assurance of the payment of the same by Candlemas[8]," that is, February 2, 1550. And in a letter, written probably from London, about February, 1550, he exhorts Traves, "for God's sake to give hearty thanks for the great benefit of restitution[9]."

It has been supposed, that bishop Latimer, in the remarkable instance of "restitution," recorded in his last sermon before Edward VI., A.D. 1550, refers to the case of Bradford and Sir John Harrington[10]. This appears highly probable, as the dates and circumstances seem to coincide: and, if this

[5] Pp. 5, 6.
[6] Letter IV. pp. 10—12.
Letter VI. p. 17.
[8] Letter XI. p. 27.
[9] Letter XIV. p. 34.
[10] Biographia Britannica, article Bradford, ed. 1748.

conjecture be correct, Latimer's statement supplies details, not to be found elsewhere. The bishop says:

"I have now preached three Lents. The first time I preached restitution. . . . At my first preaching of restitution, one good man took remorse of conscience, and acknowledged himself to me, that he had deceived the king; and willing he was to make restitution: and so the first Lent came to my hands twenty pounds to be restored to the king's use. I was promised twenty pound more the same Lent, but it could not be made, so that it came not. Well, the next Lent came three hundred and twenty pounds more. I received it myself, and paid it to the king's council. So I was asked, what he was that made this restitution? But should I have named him? Nay, they should as soon have this wesant of mine. Well, now this Lent came one hundred and fourscore pounds ten shillings, which I have paid and delivered this present day to the king's council: and so this man hath made a godly restitution. 'And so,' quoth I to a certain nobleman that is one of the king's council, 'if every man that hath beguiled the king should make restitution after this sort, it would cough the king twenty thousand pounds, I think,' quoth I. 'Yea, that it would,' quoth the other, 'a whole hundred thousand pounds[1].'"

Sir John Harrington's agency had been Bradford's chief means of support at the Temple: but this source of income became withdrawn, in consequence of the constrained "restitution" above described[2]. The upright deportment of Bradford secured for him the intimate friendship of bishop Latimer. About February, 1550, Bradford writes to Traves: "I am as familiar with father Latimer as with you; yea, God so moveth him against me, that his desire is to have me come and dwell with him whensoever I will, and welcome[3]." And a few years later the bishop, as we shall soon see, spoke of Bradford with the highest commendation[4]. Bradford during many months had been sorely afflicted; and his integrity had been put to a severe test. The whole transaction was doubtless overruled by his heavenly Teacher, to the chastening and maturing of his Christian character.

[1] Works of Bp Latimer, p. 262, Park. Soc.—The "three Lents," to which Latimer refers, were, as in Harrington's case, in 1548, 1549, and 1550: and, as in that instance, the largest payment was in 1549, and another not so large in 1550.

[2] "I have and sustain my master's sore displeasure,......through the sequestration of such his business as tofore I had ado withal......I have moved my master by letters, to see if I shall have any living of him as hitherto I have had:" Letter VI. pp. 17, 8.—"My master which was hath denied me all his beneficence:" Lett. VII. p. 21.—"My master has in all his affairs disowned me:" Lett. X. p. 25.

[3] Letter XIV. p. 34.

[4] P. xxxiii.

In the spring of 1548, May 16, Bradford's translations from Artopœus and Chrysostom, with prefaces by himself, were published by Lynn[5]. In the summer he proceeded to Cambridge, "to study divinity[6]," and to prepare himself for the ministry, and there entered Catharine Hall. He had written to Traves, from the Temple, the 12th of May, "I am minded afore midsummer to leave London to go to my book at Cambridge, and, if God shall give me grace, to be a minister of his word[7];" and in a letter written shortly after he states, "This present day, by God's grace, I take my journey towards Cambridge," and "I will lie, God willing, this summer, at Catharine's Hall[8]." A subsequent letter is dated, "This Assumption day," that is, August 15, "in Catharine's Hall in Cambridge[9]."

In the brief space of a twelvemonth Bradford had "by God's blessing so profited in the godly course" he pursued, "that that blessed martyr, Doctor Ridley,...did as it were invite him and his godly companion, Master Thomas Horton to become fellows of Pembroke Hall[10]"—a college, "noted from the very dawn of the Reformation for scripturists and encouragers of gospel learning, and famous of old for the flourishing state of letters in it, beyond any other society in Cambridge[11]." The proposal of Ridley, then bishop of Rochester and master of Pembroke Hall, together with Bradford's "diligence in study, and profiting in knowledge and godly conversation," brought it about, "that, within one whole year after he had been in Cambridge, the university did give him

[5] See Vol. I. pp. 1—15, and Letters VI., VII., pp. 19, 21, of this volume.

[6] Vol. I. p. 31.

[7] Letter VI. p. 18.

[8] Letter VII. p. 20, 1.

[9] Letter VIII. p. 24. Carter, Hist. Univ. Camb. p. 69, Lond. 1753, and Dyer, Hist. Camb., Vol. II. p. 153, Lond. 1814, incorrectly state that Bradford was entered at Queens' College, Camb. That error was probably derived from Holland, Herωologia, p. 151, Lond. 1620, and Lupton, Modern Protest. Divines, p. 222, Lond. 1637, who severally state, without foundation, that Bradford, having been admitted into Queens' College, took degrees there, and was made master of that college.

[10] Vol. I. p. 31.

[11] Life of Bp. Ridley by Ridley, p. 142, Lond. 1763. Bp. R., in his Farewell Works, p. 406, Park. Soc., addresses Pembroke Hall, "Thou wast ever named, sithens I knew thee,...to be studious, well learned, and a great setter forth of Christ's gospel and of God's true word. So I found thee; and, blessed be God! so I left thee indeed.

the degree of a Master of Arts[1]." That this degree was conferred at that time, and for these reasons, is evident from the special entry, made in the University Grace Book, October 19, 1549, combined with the words of Bradford, in addressing Traves, October 22: "I trust I shall shortly here have a fellowship; I am so promised, and therefore I have taken the degree of Master of Art, which else I could not have attained[2]." The Grace Book entry is as follows:

Bradford admissus 19 Octob., [1549], et numeratur inter regentes superioris anni.

Item conceditur Johanni Bradforde, viro constantis jam ætatis et probatæ vitæ, ut studium octo annorum in literis humanioribus, artibus, et sacrarum literarum diligenti lectione, in quibus plurimum profecit, sufficiat ei pro completis gradu et forma magisterii in artibus; et ut hodie, si fieri potest, alioquin ad placitum, admittatur sine ulla magistrorum visitatione. Nam diutius hunc gradum sine magno suo dispendio expectare non potest, ut qui illi hoc tempore ampliorem vitæ conditionem adferre potest, quam sine eo assequi non potest. Ita ut ejus eruditio prius examinetur et approbetur per magistros Pylkington seniorem et Carre; et teneatur præterea proximis comitiis combinare cum cæteris ejus anni[3].

[TRANSLATION.]

Bradford was admitted 19 October, [1549], and is counted among the regents of the preceding year.

It is likewise granted to John Bradford, a man now of mature age and approved life, that his study for eight years in polite literature, arts, and the diligent perusal of holy scripture, in which he has made very great proficiency, be sufficient to him for completing the degree and form of a mastership in arts; and that on this day, if it can be accomplished, otherwise at his own pleasure, he be admitted without any visitation of masters. For he cannot longer await this degree without great cost to himself, as that which can obtain for him a higher condition of life, which without it he cannot reach. So that his learning be first examined and approved by Masters Pylkington senior and Carre; and that he be moreover bound to unite, at the next commencement, with the others of that year.

Bradford observes in a letter to Traves, written, it is probable, about November, 1549: "I am now a fellow of Pembroke Hall, of the which I nor any other for me did ever make any suit; yea, there was a contention betwixt the master of Catharine's Hall, [Sandys,] and the bishop of Rochester, who is master of Pembroke Hall, whether should have me.... My fellowship here is worth seven pound a year; for I have allowed

[1] Foxe, Acts, &c., ed. 1583, p. 1603, or ed. 1843-9, Vol. VII. p. 143.

[2] Letter X. p. 26.

[3] MS. Grace Book of the University of Cambridge, fol. 24, in Registrar's Office.

me eighteen-pence a week, and as good as thirty-three shillings four pence a year in money, besides my chamber, launder, barber, &c.; and I am bound to nothing but once or twice a year to keep a problem. Thus you see what a good Lord God is unto me[4]."

His friend Sampson graphically depicts Bradford's holy walk with God at this period: "His manner was, to make to himself a catalogue of all the grossest and most enorme sins, which in his life of ignorance he had committed; and to lay the same before his eyes when he went to private prayer, that by the sight and remembrance of them he might be stirred up to offer to God the sacrifice of a contrite heart, seek assurance of salvation in Christ by faith, thank God for his calling from the ways of wickedness, and pray for increase of grace to be conducted in holy life acceptable and pleasing to God. Such a continual exercise of conscience he had in private prayer, that he did not count himself to have prayed to his contentation, unless in it he had felt inwardly some smiting of heart for sin, and some healing of that wound by faith, feeling the saving health of Christ, with some change of mind into the detestation of sin, and love of obeying the good will of God.... Without such an inward exercise of prayer our Bradford did not pray to his full contentation, as appeared by this: he used in the morning to go to the common prayer in the college where he was, and after that he used to make some prayer with his pupils in his chamber: but not content with this he then repaired to his own secret prayer and exercise in prayer by himself, as one that had not yet prayed to his own mind; for he was wont to say to his familiars, 'I have prayed with my pupils, but I have not yet prayed with myself.'

"Another of his exercises was this: he used to make unto himself an ephemeris or a journal, in which he used to write all such notable things as either he did see or hear each day that passed. But, whatsoever he did hear or see, he did so pen it that a man might see in that book the signs of his smitten heart. For, if he did see or hear any good in any man, by that sight he found and noted the want thereof in himself, and added a short prayer, craving mercy and grace

[4] Letter XI. p. 27.

to amend. If he did hear or see any plague or misery, he noted it as a thing procured by his own sins, and still added, *Domine miserere mei*, 'Lord, have mercy upon me.' He used in the same book to note such evil thoughts as did rise in him; as of envying the good of other men, thoughts of unthankfulness, of not considering God in his works, of hardness and unsensibleness of heart when he did see other moved and affected. And thus he made to himself and of himself a book of daily practices of repentance[1]."

The distinguished John Whitgift, afterward archbishop of Canterbury, "was transplanted," probably about this time, to Pembroke Hall, "where Bradford that holy man and martyr was his tutor; and, upon the recommendation of him by his said tutor and Grindal...to Ridley the master,...he was made scholar of the house, and chosen Bible-clerk[2]."

At Cambridge Bradford, we are told by Sampson, "heard Doctor Martin Bucer diligently, and was right familiar and dear unto him." And Foxe writes: "Martin Bucer, that man of God so liked Bradford, that he had him not only most dear unto him, but also oftentimes exhorted him to bestow his talent in preaching. Unto which Bradford answered always, that he was unable to serve in that office through want of learning: to the which Bucer was wont to reply, saying, 'If thou have not fine manchet-bread, yet give the poor people barley-bread, or whatsoever else the Lord hath committed unto thee.'"

A Latin letter, written to Bucer by Bradford, is printed for the first time in this volume, pp. 352—54. It is addressed, "To Master Bucer, that most distinguished person, and his own most worshipful father and master, at Cambridge," and contains an elaborate apology, for having lost two letters which he had undertaken to convey from Bucer to Utenhovius[3] and

[1] Vol. I. Sampson's Preface, pp. 33—5.

[2] Strype, Life of Whitgift, Book I. chap. i. Vol. I. p. 8, Oxf. 1822.—Johannes Whitgift "sub tutela martyris sanctissimi Johannis Bradfordi educationem habuit aliquandiu in aula Pembrochiana Cantabrigiæ."—Ep. Godwin de Præsul. Angl. ed. Richardson, p. 155, Cantab. 1743. Vide also Life of Abp W. by Sir G. Paule, p. 3, Lond. 1612; Life of Hooker by Walton; Le Neve, Lives, &c., Vol. I. part I. p. 46, Lond. 1720.

[3] John Utenhovius, of a noble family of Ghent, and eminent for piety and learning, was a lay-elder of the German church in London, A.D. 1550, over which at that time the Polish reformer, a Lasco, presided. See letters of Utenhovius,

Birkman[4] in London. He states that the two letters, along with others which Bucer had committed to his care, were in his possession, in his bed-room, the night he arrived in town, but that early on the following morning, when he went to meet Pietro Bizarro of Perugia[5] at the house of Ochino[6], he had the mortification to find that the letters were missing.

In reference to the friendship existing between Bradford and Bucer, it is also mentioned by Strype, that those four eminent men, Parker, afterward archbishop of Canterbury, "Dr Sandys, master of Catharine Hall, [Cambridge, subsequently archbishop of York,] Grindal, [afterward archbishop of Canterbury,] and Bradford, fellows of Pembroke Hall, held a more particular converse and acquaintance with that great learned foreign divine," Bucer, "the king's professor of divinity in Cambridge." "And with these men Bucer held some conversation concerning his writing that book *De regno Christi*, dedicated to king Edward; as Sampson, a man of note, then in Pembroke Hall in that university, conjectured: but that they had an high esteem for the book after it was written, was certain, by certain private talk that Parker and the rest had among themselves; which Sampson was privy to, as he once signified in a letter to the lord Burghley[7]."

Nos. CCLXIX.—CCLXXVI., in Orig. Lett. pp. 583—604, and in Epist. Tigurin. pp. 379—392, Park. Soc.; Letter from Micronius to Bullinger, Oct. 13, 1550, No. CCLXIV. pp. 570—72, Park. Soc.; Index to Oxford edition of Strype, Utenhov. Joann.; and Gerdes. Hist. Reform. Tom. III. p. 234, and Append. pp. 75—77, Groning. et Brem. 1744—52.

[4] John Birkman, or Byrchman, sold books at that time both in London and Paris. See his letter to Bullinger, Dec. 10, 1549, No. CLXVII., in Orig. Lett. p. 344, and in Epist. Tigurin. p. 227, Park. Soc.; Anderson, Annals of the English Bible, Book I. sect. ii. p. 56, Lond. 1845; and Memoir of Tyndale, in Works of T., Vol. I. p. xxviii, Park. Soc.

[5] Peter or Pietro Bizarro, of Perugia (Perusinus), was the author of various works of history. See Strype, Annals, Book II. ch. viii. Vol. III. part I. p. 659, Oxf. 1824; and Correspondence of Sidney and Languet, edited by Pears, p. 2, Lond. 1845. See letter of Pietro Bizarro to Bullinger, Cambr. Feb. 10, 1550, No. CLXIV., in Orig. Lett. p. 338, and in Epist. Tigurin. p. 223, Park. Soc.

[6] This well-known Italian reformer, and friend of Peter Martyr, had with Martyr been invited to England by archbishop Cranmer in 1547. See Strype, Ecc. Mem., Edward, Book I. ch. xxiv., Vol. II. part I. p. 309, Oxf. 1822; Bayle, Dict., article, Ochinus; McCrie, Reformation in Italy, p. 422, Edinb. 1833; and Gerdes. Hist. Reform. Tom. IV. pp. 359, 60.

[7] Strype, Life of Parker, Book I. chap. vii. Vol. I. pp. 55, 6, Oxf. 1822: and see Annals, Book I. ch. xxviii. Vol. II. Part I. p. 394, Oxf. 1824.

Bucer's connection with Bradford further appears from Humfrey's life of bishop Jewel, where we read that "Bucer, accompanied beside others by John Bradford, that most excellent person and most faithful martyr, one of his most dear and intimate friends, went to Oxford, to see that university and Peter Martyr, a little before St Mary Magdalen's day, [July 22], 1550[1]." Martyr, in writing to Conrad Hubert, early in the following year, after the death of Bucer, thus adverts to this visit: "Ah, how continually had he on his lips the church of Strasburgh; what anxieties he underwent for her!... Last summer he came hither to Oxford to visit me, and staid in my house eleven days. What discourses, what conversations passed between us respecting all of you our most excellent brethren in Christ! When we were talking together, we seem to be conversing in the midst of you all at Strasburgh; we were thinking of our return; but he has outstripped me, and betaken himself not to our Argentine [silver] church, but to the golden one of heaven[2]."

Within three weeks after Bradford's visit to Oxford, "Doctor Ridley, that worthy bishop of London and glorious martyr of Christ, according to the order that then was in the church of England, called him to take the degree of deacon: which order, because it was not without some such abuse as to the which Bradford would not consent, the bishop, yet perceiving that he was willing to enter into the ministry, was content to order him deacon without any abuse, even as he desired[3]. This being done" at Fulham, August 10, 1550[4],

[1] "Anno 1550, sub festum Magdalenæ, quod tum erat apud nos receptum et celebratum, Oxoniam visendi Petrum Martyrem et academiam causa venit clarissimus sanctæ theologiæ apud Cantabrigienses professor Martinus Bucerus, præter cæteros Joanne Bradfordo, optimo viro et constantissimo martyre, qui ei ex intimis maximeque familiaribus erat, comitatus."—Humfred. Vit. Juell. p. 42, Lond 1573.

[2] Original Letters, Vol. II. p. 491, Park. Soc. The original Latin will be found in the Epistolæ Tigurinæ, pp. 323, 4, Park. Soc.

[3] Bradford's scruple may possibly have referred to the words, "by the saints," in the oath of supremacy, which Ridley might have conceded, those words having been erased by Edward, in the presence of his council, in the case of Bp Hooper, so recently as July 20, in this year.—See letter of Micronius to Bullinger, Aug. 28, 1550, in Orig. Lett. p. 566, Park. Soc.; and Bp Burnet, Hist. Reform. Part III. book iv. Vol. III. p. 305, ed. Nares.

[4] "Die Dominica, decimo videlicet die mensis Augusti, anno Domini millesimo quingentesimo quinquagesimo,......ordines subscripti collati et celebrati fuerunt, per reverendum in Christo patrem ac dominum, Dominum Nicholaum, miseratione divina Londinensem episcopum, in capella sive oratorio infra manerium suum de

Ridley "obtained for him a license to preach[5]," made him one of his chaplains[6], and "lodged him in his own house[7]." This resulted in a very warm friendship, which Ridley maintained uninterruptedly during Bradford's lifetime. And about four years later, in the reign of Mary, the bishop wrote concerning the present period with very lively feeling: "O good brother, blessed be God in thee, and blessed be the time that ever I knew thee:" and again, addressing Bernhere, "I thank God heartily, that ever I was acquainted with our dear brother Bradford, and that ever I had such a one in my house[8]."

In the following spring, February 28, 1551, the illustrious Bucer died. Six days previous to his decease he had appended to his will a codicil, "wherein he left to his wife to take the advice of Master Bradford and the minister of Alhallows, [Sampson,] for ordering of his burial[9]." Nicolas Car, in a letter to Sir John Cheke describing Bucer's last illness, writes:

"Bucer became so afflicted with constant difficulty of breathing, that he could scarcely bear to meet or to converse with any one: not that either his friendliness to ourselves or kindness to all around was in any degree diminished, but that that excellent person, and worthy to be remembered through all ages, perceived the close of his life to be immediately at hand. Therefore he began to confer and meditate, not with others (all of whom he surpassed in knowledge), but with himself. I remember when John Bradford, a holy young man, and especially beloved by this our friend, resorted to a singular method of bringing to remembrance, and opened to him the promises of Christ our Saviour and Lord, and exhorted him to consider who he was, what he had taught, and what steadfastness, faith, and devotion, he had always exercised, and, when most troubled, then above all to cast his whole mind, thought and care, upon God; for he alone it was that paid the price of our sins, who could restore from darkness to light, from despair to hope, from death to life—I remember, I say, that Bucer then became rather more disturbed, and replied (it

Fulham, juxta morem, ritum et formam, hujus ecclesiæ Anglicanæ nuper inde saluberrime editam et ordinatam,......diaconi......Magister Johannes Bradford, socius perpetuus collegii nuncupati Penbrook Hall in universitate Cantabrigiæ, oriundus in villa de Manchester in comitatu Lancastriæ, Cestrensis diocesis."—MS. Ridley Register, St Paul's cathedral, fol. 319, b. See Strype, Eccl. Mem. Book I. ch. xxx. Vol. II. Part I. p. 403, Oxf. 1822.

[5] Foxe, Acts, &c., ed. 1583, p. 1603, or ed. 1843—9, Vol. VII. pp. 143, 4.

[6] Bp Ridley, Letters, Works, p. 331, Park. Soc. 1841.

[7] Sampson's Pref. to Bradf. Two Serm. Vol. I. p. 31.

[8] Bp Ridley, Lett. to Bernhere, Works, p. 380.

[9] Strype, Life of Cranmer, Book II. ch. xxiv. Vol. I. p. 356, Oxf. 1812.

appeared) with some warmth, that he wished his mind not to be drawn aside from the meditation which engaged it, by any man's address or exhortation; that his eyes were fixed upon Christ crucified, that God dwelt in his heart, and that he was contemplating nothing but heaven and a speedy departure from this body." Afterward, "when Bradford was about to preach, and said that he would remember him in his prayers, Bucer with tears replied: 'O Lord, cast me not away in the time of my old age, when my strength hath failed;' and then he added, 'Let him stoutly chastise me, yet he will never cast me away, he never will cast me away.'" At another time, "the physicians and his other friends being afraid lest, after an eclipse of the moon, Bucer's strength might also fail, and he might be overcome by the power of his disorder, when on the following day, being somewhat refreshed, he seemed more enlivened, Bradford having come to him as usual, and having mentioned the alarm of the physicians and anxiety of his friends on account of that lunar eclipse and disturbance of the heavenly bodies, Bucer is reported to have held out three of his fingers, and, raising his eyes to that everlasting heaven, to have exclaimed: 'It is he, it is he, who ruleth and ordereth all things[1].'"

When his beloved and learned friend "lay a-dying," Bradford, being at Cambridge, "prophesied truly" to the people there "before the sweat came[2], what would come if they repented not their carnal gospelling[3]." On that occasion no doubt, as in his solemn Farewell to Cambridge, in the reign of Mary, shortly before his martyrdom, he exhorted the university to "remember the readings and preachings of God's prophet and true preacher, Martin Bucer[3]." Archbishop, then doctor, Parker, on the occasion of the funeral of Bucer, gave a similar warning:

Matt. iii. 9, 10. "'Say not among yourselves, We have Abraham for our father:
for I say unto you, Every tree which bringeth not forth good fruit, is
hewn down and cast into the fire.' Fear the terrible words of the
Matt. xxi. 43. Lord, 'The kingdom shall be taken from you, and given to a nation
bringing forth the fruit thereof.' Look to thyself, Cambridge, to
Matt. xxiii. 34, 5. whom God hath 'sent his prophets, wise men and scribes, from the
Luke xi. 31. utmost ends of the earth,' lest 'all the righteous blood, which hath
Matt. xxiii. 37. been shed upon the earth, come upon thee.' Repent 'thou that
slayest the prophets,' and stonest with curses 'them which have been
Jer. vii. 3, 4. sent unto thee.' Hear what followeth after, 'Behold, your house is
left unto you desolate.' 'Amend therefore your ways and your

[1] Translated from the Latin of Carr. Epist. in Bucer. Script. Anglic. pp. 874, 5, Basil. 1577. Compare Humfred. Vit. Juell., p. 261, Lond. 1573.

[2] The sweating sickness visited England the ensuing April, 1551, and committed fearful ravages. See Vol. I. p. 61, note 2.

[3] Id. p. 445.

studies: and trust ye not in lying words, saying, The temple of the Lord, the temple of the Lord, the temple of the Lord, is here[4].'"

In the course of the following summer, August 24, 1551, twelve months after Bradford's ordination, bishop Ridley "did give him a prebend in his cathedral church of St Paul's," that of Kentishtown[5]. Shortly before, July 23, in a letter to Sir John Cheke respecting that prebend, Ridley had spoken of Bradford as "a man by whom (as I am assuredly informed) God hath and doth work wonders, in setting forth of his word. He had also described Bradford, Grindal, and Rogers, as three preachers, men of good learning, and... of excellent virtue; which were able, both with life and learning, to set forth God's word in London[6]."

A few months later Bradford was appointed one of the six chaplains of Edward VI., chosen "to be itineraries, to preach sound doctrine in all the remotest parts of the kingdom, for the instruction of the ignorant in right religion to God, and obedience to the king[7]." We read in the "Diary" of king Edward, December 18, 1551:

"It was appointed, I should have six chaplains ordinary, of which two ever to be present, and four always absent in preaching: one year two in Wales, two in Lancashire and Derby; next year two in the marches of Scotland, two in Yorkshire; the third year two in Devonshire, two in Hampshire; fourth year two in Norfolk and Essex,

[4] See Concio Matt. Parker., in Bucer. Script. Angl. p. 898, Basil. 1577.

[5] "Vicesimo quarto die mensis Augusti, [anno millesimo quingentesimo quinquagesimo primo,] idem reverendus pater Dominus Nicholaus, Londinensis episcopus, canonicatum et prebendam in ecclesia cathedrali Divi Pauli London. dictam Cantlers, alias Kentyshetowne, per mortem naturalem Willielmi Layton clerici ultimi canonici et prebendarii eorundem vacantes, et ad collationem ejusdem reverendi patris pleno jure spectantes, dilecto sibi magistro Johanni Bradford, artium magistro, contulit caritatis intuitu; eumque canonicum et prebendarium dictorum canonicatus et prebendæ, de expresse renunciando pretensæ et usurpatæ jurisdictioni, auctoritati et potestati episcopi Romani, ac supremitatem serenissimæ regiæ majestatis juxta leges, &c., fideliter agnoscendo, necnon de fideliter observando statuta, ordinationes, provisiones ac laudabiles dictæ ecclesiæ cathedralis consuetudines, quatenus eum ratione ipsorum canonicatus et prebendæ tangunt et concernunt, ac quatenus legibus et statutis ac provisionibus hujus regni Angliæ non adversantur, &c., primitus juratum, rite et legitime instituit et investivit, &c.; et recepta ejus obedientia legitima scriptum fuit decano et capitulo dictæ ecclesiæ cathedralis ac eorum vicesgerentibus, &c., pro ejus inductione et installatione suis."—MS. Ridley Register, St Paul's cathedral, fol. 312, b.

[6] Bp Ridley, Lett. to Sir J. Cheke, Works, p. 331, 2, Park. Soc.

[7] Strype, Life of Cranmer, Book II. ch. xxxv. Vol. I. p. 432, Oxf. 1812.

and two in Kent and Sussex, &c.: these six to be Bill, Harley, Perne, Grindal, Bradford, and Knox[1]."

Bradford performed this most important duty with great diligence. He "truly taught and preached the word of God" in "Manchester, Ashton-under-line, Bolton, Bury, Wigan, Liverpool, Mottrine, Stepport, Winsley, Eccles, Prestwich, Middleton, Radcliffe, and the city of West-chester[2]," in Lancashire and Cheshire, and in Walden in Essex[3]. "And God gave good success to the ministry of the word, and both raised up to himself and preserved a faithful people in Lancashire, especially in and about Manchester and Bolton[4]." In the summer of 1552, "as he was abroad preaching in the country, his chance was to make a Sermon of Repentance, the which was earnestly of divers desired of him, that he should give it them written, or else put it forth in print. The which thing to grant as he could not (for he had not written it), so he told them that had so earnestly desired it. But, when no way would serve but he must promise them to write it as he could, he consented to their request that they should have it at his leisure." This was Bradford's memorable Sermon which, "for the satisfying of his promise, and profiting of the simple, ignorant and rude," he "caused to be printed[5]," July 12, in the following year. Foxe observes: "In this preaching office, by the space of three years, how faithfully Bradford walked, how diligently he laboured, many parts of England can testify. Sharply he opened and reproved sin; sweetly he preached Christ crucified; pithily he impugned heresies and errors; earnestly he persuaded to godly life[6]."

It appears from the MS. Council Books of Edward VI., that early in 1552, February 11, Bradford was directed by a

[1] Diary of Edward VI., in Ref. Records, in Bp Burnet, Hist. Reform., Part II. book i. Vol. IV. p. 225, ed. Nares. Compare Strype, Ecc. Mem. Book II. ch. vii. Vol. II. pp. 522, 4, with McCrie, Life of Knox, p. 68, Lond. 1812. Bradford "was sworn to serve the king a little before" Edward's death: Vol. I. p. 468. This may probably have been upon the present occasion.

[2] Vol. I. Farewell to Lancashire and Cheshire, p. 453.

[3] Id. Farewell to Walden, p. 455.

[4] Hollingworth's Chronicle of Manchester, p. 74, Manch. 1839, written about A.D. 1650.

[5] Vol. I. Preface to Sermon on Repent., pp. 41, 2.

[6] Foxe's Acts, &c., ed. 1583, p. 1603, or ed. 1843-9, Vol. VII. p. 144.

special order of the Privy Council, to fulfil the painful task of attending upon Sir Miles Partridge, who was then confined in the Tower, and was soon afterward executed (on account of the political troubles connected with the duke of Somerset), "to instruct him to die well[7]."

It had been intended, in the autumn of 1552, to divide the bishopric of Durham into two sees. Writing to Sir John Gate and Sir W. Cecil, November 18, upon matters dependent on that arrangement, Ridley described Grindal, Bradford and Rogers, as "men known to be so necessary to be abroad in the commonwealth, that he could keep none of them with him in his house." And, as he "had daily need of learned men's counsel and conference," he entreated that the King might grant him the collation of the chantership of St Paul's, "that he might therewith call some learned man, whom hereafter by God's grace his highness shall think meet to promote" to a bishopric; enumerating, beside others, "Master Bradford, whom in my conscience I judge more worthy to be a bishop, than many of us that be bishops already to be a parish-priest[8]."

The division however of the bishopric of Durham, though passed into law, March 1553[9], was not acted upon during the short remainder of the reign of Edward. Bradford continued therefore, for that brief space, prebendary of St Paul's, as well as chaplain to bishop Ridley.

At the close of 1552, when Bradford was at Manchester, he "treated of Noe's flood," and often forewarned the people of "those plagues" which would be "brought to pass." And on the twenty-sixth of December, St Stephen's day, "the last time that he was with them," he preached a remarkable sermon from the twenty-third chapter of St Matthew. The last six verses, the gospel for the day, was the text no doubt he selected on that occasion—a passage eminently suggestive of that solemn and prophetic warning which he then de-

7 Addit. MSS. 14,026, Council Books of Edward VI., Transcripts, British Museum. See also the originals in the Privy Council Office.

8 Bp Ridley, Letters, Works, pp. 336, 7, Park. Soc.

9 Strype, Eccl. Mem. Book II. ch. xix. Vol. II. part ii. p. 66, Oxf. 1822; Bp Burnet, Hist. Reform. Part II. book i. Vol. II. pp. 342, 3, ed. Nares; Ridley's Life of Bp Ridley, pp. 383—6, Lond. 1763.

livered[1]. Local tradition even yet points to the spot in Blackley, where the country-people say that Bradford, during that last visit to Manchester, knelt down and made solemn supplication to almighty God. His request at the throne of grace was, that the everlasting gospel might be preached in Blackley, to the end of time, by ministers divinely taught to feed the flock with wisdom and knowledge. The martyr's prayer, it is alleged, has been answered in the continuance, with scarcely an exception, of faithful men in that place.

Sampson informs us, that "besides often preaching in London and at Paul's Cross, and sundry places in the country, and especially in Lancashire, Bradford preached before King Edward the sixth, in the Lent, the last year of his reign, upon the second Psalm: and there in one sermon, showing the tokens of God's judgment at hand for the contempt of the gospel, as that certain gentlemen upon the Sabbath-day going in a wherry to Paris Garden, to the bear-baiting, were drowned, and that a dog was met at Ludgate carrying a piece of a dead child in his mouth, he with a mighty and prophetical spirit said, 'I summon you all, even every mother's child of you, to the judgment of God, for it is at hand:' as it followed shortly after in the death of king Edward[2]." This was perhaps the occasion which John Knox so well describes in his "Godly Letter," 1554: "Master Bradford...spared not the proudest, but boldly declared that God's vengeance shortly should strike those that then were in authority, because they loathed and abhorred the true word of the everlasting God; and amongst many other willed them to take ensample by the late duke of Somerset, who became so cold in hearing God's word, that, the year before his last apprehension, he would go to visit his masons, and would not dingy[3] himself from his gallery to go

[1] Vol. I. Farewell to Lancashire and Cheshire, p. 453. Hollingworth, in his Chronicle of Manchester, pp. 75, 6, records a popular tradition: "It is reported and believed, that John Bradford, preaching in Manchester, in king Edward's days, told the people, as it were by a prophetical spirit, that because they did not readily embrace the word of God, the mass should be said again in that church, and the play of Robin Hood acted there; which accordingly came to pass in queen Mary's reign."

[2] Vol. I. Sampson's Preface, p. 31.

[3] "Dingy:" vex or trouble. See Vol. I. p. 111, note 4.

to his hall for hearing of a sermon. 'God punished him,' said that godly preacher, 'and that suddenly: and shall he spare you that be double more wicked? No, he shall not. Will ye or will ye not, ye shall drink the cup of the Lord's wrath. *Judicium Domini, judicium Domini!* The judgment of the Lord, the judgment of the Lord!' lamentably cried he with a lamentable voice and weeping tears[4]."

Bishop Ridley moreover, writing from prison in the reign of Mary, speaking of Bradford, Latimer, Lever, and Knox, bears the strongest testimony to the boldness and faithfulness with which they addressed the courtiers of Edward: "Their tongues were so sharp, they ripped in so deep in their galled backs, to have purged them, no doubt, of that filthy matter that was festered in their hearts of insatiable covetousness, of filthy carnality and voluptuousness, of intolerable ambition and pride, of ungodly loathsomeness to hear poor men's causes and to hear God's word, that these men of all other these magistrates then could never abide[5]."

Sampson also represents forcibly Bradford's habits in private life:

"They which were familiar with him might see how he, being in their company, used to fall often into a sudden and deep meditation, in which he would sit with fixed countenance and spirit moved, yet speaking nothing a good space. And sometimes in this silent sitting plenty of tears should trickle down his cheeks: sometime he would sit in it and come out of it with a smiling countenance. Oftentimes have I sitten at dinner and supper with him, in the house of that godly harbourer of many preachers and servants of the Lord Jesus, I mean Master Elsyng, when, either by occasion of talk had, or some view of God's benefits present, or some inward cogitation and thought of his own, he hath fallen into these deep cogitations: and he would tell me in the end such discourses of them, that I did perceive that sometimes his tears trickled out of his eyes, as well for joy as for sorrow. Neither was he only such a practiser of repentance in himself, but a continual provoker of others thereunto, not only in public preaching, but also in private conference and company. For in all com-

[4] Vol. I. p. 111.

[5] Bp Ridley, Piteous Lamentation, Works, p. 59, Park. Soc.

panies where he did come he would freely reprove any sin and misbehaviour which appeared in any person, especially swearers, filthy talkers, and popish praters. Such never departed out of his company unreproved. And this he did with such a divine grace and Christian majesty, that ever he stopped the mouths of the gainsayers. For he spoke with power and yet so sweetly, that they might see their evil to be evil and hurtful unto them, and understand that it was good indeed to the which he laboured to draw them in God[1]."

"Edward, the star of the reformers, had set," July 6, 1553, "and Bradford's lamentation over him is full of historical interest and tenderness[2]." It would appear he disapproved the attempt then made to set aside the lawful succession of Mary[3]. He published, July 12, that noble discourse upon Repentance, which had been preached the year before, and "which had lien by him half a year at the least, for the most part of it[4]." A few days later he brought out a "Treatise of Prayer, the which had been a good space translated[5]" from the Common-places of Melancthon. His prefaces to these publications, and portions of the sermon on Repentance, indicate his full sense of the "bitter cup of God's vengeance, ready to be poured out for Englishmen to drink of[6]."

Mary was proclaimed, July 19, and reached London, August 3; and Bradford "still continued diligent in preaching, until he was unjustly deprived, both of his office and liberty, by the queen and her council. To the doing whereof because they had no just cause, they took occasion to do this injury, for such an act as amongst Turks and infidels would have been with thankfulness rewarded, and with great favour accepted, as indeed it did no less deserve.

"The fact was this: the 13th of August...Master Bourn, then bishop of Bath, made a seditious sermon at Paul's Cross, ...to set popery abroach[7], in such sort that it moved the people to no small indignation, being almost ready to pull him

[1] Vol. I. Preface of Sampson, pp. 35, 6.

[2] Haweis, Sketches of Reformation, p. 93, Lond. 1844. See the passage referred to in Bradf. Vol. I. Serm. on Repentance, pp. 61, 2.

[3] See pp. 87, 9, and Vol. I. p. 62, note 3.

[4] Vol. I. p. 41. See p. xvi, above.

[5] Id. p. 20.

[6] Id. p. 38.

[7] "Abroach:" in a posture to run out.

out of the pulpit. Neither could the reverence of the place, nor the presence of bishop Bonner, who then was his master, nor yet the commandment of the mayor of London, whom the people ought to have obeyed, stay their rage; but, the more they spake, the more the people were incensed. At length Bourn, seeing the people in such a mood, and himself in such peril... fearing lest (against his will) he should there end his wretched life, desired Bradford, who stood in the pulpit behind him, for the passion of Christ[8], to come forth, and to stand in his place and speak unto the people. Good Bradford, at his request, was content, and[9]" "coming into the pulpit had like to have been slain with a naked dagger, for it touched his sleeve[10]:" and he "there spake to the people of godly and quiet obedience: whom, as soon as the people saw to begin to speak unto them, so glad they were to hear him, that they cried with a great shout, 'Bradford, Bradford, God save thy life, Bradford!' well declaring, not only what affection they bare unto him, but also what regard they gave to his words. For after that he had entered a little to preach unto them, and to exhort them to quiet and patience, eftsoons all the raging ceased, and they in the end quietly departed each man to his house. Yet in the mean season (for it was a long time before that so great a multitude could all depart) Bourn thought (and truly) himself not yet full sure of his life, till he were safely housed, notwithstanding that the mayor and sheriffs of London were there at hand to help him. Wherefore he desired Bradford not to depart from him till he were in safety; which Bradford, according to his promise, performed. For while the mayor and sheriffs did lead Bourn to the schoolmaster's house, which is next to the pulpit, Bradford went at his back shadowing him from the people with his gown, and so to set him safe.

"Let the reader now consider the peril of Bourn, the charity of Bradford, and the headiness of the multitude, and also the grudging minds of certain, which yet still there remained behind, grieved not a little in their minds, to see that so good a man should save the life of such a popish priest, so

[8] "for the passion of Christ," inserted from Vol. I. Third Exam. p. 485.

[9] Foxe, Acts, &c., ed. 1583, p. 1604, or ed. 1843-9, Vol. VII. p. 144.

[10] Vol. I. Third Exam. p. 485.

impudently and openly railing against king Edward. Among whom one gentleman said these words: 'Ah, Bradford, Bradford! thou savest him that will help to burn thee. I gave thee his life: if it were not for thee, I would, I assure thee, run him through with my sword.' Thus Bourn for that time, through Bradford's means, escaped bodily death....The same Sunday in the afternoon, Bradford preached at the Bow Church, in Cheapside[1]:" "and there, going up into the pulpit, one willed him not to reprove the people: 'for,' quoth he, 'you shall never come down alive if you do it.' And yet notwithstanding Bradford did in that sermon reprove this fact, and called it 'sedition' twenty times[2]."

"After this he did abide still in London, with an innocent conscience, to try what should become of his just doing. Within three days after, he was sent for to the Tower of London, where the queen then was, to appear there before the council. There was he charged with this act of saving of Bourn, which act they there called seditious, and also objected against him for preaching: and so by them he was committed, first to the Tower, then unto other prisons[1]."

From the Tower Bradford wrote to a friend: "God most justly hath now cast me into a dungeon, but much better than I deserve; wherein I see no man but my keeper, nor can see any except they come to me. Something in the earth my lodging is[3]." Soon afterward he was put "into Nun's-bower, a better prison," in the Tower, where Sandys was confined. "One John Bowler was their keeper, a very perverse papist: yet, by often persuading of him (for he would give ear), and by gentle using of him, at the length he began to mislike popery, and to favour the gospel, and [was] so persuaded in true religion, that on a Sunday, when they had mass in the chapel, he bringeth up a service-book, a manchet, and a glass of wine; and there Doctor Sandys ministered the communion to Bradford and to Bowler. Thus Bowler was their son begotten in bonds[4]." Bradford, while "prisoner in the Tower[5],"

[1] Foxe, Acts, &c., ed. 1583, p. 1604, or ed. 1843—9, Vol. VIII. pp. 144, 5.

[2] Vol. I. Third Exam. p. 485.

[3] Letter XVI. to William Punt, pp. 38, 9.

[4] Foxe, Acts, &c., ed. 1583, p. 2087, or ed. 1843—9, Vol. VIII. p. 593.

[5] Title of "Hurt of hearing mass," p. 299.

took the opportunity of writing his learned treatise on "The hurt of hearing mass."

Sandys and Bradford continued to be fellow-prisoners until Wyat's rebellion. At that time Sandys, after having been in prison "twenty-nine weeks," reckoning from "St James's day," July 25, 1553, to February 6, 1554, the date of the suppression of that revolt, "was sent unto the Marshalsea," in order "that room might be made in the Tower for Wyat and other his complices[4]." And, for the same reason, Ridley states, "My lord of Canterbury, Master Latimer, Master Bradford and I, were put all together in one prison, where we remained till almost the next Easter[6]." It was an occasion of devout thankfulness to those champions of Christian truth, that they could enjoy mutual conference, reading the holy scripture, and uniting in prayer. Fourteen months later, April 18, 1554, Latimer, in a public protest, addressed to Mary's commissioners at Oxford, thus describes this most interesting scene:

"The providence of God...did bring this to pass that—where these famous men, viz. Master Cranmer, archbishop of Canterbury, Master Ridley, bishop of London, that holy man, Master Bradford, and I, old Hugh Latimer, were imprisoned in the Tower of London for Christ's gospel preaching, and for because we would not go a massing, every one in close prison from other; the same Tower being so full of other prisoners, that we four were thrust into one chamber, as men not to be accounted of, but, God be thanked, to our great joy and comfort—there did we together read over the New Testament with great deliberation and painful study. And I assure you, as I will answer at the tribunal throne of God's majesty, we could find in the testament of Christ's body and blood no other presence but a spiritual presence, nor that the mass was any sacrifice for sins: but in that heavenly book it appeared that the sacrifice, which Christ Jesus our Redeemer did upon the cross, was perfect, holy and good; that God the heavenly Father did require none other, nor that never again to be done, but was pacified with that only omnisufficient and most

[6] Bp Ridley, Letter to Grindal, Works, p. 390, Park. Soc.

painful sacrifice of that sweet slain Lamb, Christ our Lord, for our sins[1]."

A few weeks after Wyat's insurrection "bishop Ferrar, being in the King's Bench, prisoner, was pressed withal of the papists, in the end of Lent, to receive the sacrament at Easter in one kind, who after much persuading yielded to them, and promised so to do. Then (so it happened by God's providence), the Easter-even," Saturday, March 24, 1554, "the day before he should have done it, was Bradford brought to the King's Bench prisoner, where the Lord, making him his instrument, Bradford only was the mean that the said bishop Ferrar revoked his promise and word, and would never after yield to be spotted with that papistical pitch: so effectually the Lord wrought by this worthy servant of his; such an instrument was he in God's church, that few or none there were that knew him, but esteemed him as a precious jewel and God's true messenger[2]."

It deserves to be particularly noted, that both in the King's Bench, Southwark, and in the Compter in the Poultry, London, "for the time he did remain prisoner, he preached twice a day continually, unless sickness hindered him; where also the sacrament was often ministered; and through his means (the keepers so well did bear with him) such resort of good folks was daily to his lecture, and to the ministration of the sacrament, that commonly his chamber was well nigh filled therewith[2]." This may perhaps have been specially allowed at the King's Bench, through the favour of Sir William Fitzwilliam, then knight marshal of that prison, who was "a lover of the gospel," and afterward rose to great eminence in the reign of Elizabeth[3]. Bradford was "in so good credit with his keeper, that at his desire in an evening...he had license, upon his promise to return again that night, to go into London without any keeper, to visit one that was sick, lying by the Steel-yard. And he, that sweet Bradford, going thither with his friend, and the time of his return drawing nigh, he,

[1] Bp Latimer, Protest in Disput. at Oxf., Works, Vol. II. pp. 258, 9, Park. Soc.

[2] Foxe, Acts, &c., ed. 1583, p. 1604, or ed. 1843—9, Vol. VII. pp. 145, 6.

[3] See account of Sir William Fitzwilliam, p. 135, note 5, and Letter XLIX. from Bradford to that person.

having respect to fidelity therein more than life itself, went to prison again that night according to his promise, so trusty was he in word and deed[4]."

"While he was in the King's Bench, and Master Saunders in the Marshalsea, both prisoners, on the backside of those two prisons they met many times, and conferred together when they would: so mercifully did the Lord work for them, even in the midst of their troubles: and the said Bradford was so trusted with his keeper, and had such liberty in the backside, that there was no day but that he might have easily escaped away if he would, but that the Lord had another work to do for him. In the summer-time, while he was in the said King's Bench, he had liberty of his keeper to ride into Oxfordshire, to a merchant's house of his acquaintance, and horse and all things prepared for him for that journey, and the party in readiness that should ride with him: but God prevented him by sickness that he went not at all.

"One of his old friends and acquaintance came unto him while he was prisoner, and asked him, if he sued to get him out, what then he would do, or whither he would go? Unto whom he made answer, as not caring whether he went out or no: but, if he did, he said he would marry, and abide still in England secretly, teaching the people as the time would suffer him, and occupy himself that way. He was had in so great reverence and admiration with all good men, that a multitude, which never knew him but by fame, greatly lamented his death: yea, and a number also of the papists themselves wished heartily his life. There were few days in which he was thought not to spend some tears before he went to bed, neither was there ever any prisoner with him but by his company he greatly profited; as all they will yet witness, and have confessed of him no less, to the glory of God, whose society he frequented....He was no niggard of his purse, but would liberally participate that he had, to his fellow-prisoners. And commonly once a week he visited the thieves, pick-purses, and such others that were with him in the prison where he lay, on the other side; unto whom he would give godly exhortation, to learn the amendment of their lives by their

[4] Foxe, Acts, &c., ed. 1563, p. 1174. See ed. 1843—9, Vol. VII. p. 145.

troubles; and, after that so done, distribute among them some portion of money to their comfort[1]."

Fully to write the life of Bradford, at this period, would be to transcribe the greater part of the many affecting letters which he penned during his imprisonment. All his letters, known to exist are furnished in the present volumes. They are addressed to persons of different positions in life. There are letters to his mother—to Saunders and Philpot—to bishop Ridley, archbishop Cranmer, and bishop Latimer — to Sir William Fitzwilliam and Lord Francis Russell—to Sir James Hales—to Humphry Hales and his wife, and Mistress Joyce Hales—to Mistress Wilkinson, Mistress Warcup, Mistress Honywood, and Lady Vane—to Dr Hill—to Harrington—to Careless, and Bernhere, and many others[2]. His epistles have long been greatly esteemed for their spirituality and other excellencies. They deserve a careful perusal from those who desire to study his mind or temper, and to acquaint themselves with the theology of the fathers of the English Reformation.

There is one topic of peculiar moment, which is connected with some of these letters, the discussion then going forward upon the divine election and man's free-will[3]. In the treatises and letters of Bradford, and in the references to other authorities which these volumes contain, ample material will be found, to enable the intelligent reader, while he appreciates the reverential caution and loving spirit of this holy man, to form an impartial judgment of the views he held relative to that important subject.

The lamentable period at length drew nigh, when the splendour of the English "Reformation, scarce yet appearing above the horizon, almost instantly set in blood[4]." The royal assent was given, January, 16, 1555, to the "Act for the

[1] Foxe, Acts, &c. ed. 1583, p. 1604, or ed. 1843—9, Vol. VII. p. 146.

[2] Accounts of many of Bradford's correspondents will be found in the editorial footnotes to his letters: and every letter, known to exist, addressed by any one to Bradford, including several from bishop Ridley, will be found in its place in this volume, among Bradford's own letters.

[3] See Strype, Life of Cranmer, Book III. ch. xiv. pp. 502—5, Oxf. 1812; Stow, Life of Rowland Taylor, ch. vi. pp. 179—213, Lond. 1833; and Vol. I. references in p. 306.

[4] Abp. Laurence, Introd. to Authentic Documents, p. xiv, Oxf. 1819.

revival of three statutes made for the punishment of heresy[5]." Within six days, January 22, Bradford's first examination took place, before bishop Gardiner. At the commencement "the lord chancellor," Gardiner, "earnestly looked upon him, to have, belike, over-faced him: but Bradford gave no place; that is, he ceased not in like manner to look on the lord chancellor still and continually, save that once he cast his eyes to heaven-ward, sighing for God's help, and so outfaced him, as they say[6]." Bradford at first refused to plead before the court, because he "had been six times sworn, that he should in no case consent to the practising of any jurisdiction or any authority, on the bishop of Rome's behalf, within this realm of England[7]." In adopting that course he received the unqualified approbation of his beloved friend and patron, bishop Ridley[8].

At length however Bradford did plead, "saving his oath[9]." The answers he returned betoken a mind of a very high order as to depth and closeness of thought, and as to calmness and self-possession. Again and again were his judges baffled in their efforts to establish his criminality. To delineate these memorable scenes here is not possible. The three examinations he underwent, as recorded by himself, and presented in the former volume, are fraught with interest, and will receive well-merited attention from every devout or studious reader.

Sentence of condemnation was passed, January 31, 1555. It was at first intended to deliver him forthwith "to the earl of Derby, to be conveyed into Lancashire, and there to be burned in the town of Manchester, where he was born[10]." The original purpose was subsequently abandoned. The Romish "bishops, whether from secret fear of Bradford's friends (for Bradford was in favour among his own people), or from some more secret confidence of overcoming his opinion, retained him at London for some months, assailing him during that time with frequent conferences and embassies[11]." And it appears from some pages, first reprinted in the former

[5] P. 167, note 1.
[6] Vol. I. First Exam. p. 465.
[7] Id. ibid. p. 466.
[8] See Letter LXXXI. in this volume, from Bp Ridley to Bradford, p. 199.
[9] Vol. I. p. 480.
[10] Foxe, ed. 1563, p. 1199.
[11] From the Latin original of Foxe's Acts, &c., Rerum in eccles. gestar. comm. p. 484, Basil. 1559. The Latin is quoted in Bradf. Vol. I. p. 492.

volume of his works from his Examinations, Griffith, 1561, that the earl of Derby took great interest in his case, and (it was alleged) obtained from the queen the concession, that he should "have his books, and time enough to peruse them[1]." To this period belong his treatises "Against the fear of death," and on "The restoration of all things[2]."

The materials for illustrating Bradford's life and character, pertaining to this time, are exceedingly abundant and valuable: for he himself carefully recorded the various conferences that were held with him during February, March, and April, 1555, by Willerton, chaplain to bishop Bonner, Harding, archdeacon Harpsfield, archbishop Heath and bishop Day, Alphonsus a Castro and Carranza[3], and dean Weston and doctor Pendleton. These most interesting discussions manifest, on the part of Bradford, considerable learning, and intimate acquaintance with the Romish controversy. To attempt any digest of them would obviously exceed the bounds of the present memoir. They are printed as penned by Bradford, in the former volume, from the original edition, 1561.

The time of his departure from this lower world at length drew near. Foxe records, that "the night before he was had to Newgate, which was the Saturday night," June 29,1555, "he was sore troubled divers times in his sleep by dreams, how the chain for his burning was brought to the Compter gate, and how the next day, being Sunday, he should be had to Newgate, and on the Monday after burned in Smithfield, as indeed it came to pass accordingly, which hereafter shall be showed. Now he being vexed so oftentimes in this sort with these dreams, about three of the clock in the morning he waked him that lay with him, and told him his unquiet sleep, and what he was troubled withal. Then, after a little talk, Master Bradford rose out of the bed, and gave himself to his old exercise of reading and prayer, as always he had used before; and at dinner, according to his accustomed manner,

[1] Vol. I. p. 517.

[2] Id. pp. 331, 350.

[3] Carranza was confessor to Philip and Mary. Compare Vol. I. p. 530, and Bp Burnet, Hist. Reform., Part III. Suppl. book v. Vol. III. pp. 381, 2, ed. Nares. He afterward became archbishop of Toledo and primate of all Spain, but died under the charge of Lutheran opinions, at Rome, A. D. 1576. See McCrie, Reformation in Spain, ch. vii. pp. 321—3, Edinb. 1829; De Castro, Spanish Protestants, ch. ix—xii. pp. 126—91, Lond. 1851.

he did eat his meat, and was very merry, nobody being with him from morning till night, but he that lay with him, with whom he had many times on that day communication of death, of the kingdom of heaven, and of the ripeness of sin in that time.

"In the afternoon, they two walking together in the keeper's chamber, suddenly the keeper's wife came up, as one half amazed, and seeming much troubled, being almost windless, said: 'O Master Bradford, I come to bring you heavy news.'—'What is that?' said he. 'Marry,' quoth she, 'to-morrow you must be burned, and your chain is now a-buying, and soon you must go to Newgate.' With that Master Bradford put off his cap, and lifting up his eyes to heaven said: 'I thank God for it; I have looked for the same a long time, and therefore it cometh not now to me suddenly, but as a thing waited for every day and hour; the Lord make me worthy thereof;' and so, thanking her for her gentleness, departed up into his chamber, and called his friend with him, who when he came thither, he went secretly himself alone a long time, and prayed. Which done, he came again to him that was in his chamber, and took him divers writings and papers, and showed him his mind in those things, what he would have done[4]; and, after they had spent the afternoon till night in many and sundry such things, at last came to him half a dozen of his friends more, with whom all the evening he spent the time in prayer and other good exercises, so wonderfully that it was marvellous to hear and see his doings.

"A little before he went out of the Compter, he made a notable prayer of his farewell, with such plenty of tears, and abundant spirit of prayer, that it ravished the minds of the hearers. Also when he shifted himself with a clean shirt, that

[4] The following words were probably dictated or indited by Bradford at this time in reference to his writings: "I would no one read them with any great deliberation: but meseemeth that they are good and meet to be set forth." They are preceded by the following: "To Mistress Hales all the shirts he hath had of her. All his best handkerchiefs to Mistress Hales. Augustine two shirts. Two shirts to W. P[unt.] Two shirts to William his man. His books at the discretion of Master Har[rington] and W. P[unt.] A truss bed. All such as Mistress Sandys have he hath given it her. The rest of your shirts. The rest of your handkerchiefs. Your sheets. His feather-bed. Your raiment. Your spiked cap. Your hose."—This memorandum is written, in a contemporary hand, on the reverse of MS. 1. 2. 8. No. 22. 2. Emman. Coll., Cambridge, which is Bradford's Meditation on the sober use of the body, see Vol. I. p. 187.

was made for his burning (by one Master Walter Marlar's wife[1], who was a good nurse unto him, and his very good friend), he made such a prayer of the wedding garment, that some of those that were present were in such great admiration, that their eyes were as thoroughly occupied in looking on him, as their ears gave place to hear his prayer. At his departing out of the chamber, he made likewise a prayer, and gave money to every servant and officer of the house, with exhortation to them to fear and serve God, continually labouring to eschew all manner of evil. That done, he turned him to the wall, and prayed vehemently, that his words might not be spoken in vain, but that the Lord would work the same in them effectually, for his Christ's sake. Then being beneath in the court all the prisoners cried out to him, and bid him farewell, as the rest of the house had done before with weeping tears.

"The time they carried him to Newgate was about eleven or twelve o'clock in the night, when it was thought none would be stirring abroad: and yet, contrary to their expectation in that behalf, was there in Cheapside, and other places between the Compter and Newgate, a great multitude of people that came to see him, which most gently bade him farewell, praying for him with most lamentable and pitiful tears; and he again as gently bade them farewell, praying most heartily for them and their welfare. Now whether it were a commandment from the queen and her council, or from Bonner and his adherents, or whether it were merely devised of the lord mayor, alderman, and sheriffs of London, or no, I cannot tell; but a great noise there was over night about the city by divers, that Bradford should be burnt the next day in Smithfield, by four of the clock in the morning, before it should be greatly known to any ... But ... the people prevented the device suspected: for the next day," Monday, July 1, "at the said hour of four o'clock in the morning, there was in Smithfield such a multitude of men and women, that many being in admiration thereof thought it was not possible that they could have warning of his death, being so great a number in so short a time, unless it were by the singular providence of almighty God.

[1] See Letter LXX. p. 181, "to Mary Marlar, Feb. 22, 1555."

"Well, this took not effect as the people thought; for that morning it was nine o'clock of the day before Master Bradford was brought into Smithfield; which, in going through Newgate thitherward, spied a friend of his whom he loved, standing on the one side [of] the way to the keeper's houseward, unto whom he reached his hand over the people, and plucked him to him, and delivered to him from his head his velvet night-cap, and also his handkerchief, with other things besides.... After a little secret talk with him, and each of them parting from other, immediately came to him a brother-in-law of his, called Roger Beswick, which, as soon as he had taken the said Bradford by the hand, one of the sheriffs of London, called Woodrofe, came with his staff, and brake the said Roger's head, that the blood ran about his shoulders; which sight Bradford beholding with grief bade his brother farewell, willing [him] to commend him to his mother and the rest of his friends, and to get him to some surgeon betimes: and so they, departing, had little or no talk at all together. Then was he led forth to Smithfield with a great company of weaponed men, to conduct him thither, as the like was not seen at no man's burning: for in every corner of Smithfield there were some, besides those which stood about the stake. Bradford then, being come to the place, fell flat to the ground, secretly making his prayers to almighty God." And he "lying prostrate on the one side of the stake," and a young man, an apprentice, John Leaf, who suffered with him "on the other side, they lay flat on their faces, praying to themselves the space of a minute of an hour. Then one of the sheriffs said to Master Bradford, 'Arise, and make an end; for the press of the people is great[2].'

"At that word they both stood up upon their feet; and then Master Bradford took a faggot in his hand, and kissed it, and so likewise the stake. And, when he had so done, he desired of the sheriffs that his servant might have his raiment: 'for,' said he, 'I have nothing else to give him, and besides that he is a poor man.' And the sheriff said he should have it. And so forthwith Master Bradford did put off his raiment, and went to the stake: and, holding up his hands, and casting his countenance up to heaven, he said thus,

[2] See mention of Mistress Mary Honywood, p. 98, note 1, on Letter XXXVII.

'O England, England, repent thee of thy sins, repent thee of thy sins. Beware of idolatry, beware of false antichrists; take heed they do not deceive you.' And, as he was speaking these words, the sheriff bade tie his hands, if he would not be quiet. 'O Master Sheriff,' said Master Bradford, 'I am quiet: God forgive you this, Master Sheriff.' And one of the officers which made the fire, hearing Master Bradford so speaking to the sheriff, said, 'If you have no better learning than that, you are but a fool, and were best to hold your peace.' To the which words Master Bradford gave no answer, but asked all the world forgiveness, and forgave all the world, and prayed the people to pray for him, and turned his head unto the young man that suffered with him, and said, 'Be of good comfort, brother; for we shall have a merry supper with the Lord this night;' and so spake no more words that any man did hear, but embracing the reeds said thus: 'Strait is the way, and narrow is the gate, that leadeth to eternal salvation, and few there be that find it[1].'" "He endured the flame," Fuller observes, "as a fresh gale of wind in a hot summer's day, without any reluctancy, confirming by his death the truth of that doctrine he had so diligently and powerfully preached during his life[2]." One "like the Son of God" had been with him in the furnace[3]; and the Redeemer, whom he loved and served, translated "his faithful martyr[4]," as if upon the chariot of fire[5], into the heavenly Jerusalem.

No frail memorial of brass or marble has yet been erected to his memory. His "martyrdom is his monument[6];" and his name will endure through all time, revered and beloved by the English people.

His varied writings, upon "repentance," the sacrament of "the Lord's supper," "election," "the fear of death," and "the restoration of all things"—his treatises, meditations and prayers, his examinations and prison-conferences, and above all his letters—will be found, even by readers of various

[1] Foxe, Acts, &c., ed. 1583, pp. 1604, 5, 1623, or ed. 1843–9, Vol. VII. pp 146—8, 194.

[2] Fuller's Abel redivivus, p. 189, Lond. 1651.

[3] Daniel iii. 25.

[4] Rev. ii. 13.

[5] 1 Kings ii. 11. Compare the anticipations of Bradford, pp. 185, 191, 8, 249.

[6] Strype, Life of Cranmer, Book III. ch. xxi. Vol. I. p. 562, Oxf. 1812.

opinions, to repay an attentive perusal. Their peculiar and crowning excellence, like the works of archbishop Leighton, consists in pourtraying the Christian character and the life of God within the soul. During three centuries they have been eminently popular; and, in the good hand of the heavenly Physician, have many a time comforted the afflicted, strengthened the weak, and refreshed the weary.

Tenderness and sympathy were indeed prominent features of Bradford's character. Fuller remarks: "It is a demonstration to me that he was of a sweet temper, because Parsons, who will hardly afford a good word to a Protestant, saith 'that he seemed to be of a more soft and mild nature than many of his fellow[7].' Indeed he was a most holy and mortified man, who secretly in his closet would so weep for his sins, one would have thought he would never have smiled again; and then, appearing in public, he would be so harmlessly pleasant, one would think he had never wept before[8]."

The familiar story, that, on seeing evil-doers taken to the place of execution, he was wont to exclaim, "But for the grace of God there goes John Bradford," is a universal tradition, which has overcome the lapse of time. And Venning, writing in 1653, desirous to show that, "by the sight of others' sins, men may learn to bewail their own sinfulness and heart of corruption," instances the case of Bradford, who, "when he saw any drunk or heard any swear, &c., would railingly complain, 'Lord, I have a drunken head; Lord, I have a swearing heart[9].'"

His personal appearance and daily habits are graphically described by Foxe. "He was, of person, a tall man, slender, spare of body, somewhat a faint sanguine colour, with an auburn beard[10]. He slept not commonly above four hours a night; and

[7] "In his examination of J. Foxe's Martyrs."

[8] Fuller, Worthies of England, Lancashire, Vol. II. p. 193, Lond. 1840.

[9] Ralph Venning, The heathen improved, an appendix to Canaan's Flowings, sect. 110. p. 222, Lond. 1653.

[10] The best portrait of Bradford is the picture in the Chetham Library, Manchester, an excellent engraving of which is in Baines' Hist. of Lancashire, Vol. II. p. 243, Lond. 1836. See also the print in Holland's Herωologia, Lond. 1620, which is followed in Lupton's Protestant Divines, 1637, in Fuller's Abel redivivus, 1651, and in the modern painting, Pembroke Hall, Cambridge. See also Middleton's Biographia Evangelica, Vol. I. p. 352, Lond. 1779.

in his bed, till sleep came, his book went not out of his hand. ...His painful diligence, reading, and prayer, I might almost account it his whole life. He did not eat above one meal a day, which was but very little when he took it; and his continual study was upon his knees. In the midst of dinner he used oftentimes to muse with himself, having his hat over his eyes, from whence came commonly plenty of tears, dropping on his trencher. Very gentle he was to man and child.... His chief recreation was, in no gaming or other pastime, but only in honest company and comely talk, wherein he would spend a little leisure after dinner at the board, and so to prayer and his book again. He counted that hour not well-spent, wherein he did not some good, either with his pen, study, or exhortation to others[1]."

He may be said to have lived a long life in a short space of time. From his ordination as deacon to the hour of martyrdom he was only permitted to exercise the ministerial office for five years, of which no fewer than two were passed in prison. Until the great day, when the secrets of all hearts shall be revealed, it cannot be fully known to what extent England has been indebted to the labours and the prayers of this devoted man. "Certainly he was neither the least able nor the least learned[2]" of the fathers of the English church. He happily combined judgment with "learning, elocution, sweetness of temper, and profound devotion toward God: .... and of his worth the papists themselves were so sensible, that they took more pains to bring him off from the profession of religion than any other[3]." Had Edward longer occupied the English throne Bradford would have been raised to the episcopal bench. He obtained, from the great Bishop of souls, a higher promotion. By the holiness of his life and the testimony of his writings "he yet speaketh." By the flames of martyrdom "Bradford and Latimer, Cranmer and Ridley, four prime pillars of the Reformed Church of England[4]," have, through the grace of God, lighted such a candle in this country as shall never be extinguished.

[1] Foxe's Acts, &c. ed. 1563, pp. 1173, 4. See ed. 1843—9, Vol. VII. pp. 145, 6.

[2] Haweis, Sketches of Reformation, p. 92, Lond. 1844.

[3] Strype, Eccl. Mem., Mary, ch. xxviii. Vol. III. part I. pp. 363, 4, Oxf. 1822.

[4] Id. Ibid. p. 423.

LIST OF EDITIONS OF BRADFORD'S WRITINGS.

I. 1548. Translations from Artopœus and Chrysostom, printed by Lynn. See black-letter title, Vol. I. p. 2. Copies, the editor, perfect and imperfect; copy, imperfect, Bodleian, Oxford. Scarce. See Herbert, Typogr. Antiq. Vol. II. p. 755, Lond. 1785—90.

II. 1553. Sermon of Repentance, n. d. See black-letter title, and editorial preface, Vol. I. pp. 26, 8. Copy, the editor, imperfect, of exceeding rarity.

A reprint was issued by Copland, 1558 (see Herbert, I. 358), but without the printer's name or date; copy, Bodleian; and copy, imperfect, the editor. It was reprinted with the Sermon on the Lord's Supper, 1574, 1581, 1599, and 1617, see entry XIII.; and separately, 1619, copy, the late G. Stokes, Esq.; 1623, copy, the editor; 1631, copy, Bodleian; and 1652, copies, Bodleian, the editor.

III. 1553. Translation from Melancthon on Prayer, printed by Wight, n. d. See black-letter title and colophon, with editorial preface, Vol. I. pp. 16, 18. Copies, Balliol College, Oxford, the late G. Stokes, Esq.

Maunsell, Catal. of printed books, p. 86, Lond. 1595, mentions an edition by Waldegrave. Herbert, II. 1145, repeats the entry.

IV. March 15, 1559. Private Prayers and Meditations, printed by Copland. See black-letter title and colophon, Vol. I. pp. 222, 47. Copy, Bodleian, Oxford, of exceeding rarity. See Herbert, I. pp. 358, 9.

For the reprints of this collection, appended, with separate title, to the "Godly Meditations," first printed 1562, see entry IX.

V. 1559. Complaint of Verity. See editorial preface, p. 363. Copy, Rev. T. Corser, F.S.A.; imperfect copy, Bodleian; of exceeding rarity. See Herbert, III. 1600.

VI. 1561. Examinations and prison Conferences, printed by Griffith. See black-letter title, Vol. I. p. 462. Copies, the editor, and Miss Atherton (Byrom Library, Kersal Cell, near Manchester); of very great scarcity. See Herbert, I. 992, 3.

The contents of this volume were in substance reprinted in Foxe's Acts and Monuments, 1563, 1570, 1576, 1583, and after editions; and were reprinted verbatim for the first time in the present edition of Bradford's writings.

VII. Hurt of Hearing Mass, printed by Copland, n. d. See black-letter title, p. 299. Copies, British Museum, Bodleian, Cambridge University Library, the late G. Stokes, Esq. See Herbert, I. 365.

Reprints were issued by Kirkham, 1580; copies, British Museum, Dublin University Library, Rev. J. Fuller Russell, (see Herbert, III. 1321;) and 1596, copy, Chetham Library, Manchester.

VIII. Treatise against the Fear of Death, and Meditations, printed by Powell, n. d. See its title, p. 359. Copy, the late W. H. Miller, Esq., exceedingly rare.

The same collection of pieces was also published by Singleton, 1561—62, (compare Maunsell, Catal. p. 23, with Herbert, II. pp. 740, 6, and Bradf. Vol. I. p. 220), and by John Wolf, 1583, see Herbert, II. 1172. The Treatise against the Fear of Death, was reprinted by Seres, 1567, but with a different series of Meditations annexed: see next entry; and see black-letter title, and editorial prefaces, Vol. I. pp. 112, 294, 6, 331; copies, the Rev. J. Ayre, and the Rev. J. Fuller Russell: see Herbert, II. 699. Maunsell, Catal., p. 85, mentions an edition of the Treatise on Death, printed by Vautrollier, Edinburgh, 1584.

IX. 1562. Godly Meditations, printed by Hall. See black-letter title, and editorial preface, Vol. I. pp. 112, 4. Copies, Cambridge University Library, the editor, the late G. Stokes, Esq.

Parts of this collection were reprinted by Seres, 1567, see last entry; and the whole was reprinted, with the collection of 1559 appended (see entry IV.), by Allde, 1578, copy, the Rev. Canon Havergal; 1604, copies, Cambridge University Library, the editor; 1607, 1614, both editions, the editor; 1622, copy, the late G. Stokes, Esq.; and 1633, copies, Bodleian, Rev. Dr Routh, Miss Atherton (Byrom Library).

X. 1563. Acts and Monuments of Foxe, printed by Day. Copies, British Museum; imperfect copy, the editor; of great scarcity.

Eight letters were printed, for the first time, in Foxe, 1563, and were reprinted in the after editions of that work. The Examinations were reprinted in Foxe, 1563, somewhat abridged from the separate edition of Griffith, 1561.

XI. 1564. Letters of the Martyrs, arranged, and with preface, by bishop Coverdale. Copy, the editor.

Seventy-three letters of Bradford appear in this work, pp. 251—489, 650—52; of which eight were reprinted from Foxe, Acts, &c., 1563, and sixty-five were printed 1564, for the first time. Of those sixty-five twenty-nine were not reprinted either in Foxe, Acts, &c., or in any early collection of Bradford's writings, thirty-five were reprinted in the various editions of Foxe subsequent to this work, and one, the Letter on the Mass to Hopkins, pp. 345—54 (see Vol. I. pp. 389—99), was reprinted by Waldegrave, n. d. (see Maunsell, Catal. p. 23, Herb. II. 1145, and Bp Tanner, Bibliotheca, art. Bradford), and was edited by Bp Ironside, Oxford, 1688: see Vol. I. pp. 389, 583.

XII. 1570. Foxe's Acts and Monuments. Copies, Cambridge University Library, the editor, the Rev. Guy Bryan; scarce.

Three letters of Bradford, and "talk with a servant" (see Vol. I. pp. 553—56), were printed, 1570, for the first time, and were reprinted in the after editions of Foxe.

XIII. 1574. Two Sermons by Bradford, of Repentance, and of the Lord's Supper, with Preface by Sampson, printed by Awdeley and Wight. See black-letter title, and editorial preface, Vol. I. pp. 27, 8. There were two impressions of this date; copies, British Museum, the late G. Stokes, Esq., the editor.

The Sermon on the Lord's Supper was printed for the first time in this book. It was reprinted with the Sermon on Repentance, 1581, and 1599, both editions, British Museum, the editor; and 1617, copy, the late G. Stokes, Esq.

XIV. 1583. Foxe, Acts and Monuments. Copy, the editor.

Ten letters of Bradford, those to Traves and Hall, pp. 1659—64, were first printed in this edition, and were reprinted, with forty-seven other letters, making a total of fifty-seven, in the subsequent editions of Foxe.

XV. 1604. Godly Meditations, printed by Allde: see entry IX.

The Meditation on the Tenth Commandment, and "Sweet Contemplation of Heaven," seem to have appeared, for the first time, in this book. See Vol. I. pp. 112, 172, 258, 266.

XVI. 1721. Strype, Ecclesiastical Memorials.

Two letters of Bradford, to Traves, and to a person of quality, were printed for the first time in this work, reign of Mary, Originals, Nos. XXXI. and XXXII.

XVII. 1819. Authentic documents, &c., with preface by Abp Laurence, Oxford.

The second part of Bradford's "Defence of Election" was printed for the first time in this publication, but without the marginal notes and without the Dedication of that Treatise. See Bradf. Vol. I. pp. 305—30.

XVIII. 1810—32. The Collections of Bradford's Writings, published by the late Rev. Legh Richmond, "Fathers of the English Church," 1810; by the Rev. C. Bradley, 1826; and by the late G. Stokes, Esq., "British Reformers," A. D. 1827, comprise Sermons, Meditations, Letters, but do not give any piece for the first time. The Life of Bradford, by Stevens, London, 1832, contains Letters, Examinations, Conferences: the authorship of the letter "To a lady," printed from the Harleian MSS., and assigned to Bradford, no. 45, p. 143, of that work, appears doubtful: the original MS. much resembles the autograph of the martyr Philpot.

XIX. 1848—53. The present edition, issued by the Parker Society, contains, in both volumes, several pieces printed for the first time, and other pieces which are republished for the first time since the Reformation. It is the first complete edition of Bradford's writings. See the tables of contents, and various editorial prefaces.

[LETTERS.

The Letters of Bradford, eighty-two in number, together with twenty-one letters written by other persons, and chiefly addressed to Bradford, making a total of a hundred and three letters, are arranged in this edition, as closely as possible to chronological order. Seven letters of Bradford are now printed for the first time, namely, nos. (XIV.), pp. 352—54, a Latin letter to Bucer; XXVII. to his mother; XXXVIII. to Mistress Coke; XLVI. to a free-willer; LXX. to Mary Marlar; LXXVI. and LXXXIII. to Mistress Joyce Hales. Five letters by other persons, namely Traves, Rawlins, bishop Ridley, Longsho, and Careless, nos. V., XXXVI., LXIII., XCI., (XCVI.) see pp. 354—58, are published for the first time in this series. Considerable portions also of various letters, both of Bradford and others, have never before been printed.

The written sources of Bradford's letters are fifty-six MSS. in Emmanuel College, Cambridge; three in the British Museum; one that belonged to the late O. H. Williams, Esq.; and one in the possession of the editor[1]. The printed sources are, three of the early editions of Foxe's "Acts and Monuments," 1563, 1570, and 1583; the "Letters of the Martyrs," arranged by bishop Coverdale, 1564; and Strype's "Ecclesiastical Memorials," 1721, in which last publication two letters were printed for the first time. The authorities for the text of each letter are indicated upon the margin—the authority first-named being, in every instance, strictly followed, except where a deviation is mentioned in the footnotes: otherwise the various readings of different texts are, as in the former volume, only stated in particular instances.

In Foxe's Acts and Monuments, ed. 1583, pp. 1624—64, 1923, and after editions, fifty-seven of Bradford's letters are published. In bishop Coverdale's Letters of the Martyrs, 1564, pp. 251—489, 650—52, seventy-three letters are to be found. Of the aggregate of letters contained in both publications thirteen are given by Foxe, and not by Coverdale; thirty appear in Coverdale, and not in any edition of Foxe; and forty-three are common to Foxe and Coverdale, making a total of eighty-six letters of Bradford, which appear partly in Foxe and partly in Coverdale. Thirteen of these have appeared in the former volume, being classed among his public addresses (see its preface, p. ix). This leaves seventy-three letters of Bradford, printed in this volume, and derived partly from the Acts and Monuments, and partly from the Letters of the Martyrs. Those, together with the two letters that appeared in Strype, and the seven which are now printed for the first time, make a total of eighty-two letters of Bradford, printed in this volume.

Of those which had appeared in print, previously to this edition, forty-two have been carefully collated with the MSS. mentioned above: and, wherever additional matter has been found, it has been incorporated in the printed text—notice of which has usually been given in the footnotes.]

[1 The book referred to, p. 72, margin of Letter XXXVII., which contains this MS., had formerly belonged to the duke of Roxburgh. See Catalogue of the duke's library, Supplement, article 597, London, 1812.]

[1]LETTERS

OF

MASTER JOHN BRADFORD,

A FAITHFUL MINISTER AND A SINGULAR PILLAR OF CHRIST'S CHURCH, BY WHOSE GREAT TRAVAILS AND DILIGENCE IN PREACHING AND PLANTING THE SINCERITY OF THE GOSPEL, BY WHOSE MOST GODLY AND INNOCENT LIFE, AND BY WHOSE LONG AND PAINFUL IMPRISONMENTS FOR THE MAINTENANCE OF THE TRUTH, THE KINGDOM OF GOD WAS NOT A LITTLE ADVANCED; WHO ALSO AT LAST MOST VALIANTLY AND CHEERFULLY GAVE HIS BLOOD FOR THE SAME, THE 1ST[2] DAY OF JULY, IN THE YEAR OF OUR LORD 1555.[2]

I. TRAVES TO BRADFORD[3].

[Probably from LONDON, about *February*, 1548.]

MS. Harl. 416. no. 22. fol. 33, 34. British Museum.

Strype, Ecc. Mem. Mary, Originals, No. 33.

GRACE, mercy, and peace, from God the Father of our Lord Jesus Christ.

Ye shall understand that after the receipt of your letters I declared to Master Lati[mer] the sum of that ye writ to me concerning your matter with your master[4]. When I came to that place that

[1 The fourteen following lines are the inscription prefixed to Bradford's Letters, in Bp Coverdale's Letters of the Martyrs, 1564, p. 251.]

[2 This date is given by a misprint in the Letters of the Martyrs, "the fourth day of July, 1553." See Vol. I. p. 331, references in note 2.]

[3 The inscription, "Traves to Bradford," is given from internal evidence, which fully sustains the conjecture of Strype, Ecc. Mem. Vol. III. part I. p. 367, and title of letter in part II. p. 285, Originals, No. 33.

"John Traves" or "Travers" (as Foxe varies the spelling in Letters III. and XII. of this series) appears, from the inscription appended to letter XIII., to have been living at Blackley near Manchester. Strype, as above, part I. p. 364, speaks of Traves as "a learned and pious gentleman, Bradford's patron and counsellor." Foxe indeed superscribes letter XII., "To father Traves, minister of Blackley:" but it appears from III. and VIII. that Traves was married, and had children: the lists also of the clergy of the deanery of Manchester, which are still preserved, among the archives of the diocese of Chester, in the MS. visitation book of bishop Bird, who then presided over that see, do not supply the name of "Traves" or "Travers."]

[4 Bradford had been a paymaster under Sir John Harrington, of Exton, in Rutlandshire, who was treasurer of the English forces at Boulogne, A.D. 1544. See references in Vol. I. p. 32, notes 2 and 3, and pp. 486, 493. It appears

you offered yourself to be a bondman, he misliked it, and said: "Though by God's word appeareth that to make restitution we ought to sell ourselves, yet would I not," said he, "that he should go so far with his master." I asked him what counsel he would give you. He said: "Better counsel or more than I have given him I cannot: let him tarry, and committing the whole to God work by leisure." More could I not get of him; nor I durst not trouble him, for because he was studiously occupied in preparing a sermon to be preached, if God will, before the king this next Sunday. He knoweth not certainly whether he shall thereto be called, but as yet judgeth. What his counsel is, ye have heard.

Ye proceed and ask my counsel. Alas! ye know that I am but a very block, yea, more dumb than a dumb idol—as little help in me as in the block of Walsingham[1]. Earnestly I protest that I know not what nor how to counsel you: but pray, pray, and commit yourself wholly to God. Wish an increase of that desire that ye have to make restitution; and whether that God will so enrich you that ye shall be able to pay it, or that he will move your master so that he will and shall pay it, commit it to God with earnest desire and faithful prayer that at length—yet when his merciful eye shall see most meet—that he will unburden you of your check. And look for his help in peace: I mean no such beastly security as is in me, but with patient suffering, without writhing, wresting, or doubting of his promise, without desperate vows, thoughts, groanings, or woes. For the Lord knoweth when and how to deliver them that trust in him, for their best avail: yea, maugre the beards[2] of all hard hearts, God will at length, man, deliver thee. In the mean time, be neither stock nor stone, but labour for your part

from various letters of this series (Nos. I. II. IV. V. VI. VII. X. XI. XII. XIV.), that Bradford, having been cognisant of a fraud on the part of Sir John Harrington, became, when under the influence of true religion, and especially through a sermon of Bp Latimer's (see Bradford, Vol. I. p. 32), conscience-stricken on account of his own connivance, and that Sir John Harrington was, in the issue, compelled to make restitution to the government. It has been supposed, with much probability, that Bp Latimer, in the remarkable instance of "restitution" recorded in his last sermon before Edward VI. A.D. 1550 (Works of Bp Latimer, Vol. I. p. 262, Park. Soc.), refers to the case of Bradford: see Biographia Britannica, Vol. II. ed. 1748, article, "Bradford."]

[1 'The block of Walsingham:' the famous image of the virgin Mary, at Walsingham, in Norfolk, which had been burnt at Chelsea, in the 30th of Henry VIII. A.D. 1539, and to which until that time constant pilgrimages had been made, even by foreigners. Vide Dugdale's Monasticon, Vol. VI. p. 71, Lond. 1846; Bloomfield's Hist. Norfolk, Vol. V. pp. 835, 840, Lond. 1739—75. See also the description of Walsingham in the "Peregrinatio Religionis ergo" of Erasmus, translated and illustrated by J. G. Nichols, F.S.A., London, 1849.]

[2 Compare Vol. I. p. 421, lines 23, 24.]

towards the ending of it as opportunity shall shew, whether in moving him again (as I would surely wish to do), or labouring to gather of your own for the payment thereof. Do it freely, but do all in the name of the Lord, "in all things giving thanks to God the Father through Jesus Christ:" and the most mighty God move that heart of your master to enrich you to your unburdening, even when his will shall be.

Despair not, though all in haste it be not repaid, as though ye were a man forlorn for that the payment is not made; but rather give thanks to God even heartily, for that he hath opened that fault unto you, and hath given you a conscience in it. For he might have given you up into a lewd mind, which should, nothing regarding it, have still "cried, Peace, peace," until sudden destruction had come. But God of his mercy hath opened it to you, not that ye should delight in it—as, O forgive me, that I do, in commemoration of my iniquity, much more delight than sorrow—but that it should be a school, a cross, a vexation and perturbation of mind unto you; *ita tamen* that ye must be void from that desperate solicitude, and with this, that God hath given you an earnest desire to recompense; which is a great comfort, a signifying that, though ye be a wretch and a sinner, yet God is with you and in you. Who can then harm you?

"But how shall I do, if I die," say you, "this being unpaid?" —I say, God hath given you a desire to pay it, but not a power. Is God so cruel, trow ye, that he will exact of you to do that that is impossible for you to do? Are ye able to pay it? Then pay it. Are ye not able? Have a continual desire, which is to be begged of God, to pay; and in the name of God work so long as ye live, as God shall lead you towards the payment of it. And, if ye die before the satisfaction, yet I think ye shall go without peril; for I believe the sin is forgiven already for Christ's sake.

There remaineth then by the doctor's mind but restitution; and I believe that you have *animum restituendi;* and [he that] earnestly laboureth and followeth upon God's preparation toward the restitution, the same hath made a good restitution, if he die before a full restitution.

But indeed that substance that ye have at that time gathered together must go fully towards it. But what talk ye of death? God is able to make you to make restitution, even to-morrow. Pray continually for his help and ease, to unburden that way which he knoweth to be best for you: and I dare say that for Jesus' sake he will both hear and help you. But pray, not appointing God any time; *sed expecta Dominum donec misereatur tui,* [rather wait on the Lord, until he have mercy upon you,] with full submission, even in a patient faithful mind, to his will.

O how arrogantly take I upon me to babble! but, as I scribble, so do I but partly. Follow not me, Bradf[ord,] follow not me, for I am a very impenitent beast. I tell you of restitution, and am not moved there[at.] O Lord, spare me, give me not up altogether to a lewd impenitent heart, in which I procure heaps of wrath. Lord, help, for Christ's sake help me. All that I do I do it in sin and vain glory: yet shall not the devil let me to write; for out of the wild fig-tree some profit may come; but no thank to the tree but the Creator.

Now foolishly further will I go. I would not offer myself into bondage to that earthly master. Ye know not what bondage meaneth. Be it that I speak but carnally; I speak as I am. I would not but think assuredly that, as God hath given me that grace to knowledge my debt, being free, that the same Lord of his mercy will and is able at ease to work in my freedom the discharge of [my debt.]

II. TO TRAVES.

[The Temple, LONDON, 1548, perhaps early in *March.*]

Foxe, Acts, &c. ed. 1583, p. 1661; and after editions.

Gratia, misericordia, et pax, a Deo Patre nostro et Domino, [*et*] *Jesu Christo Domino nostro:* [Grace, mercy, and peace, from God our Father and Lord, and Jesus Christ our Lord.]

If mine heart were not altogether adamantine, your kind letters to me unkind miser would cause me, from the bottom of the same, to confess mine ingratitude towards you, upon your behalf, anempst[1] me, so much deserved: but, as I am to do, so shew I myself to write; and, as I am unable in the one, so am I foolish in the other. In all those unkindnesses, rudeness, &c., whereof you accuse yourself, I am enforced to acknowledge myself most justly condemned, not so feignedly by me confessed, as most truly by you experienced. In your letters, as in a glass, I may learn by you, in dejecting yourself, to espy my nakedness, which tofore I thought clothed *duplici vestitu,* [with double covering], now only but with fig-

[1 'Anempst' or 'anent': about, concerning.]

leaves hypocritically gilded. Of which dejection, wrought in you by the Holy Ghost, be not proud: for "what have you that ye have not received?" but be thankful to the Lord, not only therefore, but also for those surges which you feel, now through the cares accompanying marriage, now through education and bringing up of your children and family, now through that cross of the common accustomed trade of living: for [*per*] *multas tribulationes oportet ingredi regnum Dei;* "through many tribulations we must enter into the kingdom of heaven:" yea, they be the cognizances of God's election, the letter *Thau*[2], the instruments which work *suspiria æternæ vitæ* [the sighs of eternal life], and therefore to be embraced.

Believe me, it is the most excellent gift of God, a man to deject and humble himself, and to feel the crosses of Christ as crosses. But I, most hypocritical wretch, not worthy that this earth should bear me, am even a going to bed with Jezebel, and such as "commit fornication with her," which [Rev. iii. 20–22.] is *afflictio maxima.* O Lord, help me, and deliver me for Jesu's sake, "anoint mine eyes with ointment that I may see." O give me not over unto a lewd mind and reprobate sense, but awake my sleeping soul that Christ may shine in me.

You know the cross, the fatherly cross, the loving Lord hath laid upon me; but I am little or nothing moved therewith; I work therein (yet not I, but God's Spirit), not of a repentant faithful mind, but, I cannot tell how, of a slothful, blind, retchless intent. O Lord, forgive me for saying so, it is thy gift: forgive me mine unthankfulness for Jesu's sake; and grant me, as herein I blasphemed and dishonested thy holy name, so do thou by thy holy Spirit glorify by me the same. So be it, so be it.

Sithens my coming to London I was with master Latimer,

[2 An allusion to Ezek. ix. 4, "Set a *mark* upon the foreheads of the men that sigh and that cry for all the abominations that be done," the old Samaritan letter "Thau" having been imagined by some church writers to be that "mark" (Heb. תָּו), and either to have indicated, from its supposed shape, the cross of Christ, or, from that letter being the last of its alphabet, the completeness of redemption, or the salvation of those who to the end are faithful. Compare Hieron. Op. Comm. Lib. III. in Ezek. Proph. cap. ix. Tom. V. col. 95, 96, stud. Vallars. Veron. 1734–42. Vide also Poli Synops. in Ezek. ix., and Gibbings on Calfhill's Answ. to Martiall, p. 107, 8, Park. Soc.]

whose counsel is as you shall hear; which I purpose by God's grace to obey (if it be thy will, O Lord, *fiat*). He willed me, as I have done, to write to my master, who is in the country, and to shew him that if within a certain time, which I appointed, fourteen days, he do not go about to make restitution, that I will submit myself to my lord protector and the king's majesty's council, to confess the fault and ask pardon. This life is uncertain and frail; and, when time is, it must not be deferred. And "what should it profit me to win the whole world, and to lose my own soul?" If, as I justly have deserved, I be put to death for it, God's will be done: at the least, slander, reproach, rebuke, loss of worldly friends, loss of living, &c., shall ensue. What then? Lord, "thy will be done," thine I am: if death come, welcome be it; if slander, &c., even as thou wilt, Lord, so be it. Only grant me a penitent, loving, obedient heart, and of mere love to go forwards herein and not to shrink, to stand and not to fall, that thy name only be praised herein. Amen.

Pray, pray for me, cry for me; and, when you shall hear anything, comfort my mother; to whom, for that this bringer hath not given me an hour's warning of his departure, I have not only written nothing, but also have thus prattled to you, who—as no man else would—I think you will bear with me. For, as God knoweth, to whose grace I commit you and your bed-fellow, with all your children and family, the shortness of time, and this said bringer's importance[1] is only the let I neither send you spectacles, the price of the Paraphrases[2], nor thanks for your cheese; as by the next that cometh I will, God willing, send the premises to you, and a goodly Testament for sir Thomas Hall, which is at the binding. But be not acknown[3] that I have now written to you, for so I have prayed this bringer.

God be with us; and pray for me; and abhor not my rude scribbling, which, if it were as well written as it is meant, would deserve pardon. Thus make I an end, imputing to the hastiness of this bringer all blame which you may lay unto me.

[[1] "Importance:" importunity.]

[[2] Erasmus's Paraphr. on the New Test., in English, Vol. I., had been printed by Whitchurch, Jan. 31, 1548. See Herbert, Typogr. Antiq. Vol. I. p. 544.]

[[3] "Be not acknown:" let it not be known.]

From the Temple, this Sunday, immediately after master Latimer's famous sermon, which this bringer, as he saith, did hear.

By your poorest friend,

JOHN BRADFORD.

It shall not be long, God willing, but you shall both have and hear from me. Keep with you Melancthon's Common Places, for I have another.

III. TO THOMAS HALL[4].

[London, *March* 20, 1548.]

The grace of God, our most merciful Father, keep your mind and soul in Christ Jesu, who alone is our full sufficient Saviour; for in him we be complete, being made, through his death and one only oblation made and offered by himself upon the cross, the children of God, and fellow-heirs with him of the celestial kingdom, which is the free gift of God, and cometh not of merits, but of the mere grace of God, given to none that putteth any manner of hope or trust in any other thing visible or invisible, than in that oblation of sweet savour which Christ himself did offer upon Good Friday, as we call it: which oblation is alway recent and new in the sight of God the Father, and maketh intercession for us—us I mean, which think that only sacrifice then offered to be sufficient, as it is, hath been, and ever shall be, for all the faithful: by the which sacrifice, if we believe, we have free pardon of all our sins. To him therefore, which was both the Offerer and offering, be all honour and praise, with the Father and the Holy Ghost, blessed for ever. Amen.

Foxe, Acts, &c., ed. 1583, p. 1660; and after editions.

Sir Thomas, the occasion of this my long silence mine old friend John Traves shall declare unto you, upon the knowledge whereof I doubt not of your pardon. I have sent unto you an English and a Latin Testament, both in one print and volume, the which, though it be not so beautiful without as I could have sent you, yet no less beautiful within, and more I think for

[[4] The inscription in Foxe, Acts, &c. p. 1660, ed. 1583, is: "Another letter of master Bradford to sir Thomas Hall and father Traves of Blakeley." Thomas Hall was a priest, whence the prefix, "sir." See Vol. I. p. 589, note E.]

your profit and better for your eyes—your eyes I mean of the body, for undoubtedly it giveth light unto the soul if she be not dead:—whereof take this for an argument and a true proof. If your soul be not delighted in it, if your soul do not hunger for it (I mean not the book, but the doctrine in the book), surely your soul is sore sick; for, as the body abhorring meat is not well, even so must the soul be, for other meat hath she none. Christ, whom you must believe afore all men, affirmeth this to be true, in the fourth of Matthew: "Not only in bread, but in every word of God, the soul doth live."

Mark well, he saith not one or two words, as an epistle or a gospel, but he saith, "every word." Take heed: believe
John viii. Christ better than any man, be he never so holy; for "he that is of God heareth the word of God." Will you have a more plain badge, whether you are the elect child of God or no, than this text? Christ saith, "He that is of God heareth the word of God:" but other word of God have we none than in the canon of the Bible; and "all things written therein are written for our learning," saith Paul, whereby he proveth—seeing that it is a learning, yea, our learning—that we must learn it.

Therefore woe be to all them which either persuade men that there is other doctrine of like authority, or that dissuade men from embracing this word, this word of God, or that think this word, especially the New Testament, is not above all other to be loved, to be read, to be chewed. This is the precious stone which, in the gospel, Christ saith, "when a man hath found, he selleth all that ever he hath, and buyeth it."

Mark now, how necessary and precious Christ maketh that which great learned men—nay, devils, but no men—think not necessary: God help them. Christ bade his disciples sell their coats, and buy a sword; which is none other thing than "the word of God;" for so St Paul calleth it, "the sword of the Spirit." "Nay," say our great learned men—(I lie, they have said so, now they are ashamed)—"fetch fire, and burn it."

This I say, sir Thomas, to the intent no ungodly hypocrite should persuade you or dissuade you from reading the holy word of God, the gospel of Jesus Christ. Follow you St Paul's lesson: "Attend reading," and "the word of God dwell in you." How much? "Plentifully," saith he; and to what end? To "feed the flock of Christ, even as much as in you is," saith Peter, not once a year or once a quarter, as a strawberry[1], but "so much as in you is."

This word of God trieth all doctrine; for we ought to have our consciences charged with nothing as touching religion, except the word of God, in the canon of the Bible, set it out; I mean not only in allegories, but even in plain words; for "no other foundation can any man lay, besides that which is laid." St Paul saith, the groundwork is laid already: even so saith he to the Ephesians: "We be his workmanship to do good works, which God hath create that we should walk in them." He saith, they were not to be made, but they are made already. What shall we think then? in such works as man's wit hath founded, which yet seem most holy? Let God's word be judge. Read the same diligently and reverently with prayer (I mean not Latin service, not understood, but with true hearty prayer): and mark what the law requireth, even that which we cannot give, the whole heart, and more if it were possible—but to this end, that we, seeing our abominable uncleanness and inability, might despair in ourselves, trembling at the justice of God, and his anger which we continually procure, and so amplect[2] Christ, in whom God the Father is "well pleased." Which "Christ is the end of the law" to "justify all that believe" and continue not in their popish ignorance, justifying themselves, and treading Christ's blood under their feet, "denying the Lord that bought them."

All such, be they never so well learned, never so holy, be nothing but hypocrites and plain antichrists, which may not abide the sword of God's mouth; for the trumpets of the army (I mean still God's word) when they blow, the high walls of Jericho, the figure of hypocrisy, falleth down. Embrace therefore God's holy word, and be not only a reader, "but a doer;" for your calling requireth you to be apt to teach such proud, hypocritical, arrogant babblers as I am now, which, if I may use this term, defile[3] God's word, God forgive me: and pray you for me, and give God thanks for me, that spareth me thus Lucifer-like, not of a true zeal, but of a foolish bragging, [Rev. i. 16; xix. 15.]

[1 Compare Bp Latimer's Sermon of the Plough, preached January 18, 1548, Works of Bp Latimer, Vol. I. p. 62, and note 1, Park. Soc.]

[2 "Amplect:" embrace.]

[3 The word in the original is changed.]

which prate of God's holy word: I wot not what I do to confess it, so it is. I have sent to you other books which I pray you read; I have written your name in them.

The Holy Ghost keep you, with your brother George, his wife and children, and with your brother James, &c., sir Laurence[1], &c.

This 20th of March.

A very painted hypocrite,

JOHN BRADFORD,

Yours in Christ for ever.

Pray for me, pray for me, give God thanks for me, and take John Traves' help to read this letter written in haste. If any thing but good be chanced to John Traves, which God forbid, I pray you burn my letters out of hand.

IV. TO TRAVES.

[THE TEMPLE, LONDON, *March* 22, 1548.]

Foxe, Acts, &c., ed. 1583, p. 1661; and after editions.

GRACE, mercy, and peace from God the Father, through our Lord Jesus Christ, with increase of all manner godly knowledge and living, be with you and all your household, now and ever. Amen.

To excuse this my long silence, within five or six days after my like foolish letters written to you by John Mosse, it pleased God to send my master hither to London; whom, as I lately tofore had advertised by letters, I moved, you know wherein, and prayed him to discharge the same, or else I would submit myself. &c. Whereunto he answered that, if the books would declare it, he would satisfy. &c. The books I shewed, whereupon he promised as much as I could ask.

But being herein something more moved than he had cause (God be praised therefore, which of his mere good pleasure wrought it), at times, as I could, I desired to know how and in what time he would discharge us both. He, thinking me to be over curious herein, was not therewith contented; and, hear-

[[1] Laurence Hall, it appears from the MS. visitation book of Bishop Bird (see p. 1, note 3, above,) was priest of Oldham near Manchester.]

ing me to allege the uncertainty of time and the fear of God's justice (which, O gracious Lord, grant me to feel indeed as much as thou knowest good for me), he answered me to be scrupulous and of a superstitious conscience, for *animalis homo non percipit ea quæ sunt Dei*, ["the natural man understandeth not the things which are of God,"] and plainly said further, that I should not know, nor by these words have his head so under my girdle. And, when I shewed him that—God witnessed with me—I went about no such thing, he said that there was no godly conscience, seeing he promised afore the face of God to discharge me and to pay the thing, but it ought so to be quieted. And thus at divers and sundry times, moving eftsoons to know of him the way and time of discharging the debt, and having none other answers than tofore, I doubting worldly wisdom, which useth delays, to reign in him with this mammon (the which, O merciful God, eradicate out of his heart, mind, and all others), I was something more sharp and told him (*non ego tamen, sed gratia tua, Domine*) I would "obey God more than man:" the which he lightly regarding as seemed, I departed and went to master Latimer, to have had him to have brought me to my lord protector, whose grace then was purposed shortly to take his journey to visit the ports. Master Latimer, I say, willed me to stay until his return, which will be not long tofore Easter.

In this mean time I bade my bedfellow, my master's son, whom my master had used as his instrument to move me carnally—(for my master discharged him of his exhibition, telling him that he could not be able to keep either house or child, for I purposed to undo both him and all his—untruly, thou knowest, good Lord—and bade him to take that as a warning, that both he and his brethren should provide for themselves as they could)—I bade, I say, my said bedfellow to shew my master, as of himself, my further purpose: which thing, when he knew, so moved and feared him, that he began something to relent, and then made fair promises, that, look what I would devise, that would he do. I devised, but my devices pleased him not.

And thus, but not vainly I trust, as I now do with you (but I know your gentleness, which ever hath borne with me), I spended the time in which I have been silent to write, nay, babble to you; and he, departing out of London tofore I knew, did send me word by another of his said sons, not so given to the gospel and a life according as my bedfellow, and therefore more to be suspected—(for though *pietas non est suspiciosa*, as I should think myself rather *impius*, yet Christ bade us to be *prudentes sicut serpentes*,)—this other brother, I say, told me that my master would do all things, only his fame and ability preserved. *Et quid prodest totum mundum lucrari, animæ vero jacturam facere?* ["And what profit is it to gain the whole world, but to lose the soul?"] And with the said brother my master sent me a little billet also, wherein he confessed that he was contented within twelve months to deliver to my hands the whole money: which bill I, thinking not so good as it might have been, have devised another, and have sent it down to him in the country, with request that he will seal and sign it (for thus master Latimer thinketh sufficient): but as yet I hear not of it, doubting worldly wisdom—which was the whore that overcame Sampson, that moved David to slay Urias, that brought wise Solomon to idolatry, that crucified Christ, the which moved me to perpetrate *hoc facinus*, the which worketh in my master's heart, having higher place there than *timor Domini* (what say I, "there?" yea, yea, with me it "sitteth in the holy place;" the Lord deliver us)—doubting, I say, worldly wisdom, I remain in that same state now for this matter, though in worse for my soul (which is more [to be] lamented; pray therefore, I beseech you, pray with me and for me, that I may do so earnestly) than I was in at my last writing unto you. And, as I then was purposed, so I doubt not (grant it, Lord) but that I shall persevere, if in the mean season I shall not hear from my master accordingly.

Thus I have, like myself, foolishly but truly, declared unto you in many babbling words (which wit, if I had it, would have shortly and briefly comprehended), arrogant, unthankful wretch, my working, nay, God's working[1] in this matter, which is and was the only cause, as I now do, I troubled you not afore, to the intent I might advertise you some certainty in this thing. And, though silence had been much better than this foolish prating, yet your fatherly kindness ever towards me, in expecting from you a correction, as I have herein given cause, may, though

[[1] The words, "nay, God's working" appear in the original edition, by an evident misprint, between "arrogant" and "unthankful."]

not to you, yet to me be profitable. In hope whereof I proceed in requiring you to continue your remembrance of me, a most unkind wretch to God and you, in your prayers with the almighty merciful Lord, that I may more regard his will and pleasure herein, than all honour or shame in this life.

But I must confess unto you that my working in this matter is not of love, as I should do, nor of fear of God's justice: mine unthankfulness, mine unthankfulness, if nothing else were, hath not only deserved it, but doth deserve more than everlasting damnation: O Lord, be merciful to me, I do not so repent it as I should do.—Why say I "so?" as though this "so" were any thing? O hypocritical wretch that I am! Alas! father Traves (let me so call upon you), I am hardhearted: there was never any so obstinate, so unkind, against so loving, so merciful, so gracious, so good, so beneficial a Lord, yea, a Father, as I wretch and most miserable sinner am. This I speak, but not of humility, but of hypocrisy, yet I speak truly. I pray thee, good Father, for Christ's sake, I may think it truly, as I write it even of arrogancy: so it is; therefore pray and cry for me.

Here be such goodly, godly, and learned sermons, which these uncircumcised ears of mine heareth at the least thrice a week, which were able (the great loving mercy of God, offered to me in them, I mean) to burst any man's heart, to relent, to repent, to believe, to love and to fear that omnipotent gracious Lord, but my adamantine, obstinate, most unkind, ingrate, unthankful heart—hearing my Lord, which is Lord over all lords, so graciously, so lovingly, vouchsafe by so many his instruments to speak, to call, to cry unto me, now by his law, now by his threats, now by his gospel, now by his promises, now by all his creatures, to come, to come even to himself: but I hide me with Adam in the garden, I play not only Samuel running to Eli, but I play Jonas running to the sea, and there I sleep upon the hatches, tumbling in Jezebel's bed, *quod est afflictio maxima*, [Rev. iii. 20–22.] until it please God to "anoint mine eyes" *collyrio* ["with eye-salve"], until it please him to raise up a tempest, to turn and look upon me, as Luke saith he did on Peter. For, O Lord, it is thy gift, and cometh of thee and of thy mere grace, it cometh not of man, it cometh not of works, to repent, to believe, to fear, and to love. Work thou therefore in me, for Jesus Christ's sake, which am thy creature and most unthankful hypocritical servant, not when I will, nor as I will, but when thou wilt, even that which may be most to the glory of thy name. Amen.

What should I write? Nay, why do I not pluck these same words and paper in pieces? for I write altogether of hypocrisy and arrogant presumption: I will confess it (thou wicked spirit, the Lord judge thee), I will confess it, it is most true, John Traves, I write it but only, for it is not I, it is hypocrisy. *Scientia*, if I had it, *inflaret*, [knowledge would puff up]. O Lord, grant me thy grace, and leave me not to mine own judgment and reason. Hypocrisy, arrogancy, and obstinate security environ me, yet I feel them not, the Lord deliver me. Pray, pray for me, give God thanks for me. O Lord, even *tua fiat voluntas*, [thy will be done,] unlock this mine heart, thou "which hast the key of David, which openest" only, that I may desire to have the desire of the glory of thy name, of repentance, faith, &c. Pray for me, and be thankful for me, O father Traves, and write to me. Your letters I desire more to see than any man's living. Let me have them therefore, as you may, but your prayer at all times, that God would open mine heart to feed and taste of these comfortable places of scripture, which to me are locked. *Memento Jesum Christum resurrexisse ex mortuis:* ["Remember that Jesus Christ has risen from the dead."] This text as a text of most comfort, as it is indeed (and when God will I shall feed on it), did Paul send to Timothy to be his comfort in all places: "for our salvation"—this day of resurrection—"is nearer now than when we believed." Therefore *qui perseveraverit salvus erit*, ["he who shall have endured shall be saved."] For *consummabitur prævaricatio*, ["the transgression shall be finished,"] saith Daniel; *finem accipiet peccatum, delebitur iniquitas, et adducetur justitia sempiterna. Deus enim ipse veniet et salvabit nos. Veniens veniet, et non tardabit; et quandocumque manifestatus fuerit vita nostra Christus, tunc et nos manifestabimur cum illo in gloria. Semel enim oblatus est ut multorum peccata tolleret: rursus absque peccato conspicietur iis qui illum expectant in salutem. Sic semper cum Domino erimus. Proinde consolemini vos invicem mutuo sermonibus his.* ["Sin shall receive an end, iniquity shall be blotted out, and everlasting righteousness brought in." For "God himself shall come and save us. He who is coming shall come, and shall not delay:" "and, whenever Christ our life shall be manifested, then shall we also be manifested with him in glory." "For he has been once offered, to take away the sins of many: again shall he be seen without sin by those who look for him unto salvation." "So shall we for ever be with the Lord." "Wherefore comfort one another mutually with these sayings."]

O Lord, open mine eyes which see nothing of the great comforts in these thy most rich words; open mine eyes, good Lord, *ne nunquam obdormiam in morte*, [lest I ever fall asleep in death.] Pray for me, and commend me to your good bedfellow, *et omnibus in Christo fratribus, osculo sancto*, [and to all the brethren in Christ, with a holy kiss.]

Thus I make an end (for it is time, you may say), and I pray you still water sir Thomas Hall, unto whom I have sent a fair Testament, both in English and Latin, if this bringer will carry it. And I have herewith sent you a letter, which first peruse and read; and, when you have so done, abhor not me but my wickedness, and pray for me. And, as you can see a meet time, seal it and deliver it to sir Nicholas Worsyncroft[1], by such policy as you can think, by God's grace, through prayer. I confess unto you, God is my witness, to my knowledge I never in my being in the country this winter at any time called it to remembrance, the Lord forgive me. I would by some occasion, if any could be had afore the delivery of the letter, by some story or communication, that he did know that abomination to be sin, for I fear me he thinketh it to be no sin. The Lord open our eyes, and forgive us. Amen.

The peace of God be with you. Amen.

From the Temple, this 22d of March 1547[—8.]

Yours in Christ most bounden,

JOHN BRADFORD.

I have sent you three pair of good spectacles I trow, and other such books as have your name written in them; which take in good worth, and pray for me, and give thanks for me.

[1 The name "Worsyncroft" is supplied from the MS. visitation book of bishop Bird. See p. 1, note 3, above, as also Letter V. The printed edition of 1583 reads "Wolstoncros."]

V. TRAVES TO BRADFORD[1].

[BLACKLEY, near Manchester, early in *April*, 1548.]

MS. Harl. 416. no. 23. fol. 34. reverse. British Museum.

YOUR letters, no less loving, kind, true and faithful, than full of eloquence and learning, written to me the twenty-second of March, on Thursday in the Easter week, I did receive.

And, as concerning the letter written to sir Nicholas Worsyn-[croft,] I did never read one word of it. I could not come by to receive, no, not to see, neither book nor letter—yet the books had been seen, and the seals of the letters broken, afore they came to my hands—until such time as sir Thomas Hall might be at leisure to be present with me. On Thursday in the Easter week I was bidden that I should meet sir Thomas Hall at your mother's, there to receive letters and books from John Bradford. There I received a book, called "The true difference between the regal power and the ecclesiastical power[2]," another to sir Thomas Hall and me, called "A godly and wholesome preservative against desperation[3]," with your letters (the seal of the which had been broken) sent to me. Whiles I was in reading the letter sent to me, sir Th. H. did take the letter written to sir Nicholas Worsyn[croft]—(I never looked within it)—and delivered it unto him. And for because ye would that I should have perused it, &c., if it please you to take so much pain as to write the principal effect (which thing I would gladly ye would do), ye may. If not, let the matter pass: but in anywise ye shall neither accuse sir Th. H., nor your mother, nor yet any other person, of breaking the seals; for ye in so doing might be an occasion of discord and hate (*quod absit*) betwixt your mother and me.

And, as concerning your Testament and a little book or two (one to both him and me), he had received [them] afore I received your letters. And, where ye did write to me that I should still water sir T. H., I cannot so do: but he must water him *qui dat*

[1 This letter is now printed for the first time.
The original is without any title or inscription.]

[2 The "Opus eximium de vera differentia regiæ potestatis et ecclesiasticæ, et quæ sit ipsa veritas et virtus utriusque," written in Latin by Edward Fox, bishop of Hereford, and printed by Berthelet, 1534, 1538, and 1544, was translated into English, and dedicated to the duke of Somerset, by Henry lord Stafford, and printed by Copland, 1548, and in an edition without date. See Herbert, Typograph. Antiq., Vol. I. pp. 354, 362, 424, Lond. 1785-90.]

[3 "A godly and wholesome preservative against desperation, at all times necessary for the soul, but then chiefly to be used and ministered when the devil doth assault us most fiercely, and death approacheth nighest. Be sober, and watch—resist stedfast in the faith. 1 Pet. 5." 1551, printed by Copland for Kele Id. ibid. p. 355.]

incrementum, ["who giveth the increase."] He was never at my house since your departure out of Manchester but thrice: at all which times he desired for no further knowledge [than] the order of the table in the New Testament, how to find the epistles and gospels on the Sundays and other holydays: but in anywise ye shall not accuse him of this thing, for ye in so doing might make discord and emulation betwixt him and me.

And, as concerning your business, ah, alas! I know not what I should either say or write. I am one member, although unprofitable to the whole body, even as ye be another. Therefore, *sive patitur unum membrum, simul patiuntur omnia membra; sive glorificatur unum membrum, simul gaudent omnia membra:* ["whether one member suffereth, all the members suffer with it; or one member is glorified, all the members rejoice with it."] O when shall that day come that I shall have your letters, wherein ye shall write that ye have absolutely and consummately finished (your master's consciences and yours fully discharged) your business most weighty! And, unto that day or time be comen, if I be a natural member to the whole body, I can never be pacified nor quite quieted within myself.

VI. TO TRAVES.

[The Temple, LONDON, *May* 12, 1548.]

GRATIA, misericordia, et pax, [Grace, mercy, and peace,] &c. Foxe, Acts, &c., ed. 1583, p. 1662; and after editions.

My chance is not by this bringer to have any warning in manner of his farewell, so that I am constrained, time coarcting[4] me, to write not so much of things (which I will omit) as my desire was. Concerning the great matter you know of, it hath pleased God to bring it to this end, that I have a bill of my master's hand, wherein he is bound to pay the sum afore Candlemas next coming. This thinks Master Latimer to be sufficient. Therefore I pray you to give that gracious Lord thanks, and thanks, and thanks upon it, for me a most wretched ingrate sinner, which have also in other things no less cause to praise God's name, as for that I have and sustain my master's sore displeasure; the which hath brought me—God, I should say, through it—unto a more contempt of worldly things, through the sequestration of such his busi-

[4 "Coarcting": straitening.]

ness as tofore I had ado withal. I call it a "contempt:" well, take the word even as it is hypocritically and vain-gloriously spoken: for the which fault, amongst my others innumerable, I trust you remember in your prayers, whereof I have, I would I knew how much, need.

There is yet another thing whereof I will advertise you, even to this end, that you might pray, if it be God's will, that, as I trust shortly to begin, so he may vouchsafe to confirm that he hath begun; as, if I be not deceived, I believe it is his working. If the thing seem by God's Spirit in you that I presume, then, for the Lord's sake, advertise me; for I am much given to that disease, the Lord deliver me. I have moved my master therein already by letters, to see if I shall have any living of him as hitherto I have had; but I have thereof no answer, nor, as our natural speech is, any likelihood of any grant. Yet that I have already, I trust, [will] be able for me for three years: you look what my purpose meaneth, I am so long afore I come to it. Therefore I do it, because my long babbling should be less tedious. Now shall you have it. If God's will be (whereunto pray I may be obedient), I am minded afore midsummer to leave London to go to my books at Cambridge, and, if God shall give me grace, to be a minister of his word. Thus you have of a fly an elephant. Well, take it in good part, though you see my *etiam, non,* ["yea, nay,"] and not *etiam, etiam.* ["yea, yea."]

A tumbling stone gathereth no moss: so therefore pray for me. Perchance I do foolishly to forsake so good a living as I have. I will say no more hereof, but pray for me. I trust, as I said, for three years' study I have sufficient, if my master take all from me; and when this is spent, God will send more. I do not write this that you should think me to be in need of worldly help, and therefore, as friars were wont, secretly to beg. No, in the Lord's name I require you not to take it so; for I had rather never send letter, afore I should be herein a cross to you, for *sufficit sua diei afflictio,* ["sufficient to a day is its own trouble:"] we "are more set by than many sparrows."

But if my mother or sir Thomas Hall murmur at it, or be offended with me, as you can, remedy it with your counsel.

Howbeit, as yet I will not write to them of it, until such time as I be going. I am something fickle-minded and inconstant, therefore pray for me, that my "hand being put to the plough"—presumptuously spoken!—I "look not back." You may gather by my words in this letter the Herodical heart which lieth in me.

I have sent you a book of Bucer against Winchester[1], in English, lately translated, which I never read: therefore I cannot praise it. And, as I call to remembrance, I did send you with the other books more than you received: at the least one of them I remember which is called, "The Common Places, or the Declaration of the faith, by Urbanus Regius[2]:" ask for it, or send me word in whom the default is, you have it not. Hereafter, and that shortly by God's grace, I will send you *primitiæ laborum meorum*, [the first fruit of my labours;] a work or two which I have translated into English[3], so soon as they be printed, which will be afore Whitsuntide[4].

Pray for me, good father Traves; and God send you health of soul and body, as I would mine own or any man's living. But yet to warn you of that you know not, in writing your letters to me, you hit me home, and give me that I look for. You are deceived, and so is all that knoweth me. I never came to any point of mortification: therefore a little tickling sets me afloat: God help me, and give God thanks for me, as all men be most bounden. Thus when I once begin to write to you, I run, as the priest saith matins, for I think I may be bold on you.

[[1] "The gratulation of the most famous clerk, Master Martin Bucer, and his answer unto the two railing epistles of Stephen, bishop of Winchester, concerning the unmarried state of priests and cloisterers...translated out of Latin into English." London, R. Jugge, no date. See Herbert, Typogr. Antiq. Vol. II. p. 726.]

[[2] "A declaration of the twelve articles of the Christian faith, with annotations of the holy Scripture, where they be grounded in. And the right foundation and principal Common-places of the holy, godly Scripture, a godly short Declaration, to all Christians profitable and necessary for to come to the right understanding of holy Scripture, compiled, for the commodity of all Christian people, by D. Urbanum Regium." London, printed by Jugge for Lynne, 1548. Copy, the editor.]

[[3] The Common-places of Artopœus, and Two Homilies on prayer by Chrysostom, were translated by Bradford, and printed in one volume by Lynne, 1548. See title of that publication, and editorial preface, Vol. I. pp. 2, 3.]

[[4] Bradford's preface to the translation from Chrysostom is dated, May 16, 1548; and Whitsunday in that year fell on May 20. See Vol. I. p. 15, and p. 3, note 2.]

The Holy Ghost preserve you, your wife, and family, and persevere his grace in you unto the end. I pray you pray for me, a most (what should I call me?) miserable and blasphemous sinner. The peace of God be with us.

From the Temple, this 12th of May, 1548.

Sir Thomas Hall hath deceived me, but himself most. I desire to speak with him, as this winter it may chance, if I discharge not myself of mine office, to see him. Pray for him and for me.

A very hypocrite,

JOHN BRADFORD.

VII. TO TRAVES.

[LONDON, end of *May* or beginning of *June*, 1548 [1].]

Foxe, Acts, &c., ed. 1583, p. 1663; and after editions.

THE perseverance of God's grace, with the knowledge of his good-will, increase with you unto the end.

To declare myself, as I am a carnal man, which understandeth not the things that be of the Spirit, these my letters, though I counterfeit and meddle amongst them the spiritual words, as the devil did in his temptations to Christ, will declare no less. For I begin with carnal things in effect, and no marvel if I so end: for how can a "man gather figs of briers?" These words, as they seem, so they are spoken for a cloak to make you think otherwise: but, father Traves, you cannot think so evil of me as I am.

[Now] to the matter. This present day, by God's grace, I take my journey towards Cambridge, where, I pray God, and so earnestly pray you to pray for me, that I may circumspectly redeem this time which God hath appointed, to me unknown, to lend me: for, alas! I have spent most wickedly the time past, for the which I must account even for every hair-breadth as they say; for God hath not given here time to sin.

But if I considered this, as I do nothing less (custom of sin and pleasing myself hath so hardened my heart), I should then come to the feeling of myself, then should I hate sin which I now love, then should I fear God's wrath, which I now con-

[[1] From the allusions to the "journey towards Cambridge," and to the publication of the translations from Artopœus and Chrysostom.]

temn, then should I cry out and weep, and continually pray; as now I am as dry as a stone, as dumb as a nail, as far from praying as he that never knew any taste of it: which thing once I felt (thanks to the Lord), but now for mine unthankfulness I am almost, but most worthily, deprived. I fear me, God will take his grace from me, I am so unthankful. Alas! why do I lie in saying I fear me? Nay, God grant I may do so, for then should I pray and pray: but, seeing I cannot, speak you for me, pray for me, that the Lord would remember his old compassions towards me, for his mercies' sake draw me, yea, compel me to serve, to fear, and to love him. Thus may you see how I presume; for mine intent was to have been a minister of God's word, to have been his instrument to call from as I have called to sin: but you see how that God punisheth mine arrogancy.

Alas, what shall I do? I am an unprofitable and an idle member: I thought I should have been therein profitable; but, *Medice, cura teipsum:* ["Physician, heal thyself."] How should I, or what should I do? I cannot labour with my hands. Well, I trust God will give me grace and knowledge to translate something[2]. I fear me, yea, I distrust me, that I shall never be minister of God's word: yea, if arrogancy were not in me, how should I, of all wretches the greatest, think me to look to the highest room and vocation that is upon earth? Therefore eftsoons I desire you to pray for me, that God's will may be done in me whether I live or die, so that his name be honoured.

My master which was hath denied me all his beneficence; but I have for this life more than enough, thanks be to God, as this winter I intend by God's favour to declare more unto you.

This book which I have sent take it in good part: it is the first, I trust it shall not be the last, God hath appointed me to translate. The print is very false, I am sorry for it. I pray you be not offended at my babbling in the prologues, &c.

JOHN BRADFORD.

I will lie, God willing, this summer, at Catharine's Hall in Cambridge. Write to me.

[[2] "Nothing," orig. edit., apparently a misprint for "something."]

VIII. TO TRAVES.

[Catharine Hall, CAMBRIDGE, *August* 15, 1548.]

Foxe, Acts, &c., ed. 1583, p. 1663; and after editions.

THE loving-kindness and abundant mercy of God the Father, poured plentifully upon all the faithful, in the blood of that meek Lamb Jesus Christ, our only satisfaction and Mediator, through the working of the most Holy Spirit, be increased and perceived in you daily more and more, to the glory of God. &c.

Because I stand both in doubt of the reading and delivery of such letters as I write and send unto you, dearly beloved father Traves, I am constrained to leave off such griefs and spiritual wants as, thanks unto the Lord, I unwillingly feel; for the flesh, as you know, loveth nothing so much as security, of all enemies most perilous, and not a little familiar with me: from the which, with vain glory, hypocrisy, &c., and worldliness, the Lord deliver me.

I had not thought to have written thus much, but these I cannot keep, but commit them to your prayers. And to the intent I would you should not think any ingratitude in me, as also that I might give you occasion to write to me again, as heretofore I have done, even so do I interturb and trouble you with my babbling, but yet having this commodity, that I babble not so much as I was wont to do. The cause I have declared, which had almost been the cause I had not written at all. I did write unto you from London when I came hither: send me word what letters you have received, for from you I have received but two, and both by John Mosse, and in the latter I perceived that the Lord had visited you with sickness, his fatherly rod, whereby he declareth his love upon you, and that "he careth for you;" *ut in tempore supremo exultes, nunc ad breve tempus afflictus, quo exploratio fidei multo pretiosior auro quod perit et tamen probatur, &c., siquidem in hoc vocatus es, ut cum Christo patiaris, nam et cum illo glorificaberis. Certus enim sermo est, si sufferimus, et conregnabimus:* [" that you may rejoice in the last time, being now afflicted for a short time, that the trial of faith being far more precious than gold that perisheth and yet is tried," &c., if so be you have been called to this, "that you should suffer with Christ, for you shall also be glorified with him." For "it is a sure saying, If we suffer, we shall also reign with him."] You know that Christ, *etsi Filius Dei erat, tamen ex his quæ passus est didicit obedientiam. Patientia opus perfectum habeat, ut sitis perfecti et integri, nullaque in parte diminuti:* [" although he was the Son of God, yet learned obedience by the things which he suffered." "Let patience have her perfect work, that ye may be perfect and entire, and coming short in no part."] And doth not *patientia* come of *probatio?* The one then you had, so that you were going a school to learn the other: which learned, what want you?

The end of all God's proving is, as Paul saith, *ut impertiat nobis sanctimoniam. Igitur gratias age Deo Patri, qui idoneum te fecit ad participationem sortis sanctorum in lumine. &c. Nam qui te parumper afflixit, idem instauret te, fulciat, roboret, stabiliat:* [" that he may impart to us holiness." "Therefore render thanks to God the Father, who hath made thee meet to partake of the inheritance of the saints in light." &c. For he who hath "for a little while afflicted, the same restore, support, strengthen, establish thee."] And "the Lord knoweth how" *eripere pios e tribulatione,* ["to snatch the godly out of tribulation,"] and that *in tempore opportuno,* [in a seasonable time,] even shortly; for *haud tardat qui promisit, nam modicum tempus et videbitis me, veniens enim veniet, et non tardabit. Itaque qui consortes estis crucis Christi gaudete:* ["he doth not delay who hath promised, for yet a little while and ye shall see me, for he who is coming will come, and will not delay." "Therefore rejoice ye who partake of the cross of Christ,"] saith Peter, *ut in revelatione quoque gloriæ ejus gaudeatis exultantes:* ["that in the revelation also of his glory ye may rejoice with exceeding joy."]

O how doth my will overrun my wit! Why, Bradford, whom writest thou unto? Thou shewest thyself. Thus, father Traves, you may see my rashness to rabble out the scriptures without purpose, time, or reason. I will not blot it out, as I had thought to have done; for that hereby you shall see my need of your prayer.

Well, I look for a watch-word from you, write for God's sake; and pray for me that I may be in something profitable to the Lord's congregation, that I may be no stumbling-block, *ut non confundantur in me qui illum expectant;* ["that they who look for him may not be confounded in me."] Send me such counsel as the Lord's Spirit shall move you, how to study: my desire is in something to be profitable, if it were the Lord's will; for to be *minister verbi*, alas! I am unmeet, and my time, my time, yea, the Lord's time, I have hitherto evil, yea, most wickedly mispent it. &c.

Thus will I end. The Lord be with you and your bed-fellow, to whom have me heartily commended, and to all your children and family; the which I beseech the Lord to lighten his countenance over, and grant you his peace. Pray for me. I long for winter to speak with you. *Rescribe*, [write again.] *Ora*, pray for me.

This Assumption Day in Catharine's Hall in Cambridge.

Yours with all I have and can,

JOHN BRADFORD.

IX. TO A PERSON OF RANK.[1]

[Probably from Catharine Hall, CAMBRIDGE, *Lent*, 1549.]

MS. Harl. 416. No. 26. fol. 37, reverse. British Museum.

Strype, Ecc. Mem. Mary. Originals, No. 32.

GRACE and virtue from God the Father, through our Lord Jesus Christ, govern our minds, that sin have not the upper hand of virtue in our souls. Amen.

Whereas your mastership hath desired me to have been with you on this present day, which was never in your company, I being also a refuse, an abject, a hireling of this naughty and wretched world, yea, a worse than so, one of the most wretched sinners living—these things considered on the one side, and your humane gentleness on the other—seeing, I say, that I have disobeyed your most gentle request and desire, I am

[[1] This letter might possibly have been addressed either to Sandys (afterward archbishop of York) who was at that time master of Catharine Hall, to which Bradford belonged, or to bishop Ridley, master of Pembroke Hall (see Letter XI.), or to Bucer, then regius professor of divinity at Cambridge (see Vol. I. p. 350, references in note 4), or to some layman of rank or official position.

The superscription, which is over this letter in the Harleian MS., belongs to Letter XIII. of this series: see conclusion of that Letter.]

worthy, if ye should entreat with me according to my deserving, not alonely to go without or want all such ghostly edifying and profit, which I might have had of your mastership, but also to have you from now forth ever to be heavy master to me. But all this notwithstanding I will comfort myself with your gentleness, trusting ye will not take me at the worst. And thus, comforting myself with your gentle humanity, I humbly beseech your mastership that ye will be content this next week, or the Easter week, or any other time at your pleasure. And surely, if ye will appoint no time, I will come afore I be called. I thank you for your book.

X. TO TRAVES.

[Catharine Hall, CAMBRIDGE, *October* 22, 1549.]

THE plentiful grace of God the Father, through our only Master and Lord Jesus Christ, increase in us daily to the glory of his name. Amen.

Foxe, Acts, &c., ed. 1583, p. 1664; and after editions.

Forasmuch as I have often written to you, good father Traves, and yet have not once heard from you sithens Pentecost, I cannot now be so bold either in writing much or often as I would have been: howbeit this I say, that I much marvel that I hear not from you; but not so, for I am so wretched a sinner, that the Lord's Spirit I am certain doth not move you to write to me: yet for God's sake pray for me, and in the Lord's name I desire you give thanks to God for me. And, when it may please God to move you, write to me, though it be but two words, and counsel me how to study "the word of life," the ministry whereof I desire, if it be the Lord's pleasure, to profess: and, that I may do it both in living and learning, pray for me.

Herus meus omnibus rebus suis me abdicavit, et quæ prius concesserat jam solvere renuit, et mihi prorsus factus est inimicus: [My master has in all his affairs disowned me; and he has now refused to pay what he had before allowed; and he has become altogether my enemy.] I know not when I shall see you in body, therefore let me hear from you. I write not this that you should think me *in egestate aut angustiis esse*, [to be in poverty or straits.] No, father, the Lord giveth me *omnia affatim*, [all things in abundance,] and will do. I trust I shall shortly here have a fellowship; I am so promised, and therefore I have taken the degree of Master of Art, which else I could not have attained[1]. If I get a fellowship, I shall not need *de crastino sollicitus esse*, [to be anxious about the morrow,] as hereafter I shall more write to you by God's grace. I pray you write again, and often pray for me.

In haste as appeareth, the 22d of October.

Ne sciat mater mea quod herus meus adeo duriter mecum egit: [Let not my mother be aware that my master has dealt with me so hardly.] &c

Miserrimus peccator,

JOHN BRADFORD.

XI. TO TRAVES.

[Pembroke Hall, CAMBRIDGE, probably early in *November*, 1549.]

Foxe, Acts, &c., ed. 1583 p. 1664; and after editions.

THE peace and plenteous mercy of God our heavenly Father, in his Christ our only Lord and Saviour, be ever increased in you by the Holy Spirit, *qui efficit omnia in omnibus*, ["who worketh all things in all."] Amen.

Father Traves, though I might think myself more happy, if you would often write unto me, yet because I ought to have respect to your pains, which now that old man cannot so well sustain as it might, I had rather lose my happiness in that behalf, than will your grief, forasmuch as it can be no happiness unto me which turneth to your pain: yet, because pain is not painful when it is joined with gain, I therefore desire you for God's sake to pray often for me: for if I shall not be worthy of your prayer, as the Lord who "knoweth all things" doth right well see it, and so my conscience witnesseth, yet your good "prayer shall return into your own bosom." And know this, that "whoso converteth a sinner" by prayer, whether it be by prayer,

[[1] It appears from the Cambridge University MS. Grace Book, fol. 24, that Bradford, "vir constantis jam ætatis et probatæ vitæ," was, on account of his attainments, admitted by a special grace to the degree of M.A., October 19, 1549.]

preaching, or writing letters, &c., "the same hath saved a soul." Use therefore (for God's sake I ask it) that pains whereunto is joined profit—I mean prayer to God for me, a miserable and most wretched sinner: and, as for the gainless pain in writing to me, use it yet as you may; and surely God for whose sake you do it, in that he will reward "a cup of cold water," will in something requite you. And I know certainly that, if you did see what spiritual profit I receive by your letters, I am certain you would not think all your labour lost. For Christ's sake therefore begin again to write unto me, and reprove me sharply for my horrible unthankfulness to God.

You know how that God hath exonerated the loaden conscience of the great weighty burthen (for so I did write to you): yea, the Lord hath in manner unburthened me of the lesser burthen also; for I have an assurance of the payment of the same by Candlemas[2]. Lo, thus you see what a good God the Lord is unto me. O father Traves, give thanks for me, and pray God to forgive me my unthankfulness. But what should I rehearse the benefit of God towards me? Alas! I cannot, I am too little for all his mercies, yea, I am not only unthankful, but I am too far contumelious against God. For where you know the sun, the moon, and the seven stars did forsake me, [Gen. xxxvii. 9.] and would not shine upon me—you know what I mean, *per herum et heriles amicos*, [through my master and my master's friends]—yet the Lord hath given me here in the university as good a living as I would have wished. For I am now a fellow of Pembroke Hall, of the which I nor any other for me did ever make any suit; yea, there was a contention betwixt the master of Catharine's Hall[3], and the bishop of Rochester, who is master of Pembroke Hall[4], whether should have me: *sit hoc tibi dictum*. Thus you may see the Lord's carefulness for me. My fellowship here is worth seven pound a year; for I have allowed me eighteen-pence a week, and as good as thirty-three shillings [and] four pence a year in money, besides my chamber, launder, barber, &c.; and I am bound to nothing but once or twice a year to keep a problem. Thus you see what a good Lord God is unto me.

[2 February 2, 1550.]
[3 Edwin Sandys, afterward Archbp of York.]
[4 Nicholas Ridley, afterward Bp of London.]

But, I pray you, what do I now to God for all this? I will not speak of the great mercies he sheweth upon my soul. Surely, father Traves, I have clean forgotten God, I am all secure, idle, proud, hard-hearted, utterly void of brotherly love; I am envious, and disdain others ; I am a very stark hypocrite, not only in my words and works, but even in these my letters to you ; I am all sensual without the true fear of God, another manner of man than I have been sithens my call. Alas ! father Traves, I write this to put myself in remembrance; but I am without all sense, I do but only write it. For God's sake pray for me, which am only in name a Christian, in very deed a very worldling, and, to say to you the very truth, a most worldling of all other. I pray you, exhort my mother now and then, with my sister Margaret, to fear the Lord: and, if my mother had not sold the fox-fur which was in my father's gown, I would she would send it me: she must have your counsel in a piece of cloth.

Yours for ever,

J. BRADFORD.

XII. TO TRAVES.

[Pembroke Hall, CAMBRIDGE, Sunday, *December* 1, 1549.]

Foxe, Acts, &c., ed. 1583, p. 1659; and after editions.

THE abundant grace and rich mercy of God in Christ, our only Saviour and high Bishop, be increased in your heart through the lively Worker of all goodness, the Holy Spirit, until the day of the Lord. &c.

I have received your two letters, good father Traves, sithen that I did write any unto you, whereof, though [dis]honesty willeth to make an excuse, yet truth biddeth me otherwise, and saith, it is better with shame to confess the fault (for therein is, as a man might say, half a deserving of pardon) than without shame to lie. I might have written unto you twice (notwithstanding indeed some business wherein I have something been occupied), but yet I have not. Now the cause is, because I would not. And why would I not but because I could not? I mean, because my canning is taken away by sin, for my sins do forbid goodness unto me. Indeed, if my sinning were of infirmity, there were good hope of recovery of that which I have lost: but, seeing both willing and knowing I have too much yielded and yet do yield to my infirmities, justly I do deserve that, because I have cast away and "rejected the word of the Lord" behind my back, that "the Lord should reject me:" and, because I "would not have blessing," I am worthy, as David saith, that [Ps. cix. 17.] it be taken away from me.

I have now at length experience, that to bring a man forth of God's favour is sooner seen when a man hath received all things abundantly, than when need or the cross pincheth. Afore it pleased God to work the restitution (you know what I mean), and afore it pleased God to provide for me as he hath done, so that I can say in nothing where any want is as pertaining to my body, I was another manner of man than now I am; and yet God's deserts have otherwise bounden me: but the scripture is true, "I have advanced my children, and [Isai. i. 2.] nourished them, but they have contemned me;" I have fed them that they were "fat and gross, and they spurned against Deut. xxxii. me." Perchance you will ask me, wherein? O father Traves, I warrant you, this my style, in carnal and not in spiritual writing, doth something shew unto you, but as for it in comparison of other things is nothing. For, where the life of man is such that either it paireth[1] or amendeth, as Paul saith, "the outward man is corrupted day by day;" and therefore, except "the inward man be renewed," the shoe goeth awry: every building in Christ doth "grow to a holy temple," as the wicked on the contrary part shall proceed to worser. 2 Tim. iii.

I have made a change far otherwise in going back, than I think by letters I can persuade you. 'Wherein,' will you say? For the first, second and third, and (to be brief) in all things: as for an example, God's true fear is flown away from me, love to my brethren is exiled from me, faith is utterly taken away. Instead whereof is distrust and doubtfulness bearing rule, contempt of God's honour and of my brethren reigning, and, instead of true fear, an imagined fear according to my brain holding the principality. For I extenuate sin, and I do not consider that in sin, which a Christian ought to consider, that sin being not forgiven is such a thing for the which God

[1 "Paireth": impaireth.]

casteth his creature away; as examples not only of Saul, of Judas, of the Israelites (which were beloved indeed, and yet for sin are rejected), but also of others, on whom lately for my warning God hath shewed the same, do admonish me.

But it is but my pen which writes this; for the wicked,
Prov. xviii. [12.] saith Solomon, when they come into the depth of their sins, then they grow in security. I am I cannot tell what: I fear—but it is but blindly, or else would I awake otherwise than I do—I fear me, I say, that I am entangled of the devil, after his
2 Tim. ii. desire. Pray for me that the Lord would "give me repentance, that I may escape out of his snares." Alas! "the Spirit of prayer," which before I have felt plentifully, is taken clean away from me: the Lord be merciful unto me. "I am sold under sin," I am the bond-slave of sin; for "whom I obey, his servant I am." I am ashamed to speak oft—no, I shame not at all; for I have forgot to blush, I have given over to weep. And truly I obey—I obey, I say, mine own concupiscences—namely in eating, in drinking, in jangling and idleness: I will not speak of vain glory, envy, disdain, hypocrisy, desire of estimation, self-love; and who can tell all?

Is this the reward thou renderest to God, O Bradford? It is true, yea, too true: thou knowest it, O Lord: for thy mercy's sake pardon me. In your letters you touch me home, how that there is no man's heart, but that considering the ingratitude of this world, this belly-cheer (wherein you even take me by the nose), &c., his eyes would tumble out great gushes of tears. The Lord be praised which worketh so in you, for it is with me as with them of whom you complain. Indeed it may be so again, but, oh! it is very unlikely; for my enemies are become old, and are made by custom more than familiar, for they are as it were converted into nature in me. Yet I am not grieved therefore, although I cannot persuade myself that God will help me. O Lord, be merciful unto me for thy Christ's sake. This day I received the Lord's supper: but, how I have welcomed him, this night which I have spent in lasciviousness, in wantonness, and in prodigality, obeying my flesh and belly, doth so declare that what to say or write any more I know not; sleep doth aggravate mine eyes, and to pray I am altogether unapt. All this is come through the occasion of making this bringer a supper in my chamber: the Lord pardon me, I trust no more to be so far overseen. But this I write, not that the anger of God, which I have deserved, so feareth me: thou knowest, it O Lord. But of this perchance too much.

For God's sake pray for me, good father Traves, and write unto me as you may by your weakness: your letters do me good. By this which I have now written you may consider more: touch me therefore home in your letters, and the Lord, I trust, shall and will reward you. If God lend me life, of which I am most unworthy, I will more trouble you with my letters than I have done: but bear with me, I do it not of any evil will, the Lord I take to judge: there is none whose company and talk I more desire than yours, I speak it before God.

Prove my mother's mind how she can bear it, if when I shall come down I shall shew myself another man outwardly, but, alas! feignedly, than before I have done. Marry, when my coming will be I know not. Indeed two things move me sore; the one for my mother's cause, concerning her better instruction, if the Lord would thereto use me his instrument; the other is to talk with you, and eftsoons to trouble you, as I have hitherto ever done, but always to my profit. For God's sake pray for me, for I had never so much need.

This Sunday at night, following St Andrew's Day, at Pembroke Hall.

The most miserable, hard-hearted, unthankful sinner,

JOHN BRADFORD.

XIII. TO TRAVES.

[MANCHESTER, probably about Christmas, 1549.]

GRACE and mercy from God the Father, through our Lord Jesus Christ, govern our minds, *ne dominetur in nobis peccatum*, [" that sin may not have dominion in us."] Amen.

MS. Harl. 416. no. 25. fol. 37. Original. Holograph. British Museum.

Yesternight a little before supper, I was desired by a neighbour, my mother's friend, ayenst[1] this day to dinner: unto whom, for that a refusal would have been imputed disdainful stateliness, I unwillingly (God to witness) but not unadvisedly,

Strype, Ecc. Mem. Mary. Originals, No. 31.

[[1] "Ayenst:" an old form of 'against.']

yet foolishly, granted to the same: which I advertise you, as mine excuse of not coming this day. And, for mine absence yesterday, my vain looking for you to have come with your nearest neighbour (the rather for that I heard him commit to you the survey of his will) hath with some repentance deceived me, though to my hurt and loss, yet to your profit which else, by my coming and troubling you, should have been contrary. If you come not to-morrow hither, send me word by this bringer; and if there be no sermon, I will come to you to have your counsel in such things as by letters I will not now write.

In the mean season, in your communication with God, I pray you have me, of all sinners a most negligent, unthankful, and wretched, (O that from the bottom of my heart I confessed the same unfeignedly!) in remembrance; that at length I might truly convert, and return from these greasy flesh-pots of Egypt, to feed with his manna, patiently and assuredly expecting his mercy, joyfully sighing for and bearing the badge of his disciples and servants—the cross I mean—to crucify this Luciferous[1] and gluttonous heart, more than most worthy of
[Luke xvi. Acts xii.] the rich *epulo* [glutton] his unquenchable thirst, and gnawing worms of Herod. This paper, pen and ink, yea, the marblestone, weepeth, to see my slothful security, and unthankful hardness to so merciful and long-suffering a Lord. I confess it, I confess it—though not tremblingly, humbly, or penitently, yet I confess it—oh, hypocritically I confess it!

Therefore pray, pray for me, *ut resipiscam et ad Deum convertar, non contemnens iram ejus et mortem Filii sui Jesu Christi, sed ut Spiritu incedam et Spiritu vivam;* [that I may repent and be turned to God, not despising his anger and the death of his Son Jesus Christ, but that I may "walk in the Spirit, and live in the Spirit,"] evermore to bewail my carnal security, and this *philautiam*, [self-love;] that I may be made "a new creature" through grace, made meet to receive the "new wine" of the gospel into a "new vessel," purified by faith, wrought by "the Spirit of consolation:" which may vouchsafe to "lead us into all truth" and godly living, *ut in ipso cognoscamus Deum Patrem, solum verum Deum, et quem misit Jesum Christum;* [that in him we may

[[1] "Luciferous": Lucifer-like (see p. 9, last line), boastful, proud.]

know God the Father, "the only true God, and Jesus Christ whom he hath sent."] To which most blessed Trinity be all honour and glory for ever. Amen.

From Manchester, in haste, this Thursday in the morning.

Yours as his own,

JOHN BRADFORD.

To my very loving friend, John Traves,
in Blakely.

XIV. TO TRAVES.

[Probably from LONDON, about *February*, 1550.]

Foxe, Acts, &c., ed. 1583, p. 1664; and after editions.

THE self-same mercy, grace, and peace, which heretofore I have felt plenteously—though now, through mine unthankfulness and wilful obedience to the pleasure of this outward man, I neither feel, neither can be persuaded that I possess, yea, if I shall truly write, I in manner pass not upon the same, so far am I fallen, the Lord help me—the same mercy, &c., I say, I wish unto you as I can, with all increase of godliness—hypocritically with my pen and mouth beseeching you, in your earnest prayers to God, to be an earnest suitor unto God for me which am fallen into such a security, and even an hardness of heart, that neither I sorrow my state, neither with any grief or fear of God's abjection[2] do write this: before the Lord, "which knoweth the hearts of all men," I lie not.

Consider for Christ's sake therefore, good father Traves, my necessity, though I myself do it not; and pray for me, that God cast me not off, as I deserve most justly. For where I ought to have well proceeded in God's school, by reason of the time, I confess it to my shame, I am so far gone back, as, alas! if shame were in me, I might be ashamed to write it, but much more to write it and to think it not: such is the reward of unthankfulness. For, where God wrought the restitution of the great thing you know of (the which benefit should bind me to all obedience), alas! father Traves, I am too unthankful, I find no will in heart (though by my writing

[2 'Abjection:' casting away.]

it will be hard to persuade you) either to be thankful, either to begin a new life in all things to mortify this outward man, and heartily to be well content to serve the Lord "in spirit and verity," and withstand mine affections, and especially my beastly sensuality in meat and drink; wherewith I was troubled at my being with you, but now, through my licentious obeying that affect, I am fallen, so that a whole legion of *spirituum malorum* possesseth me.

The Lord, whom I only with mouth, my heart still abiding both in hardness and wilfulness, call upon, deliver me and help me. And for God's sake give you hearty thanks for the great benefit of restitution: pray to the Lord that at the length I may once return to the obedience of his good will. Amen.

I thank you for your cheese, and so doth father Latimer as unknown; for I did give it him, and he saith he did never eat better cheese, and so I dare say he did not. I thank him I am as familiar with him, as with you; yea, God so moveth him against me, that his desire is to have me come and dwell with him whensoever I will, and welcome.

This do I write yet once more, to occasion you to be thankful for me to the Lord, which by all means sheweth nothing but most high love to me, and I again a very obstinate rebellion. Pray therefore for me.

In haste, the sinful

J. BRADFORD.

XV. TO BERNHERE, CARELESS[1], &c.

[Between *July* 19[2] and *August* 16, 1553, probably from LONDON.]

Foxe, Acts, &c., ed. 1563, p. 1184; and after editions.

Bp Coverdale, Letters of the Martyrs, 1564, p. 330.

To my loving brethren, B., C., &c., their wives and whole families, J. Bradford.

I beseech the everliving God to give you all, my good bre-

[1 The Letter being addressed to "B" and "C," in the early printed editions, it seems probable that the names of Bernhere and Careless, who were Bradford's especial friends, may be those intended.]

[2 Queen Mary was proclaimed July 19, 1553, and Bradford was imprisoned August 16 following, to which last event he refers as probable in the fourth paragraph of this letter: "Our bodies are like to be laid in prison." Compare Vol. I. p. 16, note 3, et seq., and pp. 38—42.]

thren and sisters, the comfort of the Holy Spirit, and the continual sense of his mercy in Christ our Lord, now and for ever. Amen.

The world, my brethren, at this present seemeth to have the upper hand, iniquity overfloweth, the truth and verity is seeming to be suppressed, and they which take part therewith are unjustly entreated, as they which love the truth lament to see and hear as they do. The cause of all this is God's anger and mercy: his anger, because we have grievously sinned against him, his mercy, because he here punisheth us, and as a father nurtureth us.

We have been unthankful for his word; we have contemned his kindness; we have been negligent in prayer; we have been too carnal, covetous, licentious, &c.; we have not hastened to heaven-ward, but rather to hell-ward; we were fallen almost into an open contempt of God and all his good ordinances. So that of his justice he could no longer forbear, but make us to[3] feel his anger, as now he hath done, in taking his word and true service from us, and permitted Satan to serve us with antichristian religion, and that in such sort, that if we will not yield to it, and seem to allow it[3] in deed and outward fact, our bodies are like to be laid in prisons, and our goods given, we cannot tell to whom. This should we look upon as a sign of God's anger, procured by our sins; which, my good brethren, every one[3] of us should now call to our memories oftentimes, so particularly as we can, that we might heartily lament them, repent them, hate them, ask earnestly mercy for them, and submit ourselves to bear in this life any kind of punishment, which God will lay upon us for them. This should we do, in consideration of God's anger in this time.

Now his mercy in this time of wrath is seen, and should be seen of us, my dearly beloved, in this, that God doth vouchsafe to punish us in this present life. If he should not have punished us, do not you think that we would have continued in the evils we were in? Yes, verily, we would have been worse, and have gone forwards in hardening our hearts, by impenitency and negligence of God and true godliness: and then, if death had come, should not we have perished, both soul and body, into eternal fire and perdition?

[[3] 'to,' 'it,' 'one,' 1564: not in 1563.]

Alas, what misery should we have fallen into, if God should
have suffered us to have gone on forward in our evils! No
greater a sign of damnation there is, than to live in evil and
sin, unpunished of God; as now the papists, my dearly beloved,
Rev. ii. are cast into Jezebel's bed of security, which of all plagues is
Heb. xii. the most grievous[1] plague that can be. They "are bastards
and not sons," for they are not under God's rod of correction.
A great mercy it is therefore, that God doth punish us; for, if
he loved us not, he would not punish us. Now doth he chastise
1 Cor. xi. us, "that we should not be damned with the world." Now doth
he nurture us, because he favoureth us. Now may we think
1 Pet. iv. ourselves God's household[1] and children, because he beginneth
his chastising at us. Now calleth he us to remember our sins
past. Wherefore? That we might repent, and ask mercy.
And why? That he might forgive us, pardon us, justify us,
Rom. viii. and make us his children, and so begin to make us here like
unto Christ; that we might be like unto him elsewhere, even
in heaven, where already we are set by faith with Christ, and
at his coming, in very deed, shall enjoy his presence[2], when
Phil. iii. our sinful and "vile bodies shall be made like to Christ's glorious body, according to the power whereby he is able to make
all things subject to himself."

Therefore, my brethren, let us in respect hereof not lament
but laud God, not be sorry but be merry, not weep but rejoice
and be glad, that God doth vouchsafe to offer us his cross,
thereby to come to him to endless joys and comforts. For,
Rom. viii. "if we suffer, we shall reign;" if we "confess him before men,
2 Tim. ii. Matt. x. he will confess us before his Father in heaven;" if we be not
ashamed of his gospel now, he will not be ashamed of us in
the last day, but will be glorified in us, crowning us with
Matt v. crowns of glory and endless felicity: for "blessed are they that
suffer persecution for righteousness' sake, for theirs is the king-
1 Pet. iv. dom of heaven." "Be glad," saith Peter, "for the Spirit of
1 Pet. v. God resteth upon you:" "after that you are a little while
afflicted, God will comfort, strengthen, and confirm you." And
therefore, my good brethren, be not discouraged for cross, for
prison or loss of goods for confession of Christ's gospel and

[[1] 'grievousest,' 'house,' 1563: 'most grievous,' 'household,' 1564.]

[[2] 'We shall then most joyfully enjoy,' 1563: 'shall enjoy his presence,' 1564.]

truth, which ye have believed, and lively was taught amongst you, in the days of our late good and most holy prince, king Edward.

This is most certain. If you lose any thing for Christ's sake, and for contemning the antichristian service set up again among us, as you for your parts, even in prison, shall[3] find God's great and rich mercy far passing all worldly wealth, so shall your wives and children, in this present life, find and feel God's providence more plentifully than tongue can tell; for he will "shew merciful kindness on thousands of them that love him." "The good man's seed shall not go a begging his bread." You are good men, so many as "suffer for Christ's sake."

Matt. xix.

Psal. xxxvii.

I trust you all, my dearly beloved, will consider this gear with yourselves, and in the cross see God's mercy, which is more sweet and to be set by than life itself, much more then than any muck or pelf of this world. This mercy of God should make you merry and cheerful, for "the afflictions of this life are not to be compared" to the joys of the life prepared for you. You know the way to heaven is not "the wide way" of the world, which windeth to the devil, but it is a "strait way" which few walk in: for few "live godly in Christ Jesu," few regard the life to come, few remember the day of judgment, few remember how Christ "will deny them before his Father that do deny him" here, few consider that Christ "will be ashamed" of them in the last day which are ashamed now[4] of his truth and true service, few cast their accounts what will be laid to their charge in the day of vengeance, few regard the condemnation of their own consciences, in doing that which inwardly they disallow, few love God better than their goods. But I trust yet you are of these few, my dearly beloved; I trust you be of the "little flock, which shall inherit the kingdom of heaven;" I trust you are of[4] the mourners and lamenters, which shall be comforted with "comfort which never shall be taken from you," if you now repent your former evils, if now you strive against the evils that are in you, if now you continue to call upon God, if now you defile not your bodies with any idolatrous service, used in the antichristian churches, if you "molest not the good Spirit of God," which is given you

Rom. viii.

Matt. vii.

2 Tim. iii.

2 Cor. v.

Matt. x.

Rom. xiv.

Luke xii.

Eph. iv.

[[3] 'ye shall,' 1563: 'shall,' 1564.]
[[4] 'now,' 'of,' 1564: not in 1563.]

as a gage of eternal redemption, a Counsellor and Master to "lead you into all truth." Which good Spirit I beseech the Father of mercy to give to us all, for his dear Son's sake,
Acts xx. Jesus Christ our Lord: "to whom I commend you all, and to the word of his grace," which is able to help you all, and save you all that believe it, follow it, and serve God there-
Matt. x. after. And of this I would you were all certain, that all "the hairs of your heads are numbered," so that not one of them
Matt. viii. Job i. shall perish, neither shall any man or devil be able to attempt anything, much less to do anything to you or any of you, before your heavenly Father, which loveth you most tenderly, shall give them leave. And, when he hath given them leave,
Psal. civ. Psal. xxxi. they shall go no further than he will, nor keep you in trouble any longer than he will.

1 Pet. v. Therefore "cast on him all your care, for he is careful for you." Only study to please him, and to keep your consciences clean, and your bodies pure from the idolatrous service, which now everywhere is used; and God will marvellously and mercifully defend and comfort you. Which thing he do for his name's sake, in Christ our Lord. Amen.

XVI. TO WILLIAM PUNT[1].

[The Tower, LONDON, about *August*, 1553.]

Bp Coverdale, Letters of the Martyrs, 1564, p. 305. Foxe, Acts, &c., ed. 1570, p. 1822; and after editions.

GRACE and peace from God the Father, through our Lord Jesus Christ. Amen.

Dear brother, God most justly hath cast me now into a dungeon, but much better than I deserve; wherein I see no man but my keeper, nor can see any except they come to

[1 This Letter being inscribed, in the early printed editions, to "W. P." it seems likely that the name of "William Punt" may be that intended, who is mentioned in various letters by Bradford, and to whom, having conveyed writings from Bradford and Bp Hooper to Bps Ridley and Latimer and Abp Cranmer, at Oxford, 1554, a letter was addressed by Bp Ridley, No. XX. p. 376, Park. Soc.: vide also Foxe, Acts, &c., p. 1605, ed. 1563, or Vol. VIII. p. 384, ed. 1843—9.

The initials "W. P.", however, might possibly stand for "William Porrege," who is mentioned in the postscript to Bradford's letter to Joyce Hales, August 8, 1554, and was afterward a minister in the reign of Elizabeth: see Foxe, p. 2081, ed. 1583, or Vol. VIII. p. 576, ed. 1843—9.]

me. Something in the earth my lodging is; which is an example and memorial of my earthly affections, which God, I trust, will mortify—and of my sepulchre, whereunto I trust my Lord God will bring me in peace, in his good time. In the mean season he give me patience, lively hope, and his good Spirit. I pray you, pray for me, for the prayer of the godly, if it be "effectual, worketh much" with God.

I thank God, my common disease doth less trouble me now than when I was abroad, which doth teach me the merciful providence of God towards me. Commend me to Mistress Wilkinson, whom we pray God to strengthen in his truth and grace unto the end[2]. Use true and hearty prayer, and you shall perceive, God at length will declare himself to see, where now many think he sleepeth.

This disease was a rheum with a feebleness of stomach, wherewith he was much troubled whiles he was at liberty.—[Coverdale and Foxe.]

Out of the Tower, by the Lord's prisoner,

JOHN BRADFORD.

XVII. TO MISTRESS WILKINSON[3] AND OTHERS.

Bp Coverdale, Letters of the Martyrs, 1564, p. 343.

MS. 1. 2. 8. No. 80. Transcript. Emman. Coll. Cambridge.

THE Lord of mercy, in Christ his Son our Saviour and only Comforter, be with you all now and for ever. Amen.

Although presently I have little time, by reason of this

[2 The last sentence, "Commend me...the end," is in 1564, but not in 1570, or after editions of Foxe.]

[3 Mistress Wilkinson was "a godly matron and...singular patroness to the good saints of God and learned bishops, as to Master Hooper, to the bishop of Hereford [John Harley], to Master Coverdale, Master Latimer, Doctor Cranmer, with many other:" (Foxe, Acts, &c., ed. 1583, p. 1756, or ed. 1843—9, Vol. VII. p. 517.) Bp Ridley too speaks gratefully of her "charitable and friendly benevolence:" (Works, pp. 360, 385, Park. Soc.) See also Bp Latimer's short and affecting letter "to Mistress Wilkinson of Soper Lane*, in London, widow, she being at the manor of English in Oxfordshire," in Works of L. p. 444, Vol. II. Park. Soc. Abp Cranmer in a letter exhorted her "to withdraw herself from the malice of her and God's enemies, into some place where God is most truly served:" (Works of C. p. 444, Vol. II. Park. Soc.) Foxe states, on the margin of a letter to her from Bp Hooper, that she "died in exile at Frankfort:" Acts, &c., ed. 1570, p. 1691, or ed. 1843—9, Vol. VI. p. 672.]

[* "Now New Queen-street in Cheapside."—Stow's London, Vol. I. book III. p. 15, 25, 50, ed. Strype, Lond. 1720.]

bringer's short departing, and less occasion of necessary matter, to write unto you, yet in that it hath pleased God to offer me more liberty to write than before I had, as this reader can report, I thought good to signify unto you the same, with the acknowledging of the receipt of your tokens: for the which I neither can nor will go about to flatter you with thanks, in that I know you look for none at mine hands, God being the cause, and his word the end, wherefore you did so. To him I know you would have me thankful, and I beseech you pray that I may so be, and not only thankful for myself and his benefits towards me, but also thankful for you, to whom God hath given to fear his name and love his truth. The which gifts far pass the riches of the world, for they shall perish, and be left we know not unto whom; but these gifts of God, as they last for ever, so they make happy the possessors of the same.

Go to therefore, and pray God to increase them of his goodness, as of his mercy he hath begun them in you, and indeed so he will: for to whom he giveth the earnest of willing, to the same he will give the grace of continuing, if we reject not the same; as we do when we be double-hearted, and part
2 Kings xvii. our fear and love; as did the Samaritans, which feared God and their Adrammelech, loved God's religion and their old country customs, &c. If this doubleness come on us, that we fear more the world, and couple it with the fear of God; if we love the muck of this mould, and couple it with the love of God's religion, then part we stake, then mar we the market, then the Spirit of God will depart, then play we as Ananias
Acts v. and Sapphira did, and so sooner or later shall fall to perdition with them.

But, as I said, I think no such thing of you; I think of you as of God's dear children, whose hearts are whole with the Lord. And therefore I write not this as though you were such, but because it is God's goodness you be not such, because Satan would have you such, and because many that were as you now be are such. Therefore to make you, as thankful, so careful to continue, but yet so that your care be cast all on the Lord, is the only cause I write this, and would write more, but that the bringer cannot tarry. And therefore hastily and abruptly I make an end, beseeching almighty God, in our Redeemer Jesus Christ, to be with you, and with his holy Spirit comfort you all, and help my good sister Mistress W[arcup][1], to be a happy and a good mother of the child, of which as yet I hear God hath not delivered her.

By your own to use in the Lord for ever,

JOHN BRADFORD.

XVIII. TO HIS MOTHER AND OTHERS[2].

[Tower of LONDON, *October* 6, 1553.]

OUR dear and sweet Saviour Jesus Christ, whose prisoner at this present (praised be his name therefore) I am, preserve and keep you, my good mother, with my brothers and sisters, my father John Traves, Thomas Sorrocold, Laurence and James Bradshaw, with their wives and families, &c., now and for ever. Amen.

Bp Coverdale, Letters of the Martyrs, 1564, p. 290.

Foxe, Acts, &c., ed. 1570, p. 1805; and after editions.

MS. 2. 2. 15. No. 62. Transcript. Emman. Coll. Cambridge.

I am at this present in prison sure enough for starting to confirm that I have preached unto you; as I am ready, I thank God, with my life and blood to seal the same, if God vouch me worthy of that honour. For, good mother and brethren, it is a most special benefit of God "to suffer for his name's sake" and gospel, as now I do; I heartily thank him for it, and am sure that with him I shall be partaker of his glory, as Paul saith, "If we suffer with him we shall reign with him." Therefore be not faint-hearted, but rather rejoice, at the least for my sake, which now am in the right and high way to heaven; for "by many afflictions we must enter into the kingdom of heaven."

2 Tim. ii.

Acts xiv.

Now will God make known his children. When the wind doth not blow, then cannot a man know the wheat from the chaff; but, when the blast cometh, then flieth away the chaff, but the wheat remaineth, and is so far from being hurt, that by the wind it is more cleansed from the chaff, and known to be wheat. Gold, when it is cast into the fire, is the more precious: so are God's children by the cross of affliction. Always God "beginneth his judgment at his house." Christ and the

[1 See first note to Letter XIX.]

[2 The inscription of this letter in Bp Coverdale and Foxe is: "To his mother, a godly matron dwelling in Manchester, and to his brethren and sisters, and other of his friends there."]

apostles were in most misery in the land of Jewry, but yet the whole land smarted for it after: so now God's children are first chastised in this world, that they should not be damned with the world, for surely great plagues of God hang over this realm.

Ye all know, there was never more knowledge of God, and less godly living and true serving of God. It was counted a foolish thing to serve God truly, and earnest prayer was not past[1] upon. Preaching was but a pastime. The communion was counted too common. Fasting to subdue the flesh was far out of use. Alms was almost nothing. Malice, covetousness, and uncleanness, was common everywhere, with swearing, drunkenness, and idleness. God therefore now is come, as you have heard me preach; and, because he will not damn us with the world, he beginneth to punish us, as me for my carnal living: for as for my preaching I am most certain it is and was God's truth, and I trust to give my life for it by God's grace. But, because I lived not the gospel truly but outwardly, therefore doth he thus punish me, nay, rather in punishing bless me: and indeed I thank him more of this prison than of any parlour, yea, than of any pleasure that ever I had, for in it I find God, my most sweet good God always. The flesh is punished, first to admonish us now heartily to live as we profess, secondly to certify the wicked of their just damnation, if they repent not.

Perchance you are infirmed and weakened of that which I have preached, because God doth not defend it, as you think, but suffereth the old popish doctrine to come again and prevail. But you must know, good mother, that God by this doth prove and try his children and people, whether they will unfeignedly and simply hang on him and his word. So did he with the Israelites, bringing them into a desert, after their coming out of Egypt, where (I mean the wilderness) was want of all things in comparison of that which they had in Egypt.

Christ, when he came into this world, brought no worldly
John xvi. wealth nor quietness with him, but rather war. "The world," saith he, "shall rejoice, but ye shall mourn and weep, but your weeping shall be turned into joy:" and therefore "happy are they that mourn and weep, for they shall be comforted:"

[1 'Past upon:' cared for.]

they are marked then with God's mark in their foreheads, and not with the beast's mark (I mean the pope's shaven crown), who now with his shavelings rejoice. But woe unto them, for they shall be cast down, they shall weep and mourn! The rich glutton had here his joy, and Lazarus sorrow, but afterwards the time was changed. The end of carnal joy is sorrow. Now let the whoremonger joy, with the drunkard, swearer, covetous, malicious, and blind buzzard sir John; for the mass will not bite them, neither make them to blush, as preaching would. Now may they do what they will, come devils to the church, and go devils home, for no man must find fault: and they are glad of this, now have they their hearts' desire, as the Sodomites had when Lot was gone: but what followed? Forsooth when they cried, "Peace, all shall be well," then came God's vengeance, fire and brimstone from heaven, and burnt up every mother's child. Even so, dear mother, will it do to our papists.

Of this place the earl of Derby seemeth to take hold, complaining that he curseth them that teacheth any false doctrine.—[Foxe, ed. 1570, p. 1806. See Bradf. Vol. I. p. 469.]

Wherefore fear God; stick to his word, though all the world would swerve from it. Die you must once, and when or how you cannot tell. Die therefore with Christ; suffer for serving him truly and after his word; for sure may we be, that of all deaths it is most to be desired to die for God's sake. This is the most safe kind of dying: we cannot doubt but that we shall go to heaven if we die for his name's sake. And, that you shall die for his name's sake, God's word will warrant you, if you stick to that which God by me hath taught you.

You shall see that I speak as I think; for, by God's grace, I will drink before you of this cup, if I be put to it. I doubt not but God will give me his grace, and strengthen me thereunto. Pray that he would, and that I refuse it not. I am at a point, even when my Lord God will, to come to him. Death nor life, prison nor pleasure, I trust in God, shall be able to separate me from my Lord God and his gospel.

In peace, when no persecution was, then were you content and glad to hear me, then did you believe me: and will you not do so now, seeing I speak that, which I trust by God's grace, if need be, to verify with my life? Good mother, I write before God to you, as I have preached before him. It is God's truth I have taught. It is that same infallible word, whereof he hath said, "Heaven and earth shall pass, but my word shall not pass."

The mass and such baggage as the false worshippers of God and enemies of Christ's cross—the papists, I say—have brought in again to poison the church of God withal displeaseth God highly, and is abominable in his sight. Happy may he be, which of conscience suffereth loss of life or goods in disallowing it. Come not at it. If God be God, follow him. If the mass be God, let them that will see it, hear or be present at it, go to the devil with it. What is there as God ordained? His supper was ordained, to be received of us in the memorial of his death, for the confirmation of our faith that his body was broken for us, and his blood shed for pardon of our sins: but in the mass there is no receiving, but the priest keepeth all to himself alone. Christ saith, "Take, eat:" "No," saith the priest, "gape, peep." There is a sacrificing, yea, killing of Christ again, as much as they may. There is idolatry in worshipping the outward sign of bread and wine. There is all in Latin: you cannot tell what he saith. To conclude, there is nothing as God ordained. Wherefore, my good mother, come not at it.

Oh, will some say, it will hinder you if you refuse to come to mass, and to do as other do. But God will further you, be you assured, as you shall one day find; who hath promised to them that suffer hindrance or loss of anything in this world his great blessing here, "and in the world to come life everlasting."—You shall be counted an heretic—but not of others than of heretics, whose praise is a dispraise.—You are not able to reason against the priests; but God will, that all they shall not be able to withstand you.—Nobody will do so but you only? Indeed no matter, for "few enter into the narrow gate" which bringeth to salvation. Howbeit you shall have with you, I doubt not, father Traves and others, my brothers and sisters, to go with you therein: but, if they will not, I your son in God, I trust, shall not leave you an inch, but go before you. Pray that I may, and give thanks for me. Rejoice in my suffering, for it is for your sakes, to confirm the truth I have taught.

Matt. xix. [Mark x. 30.]

Howsoever you do, beware this letter come not abroad, but into father Traves his hands: for, if it should be known that I have pen and ink in the prison, then would it be worse with me. Therefore to yourselves keep this letter, commending me to God and his mercy in Christ Jesus; who make me worthy,

For all this *caveat*, yet this letter came to the earl of Derby's knowledge.—[Foxe, ed. 1570, p. 1806.]

for his name's sake, to give my life for his gospel and church sake.

Out of the Tower of London, immediately after I had read my brother's letter[1], the 6th day of October, 1553.

My name I write not for causes: you know it well enough. Like the letter never the worse. Commend me to all our good brethren and sisters in the Lord. Howsoever you do, be obedient to the higher powers; that is, in no point, either in hand or tongue, rebel; but rather, if they command that which with good conscience you cannot obey, lay your head on the block, and suffer whatsoever they shall do or say. "By patience possess your souls."

XIX. TO WARCUP AND HIS WIFE[2]; MISTRESS WILKINSON[3], AND OTHERS[4].

[Tower of LONDON, *November* 19, 1553.]

VERBUM Domini manet in æternum: "The word of the Lord endureth for ever[5]." Bp Coverdale, Letters of the Martyrs, 1564, p. 280.

The same peace our Saviour Christ left with his people, which is not without war with the world, almighty God work plentifully in your hearts now and for ever. Amen. Foxe, Acts, &c., ed. 1570, p. 1817; and after editions.

MS. 2. 2. 15. Nos. 18. 31. 40. 47. Four early transcripts. Emman. Coll. Cambridge.

[1 The last eight words are first printed here from the Emmanuel MS.]

[2 Mistress Anne Warcup, of the manor of English, in the parish of Nuffield, near Nettlebed in Oxfordshire (Wood's Athen. Oxon., ed. Bliss, Vol. I. col. 754), and to whom various letters by Bradford are addressed, was, with Mistress Wilkinson, distinguished for beneficence to the Marian confessors and martyrs: see Bp Ridley's mention of this lady, Works, p. 360, Park. Soc., and letter to her from Bp Hooper, Works, Vol. II. p. 602, Park. Soc. She was instrumental in saving the life of Bp Jewel, when that great divine, having fled from Oxford early in 1555, was brought, almost dead with vexation and weariness, to her mansion of English, by Augustine Bernhere. Vide Humfred. Vit. Juell. Lond. 1573, p. 82; Life of Jewel by Ayre, in Works of J., Park. Soc. Vol. IV. p. xi; Strype, Ecc. Mem. Vol. III. part 1, p. 224—7.]

[3 See p. 39, note 3, above.]

[4 Bp Coverdale and Foxe attribute this letter to Bradford: but in Strype, Ecc. Mem. Vol. III. part II. p. 302, and in MS. 1. 2. 8. no. 58, and MS. 2. 2. 15. no. 28, Emman. Coll. Camb., it is given with the signature of Bp Latimer, and the date May 15, 1555: see Works of Bp L., Vol. II. p. 435. It might possibly have been re-issued by Latimer from Oxford, in May, 1555, with slight alteration, having been originally penned by Bradford in the Tower of London, November, 1553.

Parts of this letter are closely similar to Bradford's "Exhortation to the brethren in England:" Vol. I. p. 414—33.]

[5 The Latin words occur in the Emman. MS. 2. 2. 15. no. 18., the English in no. 48.]

The time, I perceive, is come, wherein the Lord's ground will be known: I mean, it will now shortly appear, who have received God's gospel into their hearts indeed, to the taking of good root therein; for such will not shrink[1] for a little heat or sunburning weather[2], but stiffly will stand and grow on, maugre the malice of all burning showers and tempests. And—forasmuch as, my beloved in the Lord, I am persuaded of you that ye be indeed "the children of God," God's "good ground," which groweth and will grow on, by God's grace, bringing forth fruit to God's glory after your vocations, as occasion shall be offered, burn the sun never so hot—therefore I cannot but so signify unto you, and heartily pray you and every one of you, accordingly to go on forwards after your Master Christ, not sticking at the foul way and stormy weather which you are come into, and are like so to do; of this being most certain, that the end of your journey shall be pleasant and joyful, in such a perpetual rest and blissfulness as cannot but swallow up the showers that ye now feel and are soused in—if ye often set it before your eyes, after Paul's counsel in the latter end of the fourth and beginning of the fifth of the second epistle to the Corinthians. Read it, I pray you, and remember it often, as a restorative to refresh you, lest ye faint in the way.

And, besides this, set before you also that, though the weather be foul and storms grow apace, yet go not ye alone, but [1 Pet. v.] other your brothers and sisters pad[3] the same path, as St Peter telleth us; and therefore company should cause you to be the more courageous and cheerful. But, if ye had no company at all to go presently with you, I pray you tell me if, even from the beginning, the best of God's friends have found any fairer weather and way to the place whither ye are going (I mean heaven), than ye now find and are likely to do—except ye will, with the worldlings, which have their portion in this life, tarry still by the way till the storms be overpast; and then either night will so approach that ye cannot travel, either the doors will be sparred[4] before ye come, and so you shall lodge without, in wonderful evil lodgings. Read Apocalypse twenty-second. Begin at Abel, and come from him to Noah, Abraham, Isaac, Jacob,

[1 'shrink,' Emman. MSS.: not in 1564 or 1570.]
[2 'weather,' Emman. MSS.: 'wither,' 1564 and 1570.]
[3 'Pad:' travel on foot.] [4 See Vol. I. p. 417.]

Joseph, the patriarchs, Moses, David, Daniel, and all the saints in the Old Testament: and tell me whether any of them found any fairer way than ye now find.

If the Old Testament will not serve, I pray you come to the New; and begin with Mary and Joseph, and come from them to Zachary, Elizabeth, John Baptist, and every one of the apostles and evangelists; and search, whether they all found any other way into the city we travel towards, than by many tribulations.

Besides these, if ye should call to remembrance the primitive church—Lord God!—ye should see so many to have given cheerfully their bodies to most grievous torments, rather than they would be stopped in their journey, that there is no day in the year, but, I dare say, a thousand was the fewest that with great joy lost their homes here—but in the city they went unto have found other manner of homes than man's mind is able to conceive. But if none of all these were, if ye had no company now to go with you, as ye have me your poor brother and bondman of the Lord, with many other, I trust in God; if ye had none other of the fathers, patriarchs, good kings, prophets, apostles, evangelists, martyrs, and other holy saints and children of God, that in their journey to heavenward found as ye now find, and are like to find if ye go on forward as I trust ye will; yet ye have your Master and your Captain Jesus Christ, the dear, darling, and only begotten and beloved Son of God, in whom was all the Father's pleasure, joy, and delectation; ye have him to go before you, no fairer way but much fouler, into this our city of Jerusalem. I need not, I trust, to rehearse what manner of way he found. Begin at his birth, and till ye come to his burial ye shall find that every foot and stride of his journey was no better but much worse than yours now is.

Wherefore, my dearly beloved in the Lord, be not so dainty as to look for that at God's hands, your dear Father, which the fathers, patriarchs, prophets, apostles, evangelists, martyrs, saints, and his own Son Jesus Christ did not find. Hitherto we have had fair way, I trow, and fair weather also. Now, because we have loitered by the way, and not made the speed we should have done, our loving Lord and sweet Father hath overcast the weather, and stirred up storms and tempests, that we might with more haste run out our race before night come, and the doors be sparred[4]. The devil standeth now at every inn-door in his city and country of this world, crying unto us to tarry and lodge in this or that place, till the storms be overpast: not that he would not have us wet to the skin, but that the time might overpass us to our utter destruction. Therefore beware of his enticements; cast not your eyes on things that be present, how this man doth, and how that man doth; but cast your eyes on

Phil. iii. the glaive[1] ye run at, or else ye will lose the game. Ye know that he which runneth at the glaive[1] doth not look on other that stand by and go this way or that way; but altogether he looketh on the glaive[1], and on them that run with him, that those which be behind overtake him not, and that he may overtake them which be before. Even so should we do, leave off looking on those which will not run the race to heaven's bliss, by the path of persecution with us, and cast our eyes on the end of our race, and on them that go before us, that we may overtake them—and on them which come after us, that we may provoke them to come the faster after.

He that shooteth will not cast his eyes in his shooting on them that stand by or ride by the ways, I trow, but rather on the mark he shooteth at; for else he were like to win the wrong way. Even so, my dearly beloved, let your eyes be set on the

Hebr. xii. mark ye shoot at, even Christ Jesus, "who for the joy he set before him did joyfully carry his cross, contemning the shame; and therefore he now sitteth on the right hand of the throne of God." Let us follow him, for this did he, that we should not

Rom. viii. 2 Tim. ii. Matt. x. [Mark viii.] be faint-hearted; for we may be most assured, that "if we suffer with him we shall undoubtedly reign with him." But, "if we deny him, surely he will deny us:" for "he that is ashamed of me," saith Christ, "and of my gospel in this faithless generation, I will be ashamed of him before the angels of God in heaven." O how heavy a sentence is this, to all such as know the mass to be an abominable idol, full of idolatry, blasphemy and sacrilege against God and his Christ, as undoubtedly it is, and yet for fear of men, for loss of life or goods, yea, some for advantage and gain, will honest it with their presence, dis-

[[1] 'Glaive:' a broad sword or a kind of halberd, which apparently was both the mark aimed at and the prize given in a race. Compare Letter XXVI., to Mistress Brown: "None receiveth the glaive, but those that run to the appointed mark." Strutt observes: "This year, 1540, by consent of the parties concerned, the ball was changed into six glaives of silver of the like value, as a reward for the best runner:" Sports and pastimes, book II. ch. iii. § 13.]

sembling both with God and man, as their own heart and conscience doth accuse them. Better it were that such had never known the truth, than thus wittingly, and for the fear or favour of man "whose breath is in his nostrils," to dissemble it, or rather, Isai. ii.
as indeed it is, to deny it. "The end" of such is like to be 2 Pet. ii. Heb. vi. x.
"worse than their beginning." Such had need to take heed of the two terrible places to the Hebrews, in the sixth and tenth chapters, lest by so doing they fall therein. Let them beware they play not wily-beguile[1] themselves, as some do, I fear me, which go to mass; and, because they worship not, nor kneel not, nor knock not as others do, but sit still in their pews, therefore they think they rather do good to others than hurt.

But, alas! if these men would look into their own consciences, there should they see that they are very dissemblers; and in seeking to deceive others (for by this means the magistrates think them of their sort) they deceive themselves. They think, at the elevation time, all men's eyes are set upon them, to mark how they do. They think, others hearing of such men going to mass do see or enquire of their behaviour there. Oh! if there were in those men, that are so present at the mass, either love to God or to their brethren, then would they for the one or both openly take God's part, and admonish the people of their idolatry. They fear man more than "him which hath Matt. x.
power to cast both soul and body into hell-fire;" they "halt on 1 Kings xviii. [21, Septuag.]
both knees;" they "serve two masters." God have mercy upon such, and open "their eyes with his eye-salve, that they may Rev. iii.
see" that they which take not part with God are against God, and that "they which gather not with Christ do scatter abroad." O that they would read what St John saith will be done to Rev. xxi.
"the fearful!" The counsel given to the church of Laodicea is Rev. iii.
good counsel for such.

But, to return to you again, dearly beloved: "be not ye 2 Tim. i.
ashamed of" God's gospel. "It is the power of God to salva- Rom. i.
tion, to all those that do believe it." Be therefore "partakers of the afflictions," as God shall make you able, knowing for certain, that "he will never tempt further than he will make 1 Cor. x.
you able to bear." And think it no small grace of God, to suffer persecution for God's truth; "for the Spirit of God rest- Phil. i.
eth upon you;" and "ye are happy," as one day ye shall see. 1 Pet. iv. Matt. v.

[[1] See Vol. I. p. 375, note 4.]

Read 2 Thess. i. and Hebrews xii. As the fire hurteth not gold, but maketh it finer, so shall ye be more pure by suffering with Christ. The flail and wind hurteth not the wheat, but cleanseth it from the chaff; and ye, dearly beloved, are God's wheat: fear not therefore the flail, fear not the fanning wind, fear not the millstone, fear not the oven; for all these make you more meet for the Lord's own tooth. Soap, though it be black, soileth not the cloth, but rather at the length maketh it more clean: so doth the black cross help us to more whiteness, if God strike with his battledore. Because ye are God's sheep, prepare yourselves "to the slaughter," always knowing that "in the sight of the Lord our death shall be precious." "The souls under the altar" look for us to fill up their number: happy are we if God have so appointed us. Howsoever it be, dearly beloved, cast yourselves wholly upon the Lord, with whom all "the hairs of your head are numbered," so that "not one of them shall perish." Will we, nill we, we must drink God's cup if he have appointed it for us. Drink it willingly then, and at the first when it is full, lest peradventure, if we linger, we shall drink at the length of "the dregs with the wicked," if at the beginning we drink not with his children; for with them his "judgment beginneth," and when he hath wrought his will on mount Sion, then will he visit the nations round about.

(1 Pet. i.; Rom. viii.; 1 Pet. v.; Matt. x. [Luke xxi. 18.]; Ps. lxxv.; 1 Pet. iv.)

"Submit yourselves therefore under the mighty hand of the Lord." No man shall touch you without his knowledge. When they touch you therefore, know it is to your weal: God thereby will work to make you like unto Christ here, that ye may be also like unto him elsewhere. Acknowledge your unthankfulness and sin, and bless God that "correcteth you" in the world, "because ye shall not be damned with the world." Otherwise might he correct us than in making us to suffer for righteousness' sake: but this he doth, because we are not of the world. Call upon his name, through Christ, for "the joy and gladness of his saving health[1]." Believe that he is merciful to you, heareth you, and helpeth you: "I am with him in trouble, and will deliver him," saith he. Know that God hath appointed bounds, over the which the devil and all the

(1 Pet. v.; Rom. viii.; 1 Cor. xi.; Ps. li. [MS. No. 18.]; Ps. l.; Ps. xcii.)

[[1] "The joy and gladness of his saving health," MS. 2. 2. 15. No. 18: "his help as he commandeth us," 1564 and 1570.]

world shall not pass. If all things seem to be against you, yet say with Job, "If he kill me, I will hope in him." Read the 91st Psalm, and pray for me your poor brother and fellow-sufferer for God's gospel's sake—his name therefore be praised, and of his mercy he make me and you worthy to suffer with good conscience for his name's sake.

Die once we must, and when we know not. Happy are they whom God giveth to pay nature's debt, I mean to die for his sake, for[2] here is not our home. Therefore let us accordingly consider things, always having before our eyes "heavenly Jerusalem," the way thither to be by persecutions. Remember[2] the dear friends of God, how they have gone it after the example of our Saviour Jesus Christ; whose footsteps let us follow even to the very gallows, if God so will, not doubting but that, as he within three days rose again immortal, even so we shall do in our time—that is, when "the trumpet shall blow," and the angel shall shout, and "the Son of man shall appear in the clouds, with innumerable saints and angels, in majesty and great glory." Then "shall the dead arise," and "we shall be caught up into the clouds to meet the Lord, and so be always with him. Comfort yourselves with these words;" and pray for me for God's sake.

Happy is that death which, seeing once it must needs be paid, is bestowed upon the Lord.—[Foxe.] Heb. xii. Rev. xxi. xxii.

E carcere [from prison], 19 November, 1553.

JOHN BRADFORD.

XX. TO EATON.

To my dear friend and brother in the Lord, master George Eaton:

Bp Coverdale, Letters of the Martyrs, 1564, p. 446.

Almighty God, our dear Father, give to you daily more and more the knowledge of his truth, and a love and life to the same for ever in all things, through Jesus Christ our Lord. Amen.

I should begin with thanksgiving to God, and to you as his steward, for the great benefits I have oftentimes received from you, and especially in this time of my most need, far above my expectation: but because thankfulness lieth not in words or

[[2] "for," "remember," MS. 2. 2. 15. No. 31: not in 1564 or 1570.]

letters, and because you look not to hear of your well-doing of man, I am purposed to pass it over with silence, and to give myself presently to that which is more profitable unto you; that is, as God shall lend me his grace, briefly to labour, or at least to shew my good will, to help you in God's gift to me, as you by your doing the like in God's gift unto you have, as already done, so occasioned me greatly hereto. I would gladly have done it heretofore, but I have been discouraged to write unto you, lest hurt thereby might come unto you; which is the only cause I have not hitherto written, nor now would not have done, but that I stand in a doubt whether ever hereafter I shall have liberty to write unto you. And therefore, whilst I something may, I thought good to do thus much, to declare unto you how that, as I think myself much bound to God for you, so I desire to gratify the same, as God should enable me.

The days are come, and more and more do approach, in the which trial will be of such as have unfeignedly read and heard the gospel; for all others will abide no trial, but as the world will. But, of you because I have better hope, I cannot but, as pray to God in him to confirm you, so to beseech you of the same. I know, it will be a dangerous thing indeed to declare that which in word you have confessed, and in heart have believed, specially concerning the papistical mass: but, notwithstanding, we must not for dangers depart from the truth, except we will "depart from God;" for, inasmuch as God is "the truth," and the truth is God, he that departeth from the one departeth from the other. Now, what a thing it is to "depart from God," I need not to tell you, because you know it is no less than a departing from all that good is, and not only so, but also a coupling of yourself to all that evil is; for there is no mean, either we depart from God and stick to the devil, or depart from the devil and stick to God.

Some men there be, which for fear of danger and loss of that they must leave—when, where, and to whom, they know not—do deceive themselves, after the just judgment of God, to believe the devil, because they have no lust to believe God, in hearkening to Satan's counsel of parting stake with God; as to be persuaded that it is not evil, or else no great evil, inwardly in heart to conceal the truth, and outwardly in fact to betray it. And therefore, though they know the mass to be abomination, yet they make it but a straw, in going to it as the world doth; in which thing the Lord knoweth they deceive themselves to damnation, dream they as they lust. For surely the body departing from the verity, and so from God, will draw and drown in damnation the soul also; for we shall "receive according to that we do in the body, good or bad:" and therefore the matter is more to be considered than men make of it; the more it is to be lamented.

But I trust, my right dearly beloved, you will consider this with yourself, and call your conscience to account, as God's word maketh the charge. Beware of false auditors, which making a false charge can get no quietness of the conscience, after God's word. Therefore cast your charge; and there shall you see that no "belief of the heart" justifieth, which hath not "confession of the mouth" to declare the same. "No man can serve two masters:" "he that gathereth not with Christ," as no mass-seer unreproving it doth, "scattereth abroad." God's chosen are such as not only have good hearts, but also kiss not their hands, nor "bow their knee to Baal." Christ's disciples are none but such as "deny themselves, take up their cross, and follow him." "He that is ashamed of Christ and his truth in this generation" must look that Christ "will be ashamed of him in the day of judgment." "He that denieth Christ before men shall be denied before God." Now two kinds of denial there be, yea, three kinds; one in heart, another in word, and the third in deed: in the which kinds all mass-gospellers be so bitten, that all the surgeons in the world can lay no healing plaster thereto, till repentance appear and draw out the matter of using the evil and resorting to the mass. For pure should we be from all spots, "not only of the flesh, but also of the spirit;" and our duty is to depart, not only from evil, that is, from the mass, but also from "the appearance of evil," that is, from coming at it.

Woe unto them that give offence to the children of God! that is, which occasion, by any means, any to tarry in the church at mass-time—much more then they which occasion any to come thereto—most of all they which enforce any thereto. Assuredly a most heavy vengeance of God hangeth upon such. "Such as decline to their crookedness God will lead on with wicked workers;" whose "portion shall be snares, fire, brimstone and stormy tempests;" whose palace and house shall be hell-fire and darkness; whose cheer shall be weeping and gnashing of teeth; whose song shall be 'Woe, woe, woe!' from the which the Lord of mercy deliver us.

My dearly beloved, I write not this as one that thinketh not well of you, but as one that would you did well: and therefore to help you thereto I write as I write, beseeching God to open your eyes to see the dangers men be in, that dissemble with God and man, to the end you do not the like; and also to open your eyes to see the high service you do to God, in adventuring yourself, and that you have, for his sake.

O that men's eyes were opened to see that "the glory of God resteth upon them" that suffer anything for his sake! O that we considered that it is happiness to suffer anything for Christ's sake, which have deserved to suffer so much for our sins and iniquities! O that our eyes were opened to see the "great reward they shall have in heaven," which suffer the loss of anything for God's sake! If we knew the cross to be as a purgation most profitable to the soul, as a purifying fire to burn the dross away of our dirtiness and sins, as an oven to bake us in to be the Lord's bread, as soap to make us white, as a stew[1] to mundify[2] and cleanse us, as God's frame-house to make us like to Christ here in suffering, that we may be so in reigning, then should we not so much care for this little short sorrow, which the flesh suffereth in it: but rather, in consideration of the exceeding endless joy and comfort which will ensue, we should run forwards in our race, after the example of our Captain Christ: who comfort us all in our distress, and give us "the Spirit of prayer," therein to "watch and pray, that we be not led into temptation." Which God grant to us for ever. Amen.

And thus much I thought good to write to you, at this present, to declare my carefulness for the well-doing of you and all your family, whom I commend with you into the hands and tuition of God our Father: so be it.

Your own in the Lord,

JOHN BRADFORD.

[1 "Stew:" a house for bathing, sweating, or otherwise cleansing the body. Todd's Johnson.]

[2 "Mundify:" make clean.]

XXI. TO ROBERT HARRINGTON AND HIS WIFE[3].

[Tower of LONDON, *December* 20, 1553.]

GOD's mercy in Christ I wish you to feel, my dear brother, with my faithful sister your wife, now and for ever. Amen.

Bp Coverdale, Letters of the Martyrs, 1564, p. 370.

Foxe, Acts, &c., ed. 1570, p. 1836; and after editions.

Having this occasion, I could not but write something, as well to put myself in remembrance of my duty to Godwards for you both, in thankfulness and prayer, as to put you in remembrance of me and your duty towards God for me in praying for me; for I dare not say in thankfulness for me. Not that I would have you to give no thanks to God for his wonderful great and sweet mercies towards me and upon me in Christ his Son, but because I have not deserved it at either of your hands. For ye both know right well, at least my conscience doth accuse me, how that I have not only not exhorted and taught you, as both my vocation and your deserts required, to "walk worthy of that vocation" which God hath made you worthy of, and "with trembling and fear to work out your salvation"—that is, in the fear of God to give yourselves to great vigilance in prayer for the increase of faith, and to a wary circumspection in all your conversation, not only in works and words, but also in thoughts, because God is a "Searcher of the heart," and "out of the heart it cometh that defileth us" in God's sight—I have, I say, not only not done this, but also have given you example of negligence in prayer, watching, fasting, talking and doing. So that woe to me for giving such offence!—Partly for this cause, dear

[[3] This letter is thus inscribed, because it is entitled by Foxe, "Another letter to N[athanael] and his wife;" and Bradford, in his letter to Robert Cole, printed later in this series (Coverd. Lett. of Mart. p. 411), applies the name "Nathanael" to his beloved friend, Robert Harrington—third son of sir Robert H. of Exton, his early patron—on account of that person's "godly simplicity and singleness of heart:" (Coverd. Lett. of Mart. p. 414). A letter from Adn Philpot to Robert Harrington expresses earnest gratitude to him for "that great gentleness and pain which he had taken for the relief of him and of other their afflicted brethren in Christ:" (Works, p. 241, Park. Soc.). Two letters of the martyr Saunders are addressed to "Mistress Lucy Harrington, a godly gentlewoman and friendly to him in his troubles," wife of Robert H. See Foxe, Acts, &c., ed. 1583, p. 1500, or ed. 1843—9, Vol. VI. p. 632. Playfair, Baronetage, Vol. I. p. 72, London, 1811. The editor possesses a copy of Œcolampadius on Daniel and the minor prophets, Basil, 1530, which has on the title, in the autograph of Bradford, "Jhon Bradforde dydde geue thys boke to Robert Harryngton."]

brother and sister, God hath cast me and keepeth me here, that I might repent me and turn to him, and that ye might also by this correction upon me be more diligent to redress these things and others, if they in your conscience do accuse you.

My dearly beloved, heavy is God's anger fallen upon us all; doleful is this day. Now hath antichrist all his power again. Now is Christ's gospel trodden under foot. Now is God's people a derision and a prey for the wicked. Now is the greatest plague of all plagues fallen, the want of God's word; and all these we have—yea, I alone have—justly deserved. O that as

1 Chron. xxi. I write, 'I alone,' I could with David and with Jonas in heart say so! But I do not, I do not, I see not how grievously I have sinned, and how great a misery is fallen for mine unthankfulness for God's word, for mine hypocrisy in professing, preaching, hearing, and speaking of God's word, for my not praying to God for the continuance of it, for my not living of it throughly, as it requireth, &c. I will speak nothing of my manifest evils, for they are known to you well enough.

Dear brother and sister, with me say ye the like for your own parts, and with me join your hearts; and let us go to our heavenly Father, and for his Christ's sake beseech him to be merciful unto us, and to pardon us:

'O good Father, it is we that have deserved the taking away of thy word, it is we that have deserved these thy just plagues fallen upon us, we have done amiss, we have dealt unjustly with thy gospel, we have procured thy wrath: and therefore just art thou in punishing us, just art thou in plaguing us, for we are very miserable. But, good Lord and dear Father of mercy, whose justice is such that thou wilt not punish the poor souls of this realm (which yet have not thus sinned against thee as we have done, for many yet never heard thy word) for our trespasses; and whose mercy is so great, that thou wilt "put our iniquities out of thy remembrance" for thy Christ's sake, if we repent and believe; grant us, we beseech thee, true repentance and faith, that we having obtained pardon for our sins may, through thy Christ, get deliverance from the tyranny of antichrist, now

Ps. cxxv. oppressing us. O good Father, which hast said, that "the sceptre of the wicked" should not long lie upon and over the just, "lest they put forth their hands to iniquity" also, make us just, we pray thee in Christ's name, and cut asunder the cords of them that hate Sion. Let not the wicked people say, "Where is their God?" "Thou, our God, art in heaven, and doest whatsoever it pleaseth thee upon earth."

'O that thou wouldest, in the meanwhiles—before thou do deliver us—that, I say, thou wouldest open our eyes to see all these plagues to come from thee, and all other that shall come, whatsoever they be, public or private, that they come not by chance nor by fortune, but that they come even from thy hand, and that justly and mercifully! Justly—because we have and do deserve them, not only by our birth-poison, still sticking and working in us, but also by our former evil life past, which by this punishment and all other punishments thou wouldest have us to call to our remembrance, and to set before us, that thou mightest put them from before thee; whereas they stand, so long as they are not in our remembrance to put them away by repentance. Mercifully, O Lord God, dost thou punish, in that thou dost not correct to kill, but to amend; that we might repent our sins, ask mercy, obtain it freely in Christ, and to begin to "suffer for righteousness sake;" to be part of thy house, whereat thy "judgment beginneth;" to be "partakers of the afflictions" of thy church and thy Christ, that we might be "partakers of the glory" of the same; to weep here, that we might rejoice elsewhere; to be judged in this world, that we might with thy "saints judge hereafter the world;" to "suffer with Christ," that we might "reign with him;" to be like to Christ in shame, that we might be like to him in glory; to receive our evils here, that we might with poor Lazarus find rest elsewhere—rest, I say, and such a rest as "the eye hath not seen, the ear hath not heard, nor the heart of man is able to conceive."

'O that our eyes were open to see this, that the cross cometh from thee to declare thy justice and thy mercy! and hereto, that we might see how short a time the time of suffering is; how long a time the time of rejoicing is, to them that suffer here; but to them that will not, how long and miserable a time is appointed and prepared; a time without time, in eternal woe and perdition, too horrible to be thought upon. From the which keep us, dear Father, and give more sight in soul to see this gear, and how that all thy dearest children have carried the cross of grievous affliction in this life; in whose company do thou place us, and such a cross lay upon us as thou wilt make us able to bear, to thy glory and our salvation in Christ: for whose sake we pray thee to shorten the days of this our great misery, fallen upon us most justly, and in the mean season give us patience, repentance, faith, and thy eternal consolation. Amen, Amen, Amen.'

And thus, dear hearts, I have talked, methinks, a little while with you, or rather we have all talked with God. O that God would give us his "Spirit of grace and prayer!" My dearly beloved, pray for it, as for yourselves, so for me, and that God would vouchsafe to make me worthy to suffer with a good conscience for his name's sake. Pray for me, and I shall do the like for you.

This 20th of December, by him whom by this bringer ye shall learn. I pray you give my commendations to all that love me in the Lord. Be merry in Christ, for one day in heaven we shall meet and rejoice together for evermore. Amen.

JOHN BRADFORD.

XXII. TO COKER[1].

[Probably from the Tower of LONDON, *January*, 1554.]

Bp Coverdale, Letters of the Martyrs, 1564, p. 388.

MS. 2. 2. 15. No. 119. Transcript. Emman. Coll. Cambridge.

To my good brother, Master Coker, at Maldon, in Essex.

Although I have presently both little time, and less opportunity otherwise, to write as I would, yet as I may I thought better to write something than utterly to be silent. For if I should not so do, having so convenient a messenger; as I might towards you incur the suspicion of ingratitude, and forgetfulness of your love-token sent to me into the Tower by my good brother William Punt[2], so might I not satisfy the desire of this my poor brother and friend, John Searchfield, which cometh unto you for help and comfort, as you can[3], in this troublesome time.

This dare I say, that the man feareth God, and for God's

[[1] The heading of the Emmanuel MS. is: "A letter that Master John Bradford sent to one Master Coker, dwelling at Hasel[eigh] by Maldon in Essex, entreating him to harbour one John Searchfield a bookbinder in London, who in queen Mary's time did wander, to keep a good conscience, *anno Domini* 1554." Vide Strype, Eccl. Mem. Vol. III. part. i. p. 227.]

[[2] The last sixteen words are now first printed from the Emmanuel MS.]

[[3] "as you can," Emman. MS.: not in 1564.]

sake and conscience towards him sustaineth both loss and labour. For our common Father's sake therefore, in Christ, help him to some hole to hide himself in, for a little time, if conveniently you may: and remember that "he that receiveth one of Christ's little ones receiveth Christ," as he himself in the last day will acknowledge. Which last day let us often look on and set before us, as the thing which most maketh to our comfort.

Now we sorrow and sigh, to see the sea swell and rage on this sort, as it doth: and, to confess the truth, we have double cause, as well because we have deserved this sour sauce, by reason of our unthankfulness and many sins (which the Lord pardon), as because God's glory is trodden under foot. But this comfort we have that, as God our good Father "will not the death of a sinner," so will he order this gear most to his glory and our joy and comfort, if we repent now and heartily lament our evils, use earnest, humble, and often, yea, continual prayer, and cast ourselves wholly on him and his goodness, still labouring to loathe this life, and longing for the life to come: for the which, we should account this, as it is, a very vale of misery, much to be mourned in, because the time of our habitation herein and exile is prolonged. God grant us his holy Spirit, to strengthen us in his truth professed, that we may persevere to the end, in the joyful and courageous confessing of his Christ. Amen.

I pray you continue, as I trust you do, to keep both soul and body pure in God's service. Strive to "enter in at the narrow gate," though you leave your lands and goods behind you. It is not lost, which for Christ's sake we leave, but lent to a great usury. Remember that this time is come but to try us. God make us faithful to the end; God keep us always as his children. Amen.

I pray you commend me to Master Osburne, and to all our good brethren in the Lord. The peace of Christ be with us all. Amen, Amen.

Yours in Christ,

JOHN BRADFORD.

XXIII. TO ROBERT HARRINGTON AND ANOTHER[1].

[Perhaps from the Tower, *January*, 1554.]

Bp Coverdale, Letters of the Martyrs, 1564, p. 363.

MS. 2. 2. 15. No. 44. Transcript. Emman. Coll. Cambridge.

"THE God of all mercies and the Father of all consolation" shew unto you more and more the riches of his mercies in Christ Jesus our Lord, and grant you a lively faith to apprehend and pull unto yourselves the same, to your everlasting comfort. Amen.

Because my mind will not let me rest to think upon, and as it were to see sore storms like to fall more felly[2] than any yet we have felt—I should rather say ye have felt, and are like to feel, if ye continue to confess Christ[3] christianly, as ye have begun—I thought it my duty to admonish you, that therefore ye should not be dismayed nor think it any strange thing. For undoubtedly you confessing Christ according to the truth taught you, yea, received of you, though trouble come, the same shall be so far from hurting you, that it shall profit you exceedingly (making you thereby like to him which for your sakes suffered much greater sorrow than all men can sustain); as well that your sorrows and afflictions, whatsoever they be that shall come unto you, should be sanctified in his cross and that which he suffered; as also that in him ye might have both example how to order yourselves in the cross, and how soon, shortly, and gloriously the end of your cross will be. Therefore, I say, be not dismayed, in that the cross cannot but conform and make us like unto Christ, not simply of itself, but by God's Spirit, which maketh it his chief mean thereto; first in putting us in mind of our corruption received of Adam, the cause of all care; then by occasioning us to remember as well our privy hid sins, as also our more manifest evils, that we

[[1] This letter is inscribed as above, its heading in the "Letters of the Martyrs" being, "To his godly friends, G. and N., encouraging them to prepare themselves to the cross, and patiently to endure afflictions for God's cause and his holy gospel;" as the initial "N." may probably stand for "Nathanael," Bradford's usual designation for "Robert Harrington:" see first note on Letter XXI. The initial "G." might possibly represent either one of the Glover family or the martyr Greene: Foxe, Acts, &c., ed. 1583, pp. 1709, 1851, or ed. 1843—9, Vol. VII. pp. 384, 731. The Emmanuel MS. has not any heading.]

[[2] "Felly:" fiercely, cruelly.]

[[3] "Christ," MS.: not in 1564.]

therethrough might be provoked to repentance and asking of mercy, the which undoubtedly God will give us for his Christ's sake, and thereto also his holy Spirit to sanctify us, if we ask the same.

Now this Spirit will not cease more and more both to mortify "the old man" with his desires, and also to renew and repair "the new man" daily, with augmentation and increase; so that at the length we shall be made so like to Christ that we cannot but be coupled unto him; I mean not by faith as now we be, but even in deed, leaving here behind us, with Elias, our cloak the flesh, which one day God will call and quicken again, to be like unto the glorious and immortal body of his Son Jesus Christ our Lord, after that it hath suffered and slept, as his hath done, the afflictions and time which God hath already appointed.

My dear brethren and sisters, this is most certain that the afflictions and crosses which ye shall suffer God hath already appointed for you, so that they are not in the power, choice, and will of your and his enemies. If ye would flee them ye cannot; but, will ye, nill ye, needs must ye have them. If ye will not carry them in the love of God, ye shall carry them in his displeasure. Therefore "cast your care on him which careth for you," and hath "counted all the hairs of your heads, so that one shall not perish," if that ye commit yourselves to his ordering; where else your heads and bodies, yea, souls too shall perish, if that ye withdraw yourselves as unwilling to take his cup and to drink of it. Not that I would have you to thrust yourselves, headlong and rashly, to take or pull unto you trouble; or that I would not have you to use such honest and lawful means as ye may, in the fear of God and with good conscience, to avoid the cross and "give place to evil;" but that I would have you willing to put forth your hand to take it, when God offereth it, in such sort as with good conscience ye cannot escape. Then take it, kiss it, and thank God for it; for it is even a very sacrament that God loveth you, as he saith: "Whom I love, them do I chastise;" "and, if ye be not partakers of correction, surely ye are no children." But if he once chastise you, if that ye kiss the rod, verily he will cast the rod into the fire, and call you and kiss you, as the mother doth her child, when she perceiveth the child to take in good part the correction. But why do I compare God your Father's love to a mother's? in that it far passeth it. For saith he, "though it be possible that a natural mother should forget the child of her womb, yet will not I forget thee, saith the Lord," our good God and Father, through Christ. Though he seem angry towards evening, yet in the morning we shall find him well pleased, if in Christ we come to him and cry, Abba, dear Father, help us, and, as thou hast promised, "tempt us not further than thou wilt make us able to bear."

Therefore, my dear hearts in the Lord, be of good comfort, be of good comfort in the Lord. Confess him and his truth, and fear not prison, loss of goods or life. Fear rather that prison, out of the which there is no deliverance; fear rather the loss of those goods which last for ever; fear rather the loss of the life which is eternal, whereunto ye are called: and the way by which God will bring you to it—in that ye certainly know not whether it will be by prison, fire, halter, &c.—whensoever these come, as I said before, let them not dismay you, nor seem strange to you. For no small number of God's children are gone that way, and we are a good company here together, which are ready to follow the same way through God's grace, if God so will.

I beseech you, make you ready, and go with us; or rather be ready, that when we come we may go with you. The journey is but short, though it be unpleasant to the flesh. Perchance, if we should die in our beds on a corporal malady, it would be much longer and also more painful: at the least in God's sight it cannot be so precious and gainful as I know this kind of death is; whereto I exhort you to prepare yourselves, mine own dear hearts in the bowels and blood of our Saviour Jesus Christ: to whose tuition, grace, governance, and protection, I heartily commend you all, and beseech you that ye would do the like unto me in your hearty prayers.

Out of the Tower of London, 1554[1], this Saturday at night[2].

By your own, to live in the Lord for ever,

JOHN BRADFORD.

[[1] "Out of the Tower of London, 1554," not in MS., but in 1564.]
[[2] "this Saturday at night," MS.: not in 1564.]

XXIV. TO ROBERT HARRINGTON AND HIS WIFE[3].

[Tower of LONDON, *February* 12, 1554[4].]

GRACIOUS God and most merciful Father, for Jesus Christ's sake, thy dearly beloved Son, grant us thy mercy, grace, wisdom, and holy Spirit, to counsel, comfort, and guide us in all our cogitations, words and works, to thy glory and our everlasting joy and peace, for ever. Amen.

Bp Coverdale, Letters of the Martyrs, 1564, p. 366.

Foxe, Acts, &c., ed. 1570, p. 1825; and after editions.

MS. 2. 2. 16. No. 35. Transcript. Emman. Coll. Cambridge.

In my last letter (which I send you herewith now, as tofore I would have done if conveniently I might[5]) ye might perceive my conjecturing to be no less towards you, than now I have partly learned. But, my dearly beloved, I have learned none other thing than before I have told you would come to pass, if ye cast not away that which I am sure ye have learned. I do appeal to both your consciences, whether herein I speak truth, as well of my telling (though not so often as I might and should, God forgive me) as also of your learning.

Now God will try you, to make others to learn by you that which ye have learned by others: and by them which suffered this day ye might learn, if already ye had not learned, that life and honour is not to be set by more than God's commandment. They in no point, for all that ever their ghostly fathers could do[6], having Doctor Death to take their part, would consent or seem to consent to the popish mass and papistical God, otherwise than in the days of our late king[7] they had received; and this their faith they have confessed with their deaths, to their great glory and all our comforts if we follow them, but to our confusion if we start back from the same.

The Lady Jane and her husband were beheaded that day.—[BpCoverdale and Foxe.]

[3 This letter is thus entitled, because it is followed in the "Letters of the Martyrs" by "another letter to the same persons," who, for the reasons stated in the first note on that letter, No. XXI. of this series, are believed to be Robert Harrington and his wife.]

[4 This date is determined by the side-note of Bp Coverdale and Foxe, in reference to the execution of the lady Jane Grey, and her husband, lord Guildford Dudley.—Strype, Eccl. Mem. Vol. III. part I. p. 141.]

[5 The last sixteen words are now first printed from the Emmanuel MS.]

[6 Fecknam had been sent two days before the death of lady Jane Grey, "to commune with her, and to reduce her from the doctrine of Christ to queen Mary's religion:" see the conference between lady Jane and Fecknam, in Foxe, Acts, &c., ed. 1583, p. 1419, or ed. 1843—9, Vol. VI. p. 415.]

[7 Edward VI.]

Wherefore I beseech you both to consider it, as well to praise God for them, as to go the same way with them if God so will. Consider not the things of this life, which is a very prison to all God's children, but the things of everlasting life, which is our very home. But to the beholding of this gear ye must open the eyes of your mind—of faith I should have said—as Moses did, which "set more by trouble with God's people, than by the riches of Egypt" and Pharaoh's court. Your house, home and goods, yea, life and all that ever ye have, God hath given to you as love-tokens, to admonish you of his love, and to win your love to him again. Now will he try your love, whether ye set more by him than by his tokens or no. If ye for his tokens' sake, that is, for your home, house, goods, yea, life, will go with the world lest ye should lose them, then be assured, your love, as he cannot but espy it to be a strumpet's love, so will he cast it away with the world. Remember that "he which will save his life shall lose it," if Christ be true; but he which adventureth, yea, "loseth his life for the gospel's sake, the same shall be sure to find it eternally." Do not ye both know that the way to salvation is not "the broad way" which many run in, but "the strait way" which few now walk in?

Before persecution came, men might partly have stand in a doubt, by the outward state of the world with us, although by God's word it was plain, whether was the highway, for there was as many pretended the gospel as popery: but now the sun is risen, and the wind bloweth, so that the corn which hath not taken fast root cannot nor will not abide: and therefore easily ye may see "the strait way" by the small number that passeth through it. Who will now adventure their goods and life for Christ's sake? which yet gave his life for our sakes. We now are Gergesites, that would rather lose Christ than our porkets. (Matt. viii.) A faithful wife is never tried so to be, but when she rejecteth and withstandeth wooers. A faithful Christian is then found so to be, when his faith is assaulted. If we be not able—I mean, if we will not forsake this world for God's glory and gospel's sake—trow ye that God will make us able or give us a will to forsake it for nature's sake? Die ye must once, and leave all ye have, God knoweth how soon and when, will ye or will ye not. And, seeing perforce ye must do this, will ye not willingly now do it for God's sake?

If ye go to mass, and do as the most part doth, then may ye live at rest and quietly; but, if ye deny to go to it, then shall ye go to prison, lose your goods, leave your children comfortless, yea, lose your life also. But, my dearly beloved, open the eyes of your faith, and see how short a thing this life is, even a very shadow and smoke. Again see how intolerable the punishment of hell-fire is, and that endless. Last of all look on the joys incomprehensible, which God hath prepared for all them, world without end, which lose either lands or goods for his name's sake. And then do ye reason thus: 'If we go to mass, the greatest enemy that Christ hath, though for a little time we shall live in quiet, and leave to our children that they may live hereafter, yet shall we displease God, fall into his hands, which are[1] horrible to hypocrites, and be in wonderful hazard of falling from eternal joy into eternal misery, first of soul and then of body, with the devil and all idolaters. Again we shall want peace of conscience, which surmounteth all the riches of the world: and, for our children, who knoweth whether God will not[2] visit our idolatry on them in this life? yea, our house and goods are in danger of losing, as our lives are, by reason of fire, thieves, and other[3] casualties; and, when God is angry with us, he can send always when he will one mean or another to take all from us for our sins, and to cast us into care for our own sakes, which will not come into some little trouble for his sake.'

On this sort reason with yourselves: and then doubtless God will work otherwise with you and in you than ye are aware of. Where now ye think yourselves unable to abide persecution, be most assured, if so be ye purpose not to forsake God, that God will make you so able to bear his cross, that therein "ye shall rejoice." "Faithful is God," saith Paul, "which will 1 Cor. x.
not tempt you further than he will make you able to bear;" yea, he "will give you an outscape" in the cross, which shall be to your comfort. Think how great a benefit it is, if God will vouch you worthy this honour, to suffer loss of anything for his sake. He might justly cast most grievous plagues upon you: and now he will correct you with that rod whereby you

[1 "are," MS.: "is" 1564 and 1570.]
[2 "not," only in MS.]
[3 "are, by reason of fire, thieves, and other," MS.: "be, through many," 1564 and 1570.]

shall be made "like to his Christ," "that for ever ye may reign with him." Suffer yourselves therefore now to be made like to Christ, for else ye shall never be made like unto him. The devil would gladly have you both[1] now to overthrow that which godly ye have of long time professed. O how would he triumph if he could win his purpose! O how would the papists triumph against God's gospel in you! O how would you confirm them in their wicked popery! O how would the poor children of God be discomforted, if now ye should go to mass and other idolatrous service, and do as the world doth!

Hath God delivered you from the sweat[2] to serve him so? Hath God miraculously restored you to health from your grievous agues for such a purpose? Hath God given you such blessings in this world and good things all the days of your life hitherto? And now of equity will ye not receive at his hands and for his sake some evil? God forbid: I hope better of you. Use prayer, and "cast your care upon God;" commit your children into his hands; give to God your goods, bodies and lives, as he hath given them or rather lent them unto you. Say with Job, "God hath given, and God hath taken away: his name be praised for ever." "Cast your care upon him," I say, "for he is careful for you;" and take it amongst the greatest blessings of God "to suffer for his sake:" I trust he hath kept you hitherto to that end.

And I beseech thee, O merciful Father, for Jesus Christ's sake, that thou wouldest be merciful unto us, comfort us with thy grace, and strengthen us in thy truth, that "in heart we may believe" and "in tongue boldly confess" thy gospel, to thy glory and our eternal salvation. Amen.

Pray for me, and I by God's grace will do the same for you.

JOHN BRADFORD.

[[1] "both," MS.: not in 1564 or 1570.]
[[2] See Vol. I. p. 61, note 3.]

XXV. TO ROYDEN AND ELSING[3].

[Probably from the Tower of LONDON, after *February* 14, 1554[4].]

To my dear friends and brethren, R[oyden] and E[lsing], with their wives and families. Bp Coverdale, Letters of the Martyrs, 1564, p. 338. Foxe, Acts, &c., ed. 1570, p. 1824; and after editions. MS. 2. 2. 15. No. 96. Transcript, Emman. Coll. Cambridge.

The comfort of Christ, felt commonly of his children in their cross for his sake, the everliving God work in both your hearts, my good brethren, and in the hearts of both your yoke-fellows, especially of good Mary, my good sister in the Lord. Amen.

If I had not something heard of the hazard which you are in for the gospel's sake, if you continue the profession and confession thereof, as I trust you do and will do, and that unto the end, God enabling you—as he will doubtless, for his mercy's sake, if you hope in him, for this bindeth him, as David in Christ's person witnesseth, "Our fathers hoped in thee, and thou deliveredst them," &c.—yet by conjectures I could not but suppose, though not so certainly, the time of your suffering and probation to be at hand. For now is the power of darkness fully come upon this realm, most justly for our sins and abusing the light lent us of the Lord, to the setting forth of ourselves more than of God's glory; that as well we might be brought into the better knowledge of our evils, and so heartily repent (which God grant us to do), as also we might have more feeling and sense of our sweet Saviour Jesus Christ, by the humbling and dejecting of us, thereby to make us, as more desirous of him, so him more sweet and pleasant unto us: the which thing the good Spirit of God work sensibly in all our hearts, for God's holy name's sake. Ps. xxii.

For this cause I thought it my duty (being now where I have some liberty to write, the Lord be praised, and hearing of you as I hear) to do that which I should have done if I had heard nothing at all; that is, to desire you to be of good cheer and comfort in the Lord (although in the world you see cause

[3 Bp Coverdale gives the initials, "R. and E." Foxe supplies the names Royden and Elsing, in a side-note. Sampson refers to Elsing as a harbourer of godly and faithful men, in his preface to Bradford's Sermon on Repentance: Vol. I. p. 36.]

[4 From the allusion, in the last paragraph but two, to men "dying as rebels," which probably may refer to the executions, February 14, 1554, after Wyatt's rebellion.]

rather to the contrary), and to go forwards in the way of God, whereinto you are entered; considering that the same cannot but so much more and more wax strait to the outward man, by how much you draw nearer the end of it Even as in the travail of a woman, the nearer she draweth to her delivery, the more her pains increase, so it goeth with us in the Lord's way, the nearer we draw to our deliverance by death to eternal felicity. Example whereof we have—I will not say in the holy prophets and apostles of God, which "when they were young girded themselves and went in manner whither they would, but when they waxed old they went girded of others whither they would not," concerning the outward man—but rather and most lively in our Saviour Jesus Christ, whose life and way was much more painful to him towards the end, than it was at the beginning. And no marvel, for Satan can something abide a man to begin well and set forwards, but rather than he should go on to the end he will vomit his gorge, and cast floods to overflow him, before he will suffer that to come to pass.

John xxi.

Therefore—as we should not be dismayed now at this world, as though some strange thing were happened unto us, in that it is but as it was wont to be to the godly, in that the devil declareth himself after his old wont; in that we have professed no less but to forsake the world and the devil, as God's very enemy; in that we learned no less at the first, when we came to God's school, than to "deny ourselves, and to take up our cross, and follow" our Master, which leadeth us none other way than he himself hath gone before us—as, I say, we should not be dismayed, so we should with patience and joy go forwards, if we set before us as present the time to come, like as the wife in her travail doth the deliverance of her child, and as the saints of God did, but especially our Saviour and pattern Jesus Christ; for the apostle saith, "He set before him the joy and glory to come, and therefore contemned the shame and sorrow of the cross." So if we did, we should find at the length as they found. For whom would it grieve, which hath a long journey to go, to go through a piece of foul way, if he knew that after that the way should be most pleasant, yea, the journey should be ended, and he at his resting-place most happy? Who will be afraid or loath to leave a little pelf for a little time, if he knew he should shortly after receive most plentiful riches?

Heb. xii.

Who will be unwilling for a little while to forsake his wife, children, or friends, &c., when he knoweth he shall shortly after be associated unto them inseparably, even after his own heart's desire? Who will be sorry to forsake this life, which cannot but be most certain of eternal life? Who loveth the shadow better than the body? Who can love this life, but they that regard not the life to come? Who can desire the dross of this world, but such as be ignorant of the treasures of the everlasting joy in heaven? I mean, who is affeared to die, but such as hope not to live eternally?

Christ hath promised pleasure, riches, joy, felicity, and all good things, to them that for his sake lose anything or suffer any sorrow. And is he not true? how can he but be true? for "guile was never found in his mouth." Alas, then, why are we so slack and slow, yea, hard of heart, to believe him promising us thus plentifully eternal blissfulness, and are so ready to believe the world, promising us many things, and paying us nothing? If we will curry favour now, and "halt on both knees"—if so—then it promiseth us peace, quietness, and many things else. But how doth it pay this gear? or, if it pay it, with what quietness of conscience? or if so, how long? I pray you. Do not we see before our eyes men to die shamefully—I mean, as rebels and other malefactors—which refuse to die for God's cause? What way is so sure a way to heaven as to suffer in Christ's cause? If there be any way on horseback to heaven, surely this is the way. "By many troubles," saith the apostle, "we must enter" into heaven. "All that will live godly in Christ Jesu must suffer persecution." For the world cannot love them that are of God; the devil cannot love his enemies; the world will love none but his own: but you are Christ's, therefore look for no love here. Should we look for fire to quench our thirst? and as soon shall God's true servants find peace and favour in antichrist's regiment.

Matt. xix.

1 Pet. ii.

[1 Kings xviii. 21, Septuag.]

Acts xiv.

2 Tim. iii.

Therefore, my dearly beloved, "be stout in the Lord, and in the power of his might. Put on you his armour;" "stand in the liberty of Christ" which you have learned; rejoice that you may be counted worthy to suffer anything for God's cause. To all men this is not given. "Your reward is great in heaven," though in earth you find nothing. The journey is almost past, you are almost in the haven. Hale on apace, I beseech you and merrily hoist up your sails. Cast yourself on Christ, who "careth for you." Keep company with him now still to the end. "He is faithful," and will never leave you, "nor tempt you further than he will make you able to bear;" yea, in the "midst of the temptation he will make an outscape."

Now pray unto him heartily, be thankful of his dignation, rejoice in hope of the health you shall receive; and be mindful of us which are in the vaward[1] and by God's grace trust in Christ to be made able to break the ice before you, that you following may find the way more easy. God grant it may so be. Amen, Amen.

Out of prison, by your brother in Christ,

JOHN BRADFORD.

XXVI. TO MISTRESS BROWN[2].

Bp Coverdale, Letters of the Martyrs, 1564, p. 412.

Foxe, Acts, &c., ed. 1570, p. 1832; and after editions.

MS. 1. 2. 8. No. 91. Transcript, imperfect, Emman. Coll. Cambridge.

To my good sister, Mistress Elizabeth Brown.

Good sister, God our Father make perfect the good he hath begun in you, unto the end.

I am afraid to write unto you, because you so overcharge yourself at all times, even whensoever I do but send to you commendations. I would be more bold on you than on many others; and therefore you might suspend so great tokens, till I should write unto you of my need: which thing doubtless I would do, if it urged me.

Dear sister, I see your unfeigned love to mewards in God, and have done of long time; the which I do recompense with the like, and will do by God's grace, so long as I live; and therefore I hope not to forget you, but in my poor prayers to have you in remembrance, as I hope you have me. Otherwise I can do you no service, except it be now and then by my writing, to let you from better exercise; where yet the end of my writing is to excite and stir up your heart more earnestly to go on forwards

2 Tim. ii. in your well-begun enterprise. For you know, "none shall be

[1 "Vaward:" van, foremost rank.]

[2 Foxe, Acts, &c., ed. 1570, p. 1832, and ed. 1576, p. 1567, has the side note: "A letter of Master Bradford to Mistress Brown, now called Mistress Bettes." The edition of 1583, p. 1649, has "Now called Mistress Rushbrough."]

crowned but such as strive lawfully;" and none receiveth the glaive[3] but those that run to the appointed mark. None shall be saved but such as persist and continue to the very end. Therefore, dear sister, remember that we "have need of patience, that when we have done the good will of God we may receive the promise." Heb. x. Patience and perseverance be the proper notes, whereby God's children are known from counterfeits. They that persevere not were always but hypocrites. Many make godly beginnings, yea, their progress seemeth marvellous; but yet after the end they fail. "These were never of us," saith St John; "for, if they had been of us, they would have continued" unto the very end.

Wholesome lessons of life.—[Foxe.]

Go to therefore, mine own beloved in the Lord; as you have well begun, and well gone forward, so well persist and happily end, and then all is yours. Though this be sharp and sour, yet it is not tedious or long. Do all that ever you do simply for God, and as to God: so shall never unkindness, nor any other thing, make you to leave off from well-doing, so long as you may do well. Accustom yourself now to see God continually, that he may be "All in all" unto you. In good things behold his mercy, and apply it unto yourself. In evil things and plagues behold his judgments; wherethrough learn to fear him. Beware of sin, as the serpent of the soul, which spoileth us of all our ornature and seemly apparel in God's sight. Let "Christ crucified" be your book to study on, and that both night and day. Mark your vocation, and be diligent in the works thereof; use hearty and earnest prayer, and that in spirit. "In all things give thanks" to God our Father, through Christ. Labour to have here life everlasting begun in you; for else it will not be elsewhere enjoyed. Set God's judgment often before your eyes, that now examining yourself you may make diligent suit, and obtain never to come into judgment. Uncover your evils to God, that he may cover them. Beware of this antichristian trash, defile not yourself in soul or body therewith; but "accomplish holiness in the fear of God," and "bear no yoke with unbelievers." Look for "the coming of the Lord," which "is at hand:" by earnest prayer and godly life hasten it. God our Father accomplish his good work in you. Amen.

[[3] See p. 48, note 1, above.]

Commend me to my good mother, Mistress Wilkinson, and to my very dear sister, Mistress Warcup. I shall daily commend you all to God, and I pray you to do the like for me.

JOHN BRADFORD.

XXVII. TO HIS MOTHER[1].

[Tower of LONDON, *February* 24, 1554.]

MS. on reverse of colophon of "A declaration of Christ," &c., by Bp Hooper, printed at Zurich, 1547, Holograph, in possession of the editor.

GOOD mother and right dear to me in the Lord, I wish to you for ever God's peace in Christ. But this cannot be had or kept without war with ourselves, with the world, and with the devil: therefore accordingly prepare yourself, though you be a woman, to take unto you a man's heart, that valiantly you may "fight a good fight," and receive a crown of victory, which none shall have but he that fighteth lawfully. If in yourself you feel weakness, let the same be so far from making you faint-hearted, that thereby you rather gather matter of courage and comfort, because God's power is never so much seen and known as to them and by them which see and lament their weakness: as Paul testifieth, who said he would "gladly rejoice in his infirmities," that God's virtue and power might dwell in him; thereby teaching, none to be so fit for God to choose as his instruments to work by and set forth his power, as those which be most weak, that all power and glory might be ascribed to the Lord, and "he that rejoiceth might rejoice in him" which "triumpheth by the weak against the mighty of the world."

Therefore, my good mother, of your infirmities and weakness gather rather matter to comfort you and to cause you to be courageous, than to discomfort you, and to make you faint-

[[1] This letter is now first printed.

The original has not any inscription. It is probably the same that Bradford mentions to his mother in the next letter, No. XXVIII., p. 76: (see margin there:) for the present letter treats of the same topics with that hitherto missing, namely prayer and trust in God under trial; and it begins, "Good mother and right dear to me in the Lord."

It is possible however, that this letter might have been intended for Mistress Wilkinson, of whom Bradford speaks, at the close of the last letter, as "my good mother," and whom he addresses in a letter probably written in February, 1555, as "good mother and dear mistress in the Lord," "right dear mother."]

hearted. That you may have hereof more experience, do as I know you do in your trouble and temptations, "call upon the Lord," upon whose back you are commanded to "cast your burthen" (for he will bear it), and, as Peter teacheth, "all your care:" "Cast all your care on him," saith he: and then doubtless you shall find it true that he is "with you in trouble, will deliver you, and glorify you." Call therefore, I say, on him in your trouble and terror, for so he commandeth you to do; and doubtless, according to his promise, he will so help you that you shall glorify and praise him at the length. For oftentimes at the first he maketh as though he heard us not: whereas of truth it is otherwise, according to this, "Before they call on me I hear them, whilst they are in speaking I grant them their petitions."

But he doth so put off, and as it were dissemble, as though he heard not, for three causes. First, thereby to try our faith, that is, that we might thereby better see our faith, the which, the more it is tried, the more it shall be found praiseworthy, as gold, the oftener and more it is cast into the fire, the more it is pure and to be esteemed. Secondly he lingereth to grant our requests, to make us to call more earnestly, and that we might acknowledge his gifts with more gratitude and thankfulness when we shall obtain the same. Last of all he doth put off our prayers, that he might recompense it with abundance, that is, that he might more plentifully pour upon us the effect of our petitions.

Whensoever therefore we pray, and be not forthwith heard as we think, let us remember these three things; and then, as we shall persevere in prayer, so we shall indeed have lively experiment of that which I spake—I mean, how that God careth for our weakness in such sort, that the weaker we be the dearer we should think ourselves to be unto God; as we commonly see parents have a great deal more care for their children that be sickly and weak, than they have for the others that be whole enough, that be in good plight and liking.

These things I write unto you, good and most dear mother, not so much doubting your weakness, as to declare thereby the comfort you may gather, and I do well know you feel, at the hands of your dear Father and most tender-hearted

Husband, Jesus Christ, who hath married you to himself in mercy and great compassion, and hath endowed you with the dowry of his deserts, wherethrough you are enriched and invested in all the goods he hath, which be such as "the eye hath not seen, the ear hath not heard, nor the heart of man is able to conceive:" whither he soon bring us for his own mercies' sake. Amen.

E carcere [from prison], 24 *Februarii*, 1554.

JOHN BRADFORD.

XXVIII. TO HIS MOTHER.

[Probably the Tower of LONDON, about *February* 24, 1554[1].]

Bp Coverdale, Letters of the Martyrs, 1564, p. 451.

Foxe, Acts, &c., ed. 1570, p. 1838; and after editions.

THE Lord of life and Saviour of the world, Jesus Christ, bless you and comfort you, my good and dear mother, with his heavenly comfort, consolation, grace and Spirit, now and for ever. Amen.

If I thought that daily, yea, almost hourly, you did not cry upon God the Father, through Jesus Christ, that he would give me his blessing, even the blessing of his children, then would I write more hereabouts. But forasmuch as herein I am certain you are diligent—and so I beseech you, good mother, to continue—I think it good to write something, whereby this your crying might be furthered: furthered it will be, if those things which hinder it be taken away; among the which in that I think my imprisoment is the greatest and chiefest, I will thereabout spend this letter, and that briefly, lest it might increase the let, as my good brother, this bringer, can tell you.

He meaneth the danger of more strait imprisonment that might hereby follow.—[Coverdale and Foxe.]

You shall know therefore, good mother, that for my body, though it be in a house out of the which I cannot come when I will, yet, in that I have conformed my will to God's will, I find herein liberty enough, I thank God; and for my lodging, bedding, meat, drink, godly and learned company[2], books and all

[1 From the supposed allusion in this to the last letter: see p. 72, note 1, above.

[2 Bradford in the King's Bench was imprisoned with Bp Ferrar, Rowland Taylor, and Adn Philpot, as in the Tower he had for a time been imprisoned with Abp Cranmer and Bps Ridley and Latimer. See Letter XXXV. of this series to Lady Vane; Bp Ridley's Works, p. 390, Park. Soc.; Bp Latimer's Works, Vol. II. pp. 258, 9, Park. Soc.]

other necessaries for mine ease, comfort, and commodity, I am in much better case than I could wish; and God's merciful providence here is far above my worthiness. Worthiness quoth I? Alas! I am worthy of nothing but damnation.

But, besides all this, for my soul I find much more commodity; for God is my Father, I now perceive, through Christ: therefore, in prisoning me for his gospel, he maketh me like to the image of his Son Jesus Christ here, that, when he cometh to judgment, I might then be like unto him, as my trust and hope is I shall be. Now he maketh me like to his friends the prophets, apostles, the holy martyrs and confessors. Which of them did not suffer, at the least, imprisonment or banishment for his gospel and word?

Now, mother, how far am I unmeet to be compared to them! I—I say—which always have been and am so vile an hypocrite and grievous a sinner. God might have caused me, long before this time, to have been cast into prison as a thief, a blasphemer, an unclean liver, and an heinous offender of the laws of the realm: but, dear mother, his mercy is so great upon both you and me and all that love me, that I should be cast into prison as none of these, or for any such vices, but only for his Christ's sake, for his gospel's sake, for his church's sake, that hereby, as I might learn to lament and bewail my ingratitude and sins, so I might rejoice in his mercy, be thankful, look for eternal joy with Christ, for whose sake (praised be his name for it!) I now suffer, and therefore should be merry and glad. And indeed, good mother, so I am, as ever I was: yea, never so merry and glad was I, as I now should be, if I could get you to be merry with me, to thank God for me, and to pray on this sort: 'Ah, good Father! which dost vouchsafe that my son, being a grievous sinner in thy sight, should find this favour with thee, to be one of thy Son's captains and men of war, to fight and suffer for his gospel's sake, I thank thee, and pray thee, in Christ's name, that thou wouldest forgive him his sins and unthankfulness, and make perfect in him that good which thou hast begun: yea, Lord, I pray thee, make him worthy to suffer, not only imprisonment, but even very death, for thy truth, religion, and gospel's sake. As Hannah did apply and give her first child, Samuel, unto thee, so do I, dear Father, beseeching thee, for Christ's sake, to accept this my gift, and give my son John Bradford grace, always truly to serve thee and thy people, as Samuel did. Amen.'

If on this sort, good mother, from your heart you would pray, as I should be the most merryest man that ever was, so am I certain the lets of your prayer for my imprisonment would be taken away. Good mother, therefore mark what I have written, and learn this prayer by heart, to say it daily; and then I shall be merry, and you shall rejoice, if that you continue, as I trust you do, in God's true religion, even the same I have taught you, and my father Traves, I trust, will put you in remembrance of: my brother Roger also, I trust, doth so daily. Go to therefore, and learn apace. Although the devil cast divers lets in the way, God, in whom you trust, will cast them away for his Christ's sake, if you will call upon him; and never "will he suffer you to be tempted above that he will make you able to bear." But how you should do herein, the other letter[1] I have written herewith shall teach you, which I would none should read till my father Traves have read it; and he will give you, by God's grace, some instructions.

This letter cometh not to our hands.—[Coverdale and Foxe.]

Now therefore will I make an end, praying you, good mother, to look for no more letters; for if it were known that I have pen and ink and did write, then should I want all the foresaid commodities I have spoken of concerning my body, and be cast into some dungeon in fetters of iron: which thing I know would grieve you: and therefore, for God's sake, see that these be burned, when this little prayer in it is copied out by my brother Roger, for perchance your house may be searched for such gear when you think little of it; and look for no more, sweet mother, till either God shall deliver me and send me out, either you and I shall meet together in heaven, where we shall never part asunder. Amen.

I require you, Elizabeth and Margaret, my sisters, that you will fear God, use prayer, love your husbands, be obedient unto them, as God willeth you, bring up your children in God's fear, and be good housewives. God bless you both, with both your husbands, my good brethren, whom to do good because I now cannot, I will pray for them and you. Commend me to my sister Ann, mother Pike, T. Sorocold and his wife, R. Shalcross and his wife, R. Bolton, J. Wild, M. Vicar, the parson

[[1] See p. 72, note 1, above.]

of Mottram, sir Laurence Hall, with all that love and I trust live the gospel: and God turn sir Thomas his heart. Amen. I will daily pray for him.

I need not to set my name: you know it well enough. Because you should give my letters to father Traves to be burned, I have written here a prayer for you to learn to pray for me, good mother, and another for all your house, in your evening prayer, to pray with my brother. These prayers are written with my own hand: keep them still, but the letters give to father Traves to burn, and give father Traves a copy of the latter prayer.

XXIX. TO LORD RUSSELL[2].

Bp Coverdale, Letters of the Martyrs, 1564, p. 275.

Foxe, Acts, &c., ed. 1570, p. 1816; and after editions.

MS. G. g. iv. 13. p. 158. Transcript, University Library, Cambridge.

MS. 1. 2. 8. No. 14. Transcript, Emman. Coll. Cambridge.

THE everlasting and most gracious God and Father of our Saviour Jesu Christ bless your good lordship with all manner of heavenly blessings, in the same Christ our only comfort and hope. Amen.

Praised be God our Father which hath vouched you worthy, as of faith in his Christ, so of his cross for the same. Magnified be his holy name, who as he hath delivered you from one cross, so he hath made you willing, I trust, and ready to bear another, when he shall see his time to lay it upon you. For these are

[2 The inscription of this letter in Coverdale and Foxe is: "To the Honourable Lord Russell, now Earl of Bedford, being then in trouble for the verity of God's gospel."

Lord Francis Russell "was committed to the sheriff of London's custody," July 30, 1553: Foxe, Acts, &c., ed. 1583, p. 1465, or ed. 1843—9, Vol. VI. p. 537. He became the second earl of Bedford, on the death of his father, March 20, 1555. He addressed a letter to Bullinger from Venice, April 26, 1556, (Pellican having died the first of that month). Original Letters, No. LXIX. p. 138, Park. Soc. He was one of the four of Elizabeth's Council, who were made privy to the revision of the Prayer-Book, 1559, and, holding under the Crown various offices of trust and dignity, was distinguished for piety and many excellences. See the interesting "Mirror of true honour and Christian nobility, exposing the life, death, and divine virtues of the most noble and godly lord Francis, earl of Bedford," by George Whetstone, London, Jones, 1585, reprinted in Park's Heliconia, Vol. II. Longmans, 1815. Various letters from this nobleman to Gualter and Bullinger are printed in the Zurich Letters, Vol. II. Park. Soc. He died, aged 58, in 1585. Vide Collins' Hist. of English Peerage, Vol. I. p. 270—72, Lond. 1812.]

the most singular gifts of God, given as to few, so to none else but to those few which are most dear in his sight.

Faith is reckoned, and worthily, among the greatest gifts of God; yea, it is the greatest itself that we enjoy, for by it, as we be justified and made God's children, so are we temples and possessors of the Holy Spirit, yea, of Christ also, and of the Father himself. By faith we drive the devil away, we "overcome the world," and are already citizens of heaven and fellows with God's dear saints. But who is able to reckon the riches that this faith bringeth with her unto the soul she sitteth upon? No man, nor angel. And therefore, as I said, of all God's gifts she may be set in the top, and have the uppermost seat. The which thing if men considered, in that she cometh alonely from God's own mercy-seat, by the hearing, not of mass or matins, diriges[1], or such draff, but of the word of God, in such a tongue as we can and do understand—as they would be diligent and take great heed for doing or seeing anything which might cast her down, for then they fall also—so would they with no less care read and hear God's holy word, joining thereto most earnest and often prayer, as well for the more and better understanding, as for the loving, living, and confessing of the same, maugre the head of the devil, the world, our flesh, reason, goods, possessions, carnal friends, wife, children, and very life here, if they should pull us back to hearken to their voice and counsel, for more quiet, sure, and longer use of them.

Ephes. v. John xiv. 1 Pet. v. 1 John v.

Now, notwithstanding this excellency of faith, in that we read the apostle to match therewith, yea, as it were, to prefer suffering persecution for Christ's sake, I trow no man will be so fond as to think otherwise but that I and all God's children have cause to glorify and praise God, which hath vouched you worthy so great a blessing. For, though the reason or wisdom of the world think of the cross according to their reach, and according to their present sense, and therefore fleeth from it as from a most great ignominy and shame, yet God's scholars have learned otherwise to think of the cross, that it is the frame-house in the which God frameth his children like to his Son Christ, the furnace that fineth God's gold, the high-

Phil. i.

[[1] See Vol. I. p. 589, note D.]

way to heaven, the suit and livery that God's servants are served withal, the earnest and beginning of all consolation and glory. For they—I mean God's scholars, as your lordship is, I trust—do "enter into God's sanctuary," lest "their feet slip." Psal. lxxiii.
They look not, as beasts do, on things present only, but on things to come, and so have they as present to faith the judgment and glorious coming of Christ; like as the wicked have now their worldly wealth wherein they wallow and will wallow, till they tumble headlong into hell, where are torments too terrible and endless. Now they follow the fiend, as the bear doth the train of honey, and the sow the swillings, till they be brought into the slaughter-house, and then they know that their prosperity hath brought them to perdition. Then cry they, 'Woe, woe, we went the wrong way; we counted these Wisd. v.
men'—I mean such as you be, that suffer for God's sake loss of goods, friends and life, whom they shall see endued with rich robes of righteousness, crowns of most pure precious gold, and palms of conquest, in the goodly glorious palace of the Lamb, where is eternal joy, felicity, &c.—'we counted,' will they then say, 'these men but fools and madmen; we took their conditions to be but curiosity.' &c. But then will it be too late, then the time will be turned, laughing shall be turned into weeping, and weeping into rejoicing. Read Wisdom ii. iii. iv. v.

Therefore, as before I have said, great cause have I to thank God which hath vouched you worthy of this most bountiful blessing: much more then you have cause, my good lord, so to be, I mean, thankful. For look upon your vocation, I pray you, and tell me how many noblemen, earl's sons, lords, knights, and men of estimation, hath God in this realm of England dealt thus withal. I dare say you think not that you have deserved this. Only God's mercy in his Christ hath wrought this on you, as he did in Jeremy's time on Abimelech, [Jer. xxxviii. xxxix.
in Ahab's time on Abdias, in Christ's time on Joseph of Arimathea, 1 Kings xviii. John xix.
in the apostles' time on Sergius Paulus and the queen Acts xiii. viii.]
Candace's chamberlain. Only now be thankful and continue, continue, continue, my good lord, continue to confess Christ. "Be not ashamed of him before men," for then "will not he be ashamed of you." Now will he try you: stick fast unto him,

Psal. xci. and he will stick fast by you; "he will be with you in trouble and deliver you." But then must you cry unto him, for so it precedeth: "He cried unto me, and I heard; I was with him in trouble." &c.

Remember Lot's wife which looked back; remember Francis Spira[1]; remember that "none is crowned, but he that striveth lawfully." Remember that all you have is at Christ's commandment. Remember, he lost more for you than you can lose for him. Remember, you lose not that which is lost for his sake, for you shall find much more here and elsewhere. Remember, you shall die; and when, where, and how, you cannot tell. Remember, the death of sinners is most terrible. Remember, "the death of God's saints is precious in his sight." Remember, the multitude goeth "the wide way," which windeth to woe. Remember, that "the strait gate," which leadeth to glory, hath but few travellers. Remember, Christ biddeth you "strive to enter in thereat." Remember, "he that trusteth in the Lord" shall receive strength to stand against all the assaults of his enemies.

Be certain, "all the hairs of your head are numbered." Be certain, your good Father hath appointed bounds, over the which the devil dare not look. Commit yourself to him: he is, hath been, and will be your keeper: "cast your care on him, and he will care for you." Let Christ be your scope and mark to prick at; let him be your pattern to work by; let him be your ensample to follow; give him as your heart so your hand, as your mind so your tongue, as your faith so your feet; and let his word be your candle to go before you, in all matters of religion.

Psal. i. "Blessed is he that walketh not" to these popish prayers,
1 Cor. vi. "nor standeth" at them, "nor sitteth" at them. "Glorify God in both soul and body." "He that gathereth not with Christ scattereth abroad." Use prayer, look for God's help, which is at hand to them that ask and hope thereafter assuredly. In which prayer I heartily desire your lordship to remember us, who as we are going with you right gladly, God therefore be praised, so we look to go before you, hoping that you will fol-

[[1] See Vol. I. p. 433, note 6. The life of Spira was originally published at Geneva, 1550: "Exemplum memorabile desperationis in Francisco Spira, propter abjuratam fidei confessionem, cum præfatione D. Joannis Calvini."]

low, if God so will, according to your daily prayer: "Thy will be done on earth," &c.

The good Spirit of God always guide your lordship unto the end. Amen.

Your lordship's own for ever,

JOHN BRADFORD.

XXX. TO A FRIEND.

A letter of thanks to a good benefactor of his.—[Foxe.]

Bp Coverdale, Letters of the Martyrs, 1564, p. 456.

Foxe, Acts, &c., ed. 1570 p. 1835; and after editions.

THE mercy of God in Christ, peculiar to his children, be evermore felt of you, my dearly beloved in the Lord. Amen.

When I consider with myself the benefits which God hath shewed unto me by your means, if I had so good and thankful a heart as I would I had, I could not with dry eyes give him thanks, for certainly they are very many and great; and now, being yet still the Lord's prisoner, I perceive from him more benefits by you; for the which I think myself so much bound to you, my good brother (although you were but the instrument by whom God wrought and blessed me), that I look not to come out of your debt, by any pleasure or service that I shall ever be able to do you in this life. I shall heartily pray unto God therefore, to requite you the good you have done to me for his sake; for I know that which you have done, you have done it simply in respect of God and his word. He therefore give you daily more and more to be confirmed in his truth and word, and so plentifully pour upon you the riches of his holy Spirit and heavenly treasures, laid up in store for you, that your corporal and earthly riches may be used of you as sacraments and significations thereof, the more to desire the one, that is, the heavenly, and the less to esteem the other, that is, the earthly. For Satan's solicitation is, so to set before you the earthly, that therein and thereby you should not have access to the consideration of the heavenly, but as one bewitched should utterly forget them, and altogether become a lover and worshipper of the earthly mammon, and so to fall to covetousness and a desire to be rich, by that means to bring you into many noisome and hurtful lusts; as now-a-days I hear of many which have utterly forsaken God and all his heavenly riches, for antichrist's pleasure and the preserving of their worldly pelf, which they imagine to leave to their posterity: whereof they are uncertain, as they may be most certain they leave to them God's wrath and vengeance, in his time to be sent by visitation, if they in time heartily repent not, and prevent not the same by earnest prayer. Wherein, my good brother, if you be diligent, hearty, and persevere, I am sure God will preserve you from evil, and from yielding yourself to do as the world now doth, by allowing in bodily fact, in the Romish service, that which the inward cogitation and mind doth disallow. But if you be cold in prayer, and come into consideration of earthly and present things simply, then shall you fall into faithless follies and wounding of your conscience. From which God evermore preserve you, with your good wife, and your babe Leonard, and all your family, to the which I wish the blessing of God, now and for ever, through Christ our Lord. Amen.

I pray you give thanks for me to your old bedfellow, for his great friendship, for your sake shewed to me when I was in the Tower.

JOHN BRADFORD.

XXXI. BP RIDLEY TO BRADFORD.

[Bocardo in OXFORD, probably the beginning of *April*, 1554[1].]

Foxe, Acts, &c., ed. 1563, p. 1294; and after editions.

Bp Coverdale, Letters of the Martyrs, 1564, p. 58.

WELL beloved in Christ our Saviour, we all with one heart wish you, with all those that love God in deed and truth, grace and health, and specially to our dearly beloved companions which are, in Christ's cause and the cause both of their brethren and of their own salvation, ready and willing to put their neck[2] under the yoke of Christ's cross.

How joyful it was unto us all to hear[3] the report of Doctor Taylor and of his godly confession, &c., I ensure you it is hard for me to express. Blessed be God which was, and is, the Giver of that and of all godly strength and stomach in the time of

[[1] From the allusion to Rowland Taylor's "godly confession," apparently when he first appeared before Gardiner, early in April 1554, the letter from the Council for his arrest having been issued, March 26. See Foxe, Acts, &c., ed. 1583, p. 1428, 1520, or ed. 1843—9, Vol. VI. p. 439, 681.]

[[2] "to put their neck willingly," 1563: "ready and willing to put their neck," 1564.]

[[3] "to hear," 1564: not in 1563.]

adversity. As for the rumours that have or do go abroad, either of our relenting or massing, we trust that they, which know God and their duty towards their brethren in Christ, will[4] not be too light of credence. For it is not the slanderer's evil tongue, but a man's own evil deed, that can with God "defile a man:" and therefore, by God's grace, ye shall never have cause[4] to do otherwise than ye say ye do, that is, not to doubt but that we will by God's grace continue. &c.

Like rumour as you have heard of our coming to London hath been here spread of the coming of certain learned men prisoners hither from London: but as yet we know no certainty whether of these rumours is or shall be more true. Know you, that we have you in our daily remembrance, and wish you and all the rest of our foresaid companions well in Christ. It should do us much comfort, if we might have knowledge of the state of the rest of our most dearly beloved, which in this troublesome time do stand in Christ's cause, and in the defence of the truth thereof. Somewhat we have heard of Master Hooper's matter[5], but of the rest never a deal. We long to hear of father Crome, Doctor Sandys, Master Saunders, Veron, Becon, Rogers, &c.[6]

We are in good health, thanks be to God, and yet the manner of our entreating doth change as sour ale doth in summer. It is reported to us of our keepers, that the university beareth us heavily[7]. A coal chanced to fall in the night out of the chimney, and burnt a hole in the floor, and no more harm was done, the bailiffs' servants sitting by the fire. Another night there chanced, as master bailiffs told us, a drunken fellow to multiply words, and for the same he was set in Bocardo. Upon these things, as is reported, there is risen a rumour in the town and country about, that we would have broken the prison with such violence as, if master bailiffs had not played the pretty men, we should have made a scape. We had out of our prison a wall that we might have walked upon, and our servants had liberty to go abroad in the town or fields: but now both they and we are restrained of both. My lord of Worcester[8] passed by through Oxford, but he

Bocardo is a stinking and filthy prison for drunkards, whores and harlots and the vilest sort of people.—[Coverdale.]

[[4] "they will," "other cause," 1563: "will," "cause," 1564.]

[[5] This may probably have been the deprivation of Hooper of the bishoprics of Worcester and Gloucester, March 19, 1554: Foxe, Acts, &c., ed. 1583, p. 1505, or ed. 1843—9, Vol. VI. p. 645.]

[[6] The last two sentences occur in Foxe, 1563, and after editions, but not in Coverdale, 1564.]

[[7] "Beareth heavily:" regardeth with ill-will.]

[[8] Richard Pates. Vide Godwin De Præs. Angl. ed. Richardson, Tom I. p. 50, Cantab. 1743.]

did not visit us. The same day began our restraint to be more, and the Book of the Communion was taken from us by the bailiffs at the mayor's commandment, as master bailiffs did report to us. No man is licensed to come unto us. Afore they might, that would, see us upon the wall: but that is so grudged at, and so evil reported, that we are now restrained. &c.

Sir, blessed be God, with all our evil reports, grudgings and restraints, we are merry in God; and all our cure and care is and shall be, by God's grace, to please and serve him, of whom we look and hope, after these temporal and momentary miseries, to have eternal joy and perpetual felicity with Abraham, Isaac and Jacob, Peter and Paul, and all the heavenly company of the angels in heaven, through Jesus Christ our Lord. As yet there was never learned man, or any scholar or other, that visited us since we came into Bocardo, which now in Oxford may be called a college of quondams[1]; for, as ye know, we be no fewer there than three, and I dare say every one well contented with his portion, which I do reckon to be our heavenly Father's fatherly, good and gracious gift.

Thus fare you well. We shall, with God's grace, one day meet together and be merry: the day assuredly approacheth apace. The Lord grant that it may shortly come; for, before that day come, I fear me the world will wax worse and worse. But then all our enemies shall be overthrown and trodden under foot, righteousness and truth then shall have the victory, and bear the bell[2] away; whereof the Lord grant us to be partners, and all that loveth truly the truth.

We all pray you, as ye can, to cause all our commendations to be made to all such as ye know did visit us and you when we were in the Tower with their friendly remembrances and benefits. Mistress Wilkinson and Mistress Warcup[3] have not forgotten us, but even since we came into Bocardo with their charitable and friendly benevolence have comforted us: not that else we did lack (for God be blessed, which ever hitherto hath provided sufficiently for us); but that is a great comfort and an occasion for us to bless God, when we see that he maketh them so friendly to tender us, whom some of us were never familiarly acquainted withal.

Yours in Christ,

NICHOLAS RIDLEY.

[1 "Quondams:" persons formerly in office.—Nares' Glossary.]

[2 See Vol. I. p. 480, note 2.]

[3 See p. 39, note 3, and p. 45, note 2, above.]

XXXII. TO SIR JAMES HALES[4].

[King's Bench prison, *April* 12, 1554.]

"THE God of mercy and Father of all comfort" plentifully pour out upon you and in you his mercy, and with his consolations comfort and strengthen you to the end, for his and our Christ's sake. Amen.

Foxe, Acts, &c., ed. 1570, p. 1818; and after editions.

Bp Coverdale, Letters of the Martyrs, 1564, p. 286.

MS. 2. 2. 15. No. 8. Original, Transcript, with corrections in Bradford's autograph Emman. Coll. Cambridge.

Although, right worshipful sir, many causes might move me to be content with crying for you to your God and my God, that he would give you grace to persevere well, as he hath right notably begun, to the great glory of his name and comfort of all such as fear him—as lack of learning, of familiarity, yea, acquaintance (for I think I am unknown to you both by face and name) and other such like things—yet I cannot content myself, but presume something to scribble unto you: not that I think my scribbling can do you good, but that I might hereby declare my συμπάθειαν [sympathy] and compassion, love and affection I bear towards your mastership; which is contented, yea, desirous with us poor misers[5] to confess Christ's gospel in these perilous times and days of trial. O Lord God, how good art thou, which dost thus glean out grapes, I mean children for thyself, and brethren for Christ!

Look, good Master Hales, on your vocation: not many judges, not many knights, not many landed men, not many rich

[[4] The history of Sir James Hales (of Tenterden in Kent, Justice of the Common Pleas) is especially melancholy. He "did excel all others in virtue, prudence, gravity, and true ministering of justice:......the law itself seemed no less to be printed and written in his life and doings, than in the very volumes or papers; and he had like hearty affection to the gospel of Christ." Though a zealous Protestant, he alone among the judges and council of Edward VI. refused to subscribe the deed by which the crown was bequeathed to the heirs of the duchess of Suffolk. Nevertheless he was committed to the King's Bench, October 6, 1553, because, when indictments against priests for saying mass were brought before him, he "gave order therein as the law required." He was afterward removed to other prisons; and it is believed, he was led to make some concession of his principles. He was so troubled, that he made, while in confinement, an attempt upon his life, April 13, 1554, and, after being discharged, "casting himself into a shallow river, was drowned therein," early in August, 1554. Bradford's letter had been sent, April 12, the day before Hales' attempt on his own life, while in the Bread-compter prison.—Foxe, Acts, &c., ed. 1563, p. 1113, and ed. 1583, p. 1532, or ed. 1843—9, Vol. VI. pp. 384, 394, 710; Bp Hooper's Works, Vol. II. p. 377, Park. Soc.; Strype, Ecc. Mem. Vol. III. part I. p. 274; and Carte's England, reigns of Edward VI. and Mary, Vol. III. pp. 277, 293, Lond. 1747—55. See also the last note on this letter.]

[[5] "Misers:" unhappy ones.]

men and wealthy to live, as you are, hath God chosen to suffer for his sake, as he hath now done towards[1] you. Certainly, I dare say, you think not so of yourself, as though God were bound to prefer you, or had need of you, but rather attribute this, as all good things, unto his free mercy in Christ. Again I dare say that you, being a wise man, do judge of things wisely; that is, concerning this your cross (which I call a preferment[2]), you judge of it not after the world and people, which is *magnus erroris magister*, [a great teacher of error,] nor after the judgment of reason and worldly wisdom, which is foolishness to faith, nor after the present sense, to the which

Heb. xii. *non videtur gaudii sed molestiæ*, "it seemeth not to be joyous, but grievous," as Paul writeth—but after the word of God, which teacheth your cross to be, in respect of yourself, between God and you, God's chastising and your Father's correction, nurture, school, trial, pathway to heaven, glory and felicity, and the furnace to consume the dross and mortify the relics of old Adam which yet remain, yea, even the frame-house to fashion you like to the dearest saints of God here, yea, to Christ the Son of God, that elsewhere you might be like unto him.

Now concerning your cross, in respect of the world, between the world and you, God's word teacheth it to be a testimonial of God's truth, of his providence, of his power, of his mercy[3], of his justice[3], of his wisdom, of his anger against sin, of his goodness, of his judgment, of your faith and religion: so that by it you are to the world a witness of God, one of his *testes*, [witnesses,] that he is true, he ruleth all things, he is just, wise, and at the length will judge the world, and cast the wicked into perdition, but the godly he will take and receive into his eternal habitation.

All this and much more you know by the word of God better than I, and therefore I do omit the quotations of places[4]. I know you judge of things after faith's fetch and

2 Cor. iv. the effects or ends of things; and so you see *æternum pondus gloriæ*, "an eternal weight of glory," which this cross shall bring unto you, *dum non spectas ea quæ videntur, sed ea quæ*

[1 "done," 1570, not in MS.: "towards," MS., not in 1570.]
[2 "which I call a preferment," "worldly-wise," "I trust," MS.: not in 1570.]
[3 "of his mercy," MS., not in 1570: "of his justice," 1570: not in MS.]
[4 The last twenty-four words now are first printed from the MS.]

non videntur, "while you look not on the things which are seen, but on the things which are not seen." Let the worldlings weigh things, and look upon the affairs of men with their worldly and corporal eyes, (as did many in subscription of the king's last will, and therefore they did that for the which they beshrewed themselves:) but let us look on things with other manner of eyes, as, God be praised, you did, in not doing that which you were desired, and driven at to have done[5]. You then beheld things not as a worldly-wise[2] man, but as a man of God; and so you do now in religion, I trust[2], at the least hitherto you have done: and, that you might do so still, I humbly beseech and pray you, say with David, *Defecerunt oculi mei in* Ps. cxix. [82.] *eloquium tuum: quando consolaberis me?* "Mine eyes fail for thy word, saying, when wilt thou comfort me?" Though you be as *uter in fumo*, "like a bottle in the smoke," (for I hear say[6] you want health), yet *ne obliviscaris justificationes Dei*, "do not forget the statutes of the Lord;" but cry out with David[6], *Quot sunt dies servi tui? quando facies de persequentibus me judicium?* "How many are the days of thy servant? when wilt thou execute judgment on them that persecute me?" And be certain, *quod Dominus veniens veniet, et non tardabit. Si* Habak. ii. *moram fecerit, expecta illum:* "The Lord will surely come, and not stay: though he tarry, wait for him:" for he is but *ad momentum in ira sua, et vita in voluntate ejus. Ad vesperam* Ps. xxx. *demorabitur fletus, et ad matutinum lætitia:* "He is but a while in his anger, but in his favour is life. Weeping may abide at evening, but joy cometh in the morning." Follow therefore Esay's counsel, *Abscondere ad modicum, ad momen-* Isai. xxvi. *tum, donec pertranseat indignatio ejus:* "Hide thyself for a very little while, until the indignation pass over," which is not *indignatio* indeed, but to our sense: and therefore, in the twenty-seventh chapter of that prophet, God saith of his church and people, that, as he "keepeth night and day," so Isai. xxvii. *non est indignatio mihi*, saith he.

The mother sometime beateth the child, but yet her heart melteth upon it even in the very beating; and therefore she casteth the rod into the fire, and colleth[7] the child, giveth it an apple, and dandleth it most motherly. And, to say the truth,

[[5] See p. 85, note 5, above.] [[6] "say," "with David," MS.: not in 1570.]

[[7] "Colleth:" embraces or clasps about the neck.—Nares' Glossary.]

the love of mothers to their children is but a trace to train us to behold the love of God towards us: and therefore saith he, Isai. xlix. "Can a mother forget the child of her womb?" as who say, No; but, "if she should do so, yet will not I forget thee, saith the Lord of hosts." Ah, comfortable saying! "I will not forget thee, saith the Lord."

Indeed the children of God think oftentimes, that God Ps. xxvii. lxix. cxix. xxxviii. hath forgotten them; and therefore they cry, *Ne abscondas faciem tuam a me, &c.*: "Hide not thy face from me," &c.; *Ne derelinquas me, Domine, &c.*, "Leave me not, O Lord," Ps. xxxi. &c.; whereas in very truth it is not so, but to their present sense; and therefore David said, *Ego dixi in excessu meo, projectus sum a facie tua:* "I said in my agony, I was clean cast away from thy face[1]." &c. But was it so? Nay, verily, read his psalm, and you shall see. So writeth he also in other places very often, especially in the person of Christ; as when Ps. xxii. he saith, *Deus meus, Deus meus, ut quid dereliquisti me?* "My God, my God, why hast thou forsaken me?" He saith not, *Ut quid derelinquis?* "Why dost thou forsake me?" or, *Derelinques me?* "Why wilt thou forsake me?" but, *Ut quid dereliquisti me?* "Why hast thou forsaken me?" Where indeed God had not left him, but that it was so to his sense, and that this psalm telleth full well: which psalm I pray you now and then read; it is the 22nd: and thereto join the 30th, and the 116th, with divers others.

The same we read in the prophet Esay, in his 40th chapter, where he reproveth Israel for saying, God had forgotten Isai. xl. them. *Nunquid nescis?* (saith he) "Knowest thou not?" *An non audivisti? &c.* "Hast thou not heard?" &c. *Qui sperant in Domino mutabunt fortitudinem:* "They that trust in the Lord shall renew their strength." And in his 54th chapter: *Noli timere, &c. Ad punctum enim in modico dereliqui te, at in miserationibus magnis congregabo te. In momento indignationis abscondi faciem meam parumper a te, at in misericordia sempiterna misertus sum tui, dixit Redemptor tuus Dominus. Nam istud erit mihi sicut aquæ Noe. Ut enim juravi ne porro aquæ Noe pertransirent terram, sic juravi*

[[1] Instead of "David said......from thy face," the MS. has: "Hezekias writeth, as Jonas being in the whale's belly, *Ego dixi*, &c., 'I said, O Lord, that thou hadst forsaken me,' &c."]

ut non irascar tibi, et non increpem te. Montes enim commovebuntur et colles contremiscent, misericordia autem mea non recedet a te, et fœdus pacis meæ non movebitur, dicit miserator tuus Dominus: "Fear not," &c. "For a little while I have forsaken thee, but with great compassion will I gather thee. For a moment in mine anger I hid my face from thee for a little season: but in everlasting mercy have I had compassion on thee, saith the Lord thy Redeemer. For this is unto me as the waters of Noe; for, as I have sworn that the waters of Noe should no more go over the earth, so have I sworn that I would not be angry with thee nor rebuke thee. For the mountains shall remove, and hills shall fall down; but my mercy shall not depart from thee, neither shall the covenant of my peace fall away, saith the Lord that hath compassion on thee."

But the scriptures are full of such sweet places to them that will *portare iram Domini, et expectare salutem et auxilium ejus*, "bear the wrath of the Lord, and wait for his health and help." As of all temptations this is the greatest, that God hath forgotten or will not help us through the pikes, as they say, so of all services of God this liketh he best, to hope assuredly on him, and for his help always, which is *adjutor in tribulationibus*, "an helper in tribulations," and doth more gloriously shew his power by such as be weak, and feel themselves so. For, *quo infirmiores sumus, eo sumus in illo robustiores. Sic oculi Domini:* "the weaker we are, the more strong are we in him." Thus "the eyes of the Lord be on them" that tremble and fear. *Voluntatem eorum faciet*, "he will accomplish their desire: he is with them in their trouble, he will deliver them:" *antequam clamaverint exaudit eos*, "before they cry he heareth them;" as all the scriptures teach us. To the reading whereof and hearty prayer I heartily commend you, beseeching almighty God, that of his eternal mercies he would make perfect the good he hath begun in you, and strengthen you to the end, that you might have no less hope, but much more, of his help to your comfort now against your enemies, than already he hath given you against the duke of Northumberland[2], for not subscribing to the king's will.

Micah vii.

1 Cor. xii.

Ps. cxlv.

Be certain, be certain, good Master Hales, that all the hairs of your head your dear Father hath numbered, so that

[[2] "N." 1570: "the duke of Northumberland," MS. See p. 85, note 5, above.]

one of them shall not perish: your "name is written in the book of life." Therefore upon God "cast all your care," which will comfort you with his eternal consolations, and make you able to go through the fire, if need be, which is nothing to be compared to the fire whereinto our enemies shall fall and lie for ever. From the which the Lord deliver us, though it be through temporal fire, which must be construed according to the end and profit that cometh after it: so shall it then not much dare[1] us to suffer for our Master Christ's cause, the which the Lord grant for his mercy's sake. Amen.

[2]The Lord hath appointed you with us to be in the vaward of his battle: and therefore, as he is now to be thanked, so ought we, for the trust he putteth in us, to be more stout. And why should not we be so? Is not our cause God's cause? Is there any so sure way to heaven as this is? The apostles rejoiced that they were counted worthy to suffer anything for Christ's sake. We have deserved prison for our sins. And is not this a great benefit, to suffer as God's friends? who suppresseth our sins under our feet, as though we were righteous. All men have not found this grace. Therefore be thankful, be cons[tant.][3] Fear not "men whose breath is in their nostrils:" they have no power over our souls. Sure we are of heaven if we suffer here. God will offer himself unto us as unto children, if we patiently abide it. That we may e[ach][3] thus do, let us pray to him which is Emmanuel, "God with
Ps. l. xci. us," which will hear us, he[lp] and comfort us. "Rich is he
Rom. x. in mercy to all that call upon him"...[4]that put their trust in
Ecclus. ii. Ps. cxxv. him...[4]Put therefore your trust in him, who commandeth his angels to pitch their tents about you. Give over yourself to him which hath given himself to you and for you. You are called unto Christ's company: leave him not now for the storms which are to arise. But, as the shipmen in storms make more haste to hale into the haven, so, good Master Hales, hale into the haven of heaven; to the which God safely bring you by suffering (for that is the means), according to his good will. Amen.

[[1] "Dare," to frighten, alarm, Nares: or to harm, pain, grieve, Bailey's Dict., and Holloway's Provinc. Dict.]

[[2] The remainder of this letter, namely the last thirty-three lines, now are first printed from Bradford's autograph. The printed editions, after the words "mercy's sake. Amen," end with "From the King's Bench, your humble John Bradford."]

[[3] MS. torn.] [[4] One or two lines wanting, the MS. being torn.]

I pray you take in good part my poor writing, which cometh of a good will to you, which deserveth acceptance, though otherwise it requireth pardon. Pray for me; as God give me grace to give thanks and pray for you, that you never look back with Lot's wife, that you never pull your hand from the plough to the which you have put it, God's name be praised therefore.

This bringer shall tell you my name[5].

XXXIII. TO LADY VANE[6].

[King's Bench, LONDON[7].]

Bp Coverdale, Letters of the Martyrs, 1564, p. 336.

MS. 1. 2. 8. No. 43. Transcript. Emman. Coll. Cambridge.

THE everlasting and most merciful God, which is the Father of our Saviour Jesus Christ, increase in your ladyship the knowledge and love of his truth, with the gift of perseverance to continue therein to the end. Amen.

Albeit at this present I have no convenient leisure to write as should be seemly to send to your personage, yet, considering your gentle good-will for God's cause towards me, I thought I might be the more bold to write something, although not in such sort as I would, and perchance on your behalf might be looked for.

[[5] The Emmanuel MS. adds, in a different hand from those in the letter, the following memorandum:

"Master Bradford, being desired to write unto Judge Hales in the Fleet, before he made his answer unto his examiners, wrote this letter: but it came to him after he had agreed to his examiners. Upon the delivery of this letter, he said to the bringer, 'It came too late;' and the very same night following he attempted to have killed himself with a knife."]

[[6] Elizabeth lady Vane "seems to have been Sir Ralph Vane's widow, who was beheaded with the duke of Somerset," in 1552.—Strype, Ecc. Mem. Vol. III. part I. p. 226. She "was a special nurse and a great supporter, to her power, of the godly saints which were imprisoned in queen Mary's time: unto whom" various letters were addressed by Adn Philpot (Works, p. 259, et seq., Park. Soc.), Bradford, and others,' commending her "Christian zeal toward God's afflicted prisoners and the verity of his gospel. She departed...at Holborn, [London], 1568; whose end was more like a sleep than any death, so quietly and meekly she deceased and departed hence in the Lord."—Foxe, Acts, &c., ed. 1583, p. 1642, or ed. 1843—9, Vol. VII. p. 234. An interesting letter from this lady occurs in Writings of Adn Philpot, p. 155, Park. Soc.]

[[7] This letter, being "from the King's Bench," must have been written after March 23, 1554, Bradford having been brought to that prison on Easter-eve, which in that year fell on March 24. See Foxe, Acts, &c., ed. 1583, p. 1604, or ed. 1843—9, Vol. VII. p. 146; and tables in Sir H. Nicolas' Chronology, Lond. 1838, p. 67.]

I doubt not but that your ladyship considereth often with yourself, that you are the child of God, and a citizen of heaven by Christ, in whom God the Father, before the world was made, hath chosen you of his own mere mercy, and not of your deserts done or to be done. That you should with thankfulness call this to mind often, thereby to excite and stir up yourself to the love of God in his sight, and to all holiness of life in the sight of man, many things should move and occasion you justly; as that you were born of christian parents, that the name of God was called upon you in baptism, which is a sacrament of regeneration and adoption into the children of God, with all other benefits which hitherto you have received. Amongst which surely your ladyship should not think the least, even the crosses that God hath hitherto exercised you withal, as the loss of your good husband[1], lands, and other worldly commodities, &c. But above all, next to Christ crucified, this is most thankfully to be considered, that God, as he hath given you patience, I trust, in your trouble, so in these dangerous days he hath given you a desire to know him, and to help them which for his sake be in trouble; for this I gather and evidently see by your twice sending to me, which am not otherwise known to you but by name. I pray God, I may be heartily thankful to him for you, and so dispose your benefits as you desire. My best I will do by God's grace: but enough of this.

My desire is, good madam, although I have no doubt, as I said, but that you be diligent herein, that you would often call to mind your state before God, I mean, how that you be his child through Christ; and this I would you did for divers causes. First, that you might be quiet in conscience before him in this troublesome world, as we never can be until this be something settled. Secondly, that you might be careful to appear in his sight, and in the sight of man, as one of God's children. Thirdly, that you might in all troubles, boldly by prayer through Christ, go to him and call him by the name of Father, with hope of his help always to your comfort. Fourthly, that you might not be dismayed if trouble come unto you, as it cannot be but more or less it must needs come; for the world loveth none but such as be his, the devil

[[1] See previous page, note 6.]

can never suffer the children of God to be quiet: I will not speak of our mortal and familiar enemy "the flesh," which ceaseth not to "fight against the spirit." But God your Father being heartily called upon, in and through Christ, as he will with his holy Spirit help you, so will he give you the victory at the length to your singular comfort; which, I pray God, you may daily more and more feel. Amen.

From the King's Bench in haste as appeareth.

Your ladyship's own in Christ to command,

JOHN BRADFORD.

XXXIV. BP RIDLEY TO BRADFORD.

[OXFORD, early in *May*, 1554[2].]

DEARLY beloved, I wish you "grace, mercy, and peace."

According to your mind I have run over all your papers[3]; and what I have done (which is but small) thereat may appear. In two places I have put in two loose leaves. I had much ado to read that was written in your great leaves; and I ween somewhere I have altered some words because I could not read perfectly that which was written[4]. Sir, what shall best be done with these things now ye must consider: for, if they come in sight at this time, undoubtedly they must to the fire with their father; and, as for any safeguard that your custody can be unto them, I am sure you look not for it: for, as ye have been partner of the work, so, I am sure, ye look for none other but to have and receive like wages, and to drink of the same cup. Blessed be God, that hath given you liberty in the mean season, that you may use your pen to his glory, and to the comfort, as I hear say, of many. I bless God daily in you and all your whole company, to whom I beseech you to commend me heartily. Now I love my countryman[5] in deed and

Foxe, Acts, &c., ed. 1563, p. 1295; and after editions.

Bp Coverdale, Letters of the Martyrs, 1564, p. 60.

[3]This was a treatise of the communion, with other things, which Master Bradford sent to him to peruse and to give his judgment thereof.—[Bp Coverdale.]

[[2] This date is obtained from the remarks, in this letter, upon the design of a Public Disputation at Cambridge, Bp Hooper's letter to Bp Ferrar and others being dated May 6, and the "Declaration concerning religion" being dated May 8, 1554: see references in next page, note 2.]

[[3] These, from the side-note of Bp Coverdale above, were probably Bradford's Sermon on the Lord's Supper: see Vol. I. p. 28, 82.]

[[4] The last two sentences occur in Foxe, 1563, and after editions, but not in Coverdale, 1564.]

[[5] Bp Ridley was born at Willowmontwick—Dr Rowland Taylor was born at Rothbury—in Northumberland. See Dr Turner's letter in Works of Bp Ridley, Append. no. III. p. 487—95, Park. Soc.]

in truth, I mean Doctor Taylor, not now for my earthly country's sake, but for our heavenly Father's sake, and for Christ's sake, whom, I heard say, he did so stoutly in time of peril confess[1]; and yet also now for our country's sake, and for all our mother's sake, but I mean of "the kingdom of heaven" and of "heavenly Jerusalem," and because of the Spirit which bringeth in him, in you, and in your company, such blessed fruits of boldness in the Lord's cause, of patience and constancy. The Lord, which hath begun this work in you all, perform and perfect this his own deed until his own day come. Amen.

As yet I perceive ye have not been baited[2]; and the cause thereof God knoweth, which will let them do no more to his, than is his pleased will and good pleasure to suffer them to do for his own glory, and to the profit of them which be truly his. For "the Father," which doth guide them that be Christ's to Christ, "is more mighty than all they; and no man is able to pull them out of the Father's hands." Except, I say, it please our Father, it pleaseth our Master Christ, to suffer them, they shall not stir one hair of your heads.

My brother Punt, the bearer hereof and Master Hooper's letters[2], would that we should say what we think good concerning your mind, that is, not for to answer, except ye might have somewhat indifferent judges.—We are, as ye know, separated, and one of us cannot in any thing consult with another, and much strait watching of master bailiffs is about us, that there be no privy conference amongst us: and yet, as we hear, the scholars beareth us more heavily than the townsmen. A wonderful thing! among so many never yet scholar offered to any of us, so far as I know, any manner of favour, either for or in Christ's cause.

Now, as concerning your demand of our counsel, for my part I do not mislike that which I perceive ye are minded to do: for I look for none other but, if ye answer afore the same commissioners that we did, ye shall be served and handled as we were, though ye were as well learned as ever was either Peter or Paul. And yet, further, I think that occasion afterward may be given you; and the con-

[[1] See p. 82, note 1, above.]

[[2] An allusion to the design of holding a Public Disputation at Cambridge, between the Romish divines, and Bps Hooper and Ferrar, Adn Philpot, Bradford and others, similar to that which had been held at Oxford, with Abp Cranmer, and Bps Ridley and Latimer, April 1554. See, in Vol. I. p. 367—74, "Declaration concerning religion" by Bradford and others; Bp Hooper's letter to Ferrar, Taylor, Bradford, and Philpot, Let. xxx. in Works, p. 592, Park. Soc.; Foxe, Acts, &c., ed. 1583, p. 1469, or ed. 1843—9, Vol. VI. p. 550; Soames' Hist. Reform., Lond. 1826—8, Vol. IV. p. 207—15.]

sideration of the profit of your auditory may perchance move you to do otherwise. Finally, determinately to say what shall be best I am not able[3]: but I trust he, whose cause ye have in hand, shall put you in mind to do that which shall be most for his glory, the profit of his flock, and your own salvation.

This letter must be common to you and Master Hooper, in whom and in his prison-fellow, good father Crome[4], I bless God even from the bottom of my heart; for I doubt not but they both do to our Master Christ true, acceptable, and honorable service, and profitable to his flock, the one with his pen, and the other with his fatherly example of patience and constancy and all manner of true godliness. But what shall I need say to you, "Let this be common among all your brethren?" among whom, I dare say, it is with you as it is with us, among whom all things here are common, meat, money, and whatsoever one of us hath that can or may do another good.

Although I said, master bailiffs and our hosts straitly watch us, that we have no conference or intelligence of anything abroad, yet hath God provided for every one of us, in the stead of our servants, faithful fellows which will be content to hear and see, and to do for us whatsoever they can. It is God's work surely: blessed be God for his unspeakable goodness. "The grace of our Lord Jesus Christ, and the love of God, and the communication of the Holy Ghost be with you all. Amen, Amen."

As far as London is from Oxford, yet thence we have received of late both meat, money, and shirts, not only from such as are of our acquaintance, but of some (whom this bearer can tell) with whom I had never to my knowledge any acquaintance. I know for whose sake they do it: to him therefore be all honour, glory, and due thanks: and yet I pray you do so much as to shew them that we have received their benevolence, and (God be blessed) have plenty of all such things. This I desire you to do, for I know they be of Master Hooper and your familiar acquaintance.

Master Latimer was crazed[5]; but I hear now, thanks be to God, that he amendeth again.

Yours in Christ[6],

NICHOLAS RIDLEY.

[3 "not able to say," 1563: "not able," 1564.]

[4 See the history of Crome, in Strype, Ecc. Mem. Vol. III. part I. pp. 157—67.]

[5 "Crazed:" ill, sickly.]

[6 "Yours in Christ," 1564: not in 1563.]

XXXV. TO LADY VANE.

Bp Coverdale, Letters of the Martyrs, 1564, p. 335.

Foxe, Acts, &c., ed. 1570, p. 1824; and after editions.

MS. 1. 2. 8. No. 42. Transcript, imperfect. Emman. Coll. Cambridge.

As to mine own soul, I wish to your ladyship grace and mercy, from God our dear Father in Christ our Lord and Saviour.

I thank God that something he hath eased you, and mitigated his fatherly correction in us both. I would to God he had done so much in the behalf of the grief of the body to you, as he hath done to me: for, as for the soul, I trust you feel that which I pray God increase in you (I mean his fatherly love), and grant that I may with you feel the same in such degree as may please him: I will not say, as you feel, lest I should seem to ask too much at one time. God doth often much more plentifully visit with the sense of his mercy them that "humble themselves under his mighty hand," and are sore exercised, as you long have been, than others which to the face of the world have more shew and appearance. Therefore I wish as I do, and that not only for mine own commodity, but also that I might occasion you to the consideration of the goodness of God, which I by your letters do well espy, which is indeed the high-way whereby, as God increaseth his gifts, so sheweth he more lively his salvation. Ps. l. cvii.

I have received God's blessing from you, the which I have partly distributed unto my three fellow-prisoners, Master Ferrar, Master Taylor, Master Philpot; and the residue I will bestow upon four poor souls, which are imprisoned in the common jail for religion also. As for mine own part, if I had had need, I would have served my turn also: but because I had not, nor, I thank God, have not, I have been and will be your almoner, in such sort as I have already advertised you: God reward you, and give you to find it spiritually and corporally. Because otherwise I cannot talk with you, therefore on this sort, as occasion and opportunity will serve, I am ready to shew my good-will, and desire of your help and furtherance in the Lord to everlasting life, whereunto God bring us shortly for his mercy's sake. Amen.

Good madam, be thankful to God, as I hope you be, be earnest in prayer, continue in reading and hearing God's word; and, if God's further cross come, as therein God doth serve his providence, for else it shall not come unto you, so be certain the same shall turn to your eternal joy and comfort. Amen.

JOHN BRADFORD.

XXXVI. RAWLINS TO BRADFORD[1].

[ANTWERP, *July* 31, 1554.]

ALTHOUGH, my dearly beloved, and beloved again, in Christ, I want time to utter by writing the state of God's church on this side, yet I thought it good to write these few lines, and it were no more, but to put you in remembrance to pray for the same, which I do nothing doubt of your diligence therein; and, as a poor member of the same, I beseech you be mindful of me. MS. 2 2. 15. No. 49. Transcript. Emman. Coll. Cambridge.

Ah! my beloved, my wounds and sores break out in great abundance, that woe be unto me. Ah, good Lord, good Lord, what a heaviness is this! that—whereas he delivered me from seeing and feeling so great a number of miseries which both you and other of my brethren have felt, to the end I should not only have sought for the curing of my own wounds and sores (which are diffidence of his promises, not loving him, not fearing him, not obeying him, and a number of others), but also I should have been as one to have come before him in the gap, to have intreated his mercy for my brethren and country—but unto God only is it known, I have neither sought amendment in myself, nor yet did I so much as once bring one little stick to the stopping of the gap. Notwithstanding, so good is God my heavenly Father, even in the writing hereof, that he certifieth my conscience, he will for his sweet Son's sake pardon and forgive these faults past, and will give his holy Spirit to work the amendment. Oh! praised be his holy name for ever and ever: I doubt nothing of your 'Amen.'

Now farewell, as one for whom the almighty Lord is to be magnified, which not only endued you with many of his graces, to the teaching and learning of your brethren in prosperity, but now as I understand hath doubled them upon you in the confirming of

[[1] This letter is now printed for the first time.
The heading in the MS. is: "A godly letter sent from one Erkynnold Rawlins, being beyond the seas at Antwerp, to Master John Bradford, being prisoner in the King's Bench in Southwark, the 31st day of July, *anno* 1554." A contemporary memorandum written on Emmanuel MS. 2. 2. 15. No. 50 (Letter from Rawlins to Punt), states that Rawlins "since queen Elizabeth came in died in Germany."]

your brethren in adversity. Ah, what can a piece of earth do in the extolling and magnifying of this good God? But yet so humbly doth he abase himself for Christ's sake, that he looketh not on earth, but upon his own mercy. Oh! praised be his name for ever and ever, who not only hath given me sorrow in writing hereof, but hath also given me comfort in sweet Christ. O what joy should it be above, if God would send you amongst us! But his good will be done.

All do salute you in Christ, and amongst other my poor Dorithee.

Yours to use in Christ,

ERKYNNOLD RAWLINS.

XXXVII. TO MISTRESS MARY HONYWOOD[1].

[King's Bench, LONDON[2].]

Bp Coverdale, Letters of the Martyrs, 1564, p. 303.

Foxe, Acts, &c., ed. 1570, p. 1821; and after editions.

MS. 2. 2. 15. No. 24. Fragment of transcript. Emman. Coll. Cambridge.

THE good Spirit of God, which guideth his children, be with you, my good sister in the Lord, for ever. Amen.

Although, as I to you, so you unto me in person are unknown, yet to him whom we desire to please we are not only in persons, but also in hearts, known and thoroughly seen. And therefore, as for his sake you would by that you sent of me be perceived, how that in God you bear to me a good-will, so, that I to you might be seen in God to bear you the like, I send to you these few words in writing, wishing that in all your doings and speech, yea, even in your very thoughts, you would labour to feel that they are all present and open before the sight of God, be they good or bad. This cogitation often

[1 This letter, being addressed in Bp Coverdale and Foxe "to Mistress M. H., a godly gentlewoman," is inscribed in this edition as above, because of the probable conjecture of the "Biographia Britannica," that those initials represent "Mary Honywood:" (Biogr. Britan. ed. 1740, Vol. II. article Bradford.) Fuller records that this lady attended the martyrdom of Bradford, when, so great was the crowd, her shoes were trodden off; and she had to walk to St Martin's before she could obtain a pair. Mistress H. suffered in after years from religious depression; and it was in her case that the well-known story of the Venice-glass occurred. See Fuller (who received the story from Bp Morton, to whom it had been given by Mistress Honywood herself) in Fuller's Worthies of England, Kent. Vide also Life of Foxe by his son, prefixed to Foxe, Acts, &c., ed. 1641, Vol. II. Dame Honywood died in 1620, aged 92 years, and numbering at that time 367 descendants. See inscription on the tomb of Mistress H., in Markshall church, given in Fuller, as above, and in Hakewill's Apology, pp. 252, 3, Oxford, 1635.]

[2 See p. 91, note 7, above.]

had in mind, and prayer made to God for the working of his Spirit, thereby, as a mean, you shall at the length feel more comfort and commodity, than any man can know but such as be exercised therein. Howbeit this is to be added, that in thinking yourself and all that you have and do to be in the sight of God—this, I say, is to be added—that you think his sight is the sight, not only of a Lord, but rather of a Father, which tendereth[3] more your infirmities, than you can tender the infirmities of any your children. Yea, when in yourself you see a motherly affection to your little one that is weak, let the same be unto you a trace, to train you to see the unspeakable kind affection of God your Father towards you. And therefore, upon the consideration of your infirmities and natural evils, which continually cleave unto us, take occasion to go to God as your Father, through Christ; and before his merciful heart lay open your infirmities and evils, with desire of pardon and help after his good-will and pleasure, but in his time and not when you will, and by what means he will, not that way that you would. In the mean season hang on hope of his fatherly goodness, and surely you shall never be ashamed. For if a woman that is natural cannot finally "forget the child of her womb," be sure God, which is a Father supernatural, cannot nor will not forget you. Yea, if a woman could be so Isai. xlix.
forgetful, yet God himself saith, he will not be so.

This opinion, yea, rather certain persuasion of God your Father through Christ, see that you cherish, and by all means, as well by diligent consideration of his benefits, as of his loving corrections, whether they be inward or outward, see that you nourish; knowing for certain that, as the devil goeth about nothing so much as to bring you in a doubt, whether you be God's child or no, so whatsoever shall move you to admit that dubitation, be assured the same to come from the devil. If you feel in yourself, not only the want of good things, but also plenty of evil, do not therefore doubt whether you be God's child in Christ or no: for, if for your goodness' or illness' sake, which you feel or feel not, you should believe or doubt, then should you make Christ Jesus, for whose sake only God is your Father, either nothing or else but a half Christ. But rather take occasion of your wants in good, and of your plenty in evil,

[[3] "Tendereth:" regards or treats with tenderness.]

to go to God as to your Father, and to pray him that, inasmuch as he commandeth you to believe that he is your God and Father, so he would give[1] you his good Spirit, that you might feel the same, and live as his child, to his glory. And cease not upon such prayers to look for comfort in God's good time, still hoping the best, and rejecting all dubitation, and so all evil works, words, and cogitations, as the Lord shall enable you by his good Spirit and grace; which I beseech him to give unto you, my good sister, for ever. And further I pray you that, as he hath made you to be a helper unto your husband, so you would endeavour yourself therein to shew the same as well in soul as body, and beg grace of God, that your endeavours may be effectual to both your comforts in Christ. Amen.

Out of the King's Bench, by the Lord's prisoner[2],

JOHN BRADFORD.

XXXVIII. TO MISTRESS COKE[3].

[*July* 23, 1554.]

MS. 2. 2. 15. No. 68. Original. Emman. Coll. Cambridge.

THE eternal mercy of God in Christ toward you, my dear sister, [be] more and more perceived and felt in your heart, by the working of the Holy Spirit, the earnest of our redemption and purchase of our inheritance, by the merits of Jesu Christ our Lord. Amen.

The 23rd of July.—[MS.]

This day, immediately after my rising, which was about twelve of the clock, I received your loving letters, how safely I cannot tell, because the letters wherein mine was inclosed were opened before they were delivered to your friend [to whom] you sent them: but enough of this, to make you more circumspect in sealing, yea, in sewing your letters, that no man will ever deliver them if he once break them. At this

[[1] The MS. begins with the words "you his good," being only a fragment.]

[[2] The last nine words are in the MS., but not in the printed editions.]

[[3] This letter is now first printed.

The original MS. has no heading, but on a blank page has an inscription, "The copy of a letter sent to M. Cok." The name "Margery Coke" occurs subsequently in Letter LXXX., Feb. 16, 1555, to Hart and others, on election.]

present, lying in my bed betwixt my heat and cold of my fever, which is even a quotidian or a double quartan, I speak with my tongue that, by the help of another, I send written unto you.

I perceive by your letters the blessing of God, and his fatherly providence towards you, in staying your husband's mind above your expectation. Therefore, I exhort you to be thankful, and confirm your faith, by this providence past, of the continuance of his fatherly providence to come towards you for ever. As concerning the diabolical doctor before whom ye are like to come, two things I would wish ye did note and forget not: one, to do as Moses did, Hebrews xi, that is, as with your corporal eyes you see the commissary and his accomplices, so with your spiritual eyes you cease not to look upon the presence, power, justice, truth, and the goodness of God: the other, that ye forget not to put God diligently in remembrance of his most comfortable promise, made to you there (the which I pray you look upon), Matthew x. These two things if you remember, as by God's grace ye shall not faint for fear of man, so shall ye not be put to shame for lack wherewith and how to answer them. Howbeit, because I will do my best to satisfy your request in this behalf, lo, I have sent you that which God hath given me to the profit of his church, I trust, in this thing. Read it as you can: and, when you have weighed it, and have the substance of the thing in your mind, I pray you send it again, because it is not mine: I speak not of the work, but of the written paper.

Your other temptations of election, as well inwardly by your infirmity and natural corruption, as also outwardly by the devil and his instruments, which sometime may be the children of God, and the scriptures also, as we see, Matthew xv., of Peter, and Matthew iv., of Christ's temptations—for these
your temptations, I say, I know no other remedy but, first, to 1.
be very heedful ye consent not to them or to any of them;
secondly, you lament them; thirdly, ye pray to God your 2. 3.
Father for Christ's sake to pardon them, and to put them away; and, last of all, to meditate and feed upon those most plain places of scripture, which make so manifestly therewith, that no man can put away, but such as would not have Jesus

to be a perfect and an alone omnisufficient Saviour. For, if our salvation depend upon anything else, in part or in whole, but in the grace of God, not in us but in Christ only and alone, then is Christ not our whole justice, salvation and redemption. Not that by these words thus spoken I would any man should gather any other to be saved, but such as be members of Christ and have Christ dwelling in them; howbeit by faith, which only in the quieting of conscience looketh clean out of ourselves into the mercy and grace of God in Christ, not only sithen our vocation, or Christ's incarnation,
1 Pet. i. but also in his pre-ordination before the world was made: and therefore, the more we are fully persuaded hereof, the more we are transformed into the holy image of God which cannot but, according to the portion thereof in us by faith, through the operation of God's Spirit, detest[1] and flee from all kind of evil, and have our whole delectation in God and his word. And the cause why we are so faint in fleeing evil and diligent doing good is the wavering of this certainty of God's election, which were not to the glory of his grace if we should doubt of it, by reason in part or whole of anything in us.

This I speak to you, good sister, now as a sick woman in the Lord, to use it as sick folks' meat: if otherwise, your blood will light on your own head[2]. Not that I think so of you—God forbid, I take you as my dear sister in the Lord—but lest any man should read these letters, and they be taken not so as I mean, and to the godly plainly write. As for the "angels that kept not [their first estate[3],"] their fall—how this can make to weaken the faith of election and certainty thereof, I see not, but rather for it. For, as Adam's fall, although he was created to life, hindered not, but more lively sets forth, God's glory and election (no thanks to Adam therefor, for he did not eat the apple to that end), even so the fall of "the angels that fell" sets forth unto us, in them that fell not, the certainty of God's election concerning them, that all creatures in heaven and in earth might stand in fear of the

[[1] "but" is written over the line, before "detest" in the MS.]

[[2] The remainder of this letter is in Bradford's autograph in the MS.]

[[3] These three words are inserted to complete the sense, otherwise imperfect.]

Lord, and cry out with Paul, "How unsearchable are his ways!" &c.

But of this matter you shall hear more if God send health, so soon as possible can be.

Your unfeigned brother in the Lord,

J. B.

XXXIX. TO HUMPHREY HALES[4].

[*August* 5, 1554.]

To my good friend in God, Master Humphrey Hales.

As to my dear friend, I wish unto you, gentle Master Hales, health of soul and body, to God's glory and your everlasting comfort. Amen.

Bp Coverdale, Letters of the Martyrs, 1564, p. 310.

Although it be commonly spoken, and as commonly verified, that seldom seen is soon forgotten, yet it is not so commonly seen or experienced amongst them whose friendship is in God the Father through Christ, as ours is, but in those whose friendship is begun in respect of some earthly commodity. And therefore, lest I should incur this suspicion at your hands, which have so many ways deserved the contrary, I thought it my duty to refresh (if it need refreshing) the amity in God begun betwixt us, which I doubt not shall continue so long as we live, or else I would be sorry: in consideration whereof, both mindful of my promise made unto you, and careful for your safety, I have caused a place to be provided for your wife's deliverance, where she may so quietly and safely remain, that for the avoiding of the perils and dangers of these days I see none more convenient: I mean it in Hadley[5] at Doctor Taylor's house, where I trust there is no peril to youward, nor to any that feareth or regardeth any peril that thereby may happen. And herein of very love and good-will I am the more familiar and bold to admonish you, not as distrusting you—God forbid, for I think of you as of a very child of God—but as one careful for you, lest

[4 Master Humphrey Hales was eldest son of Sir James Hales (see p. 85, note 5, above), and married Joan, daughter and coheiress of Robert Atwater, by whom he had two sons, James and Humphrey, and one daughter, Abigail. See Betham's Baronetage, Vol. I. p. 131, and Vol. II. p. 112.]

[5 Hadleigh Rectory in Suffolk, to which Doctor Rowland Taylor had been presented by Abp Cranmer, 1544, and where he suffered martyrdom, February 9, 1555. Vide Life of Taylor by Stow, London, 1833, pp. 15, 250.]

you should at length, through the common infirmity of our frail flesh and the manifold offences given of the world, do exteriorily as the world doth, to save your sleeve and maim your arm for ever; as those do, which for the saving of their goods jeopard goods of body and soul, in the peril of eternal damnation.

If I suspected any such thing in you, gentle Master Hales, I then would go about to tell you what this life is, a smoke, a shadow, a vapour, &c.; what the glory of this life is, grass, hay; yea, how full of misery it is, and hath more aloes than honey. If I suspected anything your conscience, I would then set before you—on the one part, the judgment of Christ, which shall be most assuredly the terrible sentence to them which are ashamed to confess his gospel, the eternal woe and misery which they shall be cast into that will not obey his gospel here—and, on the other part, the most pleasant shout of the angel, to summon all men to come before our Captain and Brother Christ, the collection and catching of us up in the clouds to meet our Master, the eternal joy and felicity which we shall receive that here confess him, here suffer with him, here lose any thing for his sake. If I did in any point so much as think that you would defile your body in the antichristian service now used, then would I go about to set forth these things, briefly spoken, more at large. But, as I said before, I say again, because I am as well persuaded of you, my dearly beloved brother, as of any in your profession and state, I cannot but pray God to make perfect the good which he hath begun in you, and desire you, as you have begun in God, so to go forward.

Job vii.

As your example hath done good to many, so cast not all down with a tip[1]. Terrible is that woe which Christ threateneth to them "by whom offences do come." You know that the way of salvation is straiter than men make it. You know the soul is to be considered above all things. Happy is the loss of that bodily life, liberty, and goods, by the which a spiritual life, freedom, and felicity is purchased. "What should it profit a man to win the whole world, and to lose his own soul?" Who would desire a two years' merry life for an eternal sorrow? as these mass-gospellers do, which yet are uncertain of two years' life; and God knoweth what wounds their consciences have. Hard is it to recover health to the conscience: and, because I am

[[1] "tip:" a fall.]

careful for it to youwards, as to mine own brother and dear friend, therefore I write thus. We are in God's power, and not in the power of our enemies: he it is that hath "all our hairs numbered:" before he say, 'Amen,' no man shall once touch you. Into his hands commit yourself; "cast your care on him;" have a care to please him: and then he will care to keep you.

You know the oath the *Athenienses* did make, *Pugnabo pro sacris, et solus, et cum aliis;* "I will fight for the defence of religion, both alone and with others." Which saying of the heathen will be to our condemnation, if for his holy word and gospel's sake we dare not adventure the loss of that he hath lent us, keepeth for us, and can when he will take away from us, or us from it. If worldly men dare jeopard a joint with God, rather than they would lose worldly things, as experience teacheth, certainly it should be much to our shame, which in baptism have vowed and solemnly sworn to forsake the world, if we dare not jeopard a joint with man, rather than we would lose a good conscience and spiritual treasures. He that will not have God's [Ps. cix. 17. blessing, it shall be taken from him, saith David.

Therefore, my dearly beloved, beware. You are now "the temple of the Holy Ghost." Defile it not for the Lord's sake, but keep it pure, not only "from all uncleanness of 2 Cor. vii. the spirit, but also of the flesh," as I trust you will: and cry unto your Father for his strength and aid; which I beseech him, of his mercy, always to give unto you, my own good friend, even as I desire to myself.

If in anything I could help you, you may be assured thereof, as of your brother. My prayer to God, night and day, you shall have, that for his holy name's sake he would bless you in all things, and keep you, with my good sister your wife, unto the very end, as his dear elect children. Amen, Amen.

From my lodging, you know where, this fifth of August.

By your own to use in the Lord for ever,

JOHN BRADFORD.

XL. TO HUMPHREY HALES[1] AND HIS WIFE.

[*August* 8, 1554.]

Bp Coverdale, Letters of the Martyrs, 1564, p. 312.

THE everliving and merciful God, our dear Father through Christ, be with you both, my most dearly and entirely beloved in the Lord, now and for ever.

I cannot forbear but signify unto you both, that my heart is careful and heavy for the cross which is come upon you by the heavy and fearful judgment of God fallen upon your father[2] justly, for his denying of God for fear of men and love of these things which he hath left behind him unto you and others. God grant his fact be so imprinted in the hearts of all men, especially of you both, that his fall may be unto you, I will not say a rising (for yet I trust ye are not fallen), but an establishing in the verity of God, whereof whoso is ashamed shall at length feel such shame as I beseech God keep us all from. Happy are they that mark the judgments of God upon others, to come and increase in repentance, to fear God's wrath and judgments, which is always like himself, if we follow the steps of them on whom he taketh punishment.

Luke xiii.

I need not tell you the cause of this that hath happened unto your father, if it be as I with sorrow have heard. For you know well enough, that till he forsook God, gave ear to the serpent's counsel, began to mammer[3] of the truth, and to frame himself outwardly to do that which his conscience reproved inwardly—for that which he mingled with the love of God, I mean the love of the world, cannot be in any man without the expulsion of God's love—till then, I say, God did not depart and leave him to himself, to the example of you and me, and all others; that we should fear even ourselves and our own hands, more than man and all the powers of the world, if we therefore should do anything which should wound our conscience.

The conscience, I tell you, is soon wounded, yea, sooner than we be ware of. The devil useth all kind of deceit to blind us from seeing that which might wound it: but, when the stripe is given, then either shutteth he still up our eyes with contempt to

[1 See p. 103, note 4, above.] [2 See p. 85, note 5, above.]
[3 "Mammer:" hesitate or be in doubt.—Nares' Glossary.]

our hardening, or else openeth them to bring us to utter despairing. In your father as ye may see the latter, so in many worldly gospellers you may, if you will, see the other. God might deal with all such, as he hath done now with your father: but, because the time of his judgment is not yet come, his wisdom hath thought good to set your father forth as an example to all men; as he did in the first world Cain, in the second world Cham, in the third age Korah, &c., in Christ's time Judas, in the apostles' time Ananias, &c., although none will heartily consider it, but such as be God's children indeed.

But here, in comparing your father thus, my dearly and unfeignedly beloved in the Lord, I must pray you not to be offended, or think that I do determinately judge (to God I leave all judgment): but, because the fruit to us declareth no less, to the admonishment of us all, I trust ye will accordingly consider my collation. For your parts as I think godly of you both, that indeed ye are both the children of God, so I pray you comfort yourselves as David did, though his son Absalom perished so desperately, and though his father-in-law Ahithophel, father to Bathsheba, as the Hebrews write, perished so miserably. Ye know, Jonathan was not the worse, because his father slew himself, nor Bathsheba, because of her father Ahithophel: they both were the children of God; and so I am assured, as man can be, that ye are. As they used God's judgments upon their parents, so do ye, to fear God and love God the more, and to flee from those things, which in your father ye did see displeased God.

O that I were with you but one half hour! not only with you to lament, but also, as God should lend me his grace, to comfort you—who by this judgment doth tempt your patience and faith, to the comfort of you both, as you shall find, I am assured. My dear hearts in the Lord, if I could by any means comfort you, certainly, if my life lay on it, I think you should forthwith perceive it: but, because I can do no more than I can, therefore as I can I do, that is, as to write, so to send this messenger, my good friend and brother, with the same, to learn certainly the truth herein and the condition of your estate. My other letter was made before I knew of this matter. I pray God this, which by report I understand, be otherwise: but God's good will be done; who give us patience and comfort in him.

To whom I commend you both, even as heartily as any friends I have in this life of your estate.

From my lodging you know where, this eighth of August, *anno Domini* 1554.

By your own to use in the Lord for ever,

JOHN BRADFORD.

XLI. TO MISTRESS JOYCE HALES[1].

[*August* 8, 1554.]

Bp Coverdale, Letters of the Martyrs, 1564, p. 322.

Foxe, Acts, &c., ed. 1570, p. 1822; and after editions.

MS. 2. 2. 15. No. 38. Original, Holograph. And No. 13, Transcript. Emman. Coll. Cambridge.

Ah, my dearly beloved, and most dearly beloved in the Lord, how pensive is my heart presently for you by reason of the terrible and[2] fearful judgment of our God! which even now I heard for truth by Richard Proude[3], where tofore I did not believe it, because your last letters, delivered safely to me upon Monday last past, did thereof speak nothing[4]. God, our good Father, for his great mercies' sake in Christ, have mercy upon us, and so with his eternal consolation comfort you, my dear heart, as I desire in my most need to be of him comforted. Amen.

The cause why hitherto, sithen I received[5] your letters by William Porrege (which I received safely, on Sunday was seven-night, with both your tokens[6]), I have not sent unto you again, this bringer can tell you: yea if I had not heard for

[1 The autograph MS. has, on the margin, in another hand: "To Mistress Joyce Hales, comforting her upon the death of her father-in-law." The "Defence of election," and the treatise on "The restoration of all things," Vol. I. pp. 307, 351, are severally inscribed to this lady: she was daughter-in-law of Sir James Hales, Justice of the Common Pleas. See Vol. I. p. 248, and p. 85, note 5, of this volume, on Letter XXXII. to Sir James Hales.

The heading of this letter in Bp Coverdale, 1564, and in other printed editions, is: "A letter which he wrote to a faithful woman in her heaviness and trouble, most comfortable for all those that are afflicted and broken-hearted for their sins."]

[2 "terrible and," "again," autogr. MS.: not in MS. No. 13, or printed editions.]

[3 "Ah my......Proude," both MSS. and 1564: not in Foxe, 1570, or after editions.]

[4 The last twenty-three words now are first printed from the autogr. MS. in which they are scored across.]

[5 "hitherto, sithen I received," autogr. MS.: "since the receipt of your letter," MS. No. 13, and 1564.]

[6 The last fifteen words now are first printed from the autogr. MS.]

truth of this heavy chance, as yet you had not thus soon heard from me. For I began upon Monday at night[7] a piece of work for your comfort, whereof I send you now a piece, and that of the midst of it[8], because my heart is heavy for your sake, and I cannot be quiet till I hear how you do in this cross: wherein, my dear sister, I beseech you to be of good comfort, and to be no more discouraged than was David of Absalom's death, the good Jonathan of his father Saul's fearful end, Adam of Cain, Noah of Cham, Jacob of Reuben, and the godly Bathsheba of the terrible end of her father, or at the least her grandfather's death, Ahithophel. Not that I utterly condemn and judge your father (for I leave it to God); but because the fact of itself declareth God's secret and fearful judgment and justice towards him and all men, and his great mercy towards us; admonishing all the world how that he is to be dread and feared, and Satan not to sleep, and us his children especially, how weak and miserable we be of ourselves, and how happy we are in him, which have him to be our Father, Protector, and Keeper, and shall have for evermore, so that no evil shall touch us, further than shall make to our Father's glory and to our everlasting commodity. And therefore let this judgment of God be an occasion to stir us up more carefully to walk before God, and unfeignedly to[9] cast our whole care upon our dear Father, which never can nor will leave us; for "his calling and gifts be such that he can never repent him of them:" "whom he loveth he loveth to the end;" none of his chosen can perish, of which number I know you are, my dearly beloved sister. God increase the faith thereof daily more and more in you; he give unto you to hang wholly on him, and on his providence and protection; for, "whoso dwelleth under that secret thing" and help of the Lord, he shall be cocksure for evermore. "He that dwelleth," I say; for if we be flitters and not dwellers, as was Lot a flitter from Segor, where God promised him protection if he had dwelled there still, we shall remove to our loss, as he did into the mountains.

Rom. xi.

Ps. xci. xxxi.

Gen. xix. [Septuag. and Vulg.]

[7 "upon Monday at night," autogr. MS., scored across, with "of late" written over, which is the reading in MS. No. 13, and 1564.]

[8 "a piece and that of the midst of it," autogr. MS., scored across, with "but a part," written over it, which is the reading in MS. No. 13, and 1564.]

[9 The former part of this paragraph, "The cause why hitherto.........and unfeignedly to," does not occur in Foxe 1570, or after editions.]

Dwell therefore, that is, "trust," and that finally unto the end, in the Lord, my dear sister, and you "shall be as mount Sion." "As mountains compass Jerusalem, so doth the Lord all his people." How then can he forget you, which are "as the apple of his eye," for his dear Son's sake? Ah, dear heart, that I were now but one half hour with you, to be a Simon to
[Luke xxiii. 26.] help to carry your cross with you! God send you some good Simon, to be with you and help you. I will be a Simon absent to carry, as I can learn, your cross, which you have promised not to hide from me. O that God would hereby[1] touch your husband's heart, so that he would get him beyond the seas! although by that means I should never more corporally see you, as indeed I fear it, I fear it; but God's good will be done. I have written to him, as this bringer can tell you[2]: God for his mercy's sake turn it to your and his good. Amen.

But—to come again to that from whence I have digressed, whereunto you occasion me also[3] by your letters, complaining to me of the blindness of your mind, and of the troubles you feel through talk with some—my dearly beloved, God make you thankful for that which he hath given unto you; he open your eyes to see what and how great benefits you have received, that you may be less covetous or rather impatient (for so, I fear me, it should be called), and more thankful. Have not you received at his hands sight to see your blindness, and thereto a desirous and seeking heart to see where he lieth in the mid-day? as his
[Cant. i. 7.] dear spouse speaketh of herself in the Canticles. O Joyce, my good Joyce, what a gift is this! Many have some sight, but none this sobbing and sighing, none this seeking which you have, I know, but such as he hath married unto him in his
[Luke vii. 38.] mercies. You are not content to kiss his feet with the Mag-
Cant. i. dalen, but you would be "kissed even with the kiss of his mouth." You would see his face with Moses, forgetting how
Ps xxvii. cv. he biddeth us "seek his face," yea, and that "for ever;" which signifieth no such sight as you desire to be in this present life, which would see God now "face to face:" whereas he cannot be seen but covered under something, yea, sometime in that

[1 "hereby," autogr. MS.: "heartily," MS. No. 13, and 1564.]

[2 "as this bringer can tell you," only in autogr. MS.]

[3 The last twelve lines, "Ah, dear heart, that I were......you occasion me also," do not occur in Foxe 1570, or after editions.]

which is, as you would say, clean contrary to God, as to see his mercy in his anger. In bringing us to hell faith seeth him to bring us to heaven; in darkness it beholdeth brightness; in hiding his face from us it beholdeth his merry countenance. How did Job see God, but, as you would say, under Satan's cloak? For who cast the fire from heaven upon his goods? who overthrew his house, and stirred up men to take away his cattle, but Satan? and yet Job pierced through all these, and saw God's work, saying, "The Lord hath given, the Lord hath taken away." &c. In reading of the Psalms, how often do you see that David, in the shadow of death, saw God's sweet love! And so, my dearly beloved, I see that you, in your darkness and dimness, by faith do see clarity and brightness: by faith, I say, because faith is of things absent, "of things hoped for," of things which, I appeal to your conscience, whether you desire or not. And can you desire any thing which you know not? and is there of heavenly things any other true knowledge than by faith?

Therefore, my dear heart, be thankful, for (before God I write it) you have great cause. Ah, my Joyce, how happy is the state wherein you are! Verily you are even in the blessed state of God's children, for "they mourn:" and do not you so? and that not for worldly weal, but for spiritual riches, faith, hope, charity, &c. Do you not "hunger and thirst for right- Matt. v.
eousness?" And I pray you, saith not Christ who cannot lie, that happy are such? How should God wipe away the tears from your eyes in heaven, if now on earth with your handkerchiefs you could do it[4]? How could heaven be a place of rest, if on earth you did find it? How could you desire to be at home, if in your journey you found no grief? How could you so often call upon God, and talk with him, as I know you do, if your enemy should sleep all day long? How should you elsewhere be made like unto Christ—I mean in joy—if in sorrow you sobbed not with him? If you will have joy and felicity, you must first needs feel sorrow and misery. If you will go to heaven, you must sail by hell. If you will embrace Christ in his robes, you must not think scorn of him in his rags. If you will sit at Christ's table in his kingdom, you must first abide with

[[4] "with your handkerchiefs you could do it," autogr. MS.: "ye shed no tears," MS. No. 13, and printed editions.]

him in his temptations. If you will drink of his cup of glory, forsake not his cup of ignominy.

Can the head Corner-stone be rejected, and the other more base stones in God's building be in this world set by? You are one of his "lively stones:" be content therefore to be hewn and snagged at, that you might be made the more meet to be joined to your fellows, which suffer with you Satan's snatches, the world's wounds, contempt of conscience, and frets of the
Rom. vii. flesh; wherethrough they are enforced to cry, "O wretches that we are, who shall deliver us?" You are of God's corn: fear not therefore the flail, the fan, millstone, nor oven. You are one of Christ's lambs: look therefore to be fleeced, haled at, and even slain.

If you were a market-sheep, you should go in more fat and grassy pasture. If you were for the fair, you should be stall-fed, and want no weal. But, because you are for God's own occupying, therefore you must pasture on the bare common, abiding the storms and tempest that will fall. Happy, and
John xxi. twice happy are you, my dear sister, that God now haleth you whither you would not, that you might come whither you would. Suffer a little, and be still. Let Satan rage against you, let the world cry out, let your conscience accuse you, let the law load you and press you down, yet shall they not prevail, for
Rom. viii. Christ is "Emmanuel, that is, God with us." "If God be with us, who can be against us?" The Lord is with you; your Father cannot forget you; your Spouse loveth you. If the
Matt. viii. [xiv.] waves and surges arise, cry with Peter, "Lord, I perish;" and he will put out his hand and help you. Cast out your anchor of hope, and it will not cease for all the stormy surges, till it take hold on the rock of God's truth and mercy.

Think not that he which hath given you so many things corporally, as inductions of spiritual and heavenly mercies, and that without your deserts or desire, can deny you any spiritual
Phil. ii. comfort, desiring it: for, if he give to desire, he will give you to have and enjoy the thing desired. The desire to have, and the going about to ask, ought to certify your conscience, that they be his earnest of the thing which, you asking, he will give
[Isai. lxv.24.] you: yea, before you ask, and whilst you are about to ask, he will grant the same, as Esay saith, to his glory and your eternal
Rom. viii. consolation. "He that spared not his own Son for you" will

not, nor cannot think anything too good for you, my heartily beloved.

If he had not chosen you (as most certainly he hath), he would not have so called you; he would never have justified you; he would never have so glorified you with his gracious gifts, which I know, praised be his name therefore; he would never have so exercised your faith with temptations, as he hath done and doth—if, I say, he had not chosen you. If he have chosen you—as doubtless, dear heart, he hath done in Christ, for in you I have seen his earnest, and before me and to me you could not deny it, I know both where and when—if, I say, he have chosen you, as most certainly he hath[1], then neither can you nor shall you ever perish; for, if you fall, he putteth under his hand; you shall not lie still, so careful is Christ your Keeper over you. Never was mother so mindful over her child as he is over you: and hath not he always been so? Speak, woman, when did he finally forget you? And will he now, trow you, in your most need do otherwise, you calling upon him, and desiring to please him? Ah! my Joyce, think you God to be mutable? is he a changeling? doth he not love to the end them whom he loveth? are not his "gifts and calling such that he cannot repent him of them?" for else were he no God. If you should perish, then wanted he power, for I am certain his will towards you is not to be doubted of. Hath not the Spirit, which is "the Spirit of truth," told you so? And will you now hearken with Eve to the lying spirit? which would have you—not to despair, no, he goeth more craftily to work, howbeit to that end, if you should give ear unto it, which God forbid—but to doubt and stand in a mammering[2]: and so should you never truly love God, but serve him of a servile fear, lest he should cast you off for your unworthiness and unthankfulness, as though your thankfulness or worthiness were any causes with God, why he hath chosen you or will finally keep you. Ah! mine own dear heart, Christ only, Christ only, and his mercy and truth, in him and for him is the cause of your election. This Christ, this mercy, this truth of God, remaineth for ever, is certain for ever: and so is your election certain for ever, for ever, for ever—I say, for ever. If

Rom. xi.

[1 "as most certainly he hath," only in autogr. MS.]
[2 "Mammering:" hesitation, uncertainty.]

"an angel from heaven" should tell you the contrary, "accursed be he," "accursed be he." Your thankfulness and worthiness are fruits and effects of your election; they are no causes. These fruits and effects shall be so much more fruitful and effectual, by how much you waver not.

Therefore, my dearly beloved, arise, and remember from
Ps. cxxi. whence you are fallen. You have a Shepherd which "neither slumbereth nor sleepeth;" no man nor devil can "pull you out of his hands." Night and day he commandeth his angels to keep you. Have you forgotten what I read to you out of
Ps. xxiii. the psalm, "The Lord is my Shepherd, I can want nothing"? Do you not know that God sparred[1] Noah in the ark on the outside, so that he could not get out? So hath he done to
Ps. xci. you, my good sister, so hath he done to you. "Ten thousand shall fall on your right hand, and twenty on your left hand, yet
Ps. cxxix. no evil shall touch you." Say boldly therefore, "Many a time from my youth up they have fought against me, but they have
[Ps. cxxv. 2.] not prevailed," no, nor never shall prevail, for "the Lord is round about his people:" and who are the people of God, but such as hope in him? Happy are they that "hope in the Lord;" and you are one of those, my dear heart, for I am assured you have "hoped in the Lord;" I have your words to shew most manifestly, and I know they were written unfeignedly. I need not to say, that even before God you have simply confessed to me, and that oftentimes, no less. And once if you had this hope, as you doubtless had it, though now you feel it not, yet shall you feel it again; for "the anger of the Lord lasteth but a moment," but "his mercy lasteth for ever."

Tell me, my dear heart, who hath so weakened you? Surely
Gal. v. "not a persuasion which came from him who called you:" for why should you waver and be so heavy-hearted? Whom look you on? on yourself, on your worthiness, on your thankfulness, on that which God requireth of you, as faith, hope, love, fear, joy, &c.? Then can you not but waver indeed: for what have you as God requireth? Believe you, hope you, love you, &c., as much as you should do? No, no, nor never can in this life. Ah, my dearly beloved, have you so soon forgotten that which ever should be had in memory? namely that, when

[[1] See Vol. I. p. 417.]

you would and should be certain and quiet in conscience, then should your faith burst throughout all things, not only that you have in you, or else are in heaven, earth, or hell, until it come to "Christ crucified," and the eternal sweet mercies and goodness of God in Christ? Here, here is the resting-place, here is your Spouse's bed: creep into it, and in your arms of faith embrace him. Bewail your weakness, your unworthiness, your diffidence, &c.: and you shall see he will turn to you. What, said I, you shall see? Nay, I should have said, you shall feel he will turn to you[2]. You know that Moses, when he went into the mount to talk with God, he entered into a dark cloud; and Elias had his face covered when God passed by. Both these dear friends of God heard God, but they saw him not; but you would be preferred before them. See now, my dear heart, how covetous you are. Ah! be thankful, be thankful. But God be praised, that your covetousness is Moses' covetousness. Well, with him you "shall be satisfied." [Exod. xxxiii. 18.] But when? Forsooth, "when he shall appear." Here is not Ps. xvii. the time of seeing, but, as it were, "in a glass." Isaac was deceived, because he was not content with hearing only.

Therefore, to make an end of these many words—wherewith, I fear me, I do but trouble you from better exercises—inasmuch as you are indeed the child of God, elect in Christ before the beginning of all times; inasmuch as you are given to the custody of Christ, as one of God's most precious jewels; inasmuch as Christ is faithful, and thereto hath all power, so that you shall "never perish," no, one hair of your head shall not be lost, I beseech you, I pray you, I desire you, I crave at your hands with all my very heart, I ask of you with hand, pen, tongue and mind, in Christ, through Christ, for Christ, for his name, blood, mercies, power and truth's sake, my most entirely beloved sister, that you admit no doubt of God's final mercies towards you, howsoever you feel yourself, but complain to God, and crave of him, as of your tender and dear Father, all things: and, in that time which shall be most opportune, you shall find and feel, far above that your heart or the heart of any creature can conceive, to your eternal joy. Amen, Amen, Amen.

[[2] Twelve words occur here, scored across in the autogr. MS.]

[1]Your tokens I heartily thank you for: and here I have sent you that which I pray y[ou to[2]] use as you will. Yours I will use myself as God will. [Mine[2]] came from one of good-will to me: and even so doth it now to you. My book of "The hurt of hearing[3]," &c., I did give unto you: howbeit, if you be weary of it, you may re-send it again. Your token at your departing I perceive now deceived me, I will not say you. &c.

If in my letters, or in the preface of the meditation, &c., I write any foolish words, you may rase them out: for perchance —nay, without perchance—I offend you in some my terms: and therefore I will hereafter (if I can remember, as I have not done in this letter) be more wary. What I have written to your husband this bringer can tell you, for they be of his writing. Many other things I had in my mind to have written, but I have now forgotten them. If God will that you come hither— I mean not to this place, God forbid—I shall utter more at large, and better remember them. If you come not hither (as indeed I fear it), as occasion shall serve, so will I, if I can, send unto you. At the least, be wheresoever you shall be, in spirit I shall oftener see you than you think.

This bringer, if you come hither, shall come for you when you will and whither you will, and now tarry with you as long as you will, although I desire indeed to know how you do. My body is in very good health, I thank God, for I cannot be long crazed[4]: one way shall I go shortly, if sickness come. Pray God to forgive me mine unthankfulness for all his mercies. The good Spirit of God always keep us as his dear children: he comfort you as I desire to be comforted, my dearly beloved, for evermore. Amen.

I break up this abruptly, because our common prayer-time[5]

[1 The next three paragraphs, being twenty-six lines, "your tokens......mine unthankfulness for all his mercies," now are first printed from the autograph MS., in which alone they occur.]

[2 MS. torn.]

[3 Bradford's treatise on "The hurt of hearing mass," printed in this volume.]

[4 See p. 95, note 5, above.]

[5 This letter being dated August 8, which in 1554 fell on a Wednesday, the allusion to "common prayer-time," confirms the remarkable statement of Foxe, that while Bradford was in prison "he preached twice a day continually." See Vol. I. p. 83, note 4.]

calleth me. The peace of Christ dwell in both our hearts for ever. Amen.

This eighth of August, by him that in the Lord desireth to you as well and as much felicity as to his own heart.

JO. B.[6]

As for William Porrege's[7] report[8], if it be as you hear, you must prepare to bear it. It is written on heaven's door, 'Do well and hear evil.' Be content therefore to hear whatsoever the enemy shall imagine to blot you withal. God's good[9] Spirit always comfort and keep you. Amen, Amen[10].

XLII. TO ROBERT HARRINGTON[11] AND HIS WIFE.

Bp Coverdale, Letters of the Martyrs, 1564, p. 414.

Foxe, Acts, &c., ed. 1570, p. 1835; and after editions.

THE merciful God, and Father of our Saviour Jesus Christ, which loveth us as a most dear father, and hath put upon him towards us the affection of a most tender mother towards her children—so that he can no less think upon us (although of ourselves we be most unworthy, and deserve nothing less), than she can think on her only-begotten child in his distress: yea, if she should forget her child, as some unnatural mother will do, yet will he never forget us, although for a time he seem to sleep, that we might be occasioned to call loud and awake him—this good God keep you, my dear brother Nathanael and your good yoke-fellow, my heartily beloved sister in the Lord, in all things now and for ever, to his glory and your eternal comfort; and also of his goodness he grant you both the feeling of that hope, which undoubtedly he hath laid up in store for you both, far

Note that this Nathanael was not his proper name, but was so called for his unfeigned simplicity and truth.—[Foxe.]

[6 "Jo. B.," autogr. MS.: "John Bradford," 1564, 1570, and after editions.]

[7 See p. 38, note 1, above.]

[8 "William Porrege's report," autogr. MS.: "the report of W.P.," MS. No. 13, and printed editions.]

[9 "good," autogr. MS.: "holy," MS. No. 13, and printed editions.]

[10 This paragraph closes the letter as a postscript, as above, in autogr. MS., and MS. 13, but occurs before "This eighth of August," &c., in the printed editions.]

[11 See p. 55, note 3, above. The inscription of this letter in Bp Coverdale is: "To a faithful friend of his, whom, for his godly simplicity and singleness of heart in the ways of the Lord, he called Nathanael, as he doth also here in this letter." Its title in Foxe is: "To a faithful friend of his and his wife, resolving their doubt why they ought not to come to auricular confession.]

passing the store and provision, not only which you had made, but all the world is able to make, as I trust already he hath wrought it in you; but I beseech him to increase it more and more, and kindle in you a hearty longing for the enjoying of the same. The which once felt and had indeed, then the means by the which we come thereto cannot be so greatly dreaded, as most men do dread them; because either they want this feeling (I mean it of altogether), or else because the sense of this present time and things therein are as a mist to the hiding of those things from our sight, lest we should run and embrace them by hearty prayer: the Spirit whereof God grant us, and indeed we should attain enough in this behalf, if we continued therein.

As for auricular confession, wherein you desire my advice for your good yoke-fellow and family, my most dear brother, I am as ready to give it as you to desire it, yea, more glad, forasmuch as half a suspicion was in me, at the least touching my dear sister your wife, of a loathing of my advice, that too much had been given; where indeed I should lament my too little feeding you spiritually, as both you out of prison and in prison have fed me corporally. But, as I always thought of her, so I yet think, that she is the child of God, whom God dearly loveth, and will in his good time, to her eternal comfort, give her her heart's desire in sure feeling and sensible believing of this, which I would she had often in her mind; namely, that he is her God and Father, through Christ Jesus, our dear Lord and Saviour. A greater service to God she cannot give than to believe this. If Satan say, she believeth not, to answer, not him, but the Lord, and to say, 'Yea, Lord, help my unbelief, and increase my poor faith, which Satan saith is no faith; make him a liar, Lord, as always he hath been, is and shall be.' Undoubtedly, sooner or later, God will graciously hear her
[Ps. lvi. 8.] groans, and keep all "her tears in his bottle," yea, write them in his counting-book; for he is a righteous God, and hath no pleasure in the death of his creature. He loveth mercy, he will return and shew her his mercy; he "will cast all her sins and iniquities into the bottom of the sea;" and the longer that he tarrieth, as he doth it but to prove her, so the more liberally will he recompense her long looking, which no less pleaseth him than it grieveth now her outward Adam, for the mortifica-

tion whereof God useth this cross: and therefore, if she desire to bear the same, doubtless God will make her able to bear it; and, in presumption of his goodness and strength, let her cast herself wholly upon him, for he is faithful, and will assuredly confirm and bring to a happy end that good which graciously he hath begun in her. The which thing I desire him to do for his own glory and name's sake. Amen, Amen.

And now to the matter: confession auricular, as it was first used and instituted, which was by the way of a counsel-asking[1], I take to be amongst those traditions which are indifferent, that is, neither unlawful nor necessarily binding us, except the offence of the weak could not be avoided. But, to consider it as it is now used—I write to you but as I think, and what my mind is, the which follow no further than good men, by God's word, do allow it—to consider it, I say, as it is now used, methinks it is plainly unlawful and wicked, and that for these causes:

First, because they make it a service of God, and a thing which pleaseth God of itself, I will not say meritorious. This bringer my brother can tell you at large, how great an evil this is.

Secondly, because they make it of necessity, so that he or she that useth it not is not taken for a good Christian.

Thirdly, because it requireth of itself an impossibility, that is, the numbering and telling of all our sins, which no man perceiveth, much less can utter.

Fourthly, because it establisheth and confirmeth, at the least alloweth, praying to saints. *Precor sanctam Mariam* you must say, or the priest for you.

Fifthly, because it is very injurious to the liberty of the gospel, the which to affirm in example and fact I take to be a good work, and dear[2] in God's sight.

Sixthly, because, as it is used, it is a note, yea, a very sinew of the popish church: and therefore we should be so far from allowing the same, that we should think ourselves happy to lose anything, in bearing witness thereagainst.

Seventhly, because instead of counsel thereat you should

[1 Compare Sermon on Repentance, Vol. I. p. 51.]
[2 "a dear" 1564: "dear" 1570, and after editions.]

receive poison; or, if you refuse it under Sir John's[1] *benedicite*, you should no less there be wound in the briers.

Eighthly, because the end and purpose why we go thither is for the avoiding of the cross, that is, for our own cause, and not for Christ's cause or for our brethren's commodity: for, in that they make it so necessary a thing and a worshipping of God, it cannot but be against Christ and the freedom of his gospel; and the same thing teacheth us, that it is against the commodity of our brethren, which either be weak, either be strong, either be ignorant, either be obstinate. If they be weak, by your resorting to it they be made more weak; if they be strong, you do what you can to infirm[2] their strength; if they be ignorant, therein you help to keep them by your fact; if they be obstinate, your resorting to it cannot but rock them asleep in their obstinate error of the necessity of this rite and ceremony.

These causes recited do shew you what I think in this: but my thinking must no further bind you than a man's thought should do, except the same be grounded upon God's word, which bindeth indeed, as I think they do. I doubt not but you, weighing these causes, and especially two of the first and the last, if you pray to God for his Spirit to direct you, and thereto ask the advice of this my good brother and other godly learned men—I doubt not, I say, but you should be guided to do that which is best in God's sight, although, in the sight of the world, perhaps you should be counted foolish and precise. But be at a point with yourselves, as the disciples of Christ which had forsaken themselves, to follow not your will but God's will, as you daily pray in the Lord's Prayer.—The cross of Christ be willing to carry, lest you carry the cross of the world, the flesh, or the devil. One of these four crosses you must carry: three of them bringeth to hell: and therefore the more part goeth that way which is "a broad way." Only the fourth bringeth to heaven: but few go that way, as well because "the way is strait," as also because few walk in it. Howbeit, though it be strait, it is but short, and the few are many, if you consider the godly, as the patriarchs, prophets, apostles, martyrs, confessors, and Christ Jesus, with all his guard and train. Think not scorn to come after them which are gone before you, and after them which now go before you; in whose

[1 See Vol. I. p. 589, note E.] [2 "Infirm:" weaken.]

number I trust I am appointed to be one, and I beseech you pray for me, that God would vouch me worthy that honour. Our sins deserve plagues, prison, and the loss of all that ever we have: therefore, if God remove our sins out of sight, and send us prison, or loss of goods and living, for his name's sake, O how happy are we! My dear hearts in the Lord, consider this gear; and be assured that he which loseth anything for Christ's sake the same in his posterity shall find it here, and in heaven elsewhere.

As for unableness to answer for your faith, it shall be enough to will them to dispute with your teachers. Faith standeth not in disputing: I think few, if it came to disputing, could defend the Godhead of Christ and many other articles; I speak it for the simple sort. Pray for me.

Lack of paper maketh this end. Commend me to my good brother Richard Bleacher, and my good sister his wife: I pray them to pray for me. I trust by this bearer to hear how you do.

JOHN BRADFORD.

XLIII. TO MISTRESS WILKINSON[3] AND MISTRESS WARCUP[4].

To my dearly beloved in the Lord, Mistress W[ilkinson] and Mistress W[arcup.] Bp Coverdale, Letters of the Martyrs, 1564, p. 423.

Almighty God, our dear and most merciful Father, be always with you both, my entirely beloved mother and sister in the Lord; and as his babes he for ever keep you unto his eternal kingdom, through Christ our Saviour. Amen.

I purpose not to go about to render thanks to you for God's great goodness towards me by you, because I cannot. Either of you hath so heaped upon me benefits, that it were hard for me to reckon the tithes. He, for whose sake you have done it and all the good you do, one day recompense you after your heart's desire in him. In the mean season I beseech him to reveal unto you, more and more, the riches of his grace and love in Christ, by whom ye are beloved and were, before the world was, and shall be doubtless world without end.

[[3] See p. 39, note 3, above.] [[4] See p. 45, note 2, above.]

According to the revelation and your sense or faith herein, so will you contend to all piety and godliness, as St John saith:
1 John iii. "He that hath this hope will purify himself as Christ is pure." For how should it otherwise be but, if we be certainly persuaded that heaven is ours, and we citizens thereof—but, I say, we should desire the dissolution of our bodies, and death to despatch us, and to do his office upon us? If we did certainly believe we were members of Christ and God's temples, how should we but flee from all impurity and corruption of the world, which cometh by concupiscence? If we did certainly believe, that God indeed of his mercy in Christ is become our Father, in that his good-will is infinite, and his power according thereto, how could we be afraid of man or devil; how could we doubt of salvation, or any good thing which might make to God's glory and our own weal?

Now, that we should be certain and sure of this, that we are God's children in Christ, mark whether all things teach us not. Behold the creation of this world, and the gubernation[1] of the same: do not these teach us that God loveth us? and is God's love out of Christ the beloved? is not his love, as he is, un-
John xiii. changeable? doth not St John say, that "he loveth to the end" whom he loveth? Therefore, I say, the very creatures of God, concerning both their creation and conservation, tell us that God loveth us, that is, that we in Christ be his children and darlings, although in ourselves and of ourselves we be otherwise, namely children of wrath.

Again, look upon the law of God, and tell me whether it do not require this certainty of you, namely, that you be God's dear children in Christ. Doth not God plainly affirm and say, "I am the Lord thy God?" doth he not charge you "to have none other Gods but him?" How then can you perish, if God be your God? doth not that make God no God? doth not
Ps. cxliv. David say, that "those people be happy, which have the Lord for their God?"

Besides this, look on your belief: do you not profess that you 'believe in God your Father almighty?' which wanteth no power to help you, as he wanted no good-will in Christ to choose you. Do you not say that you 'do believe remission of sins, resurrection of the body, life everlasting, fellowship

[[1] "Gubernation:" government.]

with the saints,' &c.? But how do you say you believe this gear, and be not certain thereof? Is not faith a certainty? Is not doubting against faith? as St James saith, "Pray in faith and doubt not," for he that doubteth obtaineth nothing. When Peter began to doubt, he had like to have been drowned: beware of it therefore. Matt. xiv.

Moreover, for to certify your consciences that you be God's children and shall never finally perish, through God's goodness in Christ, behold your Head, your Captain, I mean Christ Jesus. Wherefore came he into this world, but to redeem you, to marry you unto himself, to destroy the works of Satan, to save and seek that which was lost? Wherefore suffered he so great and bitter passions? did he it not to take away your sins? Wherefore did he rise from death? did he it not to justify you? Wherefore did he ascend into heaven? did he it not to take possession there for you, to "lead your captivity captive," to prepare and make ready all things for you, to appear before the Father, always praying for you? If these be true, as they be most true, why then stand you in a doubt? do you not thereby deny Christ? Wherefore were you born of christian parents and in God's church, but because you were God's children by Christ before you were born? For this cause you were baptized: and hitherto the Lord hath thus dealt with you, sparing you, correcting you, and blessing you. But why? Verily because you be his children, and shall be for ever, through Christ.

Tell me, why hath God kept you till this time, but that he will for his sake have you even here made like unto Christ, that elsewhere you may so be? Why hath he opened your eyes from popery, but because you be his children indeed? When you do pray, do you not call him Father? why do you doubt of it then? why will you believe the devil more than God your Father, the Son, and the Holy Ghost; more than the holy word of God, both in the law and in the gospel; more than all the blessings and castigations of God? do not all these preach to you and tell you, that you are God's babes through Christ? Therefore, my dearly beloved, believe it, and give not place to the devil, but withstand him strong in faith; say with the poor man: "I believe; Lord, help my unbelief;" Mark ix.
say with the apostles: "Lord, increase our faith." Luke xvii.

This, mine own hearts in the Lord, I write not that you should live more securely and carnally, doing as the spiders do which gather poison where bees gather honey, but that, as the elect of God, you might live in all purity, godliness, and peace: which God increase in us all for his Christ's sake. Amen.

I pray you heartily, pray for us, that to the very end we may, as I hope we shall, go lustily and cheerfully whithersoever our heavenly Father shall bring and lead us. His will, which is always good, be done on earth as it is in heaven. Amen.

Your brother in bonds, for the testimony of Jesus Christ,

JOHN BRADFORD.

XLIV. TO ROYDEN[1] AND HIS WIFE.

[Probably in the Autumn of 1554[2].]

Bp Coverdale, Letters of the Martyrs, 1564, p. 383.

MS. 2. 2. 15. No. 15. Original, Holograph. Emman. Coll. Cambridge.

To my good friends in the Lord, Master R[oyden] and his wife.

My dearly beloved, I heartily commend me unto you in our common Christ, whom I so call, not that I would make him as common things be, that is, nothing set by, but because by him we are brought into a communion, and that as with him so with his Father, and as with his Father so with all God's people, if we be his people, as I trust we are; and therefore write I unto you, as one careful, but not so much as I should be, for you, as for them whose well-doing comforteth me and is profitable to me, and whose evil-doing maketh me heavy and woundeth me.

The days are come, in the which we cannot but declare what we be, if we be indeed as we should be, as I trust we are, that is, if we be Christ's disciples: I mean, we cannot now do as the world doth, or say as it saith, but as God's church doth and saith. The world seeketh itself, and speaketh thereafter: the church of God seeketh Christ's glory, and speaketh accordingly. The worldlings follow the world: the church-children follow their Captain Christ; and therefore, as of the world they are not known to be as they be, so are they hated, and if

[1 The words "Master Royden," are inscribed on the last blank page of the MS.]

[2 From the allusion to the case of Sir James Hales, who died early in August, 1554. See p. 85, note 5, above.]

God permit it are persecuted and slain: the which persecution is the true touchstone, which trieth the true church-children from hypocrites, as the wind doth the wheat from the chaff.

And of this gear this our time and age setteth very many forth for example, doctrine, and fear, which once were hearty and very zealous, and now are so cold that they smell nothing of the Spirit; for they are not only afraid to seem to speak with a church-child, but also ashamed; and not only ashamed of them, and so of that they profess, but also frame and fashion themselves in all outward behaviour, as in coming to church and hearing mass, so as no man can accuse them for not allowing it, or not honouring it, as well as the papists, where in their hearts they disallow it, and know the same to be naught, at the least they have known it. But halting out of the way may perchance have brought them so far, that now they cannot see the way, they are so far and so long gone astray; for, the further and longer a man goeth wide, the harder shall it be to recover and see the way: and therefore the apostle giveth warning thereof, Hebrews twelfth, as doth Moses, Deuteronomy twenty-ninth, speaking of men that bless themselves, inwardly cursing themselves.—Read both the chapters, I pray you: and mark the example of Master Hales[2], which, after that he consented to seem to allow in outward fact that which he knew once was evil, was fearfully left of God, to our admonition. For, albeit God hath not done thus to all that have indeed done that he purposed to do, yet in this example God teacheth us how fearful a thing it is to wound our conscience and do anything thereagainst, to the offence of the godly and comfort of the obstinate.—I write not this, as thereof to accuse you or either of you; for, as I cannot lightly be persuaded of any such thing of you, so I am assured you hitherto would not do any such thing; for I ween there be yet no great penalty to punish you for not so doing, if thereof you should have been accused; for he that will do a thing unforced, I cannot hope anything of the same, but that he will run apace when he is forced. But of this enough to you, which are to be comforted and exhorted to continue in that pureness of religion, which you have, as I think, hitherto received and by your open conversation protested.

Howbeit, considering how you have heard and read as much

as in manner can be spoken herein (for the scriptures, which of themselves are most perfect herein, you have read and read again), I think it good to exhort you to use earnest and hearty prayer, as I trust you do: and then doubtless God will so write that you have read in your hearts, as shall be both comfortable and profitable unto you and others plentifully: you shall rejoice
Matt. vii. in "the strait way," which few find, and fewer walk in, but
Heb. x. most few continue therein to the end. You shall "suffer with joy the direption[1] of your goods," because the best part of your substance is in heaven. You will set before you the example
Heb. xii. of Christ, "the Beginner and Ender of your faith," who suffered much more than we can suffer, that we should not be
Matt. v. faint-hearted. You will "rejoice, and greatly, because great
Acts v. is your reward in heaven." You will be glad that God "accounteth you worthy to suffer" anything for his sake. You will
2 Cor. iv. set before you the end of this your short cross, and the great glory which will ensue the same. You will know, that it is
2 Thess. i. no small benefit of God, "to suffer for his sake." You will
Phil. i. John xiv. xvi. know, that your sorrowing shall be turned to joying. You will know that, as God doth make you now like to Christ in
Rom. viii. suffering, so shall you be in reigning; and, if you be partakers of affliction, you shall be also of glory, &c. *Summa* you will know that this is the surest and safest way to heaven, which is
Rev. i. called "the kingdom of patience."

But because I have written a little treatise hereof[2], and of the harm of halting with the world, in coming to mass[3], I send them both unto you to peruse and read them, and then at your leisure to re-deliver them to this bringer or my man, when I shall send to you for the same. In the mean season I shall as heartily as I can pray to God for you both, my most dear members in the Lord. What said I, as heartily as I can? God forgive me, for I do nothing so well as I might, in that I flatter myself too much: God lay it not to my charge. Indeed I have most cause to pray night and day, and to give thanks night and day, for you both.—The Lord of mercy in Christ bless you both, keep you both, and send you both, as well to

[[1] "Direption:" plundering.]

[[2] This may have been either the "Exhortation to patience," Vol. I. pp. 375—78, or the "Exhortation to the brethren in England," Vol. I. pp. 414—33.]

[[3] The "Hurt of hearing mass," printed in this volume.]

do as I wish to my dearest and best beloved friends and brethren in the Lord.

I pray you to continue to pray for me, as I doubt not you do; and so give thanks to God for me, "for he is good, and his mercy endureth for ever." The day will come, when we shall meet together and never depart. God send it shortly. Amen.

JOHN BRADFORD.

XLV. TO MISTRESS BROWN.

Good sister, I beseech God to make perfect the good which he hath begun in you, unto the very end. Amen.

Bp Coverdale, Letters of the Martyrs, 1564, p. 413.

This life more and more waxeth unto us as it should be, that is, a miserable life, a weeping life, a woeful life: and therefore let us long for our happy life, our laughing life, our joyful life, which we shall enjoy, and then have in very deed, when we depart by death out of this dangerous state, wherein we now are by reason of this sinful flesh which we carry about us. Therefore let us prepare ourselves accordingly, and in misery and sorrow be glad through hope. Now we are dispersed, but we shall be gathered together again there, where we shall never part, but always be together in joy eternal. In hope hereof let us bear with better will our bitter burdens, which we feel and shall feel in this miserable world. We have cause to thank God, that maketh this world unto us a wilderness. If so be therein we be patient, kiss God's rod, and humble ourselves before God, assuredly we shall come into the most pleasant land of rest.

Wherefore, good sister, as I said, I say again, be merry with sorrow, rejoice in hope, be patient in trouble, pray in affliction: and amongst others I pray you heartily pray for me, that God would forgive me my unthankfulness, not only against you, which is great indeed, but also against all his people, but specially against his majesty. As I can, I shall commend you unto the tuition of our Shepherd Christ; who always keep us as his lambs, for his holy name's sake. Amen.

Your afflicted brother,

JOHN BRADFORD.

XLVI. TO A FREE-WILLER[1].

1554.

MS. 2. 2. 15. No. 74. Transcript. Emman. Coll. Cambridge.

The Lord of mercy grant us his wisdom and grace to guide us in all things as his dear children through Christ for evermore. Amen.

I have received from you the schedule I lent you with increase, that is, with three letters, one from my brother Simson[2], another from Henry Hart[3], and another from you. Concerning the first, because I hope it require none answer (for yet I have not read it), I need not to write no more. Concerning the second, which I have not read also, hereafter I trust shortly to answer, and that in such sort that I doubt not to have the hands of all prisoners in England to subscribe to the condemnation of them all of error: I speak it of the prisoners that be of any learning.

Concerning your letter, I answer thus: first, that silence cannot cease controversies, as you write; secondly, that I kept promise with you, for, though I wrote many words (and yet not many more than you did write to me), yet I would have thought that your wisdom could in few words have found out easily, as well my belief and judgment in that which you call into controversy, as an answer to your request. I pray you, do not the three rules, written briefly in the latter end of my schedule, set forth in short and plain words that which you required of me? Again, do not the twelve first articles, as correct your writing, so plainly tell you my meaning? Last of all, the thirteenth article would make a wise man soon to see my judgment in this matter: for, although I rehearse St Augustine's word, yet do not I rehearse them as his words only. Therefore I much marvel that you will find fault, where none is, except herein, that I have both satisfied your request according to my promise, and also answered and corrected your articles: which perchance so moved you that you could not well see that which another man that readeth my writing without prejudice cannot but see.

[1 This Letter is now printed for the first time.] [2 See Vol. I. p. 434.]

[3 A leader at that time of the sect called "Freewillers." See Vol. I. pp. 306, 318; also Letter LXII. to Abp Cranmer and Bps Ridley and Latimer, Jan. 18, 1555; Letter LXIII. from Bp Ridley to Bernhere, p. 173, note 6; and Strype, Cranmer, Vol. I. p. 502—5.]

Last of all—where you write that my doctrine is not simple nor plain, nor agreeth with itself so far as you see, and therefore you cannot be edified thereby, if you shall speak without flattery—to this I will say no more presently but that, to speak flatly, methinks you go not so simply to work with me as I thought you would, in that you accuse my doctrine and writing and not the matter. Until you shall send me word, wherein it is not simple, and wherein it varieth with itself, I shall not be utterly free from suspicion of calumniation on your behalf. As concerning your request for me to judge well of you, I would be sorry you had so much cause to think otherwise towards me, as I have towards you: I speak this plurally, and not simply to your own person, according to your own writing, saying, 'Judge well of us.'

With your letters I received this which is imprinted. What you mean thereby I will not judge; for I trust you will advertise me your meaning, and send it me, with the same again, by my brother Punt, this bringer, or at your more leisure. Indeed you should do me more pleasure to send me this imprinted thing and your meaning by this bringer, rather than to take more leisure.

As for your confession, that God is omnipotent, and that his will is certain and unresistible, whereto you add that the same is mutable, because you read him to change his works often at the prayers and peevishness of men, I cannot but see a contrariety in this your assertion. Yea, methinks you, making the will of God mutable and not mutable, either make two wills in God, or two gods, or rather no God, for a thing in danger to mutation is not God: but of this more another time. For salvation and damnation, methinks you in words agree with me, save that expressly you do not tell, who it is that damneth and pronounceth the sentence to the wicked: I doubt not but you mean none other than God: and therefore, as I said, you consent with me, that damnation cometh from the justice of the Lord on the wicked, through their own just deserts. As for Master Philpot, I think he himself will answer you for his book.

Thus briefly and in haste I have written unto you my mind as appeareth. If you take it as I mean it, then doubt I not of displeasing, or rather fear it not. God's peace be with us in Christ for ever.

Yours, to do you the good I can,

JOHN BRADFORD.

God's will concerning the salvation of those that he have given to Christ is determined, and therefore immutable. Now

this is not infirmed because we read how God doth seem in some things to alter his will, before not determined, but dependant upon man's behaviour: which will is not altered in respect of himself, but in respect of us which judge of God and his will after his word and works: whereby we see that his will indeed is always wrought. If he would not have had the Ninevites saved, would he have sent Jonas thither? If Hezekias' death was determined, whereto sent he Esay to tell him? Did not Jonas, going to Nineveh, declare that God's sentence pronounced was not determined but hanged upon condition? Did not Hezekias' prayer granted declare Esay's denunciation of his death to depend upon condition? as by the alteration of it we perceive. Sentences determined with God are immutable, as is the sentence of God for those which he hath given to Christ, for whom Christ's prayer, John seventeenth, is heard undoubtedly. Sentences simply spoken and undetermined are mutable, as that of the destruction of Nineveh, of Hezekias'
Gen. xx. death, of Abimelech, Genesis twentieth. When they be determined and when not, we may judge by the word and of the end. Some things depend partly on us, and some upon God wholly and altogether. Those that depend partly upon us are mutable to us, because we ourselves of ourselves be so; but that depend wholly upon God are immutable, because he is so.

Now, if you will say that salvation dependeth partly on ourselves, and not simply, wholly and altogether on God's mercy and truth in Christ and his merits, you deny salvation to come of grace, contrary to the prophets and apostles; for grace to us is not but in respect of grace to Christ. And hereof I half suspect you all, that indeed you are adversaries to grace by maintaining free-will, though in words you deceive yourselves and others. Wherefore I pray you weigh this with yourself the better, and see whether you can espy how your doctrine is doubtful—I mean, how that you are never certain of your salvation, because you are never certain of your power how much and free it is.

Now, as a beastly[1] man will gather hereout perchance, that, seeing salvation dependeth wholly and altogether upon God and his grace in and for Christ, it forceth nothing what we do, whether we pray or not pray, live well or evil, so the godly

[[1] "Beastly:" obstinate, mulish, or sensual, carnal.]

will gather hereout that, as God's providence bindeth not our hands, so it hindereth not in us any good thing, but rather provoketh us thereunto mightily: for the godly, though they hang on God's providence and grace wholly and continually, yet do not they at any time separate those things which God hath coupled together. Therefore they till the earth, and yet still hang on God and his providence, knowing full well that God can and will, if need be, provide for them without their tilling: they pray, watch and fast, and do good deeds, and yet still hang on God's eternal and immutable decree and grace in Christ altogether, using none of these things to infirm their faith in this behalf, but, knowing them to be God's instruments to their salvation, do use them accordingly, although they be certain that without all these God can and will make his counsel to stand for ever, as we see he doth it in the elect infants without these things.

This I thought good to write to you, more than I was purposed (for I thought out of hand to have sent you that which is written on the other side): but, because it was past time yesternight so to do, that you might see I desire to do you good, I have added this, which I have written with some more haste than I would have sent forth thus to one of whom I think not well.

As concerning Henry Hart's errors, which I have now read, that he by blanching[2] goeth about to defend, if after the doings of some things I have in hand I do not by God's grace evidently make them to appear to such as will not shut their eyes, then suspect me to have slandered him; as methinks you have done me, till you shall shew me wherein I am at variance with myself in doctrine.

Fare ye well.

XLVII. TO MISTRESS MARY HONYWOOD[3].

To my good sister, Mistress H[onywood.] The peace of God, with increase of faith and feeling of his mercy to your comfort in Christ, the Holy Ghost work in your heart now and for ever. Amen. Bp Coverdale, Letters of the Martyrs, 1564, p. 426.

[[2] "Blanching:" evading, shifting.—Todd's Johnson's Dict.]
[[3] See p. 98, note 1, above.]

As it is much to my comfort, that God hath given you such a love and zeal to his truth, so I exhort you, my good sister, diligently to labour, as by continual reading and meditation of God's holy word, so by earnest prayer and other godly exercises to maintain and increase the same, that, by the feeling of God's gracious Spirit working in you such good fruits as witnesses of your faith, you may grow in strength thereof and certainty of God's favour and good-will towards you. For, above all things, of this I would have you to be most assured, that you are beloved of God, that you are his dear child, and shall be for evermore through Christ, in whom you are by faith, and he in you. Out of this certainty (the cause whereof is God's own goodness, grace, and truth) springeth true love, and loving fear, and obedience to God continually and in all things. Where it is (I mean this faith, certainty and persuasion of God's eternal goodness to you in Christ), there no sins are imputed to you, or laid to your charge, to condemnation, nor shall be, though for correction sake now and then your heavenly Father visit them fatherly, or rather you for them. Where it is not, there is nothing, be it never so well done, that pleaseth God.

Labour therefore for this certainty of faith through Christ: whensoever you doubt, you heap sin upon sin. If Satan, your conscience, or God's law do accuse you, confess your fault, and hide it not before the Lord: but, when they would infer that because of your sin you are condemned, you are cast away, then answer them, that it is but their office to accuse and witness, not to give sentence and judge: it only appertaineth to God to give judgment. Paul saith, "It is God that absolveth, who then shall condemn us?" God himself promiseth, before he demand anything of us, that he is our Lord and our God: and are not they happy which have the Lord for their God? is he God to any whose sins he remitteth not? Through Christ he is our Father; and therefore we are commanded so to call him: and can there want any fatherly kindness in him towards us which be his children? No, verily: therefore be sure, and waver not of God's love and favour towards you in Christ. The cause of his love is his own goodness and mercy: this lasting for ever, his love lasteth for ever. How can you then but be quiet and happy? Use this gear to comfort the weak conscience, and not to unbridle the mighty affections of the flesh or old Adam, which must have other meat.

Your own in the Lord,

JOHN BRADFORD.

XLVIII. TO COLE AND SHETERDEN.

To my friends and brethren in the Lord, R[obert] Cole and N[icholas] Sheterden: I wish to you, my good brethren, the same grace of God in Christ, which I wish and pray "the Father of mercies" to give to me for his holy name's sake. Amen.

Bp Coverdale, Letters of the Martyrs, 1564, p. 409.

Foxe, Acts, &c., ed. 1570, p. 1840; and after editions.

MSS. 2. 2. 15. No. 92. And 1. 2. 8. No. 48. Transcripts. Emman. Coll. Cambridge.

Your letter though I have not read myself, because I would not alienate my mind from conceived things to write to others, yet I have heard the sum of it, that it is of God's election; wherein I will briefly write to you my faith, and how I think it good and meet for a christian man to wade in it. I believe that man, made after the image of God, did fall from that blessed state, to the condemnation of himself and all his posterity. I believe that Christ, for man being thus fallen, did oppose himself to the justice of God, a Mediator, paying the ransom and price of redemption for Adam and his whole posterity that refuse it not finally. I believe that all that believe in Christ (I speak of such as be of years of discretion) are partakers of Christ and all his merits. I believe that faith, and to believe in Christ—I speak not now of faith that men have by reason of miracles, or by reason of earthly commodity, custom and authority of men, which is commonly seen, the hearts of them that so believe being not right and simple before God, but I speak of that faith which indeed is the true faith, the justifying and regenerating faith—I believe, I say, that this faith and belief in Christ is the work and gift of God, that is, to those whom God the Father, before the beginning of the world, hath predestinate in Christ unto eternal life.

John ii. xii. Acts viii. Matt. xiii.

Exod. xiv.

Search your hearts whether you have this faith[1]. If you

[[1] "Search......faith," MS. 15. No. 92: "For the certainty of this faith search your hearts," MS. 8. No. 48, and printed editions.]

have it, praise the Lord, for you are happy, and therefore cannot finally perish; for then happiness were not happiness if it could be lost. When you fall, the Lord will put under his hand, that you shall not lie still. But, if you feel not this faith, then know that predestination is too high a matter for you to be disputers of it[1], until you have been better scholars in the school-house of repentance and justification, which is the grammar-school, wherein we must be conversant and learned, before we go to the university of God's most holy predestination and providence[2].

Thus do I wade in predestination, in such sort as God hath patefied and opened it. Though in God it be the first, yet to us it is last opened: and therefore I begin with creation, from thence I come to redemption, so to justification, and so to election. On this sort I am sure, that warily and wisely a man may walk in it easily by the light of God's Spirit, in and

2 Thess. iii. by his word, seeing this faith not to be given to all men, but to such as are born of God, predestinate before the world was made, after the purpose and good will of God. Which will we may not call into disputation, but in trembling and fear submit ourselves to it, as to that which can will none otherwise than that which is holy, right and good, how far soever otherwise it seem to the judgment of reason: which must needs be beaten down, to be more careful for God's glory than for man's salvation, which dependeth only thereon, as all God's children full well see; for they seek not the glory which cometh

Jer. ix. John v. of men, but "the glory which cometh of God." They know God to be a God which doeth on earth, not only mercy, but also judgment; which is justice and most justice, although our foolish reason cannot see it; and in this knowledge they glory and rejoice, though others, through vain curiosity, grudge and murmur thereagainst.

Thus briefly I have sent you my mind and meaning concerning this matter. Hereafter you shall have, I think, your letter particularly answered by Master Philpot, as also if I have

[1 "it," only in MS. 15. No. 92.]

[2 The preceding paragraph is given in the body of this letter as above in the Emmanuel MS. 1. 2. 8. No. 48, but on its margin in MS. 2. 2. 15. No. 92, and in Bp Coverdale and Foxe.]

time, and you so require it, I will do, after that I have answered my father Hart[3], the which thing hitherto to do God by sickness hath letted[4].

JOHN BRADFORD.

XLIX. TO SIR WILLIAM FITZWILLIAM[5].

THE peace of God proper to his people the Holy Ghost work daily and deeply in your heart, through Jesus Christ our Lord. Amen. Bp Coverdale, Letters of the Martyrs, 1564, p. 386.

I thank my Lord and God, through his Son our Mediator and Saviour, for his mercies and graces given to your mastership, the which I beseech his goodness to increase in you continually, to your everlasting comfort in him. By his mercies towards you I mean not in your lands, possessions, offices, natural wisdom, rights, health, form, &c., which indeed be gifts of God given to you of his mercy without your deserts; and therefore should he be daily of you praised for the same, as I doubt not but he is (for else your ingratitude would provoke him to punish you in them and by them, if he love you); but I mean his mercies towards you, in the knowledge and love of his truth in religion.

The which benefit in that you, amongst the not many of your estate and condition, as St Paul witnesseth, have received as a very testimonial of your election in Christ, I would be sorry that you should need any such as I am to move you to thankfulness; for I am not in a mammering whether you be thankful to God for this great mercy, which is much more to be esteemed than all that ever you have. I humbly beseech God in his Christ to increase the same in you to the very end: 1 Cor. i.

[3 See p. 128, note 3, above.]

[4 The last nineteen words now are first printed from MS. 15. No. 92.]

[5 The inscription in Bp Coverdale is: "To the worshipful Sir William Fitzwilliam, then being knight-marshal of the King's Bench," to which office he had been appointed by Edward VI. He was of Milton in Northamptonshire, and was "a good man and a lover of the gospel:" Strype, Ecc. Mem. Vol. III. part I. p. 124. He was a person of much distinction, and in the reign of Elizabeth, between 1560 and 1594, was three times lord-deputy of Ireland, where his vigilance was conspicuous in the year of the Spanish invasion, 1583. He married Ann, daughter of Sir William Sidney, of Penshurst, and died, aged 73, June 22, 1599. He was the lineal ancestor of the present earl Fitzwilliam.—See Fuller's Worthies, Northamptonshire, ed. 1840, Vol. II. p. 508; and Collins' Hist. of Peerage, ed. 1812, Vol. IV. p. 392.]

and, that by me he might do the same in some part, I thought it good and also my bounden duty, deeply deserved on your behalf towards me, for the which I beseech the Lord to reward you, to send to you this Treatise of the doings of Master Ridley at Oxford, concerning his Disputation about the sacrament[1]. I know that there hath gone divers copies abroad, but none of them were as I know this is; for I have translated it out of that copy in Latin which was corrected with his own hand, which came unto me not without his own consent; and therefore dare I be bold to say, that this hath not before been seen on this sort. In reading whereof you shall well see this I speak to be most true, and also that which causeth me to suppress commendations of the thing—the excellency and worthiness thereof I mean—because I think I cannot speak anything so worthily as undoubtedly these his doings do deserve. Unto your mastership I send them as a token of my duty towards you, thereby to declare that, as you deserve much of me, so I would shew myself willing to recompense the same if I could: but in that I cannot, and also your doing is simply in respect of God and his cause, I will according to your expectation leave the recompense unto him; in the mean season praying him that of his goodness he would, as increase the knowledge and love of his truth in you, so strengthen you after your vocation, both purely to walk and manfully to confess his gospel, if he shall think it needful to call you to that honour—for surely of all honours it is the greatest to suffer anything for Christ's sake. Most happy may that man think himself, that hath anything for his cause to lose. As he shall be sure to find for his own part eternal felicity and honour endless, so shall his posterity, even temporally, prove this to be most true.

This Treatise of Master Ridley's Disputation, which he sent to him, you shall read in the Book of Martyrs, fol. 963. [ed. 1563, or ed. 1843—9, Vol. VI. p 469.—Bp Coverdale.]

For God's sake therefore, right worshipful sir, consider well this gear, and weigh it not as the world and your motherwit will move you to do, but as the word of God doth teach you: there shall you see this I speak of to be matter of much mirth, joy and glory, though to the world it seem clean contrary. God's "good Spirit" always guide you to his glory, and give you "the Spirit of prayer," continually to pray that God never further tempt you, than he will make you able to bear. Amen.

[[1] See Works of Bp Ridley, Park. Soc. pp. 189—252, 433—85.]

In that this copy is not so fair written as I wish and would have had it, I shall desire you to consider where I am, and how I cannot have things so done as I would; and therefore you have it as may be, when it may not be as I would it were and should be.

From the King's Bench.

Your humble

JOHN BRADFORD.

L. LEVER[2] TO BRADFORD[3].

[ZURICH, *October* 25, 1554.]

Bp Coverdale, Letters of the Martyrs, 1564, p. 688.

MS. 2. 2. 15. No. 113. Transcript. Emman. Coll. Cambridge.

THE grace of God be unto you, with my hearty commendations. I have seen the places, noted the doctrine and discipline, and talked with the learned men of Argentine[4], Basil, Zurich, Bern, Lausan, and Geneva; and I have had experience in all these places of sincere doctrine, godly order and great learning, and especially of such virtuous learning, diligence and charity, in Bullinger at Zurich, and in Calvin at Geneva, as doth much advance God's glory, unto the edifying of Christ's church, with the same religion for the which you be now in prison. And, as I doubt not but you in reading of their books have found much godly and comfortable knowledge, so I am sure that they in hearing of your constancy and patience take occasion greatly to rejoice with thanksgiving unto God, which doth testify his truth unto the world, not only by their writing, but also by your suffering. The Lord therefore, which useth this your suffering, joined with godly learning, to set forth his glory, not only unto the comfort of simple souls in England, but also unto the great rejoicing and encouraging of the most godly, learned men in all countries, will, as I desire and trust, give you such comfort in conscience as shall easily bear the pains of your imprisonment.

If you desire to suffer or do that thing which might testify the truth, advance the glory, and edify the church of Christ, truly you have your desire: yea, and I ensure you, very many godly men in divers places give daily thanks unto God in prayer for you. You know your cause is good: your friends be in favour and your adver-

[2 See Vol. I. p. 565, note 7.]

[3 The title of this letter in Bp Coverdale is: "A letter of Master Thomas Lever, being then in exile for the testimony of God's gospel, to Master Bradford, prisoner in the Tower of London."]

[4 Argentine: Strasburgh.]

saries in displeasure with the almighty God, your heavenly Father: your suffering for the truth shall not be unrewarded; your hope in Christ shall never be confounded. For, although your bodies be kept within prisons, yet your testimony unto the truth shineth far abroad in the world; and your faithful prayers, in charitable unity joined with many others, be continually presented afore the throne of God.

God grant you grace to find and use comfortable meditation of his word, in diligent obedience unto his will: Christ be your Keeper in comfort. Amen.

Scribbled at[1] Zurich, the 25th of October, by yours faithfully in Christ,

THOMAS LEVER.

LI. TO LORD RUSSELL[2].

Bp Coverdale, Letters of the Martyrs, 1564, p. 278.

The eternal mercies of God, in his dear Son our Saviour Jesus Christ, be more and more felt and heartily perceived of you, my good lord, to your endless joy and comfort. Amen.

Because your lordship looketh not for thanks of me for God's benefits ministered by you, and in few words I cannot duly declare that I would do, I will omit the same, praying God our dear Father, in the day of his retribution, to remember it, and in the mean season to assist, counsel and comfort you as his child, for ever in all things.

I doubt not but that you have that childlike opinion, yea, persuasion of his goodness in Christ towards you, than which blessing, my good lord, none is greater given to man upon earth. For assuredly he that hath it is the very child of God, elect before all time in Christ Jesu our Lord, and therefore shall enjoy everlasting felicity, although he be here afflicted and tossed in trouble and temptation to his trial, that when he is found faithful he may receive the crown of glory. The only thing that discerneth the child of God from the wicked is this faith, trust, and hope in God's goodness, through Christ, the which I trust you have: God increase it in you, and make you thankful. Certainly such as enjoy it be happy. If they be happy, and that happiness is not where anything is to be de-

[[1] "Scribbled at," MS.: "From," 1564.]
[[2] See p. 77, note 2, above.]

sired, they cannot but for ever be most assured of perseverance to salvation: for, if they fall, the Lord putteth under his hand that they shall not perish; they are beloved of Christ, which "loveth them to the very end."

God for his mercy sake in Christ open more and more your eyes to see this his sweetness in Christ, to make you secure in him, and awake the flesh from her security, to be vigilant and heedful how you may most behave yourself in thankful obedience to God, and careful help and service to his people; that all your whole life may tend to this, how by example and otherwise you may do good to others, and still confirm his true service and religion by your constancy: wherein if you continue to the end, you shall receive an incorruptible crown of immortal and unspeakable glory. But if, for because of God's tarrying, which is only to prove you, you relent (which God forbid), thinking it enough in heart to serve God, and in body to do as may make most to your commodity temporally, as many do, then undoubtedly your standing hitherto (wherefor God's holy name be praised) shall make much more for the papistical kingdom and glory thereof, than if you had never done as you have done. Whereof, my good lord, be not weary nor unthankful; for with the godly and in the church of God you are and shall be had, as a worthy member of Christ, worthy of double honour, because God of his goodness hath vouched you worthy without your deserts. In the one, that is, for lands and possessions, you have companions many: but in the other, my good lord, you are A *per se* A [3] with us, to our comfort and joy unspeakable, so long as you continue, as I trust you will do to the end, and to our most heavy sorrow (which God forbid) if you should relent in any point.

Therefore I beseech your lordship, in the bowels and blood of our Saviour Jesus Christ, to persevere and continue to the end. He that hath not tempted you hitherto above your strength will continue so to the end. If for a time "he hide his face" from you, yet he doth it "but for a moment," to make you the more heartily to cry to him: and surely he will

[[3] "A *per se* A." This form was applied, in spelling, to the letter A (in common with the other vowels), as being in itself a complete vocal sound, and hence was used to imply pre-eminent excellence. See examples from Chaucer and other authors in Nares' Glossary.]

hear you, not only when you are in crying, but also whilst you are in thinking how to cry. "He is with you in trouble, and will indeed deliver you." The longer he tarrieth, the more pleasantly and comfortably will he appear. Only believe and look for his help, and you shall have peace, such peace as the world knoweth not nor can know: the which God give us a true feeling of; and then we shall not be grieved with afflictions, but rather rejoice in them, because they are but exercises and trials of faith, to the increase of faith and patience, with many godly virtues, &c.

As concerning the number and charges of us here, which this day I heard your lordship desired to understand, this is, so much as I know, that we are four in number together, whose names this bearer shall tell you[1]: the charges of the least is twelve shillings a week. There are five others, whose charges be not so great, but as they will themselves—I mean, they pay daily as they take, and that to the uttermost: these were never ministers. I trust there is no urgent need in any of us all, and I think least in myself, through God my Father's providence, the which I have and do daily wonderfully feel, his name therefore be praised.

Other things I would write; but, because they may be more safely told by this bringer, I have omitted the same for that purpose.—God of his goodness ever be with you, and keep your lordship to the very end, as his dear child. Amen, Amen.

Your humble to command,

JOHN BRADFORD.

LII. TO LADY VANE[2].

Bp Coverdale, Letters of the Martyrs, 1564, p. 334.

Foxe, Acts, &c., ed. 1570, p. 1824; and after editions.

To my good lady Vane. The true sense and sweet feeling of God's eternal mercies in Christ Jesus be ever more and more lively wrought in your heart by the Holy Ghost. Amen.

I most heartily thank you, good madam, for your comfort-

[1 It appears from Letter XXXV., p. 96, above, that Bradford's three fellow-prisoners, at this time, in the King's Bench, were Bp Ferrar, Adn Philpot, and Dr Rowland Taylor.]

[2 See p. 91, note 6, above.]

able letters: and, whereas you would be advertised what were best to be done on your behalf, concerning your three questions, the truth is, that the questions are never well seen nor answered, until the thing whereof they arise be well considered: I mean, until it be seen, how great an evil the thing is. If it be once indeed in your heart perceived, upon probable and pithy places gathered out of God's book, that there was never thing upon the earth so great and so much an adversary to God's true service, to Christ's death, passion, priesthood, sacrifice and kingdom, to the ministry of God's word and sacraments, to the church of God, to repentance, faith, and all true godliness of life, as that is whereof the questions arise, as most assuredly it is indeed, then cannot a christian heart but so much the more abhor it and all things that in any point might seem to allow it or anything pertaining to the same, by how much it hath the name of God's service.

These questions were concerning the mass, wherein she desired his judgment.—[Bp Coverdale and Foxe.]

Again your ladyship doth know that, as all is to be discommended and avoided, which is followed or fled from in respect of ourselves, in respect of avoiding Christ's cross, so the end of all our doings should be to Godwards, to his glory, to our neighbours, to edification and good example, whereof none can be given in allowing any of the three questions by you propounded.

But, because this which I write now is brief, and needeth the more consideration or explication, as I doubt not of the one in you, so from me by God's grace you shall receive the other shortly. For I have already written a little book of it which I will send unto you, in the which you shall have your questions fully answered and satisfied; and therefore I omit to write any more hereabouts presently, beseeching God our good Father to guide you, as his dear child, with his "Spirit of wisdom," power, and comfort, unto eternal life, that you may be strong, and rejoice in him and with his church, to carry Christ's cross if he shall so think it need: which is a thing to be desired, wished, and embraced, if we looked on things after the judgment of God's word, and tried them by that touchstone.

He meaneth his book which he calleth the "Hurt of hearing mass."—[Bp Coverdale and Foxe.]

1 Pet. ii.

If you be accustomed to think on the brevity, vanity and misery of this life, and on the eternity, truth and felicity of everlasting life; if you look on things after their ends, and not after their present appearance only; if you use yourself to set

God's presence, power and mercy, always before your eyes, to see them as God, by every creature, would you should; I doubt not but you shall find such strength and comfort in the Lord, as you shall not be shaken with all the power of Satan.

God's mercy in Christ be with you, and his good Spirit guide you for ever. Amen.

LIII. TO LADY VANE[1].

Bp Coverdale, Letters of the Martyrs, 1564, p. 403.

Foxe, Acts, &c., ed. 1570, p. 1829; and after editions.

MS. 2. 2. 15. No. 105. Transcript. Emman. Coll. Cambridge.

To the worshipful, and in God my most dear friend, the lady Vane. The good Spirit of God our Father be more and more plentifully perceived of your good ladyship, through the mediation and merits of our dear Saviour Jesus Christ. Amen.

Although your benefits towards me have deserved at my hands the service I can do for you, yet, right worshipful and dearly beloved in the Lord, the true fear of God and the love of his truth, which I perceive to be in you, especially and above all other things doth bind me hereunto. This bearer hath told me, that your desire is to have something sent to you concerning the usurped authority of the supremacy of the bishop of Rome, which is undoubtedly that great Antichrist, of whom the apostles do so much admonish us; that you may have as well something the more to stay you on, as also wherewith to answer the adversaries, because you may perchance therein be something apposed. To satisfy this your desire I will briefly go about, and so that I will, by God's grace, fully set forth the same, to enarm you to withstand the assaults of the papists herein, if you mark well and read over again that which I now write.

The papists do place in pre-eminence over the whole church the pope, thereby unplacing Christ which is the Head of the church, that giveth life to the whole body, and by his Spirit doth make lively every member of the same. This they do without all scriptures; for where they bring in this spoken to Peter, "Feed my sheep," I would gladly know whether this was not commanded unto others also?—As for that which perchance they will urge, that he spake to Peter by name, if they had any learning, they would easily perceive how that

[[1] See p. 91, note 6, above.]

it was not for any such cause as they pretend, but rather, by a threefold commandment, to restore to him the honour of an apostle, which he had lost by his threefold denial.

And how dare they interpretate these words, "my sheep," "my lambs," to be the universal church of Christ? I trow a man might easily by the like reason prove that Peter himself had resigned that which Christ had given to him, in exhorting his fellow-pastors to "feed the flock of Christ." Is not this pretty stuff? Because Christ saith to Peter, "Feed my sheep," therefore he ought to rule the universal and whole church of Christ. If Peter do truly write unto others that they should do the like, that is, "feed Christ's flock," either he translateth his right and authority committed to him upon them, or else he doth participate and communicate it with them. So that foolishly they go about to establish that which hath no ground.

Peter indeed was a "shepherd of the sheep," but such a one as bestowed his labour on them, so far as he could stretch out himself by his ministry. But the papists prate that he had full power over all churches; wherein they may see Paul to improve[2] them, for else he had done unjustly in denying him the superior place. Howbeit, who ever yet read that Peter did take anything upon him over churches committed unto other men? Was not he sent of the church, and sent as one not having rule over the rest? I grant that he was an excellent instrument of God; and, for the excellency of his gifts, whensoever they met together, place therefore was commonly given unto him. But what is this to the purpose, to make him ruler and head over all the whole church, because he was so over a small congregation?

But be it so, that Peter had as much given to him as they do affirm, who yet will grant that Peter had a patrimony given for his heirs? 'He hath left,' say the papists, 'to his successors the self-same right which he received.' O Lord God! then must his successor be a Satan; for he received that title of Christ himself. I would gladly have the papists to shew me one place of succession, mentioned in the scriptures. I am sure that, when Paul purposely painteth out the whole administration of the church, he neither maketh one head, nor any

Matt. xvi.

[[2] "Improve:" disprove.]

inheritable primacy; and yet he is altogether in commendation of unity. After he hath made mention of "one God the Father," of "one Christ," of "one Spirit," of "one body" of the church, of "one faith," and of "one baptism," then he describeth the mean and manner how unity is to be kept; namely, because unto every pastor "is grace given, after the measure wherewith Christ hath endowed them." Where, I pray you, is now any title of *plenitudinis potestatis*[1], "of fulness of power?" When he calleth home every one unto a certain measure, why did he not forthwith say, 'one pope?' Which thing he could not have forgotten, if the thing had been as the papists make it.

But let us grant that perpetuity of the primacy in the church was established in Peter, I would gladly learn why the seat of the primacy should be rather at Rome, than elsewhere. 'Marry,' say they, 'because Peter's chair was at Rome.' This is even like to this, that, because Moses the greatest prophet, and Aaron the first priest, exercised their offices unto their death in the desert, therefore the principallest place of the Jewish church should be in the wilderness.

But grant them their reason, that it is good, what should Antioch claim? for Peter's chair was there also; wherein Paul gave him a check, which was unseemly and unmannerly done of Paul, that would not give place to his president and better. 'No,' say the papists, 'Rome must have this authority, because Peter died there.' But what and if a man should by probable conjectures shew, that it is but a fable, which is feigned of Peter's bishopric at Rome? Read how Paul doth salute very many private persons, when he writeth to the Romans. Three years after his epistle made, he was brought to Rome prisoner. Luke telleth, that he was received of the brethren: and yet in all these no mention at all of Peter, which then by their stories was at Rome. Belike he was proud, as the pope and prelates be, or else he would have visited Paul! Paul being in prison in Rome did write divers epistles, in which he expresseth the names of many which were in com-

[[1] ......alii in partem solicitudinis, tu in plenitudinem potestatis vocatus es.—Bernard. De Consid. Lib. II. cap. viii. 16. Op. Vol. I. Tom. II. col. 422, ed. Bened. Par. 1690. ......pontifex......de ejus plenitudine omnes accipiunt, quos ipse vocat in partem solicitudinis, non in plenitudinem potestatis.—Durand. Rat. Div. Offic. Lib. II. fol. xxv. b. col. 2, Argentin. 1486.]

parison of Peter but rascal personages; but of Peter he speaketh never a word. Surely, if Peter had been there, this silence of him had been suspicious. In the second epistle to Timothy Paul complaineth, that no man was with him in his defence, but all had left him. If Peter had been then at Rome, as they write, then either Paul had belied him, or Peter had played his Peter's part. In another place how doth he blame all that were with him, only Timothy excepted! Therefore we may well doubt whether Peter was at Rome, bishop, as they prate, for all this time and long before they say that Peter was bishop there.

2 Tim. iv.

Luke xxii.

Phil. ii.

But I will not stir up coals in this matter.—If Rome be the chief seat, because Peter died there, why should not Antioch be the second? why should not James and John, which were taken with Peter "to be as pillars"—why, I say, should not their seats have honour next to Peter's seat? Is not this gear preposterous, that Alexandria, where Mark which was but one of the disciples was bishop, should be preferred before Ephesus, where John the evangelist taught and was bishop—and before Jerusalem, where not only James taught and died bishop, but also Christ Jesus our Lord and High Priest for ever? by whom being Master, I hope, honour should be given to his chair, more than to the chair of his chaplains.

[Gal. ii. 9.]

I need to speak nothing, how that Paul telleth Peter's apostleship to concern rather circumcision or the Jews, and therefore properly pertaineth not to us. Neither do I need to bring in Gregory the sixtieth bishop of Rome, which was about the year of our Lord 600; who plainly in his works doth write, that this title of primacy, and to be head over all churches, under Christ, is a title meet and agreeing only to antichrist[2]; and therefore he calleth it a profane, a mischievous and a horrible title[3]. Who should we believe now, if we will neither believe apostle nor pope?

[[2] See Vol. I. p. 538, note 3.]

[[3] In isto enim scelesto vocabulo consentire, nihil aliud est quam fidem perdere. —Gregor. Magni Papæ I. Epist. Lib. v. Indict. XIII. Ad Sabin. Diac. Epist. xix. Op. Tom. II. col. 747, ed. Bened. Par. 1705. Compare Epist. Lib. VII. Indict. XV. Ad Anastas. Episc. xxvii. col. 873; and see references in Bp Jewel, "Of the Supremacy," Works, Park. Soc. Vol. I. p. 345, and in the very learned "Treatise of the Pope's Supremacy," by Barrow, edited by Abp Tillotson, Lond. 1680, p. 180.]

If I should go about to tell how this name was first gotten by Phocas[1], I should be too long. I purpose, God willing, to set it forth at large in a work which I have begun, "Of Antichrist," if God for his mercy's sake give me life to finish it. For this present therefore I shall desire your ladyship to take this in good part. If they will needs have the bishop of Rome to be acknowledged for the head of the church, then will I urge them that they shall give us a bishop. But they obtrude unto us a butcher rather, or a bitesheep, than a bishop.

They brag of Peter's succession, of Christ's vicar; this is always in their mouth: but, alas! how can we call him 'Christ's vicar' that resisteth Christ, oppugneth his verity, persecuteth his people, and like a prelate preferreth himself above God and man? how or wherein doth the pope and Christ agree? how supplieth he Peter's ministry, that boasteth of his succession? Therefore, to begin withal, which I will use presently for a conclusion, if the papists will have the bishop of Rome supreme head of the church of Christ in earth, they must, afore they attain this, give us a bishop in deed, and not in name. For, whosoever he be that will make this the bond of unity, whatsoever the bishop of Rome be, surely this must needs follow, that they do nothing else but teach a most wicked defection and departing from Christ. But of this, if God lend me life, I purpose to speak more at large hereafter.

Of this matter he wrote afterwards a godly treatise, which he calleth "Antichrist."—[MS.]

Now will I betake your ladyship unto the tuition of God our Father, and Christ our only Head, Pastor, and Keeper: to whom see that you cleave by true faith, which dependeth only upon the word of God; which if you do follow as "a lantern to your feet, and a light to your steps," you shall then avoid darkness and the dangerous deeps, whereinto the papists are fallen by the just judgment of God, and seek to bring us into the same danger with them, that, "the blind following the blind, they both may fall into the ditch." Out of the which God deliver them according to his good will, and preserve us for his name's sake, that we being in his light may continue therein, and walk in it "whilst it is day:" so shall the night never oppress us, we going from light to light, from virtue to virtue,

[[1] The edict of Phocas is commonly assigned to A.D. 606. Vide Mosheim, Eccl. Hist., Cent. VII., part II. ch. ii. sect. 1.]

from faith to faith, from glory to glory, by the governance of God's good Spirit, which God our Father give unto us all, for ever and ever. Amen.

From the King's Bench.

Your brother in bonds, for the testimony of Jesus Christ,

JOHN BRADFORD.

LIV. TO MISTRESS JOYCE HALES[2].

My dearly beloved, I beseech our merciful Father to comfort your heavy and pensive heart with his own consolations in Christ, as I am assured he will in his good time. Which with patience look for, good sister, after the example of Job, Elias, Abraham, and all the dear saints of God, which are set forth unto us "for patterns of patience." God grant us well to cut our cloth after them; for God is the same God now, and the end will shew that he is a merciful Lord and full of compassion. My dear sister, you shall unfeignedly feel it at the length, though presently it seemeth otherwise unto your sense; you shall, "after you be a little exercised herein, find a quiet fruit of righteousness," "the God of grace, which hath called you unto his eternal glory, confirming and strengthening you," being somedeal afflicted with your brethren and sisters "that be in the world;" for alone you suffer not, as I trust you know.

[Bp Coverdale, Letters of the Martyrs, 1564, p. 306.]

[James v.]

[Heb. xii.]

[1 Pet. v.]

It comforted me to read in your letters, that no displeasure of father, mother, husband, children, &c., doth move you to be ruled after the counsel of the world; and therefore you will me not to be affeared for you. O, my beloved, what thanks should I give to our God and dear Father, for this his exceeding kindness towards you! His name be magnified for you for ever, his mercy be more and more multiplied unto you, in you, and upon you, for ever and ever. Amen. God make me thankful herefor.

But you add, that the fear of death doth now and then

[2 The title of this letter in Bp Coverdale is: "To Mistress J. H., a faithful woman, and fearing God, whom he exhorteth to be patient under the cross, and not to fear death," who is addressed in the second paragraph by the name, "Joyce." Mistress Joyce Hales, daughter-in-law of Sir James Hales, is evidently the person addressed. See p. 108, note 1, above, on letter XLI.]

move you a little: howbeit you say that, as I have counselled you, you will strive thereagainst. My good Joyce, I take you at your word; keep promise, I pray you, that is, strive against it; and I promise you, in the name of the Lord, that you shall have the victory, which I would wish you to set before your eyes also, and so shall the terror of death trouble you the less. Soldiers going to war set not before their eyes simply the strife, but rather the victory: and, my good sister, will not you herein follow them? In your travail with child, doth not the hope of the babe to be delivered mitigate the malady? Doth not the sick, in taking bitter and loathsome physic, set before him the commodity which will ensue? And, my dear sister, will not you by these be something informed?—Consider what this life is, consider what death is, consider what is prepared for you after death.

Concerning this life, you know that it is full of misery, vanity and woe: it is a plain exile, and hath nothing in it permanent: it is therefore compared to a vapour, to a smoke, to a shadow, yea, to a warfare, a wilderness, a vale of wretchedness, wherein we are compassed on every side with most fierce and fearful enemies. And should we desire to dwell here? should we lust to live in this loathsome and laborious life? should we wish to tarry in this wretchedness? should we have pleasure to remain in this perilous state? Daniel's den is not so dreadful as is this dungeon we dwell in.

Concerning death, to them that be (as I know you are) God's dear children, my tenderly beloved sister, what other thing is it than the despatcher of all displeasure, the end of all travail, the door of desires, the gate of gladness, the port of paradise, the haven of heaven, the rail of rest and quietness, the entrance to felicity, the beginning of all blissfulness? It is the very bed of down (and therefore well compared to a sleep), for the doleful bodies of God's people to rest in, out of the which they shall rise and awake, most fresh and lusty to life everlasting. It is a passage to the Father, a chariot to heaven, the Lord's messenger, a leader unto Christ, a going to our home, a deliverance from bondage and prison, a dismission from war, a security from all sorrows, and a manumission from all misery. So that the very heathen did in some places cause the day of their death to be celebrated with mirth, melody and minstrelsy. And should we be dismayed at it, should we be afraid of it, should we tremble to hear of it? Should such a friend as it is be unwelcome? should the foulness of his face fear us from his good conditions? should the hardness of his husk hinder us from his sweet kernel? Should the roughness of the tide tie us to the bank and shore, there to be drowned, rather than the desire of our home drive us to go aboard? Should the hardness of the saddle set us on our feet to perish by the way, rather than to leap up and endure the same a little, and so to be where we would be?

Concerning that which is prepared for you after death, if I should go about to express it, the more I should so do, the further I should be from it: for "the eye hath not seen, neither the ear hath heard, nor the heart of man is able to conceive" in any point the joy, mirth, melody, pleasure, power, wealth, riches, honour, beauty, fellowship, dainties, odours, glory, wisdom, knowledge, treasures, security, peace, quietness and eternal felicity, which you shall have and enjoy, world without end, with God the Father, the Son, and the Holy Ghost, with the angels, archangels, with the patriarchs and prophets, with the apostles and evangelists, with the martyrs and confessors, and with all the saints of God, in the palace of the Lord in heaven, the kingdom of God, the glory of the Father. O woe to the blindness of our eyes that see not this! woe to the hardness of our hearts that feel not this! woe to the deafness of our ears that hear not this, in such sort as we should do! wherethrough we might be so far from fearing death, that rather we should wish it, crying with Simeon, "Now let thy servant depart in peace"—with Paul, "I desire to be dissolved, and to be with Christ"—with David, "When shall I come and appear before thee?"—and again, "O woe is me that my habitation is thus prolonged!" &c. Ps. cxx.
But, alas! dear sister, great is our unbelief; full faint is our faith, or else "night and day tears should be our bread and Ps. xlii.
drink, while it is said unto us, Where is your God?"

It is a token of little love to God, to be loath to go unto him when he calleth. If my dearest friend, of a special favour and tender good-will, should send a horse for me to come unto him, should I be displeased thereat? yea, should I not be willing and glad to come unto him? And, alas! yet if death, the Lord's palfrey, the Lord's messenger, should come, I think I should not be so ready, but be fearful, as you foresee yourself to be: wherethrough I doubt not you take occasion to lament the weakness of your faith, and, seeing your need, to prepare for remedy against the time of need, and to beg of God his aid, strength, and comfort, against that pinch: which undoubtedly you shall have, and find his promise true, that in an acceptable time he heard your prayer. Such as I am have no such foresight of death, and therefore are less presently dismayed, which will turn to our greater grief in the plunge, save that for my part I hope he will "never tempt me further than he will make me able to bear." Into his hands I offer myself, beseeching him for his Christ's sake to keep me, soul and body, to his kingdom and glory, and to lead me, order me, and dispose me as he will, in all things, in all places, and for ever, that at the length I may come whither I will, that is, into his own blessed presence and fruition of immortality, with you and his saints. Amen.

Thus much I thought good to write unto you for this present, to occasion you the less to fear death, which either needeth not or booteth not: and therefore even reasonable men, much more spiritual men, labour to strive against the fear of that which they can by no means avoid: but of this hereafter I trust mouth to mouth to speak with you.

Now as to my soul I pray and wish unto you, my most dear sister in the Lord, whose grace guide you, and his mercy embrace you on every side for ever. Amen.

Yours,

JOHN BRADFORD.

LV. TO MISTRESS MARY HONYWOOD[1].

JESUS IMMANUEL[2].

Bp Coverdale, Letters of the Martyrs, 1564, p. 298.

Foxe, Acts, &c., ed. 1570, p. 1820; and after editions.

MS. 1. 2. 8. No. 87. Transcript. Emman. Coll. Cambridge.

I HUMBLY and heartily pray the everliving good God and "Father of mercy," to bless and keep your heart and mind in the knowledge and love of his truth, and of his Christ, through the inspiration and working of the Holy Spirit. Amen.

Although I have no doubt, but that you prosper and go forwards daily in the way of godliness, more and more drawing towards perfection, and have no need of anything that I can write, but rather might write to me thereabouts, yet because of this messenger and of her request, also[3] because my desire is, that you might be more fervent and persevere to the end, I could not but write something unto you, beseeching you both often and diligently to call unto your mind, as a mean to stir you hereunto, yea, as a thing which God most straitly requireth you to believe, that you are beloved of God, and that he is your dear Father, in, through and for Christ and his death's sake. This love and tender kindness of God towards us in Christ is abundantly herein declared, in that he hath, to the goodly work of creation of this world, made us after his image, redeemed us being lost, called us into his church, sealed us with his mark and sign-manual of baptism, kept and conserved us all the days of our life, fed, nourished, defended and most fatherly chastised us, and now hath poured, or at the least instilled and dropped[4] in our hearts the sparkles of his fear, faith, love and knowledge of his Christ and truth. And therefore we lament, because we lament no more our unthankfulness, our frailness, our diffidence and wavering, in things wherein we should be most certain.

All these things we should use, as means to confirm our faith of this, that God is our God and Father, and to assure us

[1 See p. 98, note 1, above. The inscription of this letter in Bp Coverdale and Foxe is: "To Mistress M. H., a godly gentlewoman, comforting her in that common heaviness and godly sorrow, which the feeling and sense of sin worketh in God's children."

The Emmanuel MS. has, in a different hand from that of the transcriber, the inscription, "To Mistress A. Warcup."]

[2 "Jesus Immanuel," only in MS.]

[3 The last seventeen words "but rather......request also," occur only in the MS.: "yet" 1564 and 1570.]

[4 "poured or......and dropped," MS.: "kindled" 1564 and 1570.]

that he loveth us as our Father in Christ. To this end, I say, we should use the things before touched, especially in that of all things God requireth this faith and persuasion of his fatherly goodness, as his chiefest service: for, before he ask anything of us, he saith, "I am the Lord thy God," giving himself, and then all he hath, to us, to be our own; and this he doth in respect of himself, of his own mercy and truth, and not in
[Rom. xi. 6.] respect of us, "for then were grace no grace." In consideration whereof, when he saith, "Thou shalt have none other gods but me," "thou shalt love me with all thy heart," &c., though of duty we are bound to accomplish all that he requireth, and are culpable and guilty of sin[1] if we do not the same, yet he requireth not these things further of us, than to make us more in love, and more certain of this his covenant, that he is our Lord and God. In certainty whereof, as he hath given this whole world to serve to our need and commodity, so hath he given his Son Christ Jesus, and in Christ himself, to be a pledge and gage, whereof the Holy Ghost doth now and then give us some taste and smell, to our eternal joy.

Therefore, as I said, I say again[2], because God is your Father in Christ, and requireth of you straitly to believe it, give yourself to obedience, although you do it not with such feeling as you desire. First must faith go before, and then feeling will follow. If our imperfection, frailty, and many evils should be occasions whereby Satan would have us to doubt, as much as we can, let us abhor that suggestion, as of all others most pernicious, for so indeed it is. For when we stand in a doubt, whether God be our Father, we cannot be thankful to God, we cannot heartily pray, or think anything we do acceptable to God; we cannot love our neighbours, and give over ourselves to care for them, and do for them as we should do: and therefore Satan is most subtle hereabouts, knowing full well that, if we doubt of God's fatherly, eternal mercies towards us through Christ, we cannot please God, or do anything as we should do to man. Continually casteth he into our memories our imperfection, frailty, falls and offences, that we should doubt of God's mercy and favour towards us.

Therefore, my good sister, we must not be sluggish herein;

[[1] "of sin," only in MS.] [[2] "I say again," only in MS.]

but, as Satan laboureth to loosen our faith, so must we labour to fasten it, by thinking on the promises and covenant of God in Christ's blood; namely, that God is "our God" with all that ever he hath. Which covenant dependeth and hangeth upon God's own goodness, mercy, and truth only, and not on our obedience or worthiness in any point, for then should we never be certain. Indeed God requireth of us obedience and worthiness, but not that thereby we might be his children and he our Father; but, because he is our Father and we his children, through his own goodness in Christ, therefore requireth he faith and obedience. Now, if we want this obedience and worthiness which he requireth, should we doubt whether he be our Father? Nay, that were to make our obedience and worthiness the cause, and so to put Christ out of place, for whose sake God is our Father. But rather, because he is our Father, and we feel ourselves to want such things as he requireth, we should be stirred up, not to a doubtfulness whether he be our Father (for all that maketh hereto cometh of the devil, which is a liar), but[3] to a shamefacedness and blushing, because we are not as we should be: and thereupon should we take occasion to go to our Father in prayer, on this manner:

'Dear Father, thou of thine own mercy in Christ hast chosen me to be thy child; and therefore thou wouldest I should be brought into thy church and faithful company of thy children, wherein thou hast kept me hitherto—thy name therefore be praised. Now I see myself to want faith, hope, love, &c., which thy children have, and thou requirest of me: wherethrough the devil would have me to doubt whether thou art my Father: by which means I call into doubt, whether thy word be thy word, whether Christ, which died for mankind, be dead for me or no, to thy great dishonour and mine own destruction[4]. Therefore I come to thee, as to my merciful Father, through thy dear Son Jesus Christ, and pray thee to help me. Good Lord, help me, and give me faith, hope, love, &c.; and grant that thy holy Spirit may be with me for ever, and more and more to assure me that thou art my Father, that this merciful

[[3] The last twenty-three words only occur in the MS.]

[[4] The last thirty-eight words, "whether thou art......my destruction," now are first printed from the MS. The printed editions read instead, "yea, utterly to despair of thy fatherly goodness, favour, and mercy."]

covenant thou madest with me in respect of thy grace, in Christ and for Christ, and not in respect of any my worthiness, is always true to me.' &c.

On this sort, I say, you must pray and use your cogitations, when Satan would have you to doubt of salvation. He doth all he can to prevail herein: do you all you can to prevail herein against him. Though you feel not as you would, yet doubt not, but "hope beyond all hope," as Abraham did. Faith always, as I said, goeth before feeling. As certain as God is almighty, as certain as God is merciful, as certain as God is true, as certain as Christ was crucified, is risen, and sitteth on the right hand of the Father—as certain as this is God's commandment, "I am the Lord thy God"—so certain ought you to be that God is your Father. As you are bound to "have none other gods but him," so are you no less bound to believe that God is "your God." What profit should it be to you to believe this to be true, "I am the Lord thy God," to others, if you should not believe that this is true to yourself? The devil believeth on this sort. And whatsoever it be that would move you to doubt of this, whether God be your God through Christ, that same cometh undoubtedly of the devil. Wherefore did God make you, but because he loved you? Might not he have made you blind, dumb, deaf, lame, frantic, &c.? might not he have made you a Jew, a Turk, a papist, &c.? And why hath he not done so? Verily because he loved you. And why did he love you? what was there in you to move him to love you? Surely nothing moved him to love you, and therefore to make you, and so hitherto to keep you, but his own goodness in Christ. Now then, in that his goodness in Christ still remaineth as much as it was—that is, even as great as himself, for it cannot be lessened—how should it be but that he is your God and Father? Believe this, believe this, my good sister; for God is no changeling, them whom he loveth "he loveth to the end."

Ecclus. ii. [16. "As his majesty is, so is his mercy."]

Cast therefore yourself wholly upon him; and think without all wavering that you are God's child, that you are a citizen of heaven, that you are the daughter of God, "the temple of the Holy Ghost," &c. If hereof you be assured, as you ought to be, then shall your conscience be quieted, then shall you lament more and more that you want many things which God loveth; then shall you labour to be holy both[1] in soul and body, then shall you go about that God's glory may shine in you in all your words and works; then shall you not be afraid what man can do unto you, then shall you have such wisdom to answer your adversaries, as shall serve to their shame and your comfort; then shall you be certain that no man can touch one hair of your head, further than shall please your good Father to your everlasting joy; then shall you be most certain that God as your good Father will be more careful for your children, and make better provision for them, if all you have were gone, than you can; then shall you, being assured, I say, of God's favour towards you, give over yourself wholly to help and care for others that be in need; then shall you contemn this life, and desire to be at home with your good and sweet Father; then shall you labour to mortify all things that would spot either soul or body. All these things spring out of this certain persuasion and faith, that God is our Father, and we are his children by Christ Jesus. All things should help our faith herein; but Satan goeth about in all things to hinder us.

Therefore let us use earnest and hearty prayer. Let us often remember this covenant, "I am the Lord thy God;" let us look upon Christ and his precious blood, shed for the obsignation[2] and confirmation of this covenant; let us remember all the free promises of the gospel. Let us set before us God's benefits generally in making this world, in ruling it, in governing it, in calling and keeping his church, &c. Let us set before us God's benefits particularly, how he hath made us creatures after his image; how he hath made us of perfect limbs, form, beauty, memory, &c.; how he hath made us Christians, and given us a right judgment in his religion; how he hath ever sithen we were born blessed, kept, nourished and defended us; how he hath often beaten, chastised and fatherly corrected us; how he hath spared us, and doth now spare us, giving us time, space, place, grace. This if you do, and use earnest prayer, and so flee from all things which might wound your conscience, giving yourself to diligence in your vocation, you shall find at the length, that which God grant to me with you,

[1 "both," only in MS.]

[2 "Obsignation:" sealing.]

a sure certainty of salvation, without all such doubt as may trouble the peace of conscience, to your eternal joy and comfort. Amen, Amen.

Yours to use in Christ,

JOHN BRADFORD.

LVI. TO A FRIEND[1].

Bp Coverdale, Letters of the Martyrs, 1564, p. 389.

Foxe, Acts, &c., ed. 1570, p. 1832; and after editions.

My good brother, our merciful God and dear Father through Christ open your eyes effectually to see, and your heart ardently to desire, the everlasting joy which he hath prepared for his slaughter-sheep, that is, for such as shrink not from his truth, for any storm's sake. Amen.

When you shall come before the magistrates, "to give an answer of the hope which is in you," do it with all reverence and simplicity: and, because you may be something afraid by the power of the magistrates, and cruelty which they will threaten against you, I would you set before you the good father Moses, to follow his example; for he set the invisible God before his eyes of faith, and with them looked upon God and his glorious majesty and power, as with his corporal eyes he saw Pharaoh and all his fearful terrors. So do you, my dearly beloved: let your inward eyes give such light unto you that, as you know you are before the magistrates, so and much more you and they also are present before the face of God: which will give such wisdom to you, fearing him and seeking his praise, as the enemies shall wonder at; and further he will so order their hearts and doings, that they shall, will they nill they, serve God's providence towards you (which you cannot avoid though you would), as shall be most to his glory and your everlasting comfort.

Therefore, my good brother, let your whole study be only to please God; put him always before your eyes, for "he is on your right hand, lest you should be moved." "He is faithful, and never will suffer you to be tempted above that he will make you able to bear:" yea, every hair of your head he hath

[[1] The inscription in Bp Coverdale and Foxe is: "To a friend of his, instructing him how he should answer his adversaries."]

numbered, so that one of them shall not perish without his good will, which cannot be but good unto you, in that he is become your Father through Christ: and therefore, as he hath given you "to believe in him" (God increase this belief in us all), so doth he now graciously give unto you "to suffer for his name's sake." The which you ought with all thankfulness to receive, in that you are made worthy to drink of the self-same cup, which not only the very sons of God have drank of before you, but even the very natural Son of God himself hath brought you good luck. O he of his mercy make us thankful to pledge him again! Amen.

Because the chiefest matter they will trouble you, and go about to deceive you withal, is the sacrament, not of Christ's body and blood, but of the altar, as they call it, thereby destroying the sacrament which Christ instituted, I would you noted these two things: first, that the sacrament of the altar, which the priest offereth in the mass, and eateth privately with himself, is not the sacrament of Christ's body and blood, instituted by him; as Christ's institution, plainly written and set forth in the scriptures, being compared to their using of it, plainly doth declare.

Again, if they talk with you of Christ's sacrament instituted by him, whether it be Christ's body or no, answer them that, as to the eyes of your reason, to your taste and corporal senses, it is bread and wine (and therefore the scripture calleth it after the consecration so), even so to the eyes, taste, and senses of your faith, which ascendeth to the right hand of God in heaven, where Christ sitteth, it is in very deed Christ's body and blood, which spiritually your soul feedeth on to everlasting life, in faith and by faith, even as your body presently feedeth on the sacramental bread and sacramental wine.

By this means, as you shall not allow transubstantiation, nor none of their popish opinions, so shall you declare the sacrament to be a matter of faith, and not of reason, as the papists make it; for they deny God's omnipotency, in that they say, 'Christ is not there, if bread be there;' but faith looketh on the omnipotency of God joined with his promise, and doubteth not but that Christ is able to give that he promiseth us spiritually by faith, the bread still remaining in substance, as well as if the substance of bread were taken away;

for Christ saith not in any place, 'This is no bread.' But of this gear God shall instruct you, if you hang on his promise, and pray for the power and wisdom of his Spirit; which undoubtedly, as you are bound to look for, praying for it, so he hath bound himself by his promise to give it. The which thing he grant unto us both and to all his people, for his name's sake, through Christ our Lord. Amen.

JOHN BRADFORD.

LVII. BP RIDLEY TO BERNHERE[1].

[OXFORD, probably about *December* 18, 1554 [2].]

MS. 2. 2. 15. No. 148. Original, Holograph. Emman. Coll. Cambridge.

MS. Harl. 416. No. 20. p. 32. Transcript, Fragment. British Museum.

Bp Coverdale, Letters of the Martyrs, 1564, p. 70.

BROTHER Austin, you are heartily welcome to Oxford again: ye have made good speed indeed. That all our dear beloved brethren in Christ are in good comfort, and hearty in Christ's cause, it comforteth and rejoiceth, I ensure you, my heart in God to hear of it[3]. I trust, the tidings which were spread abroad since your departure, that Master Grimbold should have been arraigned and condemned for treason to be hanged and quartered, was not true; or else I think ye would have said something of it[4]: let me know if there be anything.—The tokens sent on to me and to my brother ye shall deliver to the bearer. N.[5] R. I would know by him how long ye intend to tarry here or hereabouts[6].

Now not two or three days ago there was given me first a privy warning from a man of God, one Lifley, a glover, and since that mine hostess Mistress Irish hath told me the same[7], that we prisoners here all three should be shortly and suddenly conveyed into three several colleges; for what purpose, and how to be ordered,

[1 Parts of this letter now are first printed from Bp Ridley's autograph.

It is given here, partly on that account, and partly because of its intimate connexion with the letters between Bradford and Ridley.]

[2 This date is approximately conjectured from the connexion of this and the ensuing letter with No. LXI., the date of which must have been about January 18, 1555, from its allusion to the dissolution of parliament, which was on January 16.]

[3 The printed edition of 1564 interpolates here a sentence, "This day was...... of Master Hooper," which belongs to Letter LXIII. of this series, now first printed from Bp Ridley's autograph. That edition likewise inserts a few words between the first two sentences of this letter, which also belong to No. LXIII.]

[4 The last eleven words only occur in the autograph MS.]

[5 The letter "N." in the autograph is doubtful, being almost blotted out.]

[6 The last thirty-two words are supplied from Ridley's autograph.]

[7 The autograph MS. gives the last twelve words.]

God knoweth. At the which time, and at the earnest request of that fore-named man of God—which request came, as God knoweth, of himself, without any motion or mention made of me of any such thing[8]—I did deliver unto him[9] some of the things I said I had in hand: and I ween he hath written some of them out already. What they be ye shall see by him. If ye be not acquaint with him, these my letters shall suffice to acquaint you: for by all experience that I have—and I have some of him, and surely much cause to thank him—there is one spirit in you both, although ye [were] born in divers countries[10]: nor, I dare say, he will reckon of no diversity of country, where there is unity in spirit.

I pray you let me know if he spake with Master Hooper and his company, and how they do; and whether Master Hooper doth deliver his doings as he said he would do; and, if he have, what hear ye of them[11].—Master Bradford desireth that thanks should be rendered unto you for your comfortable aid wherewith ye comfort him: but ye must tell him that he speak and bid them thank you for him, which are not bound to thank you for themselves: and, if he do so, then I ween all we prisoners of Oxford shall so stop his mouth[12].

Beside the things which Lifley hath, I have some things else, which, if it please God, I would wish might come to light, if perchance any thereby might receive any light to love the truth the better, and to abhor the falsehood of antichrist. I have written annotations *in priorem librum Tonstalli*[13] *Latine*[14] *plenius, in secundum vero parcius: optarem ut transcriberentur, ne fortassis una mecum fiant subito Vulcani cibus:* [in Latin more fully on the first book of Tonstal, but more sparingly on the second: I would wish that they were transcribed, lest perchance they should, together with myself, suddenly become food for fire.] I have also many things, but as yet confused, set together of the abominable usurpation, arrogance and wickedness of the see and bishop of Rome, and all gather[ed] together in Latin. If those things were written out, I would wish that Master Bradford would take them, and translate and order them as he should think might best help

[8 The last twenty words now are first printed from the autograph MS.]

[9 "unto him," 1564: not in autograph MS.]

[10 Bernhere, to whom this letter was addressed, being a Swiss.]

[11 The last ten lines, "and I ween he hath......have, what hear ye of them," now are first printed from Bp Ridley's autograph.]

[12 The last sentence is placed, in 1564, nearly at the end of the letter.]

[13 This probably was the well-known work of Tonstal, then bishop of Durham, on the Eucharist. See Vol. I. p. 510, note 5.]

[14 "Latine," Autogr. MS., and Harl. MS.: not in 1564.]

to open the eyes of the simple, for to see the wickedness of the synagogue of Satan.

But that at your last being here you cast cold water upon mine affection towards Grimbold, else methink I could appoint wherein he might occupy himself to his own profit in learning which he liketh, and to no small profit which might ensue afterward[1] to the church of Christ in England: as, if he would take in hand and interpretate Laurentius Valla[2] (which, as he knoweth, is a man of singular eloquence), I say, his book, which he made and wrote against that false feigned fable, forged of Constantinus Magnus, and his dotation and glorious exaltation of the see of Rome[3]: and, when he hath done that, let him translate a work of Æneas Sylvius, *De gestis Basiliensis Concilii*[4]. In the which although there be many things that savoureth of the pan[5], and also he himself was afterward a bishop of Rome, yet, I dare say, the papists would glory but a little to see such books go forth in English. If ye will know where to have these books or treatises, ye may have them both together, and many like treatises, which painteth out the wickedness of the see of Rome, in a book set forth by a papist called Ortwinus Gratius, called, *Fasciculus rerum expetendarum et fugiendarum*[6]. In

[[1] "afterward," Autogr. MS., and Harl. MS.: not in 1564.]

[[2] Laurentius Valla, canon of St John of Lateran, a distinguished scholar and critic, died at Rome, 1465. His learned treatise upon the forged Donation of Constantine—"De falso credita et ementita Constantini Donatione Declamatio"—was printed separately in various editions, and in his Works, Basil, 1540, and in the "Fasciculus" of Orthuinus Gratius, Colon. 1535, and Lond. 1690, Tom. I.]

[[3] Constantin. Mag. Donat. privileg., in the "Fasciculus" as above; Fabric. Biblioth. Græc., Tom. VI. pp. 697—700, Hamburg, 1790—1809; Mosheim, Eccl. Hist., Cent. VIII. Part II. ch. ii. 11; Gibbings on Fulke's Answers, p. 360, note 4, Park. Soc.]

[[4] Æneas Sylvius (Piccolomini), subsequently Pius II., had been a zealous opponent of the papal claims at the memorable Council of Basil, 1431—35. His valuable "Commentaria de gestis Basil. Concil." will be found in his Works, printed at Basil, 1551 and 1571, and in the "Fasciculus" of Orthuinus Gratius—and are also (possibly on account of Bp Ridley's suggestion) printed by Foxe, Acts, &c., ed. 1563, pp. 281—346, or ed. 1843—9, Vol. III. pp. 605—99, and in an abridged form in the intermediate editions. Vide Gibbings on Fulke's Answers, p. 302, Park. Soc.; Ayre on Bp Jewel's Defence of Apol., Works, Vol. IV. p. 678, note 3, Park. Soc.; and Bayle, Dict., article, Æneas Sylvius.]

[[5] Nix, bishop of Norwich, 1501—36, used to call the persons whom he suspected of heresy, "men savouring of the frying-pan:" the French had an equivalent phrase, "sentir le fagot."—Southey, Book of the Church, end of ch. XI. p. 235, Lond. 1841.]

[[6] Orthuinus Gratius (Graes), a learned German, published his remarkable collection of church documents, "Fascic. rer. expet. et fugiend.", 1535, at Cologne, where he died 1542: Chalmers, Biog. Dict. The "Fasciculus" was reprinted, London, 1690, with an extensive Supplement of Documents, arranged by Brown, rector of Sundridge, Kent.]

that book ye shall have *Confessionem fratrum Waldensium*[7], men of much more[8] learning, godliness, soberness and understanding in God's word, than I would have thought them to have been in that time, before I did read their works. If such things had been set forth in our English tongue heretofore, I suppose surely great good might have comen to Christ's church thereby.

To my good lady's grace, and to my lady Vane, what thanks can I give, but desire almighty God to lighten, comfort and strengthen them evermore in his ways? Of two other whom Sharp speaketh of, the one I know, the other whom ye name Person, I cannot tell who he is[9], but God knoweth him: to whom in them all and for all their kindness I render hearty thanks.

Brother Austin, ye for our comfort run up and down; and who beareth your charges God knoweth. I know ye must need in so doing take much pains. I pray you take of my tokens three shillings, four pence[10], toward your charges.

N. R.

LVIII. BP RIDLEY TO BRADFORD.

[Bocardo, OXFORD, probably about *December* 20, 1555[11].]

BROTHER Bradford, I wish you and your company in Christ, yea, and all the holy brotherhood, that now with you in divers prisons suffereth and beareth patiently Christ's cross for the maintenance of his gospel, "grace, mercy, and peace from God the Father, and from our Lord Jesus Christ."

MS. 2. 2. 15. No. 53. Original, Holograph, Imperfect. Emman. Coll. Cambridge.

MS. Harl. 416. No. 21. fol. 32, reverse Transcript. British Museum.

Bp Coverdale, Letters of the Martyrs, 1564, p. 62.

Foxe, Acts, &c., ed. 1570, p. 1897; and after editions.

Sir, considering the state of this chivalry and warfare, wherein I doubt not but we be set to fight under Christ's banner and his cross against our ghostly enemy "the devil, the old serpent Satan," methink I perceive two things to be his most perilous and most dangerous engines which Satan hath to impugn Christ's verity,

[7 "Profess. fid. fratr. Waldens. regi Uladislao ad Hungariam missa," and "Respons. excusat. fratr. Waldens. contra binas literas R. P. August. sacr. theol. doct. ad eund. reg. datas," Tractat. 19 and 20 in the "Fasciculus," as above.

These early apologies of the Moravian United Brethren, who were persecuted under the appellation of Waldenses and Picards or Beghards, were addressed, 1507—8, to the Polish prince, Wladislas or Vladislav, who became king of Bohemia 1471, and of Hungary 1490, and died 1516. See Mosheim, Eccl. Hist. Cent. xv. Part II. ch. iii. 7; and Elliott, Horæ Apocalypt., Lond. 1851. Vol. II. Append. VI. "on the Calixtines and the United Brethren," pp. 536—39. These Apologies are quoted by Foxe, Acts, &c., ed. 1583, p. 230, or ed. 1843—9, Vol. II. p. 264, et seq.] [8 "more," 1564: not in autogr. MS.]

[9 The last nineteen words now are first printed from the autograph MS.]

[10 "three shillings and four pence" only occur in the autograph MS.]

[11 See p. 158, note 2, above.]

his gospel, his faith, and the same two also to be the most massy posts and mighty pillars, whereby he maintaineth and upholdeth his Satanical synagogue. These two, sir, are in my judgment, the one his false doctrine and idolatrical use of the Lord's supper, and the other the wicked and abominable usurpation of the primacy of the see of Rome. By these two Satan seemeth to me principally to maintain and uphold his kingdom; by these two he driveth down
Rev. viii. mightily (alas! I fear me) "the third part of the stars" in heaven. These two poisonful rotten posts he hath so painted over with such a pretence and colour of religion, of unity in Christ's church, of the catholic faith and such like, that the wily serpent is able to "deceive,
Rev. ii. if it were possible, even the elect" of God. Wherefore John said, not without great cause, "If any know not Satan's subtleties and the dungeons thereof, I will wish him[1] none other burden to be laden withal."

Sir, because these be[1] his principal and main posts whereupon standeth all his falsehood, craft and treachery, therefore, according to the poor power that God hath given me, I have bended mine artillery to shoot at the same. I know it is but little, God knoweth, that I can do; and of my shot I know they pass not. Yet will I not, God willing, cease to do the best that I can to shake those cankered and rotten posts. The Lord grant me good success, to the glory of his name, and the furtherance of Christ's gospel. I have almost, I thank God, for this present time spent a good part of my powder[2] in these scribblings, whereof this bearer shall give you knowledge.

Good brother Bradford, let the wicked surmise and say what they list; know you for a certainty by God's grace, without all doubt, that in Christ's gospel's cause, against and upon the foresaid God's enemies, I am fully determined to live and die. Farewell, dear brother; and I beseech you and all the rest of our brethren, to have good remembrance of the condemned heretics (as they call them) of Oxford in your prayers. The bearer shall certify you of our state. Farewell in the Lord.

From Bocardo.

Yours in Christ,

N. R.

[[1] "him," "be," not in autograph MS., because torn, but in Harl. MS., 1564, and 1570.]

[[2] The autograph MS. being torn, only supplies a few words after "my powder."]

LIX. TO MISTRESS WARCUP.

JESUS IMMANUEL[3].

To my dearly beloved sister, Mistress A[nne] W[arcup.][4] The everlasting peace of Christ be more and more lively felt in our hearts, by the operation of the Holy Ghost, now and for ever. Amen.

Foxe, Acts, &c., ed. 1563, p. 1194; and after editions.

Bp Coverdale, Letters of the Martyrs, 1564, p. 457.

MS. 1. 2. 8. No. 90. Transcript, Imperfect. Emman Coll. Cambridge.

Although I know it to be more than needeth, to write anything unto you, good sister, being, as I doubt not you be, diligently exercised in reading of the scriptures, meditating the same, and in hearty prayer to God for the help of his holy Spirit, to have the sense and feeling especially of the comforts you read in God's sweet book; yet having such opportunity, and knowing not whether hereafter I shall ever have the like, as this bringer can declare, I thought good in few words to take my farewell in writing, because otherwise I cannot.

And now, methinks, I have done it: for what else can I, or should I, say unto you, my dearly beloved in the Lord, but, Farewell? Farewell, yea, farewell[5] dear sister, farewell: howbeit in the Lord—our Lord I say—fare well: in him shall you fare well, and so much the better, by how much in yourself you fare evil and shall fare evil. When I speak of yourself, I mean also this world, this life, and all things properly pertaining to this life. In them as you look not for your welfare, so be not dismayed when accordingly you shall not feel it. To the Lord our God, to the Lamb our Christ, which hath borne our sins on his back, and is our Mediator for ever, do I send you. In him look for welfare, and that without all wavering, because of his own goodness and truth, which our evils and untruth cannot take away. Not that therefore I would have you to flatter yourself in any evil or unbelief, but that I would comfort you, that they should not dismay you. Yours is our Christ wholly: yours, I say, he is, with all that ever he hath. Is not this welfare, trow you? "Mountains shall move and the earth shall fall," before you find it otherwise, say the liar Satan what he list. Therefore, good sister, farewell, and be merry

[3 "Jesus Immanuel," MS.: not in 1563 or 1564.]
[4 The last eight words are in 1564, not in 1563.]
[5 "yea, farewell," MS.: not in 1563 or 1564.]

in the Lord; be merry, I say, be merry[1], for you have good cause.

If your welfare, joy, and salvation hanged upon any other thing, than only one[1], God's mercy and truth, then might you well be sad, heavy, and stand in a doubt. But, in that it hangeth only upon these two, tell Satan he lieth, when he would have[2] you to stand in a mammering, by causing you to cast your eyes (which only in this case should be set on Christ your sweet Saviour) on yourself in some part. Indeed look on yourself, on your faith, on your love, obedience, &c., to awake you up from security, to stir you to diligence, in doing the things appertaining to your vocation: but, when you would be at peace with God and have true consolation in your conscience, altogether look upon the goodness of God in Christ. Think on this commandment, which precedeth all other, that you must "have no other gods" but the Lord Jehovah, which is your Lord and God: the which he could not be, if that he did not pardon your sins in very deed. Remember that Christ commandeth you to call him "Father," for the same intent; and hereto call to mind all the benefits of God, hitherto showed upon you: and so shall you feel in very deed that which I wish unto you now, and pray you to wish unto me.

Farewell or well fare in the Lord Jesus: with whom he grant us shortly to meet, as his children, for his name and mercy's sake, to our eternal welfare. Amen, Amen[3].

Your own in the Lord,

JOHN BRADFORD[4].

LX. TO CERTAIN FREE-WILLERS[5].

[King's Bench prison, *January* 1, 1555.]

Bp Coverdale, Letters of the Martyrs, 1564, p. 650.

THE good Spirit of God, which is "the Spirit of truth" and guide to God's children, be with us all, and lead us into all truth. Amen.

[[1] "be merry," "one" MS.: not in 1563 or 1564.]
[[2] "have" 1564 and MS.: not in 1563.]
[[3] "Amen" once in 1563: twice in 1564.]
[[4] "Your own in the Lord, John Bradford" 1564: not in 1563.]
[[5] This letter is entitled, in Bp Coverdale: "To certain men, which maintained

Hitherto I have oftentimes resorted unto you, my friends as I thought, and by all means sought to do you good, even to mine own charges and hindrance. But now I see it happeneth otherwise; and therefore I am purposed, till I may know more than I do, to absent myself from you, but not my help, and by these letters to supply that, which by mouth patiently you cannot abide to hear.

You report me to my face that I am a great slander to the church of God; which may be two ways understand, that is, by living and doctrine. But as for living you yourselves (I thank God therefore) gave testimony with me. In doctrine therefore you mean it.

Now, in that there be many parts of the doctrine of Christ, I trow you mean not generally, but particularly; for you in generality have divers times given your commendation on my behalf, both to my face and behind my back; for the which I humbly praise my God, through Christ. In particularity therefore you mean that I am a slander; which, as far as I know, is only in this to youwards, that I believe and affirm the salvation of God's children to be so certain, that they shall assuredly enjoy the same.

You say, it hangeth partly upon our perseverance to the end; and I say, it hangeth only and altogether upon God's grace in Christ, and not upon our perseverance in any point; "for then were grace no grace." You will and do in words Rom. xi
deny our perseverance to be any cause: but yet in deed you do otherwise: for, if perseverance be not a cause, but only God's grace in Christ the whole and only cause of salvation, then the cause, that is to say, grace, remaining, the thing, that is to say, salvation, cannot but remain also. Of which thing if, with the scriptures, you would make perseverance an effect or fruit, then could you not be offended at the truth, but say as it saith, that the salvation of God's children is so certain, that they shall never finally perish, the Lord putting his hand under them that, if they fall, yet they shall not lie still. For whom he loveth he leaveth not, but "loveth them unto the end." John xii
So that perseverance is proper to them, and doth discern them from hypocrites, and such as seem to other and to themselves

the heresy of the Pelagians and papists, concerning man's free-will, which upon occasions were then prisoners with him in the King's Bench."]

also sometimes, that they be God's children. Which if they once were in deed, then, as St John saith, they "should not sin the sin to death," neither should they "go out" of God's church, but, as Paul saith, should "persevere to the end." Now to be God's child is no less, in all points, above the power of man, than to be man's child is above our own power: but so much it passeth our ability in all points to be God's child, by how much this dignity is greater.

1 John iii. v. 1 John ii. Heb. iii.

Again, once God's child indeed, and God's child for ever; that is, finally shall not he that is so perish eternally, if that God our Father be both of good-will infinite, and also of power accordingly, and if "the seed of God which remaineth in his children" can keep them from sinning—I mean, "to death," for otherwise they sin, and therefore pray daily, "Forgive us our debts," &c.

1 John iii. Matt. vi.

Moreover God's children "be under grace, and not under the law;" and therefore sin shall not damn them. "For where no law is there is no transgression:" transgression, I say, to final damnation, for the "new covenant" of God is, "never to remember their sins," but to give them such hearts and minds that, as they naturally lust and labour to do that is evil, so their inward man renewed striveth to the contrary, and at the length shall prevail; "because he is stronger that is in them, than he that is in the world;" and St Paul saith, "Who shall lay any thing to the charge of God's elect?" in that God absolveth them for Christ's sake, of whom they are kept. So that it is not possible for them to perish, in respect of their Pastor, who "is faithful" over God's people.

Rom. vi. Rom. iv. 1 John iv. Rom. viii. John vi. x. Matt. xxiv. Heb. xiii. Heb. iii.

This certainty and assurance whoso feeleth in himself, by the testimony of God's Spirit, indeed and of truth, the same is happy for ever, and cannot but, as he hopeth he shall be like to Christ in his coming, so desire it, and "purify himself" in all purity, so far will he be from carnal liberty; and, "as the elect of God," he will endue and apparel himself daily with the apparel of the elect, using prayer "night and day," which is another property of God's children. To this certainty all the creatures of God call us, concerning their creation and use. This assurance God's first commandment requireth, under pain of damnation: the gospel of God and all his promises, the sacraments and the substance of them, which is

Christ Jesus our Saviour, doth above all things require it of every one that is baptized, and brought into God's church. Nothing else doth God so require of us, as thus to be persuaded of him, for out of it floweth all godliness to God and man.

So that it cannot be but they take Satan's part, which go about to let or hinder this certainty, in themselves and in others. The which thing in that you do indeed, howsoever you mean, I cannot but, as I have done often before, admonish you of it eftsoons, that your bloods may be on your own heads, if you persevere in your obstinacy, and if you do it obstinately and not ignorantly. From the which I beseech almighty God to deliver you. Amen.

1 January. JOHN BRADFORD.

LXI. BP RIDLEY TO BRADFORD.

[OXFORD, about *January* 18, 1555[1].]

BROTHER Bradford, I wish you in Christ our Saviour "grace, mercy, and peace," and to all them which are with you or anywhere else captives in Christ: and to hear that ye be all in good health, and stand constantly in the confession of Christ's gospel, it doth heartily rejoice us. Know you likewise that we all here be—thanks be to God!—in good health and comfort, watching with our lamps light[ed] (I trust in God), when it shall please our Master, "the Bridegroom," to call us to wait "upon him unto the marriage."

Bp Coverdale, Letters of the Martyrs, 1564, p. 67.

Matt. xxv.

Now, we suppose, the day doth approach apace, for we hear that the parliament is dissolved[1]. The burgesses of Oxford are come home; and other news we hear not, but that the king is made protector to the prince to be born[2], and that the bishops have full authority, *ex officio*, to inquire of heresies. Before the parliament began, it was a rumour here, that certain from the Convocation-house was appointed, yea, ready to have come to Oxford;

[[1] This date is determined from the words in the second paragraph, "we hear that the parliament is dissolved," which had taken place, January 16, 1555, and on which day the royal assent was given to the "Act for the revival of three statutes made for the punishment of heresy." See printed Journals of the Commons, Vol. I. p. 41, and of the Lords, Vol. I. p. 491; and Soames, Hist. Reform., Vol. IV. pp. 282, 3, Lond. 1828.]

[[2] See Vol. I. p. 412, fourth paragr., note 2.]

and then there was spied out one thing to lack, for want of a law to perform their intent. Now, seeing they can want no law, we cannot but look for them shortly—I trust to God's glory, let them come when they will, &c.

Brother Bradford, I marvel greatly of good Austin[1] where he is, for that I heard say he promised his master[2] to have been here before this time; and he had from me that I would be loath to lose, yea, to want, when time shall be that it might do (nay, help me to do) my Lord and my Master Christ service: I mean my scribblings *de abominationibus sedis Romanæ et pontificum Romanorum*, [concerning the abominations of the Roman see and Roman pontiffs.] I have no copy of the same; and I look daily to be called *in certamen cum antiquo serpente*, [into conflict with "the old serpent:"] and so I told him and I ween you also, by whose means I was more moved to let him have them. I doubt not of his fidelity: I pray God he be in health and at liberty, for I have been and am careful for him. I have heard that Master Grimbold[3] hath gotten his liberty: if without any blemish of Christ's glory, I am right glad thereof. My brother-in-law[4] is where he was, that is, in Bocardo, the common gaol of the town. I have written here a letter to Master Hooper; I pray you cause it to be written to him again. Commend me to all your prison-fellows and our brethren in Christ. If Austin were here, I would have had more to say. The Lord grant that all be with him well; who ever preserve you and all that love our Saviour Christ in sincerity and truth. Amen.

Yours, by God's grace, in our Master Christ's cause, unto the stake, and thenceforth without all danger and peril for ever and ever.

I am sure you have heard of our new apparel, and I doubt not but London will have their talk of it. Sir, know you that, although this seemeth to us in our case much thanks-worthy, yet have we not that apparel that we look for: for this in time will wear; and that which we look for, rightly done on, will endure, and is called *stola immortalitatis*, [the robe of immortality.]

N. R.

[1 Augustine Bernhere: see Letter LVII.]

[2 Bp Latimer: see first note on Letter LXXIV.]

[3 Grimbold was "a young man," Bp Ridley's "chaplain, a preacher, and a man of much eloquence both in the English and also in the Latin."—Letter XI., from Bp R. to Abp Cranmer and Bp Latimer, in Works of R. p. 361, Park. Soc.]

[4 His name was Shipside or Shyphead.]

LXII. TO ABP CRANMER, AND BPS RIDLEY AND LATIMER[5].

[King's Bench prison, probably *January* 18, 1555[6].]

To my dear and most reverend[7] fathers, Doctor Cranmer, Doctor Ridley, Doctor Latimer, prisoners in Oxford, for the faithful[7] testimony of the Lord Jesus and his holy gospel.

Bp Coverdale, Letters of the Martyrs, 1564, p. 357.

MS. 2. 2. 15. No. 69. Transcript. Emman. Coll. Cambridge.

Almighty God, our heavenly Father, more and more kindle our hearts and affections with his love; that our greatest cross may be to be absent from him and strangers from our home, and that we may godly contend more and more to please him. Amen.

As always I have had great cause to praise our dear Father through Christ, so methinks I have more and more, in seeing more likely the end of my life, which is due for my sin, to be, through the exceeding grace of Christ, a testimony of God's truth. Thus the Lord dealeth not with every body: not that every body hath not more deserved at God's hands than I, which have deserved more vengeance than any other, I know, of my time and state; but that by me, I hope, the Lord will make "the riches of his grace," to his glory, to be seen more excellent. With me therefore I humbly beseech you all, my most dear fathers in God, to give thanks for me, and as you do still to pray for me; that the Lord, as for his love's sake in Christ "he hath begun his good

[[5] The original autograph of this letter, with the autograph signatures of Bp Ferrar, Rowland Taylor, Adn Philpot and Bradford, was, about the end of the sixteenth or beginning of the seventeenth century, in the library of Sir Henry Spelman, and is at present, with four other letters in Bradford's autograph, in the possession of Dawson Turner, Esq., F.R.S., late of Great Yarmouth.

Compare, in illustration of this letter, the other letters of this series that refer to its subject-matter, and "Defence of election," "treatise of election and free-will," and "brief sum of election," Vol. I. pp. 305—30, 211—20, and the various references in Vol. I. p. 306, note 3.]

[[6] See p. 167, note 1, above on Letter LXI., which it would seem that this letter crossed on the road, as Bp Ridley, in Letter LXIII. to Bernhere, which was manifestly written after the receipt of the present letter, refers to Letter LXI., as written the day before. See p. 172, note 2.]

[[7] "and most reverend," "faithful," Emman. MS., scored across: not in 1564. The Emmanuel MS., in common with many of the transcripts in that collection, having on it marks to correspond with the signatures of Bp Coverdale's printed edition of 1564, evidently was used for that edition.]

work in me," even so of and for the same his love's sake in Christ he would make it perfect, and make me to continue to the end, as I hope he will, for his "mercy and truth" "endureth for ever."

[Rev. vi. 9–11.]

As for your parts, in that it is commonly thought your staff standeth next to the door, ye have the more cause to rejoice and be glad, as they which shall come to your fellows "under the altar:" to the which society God with you bring me also in his mercy, when it shall be his good pleasure.

I have received many good things from you, my good lord, master and dear father, N. Ridley, fruits I mean of your godly labours; all which I send unto you again by this bringer: one thing except, which he can tell, I do keep upon your further pleasure to be known therein. And herewithal I send unto you a little Treatise which I have made[1], that you might peruse the same, and not only you, but also ye my other most dear and reverend fathers in the Lord for ever, to give to it your approbation as ye may think good. All the prisoners hereabouts in manner have seen it and read it; and, as therein they agree with me, nay, rather with the truth, so they are ready and will be to signify it, as they shall see you give them example.

This was the chiefest maintainer of man's free-will, and enemy to God's free grace.—[Bp Coverdale.]

The matter may be thought not so necessary as I seem to make it: but yet, if ye knew the great evil that is like hereafter to come to the posterity by these men, as partly this bringer[2] can signify unto you, surely then could ye not but be most willing to put hereto your helping hands. The which thing that I might more occasion you to perceive, I have sent you here a writing of Harry Hart's own hand, whereby ye may see how Christ's glory and grace is like to lose much light, if that your sheep quondam be not something holpen by them which love God, and are able to prove that all good is to be attributed only and wholly to God's grace and mercy in Christ, without other respect of worthiness than Christ's merits. The effects of salvation they so mingle and confound with the cause, that if it be not seen to more hurt will come by them, than ever came by the papists, inasmuch as their life

[1 This probably was the "Defence of Election," Vol. I. pp. 307—30: see its editorial preface, Vol. I. pp. 305, 6.]

[2 Augustine Bernhere.]

commendeth them to the world more than the papists. God is my witness, that I write not this, but because I would God's glory and the good of his people. In free-will they are plain papists, yea, Pelagians; and ye know that *modicum fermenti totam massam corrumpit*, ["a little leaven corrupteth the whole lump."] They utterly contemn all learning: but hereof shall this bringer show you more, what he hath seen and heard himself[3].

This is well known to all those which have had to do with them in disputations or otherwise; for the writings and authority of the learned they have utterly rejected and despised.—[Bp Coverdale.]

As to the chief captains therefore of Christ's church here, I complain of it unto you; as truly I must do of you even unto God in the last day, if ye will not as ye can help something, *ut veritas doctrinæ maneat apud posteros*, [that the truth of doctrine may continue with posterity[4],] in this behalf, as ye have done on the behalf of matters expugned by the papists. God for his mercy in Christ guide you, my most dearly beloved fathers, with his holy Spirit here and in all other things, as most may make to his glory and the commodity of his church. Amen.

Upon this occasion Master Ridley wrote a learned and godly treatise of God's election and predestination[4].—[Bp Coverdale.]

All here, God therefore be praised, prepare themselves willingly to pledge our captain Christ, even when he will and how he will. By your good prayers we shall all fare the better; and therefore we all pray you to continue to cry to God for us, as we, God willing, do and will remember you.

My brethren here with me have thought it their duty to signify this need, by their subscription[5], to be no less than I make it, to prevent the plantations which may take root by these men.

Yours in the Lord, to command[5],

ROBERT FERRAR. JOHN BRADFORD.
ROWLAND TAYLOR. JOHN PHILPOT.

[[3] "what he hath seen and heard himself," Emman. MS.: not in 1564.]

[[4] Dr Gloucester Ridley, in his Life of Bp Ridley, London, 1763, p. 554, observes: "In the Martyrs' Letters we are told by Miles Coverdale, that on this occasion Dr Ridley wrote a treatise of election and predestination, which was in the hands of some persons at that time, and he hoped would hereafter come to light: [Lett. of Mart. p. 65: see Letter LXXXV. of this series:] but I never heard that it was published; nor have I been able to meet with it in MS. The great learning and cool judgment of this prelate, and the entire subjection of his imagination to the revealed will of God, make the loss of this Treatise much to be lamented." See supposed allusion to that Treatise in Letter LXXXIX.]

[[5] "by their subscription," "to command," Emman. MS., scored across: not in 1564.]

LXIII. BP RIDLEY TO BERNHERE[1].

[OXFORD, probably *January* 19, 1555[2].]

MS. 2. 2. 15. No. 149. Original, Holograph. Emman. Coll. Cambridge.

BROTHER Austin, you are welcome to Oxford: and blessed be God for his gracious goodness, that all is well with you, and that our brethren in Christ all are in good comfort, and doth stand steadfast in the confession of Christ's true doctrine.

This day was Doctor Croke[3], the Grecian, with me at dinner; and both he and Mistress Mayoress, mine hostess, told that Master Hooper is hanged, drawn, quartered for treason: but I did believe them never one whit, for [it] is not the first tale that mine hostess hath told me of Master Hooper.

I have received Master B[radford's] angel[4] and a box of confits from his friends. Jesus! what meaneth Master B[radford] to send me such a token? knowing we have *victum et vestitum* [food and clothing] of the queen's highness: I suppose he remembered my brother: well in Bocardo it will do good indeed. I have overrun all that ye send, and do send you all again, that the rest may do the same: but your and his request I cannot for divers causes satisfy: for as yet I have not done that, for divers dangers to my own scribblings; and I suppose many harms may fall thereupon if anything be forth under the title and name of any prisoner, not to himself only, but to all the rest; as ye know I have always counselled Master Hooper not to be hasty to set forth anything under the title of his own name. I will be glad to hear and know what my lord of Canterbury and your master[5] will say; and [I] shall also think of the matter to do the best that shall lie in me. If the matter be not more for other, than for Harry Hart's scrib-

[[1] This letter now is first printed.
It is given here both on that account, and because of its close connexion with the various letters which passed between Bp Ridley and Bradford.]

[[2] See p. 167, note 1, above, on Letter LXI., which, it appears from the following allusion in the present letter, to p. 168, l. 22, was written the day before the present letter was penned: "*Yesterday* I sent to Master Bradford a letter, and told him there, if you had been here, I would have had more to say."]

[[3] Dr Richard Croke excelled in his knowledge of Greek, of which he was at one time public reader at Leipsic; he was subsequently Greek professor at Cambridge, and afterward was resident at Oxford. He was the author of various books on the Greek language. He appeared as one of Dr Story's witnesses against Abp Cranmer, September 12, 1555. He died 1558.—See Wood's Athenæ Oxon., ed. Bliss, Vol. I. cols. 259—61; and also Foxe, Acts, &c., ed. 1583, p. 1429, 1879, or ed. 1843—9, Vol. VI. p. 440, Vol. VIII. p. 63.]

[[4] "Angel:" a gold coin worth about ten shillings. The word "royal" is crossed in the original by Ridley's pen.]

[[5] Bp Latimer: see first note on Letter LXXIV., p. 186.]

bling, I would think a man might be better occupied otherwise than in confuting of them: he is a man, so far as I have heard of him (my lord of Canterbury knoweth him best of all us[6]), which hath been often monished, and, I suppose, hath in time past acknowledged certain of his follies, and yet hath not ceased, as I have heard say, to fall in them again.

Yesterday I sent to master Bradford a letter, and told him there, if you had been here I would have had more to say[7]: I mean nothing else but of two small treatises[8] I have drawn sithen your departure hence, beside that which was in writing when you were here: ye may know the matter whereof they be written, of A. Constantius[9].

When you have read this burn it[10].

N. [RIDLE]Y.

LXIV. BP RIDLEY TO BRADFORD.

[OXFORD, probably *January* 20, 1555[11].]

GRATIAM, et pacem.

Although I ween it is not yet three days ago since ye heard from me, yet having such a messenger and so diversely enforced I

MS. 2. 2. 15. No. 150. Original, Holograph. Emman. Coll. Cambridge.

Bp Coverdale, Letters of the Martyrs, 1564, p. 69.

[6 The name of Henry Hart occurs among those of Kentish sectaries, who, Strype states, "were the first that made separation from the reformed Church of England," and "held the opinions of the Anabaptists and Pelagians," and were "brought into the ecclesiastical court," 1550.—Strype, Ecc. Mem. Vol. I. part I. pp. 369—70: and Harleian MS. 421. No. 64, "Depositions of divers witnesses against some Kentish men, accused of holding erroneous tenets touching predestination."]

[7 Bp Ridley, in Letter LXI., p. 168, above, had observed: "If Austin were here, I would have had more to say."]

[8 The two treatises are probably the same as those which Bp Ridley mentions in Letter LXXXIV., and which were, at the date of that letter, being sent to Bradford.]

[9 This probably refers to the reply of Bp Gardiner, under a fictitious name, to the "Answer" of Abp Cranmer: "Confutatio cavillationum, quibus sacrosanctum eucharistiæ sacramentum ab impiis Capernaitis impeti solet, authore *Marco Antonio Constantio*, theologo Lovaniensi. Paris. 1552." A few notes on Bp Gardiner's pieces on the eucharist are printed, in Bp Ridley's Works, pp. 307—15, Park. Soc.; and these, with additions, are also attributed to Abp Cranmer: see Works of C., Vol. I. pp. 380—88, Park. Soc. The Abp, while in prison, drew up three parts of his Reply to the "Confutatio cavillationum," which are not known at present to exist. Peter Martyr however, after the martyrdoms of Bp Ridley and Abp Cranmer, replied to Bp Gardiner's "Confutatio," in his "Defens. doctr. vet. et apost. de sacr. sacram. euchar." Tiguri, 1562.]

[10 The words "nondum ita desipio" are added in the original in another hand, and apparently in allusion to the words, "When you have read this, burn it."]

[11 See p. 169, note 6, above on Letter LXII., to which it would seem that this

cannot but say something to you. What, shall I thank you for your golden token? what mean you, man? do ye not know yet that we have *victum et amictum e penario regio*, [food and clothing out of the royal storehouse]. I was so moved with your token, that I commanded it straightway to be had to Bocardo which is our common jail. I am right glad of Austin's return, for I was, as I told you, careful for him. Blessed be God that all is well.

This token was a piece of gold, which he sent to relieve his brother Shipside, prisoner in Bocardo.—[Bp Coverdale.]

I have seen what he brought from you, and shortly surveyed the whole, but in such celerity, that others also might see the same before Austin's return, so that I noted nothing but a confused sum of the matter; and as yet what the rest have done I can tell nothing at all, and it was at the writing hereof in their hands. To your request, and Austin's earnest demand of the same, I have answered him in a brief letter; and yet he hath replied again: but he must go without any further answer of me for this time[1]. I have told[2] Augustine, that I for my part, as I can and may for my tardity and dulness, will think of the matter. We are so now ordered and so straitly watched, that unneaths[3] our servants dare do anything for us; so much talk and so many tales, as is said, are told of us abroad. One of us cannot easily nor shortly be of the knowledge of another's mind; and ye know I am youngest many ways. Austin's persuasions may do more with me in that I can think I may do conveniently in this matter, armed with your earnest and zealous letters, than any rhetorick either of Tully or Demosthenes, I ensure you thereof.

He meaneth here Harry Hart, a froward free-will man, who had written a treatise against God's free election, which Bradford sent to Masters Ridley, Cranmer, and Latimer to peruse, desiring Master Ridley to answer the same.—[Bp Coverdale.]

With us as we heard say[4] that Master Grimbold was adjudged to be hanged, drawn, and quartered, of whom we hear now that he is at liberty, so we heard of late, that Master Hooper was hanged, drawn and quartered, indeed not for heresy but for treason: but, blessed be God! we hear now that all is true in like. False tongues will not cease to lie, and mischievous hearts to imagine the worst.

is a reply, as also p. 167, note 1, above on Letter LXI., which probably is the letter alluded to by Bp Ridley in the words, "Although it is not yet three days since ye heard from me."]

[1 The autograph MS. has the following side-notes added in another hand: "Of the matter of election he wrote a godly and most comfortable treatise in Latin." "That he after performed, and wrote a godly and comfortable treatise in Latin, remaining yet in the hands of some." See p. 171, note 3, above on Letter LXII.]

[2 The MS. has after "told" the words scored out by Bp Ridley, "him beside other things," "Augustine" being written above the line.]

[3 "Unneaths:" not easily, hardly, scarcely, from the Anglo-Saxon *eath*, easily. See Nares' Glossary, v. 'uneath.' "Unneaths," MS.: "scantly" 1564.]

[4 "as we heard say," MS.: "it is said," 1564.]

Farewell in Christ: and token for token now I send you not; but know this, that, as is told me, I have two scarlet gowns that scaped, I cannot tell how, in the spoil: when ye will, ye shall be bold to[5] have your part.

Commend me heartily and specially to all those whose name was in your letter[6].

N. R.

LXV. TO SAUNDERS[7].

[Probably about *January* 20, 1555[8].]

To mine own dear brother, Master Laurence Saunders, prisoner in the Marshalsea[9]. God's sweet peace in Christ be with you, my good brother in the Lord Jesus, and with all your concaptives. Amen.

Bp Coverdale, Letters of the Martyrs, 1564, p. 319.

Foxe, Acts, &c., ed. 1570, p. 1815; and after editions.

MS. 1. 2. 8. No. 45. Transcript, Emman. Coll. Cambridge.

I was letted this morning from musing on that, which I was purposed to have thought on, by reason of you, against whom I saw myself guilty of negligence even in this point, that I would not write—I should say, that I had not written unto you as yet. Therefore out of hand in manner I prepared myself to purge myself hereof: not that I will go about to excuse my fault, for that were more to load me, but, by asking both God and you pardon, to get it no more laid to my charge. Now then, as I was thus purposing and partly doing, cometh there one with a letter from you, for the which as I have cause to thank God and you (howbeit not so that you should think I give not the whole to God), so I see myself more blameworthy for thus long holding my peace. Howbeit, good brother, in this I have given a demonstration to you, to behold my negligence in all other things, and especially in praying for you and for the church of God, which for my sins and hypocrisy (hypocrisy indeed even in this writing, God deliver me from it) have deserved to be punished.

[5 "when ye will, ye shall be bold to," MS.: "whereof you shall," 1564.]

[6 "heartily and specially to all those whose name was in your letter," MS.: "to all our brethren and your fellow-prisoners in the Lord," 1564.]

[7 The English rendering of the Latin words in this Letter is inserted throughout from Foxe, Acts, &c., ed. 1570, p. 1815.]

[8 The words in the last paragraph but one, *legem habent*, shew that this letter was written after January 16, 1555, the day parliament was dissolved, and a bill was passed, to revive the sanguinary laws against protestantism. See p. 167, note 1, above.]

[9 The last twelve words are in 1564, not in 1570.]

Just is God, for we have deserved all kinds of plagues at his hands: but yet merciful is he that will on this wise chastise us with this world, *ne cum mundo condemnemur*, "that we should not be condemned with the world." He might otherwise have punished us: I mean, he might have for other causes cast us in prison, me especially, than for his gospel and word's sake. Praised therefore be his name, which voucheth us worthy this honour.

Ah! good God, forgive us our sins, and work by this thy fatherly correction on us, on me especially, effectually to love thee and thy Christ, and with joyfulness unto the end to carry thy cross through thick and thin. Always set before our eyes, not this gallows on earth if we will stick to thee, but the gallows in hell if we deny thee or swerve from that we have professed.

Ah! good brother, if I could always have God, his majesty, mercy, heaven, hell, &c., before mine eyes, then should I *obdu-*
Heb. xi. *rare*, ["endure,"] as Paul writeth of Moses: *Obduravit, inquit, perinde quasi vidisset eum qui est invisibilis:* "He endured, saith he, as he that saw him which is invisible." Pray for me, as I know you do, and give thanks also; for *in Domino spero,*
Psal. xxiii. *non nutabo. Si ambulavero per vallis medium*[1] *umbræ mortis, non timebo, quia tu, Domine, mecum es.* Amen: "In the Lord I trust, I shall not waver." "If I walk by the valley of the shadow of death, I will not fear, for thou art with me," O Lord.

I think, we shall be shortly called forth; for now *legem habent, et secundum legem*, ["they have a law, and according to the law,"] &c.: otherwise will they not reason with us; and I think their sheet-anchor will be to have us to subscribe: the which thing if we do, though with this condition, so far as the thing subscribed to repugneth not against God's word, yet this will be offensive. Therefore let us *vadere plane*, ["walk uprightly,"] and so *sane*, ["surely;"] I mean, let us all confess that we are no changelings, but *reipsa* are the same we were in religion, and therefore cannot subscribe, except we will dissemble both with God, ourselves, and the world.

Hæc tibi scribo, frater mi carissime in Domino. Jam legam tuam epistolam: These things I write to you, dear brother, in the Lord. Now I will read your epistle. Ah, brother, that I
John xv. had *practicam tecum scientiam in vite illa quam pingis! roga*

[[1] "vallis medium," MS.: "vallem" 1570 and 1564.]

Dominum ut ita vere sentiam. Amen: 'The practical understanding with you in that vine which you describe! pray the Lord, that I may think so indeed.' God make me thankful for you. *Salutant te omnes concaptivi, et gratias Domino pro te agunt: idem tu facias pro nobis, et ores ut,* &c.: 'All our fellow-prisoners salute you, and give thanks to God for you. The same do you for us, and pray that,' &c.

Your brother, in the Lord Jesus, to live and die with you,

JOHN BRADFORD.

LXVI. TO SAUNDERS[2].

[Probably about *January* 21, 1555[3].]

To mine own dear brother, Master Laurence Saunders, prisoner in the Marshalsea[4]. My good brother, I beseech our good God and gracious Father always to continue his gracious favour and love towards us, and by us, as by instruments of his grace, to work his glory and the confusion of his adversaries. *Ex ore infantium et lactentium fundet laudem ad destruendum inimicum.* &c. Amen: "Out of the mouth of infants and babes he will shew forth his praise, to destroy the enemy." &c.

Foxe, Acts, &c., ed. 1563, p. 1194; and after editions.

Bp Coverdale, Letters of the Martyrs, 1564, p. 321.

MS. 1. 2. 8 No. 46 and 76. Transcripts. Emman. Coll. Cambridge.

I have perused your letters to myself and have read them to others. For answer whereof, if I should write what Doctor Taylor and Master Philpot do think, then must I say, that they think the salt sent unto us by your friend is unsavoury: and indeed I think they both will declare it heartily, if they should come before them. As for me, if you would know what I think, my good and most dear brother Laurence, because I am so sinful and so conspurcate[5] (the Lord knoweth I lie not) with many grievous sins, which yet I hope are washed away *sanguine Christi nostri*, I neither can nor would be consulted withal, but as a cipher in agrime[6]. Howbeit, to tell you how and what I mind,

This friend moved them to subscribe, so far as it were not against God's word; and yet he after valiantly suffered.—[Foxe, 1563.]

[2 The English rendering of the Latin words in this letter is inserted throughout from Foxe, Acts, &c., ed. 1570, p. 1815.]

[3 From the allusions to approaching examination, as Bradford's first examination was on January 22, 1555. See Vol. I. p. 465.]

[4 The last twelve words are in Foxe 1570, not in 1563, nor in Coverdale 1564.]

[5 "Conspurcate:" defiled, polluted.]

[6 "Agrime:" arithmetic, contracted from algorithm.]

take this for a sum: I pray God in no case I may "seek myself;" and indeed (I thank God therefore) I purpose it not. *Quod reliquum est Domino meo committo; et spero in illum, quod*
Ps. lv. *ipse faciet juxta hoc: Jacta in Dominum curam, &c.; omni*
Ps. xxxvii. *cura vestra conjecta in illum; revela Domino viam tuam, et*
Ps. xxxii. *spera, &c.: sperantem in Domino misericordia circumdabit:* "That which remaineth I commit to my Lord God; and I trust in him that he will do according to this:" "Cast thy care on the Lord," &c.; "cast all your care upon him," &c.; "reveal unto the Lord thy way, and trust," &c.: "who that trusteth in the Lord, mercy shall compass him about."

I did not nor do not know but by your letters, *quod cras* we shall come *coram nobis:* [that to-morrow we shall come the one
Matt. x. before the other.] Mine own heart, stick still to *Dabitur vobis:*
1 Cor. x. *fidelis enim est Dominus; dabit in tentatione eventum quo possu-*
2 Pet. ii. *mus sufferre. Novit Dominus pios*[1] *e tentatione eripere. &c.*
Nahum i. *O utinam pius ego essem! Novit Dominus in die tribulationis sperantes in se, &c.:* "It shall be given you," &c.: "for the Lord is faithful; he will, in temptation, make a way that ye may be able to bear it." "The Lord knoweth how to rid out of temptation the godly," &c. "O would God I were godly!" "The Lord knoweth how to deliver out of temptation such as trust in him," &c.—I cannot think that they will offer any kind of indifferent or mean conditions: for, if we will not *adorare bestiam*, we never shall be delivered but against their will, think I.

God our Father and gracious Lord make perfect the good he hath begun in us. *Faciet, mi frater, carissime frater, quem in intimis visceribus habeo ad commoriendum et convivendum. O si tecum essem!* 'He will do it, my brother, my dear brother, whom I have in my inward bowels to live and die with. O if I were with you!'

Pray for me, mine own heart-root in the Lord.

For ever your own,

JOHN BRADFORD.

[[1] "suos," 1563: "pios," 1564, and 1570.]

LXVII. SAUNDERS TO BP FERRAR, TAYLOR, BRADFORD AND PHILPOT.

[Probably about *January* 23 or 24, 1555[2].]

"GRACE, mercy, and peace in Jesus Christ our Lord." &c. Foxe, Acts, &c., ed. 1570, p. 1671; and after editions.

Good fathers and dear brethren, be thankful unto our most gracious God, which hath preserved us, and shall, I doubt not, from blaspheming his blessed name; yea, not only that, but also *ex ore infantium et lactentium perficiet laudem, &c.*, "out of the mouths of very babes and sucklings shall he set forth his praise." Bp Coverdale, Letters of the Martyrs, 1564, p. 211. Psal. viii.

They offer us forsooth our liberty and pardon, so that we will rise with them into that faith which we with them were fallen from. 'Yea,' or 'no,' must be answered in haste. They will not admit any needful circumstances, but all, as heretofore, most detestable and abominable. Rise with them we must unto the unity.— "A pardon," say I, "of me must not be so dearly purchased: a pardon I desire, for to live with an unclogged conscience." "The Donatists[3]," say they, "sought for such singularity: but they were not meet to live in a commonwealth: no more be you, as you shall shortly understand. Wherefore away with him." Yea, the time was named—within this sevennight.— "'There be twelve hours in the day:' death shall be welcome," say I, "as being looked for long since: and yet do justice ye were best; for Abel's blood cried, ye wot what. The Spirit of God be upon you, and God save your honours."—Thus departed I from them[2]. John xi.

Pray, pray. Ah, ah! *puer sum, nescio loqui*, 'I am a child, I cannot speak.' My brother P[unt] shall shew you more herein. By him send me word what you have done. Fare ye well, and pray, pray.

I would gladly meet with my good brother Bradford on the backside about an eleven of the clock. Before that time I cannot start out, ye have such out-walkers: but then will they be at dinner.

Yours, as you know,

LAURENCE SAUNDERS.

[[2] This letter was written immediately after the first examination of Saunders, the precise date of which is not given in Foxe, but may probably have been near to or upon January 22, 1555, the day of the first examinations of Rogers and Bradford. See first Examination of Saunders in Foxe, Acts, &c., ed. 1583, p. 1498, or ed. 1843—9, Vol. VI. pp. 625, 6. See also allusions to approaching examination in the last letter.]

[[3] Mosheim, Eccl. Hist., Cent. IV., Part II. ch. v. sect. 2—8; Waddington's Ch. Hist., Part II. ch. xi. pp. 323—28, London, 1835.]

LXVIII. TO TREWE ABYNGTON, AND OTHERS[1].

[Probably about *January* 30, 1555[2].]

JESUS IMMANUEL[3].

Bp Coverdale, Letters of the Martyrs, 1564, p. 474.

MS. 1. 2. 8. No. 29. Original, Holograph. Emman. Coll. Cambridge.

YET once more, beloved in the Lord, before pen and ink be utterly by all means[3] taken from me, as I look it to be this afternoon, I thought good to write unto you, because I stand in a doubt, whether at any time hereafter, I shall see or speak with you; for within this sevennight my lord chancellor bade look for judgment.

God knoweth I lie not, I never did bear you malice, nor sought the hindrance of any one of you, but your good both in soul and body; as, when we shall all appear together before God, I am certain you shall then know, though now you doubt it, and that causeless I am right well assured. For mine own conscience can and doth bear witness with me, that I never defrauded you or any of you, of the value of one penny or pennyworth of anything, but have sought, with that which hath been given, not only in common, but also unto me and to mine own use, discretion and distribution, to do you good. Therefore disdain not the good-will of your lover in God; and, in hope that you will not, I have eftsoons even now sent unto you thirteen shillings, four pence: if you need as much more, you shall have it, or anything else I have or can do for you.

He meaneth concerning free-will, original sin, predestination, &c., wherein they are plain Pelagians and papists.—[Bp Coverdale.]

Though in some things we agree not, yet let love bear the bell away; and let us one pray for another, and be careful one for another; for I hope we be all Christ's. As you hope yourselves to pertain to him, so think of me; and, as you be his, so am I yours,

JOHN BRADFORD.

[[1] The inscription of 1564 is: "To Trewe and Abyngton, with other of their company, teachers and maintainers of the errors of man's free-will." The autograph MS. has not any inscription.]

[[2] From the allusion to Bradford's last examination, in the words, "within this seven-night my lord chancellor bade look for judgment." See Vol. I. pp. 482, 492.]

[[3] "Jesus Immanuel," "by all means," autograph MS.: not in 1564.]

LXIX. TO TREWE ABYNGTON, AND OTHERS[4].

[Probably about *January* 31, 1555.]

He that seeketh not to hinder himself temporally, that he may further his brother in more need, the same wanteth true love. I have done, do and will (except you refuse it) hinder myself this way, that I may further you, and indeed myself also, that way wherein I desire to be furthered. If I would seek mine own gains temporally, then could I have taken and used many portions of money which have been given me to mine own use[5]. I never minded to upbraid you: but that which I did write of mine own hindrance was, that you might see I loved you, and sought your weal, as I do and will be glad to do it continually.—The Lord of mercy hath forgiven us all: wherefore henceforth let us rather bear than break.

Bp Coverdale, Letters of the Martyrs, 1564, p. 475.

Yours in the Lord,

JOHN BRADFORD.

LXX. TO MARY MARLAR[6].

[*February* 2, 1555.]

To his dearly beloved sister in the Lord, Mary Marlar, John Bradford wisheth the true knowledge of Christ.

MS. 2. 2. 15. No. 95. 1. Transcript. Emman. Coll. Cambridge.

If I could recompense your kindness, so many ways shewed towards me, right dear sister in the Lord, but one way, I would think myself happy. But, inasmuch as I cannot, I must and will humbly pray to God for you, that he would otherwise gratify you with his heavenly gifts of repentance, faith, love,

[4 Bp Coverdale states, that at the preceding "letter these men were so sore offended, because he said he had hindered himself to further them, [vide Letter LX. p. 165, line 3, above,] as though he had thereby upbraided them, that in displeasure they sent it to him again. Whereupon he wrote unto them that which follows."—Lett. of Mart., 1564, p. 475.]

[5 Bp Coverdale observes: "Though he distributed to them, amongst other prisoners there, not only that which was given in common, but also to his own use, yet they suspected him of evil dealing. Thus do not they in whom the love of God dwelleth."—Ibid. p. 476.]

[6 This letter now is first printed.
Mary Marlar is probably the wife of Walter Marlar, mentioned by Foxe, who was a good nurse unto him and his very good friend, and made his shirt for his burning.—Foxe, Acts, &c., ed. 1583, p. 1605, or ed. 1843—9, Vol. VII., p. 147.]

innocency, &c., here, and with his everlasting gifts elsewhere. The which that you may the more desire and often think upon, I have sent you this which followeth, something to occasion you thereto: and, because troubles and passions are at hand towards you, as I hear, in that you be great with child, to the intent you may the better bear and patiently suffer the same, I have, to begin withal, written something of the Passion of Christ[1], [which our[2]] Captain suffered for us, that you, seeing them so many and painful, may use them as Moses did
Exod. xv. the wood, to make the bitter waters more pleasant.

God our Father make you a happy mother, and deal with you in all things as his child. Amen.

Forth of prison, the 2nd of February, *anno* 1555.

J. B.

LXXI. TO MISTRESS WILKINSON[3].

Bp Coverdale, Letters of the Martyrs, 1564, p. 342.

Foxe, Acts, &c., ed. 1570, p. 1825; and after editions.

MS. 1. 2. 8. No. 88. Transcript. Emman. Coll. Cambridge.

ALMIGHTY God, our most loving Father, increase in your heart, my good mother and dear mistress in the Lord, his true knowledge and love in Christ, to the encouraging and comforting of your faith in these stormy days, as necessary unto us, so profitable if we persist unto the end: which thing God grant unto us. Amen.

My right dearly beloved, I know not what other thing to write unto you, than to desire you to be thankful unto the Lord, in that, amongst the not many of your calling and state, it pleaseth him to give you his rare blessing—I mean, to keep you from all the filth, wherewith our country is horribly defiled. This blessing assuredly is rare as you see. But now, if he shall bless you with another blessing which is more rare, I mean, to call you forth as a martyr, and as a witness against this filth, I hope you will become doubly thankful. For a greater token commonly we have not, to judge of our election and salvation, next to Christ and faith in him, than the cross, especially when it is so glorious as on this sort to suffer anything, but chiefly loss of this life, which indeed is

[1 The Emmanuel MS. contains, after this letter, and written on the same sheet, Bradford's "meditation on the passion of Christ," and his "prayer for the presence of God:" see Vol. I. pp. 196—99, and pp. 264—66.]

[2 MS. torn.] [3 See p. 39, note 3, above.]

never found till it be so lost. "Except the grain of wheat fall and be dead, it remaineth fruitless."

You know how that he which was "rapt into the third heaven," and did know what he wrote, doth say that, as the corn liveth not except it be dead and cast into the earth, so truly our bodies. And therefore the cross should so little fear us, that even death itself should altogether be desired of us, as the tailor which putteth off our rags, and arrayeth us with the royal robes of immortality, incorruption and glory. Great shame it should be for us, that all "the whole creatures" Rom. viii. of God should desire, yea, "groan" in their kind for our liberty, and we ourselves to loathe it; as doubtless we do, if for the cross, yea, for death itself we with joy swallow not up all sorrow, that might let us from following the Lord's calling and obeying the Lord's providence: whereby doubtless all crosses and death itself doth come, and not by hap or chance.

In consideration whereof, right dear mother, in that this providence stretcheth itself so unto us and for us, that "even the hairs of our heads are numbered" with God, not one of them to fall to our hurt, surely we declare ourselves very faint in faith, if we receive not such comfort, that we can willingly offer ourselves to the Lord, and "cast our whole care" upon his back; honouring him with this honour, that he is and ever will be "careful for us" and all we have, as for his dear children. Be therefore of good cheer, even in the midst of these miseries, be thankful to the Lord, and prepare yourself for a further trial: which if God send you, as I hope, so do you believe that God therein will help and comfort you, and make you able to bear whatsoever shall happen.

And thus much, hearing you to be in the country, and one going down unto you[4], I thought good to write, praying God our Father to recompense into your bosom all the good that ever you have done, to me especially, and to many others, both in this time of trouble and always heretofore.

Your own in the Lord,

JOHN BRADFORD.

[[4] The last thirteen words are only in the MS., where they are scored across, and the words, "having this opportunity" (which is the reading in 1564 and 1570) are written over.]

LXXII. TO LADY VANE[1].

[*February 5, 1555.*]

Bp Coverdale, Letters of the Martyrs, 1564, p. 467.

OUR dear and most meek Father always be with us for his Christ's sake, and as his children guide us, for ever. Amen.

Your comfortable and necessary letters last sent to me, right worshipful and dearly beloved, do deserve at my hands, as other your benefits have done, that which I cannot give. The Lord my God recompense you, as he can and will undoubtedly. Now am I going to my good Father and your Father; now am I going to my Christ and your Christ; now am I going to my home and your home. I go before, but you shall follow; howbeit when or which way I know not; the Lord knoweth. Unto his providence and will commend yourself; for, as it cannot but come to pass, so is there nothing so good to us as it is. Happy were we that ever we were born, that God might set forth his glory by us, howsoever he do it.

Though I am led, as to Peter was said, "whither I would not," yet with me and for me give thanks, that it pleaseth my Father thus to lead me. I have deserved, yea, even since I came into this prison, many a shameful death, such and so great is my ingratitude and sins. But, lo! the tender kindness of my Father doth correct me as a child and son, making the remedy for my sins an occasion of his glory, a witnessing of his verity, a confirmation of his true religion, heretofore set forth and preached by me: wherein, good madam, persist, and you shall be safe. Be not now ashamed of it; for, though it seem to be overcome, yet by suffering it overcometh, that "God's wisdom," which is "foolishness" to the world, "God's power" which is "weakness" to the reason of man, may triumph and confound that, which with the world is wise and mighty.

Now do I begin to be Christ's disciple; now I begin to be fashioned like to my Master in suffering, that so I may be in reigning; now do I for ever take my farewell of you for this life; now commend I myself into the hands of my Father, by whose providence I came into this world, by whose providence I have been kept in this world, and by whose providence I do depart hence. And, as his providence is towards me, so doubt you nothing but it is towards you, though not in such sort exteriorly, yet in such love, solicitude and carefulness for you interiorly.

[[1] See p. 91, note 6, above.]

God, our God and Father of mercy, for the blood of his Christ wash away all our sins, comfort his church, strengthen the weak, convert or confound, as may make most to his glory, his enemies, and be with us Immanuel for ever. Amen, Amen.

In haste, out of prison, the 5th of February, 1555.

JOHN BRADFORD.

LXXIII. TO MISTRESS WARCUP[2].

[*February* 7, 1555.]

Bp Coverdale, Letters of the Martyrs, 1564, p. 458.

Foxe, Acts, &c., ed. 1570, p. 1834; and after editions.

MS. 2. 2. 15. No. 154, and MS. 1. 2. 8. No. 79. Transcripts. Emman. Coll. Cambridge.

ALMIGHTY God, our heavenly Father, for his Christ's sake increase in us faith, by which we may more and more see what glory and honour is reposed and safely kept in heaven, for all them that "believe with the heart," and "confess" Christ and his truth "with the mouth." Amen.

My dearly beloved, I remember that once heretofore I wrote unto you a *vale* or a farewell upon conjecture; but now I write my farewell to you in this life indeed, upon certain knowledge. My staff "standeth at the door;" I continually look for the sheriff to come for me, and, I thank God, I am ready for him. Now go I to practise that which I have preached. Now am I climbing up the hill: it will cause me to puff and blow before I come to the cliff. The hill is steep and high; my breath is short, and my strength is feeble. Pray therefore to the Lord for me, that, as I have now through his goodness even almost come to the top, I may by his grace be strengthened, not to rest till I come where I should be.

O loving Lord, put out thy hand and "draw me unto thee;" for "no man cometh, but he whom the Father draweth." See, my dearly beloved, God's loving mercy: he knoweth my short breath and great weakness. As he sent for Elias a fiery chariot, so sendeth he for me; for by fire my dross must be purified, that I may be "fine gold" in his sight. O unthankful wretch that I am! Lord, do thou forgive me mine unthankfulness. Indeed I confess, right dear to me in the Lord, that my sins have deserved hell-fire, much more then this fire. But, lo! so loving is my Lord, that he converteth the remedy for my sins, the punish-

[[2] See p. 45, note 2, above.]

ment for my transgressions, into a testimonial of his truth and a testification of his verity, which the prelates do persecute in me, and not my sins. Therefore they persecute not me, but Christ in me, which I doubt not will take my part unto the very end. Amen.

O that I had so open an heart, as could so receive as I should do this great benefit and unspeakable dignity, which God my Father offereth to me! Now pray for me, my dearly beloved, pray for me, that I never shrink. I shall never shrink, I hope; I trust in the Lord, I shall never shrink; for he that always hath taken my part, I am assured, will not leave me when I have most need, for his truth and mercy's sake. O Lord, help me! Into thy hands I commend me wholly. In the Lord is my trust, I care not what man can do unto me. Amen.

My dearly beloved, say you, Amen, also, and come after if so God call you. Be "not ashamed of the gospel of Christ," but keep company with him still. He will never leave you, but in the midst of temptation will give you an outscape, to make you able to bear the brunt. Use hearty prayer; reverently read and hear God's word; put it in practice; look for the cross; "lift up your heads, for your redemption draweth nigh." Know that "the death of God's saints is precious in his sight;" be merry in the Lord; pray for the mitigation of God's heavy displeasure upon our country.—God keep us for ever; God bless us with his spiritual blessings in Christ.

And thus I bid you farewell for ever in this present life. Pray for me, pray for me, for God's sake pray for me.—God make perfect his good work begun in me. Amen.

Out of prison this 7th of February[1].

Yours in the Lord,

JOHN BRADFORD.

LXXIV. TO BERNHERE[2].

[About *February* 8, 1555.]

Bp Coverdale, Letters of the Martyrs, 1564, p. 470.

To mine own good Augustine. Dear brother Augustine, I cannot but be bold of you in my need, and therefore I write as

[[1] The date "1555" is written in MS. 2.2.15. No. 154.]

[[2] Augustine Bernhere was a Swiss by birth, and was the well-known personal

I do. Come hither betimes, I pray you, in the morning, and use so to do, for then, I think, you shall speak with me. Also use to come late in the evening, and let me know, whether in the day-time I may send for you. Pray Walsh to steal you in, as I hope he will do. If he do bring you in, then shall this which followeth not need: but, doubting the worst, this do I write.

First will my man William to make all things ready for me; for I am persuaded I shall into Lancashire, there to be burned: howbeit first, they say, I must to the Fleet. Then will him to hearken early in the morning, whether I be not conveyed away, before men be ware. Also, I pray you, will Robert Harrington, who I hope will go with me, to look for that journey. Visit often my dear sister; and, although I cannot now write unto her as I would (for all things are more strange here, and cases more and more perilous), yet tell her that I am careful for her; desire her to have good comfort: God shall give us to meet in his kingdom. In the mean season I will pray for her, as my dearest sister. Of truth I never did love her half so well as I now do; and yet I love her not half so well as I would do; she is the very daughter of Abraham.

I pray thee heartily, be merry, my good brother, and desire all my friends so to be; for, I thank God, I feel a greater benefit than all the bishops in England can take from me. Praise God, and pray for me, mine own dear heart in the Lord, whom I hope I shall never forget.

Your poor brother in the Lord,

JOHN BRADFORD.

attendant on Bp Latimer, to whom we are indebted for many of the bishop's memorable sermons having been preserved. During the reign of Mary, he with surpassing diligence laboured to supply the need of the faithful confessors and martyrs: and he was, for a time, minister to those true worshippers who, during the whole of that dangerous period, used to assemble, as a congregation, in London. He was preferred, after the accession of Elizabeth, to the rectory of Southam. Three treatises by Bernhere, on election, are in MS. Bodl. 53, Bodleian Library, Oxford: and various papers, in his autograph, exist among the MSS. of Emmanuel College, Cambridge, some of which are transcripts of pieces by Bradford and others. See p. 45, note 2, above; Vol. I. p. 306, note 3; Bp Tanner's Biblioth. Britann.-Hibern. 1748, article, Bernhere; Foxe, Acts, &c., ed. 1583, p. 2074, or ed. 1843—9, Vol. VIII. p. 559; Strype, Ecc. Mem., Vol. III. part I. p. 228, and part II. pp. 132, 147; and Dedication by Bernhere, in Works of Bp Latimer, Vol. I. pp. 311—25, Park. Soc.]

LXXV. TO EATON.

[*February* 8, 1555.]

Bp Coverdale, Letters of the Martyrs, 1564, p. 449.

Foxe, Acts, &c., ed. 1570, p. 1833; and after editions.

MS. 2. 2. 15. No. 67. Original, Holograph. Emman. Coll. Cambridge.

ALMIGHTY God, our heavenly Father, recompense abundantly into your bosom, my dearly beloved, here and eternally, the good which from him by you I have continually received, sithen my coming into prison.

Otherwise can I never be able to requite your lovingkindness here, than by praying for you, and, after this life, by witnessing your faith, declared to me by your fruits, when we shall come and appear together, before the throne of our Saviour Jesus Christ; whither, I thank God, I am even now a going, ever looking when the[1] officers will come and satisfy the precept of the prelates. Whereof though I cannot complain, because I have justly deserved an hundred thousand deaths at God's hands, by reason of my sins, yet I may and must rejoice, because the prelates do not persecute in me mine iniquities, but Christ Jesus and his verity: so that they persecute not me, they hate not me, but they persecute Christ, they hate Christ. And, because they can do him no hurt, for he "sitteth in heaven" and laugheth them and their devices to scorn, as one day they shall feel, therefore they turn their rage upon his poor sheep, as Herod their father did upon the infants. Great cause therefore have I to rejoice, that my dear Saviour Christ will vouchsafe amongst many to choose me to be a vessel of grace to suffer in me (which have deserved so often and justly to suffer for my sins), that I might be most assured, I shall be a "vessel of honour," in whom he will be glorified. Therefore, my right dear brother in the Lord, rejoice with me, give thanks for me, and cease not to pray that God for his mercy's sake would make perfect the good he hath begun in me.

Matt. ii.

And, as for the doctrine which I have professed and preached, I unto you do confess in writing, as to the whole world I shortly shall by God's grace in suffering, that it is the very true doctrine of Jesus Christ, of his church, of his prophets, apostles, and all good men; so that, if an angel should come from heaven, and preach otherwise, the same were ac-

[[1] "the," autograph MS.: not in 1564 or 1570.]

cursed. Therefore waver not, dear heart in the Lord, but be confirmed in it; and as your vocation requireth, when God so will, confess it, though it be perilous so to do. The end shall evidently shew another manner of pleasure for so doing, than tongue can tell.

Be diligent in prayer, and watch therein; use reverent reading of God's word. Set the shortness of this time before your eyes; and let not the eternity that is to come depart out of your memory. Practise in doing that you learn by reading and hearing; "decline from evil, and pursue good." "Remember them that be in bonds," especially for the Lord's cause, as members of your body and "fellow-heirs of grace." Forget not the afflictions of Sion and the oppression of Jerusalem; and God our Father shall give you his continual blessing, through Christ our Lord: who guide us as his dear children for ever. Amen.

And thus I take my *vale* and farewell with you, dear brother, for ever in this present life, till we shall meet in eternal bliss; whither our good God and Father bring us shortly. Amen.

God bless all your babes for ever. Amen.

Out of prison this eighth of February.

Your afflicted brother for the Lord's cause,

JOHN BRADFORD.

LXXVI. TO MISTRESS JOYCE HALES[2].

[*February* 8, 1555.]

MS. on reverse of title of a copy of Tyndale's New Testament, Jugge, 1548, Original, Holograph[2].

BEWARE more of evil thoughts than of any evil words or deeds: for of evil words and deeds there is judgment here, and they be of such sins as precede the judgment; but of evil thoughts there is here no judgment, and they be of such sins as do follow the judgment.

[[2] This letter now is first printed.

See p. 108, note 1, above, and Vol. I. p. 248, editorial preface to "Meditations from the autograph of John Bradford," there printed for the first time, where see account of the New Testament in which this short letter was written.]

Farewell, mine own most dearly beloved sister in the Lord for ever.

Forth of prison, the 8th February, 1555, by your own most assured,

JOHN BRADFORD.

LXXVII. TO ABP CRANMER, AND BPS RIDLEY AND LATIMER[1].

[*February* 8, 1555.]

Bp Coverdale, Letters of the Martyrs, 1564, p. 466.

Foxe, Acts, &c., ed. 1570, p. 1815; and after editions.

MS. G. g. iv. 13. p. 158. University Library, Cambridge.

To my dear fathers, Doctor Cranmer, Doctor Ridley, and Doctor Latimer.

Jesus Immanuel. My dear fathers in the Lord, I beseech God our sweet Father, through Christ, to make perfect the good he hath begun in us all. Amen.

I had thought that every of your staves had stand next the door: but now it is otherwise perceived. Our dear brother Rogers hath broken the ice valiantly; and as this day, I think, or to-morrow at the uttermost, hearty Hooper, sincere Saunders, and trusty Taylor, end their course and receive their crown. The next am I, which hourly look for the porter to open me the gates after them, to enter into the desired rest. God forgive me mine unthankfulness for this exceeding great mercy, that amongst so many thousands it pleaseth his mercy to choose me to be one in whom he will suffer. For although it be most true that *juste patior*, "I justly suffer"—for I have been a great hypocrite and a grievous sinner: the Lord pardon me! yea, he hath done it, he hath done it indeed—yet *hic autem quid mali fecit?* "what evil hath he done?" Christ whom the prelates persecute, his verity which they hate in me, hath done no evil, nor deserveth death. Therefore ought I most heartily to rejoice of this dignation and tender kindness of the Lord towards me, which useth the remedy for my sin as a testimonial of his testament, to his glory, to my everlasting comfort, to the edifying of his church, and to the overthrowing of antichrist and his kingdom. O what am I, Lord, that thou shouldst thus magnify me, so vile a man and miser as always I

[[1] The English rendering of the Latin words is throughout taken from Foxe, ed. 1570, p. 1815: it is also given in the Cambridge University MS.]

have been! Is this thy wont, to send for such a wretch and an hypocrite as I have been, in a fiery chariot, as thou didst for Elias? O dear fathers! be thankful for me, and pray for 2 Kings ii.
me, that I still may be found worthy, in whom the Lord would sanctify his holy name. And, for your part, make you ready, for we are but your gentlemen-ushers. *Nuptiæ agni paratæ sunt, venite ad nuptias:* "The marriage of the Lamb has been prepared; come unto the marriage." I now go to leave my flesh there, where I received it. I shall be conveyed thither as Ignatius was to Rome, to[2] *leopardis*[3], by whose evil I hope to be made better: God grant, if it be his will that I ask, it may make them better by me. Amen.

For my farewell therefore I write and send this unto you, trusting shortly to see you, where we shall never be separated. In the mean season I will not cease, as I have done, to commend you to our Father of heaven: and, that ye would so do by me, I most heartily pray every one of you. You know now I have most need: but *fidelis Deus, qui nunquam sinet nos tentari supra id quod possumus:* "Faithful is God, which will not suffer us to be tempted above our strength." He never did it hitherto, nor now, I am assured, he will never do. Amen.

A dextris est mihi, non movebor. Propter hoc lætabitur cor Ps. xvi.
meum, quia non derelinquet animam meam in inferno, nec dabit me sanctum suum, per gratiam in Christo, videre corruptionem: "He is on my right hand: therefore I shall not fall. Wherefore my heart shall rejoice: for he shall not leave my soul in hell, neither will suffer me, his holy one, by his grace in Christ, to see corruption."

E carcere raptim, expectans omni momento carnificem: 'Out of prison, in haste, looking every moment for the tormentor,' the 8th of February, *anno* 1555.

JOHN BRADFORD.

[[2] "to," MS.: not in 1564 or 1570.]

[[3] Bp Coverdale observes in a side-note: "He meaneth that he should be conveyed by the queen's guard into Lancashire, to be burnt, as the adversaries had once determined, like as Ignatius was by a company of soldiers conveyed to Rome, and cast to the leopards. [Euseb.] Eccl. Hist. Lib. III. cap. xxxvi." Vide Ignat. ad Roman., cap. v., and Martyrium Ignat., in Patr. Apost., ed. Jacobson, Oxon. 1847, Tom. II. pp. 383, 550—79, and in Corpus Ignatianum, Cureton; London, 1849, pp. 48, 222, 231, 252.]

LXXVIII. BP RIDLEY TO BERNHERE[1].

[OXFORD, about *February* 10, 1555.]

MS. 2. 2. 15. No. 155. Original, Holograph. And No. 160, transcript in writing of Bernhere. Emman. Coll. Cambridge.

MS. Harl. 416. No. 8. fol. 16, reverse, Transcript. British Museum.

Bp Coverdale, Letters of the Martyrs, 1564, p. 72.

Foxe, Acts, &c., ed. 1570, p. 1902; and after editions.

BROTHER Augustine, I bless God with all my heart, in his manifold merciful gifts given unto our dear brethren in Christ; specially to our brother Rogers, whom it pleased him to set forth first, no doubt but of his good gracious goodness and fatherly favour towards him. And likewise blessed be God in the rest—Hooper, Saunders and Taylor, whom it hath pleased the Lord likewise to set in the fore-brunt now of battle against his adversaries, and hath endued them all, so far as I can hear, to stand in the stour[2], and to be content in his cause, and for his gospel sake, to lose their life.

And evermore and without end blessed be even the same our heavenly Father for our dear and entirely beloved brother, Bradford, whom now the Lord, I perceive, calleth for: for I ween he will no longer vouchsafe him to abide among this adulterous and wicked generation of this world. I do not doubt but that he, for those gifts of grace which the Lord hath bestowed of him plenteously, hath holpen those which are gone before in their journey, that is, hath animated and encouraged them to keep the highway, *et sic currere uti tandem acciperent premium*, [and so to run that at length they might receive the prize.] The Lord be his comfort, whereof I do not doubt: and I thank God heartily that ever I was acquainted with him, and that ever I had such a one in my house.

And yet again I bless God in our dear brother, and of this time protomartyr, Rogers, that he was also one of my calling to be a prebendary preacher in Paul's[3] of London. And now, because Grindal is gone (the Lord, I doubt not, hath and knoweth wherein he will bestow him), I trust to God it shall please him of his goodness to strengthen me to make up the trinity[4] out of Paul's church to suffer for Christ, whom God the Father hath anointed, the Holy Spirit[5] doth bear witness unto, Paul and all the apostles preached.

As for the books ye write of, ye shall have space to use them as

[[1] This letter follows the text throughout of Bp Ridley's autograph, which now has first been collated, and which supplies a short paragraph near the end, that is now first printed.

It is printed here partly on that account, and partly because, in common with the next in this series, from Bp Ridley to Bradford, it was obviously occasioned by Letter LXXVII., addressed by Bradford to Cranmer, Ridley, and Latimer.]

[[2] "Stour:" assault, onset, attack.—Nares' Glossary. "Stour," both Cambridge MSS.: "confession of his truth," 1564. The Harl. MS. has a blank, as if the transcriber had not decyphered, or had doubted the word in Ridley's autograph.]

[[3] "In Paul's," autogr. MS.: not in 1564.]

[[4] Namely himself in addition to Rogers and Bradford.]

[[5] This word is imperfect in the autograph MS., which is slightly torn.]

ye think best: only I desire that my brother Shiphead may have knowledge of them, whatsoever God shall do with me; and I pray you at last to talk with him in such things[6].

Thus fare ye now well. I had no paper; and therefore I was constrained thus to write[7].

LXXIX. BP RIDLEY TO BRADFORD.

[OXFORD, about *February* 10, 1555.]

O DEAR brother, seeing the time is now come wherein it pleaseth the heavenly Father, for Christ our Saviour his sake, to call upon you, and to bid you to come, happy are you that ever ye were born, thus to be awake at the Lord's calling. *Euge, serve bone et fidelis, quia super pauca fuisti fidelis, super multa te constituet, et intrabis in gaudium Domini:* ["Well done, good and faithful servant: because thou hast been faithful over a few things, he will place thee over many things, and thou shalt enter into the joy of thy Lord."]

Bp Coverdale, Letters of the Martyrs, 1564, p. 68.

[Matt. xxv. 21.]

O dear brother, what meaneth this, that you are sent into your own native country? The wisdom and policy of the world may mean what they will: but I trust, God will so order the matter finally by his fatherly providence, that some great occasion of God's gracious goodness shall be plenteously poured abroad amongst his, our dear brethren in that country, by this your martyrdom. Where the martyrs for Christ's sake shed their blood and lost their lives, O what wondrous things hath Christ afterward wrought to his glory and confirmation of their doctrine! If it be not the place that sanctifieth the man, but the holy man doth by Christ sanctify the place, brother Bradford, then happy and holy shall be that place wherein thou shalt suffer, and shall be with thy ashes in Christ's cause sprinkled over withal. All thy country may rejoice of thee, that ever it brought forth such a one, which would render his life again in his cause of whom he had received it.

Brother Bradford, so long as I shall understand that thou art in thy journey, by God's grace I shall call upon our heavenly Father, for Christ's sake, to set thee safely home: and then, good brother, speak you and pray for the remnant that are for to suffer

[6 This paragraph now is first printed.]

[7 The words, "I had no paper," at once receive explanation on inspecting Bp Ridley's autograph in the Emmanuel Library, Cambridge, as Ridley's letter was written, in the absence of other paper, on the reverse of that addressed to him by Bernhere, which is Letter XXIV., p. 381, in Works of Bp Ridley, Park. Soc.]

for Christ's sake, according to that thou then shalt know more clearly.

We do look now every day when we shall be called on, blessed be God! I ween, I am the weakest many ways of our company; and yet I thank our Lord God and heavenly Father by Christ, that, since I heard of our dear brother Rogers' departing and stout confession of Christ and his truth even unto the death, my heart—blessed be God!—so rejoiced of it, that since that time, I say, I never felt any lumpish heaviness in my heart, as I grant I have felt sometimes before.

O good brother, blessed be God in thee, and blessed be the time that ever I knew thee! Farewell, farewell.

Your brother in Christ, N. R.

Brother, farewell.

LXXX. TO HART, COLE, SHETERDEN AND OTHERS[1].

[*February* 16, 1555.]

Bp Coverdale, Letters of the Martyrs, 1564, p. 470.

MS. 1. 2. 8. No. 34. Transcript. Emman. Coll. Cambridge.

To his dearly beloved in the Lord, Henry Hart, John Barr, John Lidley, Robert Cole, Nicholas Sheterden, Richard Prowde[2], William Porrege[3], Roger[4] Newman, William Lawrence, John Gibson, Richard Porrege, Humphrey Middleton[4], William[4] Kemp, and to all other that fear the Lord and love his truth, abiding in Kent, Essex, Sussex and thereabout, John Bradford, a most unworthy servant of the Lord, now in bonds and excommunicate, yea, condemned to be burned for the testimony of Christ Jesus, wisheth[5] "grace, mercy and peace," with increase

[[1] The original of this letter in Bradford's autograph is in the possession of Dawson Turner, Esq. See p. 169, note 5, above. Its inscription in Bp Coverdale is: "To certain men, not rightly persuaded in the most true, comfortable, and necessary doctrine of God's holy election and predestination."]

[[2] The name, "Richard Prowde," which does not occur in the Emmanuel MS., is printed here from Bradford's autograph. That name is mentioned at the beginning of Letter XLI. above.]

[[3] See p. 38, note 1, above.]

[[4] The names "Roger," "Middleton," "William," severally do not occur in the autograph MS., blanks being left for the names "Roger," "William," which it evidently was the intention of Bradford to fill up.]

[[5] The last nine lines, from the commencement of this letter, "To his dearly beloved......of Christ Jesus wisheth," now are first printed from the Emmanuel MS.; where those lines, in common with any other words in the MS. that are not

of all godly knowledge and living, from God the eternal "Father of all consolation," through the bloody death of our alone and full Redeemer Jesus Christ, by the mighty and lively working and power of the Holy Spirit the Comforter, now[6] and for ever. Amen.

Although I look hourly for officers to come and have me to execution, yet can I not but attempt to write something unto you, my dearly beloved (as always you have been, howsoever you have taken me), to occasion you the more to weigh the things wherein some controversy hath been amongst us, especially the article and doctrine of predestination, whereof I have written a little Treatise[7], and direct it to our dear and godly sister, Joyce Hales[8], therein, as briefly shewing my faith, so answering the "enormities" gathered of some to slander the said necessary and comfortable doctrine. That little piece of work I commend unto you, as a thing whereof I doubt not to answer to my comfort before the tribunal-seat of Jesus Christ: and therefore I heartily pray you and every of you, for the tender mercies of God in Christ, that you would not be rash to condemn things unknown, lest God's woe should fall upon you, for "calling good evil, and evil good." For the great love of God in Christ, cavil not at things that be well spoken, nor construe not things to the evil part, when ye have occasion otherwise. Do not suppose that any man by affirming predestination (as in that book I have truly set it forth according to God's word and the consent of Christ's church), either to seek carnality, or to set forth matter of desperation. Only by the doctrine of it I have sought[9], as to myself, so to others, a certainty of salvation, a setting up of Christ only, an exaltation of God's grace, mercy, righteousness, truth, wisdom, power and glory, and a casting down of man and all his power; "that he that glorieth may glory only" and altogether and continually "in the Lord."

given in the "Letters of the Martyrs," 1564, are scored across, evidently to direct the printer of that work, who in all probability used, as copy, the Emmanuel transcript.]

[6 "I wish unto you now," 1564: "now," MS.]

[7 This was the "Defence of Election," all the parts of which were first brought together in one publication in Vol. I. pp. 307—30. Its second part, pp. 318—30, "answering the enormities," was first printed by the late Abp Laurence, in "Authentic Documents" on predestination, Oxford, 1819.]

[8 The last eleven words now are first printed.]

[9 "taught," 1564: "sought," MS.]

Man consisteth in two parts, the soul and the body: and every "man of God" hath, as a man would say, two men, an outward or "old man," and an inward or "new man." The devil's drift is to bring the one into a carnality, and the other into a doubt, and so to despair and hatred of God. But God for remedy hereof hath ordained his word, which is divided into two parts: the one is a doctrine which demandeth of us our duty, but giveth no power thereto; the other is a doctrine which not so much demandeth as giveth. The former is called the law, which hath its promises, conditionals, and comminations or threats accordingly: the other is called the gospel, or rather the free promises, hanging not on conditions on our behalf, but simply on God's verity and mercy, although they require conditions, but not as hanging thereon; of which promises the gospel may well be called a publication. The former, that is, the law, with her promises and comminations, tell man what he is, and shew him what he can do: the latter, that is, the gospel and free promises, tell and set forth Christ, and what mercy at God's hand, through Christ, we have offered and given unto us. The former part serveth to keep the "old man" from carnality and security, and to stir him up to diligence and solicitude: the latter part serveth how to keep the "new" and inward man from doubting and despair, and to bring us into an assured certainty and quietness with God through Christ.

The "old man" and the field he resteth in may not be sown with any other seed than is agreeable to the former doctrine: the "new man" and the field he resteth in may not be sown with any other than is agreeing to the latter doctrine. By this means man shall be kept from carnality, and from desperation also, and brought into diligence and godly peace of conscience.

It is forbidden in the old law to sow two kinds of seeds in one field, to wear linsey-woolsey petticoats, or to eat beasts that did not cleave the hoofs. God grant us to be wise husbandmen, to sow according as I have said; God grant us to be wise taylors, to cut our coats for two men of one whole cloth, as is declared; God grant us to be "clean beasts," to cleave the hoofs accordingly; that is, to give the "old man" meat meet for the mowers, that is, the law with his appurtenances, conditionals, promises and comminations, and to give to the "new man" the gospel and sweet free promises, as appertaineth. And then doubtless we

Deut. xxii. Deut. xiv.

shall walk in the right highway unto eternal life, that is, in Christ Jesu, "the end of the law" and the fulfilling of the promises, "in whom they be yea and amen."

If this my poor advice be observed, my dear brethren in the Lord, I doubt not but all controversies for predestination, original sin, free-will, &c., shall so cease that there shall be no breach of love nor suspicion amongst us: which God grant, for his mercies' sake. I am persuaded of you, that you fear the Lord; and therefore I love you and have loved you in him, my dear hearts, though otherwise you have taken it without cause on my part given, so far as I know: for hitherto I have not suffered any copy of the Treatise above specified to go abroad, because I would suppress all occasions, so far as might be.

Now am I going before you "to my God and your God, to my Father and your Father," to my Christ and your Christ, to my home and your home. I go before; but you shall come after, sooner or later. Howbeit I could not but, before I go, signify thus much unto you as I have done, that you might see my love, and thereby be occasioned to increase in love, and learn rather to bear than break.

My poor and most dear sister to me that ever I had, with whom I leave this letter, I commend unto you all and every of you, beseeching you and heartily praying you, in the bowels and blood of Jesus Christ, to care for her, as for one which is dear in God's sight, and one which loveth you all in God, and hath done, as I can and do bear her witness, although in the point of predestination it hath pleased God by my ministry to open unto her his truth: wherein as she is settled, and I trust in God confirmed, so, if you cannot think with her therein as she doth, I heartily pray you, and, as I can, in God's behalf charge you, that you molest her not, nor disquiet her, but let love abound, and therein contend who can go most before. I commend also unto you my good sister, Margery Coke[1], making for her the like suit unto you all.

Ah! dear hearts, be not faint-hearted for these evil days, which are come to try us and purify us, that we may the more "be partners of God's holiness," as to ourselves, so to the world we shall be better known. Continue to "walk in the fear of the

[[1] "M. C." 1564: "Margery Coke," MS.—Letter XXXVIII., p.100, above, is addressed by Bradford to this lady.]

Lord," as ye have well begun. "Keep yourselves pure," as I hope you do, from this rotten Romish, yea, antichristian religion. Reverently read God's word, thereto joining prayer, that, as you hear in reading God speak unto you, so in praying you may speak unto him. Labour after your callings to help others. As you have done, do still; and I pray God give you grace to continue, as I doubt not but he will, for his goodness' sake. At the length we shall meet together in Christ's kingdom, and there never part asunder, but praise the name of our good God and Father, with the patriarchs, prophets, apostles, angels, archangels, and all the saints of God.

O joyful place; O place of all places desired! My brethren, I think myself more happy than you, by how much I am now more near unto it. Elias' chariot I hourly look for to come and catch me up. My cloak, that is, my carcass, I shall leave behind me in ashes; which I doubt not my Lord will raise up and restore to me again in the last day, glorified even "like unto his own most glorious body." The portion of the good Spirit which my Father hath lent me I wish, yea, double and treble unto you all. "God the Father of mercy," in the blood of his Christ, give to every of you, my dear hearts, in him his blessing, and pour plentifully upon you his holy Spirit, that you may increase in all godly knowledge and godliness, to your own comfort and the edification of many others. Amen.

Kings ii.

Yet once more I commend unto you my foresaid most dear and beloved sister in the Lord: who always be unto her a most loving Father, Spouse, and Pastor. Amen, Amen.

Out of prison, the 16th of February, 1554[—5].

Your own heart,

JOHN BRADFORD.

LXXXI. BP RIDLEY TO BRADFORD[1].

[OXFORD, probably toward the end of *February*, 1555.]

Bp Coverdale, Letters of the Martyrs, 1564, p. 65.

DEARLY beloved brother Bradford, I had thought of late that I had written unto you your last farewell[2] (until we should have met

[1 The original of this letter, in Bradford's autograph, is in the possession of Dawson Turner, Esq.: see p. 169, note 5, above.]

[2 See Letter LXXIX., above.]

in the kingdom of heaven) by our dear brother Austin: and I sent it to meet you in Lancashire; whither, it was said here, you were appointed to be sent to suffer. But now, sith they have changed their purpose, and prolonged your death, I understand it is no other thing than that once happened to Peter and Paul. The which, although they were of the first which were cast in prison, and as little shunned peril as any other did, yet God would not have them put to death with the first, because he had more service to be done by their ministry, which his gracious pleasure was they should do. So without doubt, dear brother, I am persuaded that the same is the cause of the delay of your martyrdom.

Blessed be the Holy Trinity, the Father, the Son, and the Holy Ghost, for your threefold confession[3]. I have read all three with great comfort and joy, and thanksgiving unto God for his manifold gifts of grace, wherewith it is manifest to the godly reader that God did assist you mightily. And blessed be God again and again! which gave you so good a mind and remembrance of your oath once made against the bishop of Rome[4], lest you should be partaker of the common perjury which all men almost are now fallen into, in bringing in again that wicked usurped power of his. Which oath was made according to the prophet, "in judgment, in righteousness, and in truth," and therefore cannot without perjury be revoked, let Satan roar and rage, and practise all the cruelty he can. Jer. iv.

O good Lord, that they are so busy with you about the church! It is no new thing, brother, that is happened unto you; for that was always the clamour of the wicked bishops and priests against God's true prophets: "The temple of the Lord, the temple of the Lord, the temple of the Lord!" and they said, "The law shall not depart from the priest, nor wisdom from the elder:" and yet in them whom they only esteemed for their priests and sages there was neither God's law nor godly wisdom. [Jer. vii. 4. xviii. 18.] Ezek. vii. [26.]

It is a marvellous thing to hear what vain communication is spread abroad of you. It is said here that you be pardoned your life; and, when you were appointed to be banished and to go (I cannot tell whither), you should say that you had rather here suffer than go where you could not live after your conscience; and that this pardon should be begged for you by Bourne, the bishop of Bath, for that you saved his life[5]. Again some say, and amongst other mine hostess reported, that you are highly promoted and are

[3 Bradford's Three Examinations. See Vol. I. pp. 465—92.]

[4 See Vol. I. pp. 468, 9, and pp. 475—80, pp. 483—85.]

[5 See Vol. I. p. 485; and Foxe, Acts, &c., ed. 1583, pp. 1497, 1604, or ed. 1843—9, Vols. VI. p. 392, VII. p. 144.]

a great man with my lord chancellor. This I could not believe, but did deny it as a false lie, so surely was I always persuaded of your constancy.

What God will do with us, he knoweth. In the mean time wonderful it is to behold how the wisdom of God hath infatuated the policy of the world, and scattered the crafty devices of the worldly-wise. For, when the state of religion was once altered, and persecution began to wax hot, no man doubted but Cranmer, Latimer and Ridley should have been the first to have been called to the stake. But the subtle policy of the world, setting us apart, first assaulted them by whose infirmity they thought to have more advantage: but God disappointed their subtle purpose. For whom the world esteemed weakest—praised be God!—they have found most strong, sound and valiant in Christ's cause unto the death; to give such an onset as, I dare say, all the angels in heaven do no less rejoice to behold in them, than they did in the victorious con-
John xv. stancy of Peter, Paul, Esay, Elias or Jeremy: for "greater love no man hath than to bestow his life." &c.

Good brother, have me and us all continually in your remembrance to God in your prayers; as, God willing, we shall not be in our prayers forgetful of you.

Your own in Christ,

N. R.

LXXXII. TO A LADY[1].

[*March* 2, 1555.]

Bp Coverdale, Letters of the Martyrs, 1564, p. 401.

Foxe, Acts, &c., ed. 1570, p. 1829; and after editions.

I BESEECH almighty God, our heavenly Father, to be merciful unto us, and to increase in you, my good sister, the knowledge and love of his truth, and at this present give me grace so to write to you something of the same, as may make to his glory, and our own comfort and confirmation in him, through Christ our Lord. Amen.

Whether you may come with safe conscience to the church now, that is, to the service used commonly in part, as at matins or at evensong, or no, is your desire to have me to write something, for your further stay. My dearly beloved, although your benefits towards me might perchance make you

[[1] The inscription in Bp Coverdale and Foxe is: "To a woman that desired to know his mind whether she, refraining from the mass, might be present at the popish matins or no."]

to think, that in respect thereof I would bear with that which else were not to be borne withal, yet by God's grace I am purposed simply, and without all such respect in this matter, to speak to you the truth according to my conscience, as I may be able to stand unto, when I shall come before the Lord.

First therefore go about to learn perfectly the first lesson to be learned of all that profess Christ, that is, to "deny yourself," and in nothing to seek yourself. Secondly learn after this to begin at the next lesson to it, which is to seek God in all things you do and leave undone. Thirdly, know that then you seek God, when in his service you follow his word and not man's fantasies, custom, multitude, &c., and when with your brother you follow the rule of charity, that is, to do as you would be done by. In these is a sum of all the counsel I can give you, if that hereto I admonish you of the service now used, which is not according to God's word, but rather against God's word, directly and in manner wholly. So that your going to the service is a declaration that you have not learned the first lesson, nor never can learn it so long as you go thither: therefore the second lesson you shall utterly lose, if you cease not the seeking yourself, that is, if for company, custom, father or friend, life or goods, you seem to allow that which God disalloweth. And this that you the better may perceive, I purpose by God's grace briefly to shew.

First the matins and evensong is in a tongue forbidden publicly to be used in the congregation, that perceiveth not the tongue. Read how Paul affirmeth it, to "pray in an unknown tongue," to be against God's commandment. This one, I trow, were enough, if nothing else were: for how can God's glory be sought, where his word and commandment is wilfully broken? How can charity to man stand, when charity to God, which is obedience to his word, is overthrown? 1 Cor. xiv.

Again both in matins and in evensong, is idolatry maintained for God's service: for there is invocation and prayer made to saints departed this life, which robbeth God of that glory which he will give to none other.

Moreover this service and the setters forth of it condemneth the English service as heresy; thereby falling into

Isai. v. God's curse, which is threatened to all such as "call good evil and evil good;" whereof they shall be partakers, that do communicate with them. Besides this this Latin service is a plain mark of antichrist's catholic synagogue; so that the communicants and approvers of it thereby declare themselves to be members of the same synagogue, and so cut off from Christ and his church; whose exterior mark is the true administration of God's word and sacraments[1].

Furthermore the example of your going thither to allow the religion of antichrist (as doubtless you do in deed, howsoever in heart you think) occasioneth the obstinate to be utterly intractable, the weak papists to be more obstinate, the strong gospellers to be sore weakened, and the weak gospellers to be utterly overthrown: which things, how great offence they be, no pen is able to utter by letters.

All these evils you shall be guilty of, that company with those in religion exteriorly, from whom you are admonished to flee. If Christ be Christ, follow him: "gather with him," lest you "scatter abroad:" serve God, not only in spirit, but also in body. Make not your body, now a member of Christ, a member of antichrist. "Come out from amongst them," saith the Lord, and "touch no unclean thing." Confess Christ and his truth, not only in heart, but also in tongue, yea, in very deed, which few gospellers do. Indeed they deny him, and therefore had need to tremble, lest that Christ will deny them in the last day: the which day if it were set before our eyes often, then would the pleasures and treasures of this world be but trifles.

Therefore, good sister, often have it before your eyes, daily set yourself and your doings as before the judgment-seat of Christ now, that hereafter you be not called into judgment. Think that it will little "profit you to win the whole world, and to lose your own soul." Mark Christ's lessons well: "He that will save his life shall lose it." The Father from heaven commandeth you to hear Christ, and he saith, "Follow me:" this can you not do and follow idolatry or idolaters. "Flee from such," saith the scripture. This God grant to you, to me, and to all God's children. Amen.

[[1] See Article XIX. "Of the church," and second part of the Homily for Whitsunday, Church of England.]

Thus in haste I have accomplished your request. God grant that, as you have done me much good bodily, so this may be a little mean to do you some good spiritually. Amen.

If time would serve, I would have written more at large.

The 2nd of March, *anno* 1555.

LXXXIII. TO MISTRESS JOYCE HALES[2].

[*March* 14, 1555.]

JESUS IMMANUEL.

MS. 2. 2. 15. No. 35. Original, Holograph. Emman. Coll. Cambridge.

ALMIGHTY God, our heavenly Father, bless you and be with you, my good sister, now and for ever.

I am sorry to hear that your cross increaseth that way—I mean it of the man's behalf you brought unto me once, you know when: on whose behalf I would have thought that it would have decreased, as well for that he heard spoken of me and others, being once, as you have taken him, well-minded to the truth, as also for the singular love he, I hope yet, beareth unto you. Perchance you may be moved the rather, by reason of him, to be more faint-hearted to the truth and to the confession of it, in that also I hear how that you are something straitly handled for reading books, speaking with good men, yea, praying to God, as you would do. By all these, it is not to be marvelled, if your enemy seek to supplant you, either by waxing more cold in your purposed mind to God's truth (which God forbid), either in love to him whom you ought next under Christ to love. Therefore, when I heard of this, I could not but purpose as I could to go about something to send my help to you, whereto you even enforced me by the corporal commodity I received from you by this bringer. God for his mercies' sake use this which I write to you, a means whereby it may please him to work in you some spiritual aid and consolation. Amen.

My dear sister, forget not your profession made in baptism, which Christ requireth of all that will be his disciples, namely to "deny yourself and take up your cross:" which cross you

[[2] This letter now is first printed.
The inscription "to Mistress Joyce Hales" (see p. 108, note 1, above) is given from internal evidence, the original not having any title.]

ought so much the rather to bear, by how much it is not yours only, but Christ's also, as you were taught tofore you learned your A, B, C[1]. Remember that you are called into Christ's company; which, if you leave not here, assuredly you shall enjoy also elsewhere. Have in mind that you, as all "the elect of God," must be like in this life unto the image of Christ, "the elect and chief corner-stone" of God in his holy building: which thing you are not but by the mason-work of God, hacking and hewing from you by the cross the knobs and crooked corners, that you, "as a lively stone," might have your proportioned place in the same building, to God's eternal glory and your own everlasting joy. Though the stones which are hewn of masons to build a king's palace, if they were sensible, might complain in respect of that they suffer whiles they be a hewing, yet, in respect of the place they should serve in, they could not but rejoice. So, my dearly beloved, though it be something painful to feel God's mason-work, considering what you feel, yet, if you cast out your hope on that which you believe—and, if the Hewer all-to commenceth, God is now enforming[2] you—surely it cannot but suppress the other much, if that your faith be much. If that it be little, pray God to increase it, and strive continually to come from sense and feeling to belief and hoping; which, as it will swage something the present taste of the cross, so will it encourage you to contemn the same. And this counsel the apostle doth set forth unto us in the example of Christ, whom we ought to follow: He set beside him, saith he, "the joy, and contemned the shame;" as before him did Moses, another captain worthy to be followed, which having respect to the reward was more moved with courage to carry the cross: for, as the apostle saith, we may in no case suppose that "the afflictions of this present life may be compared in anything to the glory that shall be revealed."

O that our eyes were opened to see, or our ears opened to hear, or our hearts prepared to conceive, some little piece of the great glory God hath laid up for us that suffer any trouble for his sake! Surely, dear sister, then would we run in the scent of the sweet smell of the same: God our Father (as the spouse

[[1] See Vol. I. p. 264, note 1.]
[[2] "Enforming" or "informing:" forming, fashioning, shaping.]

in the Canticles writeth) "draw us," that we may "run after the sweet smell of his ointments." Read the eleventh to the Hebrews. How many examples you have there to occasion you the better to come from feeling presently, to the believing of that which afterwards you shall enjoy! If they before Christ's coming were so ready, doubtless it cannot but be a shame, to whom the accomplishing of the promises are so nigh, if where they were we run not apace. The nearer the hound hunting is to his game, the greater is his desire, the fresher is the scent, and the more earnestly doth he pursue. My dear friend, so shall it be unto us if so be our hounds now proceed, through heart expectance, that our nose and faith might have the more scent. God increase in us both—I mean repentance and faith.

Then doubtless, the greater crosses, the greater comforts we shall feel: and, the more sharp and heavy they be, the more like we shall be unto Christ in this life, and so in eternal life: as now, good sister, methinks your crosses are very like to Christ's, not only for the cause, but also for the party putting you to most pain, which should most ease the same. Doubtless God goeth about to try your obedience, whether you love the man for his sake or for your own. By this cross you shall better know it. If now, he being even your greatest enemy, your godly love continue, then of truth you have loved as ye should have loved; but, if it abate in respect of being your enemy, surely then it hath not been so well as it should have been[3]. I would wish displeasure to increase in you towards his evils, but more love towards his person, till you perceive him fallen an enemy unto God rather than to you. The cause in him is the "love of this world:" the cause thereof is the want of the love of the world to come. Pray therefore, good sister, for the feeling thereof; and this world's things will the less molest us.

The Lord God our Father help us, and you especially, with his grace to know and see the hope whither he hath called you through Jesus Christ our Lord. I hope God will do [so] by this your cross, wherethrough as sorrow increaseth

[[3] The following words of the original, occurring here, are scored across apparently by Bradford: "Indeed, if love be left in respect that he is God's enemy, except you saw something more."]

so shall joy; howbeit, so that this must follow, the other must go before. As summer doth follow winter, and not winter again, and winter doth follow summer, and not summer again, so sorrow in this life followeth joy eternal, and temporal joy eternal sorrow. Adam came not from paradise to paradise, but from paradise to a wilderness in comparison. So we may not think to find this world as a paradise, and to have the paradise of heaven after: but rather with the Israelites let us take this life as a wilderness, that we may with Josue and Caleb enter into paradise and the land of rest, whereinto Christ entered after his passions: whose footsteps we must follow, and not think scorn of them. God grant us so to do for his mercy's sake. Amen.

If time would have suffered, I would have written more at large; but I look hourly for the butcher, and therefore I may less attend to do as else I would. God, our good God and Father, which in his Christ hath chosen us before all times to be his everlasting saints and children, have mercy upon us, and so preserve us from all evil for evermore, to glorify his holy name, as instruments of his grace continually. Amen.

Use hearty prayer, and thereto as you may daily reading of the holy scriptures: wherein God grant you more and more to delight, and in the life of the same. Amen.

This 14th of March[1].

Your afflicted brother ready to be offered even when the Lord will,

J. B.

LXXXIV. BP RIDLEY TO BRADFORD[2].

[OXFORD, probably about the end of *March*, 1555.]

The Latin Original of this letter is MS. 2. 2. 15. No. 51. Holograph. Emman. Coll. Cambridge.

WHY, my dearest brother, do you endeavour to make out of a fly an elephant? Dismiss, I pray you, such trifling: for by

[1 The date 1555 is written on the top margin of the first page of the MS., but not in Bradford's writing.]

[2 This Letter is translated from the Latin of Bp Ridley, which has been printed in the Supplement of R's. Works, pp. 537, 8, Park. Soc. If the "two treatises written in English," mentioned in the third paragraph, are, as would seem likely, the same as the "two small treatises" on the subject of Bp Gardiner's attempted confutation of Abp Cranmer, on the eucharist, alluded to in the close of Letter LXIII., p. 173, above, then the date of this letter would certainly be after January 19, 1555.]

writing in this manner you assuredly stop my mouth, so that I can neither venture freely to acknowledge your goodness to me and to my brother, nor to thank you, lest I should seem either to acknowledge what you write, being cajoled by your error, or to afford you any opportunity, of whatever kind, for erring in time to come.

Omitting therefore all worldly flatteries of this nature, let us labour diligently, my brother, each according to his utmost power, in striving to uphold the faith. Very great thanks do I render to God, through our Lord Jesus Christ, who hath suggested this to your mind, that, what I long and earnestly prayed God might give me, you now yourself, of your own accord, come forward and offer me—nay, you do with most vehement entreaty demand of me—that is, the labour of transcribing my small treatises, such as they are, on the subject of defending our Christian faith: and you ask me to be willing to impart them to you; and by this, in which you exceedingly gratify me, you say that I shall bind you to me with a closer tie. Therefore, brother, I will readily impart to you whatever I have: and a few I do possess, some written in Latin, and some in English, but all to defend that purity of our Christian religion, which Satan is now endeavouring with such numerous and very powerful means utterly to overthrow and ruin.

I here send you two treatises written in English[3], one in a small bound book, and the other in sheets not yet bound together. But, that the copyist may not mistake, either in reading or copying out the small bound book, know that the introduction to that treatise is contained in fourteen pages, and that the annotations from Augustine which precede ought now to be put back into their own place next after Jerome[4].

I also send you here another hortatory letter, written in Latin to the brethren who are embracing Christ with the cross. Lastly I send you also those two discourses which Watson delivered at court before the queen, last year during Lent[5]; in which he ap-

[3 See last note.]

[4 The words of Ridley's original Latin, which being in contracted writing, were printed inaccurately and in italic type, p. 538, Suppl. to Works of R., Park. Soc., are: "ex Augustino debere reponi jam in suo loco proxime post Hieronymum."]

[5 Dr Thomas Watson, master of St John's Coll., Cambr., and after Bp of Lincoln, preached before queen Mary, the third and fifth Fridays in Lent, 1554, "who gave himself this task, to prove the real presence in the sacrament, and that the mass was the sacrifice of the New Testament." His sermons were printed shortly afterwards, and, being highly esteemed by the Romanists, were replied to, in 1569, by Robert Crowley, minister of Cripplegate, London. Vide Strype, Ecc.

pears to have exceedingly laboured, being a man of acute parts, to impose[1] upon the simple and delude the inexperienced, lest they should acknowledge the truth—yea, that they might embrace for light darkness, and for truth error. Now I send these to you, with my annotations, but not without a clue, which I know will easily appear to you in reading.

Now, brother, since I have, not without some labour, to the end that these writings may be of use to myself, and if possible may benefit others, collected and reduced them to order, such as they are—but how soon I shall need them I feel to be altogether[2] uncertain—I therefore pray that, as soon as you conveniently are able, if it be your wish to transcribe, you write out and return me my originals: and then you shall have whatever are still with me, should you entertain the desire of reading or transcribing them.

If I dared to send anything to my brother[3], who is now spending weary days, I think by himself, in prison, I should freely wish that he might transcribe something. But I greatly fear lest they should at length surprise him unawares, and thence take occasion for additional violence upon him. I pray you, desire him to be of good courage: for, if the rumour which they are now circulating concerning Grimbold be true, I certainly[4] grieve much for Grimbold's sake, but I know that it matters not, in ever so slight a degree, to my brother's case.

Farewell, most dear brother in the Lord.

LXXXV. TO DR HILL[5].

Bp Coverdale, Letters of the Martyrs, 1564, p. 294.

Foxe, Acts, &c., ed. 1570, p. 1822; and after editions.

MS. 2. 2. 15. No. 106. Transcript. Emman. Coll. Cambridge.

To my very friend in the Lord, Doctor Hill, physician. "The God of mercy and Father of all comfort," at this present and for ever, engraft in your heart the sense of his

Mem. Vol. III. part I. pp. 113—21, where many extracts from Watson's Sermons are given; and Herbert, Typogr. Antiq. Vol. II. pp. 791, 944, 5.]

[1 The original Latin is not "fraudem facere," as in Suppl., as above, but the equivalent, "fucum facere."]

[2 The word "omnino," before "incertum habeo," is omitted in Suppl., as above.]

[3 George Shiphead or Shipside. See pp. 168, 172, 4, 193, above; Ridley's life of Bp Ridley, p. 557; Letter XI. in Works of Bp Ridley, p. 361, Park. Soc.]

[4 The word before "Grimbaldi causa," indicated in Suppl. by two asterisks is "certe." See p. 168, note 3, above, on Grimbold.]

[5 The Emmanuel MS. has the following, written over the letter and scored across: "A godly letter sent by Master John Bradford, prisoner in the Counter in

mercy in Christ, and the continuance of his consolation, which cannot but enable you to carry with joy whatsoever cross he shall lay upon you. Amen.

Hitherto I could have no such liberty as to write unto you, as I think you know. But now in that, through God's providence, I have no such restraint, I cannot but something write, as well to purge me of the suspicion of unthankfulness towards you, as also to signify my carefulness for you in these perilous days, lest you should wax cold in God's cause—which God forbid!—or suffer the light of the Lord, once kindled in your heart, to be quenched, and so become as you were before, after the example of the world and of many others; which would have been accounted otherwise in our days, and yet still beguile themselves, still would be so accounted, although by their outward life they declare the contrary, in that they think it enough to keep the heart pure, notwithstanding that the outward man doth curry favour[6]. In which doing, as they deny God to be jealous—and therefore requireth he the whole man, as well body as soul, being both create, as to immortality and society with him, so redeemed by the blood of Jesus Christ, and now sanctified by the Holy Spirit to be the temple of God and member of his Son—as, I say, by their parting stake, to give God the heart, and the world the body, they deny God to be jealous—for else they would give him both, as the wife will do to her husband, whether he be jealous or no, if she be honest—so they play the dissemblers with the church of God, by their fact offending the godly, whom either they provoke to fall with them, or make more careless and conscienceless, if they be fallen; and so[7] occasioning the wicked and obstinate to triumph against God, and the more vehemently to prosecute their malice against such as will not defile themselves in body or soul with the Romish rags, now revived amongst us.

the Poultry in London, unto Master Doctor Hill, physician and his very friend, *in anno Domini*, 1555."]

Dr Albayn Hill was "much beloved and admired by all learned men, especially by Dr John Cay and Dr Joh. Fryer, two eminent physicians of Cambridge," and was said to be "in omni literarum genere maxime versatus." He died, December 26, 1559, and was buried in the church of St Alban's, Wood-street, London. Alice, his widow, died May 1580.—Wood's Athenæ Oxon., ed. Bliss, Vol. I. col. 308, and Vol. II. col. 174.]

[6 Alluding to those who attended, though disapproving, the Romish services.]

[7 "so," MS.: not in 1564 or 1570.]

Because of this—I mean, lest you, my dear master and brother in the Lord, should do as many of our gospellers, or
Isai. ii. rather gospel-spillers do, for fear of "man, whose breath is in his nostrils," and hath power but of the body, not fearing the Lord, which hath power both of soul and body, and that not only temporally but also eternally—I could not but write something unto you, as well because duty deserveth it, for many benefits I have received of God by your hands (for the which he reward you, for I cannot), as also because charity and love compelleth me. Not that I think you have any need: for, as I may rather learn of you, so I doubt not but you have hitherto kept yourself upright from halting; but that I might both quiet my conscience, calling upon me hereabout, and signify unto you by something my carefulness for your soul, as painfully and often you have done for my body.

Therefore, I pray you, call to mind, that there be but "two masters," two kinds of people, two ways, and two mansion-places. The masters be Christ and Satan; the people be servitors to either of these; the ways be strait and wide; the mansions be heaven and hell. Again consider that this world is the place of trial of God's people and the devil's servants: for, as the one will follow his master, whatsoever cometh of it, so will the other. For a time it is hard to discern who pertaineth to God, and who to the devil; as in the calm and peace, who is a good shipman and warrior, and who is not. But—as when the storm ariseth the expert mariner is known—as in war the good soldier is seen—so in affliction and the cross easily God's children are known from Satan's servants. For then, as the good servant will follow his master, so will the godly follow their captain, come what come will: whereas the wicked and hypocrites will bid adieu, and desire less of Christ's acquaintance. For which cause the cross is called a probation and a trial, because it trieth who will go with God, and who will forsake him; as now in England we see how small a company Christ hath, in comparison of Satan's soldiers. Let no man deceive himself, for "he that gathereth not with Christ scattereth abroad." "No man can serve two masters;" the Lord abhorreth double hearts; the "luke-warm," that is, such as
[1 Kings xviii. 21. Septuag.] are both "hot and cold, he spitteth out of his mouth." None that "halt on both knees" doth God take for his servants.

The way of Christ is "the strait way," and so strait that, as few find it and few walk in it, so no man can halt in it, but needs must go upright; for, as the straitness will suffer no reeling to this side or that side, so, if any man halt, he is like to fall off the bridge into the pit of eternal perdition.

Strive therefore, good Master Doctor, now you have found it, to enter into it. And, if you should be called or pulled back, look not on this side or that side, or behind you as Lot's wife did, but straightforwards on the end: which set before you, though it be to come, as even now present; like as you do, and will your patients to do, in purgations and other your ministrations, to consider the effect that will ensue; wherethrough the bitterness and loathsomeness of the purgation is so overcome, and the painfulness in abiding the working of that is ministered is so eased, that it maketh the patient willingly and joyfully to receive that is to be received, although it be never so unpleasant. So, I say, set before you the end of this "strait way;" and then, doubtless, as Paul saith, *æternum pondus gloriæ pariet*, ["it will bring forth an eternal weight of glory,] whilst you look not on the thing seen, for that is temporal, but on the thing which is not seen, which is eternal."

So doth the husbandman, in ploughing and tilling, set before him the harvest-time; so doth the fisher consider the draught of his net, rather than the casting in; so doth the merchant the return of his merchandise. And so should we, in these stormy days, set before us, not the loss of our goods, liberty and very life, but the reaping time, the coming of our Saviour Christ to judgment, the fire that shall burn the wicked and disobedient to God's gospel, the blast of the trump, the exceeding glory prepared for us in heaven eternally, such as "the eye hath not seen, the ear hath not heard, nor the heart of man can conceive."

The more we lose here, the greater joy shall we have there; the more we suffer, the greater triumph. For corruptible dross we shall find incorruptible treasures; for coals we shall have carbuncles[1], for gold glory, for silver solace without end, for

[[1] "Carbuncle:" a precious stone, in colour like a burning coal: it was erroneously supposed formerly to be self-luminous. The words, "for coals we shall have carbuncles," only occur in the MS., where they are scored across.]

riches robes royal, for earthly houses eternal palaces, mirth without measure, pleasure without pain, felicity endless. *Summa* we shall have God the Father, the Son, and the Holy Ghost.

O happy place! O that this day would come! Then shall the end of the wicked be lamentable, then shall they receive the just reward of God's vengeance, then shall they cry, Woe, woe, that ever they did as they have done! Read Wisdom ii, iii, iv, v; read Matthew xxv; read 1 Corinthians xv, 2 Corinthians v; and by faith (which God increase in us) consider the things there set forth. And for your comfort read Hebrews xi, to see what faith hath done; always considering the way to heaven to be "by many tribulations," and that "all they which will live godly in Christ Jesu must suffer persecution."

You know that this is our alphabet[1]: "He that will be my disciple," saith Christ, "must deny himself, and take up his cross and follow me"—not this bishop nor that doctor, not this emperor nor that king, but "me," saith Christ; for "he that loveth father, mother, wife, children or very life better than me,
Matt. viii. is not worthy of me." Remember that the same Lord saith, "He that will save his life shall lose it." Comfort yourself with this, that, as the devils had no power over the porkets, or over Job's goods, without God's leave, so shall they have none over you. Remember also that "all the hairs of your head are numbered" with God. The devil may make one believe he will drown him, as the sea in his surges threateneth to the land: but, as the Lord hath appointed bounds for the one, over the which he cannot pass, so hath he done to the other.

On God therefore cast your care, love him, serve him after his word, fear him, trust in him, hope at his hand for all help, and always pray, looking for the cross: and, whensoever it cometh, be assured the Lord, as "he is faithful, so he will never tempt you further than he will make you able to bear, but in the midst of the temptation will make such an evasion," as shall be most to his glory and your eternal comfort.

God, for his mercy in Christ, with his holy Spirit endue you, comfort you, under the wings of his mercy shadow you, and as his dear child guide you for evermore, with my good mistress your wife: whom with you and all your children and

[[1] See Vol. I. p. 264, note 1.]

family I commit to the tuition of our heavenly Father: to whom[2] I doubt not but you pray for me also; and so I beseech you to do still. Amen[3].

My brother Punt[4] telleth me, you would fain have the last part of St Hierome's works, to have the use thereof for a fortnight. I cannot for these three days well forbear it; but yet on Thursday next I will send it you, if God let me not: and use me and that I have, as your own. The Lord for his mercy in Christ direct our ways to his glory. Amen.

Out of prison by yours to command,

JOHN BRADFORD.

LXXXVI. BP RIDLEY TO BRADFORD.

[Oxford, probably about middle of *April*, 1555[5].]

Dearly beloved brother, blessed be God our heavenly Father for his manifold and innumerable mercies towards us! And blessed might he be, that hath spared us thus long together, that each one of us may bless his mercy and clemency in other unto this day, above the expectation and hope of any worldly appearance.

Bp Coverdale, Letters of the Martyrs, 1564, p. 63.

Whereas you write of the outrageous rule, that Satan our ghostly enemy beareth abroad in the world—whereby he stirreth and raiseth so pestilent and heinous heresies—as some to deny the blessed Trinity, some the Divinity of our Saviour Christ, some the Divinity of the Holy Ghost, some the baptism of infants, some original sin, and to be infected with the errors of the Pelagians, and to re-baptize those that have been baptized with Christ's baptism already—alas! sir, this doth declare this time and these days to be wicked indeed. But what can we look for else of Satan here and

[2 The last twenty-six words now are first printed from the Emmanuel MS., where they are scored across. The printed editions have instead the words: "To whose merciful tuition as I do with my hearty prayer commit you, so," which are written too on the margin of the MS.]

[3 "Amen," MS.: not in printed editions.]

[4 "P." 1564 and 1570: "Punt," MS.]

[5 The allusion, at the commencement, to being "spared above the expectation of any worldly appearance," indicates that this letter was written not only after the Act "for the punishment of heresy" was passed in Parliament, January 16, 1555, (see p. 167, note 1, above), but after Letters LXXIX. and LXXXI. of this series.]

of his ministers, but to do the worst that they can so far forth as God shall or will suffer them?

And now, methink, he is less to be marvelled at at this time, if he bestir him by all manner of means, that the truth indeed do take no place. For he seeth now—blessed be God!—that some go about in deed and in truth, not trifling, but with the loss of all that they are able to lose in this world, goods, lands, name, fame and life also, to set forth God's word and his truth—and by God's grace shall do, and abide in the same unto the end: now therefore it is time to bestir him I trow. And, as for the diversity of errors, what careth he though one be never so contrary to another? He reckoneth all, and so he may, to be his, whosoever prevail, so that truth prevail not.

Nevertheless, good brother, I suppose that the universal plague is most dangerous, which at this day is, alas! fostered and masterfully holden up by wit, worldly policy, multitude of people, power and all worldly means. As for other the devil's caltrops[1], that he casteth in our ways by some of his busy-headed younkers, I trust, they shall never be able to do the multitude so great harm. For, blessed be God! these heresies before time, when Satan by his servants hath been about to broach them, have by God's servants already been so sharply and truly confounded, that the multitude was never infected with them; or else, where they have been infected, they are healed again, that now the peril is not so great.

He meaneth here the matter of God's election, whereof he afterward wrote a godly and comfortable treatise, remaining yet in the hands of some, and hereafter shall come to light, if God so will[2].—[Bp Coverdale.]

And—where you say that, if your request had been heard, things, you think, had been in better case than they be—know you that, concerning the matter you mean, I have in Latin drawn out the places of the scriptures, and upon the same have noted what I can for the time. Sir, in those matters I am so fearful, that I dare not speak further, yea, almost none otherwise than the very text doth, as it were, lead me by the hand[2].

And where you exhort us to help, &c., O Lord, what is else in this world, that we now should list to do? I bless my Lord God, I never, as methinketh, had more nor better leisure to be occupied with my pen in such things as I can do, to set forth, when they may come to light, God's glory. And I bless my Lord God, through Jesus Christ, my heart and my work are therein occupied, not so fully and perfectly as I would, but yet so as I bless God for the same.

Farewell, dear brother: the messenger tarrieth, and I may not

[1 Instruments with spikes, formerly used in war, to wound horses' feet.]

[2 See p. 171, note 3, on Letter LXII. above, and also Letter LXXXIX.]

now be longer with you. The Lord, I trust verily, shall bring us thither, where we shall, each one with other in Christ our Saviour, rejoice and be merry everlastingly.

Your brother in Christ,

N. R.

LXXXVII. TO COLE.

To my good brother R[obert] Cole.

Bp Coverdale, Letters of the Martyrs, 1564, p. 411.

MS. 1. 2. 8. No. 49. Transcript. Emman. Coll. Cambridge.

Mine own good brother, our good and most merciful Father more and more embrace us in the arms of his mercy, as his loving and own natural children, and give us one to embrace another in the arms of love as true brethren, that with one heart and mind we may praise his holy name in Christ our Saviour, and through the grace of his Spirit may mightily every one fight against sin and all that is against the kingdom of Christ: whereunto, my beloved, we are called effectually to our everlasting felicity, I doubt not, praised be the name of our good God therefore for ever and ever. Amen.

Mine own heart in the Lord, desire our brethren that every one would bend himself to bow: let us never break. "Love suffereth long, and seeketh not herself." "We have all one Father," "we are all brethren." God keep us from dissension. If we cannot agree in all points, either the points perchance be not so necessary, or else by love we shall hereafter be brought to see that which yet is hid. If love may appear in all our doings, and that we seek one another with a simple and a single eye in God's sight, doubtless all prejudice, whereby we are letted to see manifest things, will be had away, and we will take things spoken and done in the best part; and so doubtless the name of our Father shall be sanctified in us and by us, as by instruments of grace, and God's kingdom shall increase apace in us and by us also: which thing he grant for his mercy's sake. Amen.

Commend me heartily, I pray you, to both those good women: 'good' I call them, because I am persuaded that God will deliver them, especially my good Mary[3]. I will not cease, but even as for myself to pray to God for them, and for you,

[[3] Probably Mary Marlar: see p. 181, note 7, above, on Letter LXX.]

my right dear brother in the Lord. If you were acquainted with Master Robert Harrington[1], you should find a plain Nathanael; you should see the worst at the first. I dare say for him, his only desire is to please God, and he is afraid to offend him. Pray for him, and for my good sister, J. H.[2], as I know she doth for you.

The peace of God be with you, mine own in the Lord.

JOHN BRADFORD.

LXXXVIII. TO HALL AND HIS WIFE[3].

[From the Compter in the Poultry, LONDON.]

Bp Coverdale, Letters of the Martyrs, 1564, p. 374.

Foxe, Acts, &c., ed. 1570, p. 1828; and after editions.

MS. 2. 2. 15. No. 2. Transcript. And No. 6. Transcript, in writing of Bernhere. And MS. 1. 2. 8. No. 72. Transcript. Emman. Coll. Cambridge.

To Master John Hall and his wife, prisoners in Newgate for the testimony of the gospel.

Almighty God, our heavenly Father through Jesus Christ, be with you both, my dearly beloved, as with his dear children for ever: and he so bless you with his holy Spirit, that you may in this your cross, for his cause doubtless, rejoice, and gladly take it up to bear it so long as he shall think good.

I have heard, my good brother and sister, how that God hath brought you both into his school-house (whereas you were both purposed, by his leave, to have played the truants), that thereby you might see his carefulness and love towards you. For, if it be a token of a loving and careful father for his children, to prevent the purpose and disappoint the intent of his children, purposing to depart awhile from the school, for fear of beating (which thing they would not do, if they did as much consider the commodity of learning, which there they might get), how should you take this work of the Lord, preventing your purpose, but as an evident sign of love and fatherly carefulness, that he beareth towards you? If he should have winked at your wills, then would you have escaped beating, I

[1 See p. 55, note 3, above.]

[2 Mistress Joyce Hales: see p. 108, note 1, above.]

[3 The heading of this letter in MS. 2. 2. 15. No. 2, is: "A godly letter sent by Master John Bradford, being prisoner in the Counter in the Poultry in London, unto a friend of his named Master Hall, and also to his wife, being then prisoners in Newgate, and of the company that was taken in Bow church-yard in London, upon New Year's Day, in *anno Domini*, 1555."]

mean the cross: but then should you have lost the commodity of learning, which your Father will now have you to learn and feel; and therefore hath he sent to you his cross. He, I say, hath brought you where you be: and, though your reason and wit will tell you, it is by chance or fortune or otherwise—yet, my dearly beloved, know for certain that, whatsoever was the mean, God your Father was the worker hereof, and that for your welfare, although otherwise your old Adam doth tell you, and you feel—yet, I say, of truth, that your duty is, to think of this cross, that, as it is of God's sending and cometh from him, so, although your deserts be otherwise, it is of love and fatherly affection, for your weal and commodity's sake.

What commodity is hereby? you will perchance object. You are now kept in close prison, you will say; your family and children be without good overseers; your substance diminisheth by those means; poverty will approach, and perchance more perils also, as loss of life, &c. These are no commodities, but rather[4] discommodities, and that no small ones: so that justly you would be glad to know what commodity can come to you by this cross, whereby cometh so great discommodities.

To these things I answer, that indeed it is true you say of your bodies, families, children, substance, poverty, life, &c.: which things if you would consider awhile with your inward eyes, as you behold them with outward, then perhaps you should find more ease. Do not you now, by the inward sense, perceive that you must part from all these and all other commodities in the world? Tell me then, have not you this commodity by your cross, to learn to loathe and leave the world, and to long for and desire another world, where is perpetuity? You ought, of your own head and free will, to have, according to your profession in baptism, forsaken the world and all earthly things, "using the world" as though you used it not, your heart only set upon your hoard in heaven, or else you could never be Christ's true disciples, that is, be saved, and be where he is. And trow you, my good hearts in the Lord, trow you, I say, that this is no commodity, by this cross to be compelled hereto, that you might assuredly enjoy with the Lord endless glory? How now doth God, as it were, fatherly pull you by the ears, to remember your former offences concerning these things and all other

[[4] "rather," MS. No. 6: not in printed editions.]

things, that repentance and remission might ensue? How doth God now compel you to call upon him, and to be earnest in prayer? Are these no commodities? Doth not the scripture say, that God doth correct us in the world, "because we shall not be damned with the world;" that "God chasteneth every one whom he loveth;" that the end of this correction shall be joy and holiness? Doth not the scripture say, that they are "happy that suffer for righteousness' sake," as you now do; that "the glory and Spirit of God is upon them;" that, as you are now made like unto Christ in suffering, so you shall be made like to him in reigning? Doth not the scripture say that you are now going the high and right way to heaven; that your suffering is Christ's suffering? My dearly beloved, what greater commodities than these can a godly heart desire?

Therefore ye are commanded to "rejoice and be glad" when ye suffer, as now ye do; for, through the goodness of God, "great shall be your reward." Where? Forsooth on earth, first for your children; for now they are in God's mere and immediate protection. Never was father so careful for his children, as God is for yours presently. God's blessing, which is more worth than all the world, you leave indeed to your children. Though all your providence for them should be pilled[1] away, yet God is not poor; he hath promised to provide for them most fatherly. "Cast thy burthen upon me," saith he, "and I will bear it." Do you therefore cast them and commend them unto God your Father, and doubt not that he will die in your debt. He never yet was found unfaithful, and he will not now begin with you. "The good man's seed shall not go a begging his bread;" for he "will shew mercy upon thousands" of the posterity of them that fear him. Therefore, as I said, God's reward first upon earth shall be felt by your children, even corporally: and so also upon you, if God see it more for your commodity; at the least inwardly you shall feel it by quietness and comfort of conscience. And secondly after this life you shall find it so plentifully, as "the eye hath not seen, the ear hath not heard, the heart cannot conceive," how great and glorious God's reward will be upon your bodies, much more upon your souls.

Psal. lv.

Psal. xxxvii.

God open our eyes to see and feel this indeed. Then shall

[[1] "Pilled:" plundered, robbed.—"Pilled," MSS.: "pulled," 1564 and 1570.]

we think the cross, which is a mean hereto, to be commodious. Then shall we thank God, that he would chastise us. Then shall we say with David, "Happy am I, that thou hast punished me; for before I went astray, but now I keep thy laws." This that we may do indeed, my dearly beloved, let us first know that our cross cometh from God; secondly, that it cometh from God as a Father, that is, to our weal and good. Therefore let us, thirdly, call to mind our sins, and ask pardon. Whereto let us, fourthly, look for help certainly at God's hand in his good time—help, I say, such as shall make most to God's glory, and to the comfort and commodity of our souls and bodies eternally. This if we certainly conceive, then will there issue out of us hearty thanksgiving, which God requireth as a most precious sacrifice. That we may all, through Christ, offer this, let us use earnest prayer to our God and dear Father; who bless us, keep us, and comfort us under his sweet cross for ever. Amen, Amen.

My dear hearts, if I could any way comfort you, you should be sure thereof, though my life lay thereon: but now I must do as I may, because I cannot as I would. O that it would please our dear Father shortly to bring us where we should never depart, but enjoy continually the blessed fruition of his heavenly presence! Pray, pray, that it may speedily come to pass, pray.

To-morrow I will send unto you to know your estate: send me word what are the chiefest things they charge you withal.

From the Compter, by your brother in the Lord,

JOHN BRADFORD.

LXXXIX. BP RIDLEY TO BRADFORD[1].

The Latin Original of this letter is, MS. 2. 2. 15. No. 52. Holograph. Emman. Coll. Cambridge.

THAT I have so long been silent toward you, has been caused by the rather arduous[2] labour of this my offspring which I now send you. And, although I have been a long time in travail, I nevertheless bring forth now, I acknowledge[3], a very rude thing, and shapeless, and needing much polish. Yet, because I know you to be certainly not a despiser of my labours (by which I desire, God is my witness, to benefit as many as possible, and to injure no man), I have therefore resolved to send it to you, whatever it is and such as it may be. The entire of it you now have power[4] thoroughly to know and look into: and, if you like to transcribe it, you have free power to do that likewise. Yet I shall not now send all the things which I have purposed to append to this Treatise: but, because all the passages of scripture, with which I have determined to strengthen this my Treatise, as with a wall and rampart, are not yet added, I have brought together [what I could] according to the best of my judgment. After I have completed it, I shall then read again what you have previously written, and will return you your book.

Concerning the small book you have given me the opportunity of reading, in which two writers, so much at variance, have been compared together, know that, as I am much delighted with the wit and eloquence of him that wrote it, so am I especially pleased indeed with this, that I perceive the writer of that small book to be zealous for true godliness, and to desire heartily the purity of God's word: which mind, I pray, God increase and preserve[5] in him for ever.

Farewell, most dear brother in the Lord.

You will find the index of our treatise appended to the end, fol. 47: and from its perusal you will easily see the principal point of the whole treatise, and of all the matters that are handled in it.

[1 This letter is translated from the Latin of Bp Ridley, which has been printed in the Supplement to R.'s Works, p. 539, Park. Soc. It would seem likely that the "Treatise," spoken of in the first paragraph, may be, Ridley's Treatise on election, referred to in Letter LXXXVI., p. 214, above—"I have in Latin drawn out the places of the scriptures, and upon the same have noted what I can for the time"—but which is not known now to exist. If so, the date of this letter would probably be after the middle of April, 1555, which is the supposed date of Letter LXXXVI.]

[2 The Latin is not "diffusior," as in Suppl. as above, but "difficior," probably for "difficilior."]

[3 The Latin is not "furor," as in Suppl., but "fateor."]

[4 The Latin is not "tibi licebit," but "bñ" (probably for "benigne") "licebit."]

[5 The Latin is not "confirmet," but "conservet."]

XC. TO RAWLINS[6] AND HIS WIFE.

Foxe, Acts, &c., ed. 1563 p. 1192; and after editions.

Bp Coverdale, Letters of the Martyrs, 1564, p. 314.

MS. 2. 2. 15. No. 103. Original, Holograph. And MS. 1. 2. 8. Nos. 32 and 44. Transcripts. Emman. Coll. Cambridge.

God, our dear and most merciful Father through Christ, be with you, my good brother and sister, as with his children for ever, and in all things so guide you with his holy Spirit, the Leader of his people, as may be to his glory, and your own everlasting joy and comfort in him. Amen.

Because I have oftentimes received from either of you comfort corporally, for the which I beseech the Lord, as to make me thankful, so to recompense you, both now and eternally, I cannot but go about—Lord help hereto for thy mercy's sake—to write something for your comfort spiritually.

My dearly beloved, look not upon these days and the afflictions of the same here with us, simply as they seem unto you, that is, as dismal days and days of God's vengeance, but rather as lucky days and days of God's fatherly kindness towards you and such as you be, that is, towards such as repent their sins and evil life past and earnestly purpose to amend, walking not after the will of the world and most part of men for the preservation of their pelf, which, will they nill they, they[7] shall leave sooner or later, and to whom, or how it shall be used, they know not. Indeed to such as walk in their wickedness, and wind on with the world, this time is a time of wrath and vengeance, and their beginning of sorrow is but now; because they contemn the physic of their Father, which by this purging time and cleansing days would work their weal, which they will not. And, because they will not have God's blessing, which both ways he hath offered unto them, by prosperity and adversity, therefore it shall be kept far enough from them: as, when the sick man will no kind of physic at the hands of the physician, he is left alone, and so the malady increaseth, and destroyeth him at the length. To such men indeed these days are and should be doleful days, days of woe and weeping, because their damnation draweth nigh. But unto such as be

[6 The initials, "E. R." are given in the title of this letter by Foxe, ed. 1563, and the name, "Erkinald Rawlins," by Foxe, ed. 1570, p. 1813, and after editions. Letter XXXVI. above, is addressed to Bradford by that person. The inscription of this letter in Bp Coverdale is: "To certain of his faithful friends in God, exhorting them to be joyful under the cross, as a token of God's singular favour towards them."]

[7 "they," 1564 and 1570: not in 1563.]

penitent, and are desirous to live after the Lord's will—among whom I do not only count you, but as far as man may judge I know ye are—unto such, I say, this time is and should be comfortable.

For first now your Father chastiseth you and me for our sins; for the which if he would have destroyed us, then would he have letten us alone and left us to ourselves, in nothing to take to heart his fatherly visitation, which here it pleaseth him to work presently, because elsewhere he will not remember our transgressions, as Paul writeth: He chastiseth us in the world,
1 Cor. xi. "lest with the world we should perish." Therefore, my dear hearts, call to mind your sins, to lament them, and to ask mercy for them in his sight; and withal undoubtedly believe to obtain pardon and assured forgiveness of the same, for twice the Lord punisheth not for one thing. So that, I say, first we have cause to rejoice for these days, because our Father suf-
[Rev. iii. 20—22.] fereth us not to lie in Jezebel's bed, sleeping in our sins and security, but as mindful on us doth correct us as his children: whereby we may be certain that we be no bastards, but children, for "he chastiseth every child whom he receiveth." So that they which are not partakers of his chastising, or that contemn it, declare themselves to be "bastards, and not children," as I know ye are, which, as ye are chastised, so do ye take it to heart accordingly. And therefore be glad, my dear hearts, as folks knowing certainly, even by these visitations of the Lord,
Psal. lxxxix. [33, Vulgate.] that ye are his dear elect children; whose "faults your Father doth visit with the rod of correction, but his mercy will he never take away from you." Amen.

Secondly ye have cause to rejoice for these days, because they are days of trial, wherein not only ye yourselves shall better know yourselves, but also the world shall know that ye be none of his, but the Lord's darlings. Before these days came, Lord God, how many thought of themselves, they had been in God's bosom, and so were taken, and would be taken of the world! But now we see whose they are: "for, to whom we obey, his servants we are." If we obey the world, which God forbid, and, praised be his name[1], hitherto ye have not done it, then are we the world's: but, if we obey God, then are we God's. Which thing, I mean, that ye are God's, these

[[1] "praised be his name," autogr. MS.: not in printed editions.]

days have declared both to you, to me, and to all other that know you, better than ever we knew it.

Therefore ye have no cause to sorrow, but rather to sing, in seeing yourselves to be God's babes, and in seeing that all God's children do so count you. What though the world repine thereat; what though he kick; what though he seek to trouble and molest you? My dear hearts, he doth but his kind. He cannot love the Lord, which liveth not the Lord; he cannot away with[2] the broth, that abhorreth the meat[3]; he cannot brook the child, that hateth the father; he cannot mind the servant, that careth not for the master. "If ye were of the world, the world would love you," ye should dwell quietly, there would be no grief, no molestation. If the devil dwelt in you (which the Lord forbid), he would not stir up his knights to besiege your house, to snatch at your goods, or suffer his fiends to enter into your hogs: but, because Christ dwelleth in you, as he doth by faith, therefore he stirreth up his first-begotten son the world, to seek how to disquiet you, to rob you, to spoil you, to destroy you. And perchance your dear Father, to try and to make known unto you, and to the world, that ye are destinate to another dwelling than here on earth, to another city than man's eyes have seen at any time, hath given or will give power to Satan and to the world, to take from you the things which he hath lent you, and by taking them away to try your fidelity, obedience, and love towards him (for ye may not love them above him); as by giving that ye have, and keeping it, he hath declared his love towards you.

Satan perchance telleth God, as he did of Job, that ye love God for your good's sake. What now then, if the Lord, to try you with Job, shall give him power on your goods and body accordingly, should ye be dismayed, should ye despair, should ye be fainthearted? Should ye not rather "rejoice," as did the apostles, that they were "counted worthy to suffer anything for the Lord's sake?" O! forget not the end that happened to Job; for, as it happened to him, so shall it happen unto you; for God is "the same God," and cannot long forget to shew mercy to them that look and long for it, as I know ye do: and I pray you so to do still, for the Lord loveth you, and

[[2] "Away with:" bear, endure.]
[[3] The last ten words are in the autogr. MS., but not in the printed editions.]

never can nor will forget to shew and pour out his mercy upon you. "After a little while that he hath afflicted and tried you," saith Peter, "he will visit, comfort, and confirm you." As to Jacob, wrestling with the angel, at the length morning came and the sun arose, so, dear hearts, doubtless it will happen unto you. Howbeit do ye as Job and Jacob did, that is, order and dispose your things that God hath lent you as ye may, and whiles ye have time. Who knoweth whether God hath given you power thus long, even to that end?

Go to therefore, dispose your goods, prepare yourselves to trial, that either ye may stand to it like God's champions, or else, if ye feel such infirmity in yourselves that ye be not able, give place to violence, and go where ye may with free and safe conscience serve the Lord. Think not this counsel to come by chance or fortune, but to come from the Lord: other oracles we may not look for now. As God told Joseph in a dream, by an angel, that he should flee, so, if ye feel such infirmity in yourselves as should turn to God's dishonour and your own destruction withal, know that at this present I am as God's angel, to admonish you to take time whiles ye have it, and to see that in no case God's name by you might be dishonoured. Joseph might have objected the omission of his vocation, as perchance ye will do: but, dear hearts, let vocations and all things else give place to God's name and the sanctifying thereof.

This I speak, not as though I would not have you rather to tarry and to stand to it: but I speak it in respect of your infirmity, which if ye feel to be so great in you that ye are not certain of this hope, that "God will never tempt you above your ability," flee and get you hence, and know that thereby God will have you tried, to yourselves and to others. For by it you shall know, how to take this world and your home here as no home, but that ye look for another, and so give occasion to others less to love this world, and perchance to some to doubt of their religion: wherein though[1] they be earnest, yet would not they lose so much as ye do for your religion, which ye do confirm to me and others, by your giving place to violence.

Last of all ye have cause to rejoice over these our days, because they be the days of conformation; in the which and by which God our Father maketh us like unto Christ's image

[[1] "though that," 1563: "though," 1564.]

here, that we may be like unto him elsewhere. For, "if that we suffer with him, then we shall reign also with him;" if we be buried with him, then we shall rise with him again; if we company with him in all troubles and afflictions, then we shall rejoice with him in glory; if we now sow with him in tears, we shall reap with him in gladness; if we "confess him before men, he will confess us before his Father in heaven." If we take his part, he will take ours; if we lose aught for his name's sake, he will give us all things for his truth's sake: so that we ought, I trow[2], to "rejoice and be glad," for it is not given to every one to suffer loss of country, life, goods, house, &c., for the Lord's sake.

What can God the Father do more unto us, than to call us into camp with his Son? what may Christ our Saviour do more for us, than to make us his warriors? what can the Holy Ghost do to us above this, to mark us with the cognisance of "the Lord of hosts?" This cognisance of the Lord standeth not in forked caps, tippets, shaven crowns, beads[2], or such other baggage and antichristian pelf, but in suffering for the Lord's sake. "The world shall hate you," saith Christ. Lo, there is the cognisance and badge of God's children: "The world shall hate you."

Rejoice therefore, my dearly beloved, rejoice that God doth thus vouchsafe to begin to conform you, and make you like to Christ. By the trial of these days ye are occasioned more to repent, more to pray, more to contemn this world, more to desire life everlasting, more to be holy (for holiness[3] is the end wherefore God doth afflict us), and so to[2] come to God's company. Which thing because we cannot do as long as this body is as it is, therefore by the door of death we must enter, with Christ, into eternal life and immortality of soul and body. Which God, of his mercy, and in his mercy[2], send shortly, for our Saviour Jesus Christ's sake. Amen.

[4]Thus in few words I have declared unto you my goodwill, my dearly beloved in the Lord, praying God to use it as a

[[2] "I trow," "beads," "to," "and in his mercy," autograph MS.: not in printed editions.]

[[3] "holiness," autograph MS.: "holy," printed editions.]

[[4] The two following short paragraphs, not being in the printed editions, now are first printed from the autograph MS. and MS. 1. 2. 8. No. 44.]

means to comfort you in spirit, as you have done to me in body: the which God our Father in the[1] last day give you to find eternally.

I heartily pray you to pray for us your afflicted brethren.

JOHN BRADFORD[2].

XCI. MISTRESS LONGSHO TO BRADFORD[3].

MS. 2. 2. 15. No. 117. Transcript. Emman. Coll. Cambridge.

GRACE, peace, and increase of knowledge, &c.

Dearly beloved brother in Jesus Christ, Master Bradford, in most humble and hearty commendations I christianly salute you, as heartily as heart can think or tongue express, trusting that you and your godly company be in good health.

The cause that I write is to declare the praise of God, that hath ordained you a preacher of his gospel of Christ, for whom I have great cause to magnify his name. For truly you are my greatest comfort, next unto Christ and his word, not for your person bodily, but for the holy word's sake which you have purely and godly preached unto me and others. I rejoice as much that you are absent, being in bonds for Christ's cause, as ever I did when you were present, teaching the gospel to the comfort of our souls if we could so receive it.

But, alas! we are stiff-necked Jews, whose hearts are harder than the adamant stone, and I myself one of the wickedest creatures under heaven, unthankful, blind, unwilling to virtue, and prone to vice, a babbler of his word, and no walker in the same, stubborn, hard-hearted, cruel, unmerciful, an hypocrite, and one in whom is a sea full of evils, grievously breaking the precepts of the Lord. Wherefore I desire you, for the Lord Jesus' sake[4], to remember me in your prayers, yea, your daily and fervent meditations: I trust you do and will, with the rest that be present with you, lying in bonds for the testimony of Christ. Although I did never see them, I make mention of you and all them in my groaning sighs unto God:

[[1] "the," MS. 1. 2. 8. No. 44: not in autograph MS.]

[[2] "John Bradford," 1564: not in 1563 or MSS.]

[[3] This letter now is printed for the first time.

The heading of the Emmanuel MS. is: "A letter sent to Master John Bradford by one Elizabeth Longsho, who by her letters sheweth that she stood daily in danger of imprisonment, desiring him earnestly to pray for her."]

[[4] The words "Lord Jesus' sake," are in the MS. written over the following, "blessed blood that burst out of the holy heart of Christ," which is scored across.]

and, "being absent in body, yet present in spirit," even in the midst of your bonds, I desire you yet once again, for Jesus' sake, and "for the love of the Spirit," help me with your prayers now in this persecution.

If the world reign as it doth, the one of these three things will come unto me, I know not how soon: either to flee, or abide and deny my God (which the Lord forbid), or else to be cast in prison and suffer death. O death, thou art the best and most desired! for death is life, and life is advantage to me. But "the spirit is willing and the flesh weak:" yet the Lord's will be done and not mine.

The cause why I must suffer is for not going to church and committing spiritual fornication with their strange gods. But the Lord hath assured my conscience rather to suffer the death, than to do as they would have me: for I believe all their doings to be mere vanity and abominable before God; and, touching the supper of the Lord, I believe it to be a most necessary remembrance of his glorious death and passion; I believe the scriptures contained in the book of God to be true, and, as St Paul saith, sufficient for our learning and salvation, so that we need not unwritten verities or rather vanities of Pharisees to rule the church of Christ. As for the mass, it is the most abominable idol in the whole world: the Lord open all blind, stony and hard hearts to see it. "God is a Spirit, Acts vii.
and will be worshipped in spirit and in truth," and "dwelleth not in temples made with hands." He is not eaten with the teeth[5], neither dieth he any more. But our vicar will have it to be the same body that hanged on the cross, flesh, blood, and bone[6]. To this belief of theirs say I, 'Nay:' God have the praise therefore, and for that I must suffer persecution—but, alas! not so much as my sins have deserved (for I have deserved hell-fire and everlasting torment), which the Lord, I trust, doth pardon in Christ.—The Lord grant for his Christ's sake, when trouble shall come, I may with patience suffer all rebukes, and what else for the Lord's sake shall be laid against me; for the holy word of God yet was never without persecution, nor impugners against the professors thereof; for it followeth the gospel of Christ, even as the light the sun, and the shadow the body. The pope's doctrine is "of the world," and received with the world, and seeketh nothing but the possessions of the world, and the pleasures and authority in the world, and persecut-

[[5] See Vol. I. p. 105, note 13.]

[[6] See Vol. I. p. 545, note 5; Concil. Trident. Sess. IV. Jul. Tert. ann. 1551, cap. iv. and can. ii. fol. 38, b, and 60, Antv. 1564; and Catech. Concil. Trident. ad Par. (Pars II. cap. iv. 31.) fol. 125, Paris. 1568, where occur the words, "ossa et nervos."]

eth the word of God, and with all force and subtlety draweth the people from it.

I beseech God for his tender mercies' sake to have pity upon my poor soul, that I never "run after strange gods." Pray, dear master, that I may fight against the world, the flesh, and the devil. I trust in almighty God, by the help of your prayers, to be strengthened with his holy Spirit, to the nourishing of my weak faith, for "without faith all is sin." Pray, I beseech you, that I never shrink from the truth you have taught and preached, either by word, deed, or writing, but that I may stand to it even to the fire: which fire is but temporal, and lasteth but a season.—Grant, gracious Lord, also that I may fear the fire eternal, which is "prepared for the devil and his angels," and that I may so live, to die thy servant, that, at the dreadful day of judgment when the secrets of all hearts shall be opened, 'I may be found acceptable in thy sight, and receive the blessing which thou shalt pronounce to all that love and fear thee, saying,' "Come, ye blessed children of my Father, inherit the kingdom prepared for you from the beginning of the world." Unto the which place the Lord of mercy bring both you and me. Amen.—I pray you also to say, Amen, Amen, Amen.

I have great comfort in all the holy scriptures of the Lord, and
Matt. xxiv. especially in the 24th chapter of Matthew, because it maketh mention of the coming of the Lord Jesus Christ. I pray God it may be soon, if it be his good will: or else grant us, gracious Lord, thy gospel again, and true preachers thereof, and we shall praise thy name for ever and ever. O Father, trust us, I say, once more with thy word for Christ's sake; and, if we do not then receive it more thankfully, punish us even at thy good pleasure, and according to thy blessed will.

I praise God for you, and for your book you sent me: I pray Christ I may use it to the glory of God; and I desire you to accept this my poor and simple writing. And thus making an end I bid you in Christ most hearty farewell.

Written by me,

ELIZABETH LONGSHO.

Have in remembrance in your prayers a maid of the parish of Prestige[1], whose name is Alice Sedon, which doth not cease praying for you night and day.

[[1] "Prestige:" Prestwich in Lancashire.]

XCII. TO A GENTLEWOMAN[2].

I WISH unto you, right worshipful, and my dearly beloved sister in the Lord, as to myself, the continual grace and comfort of Christ, and of his holy word, through the operation of the Holy Spirit; who strengthen your inward man with the strength of God, that you may continue to the end, in the faithful obedience of God's gospel, whereunto you are called. Amen. (Foxe, Acts, &c., ed. 1570, p. 1834; and after editions.) (Rom. i.)

I perceived by yourself, the last day when you were with me, how that you are in the school-house and trial-parlour of the Lord; which to me is, at the least it should be, a great comfort to see the number of God's elect by you increased, which is in that state whereof God hath not called many, as Paul saith. (1 Cor. i.) And, as it is a comfort to me, so should it be a confirmation unto me, that the Lord, for his faithfulness' sake, will make perfect and finish the good he hath begun in you, "to the end." If then your cross be to me a comfort, or token of your election, and a confirmation of God's continual favour, (1 Cor. i. and x.) my dearly beloved, how much more ought it to be so unto you? unto whom he hath "not only given to believe," but also to come into the trace of "suffering for his sake;" and that not commonly of common enemies, but even of your own father, mother, and all your friends, I mean kinsfolk, as you told me. By which I see Christ's words to be true, how that he came to give his children such a peace with him as the devil might not, nor may abide, and therefore stirreth up father and mother, sister and brother, rather than it should continue. (Matt. x.)

But, my dear sister, if you cry with David to the Lord, and complain to him, how that for conscience to him your "father and mother have forsaken you," you shall hear him speak in your heart, that he hath received you, and by this would have you to see, how that he maketh you here like to Christ, that (Psal. xxii.) (Rom. viii.)

[[2] Foxe (ed. 1570, p. 1834, or ed. 1843–9, Vol. VII. p. 256) observes: "In the story of Master Bradford it was above rehearsed, how a certain gentlewoman, being in trouble by her father and mother for not coming to mass, sent her servant to visit Master Bradford in prison; who, tendering the woeful case of the gentlewoman, to the intent partly to confirm her with counsel, partly to relieve her oppressed mind with some comfort, directed this letter unto her, the contents whereof are these." See Vol. I. pp. 553—56, colloquy between Bradford and the gentlewoman's servant.]

elsewhere in heaven you might be like unto him: whereof you [1 John iii.] ought to be most assured, knowing that in time, even "when Christ shall appear, you shall be like unto him." For he will make your body, which now you defile not with idolatrical [Phil. iii.] service in going to mass, "like unto his own glorious and immortal body, according to the power whereby he is able to do [Matt. x. Mark viii.] all things." He "will confess you before his Father," which do not deny his verity, in word nor deed, before your father; [2 Tim. ii.] he will make you to "reign with him," that now "suffer" for him and with him; he will reward you with himself and all the glory he hath, that now for his sake deny yourself with all that ever you have; he "will not leave you comfortless," that seek no comfort but at his hand. "Though for a little time you be afflicted," yet therein will he comfort and strengthen you, and at the length make you to be merry with him, in such joy as is infinite and endless. "He will wipe all the tears from your eyes;" he will embrace you as your dear "Husband;" he will, after he hath proved you, crown you with a crown of glory and immortality, such as the heart of man shall never be able to conceive, in such sort as the thing is. He now beholdeth your steadfastness and striving to do his good will: and shortly will he shew you how steadfast he is, and will be ready to do your will, after that you have fully resigned it to his will.

Pledge him in his cup of the cross, and you shall pledge him in the cup of his glory. Desire to drink it before it come to the dregs, whereof the wicked shall drink, and all those that, for fear of the cross and pledging the Lord, do walk with the wicked, in betraying in fact and deed that which their heart embraceth for verity. The which thing if you should do—which God forbid—then, my dear mistress and sister in the Lord, you should not only lose all that I have before spoken, and much more infinitely of eternal joy and glory, but also be a cast-away and partaker of God's most heavy displeasure, in hell-fire eternally; and so for a little ease, which you cannot tell how long it will last, to lose for ever and ever all ease and [Luke xi.] comfort. "For he that gathereth not with me," saith Christ, [2 Cor. v.] as no mass-gospeller doth, "scattereth abroad." "According to that we do in this body we shall receive, be it good or bad." [Matt. xii.] If "of our words" we shall be judged, to condemnation or salvation, much more then of our facts and deeds. You cannot

be partaker of God's religion and antichrist's service, whereof 1 Cor. x.
the mass is most principal. You cannot be a member of Christ's
church and a member of the pope's church. You must "glorify 1 Cor. vi.
God," not only in soul and heart, but also in body and deed. You may not think that God requireth less of you his wife now, than your husband did of you. If both heart and body your husband would have, shall Christ have less, trow you, which hath so bitterly and dearly bought it? If your husband could not admit an excuse, how your heart is his only, if he should have taken your body in bed with another, do you think that Christ will allow your body at mass, although your heart consent not to it?

God esteemeth his children, not only of their hearts, but of Ps. cxxv.
their pure hands and words: and therefore in Elias' time he 1 Kings xix.
counted none to be his servants and people, but such as had "not bowed their knees to Baal:" as now he doth not in England account any to be his darlings, which know the truth in heart and deny it in their deeds, as do our mass-gospellers.

We ought to desire, above all things, the sanctifying of God's holy name and the coming of his kingdom: and shall we then see his name blasphemed so horribly as it is at mass, by making it a sacrifice propitiatory, and setting forth a false Christ, of the priest's and baker's making, to be worshipped as God, and say nothing? The Jews rent their clothes asunder, on seeing or hearing anything blasphemously done or spoken against God: and shall we yet come to church where mass is, and be mute? Paul and Barnabas rent their clothes, to see the people of Lycaonia to offer sacrifice to them: and shall we see sacrifice and God's service done to an inanimate creature, and be mum? What thing helpeth more or so much antichrist's kingdom, as doth the mass? And what destroyeth preaching and the kingdom of Christ upon earth, more than it doth? And how can we then say, "Let thy kingdom come," and go to mass? How can we pray before God, "Thy will be done on earth," when we will do our own will and the will of our father or friends? How pray we, "Deliver us from evil," which knowing the mass to be evil do come to it?

But what go I about to light a candle in the noonday?—that is, to tell you that we may not go to mass, or to the congregation where it is, except it be to reprove it, in that all men, in so doing, do but dissemble both with God and man. And is dissembling now to be allowed? How long will men yet "halt on both knees?" saith God. "Halting," saith Paul, "bringeth out of the way," that is to say, out of Christ, which is "the way;" so that he which is not in him shall wither away, and be cast into hell-fire; for Christ will be ashamed of them before his Father, which be now ashamed of his truth before this wicked generation.

Therefore, my good mistress, take good heed; for "it had been better for you never to have known the truth," and therethrough to have escaped from papistical uncleanness, than now to return to it, making eftsoons your members, being members of righteousness, members of unrighteousness, as you do, if you do but go to the church where mass is. Be pure therefore, and keep yourself "from all filth of the spirit, and of the flesh;" abstain not only from all evil, but "from all appearance of evil." And so "the God of peace shall be with you," the glory of God shall govern you, the Spirit of God shall sanctify you and be with you for ever, to keep you from all evil, and to comfort you in all your distress and trouble. Which is but short, if you consider the eternity you shall enjoy in glory and felicity in the Lord: which undoubtedly you shall not fail but inherit for ever, if so be you, as the elect child of God, put your trust in his mercy, call upon his name unfeignedly, and yield not over to the wicked world, but stick still against it unto the end.

God, for his holy name's sake, which is properly "the God of the widows," be your good and dear Father for ever, and help you always, as I myself would be holpen at his hands, in all things, and especially in this his own cause. Amen, Amen.

JOHN BRADFORD.

XCIII. TO SHALCROSS AND HIS WIFE.

[From the Compter in the Poultry.]

Bp Coverdale, Letters of the Martyrs, 1564, p. 359.

To Master Shalcross and his wife, dwelling in Lancashire.

The peace of conscience in Christ and through faith in his blood, which, as it passeth and is far better than any worldly riches or joy, so is it to be redeemed with the loss of the dearest treasures we have, rather than we should lose it—this peace I wish unto you, good Master Shalcross, and unto your good yoke-fellow, my good sister in the Lord, now and for ever. Amen.

MS. 2. 2. 15. No. 87. Transcript. Emman. Coll. Cambridge.

Hitherto, although I could not write unto you, yet, as I trust you pray for me, so I have not been forgetful of you, in my poor prayers to almighty God, my dear Father through Christ: to whom I give humble praises that he hath given you grace as yet (for so I hear) to keep yourself undefiled in his service; which far differeth from the Romish rags, revived of late, and justly for our sins and unthankful using his true religion and holy ceremonies once again in place and use amongst us. In token whereof—I mean, that I have not been forgetful of you—I thought good now when I may write to signify the same, as well to renew our mutual love in God, and care one for another by hearty prayer, as to excite and provoke you both to thankfulness for God's graces hitherto, especially in the point before spoken of, and to be diligent and wary that you unto the end continue in the same; for you know that perseverance in godliness and purity is required of us, and that none other shall be "crowned but such as fight lawfully." 2 Tim. ii.

Go to therefore, and "fight on a good fight" stoutly and manfully. That is, as you know God is not to be worshipped and served but after his word written, and not after unwritten verities, or the device, fantasy and pleasures of men or women, in what state soever they be, accordingly behave yourself, as inwardly in God's sight, so outwardly before your brethren. Seem not to approve by your outward man that which the inward man detesteth. It is not enough to "believe with the heart," except the mouth and fact "confess" the same. Nor it is not enough with the mouth to acknowledge a verity, and by our fact and deed to destroy the same. Paul speaketh sometimes of deniers of God, not only with their lips and tongue, but also with their deed and life. Let not the world, or the more part of men, be an example to you to follow them or do as they do, in the service of God. Christ saith, "Follow me," speaking of himself; which is the pattern and sampler we should set before us, and not the world or more part, which windeth "the wide and broad way," whose end doth lead to perdition and everlasting woe. But rather let the example of such as walk in the "narrow and strait way," which bringeth to life endless, encourage you to walk with them, although the number of them be but few, and the personages of them be utterly contemned with the world and in the world. Which world cannot love, no, nor know indeed the children of God, because it "cannot receive the Spirit of God:" and therefore, as the ape her young ones, so it (the world I mean) doth think her own birds the fairest, contemning with deadly hate all others that will not follow her judgment.

But what saith Christ? "Be of good cheer: although the world will persecute you, yet I have overcome the world." O comfortable sentence! "I have overcome the world." This undoubtedly he meaneth for you and me and all other his children, that "he hath overcome the world" for us. But, by what means? Surely by suffering, as[1] contempt, so[1] wrong, false reports, and even very shameful and most bitter death. If he went this way, and won the victory this way, as I trust we know, let us as his servants, whose state ought not to be above our Master's, not be dismayed of contempt, of wrong, of loss of goods or life itself, but rather joyfully suffer the same, as men knowing we have better portions in heaven, and that this is the sure way to victory most victorious; for "by many tribulations must we enter into the kingdom of heaven." If we will come thither, except for tribulation sake, we will with ease and worldly quietness go to hell. You know that Paul saith, "All that will live godly in Christ Jesu must suffer persecution." Wherefore, in that you are in Christ Jesu, I dare say you will continue, though persecution come to you, being assured that it cannot come, except God have so decreed: and, if he have so decreed, then cannot you but receive it, or else a cross which will be much worse. Willingly therefore take what cross the Lord shall offer; and then the Lord will make you able to bear it, and never tempt you further than he will make you strong enough. Yea, all the hairs of your head he will number and keep, so that "one of them shall not perish." But, if you should refuse God's cross, especially in

[[1] "as," "so," MS., scored across: not in 1570.]

suffering the loss of anything for his sake, which giveth you all the good that ever you have and keepeth it—if, I say, you refuse—be certain, the plagues of God will be poured down, first on your soul and conscience, in hardening your heart and blinding your mind, either by bringing you into despair, or into a contempt and carnal security; whereafter will ensue loss of the dearest things you have, if God love you, or else he will conserve the same, to your eternal destruction.

I write not this, as distrusting your constancy in God's cause (God forbid, for methink I am assured of your godly zeal); but I do it, as I said, that you may be the more heedy, wary, diligent, and earnestly given to call upon the name of God, for his help and grace of perseverance, which is more ready to give than we to ask. I know this kind of writing is madness to the world, foolishness to reason, and sour to the flesh. But to you which are a man of God, and by profession in baptism have forsaken the world, and do consider things after the reach of faith, and have tasted of the good Spirit of [Heb. vi. 4, 5.] God, and of the life to come—unto such a one, I say, as I trust you be—this kind of writing is otherwise esteemed. For here you are but a pilgrim, your home is in heaven, your treasures are there hoarded where thieves cannot come to steal them; there is your heart: and therefore you can and will say, as the philosopher said when he was robbed of all he had, *Omnia mea mecum porto*, "I carry all with me." If he, an heathen, took his riches to be the world's rather than his, how much more should we so do? Therefore, my dear brother, accordingly prepare yourself, as you have done and do I hope. Read the second of Ecclesiasticus, how he counselleth them that will serve God, to prepare themselves to temptation. Often set before your eyes the judgment of Christ, his coming in the clouds, and the resurrection, which is now our comfort, especially in afflictions.

I write to you none otherwise than I am persuaded, I thank God, and purpose to go before you. I know there is an eternal life; I hope to be partaker of it through Christ; I know this is the way thither, I mean, by suffering; I know that, "if we suffer with him, we shall reign with him;" I know that by the cross he maketh us like to Christ here, that we might be like to him elsewhere. Therefore I write to you not words only: and hereupon I am the more earnest, as to admonish, so to pray you to cleave still to the Lord and his true religion, which you have received, and I for my part am sure that I have preached unto you. For the confirmation whereof as I am in bonds, so I trust in the goodness of God and his power to give my life in and for the same, that you and others might be certain and follow as God shall call you and vouch you worthy.

Remember that die you must; but, when as you know not, so where and how it is uncertain to you. Again all that you have you must leave behind you, for nothing shall go with you, but a good or an evil conscience. Moreover to whom you shall leave your goods it is hid from you; for you may purpose, but God will dispose. Therefore, if God will have you to die, or to lose your goods for his cause, how much are you bound then to bless God! Sure you may be, that then you cannot perish, for of all ways to heaven it is the most sure way. Your goods God will preserve, so that your children shall find them, although the wicked spoil every piece of them: for "the righteous man's seed I have not seen," saith David, "beg their bread," but God will bless them "unto a thousand generations:" the which thing I pray God to remember towards your children, for his name sake. Amen.

Thus will I betake you to God, and to his holy word; which is able, as to teach you which way to serve God, so to save you, if you believe and love it. If I thought it might do you any good, I would send you a book, which James Bradshaw[1] already hath, to teach you how you should behave yourselves, especially concerning the mass[2]: I wrote it sithen my trouble. Commend me to Thomas[3] Riddleston, although I fear me, he have defiled himself in this false service. That book I would wish he would read: as you shall advertise me, I will do in sending to him. I shall pray God to illuminate his eyes with his grace. Commend me to sir W. Charelton, who I trust

[1 See p. 41, first paragr. of Letter XVIII., above. Hollingworth in his "Chronicle of Manchester," written about A.D. 1650, and printed at Manchester, 1839, p. 73, observes, in reference to this allusion to James Bradshaw: "Possibly it is the same good man that writ to George Marsh, another of our Lancashire martyrs." See Foxe, Acts, &c., ed. 1583, p. 1573, or ed. 1843–9, Vol. VII. p. 67.]

[2 The "Hurt of hearing mass," printed in this volume.]

[3 "Thomas," MS.: "T." 1570.]

hath kept himself pure from idolatry: God grant he so continue.

Written in haste, as it appeareth, from the Compter in the Poultry, by yours in Christ,

JOHN BRADFORD.

XCIV. TO CARELESS[4].

Foxe, Acts, &c. ed. 1570, p. 2105; and after editions.

ALMIGHTY God, our dear Father, through and for the merits of his dearly beloved Son Jesus Christ, be merciful unto us, pardon us our offences; and under the wings of his mercy he protect us from all evil, from henceforth and for ever. Amen.

Dear brother Careless, I heartily pray you to pray to God for me, for the pardon of my manifold sins and most grievous offences, which need no other demonstration unto you than this; namely, that I have behaved myself so negligently in answering your godly triple letters, which are three witnesses against me. God lay not them nor none other thing to my charge, to condemnation; though to correction not my will, but his will be done.

Practice of the keys of the gospel.—[Foxe.]

Concerning your request of absolution, my dearest brother, what shall I say, but even as truth is, that the Lord of all mercy, and "Father of all comfort," through the merits and mediation of his dear Son, thy only Lord and Saviour, hath clearly remitted and pardoned all thy offences, whatsoever they be, that ever hitherto thou hast committed against his majesty: and therefore he hath given to thee, as to his child, dear brother John Careless, in token that thy sins are pardoned—he, I say, hath given unto thee—a penitent and believing heart, that is, a heart which desireth to repent and believe: for such a one is taken of him, he accepting the will for the deed, for a

[4 John Careless was a devoted confessor in the Marian time, of Coventry, who had been by employment a weaver. He died in prison, July 1, 1556. Many of his letters are printed in Bp Coverdale's Letters of the Martyrs, 1564, pp. 560—634, and in Foxe, Acts, &c., ed. 1583, pp. 1921—34, or ed. 1843—9, Vol. VIII. pp. 171—200. Many also of his letters still exist in his original autograph, in Emmanuel College, Cambridge, and in the collection of Dawson Turner, Esq.: see p. 169, note 5, above. See also Strype, Ecc. Mem. Vol. III. part. I. pp. 587, 8.]

penitent and believing heart indeed. Wherefore, my good brother, be merry, glad and of good cheer; for "the Lord hath taken away thy sins; thou shalt not die." Go thy ways: "the Lord hath put away thy sins." "The east is not so far from the west, as the Lord now hath put thy sins from thee." Look, how the heavens be in comparison of the earth, so far hath his mercy prevailed towards thee, his dear child, John Careless, through Christ the beloved. Say therefore with David: "Praise the Lord, O my soul, and all that is within me praise his holy name; for he hath forgiven thee all thy sins;" as truly he hath: and hereof I desire to be a witness. God make me worthy to hear from you the like true message for myself.

Mine own dearly beloved, you have great cause to thank God most heartily, that hath given you such repentance and faith. The Lord increase the same in you and me, a most miserable wretch, whose heart is harder than the adamant stone, or else I could not thus long have stayed from writing unto you. If I live and may, I purpose and promise you to make amends. Pray for me, my most dear brother, I heartily beseech you; and forgive me my long silence. God our Father be with us for ever. Amen.

Yours in the Lord,

JOHN BRADFORD.

XCV. CARELESS TO BRADFORD.

Bp Coverdale, Letters of the Martyrs, 1564, p. 628.

Foxe, Acts, &c., ed. 1570, p. 2104; and after editions.

MS. 2. 2. 15. No. 85. Original, Holograph. Emman.Coll. Cambridge.

JESUS IMMANUEL.

"O LORD, let the sorrowful sighing of the prisoners come before thee: and according to the greatness of thy power preserve thou those that are appointed to die[1]."

To my good brother, Master John Bradford. The peace of God in Jesus Christ, the eternal comfort of his sweet Spirit, which hath surely sealed you unto eternal salvation, be with you and strengthen you in your joyful journey towards the celestial Jerusalem, my dear friend and most faithful brother, Master Bradford, to the setting forth of God's glory, and to your eternal joy in Christ. Amen[2].

[1 "Jesus Emmanuel......to die," MS.: not in 1564 or 1570.]
[2 This paragraph is not in the MS.]

Ever since that good Master Philpot showed me your last letter, my dear heart in the Lord, I have continued in such[3] heaviness and perplexity that I cannot almost tell what I do[4]; not for any hurt or discommodity that I can perceive coming towards you, right dear in the sight of God[4], unto whom doubtless death is made life and great felicity; but for the great loss that God's church here in England shall sustain, by the taking away of so godly, worthy and necessary an instrument as the Lord hath made you to be. O that my life, and a thousand such wretched lives more, might go for yours! O! why doth God suffer me and such other caterpillars to live, that can do nothing but consume the alms of the church, and take away you, so worthy a workman and labourer in the Lord's vineyard? But woe be to our sins and great unthankfulness! which is the greatest cause of the taking away of such worthy instruments of God, as should set forth his glory and instruct the multitude of[4] his people. If we had been thankful unto God for the good ministers of his word, we had not been so soon deprived both of it and them. The Lord forgive our great ingratitude and sins, and give us true repentance and faith, and hold his hand of mercy over us, for his dear Son Christ's sake.—Take not away all thy true preachers forth of this realm, O Lord, but leave us a seed, lest England be made like unto Sodom and Gomorrah, when thy true Lots be gone.

But what go I about to mingle your mirth with my mourning, and your just joy with my deserved sorrow? If I loved you indeed, as I have pretended, I should surely rejoice with you most heartily, and praise God on your behalf from the very bottom of my heart; I should praise God day and night for your excellent election, in and through his great mercy, and should give him most humble thanks for your vocation by his gospel, and your true knowledge in the same; I should earnestly praise him for your sweet justification, whereof you are most certain by God's grace and Spirit, and should instantly pray unto him for your glorification, which shall shortly ensue; I should rejoice and be glad to see you so dignified by the crown of martyrdom, and to be appointed to that honour, to testify his truth, and to seal it with your blood; I should highly extol the Lord, who hath given you a glorious victory over all your enemies visible and invisible, and hath given you grace and strength to "finish the tower" that you have begun to build. Finally, if I loved you, I should most heartily rejoice and be glad

[3 "such," "great," 1564 and 1570.]

[4 "That I cannot almost tell what I do," "right dear in the sight of God," "the multitude of," MS.: not in 1564 or 1570.]

to see you delivered from this body of sin and vile prison of the flesh, and brought into that heavenly tabernacle, where you shall be safely kept, and never offend him more. This and much more should I do, if I had a good heart towards God, or you his dear child.

But, alas! I am an hypocrite, and do seek nothing but mine own commodity. I would have God's everlasting providence give place to my peevish will and purpose, although it were to the hindrance of his glory, and your sweet commodity.—God forgive me my horrible ingratitude, sins and offences against him: and, good brother, do you forgive me my great negligence and unthankfulness towards you: and henceforth, I promise you, I will put my will to God's will, and pray that the same may be fulfilled in you, so long as you be on this earth; and, when you are taken hence, I will most heartily praise the Lord for you, so long as I have my being in this world.

Ah! my dear heart, now I must take my leave of you, and, as I think, my *ultimum vale* in this life: but in the life to come I am right well assured we shall merrily meet together, and that shortly I trust. And in taking of my leave of you, my dear heart in the Lord, I shall desire you faithfully to remember all the sweet messages, that the Lord our good God and most dear loving Father hath sent you by me his most unworthy servant; which, as they are most true, so shall they be most truly accomplished upon you eternally: and, for the more assurance and certificate thereof to your mind and[1] godly conscience, he hath straitly charged and[1] commanded me to repeat the same unto you again, in his own name and word.

Therefore now give ear and faithful credence. Hearken, O ye heavens, and thou earth give ear, and bear me witness at the great day, that I do here faithfully and truly, without adding or minishing[1], the Lord's message unto his dear servant, his singularly beloved and elect child, John Bradford.—John Bradford, thou man so specially beloved of God, I pronounce and testify unto thee, in the word and name of the Lord Jehovah, that all thy sins, whatsoever they be, be they never so many, so grievous or so great, be fully and freely pardoned, released and forgiven thee, by the mercy of God in Jesus Christ, thine only Lord and sweet Saviour, in whom thou dost undoubtedly believe. Christ hath cleansed thee with his blood, and clothed thee with his righteousness, and hath made thee, in the sight of God his Father, "without spot or wrinkle;" so that,

Power and practice of the keys of the gospel. —[Foxe.]

[[1] "mind and," "straitly charged and," "without adding or minishing," MS.: not in 1564 or 1570.]

when the fire doth his appointed office, thou shalt be received, as a sweet burnt sacrifice, into heaven; where thou shalt joyfully remain in God's presence for ever, as the true inheritor of his everlasting kingdom, unto the which thou wast undoubtedly predestinate and ordained by the Lord's infallible purpose and decree, "before the foundation of the world" was laid. And, that this is most true that I have said, I call the whole Trinity, the almighty and eternal majesty of God the Father, the Son, and the Holy Ghost, to my record at this present: whom I humbly beseech to confirm and establish in thee the true and lively feeling of the same. Amen. *Selah.*

Farewell, dear brother, for now I have done the Lord's true message. Believe it, I charge you. I know you do believe: the Lord increase your faith. Give thanks unto the Lord: and shortly I trust we shall both sing together continual praise unto his name; to whom be all honour, glory, and praise for ever and ever. Amen, Amen[2].

As I had made an end of this simple letter, I heard some comfort both of good Master Philpot's servant and yours: but, alas! I do scarcely believe them. Well I will hope in God, and pray all night that God will send me some comfort to-morrow; and, if the Lord give you sparing to-morrow, let me hear four words of comfort from you for God's sake.

The blessing of God be with you now and for ever. Amen.

Yours for ever in the Lord Jesus, living in hope against hope[3].

Your continual orator[4],

JOHN CARELESS,

the most unprofitable servant of the Lord[4].

And[5] now, my dear brother[5], with a cheerful[6] heart and a joyful spirit, something mixed with lawful tears, I take my farewell of you, mine own dear brother in the Lord: who send us shortly a merry meeting in his kingdom, that we may both sing praises together unto him with his holy angels and blessed saints[6] for ever

[2 The last paragraph, "Farewell, dear brother......ever. Amen, Amen," now is first printed from the autograph MS.]

[3 The words, "living in hope against hope," occur as above in MS., but are printed after "John Careless" in 1564 and 1570.]

[4 "Orator:" petitioner, one who offers prayers. The words, "your continual orator," "the most unprofitable servant of the Lord," now are first printed from the autograph MS.]

[5 "And," "my dear brother," MS.: not in 1564 or 1570.]

[6 "cheerful," "saints," MS.: "merry," "spirits," 1564 and 1570.]

and ever. Farewell, thou blessed of the Lord, farewell in Christ depart unto thy rest in the Lord, and pray for me, for God's sake[1].

XCVI. TO JOHN CARELESS.

Bp Coverdale, Letters of the Martyrs, 1564, p. 373.

Foxe, Acts, &c., ed. 1570, p. 1827; and after editions.

MS. 1. 2. 8. No. 47. Transcript. Emman. Coll. Cambridge.

To my good brother, John Careless, prisoner in the King's Bench.

"The Father of mercy and God of all comfort" visit us with his eternal consolation, according to his great mercies in Jesus Christ our Saviour. Amen.

My very dear brother, if I shall report the truth unto you, I cannot but signify that, sithen I came into prison, I never received so much consolation as I did by your last letter; the name of God be most heartily praised therefore. But, if I shall report the truth unto you, and as I have begun speak still the verity, I must confess that, for mine unthankfulness to you-wards and to God especially, I have more need of God's merciful tidings, than I had ever heretofore. Ah, that Satan envieth us so greatly! Ah, that our Lord would "tread his head" "under our feet shortly!" Ah, that I might for ever, both myself beware, and be a godly example to you and others to beware, of unthankfulness!

Good brother Careless, we had more need to take heed, after a lightening, of a foil than before. God therefore is to be praised, even when he hideth, and that of long, a cheerful countenance from us, lest we, being not expert how to use it as we should do, do hurt more ourselves thereby; so great is our ignorance and corruption. This, my good brother, and right dear to my very heart, I write unto you, as to one whom in the Lord I embrace; and I thank God that you do me in like manner. God our Father more and more give us both his good Spirit, that, as by faith we may feel ourselves united unto him in Christ, so by love we may feel ourselves linked in the same Christ one to another, I to you, and you to me, we to all the

[1 The paragraph is thus placed in the MS., where it is written in a different hand from that of Careless: but in 1564 and 1570 it is printed in the body of the letter, after the paragraph that ends with, "lively feeling of the same. Amen. Selah."]

children of God, and all the children of God to us. Amen, Amen.

Commend me to our good brother Skelthrop, for whom I heartily praise my God, which hath given him to see his truth at the length, and to give place to it. I doubt not but that he will be so heedy in all his conversation, that his old acquaintance may ever thereby think themselves astray. Woe and woe again should be unto us, if we by our example should make men to stumble at the truth.

Forget not salutations in Christ, as you shall think good, to Trew and his fellows. The Lord hath his time, I hope, for them also, although we perchance think otherwise. A drop maketh the stone hollow, not with once but with often dropping: so, if with hearty prayer for them and good example you still and drop upon them as you can, you shall see God's work at the length. I beseech God to make perfect all the good he hath begun in us all. Amen.

I desire you all to pray for me, the most unworthy prisoner of the Lord.

Your brother,

JOHN BRADFORD.

XCVII. TO ADN PHILPOT.

JESUS IMMANUEL[2].

To mine own good brother, Master John Philpot, prisoner in the King's Bench. My dear brother, God our Father be praised for the good he doth daily[2] work in you and by you.

Bp Coverdale, Letters of the Martyrs, 1564, p. 408.

MS. 2. 2 15. No. 107. Original, Holograph. And No. 102, Transcript. Emman. Coll. Cambridge.

Even now I have received your loving letters, wherein I see cause to bless God for the wisdom, love and efficacy he hath and doth work in you and by you. Go on for God's sake to seek unity in Christ. If any will go to work dissemblingly, refuse it not: either shall it increase his damnation, or occasion him the sooner to conversion. Judas' dissembling turned to the hurt of himself only. If once we come into an unity and love, then shall we not suspect[3] one another, neither take

[2 "Jesus Immanuel," "daily," only in autogr. MS.]

[3 "suspect," autogr. MS.: "respect," 1564 and MS. No. 102.]

things into the worse part. Nothing hindereth them more, than for that now they hear all that ever we speak *cum prejudicio;* where, if an unity be had, this *prejudicium* will be taken away, and so then shall they see the truth the sooner. Therefore, mine own dearest brother, go on and bring it to a good end. God our Father be with thee for ever. Amen.

He meaneth here certain free will men.—[Bp. Coverdale.]

My good brother[1], Robert Cole, hath written to me in this matter, to labour to persuade them with my letters. Therefore[2] I purpose to write something to Trew and Abyngton thereabouts[1], which you shall see. I have also made a treatise of the Divinity of the Holy Ghost, which you shall shortly have. Master Gibson is here in prison upon an action of thousands pounds; I say not of a thousand but of thousands. Who knoweth whether God hath sent him hither to me (for I may twice a day speak with him), to turn him yet afore my death[3]?

Pray, my good brother, and desire mine own fellow and beloved brother, J. Careless, to do the like. I shall pray for you, both in my prayers with others and with myself alonely, as for my most dear brother upon earth. I will not forget, by God's grace, to write in the behalf of our brethren in necessity.

Jesus Christ our sweet Saviour be with us all, Immanuel for ever. Amen.

Your own in the Lord,

JOHN BRADFORD.

XCVIII. TO HOPKINS[4].

Bp Coverdale, Letters of the Martyrs, 1564, p. 354.

Foxe, Acts, &c., ed. 1570, p. 1831; and after editions.

DEARLY beloved in the Lord, I wish unto you, as unto mine own brother, yea, as to mine own heart-root, God's mercy and the feeling of the same plentifully, in Christ our sweet Saviour; who gave himself a ransom for our sins, and price for

[1 "My good brother," "thereabouts," MS. No 102: not in autogr. MS. No. 107.]

[2 "to labour to persuade them with my letters. Therefore," MS. No. 102: "and," MS. No. 107.]

[3 The preceding paragraph now is first printed from the Emmanuel autograph MS.]

[4 See Vol. I. p. 389, note 1.
The inscription of this letter in Bp Coverdale is: "To Master Richard Hopkins, then sheriff of Coventry and prisoner in the Fleet, for the faithful and constant confessing of God's holy gospel."]

our redemption, praised therefore be his holy name, for ever and ever. Amen. MS. 2. 2. 15. No. 99. Transcript. Emman. Coll. Cambridge.

I will not go about to excuse myself for not sending unto you hitherto, suffering for the Lord's sake as you do, to the comfort of me and of all that love you in the truth, but rather accuse myself both before God and you, desiring you, of forgiveness, and with me, to pray to God for pardon of this my unkind forgetting you and all other my sins; which I beseech the Lord in his mercy to do away for his Christ's sake. Amen.

Now to make amends to youward I would be glad if I could: but, because I cannot, I shall heartily desire you to accept the will, and this which I shall now write unto you thereafter; I mean, after my will, and not after the deed, to accept and take it. At this present, my dear heart in the Lord, you are in a blessed state, although it seem otherwise to you, or rather unto your old Adam (the which I dare now be so bold as to discern from you, because you would have him not only discerned, but also utterly destroyed); for, if God be true, then is his word true. Now his word pronounceth of your state, that it is happy: therefore it must needs be so. To prove this I think it need not: for you know that the Holy Ghost saith, that "they are happy which suffer for righteousness' sake," and [1 Pet. iv. 14.] that God's glory and Spirit resteth on them which suffer for conscience to God. Now this you cannot but know, that this your suffering is for righteousness' sake, and for conscience to Godwards; for else you might be out of trouble, even out of hand. I know in very deed, that you have and feel your unthankfulness to God and other sins to witness to you, that you have deserved this prisonment and lack of liberty betwixt God and yourself: and I would you so would confess unto God in your prayers, with petition for pardon, and thanksgiving for his correcting you here. But you know that the magistrates do not persecute in you your sins, your unthankfulness, &c.; but they persecute in you Christ himself, his righteousness, his verity: and therefore happy be you, that have found such favour with God your Father, as to "account you worthy to suffer for his sake," in the sight of man. Surely you shall rejoice therefore one day, with a joy unspeakable, in the sight of man also.

You may think yourself born in a blessed time, that have

found this grace with God, to be a "vessel of honour" to suffer with his saints, yea, with his Son. My beloved, God hath
1 Cor. i. not done so with many. The apostle saith, "Not many noble, not many rich, not many wise in the world hath the Lord God chosen." O then, what cause have you to rejoice, that amongst the not many he hath chosen you to be one! For this cause hath God placed you in your office, that therefore you might the more see his special dignation and love towards you. It had not been so great a thing for Master Hopkins to have suffered as Master Hopkins, as it is for Master Hopkins also to suffer as Master Sheriff. O happy day that you were made sheriff! by the which as God in this world would promote you to a more honourable degree, so by suffering in this room he hath exalted you in heaven, and in the sight of his church and children, to a much more excellent glory. When was it read that a sheriff of a city hath suffered for the Lord's sake? where read we of any sheriff, that hath been cast in prison for conscience to Godwards? how could God have dealt more lovingly with you, than herein he hath done? To the end of the world it shall be written for a memorial to your praise, that 'Richard Hopkins, sheriff of Coventry, for conscience to do his office before God, was cast in the Fleet, and there kept prisoner a long time.' Happy and twice happy are you, if herefor you may give your life. Never could you have attained to this promotion, on this sort, out of that office. How do you preach now, not only to all men, but specially to magistrates in this realm! Who would ever have thought, that you should have been the first magistrate, that for Christ's sake should have lost anything? As I said before therefore, I say again, that your state is happy. Good brother, before God I write the truth unto you, my conscience bearing me witness, that you are in a most happy state with the Lord, and before his sight.

Be thankful therefore, rejoice in your trouble, pray for
James i. patience, persevere to the end; "let patience have her perfect work." If you want this wisdom and power, ask it of God, who will give it to you in his good time. Hope still in him; yea, "if he should slay you, yet trust in him" with Job; and you shall perceive that the end will be to find him "merciful and full of compassion;" for he will not break promise with you, which hitherto did never so with any. "He is with you in trouble,"

he heareth you calling upon him: yea, "before you call," your desires are not only known, but accepted through Christ. If now and then he hide his face from you, it is but to provoke your appetite, to make you the more to long for him. This is most true: "he is a coming and will come, he will not be long." But if for a time "he seem to tarry, yet stand you still," and "you shall see the wonderful works of the Lord."

O my beloved, wherefore should you be heavy? Is not Christ Immanuel, "God with us?" Shall you not find that, as he is true in saying, "In the world you shall have trouble," so is he in saying, "In me you shall have comfort?" He doth not swear only that trouble will come, but withal he sweareth that comfort shall ensue. And what comfort! such a comfort as "the eye hath not seen, the ear hath not heard, nor the heart of man can conceive." O great comfort! who shall have this? Forsooth they that suffer for the Lord: and are not you one of them? Yea, verily are you. Then, as I said, happy, happy and happy again are you, my dearly beloved in the Lord. You now "suffer with the Lord: surely you shall be glorified with him." "Call upon God therefore now in your trouble," and he will hear you, yea, deliver you in such sort, as most shall make both to his and your glory also. And in this calling, I heartily pray you to pray for me, your fellow in affliction. Now we be both going in the high-way to heaven, for by many afflictions must we enter in thither: whither God bring us for his mercy's sake. Amen, Amen.

1 Cor. ii.

Your fellow in affliction,

JOHN BRADFORD.

XCIX. TO MISTRESS HALL[1].

Our most merciful God and Father, through Christ Jesus, our Lord and Saviour, be merciful unto us, and make perfect the good he hath begun in us unto the end. Amen.

Bp Coverdale, Letters of the Martyrs, 1564, p. 377.

[[1] The heading of this letter in Bp Coverdale is: "To Mistress Hall, prisoner in Newgate, and ready to make answer before her adversaries."

Strype records, that "on the 19th [of June 1557] was old Mrs Hall buried in the parish of St Benet Sherehog. She gave certain good gowns both for men and

Foxe, Acts, &c., ed. 1570, p. 1828; and after editions.

MS. 1. 2. 8. No. 73. Transcript. Emman. Coll. Cambridge.

Matt. v.

My dear sister, "rejoice in the Lord," rejoice, be glad, I say, be merry and thankful; not only because Christ so commandeth us, but also because our state, wherein we are presently, requireth no less, for we are the Lord's witnesses. God the Father hath vouchsafed to choose us, amongst many, to witness and testify, that Christ his Son is King, and that his word is true. Christ our Saviour, for his love's sake towards us, will have us to bear record, that he is no usurper, nor deceiver of the people, but God's ambassador, prophet and Messias; so that of all dignities upon earth this is the highest. Greater honour had not his prophets, apostles, nor dearest friends, than to bear witness with Christ, as we now do. The world, following the counsel of their sire, Satan, would gladly condemn Christ and his verity: but, lo! the Lord hath chosen us to be his champions to let this.

As stout soldiers therefore, let us stand to our Master, who is with us and standeth "on our right hand, that we shall not be much moved," if we hope and hang on his mercy: he is so faithful and true, that "he will never tempt us further than he will make us able to bear." Therefore "be not careful" (for I hear say this day you shall be called forth) what you shall answer: the Lord, which is true and cannot lie, hath promised (and will never fail nor forget it) that you shall have both what and how to answer, so as shall make his shameless adversaries ashamed. Hang therefore on this promise of God, who is an helper at a pinch, and a most present remedy to them that hope in him. Never was it heard of, nor shall be, that any hoping in the Lord was put to foil. Therefore, as I said, I say again, dear sister, be not only not careful for your answering, but also be joyful for your cause. "Confess Christ," and "be not ashamed;" and he will confess you, and never be ashamed of you. Though loss of goods and life be like here to ensue, yet, if Christ be true, as he is most true, it is otherwise in deed; for "he that loseth his life," saith he, "winneth it," "but he that saveth it loseth it."

women, and twenty gowns to poor people. Several ladies and others attended in mourning. She was memorable in being the mother of Mr Edward Hall of Gray's Inn, who set forth the chronicle called 'Hall's Chronicle:' and I conjecture she was that Mrs Hall that was a great reliever of such as were persecuted for religion in this reign, and to whom several of the martyrs wrote letters, which are extant." —Ecc. Mem. Vol. III. part II. p. 8.]

Our sins have deserved many deaths. Now, if God deal so with us, that he will make our deserved death a demonstration of his grace, a testimonial of his verity, a confirmation of his people, and an overthrow of his adversaries, what great cause have we to be thankful! Be thankful therefore, good sister, be thankful, rejoice and be merry in the Lord; be stout in his cause and quarrel; be not faint-hearted, but run out your race, and set your Captain Christ before your eyes.

Behold, how great your reward is; see the great glory and the eternity of felicity prepared for you. Strive and "fight lawfully," that you may get the crown. Run to get the game, you are almost at your journey's end. I doubt not but our Father will with us send to you also, as he did to Eli, a fiery chariot, to convey us into his kingdom. Let us therefore not be dismayed to leave our cloak behind us, that is, our bodies to ashes. God will one day restore them to us, like to the body of our Lord and Saviour Jesus Christ, whose coming is now at hand. Let us look for it, and "lift up our heads, for our redemption draweth nigh." Amen, Amen.—The Lord of mercy grant us his mercy. Amen.

2 Kings ii.

I pray you, pray for me, and so desire my brethren, which be with you. God's peace be with us all. Amen.

"Blessed be the dead that die in the Lord:" then how much more they that die for the Lord!

Your brother in bonds,

JOHN BRADFORD.

C. TO HIS MOTHER[1].

[June 24, 1555.]

God's mercy and peace in Christ be more and more perceived of us. Amen.

Bp Coverdale, Letters of the Martyrs, 1564, p. 454.

Foxe, Acts, &c., ed. 1570, p. 1839; and after editions.

My most dear mother, in the bowels of Christ, I heartily pray and beseech you to be thankful for me unto God, which thus now taketh me unto himself. I die not, my good mo-

[[1] The heading of this letter in Bishop Coverdale is: "To his mother, as his last farewell unto her in this world, a little before he was burned."]

MS. 2. 2. 15. No. 101. Transcript. Emman. Coll. Cambridge.

ther, as a thief, a murderer, an adulterer, &c.; but I die as a witness of Christ, his gospel and verity, which hitherto I have confessed, I thank God, as well by preaching as by imprisonment; and now, even presently, I shall most willing confirm the same by fire. I acknowledge that God most justly might take me hence, simply for my sins, which are many, great and grievous: but the Lord, for his mercy in Christ, hath pardoned them all, I hope. But now, dear mother, he taketh me hence by this death, as a confessor and witness, that the religion taught by Christ Jesu, the prophets and the apostles, is God's truth. The prelates do persecute in me Christ whom they hate, and his truth which they may not abide, because their works are evil, and may not abide the truth and light, lest men should see their darkness.

Therefore, my good and most dear mother, give thanks for me to God, that he hath made the fruit of your womb to be a witness of his glory: and attend to the truth, which (I thank God for it) I have truly taught out of the pulpit of Manchester. Use often and continual prayer to God the Father, through Christ. Hearken, as you may, to the scriptures; serve God after his word, and not after custom. Beware of the Romish religion in England, defile not yourself with it. Carry Christ's cross, as he shall lay it upon your back. Forgive them that kill me; pray for them, "for they know not what they do." Commit my cause to God our Father. Be mindful of both your daughters, to help them as you can.

I send all my writings to you by my brother Roger: do with them as you will, because I cannot as I would: he can tell you more of my mind. I have nothing to give you, or to leave behind me for you: only I pray God my Father, for his Christ's sake, to bless you and keep you from evil. He give you patience, he make you thankful, as for me so for yourself, that will take the fruit of your womb to witness his verity: wherein I confess to the whole world I die, and depart this life in hope of a much better; which I look for at the hands of God my Father, through the merits of his dear Son Jesus Christ.

Thus, my dear mother, I take my last farewell of you in this life, beseeching the almighty and eternal Father, by

Christ, to grant us to meet in the life to come, where we shall give him continual thanks and praise, for ever and ever. Amen.

Out of prison, the 24th of June, 1555.

Your son in the Lord,

JOHN BRADFORD.

CI. TO BERNHERE[1] AND MISTRESS HALES[2].

[The end of June, 1555 [3].]

To my good brother Augustine Bernhere. Mine own good Augustine, the Lord of mercy bless thee, my dear brother, for ever.

Bp Coverdale, Letters of the Martyrs, 1564, p. 468.

I have good hope that, if you come at night about nine of the clock[4], I shall speak with you: but come as secretly as you can. Howbeit, in the mean season, if you can, and as you can, learn of Master Bowier of the Temple, or of Master Calthrop[5], what they can report Master Green[6] hath spoken to Doctor Story[7] and others. The cause of all this trouble both to my keeper and me is through him[8], as far as Master Clayden[9] can think. He hath been with me an hour this

Foxe, Acts, &c., ed. 1570, p. 1837; and after editions.

MS. 2. 2. 15. No. 104. Original, Holograph. And 1. 2. 8. No. 31. Transcript, imperfect. Emman. Coll. Cambridge.

[[1] See p. 186, note 2, on Letter LXXIV. above. Foxe has the following side-note: "This Austin, being a Dutchman, was Latimer's servant, and a faithful minister in the time of King Edward, and in Mary's time a diligent attendant upon the Lord's prisoners."]

[[2] See p. 108, note 1, above.]

[[3] The date of Bradford's martyrdom was July 1, 1555. See Vol. I. p. 331, references in note 2.]

[[4] "late at night," 1564 and 1570: "at night about nine of the clock," autograph MS.]

[[5] The last eleven words now are first printed from the autograph MS.]

[[6] "what Master G." 1564 and 1570: "what they can report Master Green," autograph MS. Bartlett Green underwent martyrdom, January 27, 1556: but there had been at one time "slanders" concerning him: see a passage in his letter to Adn Philpot, given in Foxe, ed. 1563, p. 1459, or ed. 1843—9, Vol. VII. p. 734, but omitted in the intermediate editions. Foxe supplies a letter from Green, "To my very loving friends and masters......Master Calthorp, Master Bowier, and others my masters of the Temple," ed. 1583, p. 1855, or ed. 1843—9, Vol. VII. p. 743.]

[[7] See Writings of Philpot, pp. xxxi, 48, Park. Soc.]

[[8] "thought to come by him," 1564 and 1570: "through him," autograph MS.]

[[9] "Master Clayden" was Bradford's keeper in the Compter prison in the Poultry, where Bradford was confined after his excommunication, January 30, 1555. See Vol. I. pp. 492, 515—18, 538.]

afternoon[1]. He thinks[2] I shall be burned in Smithfield, and that shortly.

Domini voluntas fiat. Ecce ego, Domine, mitte me: 'The Lord's will be done. Behold, here I am: Lord, send me[3].' Ah! mine own sweet friend, I am now alone, lest I should make you and others worse. If I should live, I would more warily use the company of God's children than ever I have
Micah vii. done. *Iram Domini portabo, quoniam peccavi ei:* "I will bear the Lord's anger, because I have sinned against him."

Commend me to my most dear sister, for whom my heart bleedeth: the Lord comfort her and strengthen her unto the end[4]. I think I have taken my leave of her for ever in this life: but in eternal life we shall most surely meet together[5], and praise the Lord continually.

Ah! my good Joyce[6], because I cannot write to you (for I know not how, and all things are more strange here, and cases more and more perilous), I [am] on this sort since you went, that I am careful for you. Be merry, be merry, dear heart: God shall give us to meet in his kingdom. In the mean season I shall pray for thee, my dearest sister; and so I know thou doest for me[7]. I have indeed[8] taken a more certain answer of death than ever I did, and yet not so certain as I ween[8] I should do. I am now "as a sheep appointed to the slaughter."—O my God, "the hour is come, glorify thy" most unworthy child, "that he may glorify thee!"—"I have glorified thee," saith this my sweet Father, "and I will glorify thee." Amen.

Ah! mine own bowels, praise God for me, and pray for me; for I am his, I hope. I hope he will never forsake me, though I have, above all others, most deserved it; I am the

[1 The last sixteen words now are first printed from the autograph MS.]

[2 "It is said that," 1564 and 1570: "He thinks," autograph MS.]

[3 The English rendering of the Latin words in this letter is inserted, unless otherwise marked, from Foxe, Acts, &c., ed. 1570, p. 1837.]

[4 "strengthen her unto the end," 1564 and 1570, and MS. 8. No. 31: "be with her for ever," autogr. MS.]

[5 "together," only in autograph MS.]

[6 The name "Joyce" has been, in some degree, erased in the original autograph with a penknife. It seems clear however, that this is the name which had been written.]

[7 The last seven lines, "Ah! my good Joyce......thou doest for me," now are first printed from the autograph MS.]

[8 "now," "think," 1564 and 1570: "indeed," "ween," autograph MS.]

most singular example of his mercy. Dear Joyce[6], thou art his a great deal more than I am. Indeed it is so; praise thy God and Father[9]. Praised be his name for[10] ever.

But to thee again, my good Augustine. Will Robert Harrington not to come in company without Smithfield. Send me word who they be were condemned yesterday[11]. Mistress Pierpoint might[10] learn of the sheriff, Master Chester, something[12] what they purpose to do with me. Learn at Master Bowier whether any writ be[13] forth for me.

Factus sum sicut nycticorax in domicilio, et passer solitarius Ps. cii.
in lecto: "I am like to an owl in the house, and as a sparrow alone in the housetop." O my Augustine! how long shall God's enemies thus triumph?

I have sent to you, if th[at you][14] cannot come to me, this to write of baptism of inf[ants[14].] When this is done, you shall have more for[15]... Pray, pray, mine own dear friend[16], on whom I am bold[14]. The keeper telleth me it is pain of[16] death for any to speak with me: but yet I hope[16] *quod tecum sum locuturus, et fortassis si vixero cum sorore*[17]: 'that I shall speak with you, [and perhaps, if I shall live, with my sister.]' Let her look over this letter; and send me word how she doeth, for *male me habeo quod ignoro*, [it troubles me that I know not.]

To my good friend Augustine, at
Master Pierpoint's[18].

[9 The last twenty-one words now are first printed from the autograph MS.]

[10 "therefore for," "Cause Mistress Pierpoint to," 1564 and 1570: "for," "Mistress Pierpoint might," autograph MS.]

[11 The last three sentences, "But to thee again......condemned yesterday," now are first printed from the autograph MS.]

[12 "something," only in autograph MS.]

[13 "and know if you can, whether there be any writ," 1564 and 1570: "Learn at Master Bowier whether any writ be," autograph MS.]

[14 The MS. torn, and a word or two wanting.]

[15 The last twenty-seven words, "I have sent......have more for," are from the autograph MS. The printed editions of 1564 and 1570 have instead, "I have sent you this, of the baptism of children, to write out: when this is done, you shall have other things."]

[16 "heart," "that it is," "trust," 1564 and 1570: "friend," "it is pain of," "hope," autograph MS.]

[17 These ten Latin words are only in the autograph MS.]

[18 The last twenty-seven words (exclusive of the seven in brackets) now are first printed from the autograph MS.]

MEDITATION ON THE PASSION OF OUR SAVIOUR JESU CHRIST[1].

MS. 1. 2. 8. No. 21. Holograph. Emman. Coll. Cambridge.

After thou, O Lord Jesu Christ, the Son [of] God—after, I say, thou hadst supped, giving thanks, taught and prayed, the same night thou wast betrayed, thou wentest over the brook Cedron—over the which thy servant David, with his Cerethites and Pelethites, prefiguring thee and thy disciples, did go, sorrowful and heavy for the afflictions by his son Absalom, his counsellor Ahithophel, and his own servants now conspiring and risen against him; as was Judas, the bishops and the people of the Jews, conspired against thee, whereof the other was as a figure or shadow—thou, I say, dear Lord, didst pass over the brook Cedron, with thy disciples, towards the mount of Olives, whither thou wast accustomed in those days nightly to resort to pray, as in the daytime thou didst accustom to be conversant in the temple to teach. Whereby we may see that willingly thou wentest to thy passions to suffer for us; for else thou mightest have gone into some other place, which had not been so well known to Judas, that sought opportunity to betray thee.

Now as thou wast going, thy disciples did contend, as Luke writeth, who should be the greatest after thy departure, whereof they had now heard much and often, thereby declaring to our comfort and information their ambition and ignorance, that, as we might not despair for our infirmities, so we might not flatter ourselves to think us to have attained to the top when we are not passed much the toes. This their ignorance and infirmity, whereof thou hadst very often reproved them before, though yet thou didst not see it amended, yet didst thou not cast them away therefore to our consolation, but to our instruction didst most mildly and fatherly reprove them and correct them, telling them how that principality and dominion pertaineth not to their office, which was and is and for ever in this life must be a mystery, wherein he is the greatest that teacheth most, and taketh greatest pains. Therefore thou didst will them to leave that to the magistrates, which are for their

[[1] This Meditation now is first printed.]

office sake to be called, 'gracious lords;' for doubtless there they be very "gods," as the scripture calleth them, if according to their offices they behave themselves. The which thing grant thou to all, but specially to ours here in this realm, we most humbly do beseech thee.—The office of thy apostles and their successors, thou didst teach them, was another manner of thing than a principality or a lordliness: and therefore, as thou hadst commended them for tarrying with thee in thy troubles, so didst thou further admonish them of the trouble and cross which would come upon them for their office sake, shewing them that not here but elsewhere in thy kingdom they should be promoted as princes, there to sit at thy table with thee. The which thing they, not much considering, thought that they could have repelled all perils with their "two swords," which there they had with them; whereof Peter used the one to thy honour, but no thanks but blame to him therefore. By reason whereof thou, seeing so gross ignorance in them, couldst not but be something grieved; and therefore, as in way to speak more thereof, thou saidst, "Two swords were enough."

Rather they should have considered, how thou hadst told them, and that only of the testimony of the prophet Zechariah, that through thee they "should be all offended that night;" and thereto they should have remembered the comfort thou didst give them, that "after the resurrection thou wouldest go before them into Galilee;" whereby as they might have seen all things to have happened, not by chance, but by the providence of God, so they might have contained themselves thereto, and have comforted themselves with the consolation thou didst give them. But it was necessary for thee, O Lord, to admonish them of their offence, that the s[in][2] might be only their own, because they were not more ready, and that they might be more humbled in thy sight, when after their fall they might remember they had been admonished.

But—to return—thy disciples heard well and often of thee, how that "Satan had desired to sift them," thereby proving his malice and diligence; and how that indeed he should partly prevail against them, yea, wholly, if that thou, "the good Shepherd," no less loving and vigilant, hadst not prayed for them: wherethrough—I do mean thy prayer—their faith finally "fainted

[[2] MS. torn.]

not." But, alas! the corporeal Peter much regarded not thy words, but took too much upon this, as though to stand in the cross were the work of "flesh and blood." Therefore by their own experience they proved, and most specially Peter, as ever after to take better heed to thy words, so "not to think on themselves above that they should do," "lest he that standeth fall."

O good Christ, open our eyes to see and shun Satan his subtlety against us, and never to forget that "as a roaring lion" he seeketh to destroy us. O, be thou for us no less vigilant than thou wast for the disciples and Peter, but only that Satan never prevail against us; but rather protect us still with thy grace, mercy, and blessing, as thou hitherto hast done of thine own goodness, and here didst [protect] the apostles not desiring it. O give us faith, increase it in us, and grant that we may know how salutary a thing faith is, which if it faint not, Satan and all his sayings cannot prevail. O give us to feel and bewail our infinite oblivion of thy word; and enable us to stand in the cross for thy name's sake, and to find help and remedy always for the same, of thy goodness.

PRAYER ON THE TEN COMMANDMENTS[1].

MS. 2. 2. 16. No. 27. Emman. Coll. Cambridge.

O ALMIGHTY, everlasting, most righteous, fearful and merciful God, "the Father of our Lord Jesus Christ," by whom and with whom and with the Holy Ghost thou hast made and dost rule all things; thou only art "the true God," the Judge of all men, and the Governor of the world. Thou only dost "search and try the thoughts and the very bottoms of the hearts of all men." No man can hide anything from thee, for "all things are naked and bare" in thy sight. Thou hatest and abhorrest sin, and therefore thy dearest creatures infected with the same: as the rejection of the angels that fell, the abjection of mankind forth of paradise, and innumerable kinds of punishments wherewith mankind is afflicted, as mortality, ignorance, weakness,

[[1] This prayer is now printed for the first time.
On the reverse of the last page of the MS. is written: "The ten commandments drawn into a prayer by Master John Bradford." It is a contemporary transcript, which is corrected with various interlineations, that apparently are in Bradford's autograph.]

sickness, death, poverty, pestilence, wars and such like, do plainly demonstrate and open to us all which are not infidels, believing the devil who persuadeth his to think that such things come by chance and fortune.

Inasmuch as thy holy commandments, which I ought to do and obey, do accuse and condemn me of many sins, for the which thy wrath and eternal damnation hangeth over me, I know not, O Lord, what to do: for I have and do break all thy commandments.

For, concerning the first commandment, I confess that I should think in my heart truly and rightly of thee; that I should, with a sure faith, without wavering, be persuaded that thou, O Lord, which gavest these commandments, and hast opened and disclosed thyself in thy holy word given unto us, and by thy Son Jesus Christ sent from thee unto us—that thou, the one only true God, the Maker and Ruler of all things, art my Lord God in Jesus Christ; that is, for his sake dost love me, forgive me my sins, governest me with thy holy Spirit, and wilt do so still for evermore. This without all wavering I should firmly believe, and therefore be thankful to thee, love thee heartily, continually, wholly and perfectly, fear thy holy name, and be zealous for thy glory. Rejoicing I ought heartily above all things to love thee, and to feel some sparkle of a thankful heart in me towards thee; I ought to be affected and fervently moved for the greatness of thy mercy, because thou hast by thy word made thyself known unto us, because thou hast unfeignedly loved mankind, because thou wouldest indeed have us saved and not damned. I ought to be inwardly moved for the great benefits of thy dear Son our Lord Jesus Christ, because he suffered death for us, because he hath given his gospel unto us, because he hath promised that thou wilt give the Holy Ghost to us to be our Governor if we ask the same of thee in his name, and because he hath also promised us everlasting life.

The First. "Thou shalt have none other Gods but me."

But, alas! most dear Lord, thou seest my heart, how it wandereth away from thee; thou knowest that all these things do little or nothing move my mind—my heart, O Lord, is so stony. I fear thee in manner nothing; I often doubt of thine anger, of thy mercy, of thy will, of thy presence; and through this doubtfulness I am very faint in asking benefits of thee, I do wonderful coldly pray unto thee; yea, Lord, I neglect praying unto thee. I put more trust to myself and to my friends, to such things as I have and are present, than unto thee, O Lord: yea, I seek too diligently for the helps of this life, and that by other means than thou hast appointed me. How often have I offended thee in false prayer, praying unto saints and calling upon them, as though either they could have helped me, or else as though they had been more merciful than thou; and herein I have thought that I have done thee high service; I have thought that thou wouldest have rather been prayed unto at this altar or that altar, afore this image or that image than elsewhere. And even now, O Lord, I also do much offend thee when I pray, in that I do not indeed think upon thee heartily, as I should do, that is by the Mediator our Lord Jesus Christ, how that by him and through him we may come unto thee "with boldness." No, Lord, thy promises I think not upon when I pray; I am nothing so fervent in prayer as I should be.

The Second. "Thou shalt not take the name of the Lord in vain[1]."

And concerning thy second commandment[1], O Lord, how far am I from keeping it! for I ought diligently to hear and to learn the gospel, and to set it forth both in word or talking and also in example of living. But, alas! I confess to thee my negligence and slothfulness in this behalf. I sleep when thy word is read or preached, so small do I reverence it: yea, Lord, I make of thy gospel a cloak to hide my carnality and covetousness. Many evil examples and offences do I give unto others, whereby they may justly take occasion to speak evil of thy gospel. I am a hinderer of others that would do

[[1] That erroneous division of the Commandments is here followed, which reckons the first and second as one, and divides the tenth into two, which was generally in use before the Reformation, and which is still continued in the Lutheran churches, as well as in the church of Rome. See Abp Cranmer's "Catechismus," translated from Justus Jonas (printed by Lynn, 1548, and reprinted, Oxford, 1829), on first commandment, where that division is observed. See also Bullinger's Decades, Vol. I. pp. 212—14, Park. Soc., where some of the chief patristic authorities are quoted; Early Writings of Bp Hooper, pp. 349—51, Park. Soc.; Calvin. Instit. Lib. II. cap. viii. 12. Op. Tom. IX. pars I. p. 94, Amst. 1667—71; and Fowns' Trisagion, p. 451, London, 1618.

Distinction should be made between this incorrect division, which has been sanctioned by eminent names, and that fraudulent suppression of the second commandment, which frequently occurs in catechisms used in the church of Rome. See Soames' Hist. Reform. Vols. II. pp. 529—31, III. p. 298, and IV. p. 488, Lond. 1826—8; and Bp Gibson's Preservative, Vol. III. Title IX. ch., Doctrines and practices of the church of Rome, p. 302, London. 1738.]

well: and thou knowest, O Lord! how unthankful I am for my deliverance out of such errors and naughty opinions as I have been of afore I did give some ear unto thy gospel, so far am I from true repentance for my said errors.

The Third. "Remember that thou keep holy the sabbath day."

Concerning the third commandment, thou, most patient Lord, dost see how often I have and yet do lightly regard the common sermons and common prayer, in the temples on the holy-days, having no just thing to let or hinder me: whereby I am and have been an occasion that others are more negligent in the same than else they would be. O Lord! I am not thankful unto thee for the ministry of thy word and sacraments, which thou hast ordained. Alas! when did I give thee hearty thanks for preserving thy church and the holy scriptures of the Bible? When did I heartily pray unto thee for the church and for the commonweal? O how hard is mine heart, that am not moved and grieved in heart for the miseries and troubles of my brethren! and yet I know, I see, I hear wonderful great ignorance, discord, hatred, dissension, war, robbing and oppressing of thy people, the souls and bodies of many to perish. The ministers of thy word and the preachers I do not only lightly regard, but I find many faults in them, I am captious, &c.: thou seest, how unwilling I am to give them their duties. Yea, Lord, I confess that I spend the holy-days evil, in banqueting, in feasting, in idle or unhonest pastimes, by which things I provoke thine anger, not only against me, but also against many others.

The Fourth. "Honour thy father and thy mother."

Concerning the fourth, I confess, O Lord, that I am negligent concerning my vocation, in governing my household, in serving my master. I am also unthankful, &c., unto thee for our king and for the benefits of the commonweal. I murmur often, and that causeless, against the magistrates. I evil report them, so far am I from giving them due reverence from the bottom of my heart, which thing yet I ought to do. I am contentious and a busybody, I love strife, I break the orders and indifferent laws of thy commonweal, and that not without offence and hurt unto others; I am rather a hinderer than a furtherer of the commonweal. Through my foolish hastiness I keep me not in my bounds, yea, I trouble the common neighbourhood, rather than seek how to pacify and further it. I live all for myself; I seek my own profit more than the profit of the commonweal; I spy out corners to hinder and trouble others.

The Fifth. "Thou shalt not kill."

Concerning the fifth commandment, thou, Lord, dost see how greatly I offend thee; for I am angry without cause, often doth my heart boil with desire to be avenged, often do I speak roughly, bitterly, wrathfully, yea, cursingly, so great is the heat of anger in me. I am envious: it grieveth me that others prosper and do better than I; and that not of any other cause but for that I rather envy them than heartily love them. I desire to be had in favour and estimation, I am proud, I despise my fellows and them which are equal with me, I would be more set by than they. I am suspicious, I construe other men's doings and sayings to the worst. I concitate[1] displeasure against others upon light occasions, I make debate between others, I am a talebearer, whereby I occasion evil grudgings and hatred: whereas my duty is, O Lord, to be patient, to take all things to the best, so long as it is not to thy dishonour, to go about to reconcile such as be at variance. But, alas! I have not done so hitherto: no, Lord, I suffer hatred rather to increase, and that through my negligence, yea, through my maliciousness; I am a backbiter, and a favourer of backbiters, rather than a reprover of them. Finally, O Lord, I hinder my vocation and other men's, through my self-wilfulness and the haut proud stoutness of my wretched sinful heart, which is not hid in thy sight.

The Sixth. "Thou shalt not commit adultery."

And how horrible and often I break the sixth commandment, thine eyes, Lord, "which try the reins" of all men, do right well look upon. Thou seest what naughty straggling vicious thoughts and motions I have. Thou, Lord, dost see the divers and sundry vicious flames and burnings of the lusts of the flesh. I delight in seeing and in unclean cogitations[2]. And these evils do I increase and stir up in me through banqueting, sleeping, gluttony, drunkenness, gossiping, good fellowship and evil diet. And through this gear I hinder godly thoughts, meditations and prayer, making myself worse than a beast. So that I procure thine anger, O Lord, not only against myself, but also against this household, this parish and whole realm.

[1 "Concitate:" excite, arouse.]

[2 One or two words of the original are here omitted.]

Now for the seventh commandment, O Lord, I cannot excuse myself except I would heap sin upon sin. For I misspend my living, my substance, my wages, in not using them so well as I might do. Yea, Lord, I defraud other men, living by other men's sweat, and loitering myself; I deal not uprightly in buying and selling; I keep not equality for thy sake only; I pay my debts with an evil will. I exercise unlawful means and unlawful times to get money, as though my living were gotten by mine own means. I use divers pretences to borrow, but I am very slack to repay; I keep still with me that which belongeth to other men, and have been unwilling to make restitutions hitherto, as though thou wouldest forgive my sins, and wink at this my covetousness. Yea, Lord, thou seest even now, how unwilling the devil and my stubborn heart maketh me, to keep me from making restitution. I confess also, O Lord, that I am not faithful and diligent in doing my work; I sell and utter evil wares for good, and thereto I spare not to swear and to lie; I care not how I occupy and use such things as I borrow or hire. The Seventh. "Thou shalt not steal."

Finally the eighth commandment, O Lord, doth condemn me: for I use not that plainness, simplicity and truth, which thou requirest of me both in my words and deeds. I use subtlety and craft both in giving and asking counsel; and in all things I do, sometimes of obstinacy, sometimes of flattery, sometimes of fear, of displeasure, do I say or unsay things which are untrue: so that, Lord, all my trade and manners smell of nothing but even hypocrisy, seeming one thing, and indeed being another thing. The Eighth. "Thou shalt not bear false witness," &c.

As for the two last commandments, which forbid concupiscence or lusting, alas! Lord, I was never pure therefrom, no, not when I was in my mother's womb; but, even as a young toad hath always poison in it when it is never so young, even so, O Lord, I when I was conceived, straightways was this concupiscence, lusting and rebellion against thee conceived in me also; which hath put forth itself since I was able to do anything, in not ceasing from breaking outwardly thy holy commandments in open sins: which open sins, O Lord! are nothing else but the fruit of inward sin, which alway lay hid in me, and will lie so long as I am in this world and body. By reason whereof I acknowledge and confess, O gracious Lord! that I am a very The Ninth and Tenth. "Thou shalt not desire thy neighbour's," &c.

miserable and a wretched sinner. Yea, Lord, though I lie in this blindness, sinfulness and rebellion against thee, yet I do horribly and retchlessly neglect and lightly regard thy wrath hanging over my head, and over the heads of others for my sake. I do not heartily feel the multitude and huge greatness of my sins, vices and falls: but yet, Lord, unto thee do I acknowledge it and confess it, I do not hide it from thee, "for with thee is mercy and plenteous redemption." I confess, Lord, that I have deserved both present and everlasting punishments in the fire of hell, which "never shall be quenched." In true grief of heart and bitterness of mind do I cry unto thee, and say therefore, "Against thee, O Lord, I have sinned;" afore thee I have done wickedly; so that, if thou wilt damn me, thou shalt be found righteous. And even so, in shewing mercy unto me being most unworthy, thou shalt be found righteous also, because thou hast promised to have mercy freely for thy Son Jesu Christ's sake unto all that shall unfeignedly desire and ask the same. I am sorry, O Lord! that I have offended thee and procured thine anger against me and many others.

O Christ Jesu, which only art he "that takest away the sins of the world," and that by the death and once offering of thy body upon the cross! unto thee do I flee, for thou art my Redeemer and Saviour, and thou hast said, "Come unto me all you that labour and are heavy laden, and I will refresh you." And I pray thee, O eternal Father, for this thy Son's sake, that thou wouldest turn from me thy great anger, have mercy upon me, forgive me my sins, remember what thou hast said, "As surely as I live, I will not the death of a sinner, but that he should return, convert and amend." Convert me, O Lord, which hast "so loved the world, that thou wouldest not spare thy dearly beloved Son, to this end, that all that believe in him should not perish, but have life everlasting." See, Father, what thy Son hath said, namely, that thou wilt "give thy holy Spirit to them that ask thee." This Holy Spirit I ask thee in his name, most dear Father, to ascertain me that thou hast of thy great mercy forgiven me all my sins, and that thou wilt govern me for evermore.

And now, Lord, I do promise thee that I will fight more diligently against sin than I have done; I will not so sin against my conscience as I have sinned, by thy grace and help of thy holy Spirit. Which here I beseech thee for thy mercy's sake that thou wouldest plentifully pour into my heart, to rule me inwardly and outwardly, both in all my thoughts, words, and deeds, that I may henceforth live in this world to thy honour and glory, and to the help of my brethren. And after this life grant that I may be partaker of thy everlasting life, through the merits of the passion of thy dearly beloved Son our Lord and Saviour Jesus Christ, who liveth and reigneth with thee, and with the Holy Ghost, everlasting and almighty, world without end. Amen.

FRAGMENT ON ST JOHN'S GOSPEL[1].

MS. 2. 2. 16. No. 11. Original, Holograph. Emman. Coll. Cambridge.

THE cause that moved St John to write this Gospel Eusebius[2] and St Jerome[3] do witness, as they gathered out of others that were before them[4], was to affirm the Divinity of Christ against Ebion and Cerinthus: but hereof read St Jerome's Prologue[3]. This I am certain of, that the Holy Ghost hath never provided for his church by this Gospel, there only, the assertion of Christ's Godhead. Not without a mystery was it that the evangelist laid his head on Christ's bosom, in his last supper, as they that read this Gospel shall well see the very treasures and hid counsels of God most manifestly and comfortably opened by it. Though it be the last of the Gospels that be written, and therefore it is for thee last, yet I think a man should not do amiss that would begin with it, for out of it we shall best learn wherefore Christ was given. God give us

[1 This imperfect treatise now is first printed.]

[2 See, in Euseb. Hist. Eccles. Lib. VI. cap. xiv., the testimony of Clemens Alexandr., in the "Hypotyposes" or "Institutions," there quoted, to the effect that John, perceiving what respected the body to be enough detailed, encouraged also by friends, and urged by the Spirit, wrote a spiritual Gospel.]

[3 Joannes apostolus,......novissimus omnium scripsit evangelium, rogatus ab Asiæ episcopis, adversus Cerinthum aliosque hæreticos, et maxime tunc Ebionitarum dogma consurgens, qui asserunt Christum ante Mariam non fuisse.—Hieron. Lib. de vir. illustr. cap. ix. Op. Tom. II. col. 829, stud. Vallars. Veron. 1734—42. See also Hieron. Comment. in Matth. ad Euseb. Præfat. Tom. VII. cols. 3—6.]

[4 Irenæus states that the Gospel of John was written against the Nicolaitans and Cerinthus.—Iren. Cont. Hær. Lib. III. cap. xi. 1, 2. Op. Tom. I. p. 188, ed. Bened. Venet. 1734. See Du Pin. Hist. Canon. ch. ii. 6. Vol. II. p. 51. Lond. 1699-1700.]

ears to hear, eyes to see, and hearts to believe and perceive it accordingly. And hitherto for the argument.

Now to the letter and text of the Gospel. Thus it beginneth, "In the beginning was the Word, and the Word was with God, and God was the Word. This was in the beginning with God."

The scope of St John's writing is, that the restoration of mankind must be made by the Son of God. But, forasmuch as man may not be brought from God, therefore it was necessary for St John to prove that in bringing us to Christ he bringeth us not from God. For which cause be beginneth with the Divinity and Godhead of Christ, that we might know how that the benefit of life is restored to man by him which at the first gave it, and is the fountain and cause of life. Therefore he saith, "In the beginning was the Word," by this word, "beginning," sending us not to such a beginning as Moses meaneth when he saith, "In the beginning God made heaven and earth," for there is a beginning in time: whereas this with St John is rather a beginning afore all times than of any end, as full well he doth teach when he saith, "And the Word was with God:" as though he might say, 'The beginning whereof I speak is not a beginning of any end as is with Moses, but such a beginning as was before any time, that is, such a beginning as was not with man or any creatures, but such a beginning as was with God.' In which words, methinks, I see the wonderful wisdom of the Holy Ghost, which in holding his tongue and going no further in this high mystery doth teach us to be sober in ascending too far in searching and disputing of this matter of Christ's Godhead. Only we ought to be satisfied with the simple truth which after those words he plainly doth write, saying, "And that Word," or "the Word," "was God," than which words nothing can be more briefly, simply and evidently spoken. "And," saith he, "the Word," which he said "was in the beginning," "was God," teaching plainly these two things, namely, that this term, "the Word," signifieth a plain substance and person, and that this "Word," substance or person, "is God;" whereby all fond fantastical opinions against Christ's Godhead is utterly ov[erthrown[1]].

If a man would ask the question, why Christ, the Son of

[[1] MS. frayed and slightly torn.]

God, h[ath been[1]] called λόγος or *sermo*, that is, a "word," I think that a man's "word" is the show and express image of the mind, and declareth the wisdom of the same. Even so Christ is called "the Word" and "Wisdom" of God, because by him and none otherwise than by him God is known: and therefore to him is attributed, as immediately doth follow, the work of the creation and of the conservation of all things, as the redemption of mankind, by the testimony and word of God. Which word, because it cometh from this second Person, the Son of God, as from the fountain and head-spring (who so ever spake[2], wrote or ministered it), and is the chief means to bring men into the knowledge of him and so of the Father, is adorned and entitled with this glorious name, "The word of God."

Out of these things let us ever learn, that they that would know Christ or the Father must go to the word of God, written by the prophets and apostles. Again let them bear no less credence nor give no less credit unto it, than to very Christ or God himself. And, last of all, let them beware of denying Christ's Godhead and eternity, except they would make the Father at any time without wisdom and word, and so make him a foolish God and a wordless God; as they needs must do if they deny Christ to be God, and co-eternal with the Father.

As for other reasons that men may gather out of this word, λόγος, "the Word," I will neither improve nor approve further than by the testimony of God's word I am taught Servetus his folly, which thinketh that the Word, that is, the second Person, was not tofore the creation of the world[3], or but in the creation of the world (as some espied out), if men would make a distinction betwixt the two relations which the Word hath, one to Godward, another to manward: for it may not be gathered that, because the Word had no relation to usward but in the creation, therefore it had no relation to Godward: as this

[2 The word "spake" is scored across in the MS.]

[3 Id ipsum, quod in verbo et sapientia relucebat, est ipse Christus: sicut si me facie ad faciem et etiam in speculo videas, non vides nisi unam personam. Ex his plane intelligitur parabola de sapientia, Prov. viii. Persona Christi ibi ostenditur, dicens se esse ab æterno formatum. Figuratio erat Christi, relucentia, expressio quædam......Sed creatus dicitur, quia particeps creaturæ, genitus personaliter personalis Filius, atque ita personaliter creatus.—Servet. De Trin. Lib. I. Opusc. p. 13, s. l. et a.]

which followeth doth well teach, saying, "The same" (he meaneth the Word, the Son of God) "was in the beginning with God." The which repetition in that it is nothing else but that which before is spoken, we are done to wit that we should be more certain of the thing last spoken, namely, that the Word is a substance, that the beginning is not of [any] end but of eternity, that the Word is God. The which he now goeth about to prove most evidently and plenteously, saying: "All things were made by it, and without it was made[1] nothing that was made."

We may not think that we can apprehend uncreated God: and therefore he bringeth us here first to the mean, namely to the work of creation, that we might learn how that, after in our minds we[2] have conceived God, if the same conception shall be effectual [in] us, we must descend to some means, whereby we may as it were[2] tie him: for else the knowledge of God will vanish away out of our minds, so vain are they. Therefore descendeth he now to the[2] work of the creation, as though he might have said, This Word which before I have affirmed to be God his works shall declare[3]: first I affirm that "all things were made by [him[4]."]

[[1] The word "made" is scored across in the MS.]

[[2] Each of these words is uncertain, the MS. being frayed.]

[[3] A word or two is wanted here, the MS. being torn.]

[[4] The MS. ends here, being imperfect.]

[CONFUTATION OF FOUR ROMISH DOCTRINES.

The following "Confutation" formed part of a Treatise, published abroad, it would seem, by the Protestant exiles, during the reign of Mary, without any date or name of the author or printer, and now exceedingly rare. The present reprint follows a copy of that book, so issued, and possibly unique, belonging to George Offor, Esq., Hackney, and the title of which is given on the next page.

The "Confutation" is placed among Bradford's writings for the following reason. Bishop Coverdale, in 1564, attributed to Bradford a considerable portion of the entire Treatise (namely the first four chapters and part of the fourteenth), which he caused to be printed among Bradford's epistles, and with his signature, in the "Letters of the Martyrs," pp.427—46. But the complete Treatise, in its original edition, had ostensibly proceeded from one pen[5]: and, on the other hand, Coverdale not unfrequently abridged the letters he inserted—partly, it might be, for brevity's sake, and partly for the immediate objects of his publication, which seem to have been practical more than controversial. See for instance the "Defence of Election," Volume I. pp. 305—30, only a part of which had appeared in the "Letters of the Martyrs," 1564. See also Letters XXXII., XLI., LXXX., XCVII., CI., from Bradford, and Letter LVII. from bishop Ridley, above in this Volume, all of which supply matter that had been omitted by Coverdale. It appears probable therefore, that the complete Treatise had been written by Bradford. And this inference would seem to be amply sustained by close examination; because the "Confutation" is, in various parts (to which reference is made in the footnotes), closely similar to other productions which were avowedly composed by Bradford.

The "Confutation" is printed in this volume, in the desire to

[[5] Strype, not being aware that a large part of that Treatise had been attributed by Bp Coverdale to Bradford, as above stated, incorrectly supposed that the entire Treatise, being in the same type, and apparently issued at the same time, with another work, that was translated by Coverdale, was written by that prelate. See Strype, Ecc. Mem. Vol. III. part I. pp. 239, 40; and Works of Bp Coverdale, Vol. II. pp. 230—77, Park. Soc., where the complete Treatise, as originally issued in the edition without date, and of which the title is given in the next page, will be found.]

present, among Bradford's Works, every piece which, there is reason to believe, may have been written by that martyr. That portion of the original Treatise, which, after its first publication in the edition without date, re-appeared in the "Letters of the Martyrs," 1564, pp. 427—46, has already been given in Volume I. pp. 412—33, under the title of "An exhortation to the brethren throughout the realm of England," and where some sentences are supplied from the original edition.

An exhor-
tacion to the cari-
enge of Chrystes crosse, wyth a true and brefe confutacion of false and papisticall doctryne.

☞

☞ 2. Timo. 3.

☞ All, that wyll lyve godly in Chryste Jesu must suffer persecu cyon.

☞]

CONFUTATION OF FOUR ROMISH DOCTRINES.

CHAPTER I.

HOW THE PAPISTS HOLD THEIR FOUR SPECIAL ARTICLES, THAT THEY CHIEFLY PERSECUTE FOR.

[1]And here, because the persecution and cross which is come and will come upon us is specially for these four points of religion, namely, of the sacrament of Christ's body and blood, and for the sacrifice of Christ, for praying for the dead, and praying to the dead, that is, to saints, I am purposed by God's grace to write hereof a little unto you, thereby to confirm you in the truth, to your comfort in the cross about the same.

And first, concerning the first doctrine, what they would have us to believe on these points, this is their doctrine: 'The catholic church hath taught, as she hath learned and received of Christ, how that he in his last supper, according to his promise, when he promised to give a bread, even his flesh, in instituting the sacrament of the altar (as they call it) performed the same; and that, as in all things which he promised he was found true, so in this the catholic church hath believed and doth believe no less. And therefore, so soon as the priest in the mass hath fully spoken these words, "This is my body," if he purpose or his intention be as he speaketh (for that is requisite, teach they), then that which before was bread, and seemeth to the eye to be bread, is made in very deed Christ's body, flesh, blood and bone, even the selfsame which was crucified, rose again and ascended up into heaven[2]. So that he which believeth not this is a most heinous heretic, and cut off from the catholic church, and is not meet to receive this holy sacrament; because he cannot without this faith of Christ's natural, real, corporal and carnal body, under the form or accident of bread and wine, otherwise receive this sacrament than unworthily and to eternal damnation.' This is a short sum of their doctrine concerning the supper.

Of the sacrament.

John vi.

[1 See Vol. I. p. 431, note 1.] [2 See p. 227, note 6, above.]

Of the sacrifice.

Now concerning the sacrifice they teach that, 'though our Saviour himself did indeed make a full and perfect sacrifice, propitiatory and satisfactory for the sins of all the whole world, never more so, that is to say, bloodily, to be offered again, yet in his supper he offered the same sacrifice unto his Father, but unbloodily, that is to say, in will and desire; which is accounted often even for the deed, as this was. Which unbloody sacrifice he commanded his church to offer in remembrance of his bloody sacrifice, as the principal mean whereby his bloody sacrifice is applied both to the quick and dead; as baptism is the mean by the which regeneration is applied by the priest to the infant or child that is baptized. For, in that the supper of Christ is to them not only a sacrament but also a sacrifice, and that not only applicatory but also propitiatory, because it applieth the propitiatory sacrifice of Christ to whom the priest or minister will, be he dead or alive; and in that, even from the beginning, the fathers were accustomed in the celebration of the supper to have a memorial of the dead[1]; and also, in that this sacrifice is a sacrifice of the whole church, the dead being members of the church, of charity as they cannot but offer for them, even so they cannot but pray for them after the ensample of the catholic church; because "it is a wholesome thing," saith Judas Maccabeus, "to pray for the dead, that they may be delivered from their sins." Whereunto all the doctors do consent,' say they.

Prayer for the dead.

[2 Macc. xii. 44, 45.]

Prayer to saints.

Now, as for praying to saints, they teach that, 'albeit there is but one Mediator of redemption, yet of intercession the holy saints of God departed this life may well be counted mediators. And therefore it is a point of a lowly heart and humble spirit, which God well liketh, to call upon the saints to pray for us first, lest by our presumption to come into God's presence, we being so unworthy, and God being so excellent and full of majesty, we more anger and displease God: whereas by their help God may be entreated to make us more worthy to come unto him, and the sooner to grant us our petitions. For, if the holy saints of God, here being upon the earth, could and would pray for the people, obtaining many things

[[1] See Abp Usher, Answer to a Jesuit, "Of prayer for the dead," pp. 194—275, Lond. 1631; and Bingham, Orig. Eccles., Book xv. chap. iii. sect. 15—17, Works, Vol. I. pp. 756—62, Lond. 1726.]

at God's hand, it is much more to be believed now,' say they, 'that they can and will, if we pray to them, obtain for us our humble and godly desires.' And therefore to the end their sacrifice propitiatory, which in the mass they offer, may be the more available, they use about it much praying to saints.

So of these four, as of four pillars, the mass standeth. The which mass, you may see what it is, and how precious and worthy a piece of work it is, by their doctrine concerning the supper, the sacrifice, the praying for the dead and to the dead: whereof I have given you a sum in the most honest, godly and religious wise, that the best of them do set it forth in. For else, if I should have shewed you this their doctrine, as some of them set it forth, as I know you would abhor it, so the subtle papists would say that I railed and misreported them. Therefore, because they shall have no such occasion, nor you by their most subtle colours be deceived, I have, in the best manner I can, reported a sum of their doctrine. The which to the end you might the better consider and have, I will now tell you, as God's word teacheth, how these four points are to be believed and received; and then will I open the filthiness and abomination, which in this their doctrine is devilishly contained.

CHAPTER II.

HOW GOD'S WORD TEACHETH OF THE SUPPER, WITH CONFUTATION OF THE PAPISTS' HERESY OF TRANSUBSTANTIATION ABOUT THE SAME.

CONCERNING the supper of our Lord, which Christ Jesus did institute to be a sacrament of his body and blood, we believe that his words in the same supper accordingly are to be understand, that is, sacramentally, as he meant them, and not simply, contrary to his meaning, as the papists wrest them. And this is taught us, not only by innumerable such like places, as where baptism is called "regeneration," because it is a sacrament of it; circumcision is called "God's covenant," because it is a sacrament of it; but also by the plain circumstances of the text, as thereof the evangelists with the apostle

Titus iii. Gen. xvii.

Matt. xxvi. Mark xiv. Luke xxii. 1 Cor. x. xi. St Paul do write, plainly affirming that our Saviour Christ did give, and his disciples did eat, that which he took and brake and bade them divide among themselves, that is, bread and wine. For we may not think that Christ's natural body was broken, nor that his blood can be divided. And plainly our Saviour saith concerning the cup, that he would "not drink any more of the fruit of the vine" (which is not his blood, I trow, but wine), until he should "drink it new with them" after his resurrection.

Matt. xxvi. Mark xiv.

But, to make this matter more plain, like as many things in Christ's supper were figuratively done and spoken, as the washing of the disciples' feet, the paschal lamb was called the *passah*, Judas was said to have lifted up his heel against him; so doth Luke and Paul plainly alter the words concerning the cup, calling that "the New Testament[1]," which Matthew and Mark call his "blood;" yea, expressly five times the apostle calleth the sacrament of Christ's body after the consecration spoken (as they term it) "bread[2]:" "Is not the bread, which we break," saith he, "the communion of Christ's body?" Whose exposition I will more boldly stick unto, than unto all the papists' dreams, as long as I sleep not with them, by God's grace.

John xiii. Luke xxii.

1 Cor. x. xi.

They have none other sentence but these four words, "This is my body[3]." But ask them, what this is, and they will not say, as the apostle doth, namely, that it is bread. No; then they will say, that we hang all by reason, the matter being a matter of faith. Whereas they themselves altogether hang on reason, as though Christ cannot be able to do that which he promiseth, bread still in substance remaining, as the accidents do, except it be transubstantiate[4]. Is not this, trow you, to make it a matter of reason, and to hedge God's power in within the limits of reason? If Christ's words that follow, "which is given for you," be to be understand for, "which shall be given, or shall be betrayed for you," and not so precisely as they be spoken (for that were to make Christ a liar), why is it so heinous a matter with the papists, because we do not so precisely take the words immediately going before, namely, "This is my body," as to admit that, if there be bread, then Christ is a liar?

[1 Compare Vol. I. Sermon on Lord's Supper, p. 87, first paragraph.]
[2 Id. ibid. p. 86, second paragraph.] [3 Id. ibid. p. 102, lines 4, 5.]
[4 Id. Conference with Harpsfield, p. 512, second paragraph.]

Might not we reason and say, 'Then if Christ's body at the time was not betrayed (as indeed it was not), nor his blood shed, then is Christ a liar'?—But here they will say, 'All men may know that Christ by the present tense meant the future tense[5]; and in the scripture it is a most usual thing so to take tense for tense.' And, I pray you, why may not we say, that all men may know it is most common in scripture to give unto signs the names of the things which they signify? And no man is so foolish, but he knoweth that Christ then instituted a sacrament, wholly sacramentally to be understand; that is, that the sign or visible sacrament should have not only the name of the thing signified, but also some similitude therewith, or else it were no sacrament. But take bread away, as the papists do, leaving there but the accidents only, which do not feed the body: and then what shall resemble and represent unto us Christ's body broken for the food of the soul?—As wine comforteth the heart, so doth Christ's blood shed on the cross comfort the soul. But take wine away by transubstantiation, as the papists do, and tell me, what similitude remaineth? None at all, so no sacrament at all. So Christ's institution is taken away. Well do they reject God's commandment for their tradition's sake. Matt. xv.

Our faith therefore is, that the supper of the Lord is the sacrament of Christ's body and blood. These words, "This is my body, which is broken for you; This is my blood of the new testament, which is shed for your sins," are most true words and plain, according to Christ's meaning, to all them which do as he biddeth them, that is, to all such as take, eat and drink. Which words the papists keep in their purse, or else their private masses could not stand. To such, I say, as take and eat this sacrament, in sorrowing for their sinful life past, and purposing to amend, above all things remembering and believing that Christ's body was broken for their sins, and his blood shed for their iniquities—all such, I say, as verily as they see, take, taste and eat bread, and drink wine, which goeth into their body, feedeth it and nourisheth it, even so verily the soul and spirit by faith receiveth, not only Christ's body broken or his blood shed (for "the flesh profiteth nothing, it is the spirit that quickeneth," saith Christ), but even whole Christ, into John vi.

[[5] Id. Sermon on Lord's Supper, p. 102, first paragraph.]

Ephes. v. whom they are incorporate and made one with him, "flesh of his flesh, and bone of his bones." That is to say, as Christ's body is immortal and glorious, even so are theirs now by faith and hope, and at the day of the Lord they shall be in very deed. Than which thing what can be greater?

This we teach and believe concerning this sacrament, detesting and abhorring the horrible error of transubstantiation, which maketh bread and wine our God and Christ, and causeth men to be gazers, gapers and worshippers, yea, idolaters, rather than tasters and eaters, as Christ commandeth; and which maketh Christ's sacrifice of none effect, as now shall be shewed by God's grace. For this shall suffice to the declaration of our faith concerning the Lord's supper: whereunto agreeth the catholic church, and all the fathers, as full well thou mayest see in the bishop of Canterbury's book[1] (which is far from being answered either by the bishop of Winchester his book in English[2], or Marcus A. C[onstantius] in Latin[3]), that thou needest no more to confirm thy faith in this matter, but to read them with an indifferent mind, not being addict otherwise than to the desire of the truth.

As for this doctrine of transubstantiation, it is a new-found thing about a six hundred years old, even then brought out when Satan was letten loose, after a thousand years, that was bound[4]. Even then was it established, when there was more mischief among the prelates, specially the popes, about the see of Rome, who could catch it, than ever there was among the emperors for the empire. In the primitive church popes were martyred for Christ's spouse's sake, that is, the church: but now one poisoned another, and one slew another, for the rose-coloured whore of Babylon's sake, that is, the popish church.

Rev. xvii. xviii. In one hundred and sixty years there was near hard fifty popes[5]; whereas in no such time there were above thirteen[6]

[[1] "A Defence of the true and catholic doctrine of the sacrament of the body and blood of our Saviour Christ," &c., by Abp Cranmer, Wolf, London, 1550. See Works of Abp C., Vol. I. Park. Soc.]

[[2] "An explication and assertion of the true catholic faith touching the most blessed sacrament of the altar, with confutation of the same," by Bp Gardiner, 1551. Copy, Bodleian, Oxford. The whole of this treatise was reprinted by Abp Cranmer in his "Answer" to Gardiner, 1551, and will be found in the Works of Abp C., Vol. I. Park. Soc.]

[[3] See p. 173, note 9, above.]

[[4] Compare Vol. I. Sermon on Lord's Supper, p. 92, lines 1, 2.]

[[5] There were forty-nine popes, without reckoning antipopes, in 179 years,

emperors. And in the midst of this miserable state and time this doctrine of transubstantiation was the pope's beginning, as they might have leisure from conspiring against princes, and one against another, to establish it as the very principal pillar of all their power. And no marvel; for, this being admitted, then have they power over Christ the King of all kings, that he be where they will, when they will, and as long as they will, under their power. Wherethrough the other must needs follow, that if they have power over Christ, and that in heaven, to bring him down at their pleasure, much more then over all earth, emperors, kings, princes and people, yea, even over the devil, purgatory and hell, have they full power and jurisdiction, being now gods in earth, which "sit in the holy place," even "as God," yea, "above God," to make what article of faith shall please them, as they have done this of transubstantiation: which might as well be denied as granted, saith Duns[7], one of their own doctors, and Master Gabriel[8] also, if it so pleased the holy father and his spouse the church of Rome.

2 Thess. ii.

Scotus super 4. Sentent. dist. 11. Gabriel. super can. missæ.

Before this time all the fathers' diligence, labour and care, was to call men to the receiving of this sacrament for the confirmation of their faith; that, as verily as they did eat bread and drink wine here, so should they not doubt but that by faith they did feed on the body of Christ broken for their sins, and on his blood shed for their iniquities. And therefore sometimes would they call the sacrament bread 'a figure' or 'a sign;' sometime would they call it 'the body and blood of our Saviour Jesus Christ,' as the nature of sacraments is to be called with the name of the things which they do signify; that

between A.D. 882 and 1061. See tables of popes from Spanheim, in Waddington's Hist. of Church, Vol. III. p. 407, Lond. 1835; and in Sir H. Nicolas' Chronology, p. 208.]

[6 "33," orig. edit., evidently a misprint for "13."]

[7 ......sed istud corpus Christi esse in eucharistia est quoddam verum universaliter traditum nobis: iste autem intellectus, quod non sit ibi substantia panis, videretur difficilior ad sustinendum, et ad ipsum sequuntur plura inconvenientia, quam ponendo ibi esse substantiam panis.—Joann. Duns Scot. In Sentent. Lib. IV. Dist. xi. Quæst. 3. Op. Tom. II. p. 157, Antv. 1620.]

[8 Notandum quod, quamvis expresse tradatur in scriptura quod corpus Christi veraciter sub speciebus panis continetur, et a fidelibus sumitur, tamen quomodo ibi sit corpus Christi, an per conversionem alicujus in ipsum, aut sine conversione incipiat esse corpus Christi cum pane, manentibus substantia et accidentibus panis, non invenitur expressum in canone Bibliæ.—Gab. Biel, sacr. Canon. Miss. Expos. Lect. XL. fol. 94, 2, Basil. 1515.]

thereby men's minds might be withdrawn from the consideration of sensible and visible things to things heavenly, which they do signify and represent[1]. And their care and crying unto the people was to receive it; and therefore they made decrees that such as would not receive and be present should be sparred out of the church. O how earnest was Chrysostom herein! Read his sixty-first homily unto the people of Antioch[2].

But, after that this decree and doctrine of transubstantiation came in, no crying out hath there been to receive it (no, that is the prerogative of the priests and shaven shorlings): but altogether the end of their crying out was as now to believe transubstantiation, Christ to be their flesh, blood and bone at every altar, between every priest's hands, yea, in every priest's mouth, when it pleaseth them, be they never so stinking filthy[3] adulterers, drunkards, blasphemers, dicers, &c. The crying and teaching of the clergy continually hath been to believe transubstantiation, and then to come to church to see their Maker once a day[4], to hold up their hands, to knock on their breasts, to strike their faces, to mutter up their Latin prayers, to take holy water and holy bread, to live in obedience to the holy father and holy church his spouse. This was all they required. Drink, dice, card, fight, swear, steal, lie, no matter: so that in the morning they see their God, all is well—good catholic people, no man shall hurt them, or persecute them. But if any man should not allow nor worship this God of their making, although he lived a most godly life, and were a man full of charity, sobriety, and very religious, O, such is an heretic or schismatic! Nothing could please these wolves but even the blood and life of such a poor sheep, as men have felt before, and now begin to feel. Let all the pack of them burden those justly, whom now they imprison and cause to flee the realm, of any

[[1] See Vol. I. p. 87, notes 7, 8.]

[[2] Chrysost. Homil. LXI. Ad Pop. Antioch., "De sacrorum participatione mysteriorum, et quod communicare nolens nec orationi dignus est interesse," Op. Lat. Tom. V. cols. 340—46, Paris. 1588. Fifty-nine out of eighty of these Homilies are only to be found in the early Latin editions, being mere compilations from Chrysostom's genuine works. See Cave, Hist. Liter. Tom. I. p. 302, Oxon. 1740—3. Compare, in this instance, Chrysost. In Epist. ad Ephes. cap. i. Hom. iii. Op. Tom. XI. p. 23, ed. Bened. Par. 1718—38.]

[[3] A word of the original edition is here omitted.]

[[4] Compare Abp Cranmer, Works, Vol. I. p. 229, Park. Soc.; and Becon, Displaying of the Mass, in Works, Vol. III. p. 270, Park. Soc.]

other thing than only of this, that we will not serve their God of bread and wine, and then will we suffer shame.

But I have been too long herein. Now to our doctrine and belief, for the second point concerning Christ's sacrifice.

CHAPTER III.

HOW GOD'S WORD TEACHETH OF CHRIST'S SACRIFICE, AND THE POPE'S BLASPHEMY THEREIN REVEALED.

OUR doctrine and faith in this behalf is as is in the other, that is, according to God's holy word; namely, that Jesus Christ, the Son of God and second Adam, by whom we receive righteousness unto life, as by the first Adam we received sin unto death—our faith is, I say, that this Christ in our flesh, which he took of the substance of the virgin Mary, but pure and without sin, for the satisfying of God's just displeasure deserved by and in our flesh, did in the same suffer unjustly all kinds of misery and affliction, offering up himself unto his eternal Father with a most willing obedient heart and ready mind, when he was crucified upon the cross. And, thereby as he satisfied God's justice, so he merited and procured his mercy, peace, favour for all them which either before that time were dead, either were at that time present, either should afterward come and believe, by and in that offering done for them and their sins: so that God the eternal Father, I say, would be, in this their Christ, their God and Father, and not lay their sins committed to their charge to condemnation.

This doctrine the holy scripture teacheth almost everywhere: but specially in the Epistle to the Hebrews, the first, seventh, eighth, ninth chapters, this is most lively set forth, how that "by one oblation," "once offered" by this Christ himself, all that be God's people "are sanctified." For—as in respect of them that died in God's covenant and election before Christ suffered his death and offered his sacrifice, one, alone and omnisufficient, never more to be offered, he is called "the Lamb slain Rev. xiii.
from the beginning of the world," and "the one alone Mediator 1 Tim. ii.
between God and man," "whose forthcoming was from the Mic. iii. v.
beginning"—even so, in respect of the virtue and efficacy of

this one sacrifice to all God's people continually unto the world's end, the Holy Ghost doth tell us, that thereby "he hath made holy" such as be children of salvation, and saith not, 'shall make holy,' or 'doth make holy,' lest any man should with the papists indeed reiterate this satisfaction again; although in words they say otherwise, as anon we shall see, if hereunto I shew you the means whereby to apply this sacrifice: which I will do very briefly.

For in the seventeenth of St John our Saviour doth very plainly shew this in these words: "For their sakes," saith he, "I sanctify myself, that they also might be sanctified through the truth. I pray not for them alone, but for those also which shall believe on me through their preaching." Here our Saviour applieth his sacrifice in teaching and praying for them. And, as he teacheth them as ministers to do the like, that is, to preach and pray for the application of his sacrifice to the church, so doth he teach them and all the church to apply it unto themselves by believing it and by faith. The which thing the apostle St Paul in many places, but more plainly in the second to the Corinthians, the fifth chapter in the latter end, doth teach. Read it and see. So that, as ye have Christ's one only sacrifice, which he himself on the cross offered once, as sufficient for all that do believe, and never more to be reiterated, so have you, that for the applying of it to his church the ministers should preach, and pray that their preaching might be effectual in Christ. And, as Paul was ready himself to suffer death for the confirmation of the faith of the elect, so should the church and every member of the same, which is of years of discretion, by believing in Christ, through the minister's preaching, apply it to themselves. As for infants, I need not in this place to speak of God's election.

It is most certain, this kind of applying, as it killeth the papistical priests, which hate not the devil worse than true preaching, so doth it cast down all their soul-massing and foolish foundations for such as be dead and past the ministry of God's word. And also it putteth away the opinion of *opus operatum*, ['the work wrought[1],'] and of perseverance in impiety, from such as would enjoy the benefit of Christ's death.

[[1] See Bp Jewel, Reply to Harding, Art. xx. Works, Vol. I. pp. 749—57, Park. Soc.]

CHAPTER IV.

OF PRAYING FOR THE DEAD, THE TRUE DOCTRINE.

Now as concerning the third, that is, of praying for the dead and sacrificing for them, as in the other we confess, teach and believe according to God's word, so do we in this; namely, that in holy scripture, throughout the canonical books of the Old and New Testament, we find neither precept nor ensample of praying for any, when they be departed this life, but that, as men die, so shall they arise. If in faith in the Lord towards the south, then need they no prayers, then are they presently happy, and shall arise in glory; if in unbelief without the Lord towards the north[2], then are they past all help, in the damned state presently, and shall rise to eternal shame. Eccles. xi. John v.

Wherefore, according to the scripture, we exhort men to repent, and while they have time to work well. Every man shall bear his own burthen; every man shall give account for himself, and not Sir John[3] nor Sir Thomas, that sing or pray for him. "Every man shall receive according to that he himself doeth in this body, while he is here alive, be it good or bad;" and not according to that his executors, or this chantry[4] priest and that fraternity doth for him. Whereby we may well see, if we will, that, as prayer for the dead is not available or profitable to the dead, so is it not of us allowable or to be exercised. For, as they that are departed be past our prayers, being either in joy or in misery, as is above shewed, even so we, having for it no word of God, whereupon faith leaneth, cannot but sin in doing it, in that we do it "not of faith," because we have no word of God for it. Gal. v. Coloss. iii. Rom. xiv. 2 Cor. v. Rom. x. xiv.

Therefore with Abraham, Isaac, Jacob, Moses, the prophets, Christ Jesus and the apostles, we bury the dead in a convenient place, and mourn in measure, as men having hope of the resurrection—not because of them, for that were a great point of ingratitude, they being departed out of miserable condition unto a most blessed state: therefore we give thanks to God for them, praise his name for his power and might shewed in them, and pray that we may depart in the same faith, and 1 Thess. iv. Rev. xiv.

[2 See Poli Synops. in Eccl. xi. 3.] [3 See Vol. I. p. 589, note E.]

[4 "Chantry:" a chapel with an endowment for a priest to sing masses for the souls of the founder.—Todd's Johnson, Dict.]

joyfully rise with them in the resurrection; which we desire and wish the Lord would hasten—we mourn, I say, not because of them, but of ourselves, that have lost the company of such our helpers and furtherers in spiritual and temporal benefits, by them being admonished of our immortality and of the vanity of this life, that we might the more contemn it, and desire the everlasting life, where they and we shall never be separated.

This is our faith and doctrine for them that be departed; who, though they be members of the same body mystical of Christ that we be of, yet should they in this case be discerned
2 Tim. iv. from the militant members, they being at rest, and, having finished their course and fight, in no point needing any of our help, except we should too arrogantly set up our own merits and prayers, and pull down Christ, as though we were able to get pardon and higher room in heaven for others; where all our righteousness and the best thing we do is so far from helping others, that thereby we cannot help ourselves, but had need
Luke xi. to cry, *Dimitte nobis debita nostra*, ["Forgive us our debts,"]
Isai. lxiv. being no better in God's sight than a defiled woman's cloth, although to the sight of men they may seem gorgeous and gay. For, if the papists would say (as, when they are pressed with blasphemy in extolling their own merits and works of supererogation against Christ, they use), that our prayers do them no good in respect of the worthiness of their prayers, but in respect of God's goodness; in that God's goodness is not to be looked for otherwise than he hath promised, let them either shew men his promise, or else in this behalf keep silence, and exercise themselves better in doing their duties to their brethren that be alive: towards whom their charity is very cold, although, when they are dead, then they will pretend much, then will they pray for them, but yet not for nought and freely, as true charity worketh; for, no penny, no pater-noster. Give nothing, and then they will neither sing nor say *requiem* nor *placebo*[1], I warrant you. But of this sufficient.

Now to the last, of praying to the dead, or to saints departed this life.

[[1] See Vol. I. p. 589, note D.]

CHAPTER V.

OF PRAYING TO SAINTS.

HERE we confess, teach and believe, as before is said, according to God's holy word, that, as all and every good thing cometh only from God the Father by the means of Jesus Christ, so for the obtaining of the same we must call upon his holy name, as he by himself commandeth very often. But, forasmuch as God "dwelleth in light inaccessible," and "is a consuming fire," and hateth all impiety and uncleanness, and we be blind, stubble, grass, hay, and nothing but filthy, unclean and sinful; and because that therefore, as we may not, so we dare not approach to his presence; it hath pleased this good God and Father of his love to send a spokesman and Mediator, an Intercessor and Advocate between him and us, even Jesus Christ, his dearly beloved Son, by whom we might have free entrance "with boldness to come before his presence and throne of mercy, to find and obtain grace and help in time of need." For this our Mediator and Advocate is with his Father of the same substance, power, wisdom and majesty, and therefore may weigh well with him in all things; and with us he is of the same substance which we are of, even flesh and man, but pure and "without sin, in all things being tempted like unto us," and having experience of our infirmities, that he might be merciful and faithful on our behalf, to "purge us from our sins," and to bring us into such favour with the Father, that we might be not only dearly beloved through him, the only darling of the Father, but also obtain whatsoever we shall ask, according to his word and will, in the name of this same our Mediator, Saviour, Intercessor and Advocate. So that easy it is to see that, as it is an obedient service to God the Father to call always upon him in all our need, so to come to his presence through Christ is to the honour of Christ's mediation, intercession and advocateship. And therefore, as it cannot be but against the almighty God and Father to ask or look for anything elsewhere, at the hands of any that be departed this life, as though he were not the Giver of all good things, or as though he had not commanded us to come unto him, so we see it is manifestly against Christ Jesus our Lord,

James i. Psal. l. 1 Tim. vi. Heb. xii. Psal. v. Heb. ii. iv. Heb. iii. iv. 1 Pet. ii. Matt. iii. xvii. Matt. vii. 1 John v. John xiv. Psal. l.

by any other saint, angel or archangel to come and move anything at our Father's hands; as though he were not our Mediator, Advocate and Intercessor, or else not a sufficient Mediator, Advocate and Intercessor, or at least not so merciful, meek, gracious, loving, and ready to help as others: where he only so loved us, as the very hearts of all men and angels never were able to conceive any part of "the height, depth, breadth and length" of the same, as it is. If his own heart-blood was not too dear for us, being his very enemies and never desirous to do his will, how is it possible that he will contemn us for coming unto him with purpose and desire to serve him?

Ephes. iii.

Many other reasons I could give you, wherefore the saints are not to be prayed unto; for that pulleth from faith in Christ, it maketh them gods, it is idolatry. &c. But this may suffice.

So that now you see by God's word, what our faith is concerning these four things. Which that you may the more love, embrace and be content to carry with you through fire and water, I will now go about with God's grace, as briefly as I can, to shew how abominable their doctrine is, even out of the short sum thereof already before by me rehearsed.

CHAPTER VI.

THE POPISH DOCTRINE OF THE SACRAMENT CONFUTED MORE LARGELY.

FIRST, where they allege the catholic church to have taught, concerning the supper, the doctrine of transubstantiation of Christ's real and carnal presence, dearly beloved, know that this is a manifest lie. For, as the catholic church never knew of it for nine hundred years at the least after Christ's ascension, so after that time no other church did obstinately defend, cruelly maintain, and wilfully wrest the scriptures and doctors for the establishing of it, save only the popish church, as their own doctors, Duns and Gabriel, do teach[1]. Read the bishop of Canterbury's book against Winchester[2], and see.

Transubstantiation is a new doctrine.

[[1] See p. 275, notes 7 and 8, above.]

[[2] "An answer...unto a crafty and sophistical cavillation devised by Stephen Gardiner......late bishop of Winchester, against the......doctrine of the most holy sacrament of the body and blood of our Saviour Jesus Christ," by Abp Cranmer, Wolf, London, 1551. See Works of Abp C., Vol. I. Park. Soc.]

Whereas they say, that Christ in his supper by taking bread and speaking the words of consecration did make it his flesh, according to his promise in John, when he saith, "And the bread which I will give is my flesh, &c." (so that they would thereby seem to have two places of scripture for this their doctrine of transubstantiation and real or carnal presence), although diversely I could improve this; yet, for because I would not be over tedious unto you, even by the same their sentence you shall see how learnedly they lie. The sentence is this: "And the bread that I will give is my flesh, which I will give for the life of the world." First mark that he saith, "The bread is my flesh:" he saith not, "shall be my flesh," but, it "is my flesh." This, I trow, maketh against them, for the sacrament a year after at the least was not instituted. —Again he saith, that "the bread is his flesh, which he will give for the life of the world." Here would I ask them, whether Christ's death was for the life of the world, or in vain. If they say, it was for the life of the world, then why do they apply and give it to the sacrament? was it crucified? Or, if it be the same sacrifice (for so they say), either it was effectual or not. If it was effectual, then Christ's death needed not: if it was not effectual, then Christ was not God, and could not do that he would. Thus ye may see their ungodly foolishness or foolish ungodliness, I cannot tell which to call it well.

John vi.

Whereas they require the intent of the priest to consecrate Christ's body—forasmuch as we know not any man's intent (God only knoweth the heart), yea, the words we know not, they are so spoke in hugger-mugger[3]—I pray you, into what a doubtfulness are we brought, whether it be the sacrament or no! in what peril are we of worshipping a piece of bread for our Christ! Is not this, trow you, sweet and comfortable gear, that a man shall always stand in doubt whether he have received the sacrament or no?

Of the priest's intent.

Whereas they will have it bread to the eye, and not to the mouth, judge then, whether a dog may not eat Christ's body; judge, whether the devil, if he would come in the likeness of a priest, might not swallow up Christ, and so bring him into hell, from whence, because there is no redemption there, Christ's body should never come, but be damned. Judge, whether the

[[3] "Hugger-mugger:" secresy, concealment.—Nares' Glossary.]

taste of thy mouth is not as much to be credited as the sight of the eye, specially in that the scripture so often calleth it "bread" after the consecration, as before I have shewed. Judge, whether Christ's body be not very petty, that it can lie in so little a room. Judge, whether Christ hath more bodies than one, when perchance the priest hath twenty or a hundred before him. Judge, whether the priest break not Christ's body in breaking of it. Judge, whether it be seemly to chew Christ's body with the teeth. Judge, whether Christ did eat his own body, yea, or no? for Christ did eat the sacrament with his disciples. Judge, whether it be seemly that Christ should be kept so in prison, as they keep him. Judge, whether it be seemly that Christ's body should be so dindle-dandled and used, as they use it. Judge, whether the people, knocking and kneeling at the elevation of that they see—for they see but the forms of bread and wine, and not Christ's body, if it be as the papists feign—judge, I say, whether the people by the papists' own doctrine be not made idolaters.

Many more absurdities there be, which I purposely omit. This little is enough hereby to give you occasion to know the more.

Where they say that the bread is made Christ's body, flesh, blood, &c., that is, that Christ's body is made of the bread (as the bishop of Winchester in his book for this matter of the "Devil's Sophistry[1]" and elsewhere doth affirm), you may see how shamelessly, yea, blasphemously they speak. For Christ's body crucified was born of the virgin Mary, even of her substance: but they say, the supper is that body which was crucified. Now, I trow, bread is one thing, and the virgin's flesh another thing: therefore indeed they deny Christ in the flesh, that they may stablish their Christ in the bread; which is the very note of antichrist.

Last of all, whereas they say that they receive the sacrament to damnation, which do not believe their transubstantiation, if with Paul their words were conferred, you should see otherwise. For he saith, they "receive this bread (for so he calleth it after the words of consecration) unworthily," which do not esteem "Christ's body:" as indeed the papists do not,

[[1] "A detection of the devil's sophistry, wherewith he robbeth the unlearned people of the true belief in the most blessed sacrament of the altar," by Bp Gardiner, Herford, London, 1546. Copy, Bibl. Reg., British Museum.]

which would bring Christ down out of heaven for thieves and whores to chaw and eat, for moths to corrupt, and to be in danger of mowling[2]; as, if they kept their hosts long, indeed they will mould, and then will they burn them. Do these men, trow you, esteem Christ's body? Paul plainly sheweth in the same place, that the wicked man which receiveth the sacrament "unworthily" eateth not Christ's body, but "his own damnation," which I trow be not Christ's body. And this shall serve for this time to shew you, how shameless, filthy and abominable this their doctrine of transubstantiation is[3]. If in so short a sum of their doctrine there be so many abominations, I pray you, how much is in the whole sum of the same?

Now for the sacrifice.

CHAPTER VII.

THE POPISH DOCTRINE OF THE SACRIFICE CONFUTED.

First, in that they grant Christ's sacrifice on the cross, done by himself, to be full and perfect enough, we may well see that we need not this which they have found out—indeed to make the other imperfect, for else it needed no reiteration. But, seeing they reiterate it by this, and make it needful even as baptism, easily may all men know that, though they speak one thing, they mean another, and so are dissemblers and destroyers of Christ's sacrifice, little considering the great pain that Christ suffered, seeing they weigh it no better.

Whereas they say, that it is the same sacrifice which Christ offered on the cross, but unbloodily—wherein they seem to deny transubstantiation, for else I trow it must needs be bloody—I would thus reason with them. Inasmuch as Christ's sacrifice on the cross was the only perfect and all-sufficient propitiatory sacrifice "for the sins of the world," as they confess, this could not be the same, because it was done before that upon the cross. Or else the full perfect sacrifice was then in the supper finished, and so Christ's death is in vain, and a foolish thing. If Christ's death be not foolish, but indeed, as it is, the full and perfect sacrifice for the sins of the world,

[2 "Mowling," moulding.—Halliwell's Dict.]

[3 Compare Vol. I. Sermon on Lord's Supper, p. 84, last line but 12.]

then this, which they feign that he offered in his last supper, is not the same, prate what pleaseth them; or else it is not of value, take whether they will.—Whereas they prate of Christ's will, that it was accepted before his Father for the deed; as they shall never be able to shew so much as one word to prove that Christ would in his supper sacrifice himself to his Father for the sins of the world (for there is not one word thereof throughout the whole Bible), so do they belie God the Father, which would indeed have his Son to drink the cup that he prayed to be taken from him, or else make Christ's death frustrate and more than need; which is the only thing that all their doctrine tendeth unto. For, if the Father allowed his will for the deed, I pray you, who seeth not now the deed to be more than needeth?

Where they say, that Christ commanded his church to offer this sacrifice to his Father in remembrance of his bloody sacrifice, I would pray them to shew me, where he commanded it, and then good enough. But, dearly beloved, they can never shew it. If they will say, *Hoc facite*, to take *facere* for "to sacrifice," as some teach it, then will I say, that a boy of twelve year old can tell they lie. For *Hoc facite*, "Do you this," pertaineth to the whole action of Christ's supper, of taking, eating, and drinking of the sacrament, &c., and as well spoken to the laymen as the priests: but I trow they will not suffer the laymen to say mass another while now for them. No, this were too much against their honour and gain also.

But if one would ask them, what they offer to the Father, then a man should see their abominations: for, if they say, 'nothing,' then men would take them as they be, liars. If they say, 'bread and wine,' as indeed they do in their mass horribly, then in that they say they offer the same thing which Christ offered on the cross, and he offered his body, bread must needs be Christ's body, and so Christ's body is bread and wine. If they say, that 'they offer up Christ,' in that the offerer must needs be as good at the least, yea, better than the thing offered, then must they needs shew themselves open antichrists. For they make themselves equal with Christ, yea, better than he[1]: which thing indeed their holy father and grandsire the pope doth. For where Christ would take upon him to teach

[[1] Compare Vol. I., Preface to Places of Artopæus, pp. 6, 7.]

nothing but that he had received of his Father, and therefore willed men to "search the scriptures," as all his apostles did, whether their doctrine was not according thereunto, the pope and his prelates will be bold to teach what please them more than God biddeth, yea, clean contrary to that which God biddeth: as it is plain by all these four points, 'transubstantiation, sacrifice, praying for the dead, and to the dead.'

But see, I pray you, these abominations. The sacrifice of Christ for the redemption of the world was not simply "his body and his blood," but "his body broken and his blood shed," that is, all his passion and suffering in his body and flesh. In that therefore they offer, as they say, the same sacrifice which Christ offered, dearly beloved, do they not, as much as in them is, kill, slay, whip and crucify Christ again? Ah, wretches and antichrists! Who would not desire to die for his Master Christ's cause against this their heinous and stinking abomination?

Whereas they call this sacrifice of the mass, the principal mean to apply the benefit of Christ's death to the quick and dead, I would gladly have them to shew, where and of whom they learned it. Sure I am, they learned it not of Christ. For when he sent his disciples abroad to apply unto men the benefit of his death, he bade them not mass it, but preach the gospel, as the mean by the which God had appointed believers to be saved. The which thing Peter told Cornelius plainly; as Paul also teacheth almost everywhere in his epistles. But indeed preaching they may not away with, as well for that it is too painful, as for that it is nothing so gainful, nor in authority and estimation with the world. Nothing so displeaseth the devil as preaching the gospel, as in all ages easily we may well see, if we will mark, to our comfort in this age. And therefore by giving his daughter idolatry, with her dowry of worldly wealth, riches and honour, to the pope and his shaven shorlings, they have by this means in many years been begetting a daughter, which at length was delivered to destroy preaching, even the minion "Missa," "Mistress Missa[2]," who

Matt. xxviii. Mark xvi. Luke xxiv.

Acts x.

Col. i. ii. 2 Cor. v.

[[2] "Mistress Missa" is one of the speakers in "A new dialogue, wherein is contained the examination of the mass, and of that kind of priesthood which is ordained to say mass, and to offer up for remission of sins the body and blood of Christ again:" by William Turner, London, Day and Seres. Copy, Bodleian, Oxford.—See Strype, Ecc. Mem. Vol. II. part I. p. 216.]

danceth daintily before the Herods of the world, and is the cause even why John Baptist and the preachers be put into prison and lose their heads. This dancing damsel, the darling of her mother, the fair garland of her fathers (for she hath many fathers), the gaudy gallant of her grandsire, is trimmed and tricked on the best and most holy manner or wise that can be, even with the word of God, the epistle and the gospel, with the sacrament of Christ's body and blood, with the pomander[1] and perfumes of prayer and all godly things that can be, but blasphemously and horribly abused, to be a mermaid to amuse and bewitch men, sailing in the seas of this life, to be enamoured on her. And therefore, besides her aforesaid goodly apparel, she hath all kinds of sweet tunes, ditties, melodies, singing, playing, ringing, knocking, kneeling, standing, lifting, crossing, blessing, blowing, mowing, incensing, &c. Moreover she wanteth no gold, silver, precious stones, jewels and costly silks, velvets, satins, damasks, &c., and all kind of things which are gorgeous in the sight of men; as, if you call to mind the chalices, copes, vestments, crucifixes, &c., you cannot but see. And hereto she is beautified yet more, to be shewed and set forth in lying words and titles given to her; that she have all power in heaven, earth and hell, that she hath all things for soul and body, for quick and dead, for man and beast. And, lest men should think her too coy a dame, lo, sir, she offereth herself most gently to all that will come, be they never so poor, evil, stinking and foul, to have their pleasure on her. Come who will, she is "Joan good-fellow;" and that not only to make herself common to them that will, but also to ply them plentifully [with][2] most pleasant promises[2] falsely, and giving most licentious liberties to all her lovers, and great fees and wages to her diligent servants and ministers. So that there needeth no preaching of the gospel; she hath all things, she will give all things; the death of Christ she will apply and can to whom she will, and when she will. For this daughter the mother, the fathers and the grandfathers watch night and day, as the only mean whereby Herod and Herodias

[[1] "Pomander:" a ball of perfumes, which was sometimes enclosed in silver. See Nares' Glossary; Churton's Life of Nowell, p. 22, Oxford, 1809. Becon wrote a treatise entitled, "The pomander of prayer," Works, Vol. III. pp. 72-85, Park. Soc.]

[[2] Leaf torn in the copy of the original edition, which is followed.]

may live as they lust. Therefore, if any [John] Baptist dare babble one word, away will [this][2] wench bring him.

But, dearly beloved, as from [the][2] devil's darling indeed, flee from her; and know that the [true][2] and only way to apply Christ's death and sacrifice is [on][2] the minister's behalf by preaching, and on your behalf by believing.

This is a sacrament and not a sacrifice: for in this, using it as we should, we receive of God obsignation and full certificate of Christ's body broken for our sins, and his blood shed for our iniquities; as in baptism we are confirmed, and settle ourselves in possession of the promise of salvation to appertain unto us, God to be our God, Christ to be our Christ, and we to be God's people. The promise and word of God giveth and offereth, faith in us applieth and receiveth the same, and the sacraments do confirm and (as it were) seal up: baptism, that we are regenerated with the Spirit of God, made his children, brethren to Christ, and engrafted into him; the supper, that we are fed with Christ spiritually, with his body and blood, yea, that we be incorporated into Christ, to be "flesh of his flesh and bone of his bones," as he by being born of the virgin Mary was flesh of our flesh and bone of our bones.

Away therefore with their abominable doctrine, that the sacrifice of the mass is the principal means to apply Christ's death to the quick and dead; wherein all men may see that they lie boldly. For, as the word of God in the ministry pertaineth not to the dead, (for who will be so mad as to go and preach on dead men's graves, that the dead men may hear?) so likewise do not the sacraments. Little beholden were men to Christ and the apostles, if this were the principal mean to apply salvation, that they would use it so little, and preach so much. Paul, having respect to the chiefest end wherefore he was sent, said, that he was not sent to baptize, but to preach: 1 Cor. i.
and often saith he, that he was an apostle segregate of God to Rom. i. Gal. i.
preach the gospel: and the bishop Timothy did he warn to "preach in season and out of season," speaking never a word 2 Tim. iv.
of this massing or sacrificing Christ's body.

Last of all, where they make a similitude, that, as by baptism the minister applieth to the child regeneration, so in this, &c., O that this similitude were well looked on! then would it make them to bluster; for they are no more like than an apple like an oyster. In baptism the child is alive, but here the man is dead; in baptism the child is present, but here the man is perchance forty miles off, if he sacrifice for the quick, yea, a hundred miles from him; in baptism the child receiveth the sacrament, but here you must look and gape, but beware you take not; for ye may receive but once a year, and then also you must receive but the one half, the cup he will keep from you. In baptism is required God's election, if the child be an infant, or faith, if he be of age; and therefore he reciteth the promise, that it may be heard: but here is no faith required; for how can men believe, when they are dead? No promise is then preached or heard. So that even this their similitude maketh the matter plain enough; for baptism all men know to be no sacrifice. But of this I have spoken a little before, that, if applying come by the priest's massing, then were preaching in vain, believing in vain, godly life in vain; the priest were God's fellow, yea, Christ's superior, as is aforesaid.

Now for the third, of praying for the dead; wherein I will be brief.

CHAPTER VIII.

THE CONFUTATION OF THE PAPISTS' SACRIFICING AND PRAYING FOR THE DEAD.

First, when they say, this applicatory sacrifice may be called a propitiatory sacrifice, because it applieth the propitiatory sacrifice to whom the priest will, be he dead or alive; as I would have you to note, how they grant, that of itself it is not a propitiatory sacrifice, whereby they vary from that which they elsewhere teach, that it is the selfsame sacrifice which Christ offered on the cross unbloodily; so, I pray you, forget not, that the priest is God's fellow, for he may apply it to whom he will. Therefore honour Sir John, and make much of Sir Thomas: for, though God could make thee alone, yet alone, without the priest, he cannot save thee. Again, if Sir John be thy friend, care neither for God nor the devil; live as thou wilt, he will bring thee to heaven, although thou slip into hell. So they write that Gregory by massing did with Trajan the emperor[1]. It maketh

[[1] This refers to a curious but doubtful story of Pope Gregory the Great, who, it is said, was moved to offer prayer for the soul of the heathen emperor Trajan,

no matter how thou live here, so thou have the favour of the pope and his shavelings.

Whereas they say, that the fathers from the beginning were accustomed to make memorials for the dead, this I grant to be true, as we do in our communion. But, to gather that therefore they prayed for them, it no more followeth, than to say that our English Service doth allow it, where it doth not. For ye must note, that there is a memorial for the dead, as well in giving thanks to God for them, as in praying for them; for to say, to pray for the dead, is a general word, including in it giving of thanks. And therefore, when we read in the ancient fathers of the primitive church of the memorials for the dead, or praying for the dead, it is not to be understand that they prayed for to deliver them from purgatory, for that was not found out then, or from hell, as our papists do in their prayers of the mass, for there is no redemption; or for pardon of their sins, as though they had it not, for if they depart without it they are damned; or for to get them a higher place in heaven, for that were injurious to Christ, that we should purchase places and higher rooms in heaven for others: but either for the desire of the more speedy coming of Christ, to hasten the resurrection; either that they might not be thought negligent or careless over the dead; either that the living might be occasioned to increase in love to the church here in earth, who still followeth with good-will and love even men when they be departed; either to admonish the church to be diligent over such as live, and careful to extend her love, if it were possible, even to the dead. On this wise should we expound, not only the former but also the later fathers, as Austin, Chrysostom, and others; which, though in some places they seem very manifestly to allow praying for the dead, yet they are not to be understand otherwise than I have said for them[2]. For never knew they of

from reading of that monarch's clemency to a widow. ...perveniensque ad sepulcrum beati Petri apostoli, ibidem diutius oravit et flevit, atque veluti gravissimo somno correptus in extasi mentis raptus est, quo per revelationem se exauditum discit, et ne ulterius jam talia de quoquam sine baptismate sacro defuncto præsumeret petere, promeruit castigari.—Bolland. Act. Sanct., Martius, Tom. II., 12 Martii, Vita Gregor. Magni Papæ I. auctor. anon., cap. v. Oratio pro anima Trajani, p. 136, Antv. 1668.]

[[2] See p. 270, note 1, above.]

our merits and purgatory; for, if they had but dreamed thereon, surely they would have been much more circumspect in their speakings and writings of this, than they were.

Where they say that, 'because this sacrifice is the sacrifice of the whole church, whereof the dead be members, therefore they should be prayed for;' as before I have showed, that we must put a difference between the members of the church militant here on earth, and those which be now in rest and peace with God; so would I have you to note here, that they should pray for none other dead, than such as be members of Christ's church. Now, in that all such "die in the Lord," and therefore are happy, I would gladly learn, what good such prayer doeth to those so departed.—As for purgatory pick-purse[1], they pass not upon it. But, that this is a sacrifice applicatory or propitiatory, the papists can never prove.

Where they say, 'charity requireth it,' I answer that, inasmuch as charity followeth faith, and will not go a foot further than faith showeth the way, seeing faith is not but of the word of God, and God's word for this they have not, easy it is to perceive that this praying thus for the dead is not of christian charity.—But, be it that charity required it, I then marvel why they are so uncharitable, that will do nothing herein without money. Why will they not pray without pence? If the pope and his prelates were charitable, they would, I trow, make sweep-stake at once with purgatory.

Where they allege the sentence of the Maccabees, as all men of learning know, the fathers allow not that book to be [of] God's Spirit or catholic, so do I wonder that in all the Old Testament this sacrificing for the dead was never spoken of before. In all the sacrifices that God appointed we read of never one for the dead.

This gear came not up till the religion was wonderfully corrupt among the Jews; as with us it was never found out till horrible corruption of religion and ignorance of God's word came into the church of God, when preaching was put down, and massing came up. Then faith in Christ was cold, penance became popish, and trust was taught in creatures, ignorance abounded; and look, what the clergy said, that was believed. Then came up visions, miracles, dead spirits walking, and talk-

[1 "Pick-purse:" a robber. See Bp Latimer, Works, Vol. I. p. 50, Park. Soc.]

ing how they might be released by this mass, by that pilgrimage gate-going[2]. And so came up this pelf of praying for the dead, which Paul the apostle and all the prophets never spake one word of; for all men may easily see, that it is a thing which helpeth much vice, and hindereth godliness. Who will be so earnest to amend, to make restitution of that he hath gotten unjustly, and live in a godly life and true fear of God, being taught that by prayers, by masses, by founding of chauntries[3], &c., when he is gone, he shall find ease and release, yea, and come to joy eternal? Christ's doctrine is, that the way of salvation is strait: but this teaching, heaping of masses one upon another, when we are dead, maketh it wide. Christ's teaching is, that we should live in love and charity, "the sun should not go down on our wrath;" but this doctrine, to pray for the dead to be delivered out of purgatory, teacheth rather to live in little love, in wrath even to our death's day; for Sir John can and will help, Sir Thomas by a mass of *scala cœli*[4] will bring us into heaven. Christ's doctrine is, that he is "the way:" but this doctrine maketh the massing-priest the way: a way indeed it is, but to hell and to the devil. Dearly beloved, therefore take good heart unto you for this gear, rather than you would consent unto it, to lose life and all that ever you have. You shall be sure with Christ to find it, and that for ever, with infinite increase.

Last of all, where they allege the catholic church and consent of all doctors in this matter; as I wish you should know that to be the true and catholic church which is grounded upon God's word, which word they have not for them in this matter; so would I ye should know that there is no member of the church, but he may err; for they be men, and "all men be liars," as David saith. Now, if all the members may err, then you may easily see, whereto your faith ought to lean, even unto God's written word. "Hear the church" and the doctors of the church, but none otherwise than as teachers; and try their teaching by God's word. If they teach according to it, then believe and obey them: if contrary, then know they be but men, and always let your faith lean to God's word.

Howbeit, for this matter of praying for the dead, know of

[[2] "Gate:" road.—Todd's Johnson, Dict.] [[3] See p. 279, note 4, above.]
[[4] See Vol. I. p. 372, note 1; and Becon's Works, Vol. I. p. 191, note 2, Park. Soc.]

truth, that there be no doctors of four hundred or five hundred years after Christ's ascension, but, if they in some places seem to allow praying for the dead, yet they would be taken in some of the senses which I have specified. In many places do they by divers sentences declare it themselves. But of this enough.

CHAPTER IX.

THE REFUTATION OF THE HERESY OF PRAYING TO SAINTS DEPARTED OUT OF THIS WORLD.

Now to the last, of praying to saints. First, where they say, there be more mediators of intercession than Christ, making a distinction not learned out of God's book, in such sense and for such purpose as they allege, I wish they would look on the eighth to the Romans, and 1 John ii.: and there shall they learn to take better heed. The one saith, "Christ sitteth on the right hand of his Father, and prayeth for us:" the other saith, 'He is our Advocate, that is, a spokesman, comforter, intercessor, and mediator.' Now would I ask them, seeing that Christ is a mediator of intercession (as I am sure they will grant), whether he be sufficient or no. If they say, 'no,' then all men will know they lie. But if they say, 'yes,' then may I ask, why they are not content with sufficient? What fault find ye with him? Is there any more merciful than he, any more desirous to do us good than he, any that knoweth our grief and need so much as he, any that knoweth the way to help us so well as he? No, none so well. He crieth: "Ask, and ye shall have;" "come to me, and I will help you;" "ask, that your joy may be full. Hitherto ye have not asked any thing in my name." Therefore, my good brethren and sisters, let us thank God for this Mediator; and, as he is one alone Mediator for redemption, let us take him even so for intercession. For, if by his work of redemption of enemies we are made friends, surely we being friends, and having him above on the right hand of his Father, shall by him obtain all things.

Matt. vii. Matt. xi. John xvi.

Rom. v. Heb. i.

Where they call it a point of a lowly and an humble spirit to go to saints, that they may pray for them, you may easily see, it is a point of an arrogant heart and a false untrue spirit.

For, inasmuch as God plainly biddeth thee, that thou put nought to his word, nor take ought therefrom; in that his word is, "Thou shalt call upon him in thy need;" why art thou so arrogant and proud, that thou wilt go to Peter or Paul to pray for thee? Where hast thou God's word? dost thou think, God is true of his promise? why then dost thou not go unto him? Dost thou think that God at anytime receiveth thee for thy worthiness? on whom be his eyes, but "upon him that trembleth at his word?" "Blessed are they that be poor in spirit," and think themselves unworthy of God's help. Wherefore hath God sworn that he "will not the death of a sinner," but that sinners might be most certain of his love and mercy to be much greater than they be able to conceive? "His mercies are above all his works." But thou, that runnest to saints, thinkest that it is not so: for else wouldst thou go to him thyself, that thou, seeing his so much goodness, mightest the more love him; which thou canst not, if thou use other means than by Christ only.

Deut. xii. Rev. xxii. Psal. l. Isai. lxv. Matt. v. Ezek. xxxiii. Psal. cxlv.

Where they bring in the ensample of saints praying for the people, and obtaining benefits for them, whilst they were living here on earth, and so gather, that much more they will and can do it now for us, in that they be with God, if we will pray unto them—very easily may we put this away by many reasons.

First, that the cases be not like. For, when they were alive, they might know the need of the people: but now who can tell whether they know anything of our calamities and need? Esay saith, Abraham did not know them that were in his age. Again, if the people had come to them to have desired their prayers, as they would have taken this for an admonishment of their duty to the people, so would they again have warned the people of their duty, that with them they also would pray unto God themselves. Whereas there be no such reciprocal and mutual offices between the dead and the living. Now cannot we admonish them, and tell them of our needs; or, if we should go about it, surely we should still stand in a doubt, whether they did perceive us or no. But, if they did perceive the miseries of their brethren, surely their rest would not be without great grief; and of this we are sure, that they can tell us nothing also.

Isai. lxiii.

Besides this, this their reasoning smelleth, as it that went

1 Cor. i. before, of man's reason which is a fool in God's service, and of
Rom. x. a good intent which is "not according to knowledge." We may
not do after that which is good in our own eyes, but according
Deut. xi. to that which God biddeth us do. In our eyes it seemeth good,
that, as to kings and great men we use means by men, which
are of their privy chambers or near about them, either to come
to their speech, or to attain our suits, so we should do to God
by his saints. But to dream on this sort with God, to use
saints so, were and is unto faith very foolish: for God useth no
Psal. cxlv. such privy chambers to hide himself in. "He is at hand,"
saith David, "to all that call upon him." And Moses said
Deut. iv. before him, "God is near thee in all thy prayers. No nation
hath their gods so nigh unto them as our God is to us in all our
prayers." He needeth none to put him in remembrance of us;
Heb. iv. for he hath all things open to his eyes: the height of the hills
Psal. xxxiii. xcv. and the bottom of the depths are in his sight. Nothing can
hide itself from his knowledge. He hath ordained Christ Jesus
1 Tim. ii. alonely to be the mean by whom we shall speed and receive our
requests, which be according to his will, if we open our purse-
mouth, that he may pour into the same—I mean faith. For,
as a thing poured upon a vessel or other thing, the mouth being
closed, is spilt and lost, so, if we ask anything according to
God's will by Christ, the same doth us no good, except the
purse-mouth of our hearts be opened by faith to receive it.

Rom. x. But, to make an end, St Paul telleth plainly, that without
faith prayer is not made. Now, in that faith is due only to
Jer. xvii. God (for "cursed is he" that hath his faith in man, saint or
angel), to God only let us make our prayers, but by Jesus
Christ, and in his name only; for only in him is the Father
Matt. iii. xvii. "well pleased." This if we do, and that often, as Christ willeth,
Luke xviii. *Oportet semper orare*, "We must pray alway," then shall we
undoubtedly in all things be directed by God's holy Spirit,
John xiv. xv. xvi. whom Christ hath promised to be our doctor, teacher, and
Psal. xxvii. Comforter: and therefore need we not to fear what man or
devil can do unto us, either by false teaching or cruel persecu-
John x. tion; for our Pastor is such one, that "none can take his sheep
out of his hands." To him be praise for ever. Amen[1].

[[1] The last seven lines, "oportet semper......for ever. Amen," have also been printed in Vol. I. p. 432. See editorial preface, p. 268, above.]

[THE HURT OF HEARING MASS.

The "Hurt of hearing mass," in the following reprint, follows, unless it be otherwise noted, the text of the edition of Copland, without date, of which the title is given immediately after this preface. Passages in this Treatise, some of which are of considerable length, now are first printed from Lansdown MS. No. 389, fol. 38, reverse—74, in the British Museum. The text of this reprint has throughout been compared with that MS., and occasionally with another early transcript, also in the British Museum, MS. 422. No. 19, fol. 104—131, in the Harleian collection, and with the edition printed by Kirkham, 1580.

Bradford has referred to this Treatise in Letters XLI. p. 116, XLIV. p. 126, and XCIII. p. 236, above. The reasoning also in p. 513 is quoted in the very scarce first edition of Foxe's Acts and Monuments, 1563, p. 889, or ed. 1843—9, Vol. VI. p. 358.

The subject of this Treatise, being amid the fierce persecutions of the sixteenth century of deep interest, has been frequently handled both by the English and Foreign Reformers[2]. Bradford, in particular,

[[2] The names of Calvin, Viret, Bullinger, and Hooper, are referred to on the margin of p. 300. See

Calvin. Tractat. Theol. secund. part. class. tert. Advers. Pseudonicodemitas, De fugiendis impiorum illicitis sacris epistola, 1537, Excusatio ad pseudo-Nicodemos, 1545, and other Treatises, Op. Tom. VIII. pp. 409—99, Amstel. 1667—71.

Viret, "Of the principal points which are at this day in controversy concerning the holy supper of Jesus Christ, and of the mass of the Romish church,... translated by John Shut," Barker, London, 1579, referred to in Herbert, Typogr. Antiq., Vol. II. p. 1080, Lond. 1785—90; and "An epistle to the faithful, necessary for all the children of God, especially in these dangerous days, written by Master Peter Viret in French, and Englished by F. H. Esq.," Dawson for Smith, London, 1582, copy, British Museum; and see Herbert, ibid. p. 1123.

Bullinger: "Two epistles, one of Henry Bullinger, with the consent of all the learned men of the church of Tigury, another of John Calvin, chief preacher of the church of Geneva, whether it be lawful for a Christian man to communicate or be partaker of the mass of the papists, without offending God and his neighbour or not, 1 Cor. x," Stoughton, London, 1548, copy, Grenville collection, British Museum; and see Herbert, ibid. p. 750. Also "A sermon of the true confessing of Christ and the truth of the gospel, and of the foul denying of the same, made in the convocation of the clergy at Zurich, the 28th day of January, in the year of our Lord 1555, by H. B.," printed with "A treatise of the cohabitation of the faithful with the unfaithful" (this last attributed to Peter Martyr by Herbert), copy, British Museum; and see Herbert, ibid. Vol. III. p. 1581.

Bp Hooper: "Whether Christian faith may be kept secret in the heart, within addition to the general argument, has with accurate acquaintance with the chief authorities then accessible discoursed upon the origin of different portions of the Ordinary and Canon of the Mass[1]. References are given in the foot-notes chiefly to the later decisions of the most learned writers within the church of Rome, which indicate how much has been admitted upon these questions by the ablest ritualists even of that communion. To have entered upon the subject further would have exceeded the limits generally observed in the works issued by the Parker Society. Ample information and reference to various authors can be obtained by consulting the works of Gavantus and Cardinal Bona, with the additions respectively of Merati and of Sala. Abundant illustration can also be derived from the writings of learned men of Protestant communions; from the works of Hospinian[2], a distinguished divine of the sixteenth century, of Zurich; from Du Moulin's "Mass in Latin and English," London, 1641; from the writings of Bingham, 1726, which are reprinted in various editions; and from the "Origines Liturgicæ" of Palmer, London, 1845, section on the "Liturgy of Rome," and chapter on "the holy communion."

Bradford, throughout this Treatise, will be of course understood to refer to the Salisbury Missal, the book which had principally been in use in England before the Reformation—the Uses of Hereford, Bangor, York, and Lincoln having been followed in this country only within narrower limits. All these Uses, it may be proper to state, differed, in various minor particulars, at once from each other and from the Use authorized by the church of Rome, during the last two or three centuries[3]. The "Missale ad usum Sarum" is a book of

out confession thereof openly to the world as occasion shall serve; also what hurt cometh by them that hath received the gospel, to be present at mass, unto the simple and unlearned," Roan, Oct. 3, 1553, and in Bp Coverdale, Letters of the martyrs, 1564, p. 157. See Bp Hooper's Works, Vol. II. pp. 570—8, Park. Soc.]

[[1] This last-mentioned topic has been especially handled, among the English Reformers, by Barnes, "Of the original of the mass and of every part thereof," in his Works, pp. 356—58, Day, London, 1573; by Becon, Displaying of the Popish Mass, Works, Vol. III. pp. 262—70, Park. Soc., and Relics of Rome, ch. "Of the mass, and of all the parts thereof," fol. 122—38, b, Day, London, 1563; and by Foxe, Acts, &c., ed. 1563, pp. 1894—99, or ed. 1843—49, Vol. VI. pp. 368—80, and intermediate editions.]

[[2] Rodolph. Hospinian. Histor. Sacrament.... hoc est, libri quinque de cœnæ dominicæ prima institutione, ejusque vero usu et abusu in primitiva ecclesia, tum de origine, progressu, ceremoniis et ritibus missæ, &c. &c., Tiguri, 1598—1602; or Hospinian. Op. in sept. tom. distrib. Tom. III. Hist. Sacram. pars prior, Genev. 1681.]

[[3] "The distinctions of the ancient liturgies of the church of England, both

considerable rarity; and the other Missals that were formerly used in England have been very difficult of access to ordinary students; the Lincoln Missal, in particular, not being at present known to exist. The Canon of the Mass, according to Salisbury Use, it may therefore be well to add, will be found, translated into English, in Foxe's Acts and Monuments, ed. 1583, beginning of the reign of Mary, pp. 1398—1401, or ed. 1843—9, Vol. VI. pp. 362—68. The Ordinary moreover and Canon, according to the Latin Uses respectively of Sarum, Bangor, York, Hereford, and Rome, and arranged in parallel columns, have recently been printed in Maskell's "Ancient Liturgy of the Church of England." Pickering, London, 1846.]

between themselves, and the modern Roman Use, in the Ordinary and the Canon, are not only as great but greater, and more in number, and involving points of higher consequence, than a previous acquaintance with these matters, before an actual examination of the English missals, would have authorized us to expect."—Maskell, Preface to Ancient English Liturgy, p. xv., London, 1846.]

THE HVRTE OF Hering Masse. Set forth by ye faithfull seruaūt of god & constant Marter of Christ. Johñ Bradforth whē he was Prisoner in the Tower of London.

3. Kinges. 18.

¶ How long wyl ye halt betwene two opinions.

Yf ye lord be god, folowe hym.

But yf Baal be he then goo after hym.

[From a copy in the Library of the late George Stokes, Esq., Cheltenham.]

HURT OF HEARING MASS.

ALTHOUGH at this present men call this into question, whether it be lawful for a man which knoweth the truth, to be present at the celebration of the mass or no? or whether a man being in company with others at mass in body be therewith defiled, his spirit being absent and not consenting, but rather detesting and abhorring the abomination and naughtiness of the mass, or no?—although, I say, this now be come into question amongst us here in England, especially amongst many my good brethren and sisters in London, as I hear say, yet I trust it be no further, but still in question—I mean, that I trust men be not yet so persuaded, as perchance the first movers of this question either would have other so to think because they think so, or else because they yet think not so themselves fully, but would be so persuaded that, as in conscience they might be quiet, so in body and goods they might live in rest and safety. Howbeit, inasmuch as this question—if a man consider the state of the world, and reasoning or probabilities, which to a natural man cannot but seem allowable—may fortune to grow to an inconvenience to a christian conscience, and to a great offence both to God and his church, I thought it my duty, as I can, to put to my helping hand, nay, rather to beseech God in the bowels and blood of his dear Son Jesus Christ, that he would put to his helping hand, and by me as by an instrument of his grace and mercy he would work something to his glory and to the profit of his church, in and concerning this matter. Not that the matter itself needeth it, for it is very plain, and heretofore divers have written of it enough[1], if enough be enough.

Papists.

Weak gospellers.

Calvin. Viret. Bullinger. Hooper.[1]

But—because these times full of offences, Satan's great diligence and his soldiers serving at a pinch, on the one part, and the infirmities of my brethren, their ignorance and simplicity soon seduced by the subtle on the other part, seemeth to exact of me and of all charitable hearts, as the Lord hath lent his talents, so to exercise the same—the which thing, as in discharge of myself herein, so to occasion others to help the poor afflicted congregation of Christ with their learning and consola-

Matt. xxv.

[[1] See p. 297, note 2, above.]

tions learned out of God's book, I now attempt and begin in hope of God's grace, wisdom, and holy Spirit: which I desire and crave of thee, O merciful Father, in the name of thy dear child Jesus Christ, our only Saviour and Advocate, as well to guide and teach me in writing, as to work in the hearts of them to whom this shall come unto by reading, that we may know thy truth in all things, and love the same, to live it for evermore. Amen.

Whether a man or woman may, without offence to God and his church, be present at the mass with others in bodily presence, in spirit being absent, and not allowing the mass, but rather detesting it? this is the question.

That men or women may be present in body at mass, with such as take it for a God's service and a great worshipping of God, there are many reasons made; whereof these following, as they be the most probable and effectual, so be they in manner all that can be objected by any reasonable colour. Reasons to prove that a man may go to mass.

First, because "God is a Spirit," and requireth accordingly, 1.
that is to say, "in spirit" to be served, therefore the body John iv.
being at mass, if the spirit be with God, is not material, or a thing to be greatly condemned.

Again, as in the Old Testament, when much error and ido- 2.
latry was in the church, among the bishops, priests, pharisees, scribes and people, yet did neither the prophets, neither our Saviour and his apostles, abstain from coming to the temple at Jerusalem, and using of the sacrifices accustomed, as they would have done if they should have sinned in so doing; even so now it is not evil (though the mass be naught, and though they do naught which think it a God's service), if a man or woman do come to the church where mass is, and so be at it, if that in heart and mind they consent not to the wickedness and idolatry committed.

Thirdly, if when Naaman prayed the prophet Eliseus to pray 3.
that God would not be displeased with him when he should go 2 Kings v.
with his lord into the temple of Rimmon in body, although in spirit he would worship the true God of Israel—if, I say, the prophet bade him "go in peace," and all should be well, much more then it cannot be any offence to be present at mass, if so be our spirit talk with God, and allow it not.

4. Fourthly, a man being at mass, and not allowing it in his heart, as he cannot but pray to God to help his brethren, that their eyes might be open to see the evil they do in worshipping God contrary to his word (as did Astyrius who, being at the idolatrous sacrifice the people of Cæsarea used, by prayer obtained of God to have their eyes open and to see their error[1]), so by his gesture he will behave himself in such sort as rather shall make men the less to regard the mass, for he will not look up at the levation time, hold up his hands, nor strike his hands on his face, but rather kneel down in his pew or form, sadly and heavily, as one of small devotion to the mass. This reason is thought very probable.

5. Fifthly, a man being so scrupulous as to think that it is not enough to "believe well in the heart," and "with the tongue to confess" to God the christian faith, except he run out of his vocation to reprove the mass and them that come at it, as though all men were preachers—a man thus doing cannot please God, nor profit his brother, but offend both, and bring himself in great danger to lose all he hath, to be cast into prison, to undo his wife and children, &c. Therefore it cannot be but well done to go to mass, or at the least go to church where mass is[2], so that in spirit and conscience[3] we allow not the mass, but keep it pure to God[4].

Rom. x.

6. Sixthly, St Paul disalloweth them that altogether follow knowledge, where "charity is the thing edifieth, and knowledge maketh proud." Therefore in this case we ought to follow charity, and not to offend our brethren, till God reveals to them as he hath done unto us.

Cor. viii.

7. Seventhly, our Saviour sheweth "it to come from the heart, that defileth the man:" so then to come to mass in body, the heart being with God, defileth not a Christian.

Matt. xv.

8. Eighthly, it is the error of the anabaptists as it was of the Donatists[5] and other old heretics, to abstain from the ministry because of the wickedness of others: but Paul would have men

[1 The story is given from Euseb. Hist. Eccl. Lib. VII. cap. xvii., further on in this treatise, in the reply to this fourth reason.]

[2 The last ten words now are first printed from the Lansdown MS.]

[3 "and conscience," Lansd. MS : not in Copland's edition.]

[4 "it not," Copland's printed edition: "not the mass, but keep it pure to God," Lansd. MS.]

[5 See p. 179, note 3, above.]

to "prove themselves," and "not to judge of others, which 1 Cor. xi.
stand or fall to the Lord:" and even so, in this case of going Rom. xiv.
to mass, let us know the priest and people's illness do not hurt us if we in heart consent not to their evil.

Ninthly, in Samuel we read, that God bade him not look on 9.
the outward show, "for I have rejected that," saith he; "for Sam. xvi.
man looketh on that which is outward, but God beholdeth the heart." So here, if the heart be pure, it maketh no matter of the outward gesture of the body.

Tenthly, all the beauty and glory of "the king's daughter," 10.
that is, of the church and of every Christian, is "within," saith Psal. xlv.
the Psalm forty-fifth, and not without; so that, if the heart be pure, it forceth not though the body be in company at the mass with them that come to mass as to a holy thing.

11. Hereto some add the example of the three children, 11.
that they were present with others at the assembly to worship the golden image, but did not fall down to worship with others. So a man may well without sin be present in the church where and when mass is, so that he knock not and worship not there the idol, as others do.

12. This also [they] think is holpen by that which Baruch 12.
writeth to the people in the captivity, to honour God in their [Baruch vi. 4–6.]
hearts when they should see others worship stocks and stones. So, say they, when we see men at mass or worship it, let us in our hearts fear and "serve the living God," which passeth not whether in body we be in church at mass-time or no[6].

These and such like are the reasons that men make, to prove it lawful for a man or woman to be present at mass, if in spirit and heart they be absent, and allow it not. But how weak and vain all these be, yea, how far they make against that they would prove, by God's grace I trust anon to show, after that I have briefly touched the mass, what it is, and how great an evil A digression
it is. For a little thereof will I speak, and that not so much of the mass.
that men might know that it is evil (for I trust in God that very many know that, if so be they will know it), but rather that men may better consider how horrible and monstrous an evil it is: the which thing, I fear me, few do. Howbeit, because yet there are some which think reverently of the mass,

[6 The last two paragraphs now are first printed from the Lansdown MS.]

and err of simplicity and ignorance therein, to whose hands this my writing may come and perchance do them good, I doubt not but that my labour in briefly bringing in here what the mass is, and how great an evil it is, will not be thought utterly out of the way.

What the mass is of the name of it.

Concerning the mass, what it is, a man would think that of the name of it easily it might be learned; but certainly there is herein no certainty. For some call it an oblation of meal, of *mincha*[1], Leviticus vi. [14, 15,] Malachi i. [11,] Psalm cxli. [1,]; some call it a voluntary gift, of *missath*[2], Deuteronomy xvi. [10]; some say it hath the name of sending away such as was called *catechumeni*, because they were sent out of the congregation, when the Lord's supper was to be celebrated[3]; some say it cometh of sending gifts and alms for the relief of the poor, which were accustomed to be sent, and giving always tofore the receipt of the communion, at the time of the offertory, which thereof hath his name[4]; some say otherwise, and some say otherwise against them: so that there is, as I said, no certainty at all to learn what the mass is, of the name of it. And therefore I think it best to look on the parts of the mass, to learn thereout that which we cannot out of the name. Howbeit, by the way note this, that this name, *missa*, is no where read amongst the Grecians[5], with whom the primitive church did flourish, and therefore is no such ancient a relic as the

The name of the mass is not authentic nor catholic.

[1 "Mincha:" a gift, tribute, or offering to a divinity in sacrifice. Hebr. מִנְחָה. See Gesen. Lex.]

[2 "Missath:" a tribute, Deut. xvi. 10, authorised version. Hebr. מִסָּה, in construction מִסַּת. Baronius assigns this derivation to the word "mass:" ...... "missa: quod quidem......ex Hebraica vel Chaldaica nomenclatura acceptum esse videtur. Quod enim nostra vulgata legitur 'spontanea oblatio,' Hebraice et Chaldaice dicitur *missah*."—Baron. Annal. Eccl., cum cont. Rayn., ann. 34, sect. lix. Tom. I. p. 136, Lucæ, 1738—53.]

[3 The best authorities agree with Cardinal Bona, that "missa" is a Latin word, "a mittendo," and is the same as "missio," being derived first from the dismission of the catechumens and others, and secondly from the "Ite missa est," 'Depart, it is the dismission,' at the end of the Canon. See Bona, Rer. Liturg. Lib. II. cap. i. 4, 6, and notes of Sala, pp. 3—10, August. Taurin. 1747—53; Bellarmin. Disputat. De sacram. euchar. Lib. v. cap. i. 12. Tom. III. p. 411, Pragæ, 1721; and Gavant. Thesaur. sacr. rit. Pars I. in rubric. gener., Tom. I. pars I. pp. 15, et seq. ed. Merati, Rom. 1736—8.]

[4 Vide Calvin. Instit. Lib. IV. cap. xviii. 8. Op. Tom. IX. pars I. p. 384, Amst. 1667—71.]

[5 ......apud Græcos nulla est mentio hujus vocis "missa," sed pro ea λειτουργίαν dicunt.—Bellarm. ibid. cap. i. 9.]

papists make it. For the Tripartite ecclesiastical story which was written in Greek hath not this word "mass" in it, though the translator thereof into Latin[6] now and then use that word. Neither Ignatius' epistle, if in Greek they could shew it[7], would help any further than this ecclesiastical history, and Dionysius in his Hierarchy[8], notwithstanding the later translations be otherwise. As for the feigning of some, which would gladly have men persuaded of the ancience of the mass, and of the name of it, and therefore say this word *missa* is a word of the Syrians' speech[9], a man with half an eye cannot but see that therein they halt; for in that Greece is so near to Syria, and between us and it, surely it could not but have been known and written amongst the Greek authors. But, to come thither from whence I went, this shall suffice to note by the way, that the mass, whereof no certainty can be gathered out of the name of it, was never known, even but in name, to the primitive church, prate the papists as please them; and I trust shortly by the parts to demonstrate the same.

What the mass is by the parts of it.

If in speaking of the parts of the mass I observe not such an order as I should, but speak of one piece before, which should be spoken of after, I must desire pardon, as well for that (God be praised therefor) I never said mass, as also for that I have forgotten the order the priests were wont to keep, so long it is sithens I did see any.

Introit.

The *introit* (for here I ween I should begin) one Celestinus bishop of Rome ordained about the year of our Lord 430[10]: so

[6 The "Tripartite History" was compiled in Latin by Cassiodorus, about A.D. 620, from the three church-historians, Socrates, Sozomen, and Theodoret, whose writings had been rendered into Latin from the Greek by Epiphanius Scholasticus. See Cave, Hist. Liter. Tom. I. pp. 501, 2. Oxon. 1740—3.]

[7 The Greek Ignatian Epistles were first published at Dillingen in 1557, edited by Paceus; and in 1562, edited by Gesner. A shorter text, the Florentine, was first published by Vossius, Amst. 1646; the still shorter Syriac text by Cureton, Lond. 1845. See Patr. Apost. ed. Jacobson, Judic. de S. Ignat. Epist. p. xxvi, Oxon. 1847; and Corpus Ignatianum, Cureton, Introd. p. iii, Lond. 1849.]

[8 See Episc. Pearson. Vindic. Epist. S. Ignat. Pars I. cap. x. pp. 249—64, (Lib. Ang. Cath.), Oxon. 1852; and Joann. Daillæi De Script. quæ sub Dionys. Areop. et Ignat. Antioch. nomin. circumf. lib. duo, pp. 1—224, Genev. 1666.]

[9 See Bellarm. Disputat. De sacram. euchar. Lib. v. cap. i. 8, 9. Tom. III. p. 411, Pragæ, 1721.]

[10 Hic...constituit ut Psalmi David 150 ante sacrificium psallerentur, antiphonatim ex omnibus, quod antea non fiebat, sed tantum epistolæ beati Pauli recitabantur, et sanctum evangelium.—Vita Cælest. Papæ I. e Libr. Pontif. in Concil. stud. Labb. et Cossart. Tom. II. col. 1610, Lut. Par. 1671—2. Ejus institutio non

Grail.

long this piece of the mass was not catholic, nor the grail also, for some say he brought it in; howbeit others do say that Gelasius ordained the grail to be had in the mass about the year of our Lord 490; and others do write that pope Gregory, about the year of our Lord 600, did institute it[1] as many other things: so that of many [a] day the grail was [not] catholic.

Confiteor.

The *confiteor* pope Damasus brought into the mass, as it is written, about the year of our Lord 370[2]: so long the catholic church wanted it, and still should want it in that it containeth in it idolatry, invocation to saints, which is against God's word.

Kyrie eleison.

The *Kyrie eleison* nine times to be spoken in such a tongue as few priests can or do pronounce otherwise than *Kyreleson*[3], that is, "Sow have mercy," or "Pig shew mercy[3]"—this pope Gregory (though some say it was Sylvester) instituted about six hundred years after Christ[4], as he did also the antiphones[5], alleluia[6], the offertory[5], and a piece of the canon[7].

est antiquior Cælestino I. pontifice.—Merati on Gavant. Thesaur. sacr. rit. Pars I. Tit. viii. 1. Tom. I. pars I. p. 172, Rom. 1736—8.]

[1 Graduale nuncupatur...a gradibus ambonis sive pulpiti...Sunt qui...auctorem Cælestinum faciunt, sunt qui Gregorium Magnum: et Gregorius quidem [responsoria] in suo Antiphonario per ordinem digessit.—Bona, Rer. Liturg. Lib. II. cap. vi. 4. Tom. III. p. 132, stud. Sala, August. Taurin. 1747—53. ...Gregorius, Ambrosius et Gelasius composuerunt gradualia.—Durand. Ration. Div. Offic. Lib. IV. cap. xix., De graduali, fol. lxvi, Argentin. 1486.]

[2 Confessionem qua nunc utitur Romana ecclesia Pontianum Papam sive Damasum instituisse aiunt plerique recentiores [ex. gr. Platin. Hist. de vit. Pontif., Vit. Damas., fol. xxii, b, Venet. 1504], quorum assertio sine legitimo teste nullius apud me ponderis est......tacentibus hac de re priscis auctoribus.—Bona, ibid. cap. ii. 5. p. 37. See also Merati on Gavantus, ibid. Pars II. Tit. iii. 7. p. 387.]

[3 That is to say, Κύριε ἐλέησον, pronounced like, Χοῖρε ἐλέησον. See Bp Bale's "Declaration of Bp Bonner's Articles," signature O ii, 1561; and in Strype, Ecc. Mem. Vol. III. part. i. p. 178, where that passage of Bale is quoted.]

[4 Quamvis Gavantus asseveret, inhærendo Radulpho, a Græcis ad Romanos Silvestrum dictam precationem transtulisse, hoc tamen incertum est...Fere omnes Offic. Eccles. explanatores Gregorio Magno hoc tribuunt: sed multis annis ante S. Gregor. in ecclesia Latina hujus precis institutionem fuisse constat.—Merati on Gavantus, ibid. Pars I. Tit. viii. 2. p. 175. See also Bona, ibid. cap. iv. 1. p. 72.]

[5 ...Gregorius magnus unam e [Psalmis] antiphonam selegit pro introitu, et alias pro responsorio, offertorio, et communione, quas in unum congessit, et ex his librum composuit, quem Antiphonarium nuncupavit.—Bona, ibid. cap. iii. 1. p. 48.]

[6 ...Gregorius...instituit ut caneretur etiam extra tempus Paschale.—Gavant. ibid. Pars I. Tit. x. 3. p. 204.]

[7 See Vol. I. p. 513, note 9.]

Howbeit some say that Pelagius the second, his predecessor, did so first appoint *Kyrie eleison*[8].

The *gloria in excelsis* pope Symmachus ordained to be sung on the Sundays and other holydays[9], about the year of our Lord 510. Tofore this time was the mass out of order, for they write that he first brought the mass into an order: but surely the order then, as it was far from that in the primitive church was used, so was it further from the order now used; for sithen that time many things were found out and put to, as partly, if you note the years I write, you now see, but more shall see anon by God's grace. I know that some do say that Telesphorus ordained it about the year of our Lord 140[10], about which we read that Lent was commanded to be of none other but of the priests and clergy only: Isidor. Tom. I., Concil. Gratian. distinctio 6, *Statuimus*[11]. Howbeit almost all men know, that Hilarius which was about the year of our Lord 340 made this hymn, and sung it first in his church[12]: and therefore it cannot be attributed to Telesphorus.

Gloria in excelsis.

Mass first brought into order.

Lent commanded first to the priests only.

The collects who made them there is no certainty. Some say Gelasius[13], some say Gregorius[14]: so that the church could well spare them at least 490 years.

Collects.

The epistle and gospel who disposed them as they be there, there is [no] certainty, some attributing this to St Jerome,

The epistle and gospel.

[8 See Concil. Vasens. II. can. III. A. D. 529, in Concil. Tom. IV. col. 1680. The Epistle of Pelagius, Ad Episc. German. et Gall. in Concil. Tom. V. cols. 953, 4, recommending nine prefaces to be used in the Ordinary of the Mass, is considered to be spurious. See Bona, ibid. cap. x. 3. p. 232; and Merati on Gavantus, ibid. Tit. xii. 2. pp. 230, 1.]

[9 Hic constituit, ut omni die Dominico, vel natalitiis martyrum, hymnus, "Gloria in excelsis," diceretur.—Vita Symm. e Libr. Pontif. in Concil. Tom. IV. col. 1288.]

[10 Telesphorus...fecit...ut ante sacrificium hymnus diceretur angelicus, hoc est, "Gloria in excelsis."—Vita Telesph. e Lib. Pontif. in Concil. Tom. I. cols. 558, 9. See Bona, ibid. cap. iv. 4. p. 82.]

[11 ...cognoscite...statutum esse, ut septem hebdomadas plenas ante sanctum pascha omnes clerici in sortem Domini vocati a carne jejunent, quia, sicut discreta esse debet vita clericorum a laicorum conversatione, ita et in jejunio debet fieri discretio.—Telesph. Papa in Corp. Jur. Canon. Decret. Gratian. Decr. Prima Pars, Dist. IV. can. 4. p. 3, Paris. 1618.]

[12 ...recentiores...a B. Hilario...completum fuisse asseverant: sed...liquet jam eo tempore usitatum fuisse, et per varias regiones dispersum.—Bona, ibid.]

[13 Fecit...sacramentorum præfationes et orationes cauto sermone.—Vita Gelas. e Libr. Pontif. in Concil. stud. Labb. et Cossart. Tom. IV. col. 1055, Lut. Par. 1671—2.]

[14 See Vol. I. p. 513, note 9.]

some to Damasus[1], some to Telesphorus aforesaid. But this is more certain, that pope Anastasius the third ordained that men should stand up at hearing the gospel read, about the year of our Lord 405[2].

The Creed.

The creed pope Marcus about the year of our Lord 340 did ordain to be sung in the mass[3]: this pope brought in linen albs and corporasses[4], and was nothing offended that every priest should have his own wife, though now it be otherwise taken[5]. In his time there was a council called *Elibertinum Concilium*, kept in Spain, which damned all kind of images, yea, pictures in the temples[6].

I. Albs. II. Corporasses. III. Priests' marriage. IV. Images condemned.

The offertory.

The offertory, whereof now remaineth nothing but the name, is attributed to Eutychianus about the year of our Lord 280[7]. The prefaces are given to Gelasius and Gregorius[8], so that for six hundred years or thereabout after Christ they were not used.

Prefaces.

The canon.

The canon, which they have in such admiration and reverence as nothing else, was made of divers[9]. Pope Alexander

[[1] ...credibile est...Hieronymum suum lectionarium per singulos dies distributum ordinasse, jubente Damaso Papa, qui ordinem illum in Romana ecclesia servari præcepit, ex qua ad alias dimanavit.—Bona, ibid. cap. vi. 2. p. 123.]

[[2] ... Anastasii Papæ Decreto de Consecr. Dist. 1. "Apostolica," Sacerdotes et cæteri omnes ad evangelium stare debent.—Gavant. Thesaur. sacr. rit. Pars I. Tit. xvii. 2. Tom. I. pars I. p. 257, ed. Merati, Rom. 1736—8.]

[[3] Radulphus Tungrensis, prop. 23, a Marco Papa, Sylvestri successore, sancitum fuisse ait, ut symbolum Nicænum in missa diceretur. At Innocentius III. ... et alii passim scribunt, S. Damasum id recitari jussisse ad exemplum Græcorum.—Bona, ibid. cap. viii. 2. p. 171.]

[[4] ...proxima est...palla linea, sive sindon, in qua corpus Christi consecratur, cui propterea "corporalis" nomen ab ecclesiasticis scriptoribus inditum fuit.—Id. Lib. I. cap. xxv. 11. The alb was an ecclesiastical vestment, not very different from the surplice.—Palmer, Orig. Liturg., on eccl. vestures, Vol. II. p. 408, Oxf. 1845.]

[[5] Abundant evidence, from various authors will be found in Bp Jewel, Defence of Apology, Part II. chap. viii. div. 1, 2, 3, Works, Vol. III. pp. 385—429, Park. Soc. The few writings attributed to Marcus are spurious.]

[[6] Placuit, picturas in ecclesia esse non debere; ne quod colitur et adoratur in parietibus depingatur.—Concil. Eliberit. cap. 36. in Concil. Tom. I. col. 974. This council was held at Elvira, near Granada, about A.D. 305.]

[[7] ... quis ... hujus offertorii ritum instituerit, incertum est: quidam enim Pontificii Eutychiano, alii Cælestino I., et plerique Gregorio Magno, ac denique nonnulli Hadriano I. id institutum tribuunt.—Sala on Bona, Rer. Liturg. Lib. II. cap. viii. 3. Tom. III. p. 181, August. Taurin. 1747—53.]

[[8] See note 2, above; Bona, ibid. cap. x. 1. p. 227; and Merati on Gavantus, ibid. Tit. xii. 2. pp. 229, 30.]

[[9] ...ecclesia catholica sacrum Canonem multis ante seculis instituit...is enim

made one piece of it about the year of our Lord 220, *qui pridie*[10]. Pope Xistus made another piece upon a ten years after him, which he took out of the prophet Esay[11]. Pope Leo, about the year of our Lord 450, made another piece, *sanctum sacrificium*, &c.[12]. And note that this pope allowed marriage of priests[13], as all his predecessors before him have done. Pope Gregory, about the year of our Lord 600, made another piece of the canon and a great piece of the mass, as he himself witnesseth in his register[14]; for before his time it was no such hotch-potch as he made it, but now it is much worse. Pope Gregory the third, about the year of our Lord 732, put to this piece, *et eorum quorum memoria*[15], &c. And note that this pope called a council at Rome, wherein it was decreed that images should not only be had in temples but also worshipped, and that all gainsayers should be counted as heretics[16]. Innocentius the third of that name affirmeth pope Gelasius, which was about 490 years after Christ, to have made a great piece

Marriage of priests.

Images allowed, yea, commanded.

constat cum ex ipsis Domini verbis, tum et apostolorum traditionibus, ac sanctorum quoque pontificum piis institutionibus.—Concil. Trident. Sess. VI. Pii IV. ann. 1562. cap. iv. fol. 95, Antv. 1564.]

[[10] Valfridus et Micrologus opinati sunt ab Alexandro Papa additam hanc clausulam, "qui pridie:" sed rectius sentit Alcuinus etiam apostolis in usu fuisse.—Bona, ibid. cap. xiii. 1. p. 275.]

[[11] Additum...a Sixto I. plerique scribunt: sed Liber Pontif. hoc solum a Sixto constitutum ait, ut, sacerdote ipsum incipiente, etiam populus eundem cantaret.—Bona, ibid. cap. x. 4. p. 235.]

[[12] ...[verba] "sanctum sacrificium, immaculatam hostiam," S. Leo Magnus addidit: ex Innoc. [Lib. v.] cap. 4.—Gavant. ibid. Pars II. Tit. ix. 1. p. 565.]

[[13] ...is episcopus ordinetur, quem "unius uxoris virum" fuisse aut esse constiterit...—Leon. Magni Epist. XII. cap. iii. (al. I. al. LXXXVII.) Ad Episc. Afr. provinc. Maurit. Cæsar. Op. Tom. I. col. 660, Venet. 1753—57.]

[[14] Gregor. Magni Papæ I. Registr. Epist. Lib. IX. Indict. II. Ad Joann. Syracus. Epist. xii. (al. Lib. VII. Ind. II. Ep. lxiv.) Op. Tom. II. cols. 939—41, ed. Bened. Par. 1705. See Bradf. Vol. I. p. 513, note 9; and Hospinian. Hist. sacram. Lib. III. cap. ii. Gregor. I., Op. Tom. III. p. 163, Genev. 1681.]

[[15] Gregorius III...hanc clausulam in Canone post illa verba, "et omnium sanctorum tuorum," dici instituit: "Quorum solennitas hodie in conspectu tuæ majestatis celebratur, Domine Deus noster, in toto orbe terrarum." At hoc specialiter...atque...non est Canoni...adnotatum.—Bona, Rer. Liturg. Lib. II. cap. xi. 2. Tom. III. p. 246, stud. Sala, August. Taurin. 1747—53. Cardinal Bona, ibid. 3. p. 256, adds: In aliis codicibus post verba, "et omnium circumstantium," hæc adduntur: "Et eorum quorum nomina," [&c.] The two statements appear to be intermingled in the text.]

[[16] Concil. Rom. A. D. 732. in Concil. stud. Labb. et Cossart. Tom. VI. cols. 1463, 4, 85, Lut. Par. 1671—2.]

of the canon[1], as he himself did something therein[2]. About the year of our Lord 1215[3], this Innocentius ordained that the sacrament should be reserved in the churches[4]; he brought in auricular confession as a law[5]; he did constitute that no archbishop should have his pall except he were of his religion[6], and therefore we have less cause to marvel at the unity in popery. Beatus Rhenanus affirmeth that one Scholasticus which was about Gregory's time did make *Te igitur*, &c.[7]. So that we may see what an hotch-potch and how ancient a relic this canon is, which is the holiest, nay, most blasphemous piece of the mass.

Reservation of the sacrament. Auricular confession.

A palace for unity in popery.

The levation.

The levation who ordained it, I cannot tell certainly. Some attribute it to Honorius the third, about the year of our Lord 1210, and not unlikely, for indeed he ordained that the people should kneel down and worship the sacrament[8]. So long a time after Christ was it afore this gear was catholic.

Agnus.

The *agnus*, &c., pope Sergius about the year of our Lord

[1 Traditur autem quod Gelasius Papa, quinquagesimus primus a beato Petro, qui fuit post Silvestrum per clx. annos, Canonem principaliter ordinavit.—Innocent. Papæ III. Myster. Miss. Lib. III. cap. x. Op. Tom. I. p. 370, Col. 1575.]

[2 ... in Missa dicitur secunda oratio, "A cunctis," cujus est auctor Innoc. III. ex Dur[and.] Lib. IV. cap. xv. [fol. lxiii, b, Argentin. 1486.]—Gavant. Thesaur. sacr. rit., Pars I. Tit. ix. 2. Tom. I. pars I. p. 182, ed. Merati, Rom. 1736—8.]

[3 "1120," Copland's edit.: "1215," Lansd. MS.]

[4 Statuimus, ut in cunctis ecclesiis chrisma et eucharistia sub fideli custodia clavibus adhibitis conserventur.—Concil. Lateran. sub Innoc. III. cap. xx. in Concil. Tom. XI. col. 172.]

[5 Omnis utriusque sexus fidelis...omnia sua solus peccata confiteatur fideliter, saltem semel in anno...alioquin...moriens Christiana careat sepultura.—Id. ibid. cap. xxi. cols. 172, 3.]

[6 ...postquam eorum antistites a Romano pontifice receperint pallium...præstito sibi fidelitatis et obedientiæ juramento, licenter et ipsi suis suffraganeis pallium largiantur, recipientes...pro Romana ecclesia sponsionem obedientiæ ab eisdem.—Id. ibid. cap. v. col. 153.]

[7 Nam Canonem, "Te igitur cl[ementissime"] a quodam conscriptum aiunt, cui "Scholastico" nomen fuerit: et indicat hoc divus Gregorius paulo ante suam ætatem factum.—Beat. Rhenan. Annot. in Tertull. Lib. de coron. milit. cap. iii., p. 41, ad calc. Tertull. Op. Franek. 1597. See, with regard to Gregory and Scholasticus, Vol. I. p. 513, notes 10, 11.]

[8 Sacerdos vero quilibet frequenter doceat plebem suam, ut, cum in celebratione missarum elevatur hostia salutaris, se reverenter inclinet.—Honor. III. in Corp. Jur. Canon. Decretal. Greg. IX. Lib. III. Tit. xli. cap. x. pp. 640, 1, Paris. 1618. See also Const. Ric. Episc. Sar. (temp. Hon. III.) cap. xxxvii. in Concil. Tom. XI. col. 258; and Maskell on Anc. Eng. Lit., p. 92, London, 1846.]

700 brought into the mass[9]. Innocentius ordained the pax to be given to the people[10]. Pope Leo commanded the sacrament to be censed[11]. Bonifacius put in his foot for the covering of the altars[12]. Pelagius brought out the commemoration of the dead to be had in the mass[13]. Vigilius ordained that the priest should say mass with his face towards the east[14]. Platina writeth how that the first Latin mass was sung in the sixth council of Constantinople[15], which was about the year of our Lord 680[16]; and the same mass and order was there and then allowed, and so hitherto hath been with advantage, where tofore it was never so used there, nor in all the Greek churches[17].

Pax.

Censing.

Covering of altars.

Commemoration of the dead.

The first Latin mass.

But, to make an end hereof, authors do write that pope Stephanus, which would be carried and was on men's shoulders[18], pope Adrian his successor[19], and many others after them,

[[9] Sergius I. summus pontifex, teste Anastasio, statuit ut... Agnus Dei...decantaretur.—Bona, ibid. cap. xvi. 5. p. 347. See also Maskell, ibid. p. 114.]

[[10] "Pax:" an instrument, which, when the sacrifice of the mass had been offered, was kissed by the people.—Du Cange, Gloss. Its use, instead "of mutual salutation, was not until about the thirteenth century."—Maskell, ibid. p. 115. See also Bona, ibid. 7. p. 356, with Sala's additions; and, with regard to Innocent I., Bona and Sala, ibid. 6. pp. 351—54, and Innocent. Papæ I. Epist. ad Decent. episc. Eugub. cap. i. in Concil. Tom. II. col. 1246.]

[[11] ...adoletur incensum, quod a Leone I. institutum ex quibusdam chronicis scribit Radulphus, prop. 23: sed illis chronicis nulla fides adhibenda est.—Bona, ibid. cap. ix. 5, p. 218.]

[[12] Vestiendum est lineis altare ex decreto Bonifac. III., apud Polydor. Vergil. Lib. v. cap. 6. [p. 324, Amstel. 1671.]—Gavant. ibid. Tit. xx. p. 283.]

[[13] Ut scilicet pro defunctis in missa oremus, Sixto I. tribuit Platina; Pelagio I. Anselm. Ryd. in catalogo annorum; hoc est, decreto confirmaverunt.—Id. ibid. Pars II. Tit. ix. 2. p. 563. Merati, on that place, p. 568, states that the decree attributed to Pelagius is spurious.]

[[14] ...instituit...ut missa celebretur versus orientem.—Episc. Balei Acta Roman. Pontif., Vigil. Roman., p. 41, Basil. 1558.]

[[15] Joannes episcopus Portuensis octava Paschæ coram principe ac patriarcha, coramque populo Constantinopolitano in basilica sanctæ Sophiæ missam Latine celebrat.—Platin. Hist. de vit. Pontif. Vit. Agathon., fol. xli, Venet. 1504. This took place at the sixth General Council, at Constantinople, A.D. 680, 1. Compare Episc. Bal. ibid., Agath. I. p. 73.]

[[16] "750," Copland's edit.: "680," Lansd. MS.]

[[17] The last thirteen words, "where tofore...churches," now are first printed from the Lansdown MS.]

[[18] Stephanus II. ... se pontificaliter in populi medio cum summis triumphis, tanquam alter Alexander......ad Lateranensem basilicam a perferariis se gestari permisit: quod et a posteris pro magna religione observatum est, ut hominum humeris deportarentur.—Episc. Bal. ibid., Steph. II. p. 88. See also Platin. ibid., Vit. Steph. II. fol. xlviii.]

[[19] Hadrianus I. ... in officio ecclesiæ offertoria quædam versibus geminavit, et

did put something to the mass: so that by this which I have written of the parts of it—and yet I spake never a word of the private perception of the priest alone in the mass, which was not used in Gregory's time, six hundred years after Christ[1], nor at this day is used in the Greek church, nor was not catholic, as some write, in Europe above 450 years past—of the parts, I say, easily you may see that the mass is a hotchpotch and a device of man, yea, of twenty-eight popes and more, not fully found out and finished of a thousand years at the least after Christ. And yet the papists brag of it as though it had been from the apostles' time, as though Peter had sung the first mass at Antioch, and as though it were the most holy thing upon the earth, so that the church cannot be without it. Wherein they speak truly, if by the church they understand the popish church; for else Christ's church now should as well be without it, as it was of a thousand years, until the devil which was tied so long was letten loose. Read the twentieth chapter in the Revelations.

Put to the number of 308 bishops that made the former part of the creed[2].

How great an evil the mass is.

Now, the mass being known to be the device and invention of man, I will briefly shew you that it is the horriblest and most detestable device that ever the devil brought out by man.

The mass is against Christ, that is, against his priesthood. Heb. vii.

First, the mass is a most subtle and pernicious enemy against Christ, and that double, namely, against his priesthood and against his sacrifice. His priesthood is an everlasting priesthood, and such an one as cannot go to another. But the mass utterly puts him out of place, as though he were dead for ever; and so God is forsworn which said Christ should be "a priest for ever," and Paul lieth which affirmeth Christ to live, and to be "on the right hand" of the Father for us, that by him "we may come to the throne of grace to find mercy to help us in our need:" for, if these be true as they be most true, the mass priests are to be put down: for, if they be "of the order of Aaron," then resume they that which Christ hath

Psal. cx.

Heb. vii.

Heb. iv.

missarum ritus a Magno Gregorio editos, occidentalibus ecclesiis imperavit.—Episc. Bal. ibid., Hadrian. I., p. 93.]

[[1] See Bp Jewel, Reply to Harding, Art. I., "Of private mass," Vol. I. pp. 104—203, Park. Soc.]

[[2] Three hundred and eighteen bishops attended the First General Council of Nice, A. D. 325. Vide Socrat. Hist. Eccles. Lib. I. cap. viii. in Hist. Eccles. p. 23, ed. Vales., Mogunt. 1677.]

abolished; if they be "of the order of Melchisedec," then be they Christ's. Other orders of priests I read none, save that which all Christians be, to offer up themselves to God and other spiritual sacrifices by Christ, and the order of "priests of Baal," whose successors indeed the massers be: for else if they were, as they would be taken, of the order of the apostles, then should they be ministers and not massers, preachers and not traitors, as they be both to God and his church: God amend them.

Rev. i. 1 Pet. ii. Rom. xii. Heb. xiii. 2 Kings x.

Christ's sacrifice once made by himself on the tree, on the mount of Calvary, is the full and perfect propitiatory sacrifice, to the sanctification of all them that are and shall be saved, never more to be reiterated and done again, for that signifieth an imperfection. But the mass is called and had for a sacrifice propitiatory, and that such a one as fetcheth pardon *a pœna et a culpa*, ["from punishment and from guilt,"] for the quick and dead, and for whom Sir John will. In words or syllables the papists will deny this, but in very deed they do no otherwise, and in the latter end of their canon plainly they call it a propitiatory sacrifice. So that the mass, we see, is altogether against Christ alive, that is, against his priesthood, and against his death, that is, his sacrifice, and therefore a detestable evil I trow.

Christ's sacrifice. Heb. vii. ix. x.

Secondly, the mass is not only a let but also a destruction of the true worshipping of God: for, where the time is past to serve God now, as once he required, with goats, bullocks, &c., and the time is come to serve him *rationali cultu*, ["with a reasonable service,"] as Paul saith, in the offering up of our bodies by the renewing of our minds, and "serving him in spirit and truth," unfeignedly fearing his displeasure, trusting in his truth and mercy, and loving his goodness, and out of these in external obedience as he commandeth, the mass, as I say, not only letteth this, but also utterly destroyeth it. For who knoweth not that the very outward work of saying or seeing of mass is taken for a great God's service? who knoweth not that the outward work of the mass is and hath been applied for the remission of sins of the quick and the dead? And where did they ever teach that the mass was nothing worth either to the doer, or to them for whom [it] is done, without this spiritual service of God, the true fear of God, faith

The mass destroyeth God's service and all godliness of life. Rom. xii. John iv.

and love of God? No word at all was or yet is spoken hereof. All men may know therefore, if they will, the mass to let, yea, to destroy God's true service; for what needeth repentance when Sir John will save me by masses, even when the time of repentance is prevented by death? what needeth faith, what needeth goodness of life, what needeth preaching, what needeth praying, what needeth any piety at all, when that the mass hath all, and can and will serve for[1] all? For by it cometh pardon of sins, by it cometh deliverance from hell and purgatory, by it cometh fair weather, by it cometh peace and plenty, by it cometh health for man and beast.

Summa the mass is *mare malorum*, ["a sea of evil things,"] I should have said, *mare bonorum*, ["a sea of good things,"] the most singular, excellent, and incomparable jewel that can be! so that, it being gone, all is gone, the church is lost, the people perish, the faith faileth, and God is not worshipped; but, where it is, all is well, there needeth no preaching, there needeth no hearing of God's word, praying in spirit, repenting or godliness of life! If so be once a day men come to church to hear mass, to see the sacring[2], he that doth this is a good catholic, a child of the church, a man of God, although daily, after he have heard mass, he [be] all day at tavern or alehouse, at tippling, bibbing, &c. Although he use whoredom, swearing, dicing, thieving, polling, bribing, &c., if in the morrow after he come to church, take holy water, hear mass devoutly, and take altel[3] holy-bread, he is sure enough, say the papists. So that, as I said I say again, the mass utterly destroyeth all godliness of life and all God's service, as by this may something be seen, and as by experience doth now teach us; for it cannot away with that which is the root of all godliness, that is, God's word, and the true often preaching thereof. The one cannot but send the other out of the way; I mean, either the mass will put the pure preaching of God's word apart, and then "the people perish" (Proverbs xxix.), or else preaching must put it away, as once it did with us, and still would have done, if we had been thankful to God for preaching and preachers, and if we had had a lust to have lived as we have heard. Just therefore art thou, O Lord, thus to punish us, for we have deserved it. O, "in

Massing and true preach- are never together.

Prov. xix.

[[1] "save from," Copland's edit.: "serve for," Lansd. MS.]
[[2] See Vol. I. p. 160, note 1.]
[[3] "Altel:" altar.]

thine anger remember thy mercy," "be not angry with us for ever:" "turn to us again, O Lord God of hosts, look merrily upon us, and we shall be saved." "Thy will be done," and not mine.

Thirdly, the mass is not only besides Christ's institution and ordinance, but it is utterly against it, and perverteth it horribly; I mean this as concerning the supper and sacrament of Christ's body and blood: for, where he did ordain his supper to be a memorial of his death and passion, and therefore in the celebration thereof "the Lord's death should be preached out till he come," as Paul writeth, I pray you, who heareth anything hereof in the mass? Nay, they are wise enough to keep in that: for, when that is spoken of, men cannot but see thereby forgiveness of sins to come to such as believe freely, and so falleth their mart. Christ ordained his supper to be celebrated and received of the congregation; and therefore Paul willeth the Corinthians to tarry one for another, that they might all receive together: but all men see that here is no such thing. Choose the people whether they will come or no, Sir John is akin to the tide; he will tarry no man, if he have a boy to answer him, 'Amen.' Or, if he tarry for the people, yet get they no part with him, all is too little for himself, where Christ yet biddeth them, "Do this," that is, 'Distribute and give, take and eat,' as he did. Christ ordained this supper to be a taking matter, "Take, eat," saith he: but the mass is a looking matter, 'Peep, see, look, stoop down before,' &c. Christ would the celebrators of this his supper to be assured that his body was broken for them, and his blood shed for their sins, as they are assured and in possession of the bread they eat, and the wine they drink: but, lest they should be certain thereof, the mass and her minion the priest will spare nothing to the people to eat or drink with him. No, at no time the people must have their right; for the cup they may none kiss, and yet Christ bade them "all drink of it," so is his will. But our papists have another will, which the massmongers will more willingly follow than God's will, because they are of his swine, and not of Christ's sheep, which will not follow a stranger[4]. Christ never meant that one should receive the sacrament more

The mass perverteth horribly Christ's supper. 1 Cor. xi.

Matt. xxvi. Mark xiv. Luke xxii.

[[4] The last seventeen words now are first printed from the Lansdown MS.]

for another, than he would one should be baptized for another. I would wish the mass-priests were awhile in corporal food so served, as they serve their brethren in spiritual food: I mean, that the people should dine and sup for them another while, to see if that would feed them. O that men had as great a feeling of the hunger of the soul, as they have of the hunger of the body! surely they would not then be thus mocked.

But, because herein I would but touch and go, this shall suffice to the diligent for an occasion to see the mass to be a let, yea, an overthrow of Christ's institution concerning his supper: for now people think they serve God in coming to see the sacrament; but, if they knew they displeased God if they gave not themselves to the often and diligent receiving it with reverence (as divers canons compel, and the doctors cry out thereof), the mass which marreth all could not be in place.

The mass and the Lord's supper cannot be together.

For it cannot be but either the mass must drive away the right use of the Lord's supper, or the Lord's supper rightly used must drive away the mass: for the Lord's supper rightly used is when the congregation gathered together receiveth the sacrament in both kinds, as Christ instituted; but the mass is when one priest, like a churl, choppeth up all alone, and blesseth the congregation with the empty chalice, saying, *Ite missa est,* [" Depart, it is the dismission,"] after the pope's ordinance. The one of these two cannot but drive away the other, as experience teacheth us again here in England, a just punishment for our unthankfulness and horrible contempt of such an hea-

Matt. vii. 2 Pet. ii.

venly banquet: we were but "swine," and therefore not meet that such a "pearl" should long be put before us. The stink-

Exod. xvi. Num. xiv. Wisd. xvi.

ing mass with the garlic and onions of Egypt were a thousand parts more meet for us than God's pure manna, wherein was all kind of heavenly taste.—O Lord, forgive us, and be merciful unto us; and, when thy good will shall be once more, put us in trust with thy manna again. We will no more murmur, good Lord, but with thankfulness and diligence fill up our gomers[1] daily, till we come into the land of promise, thy heavenly rest and joy.

I will not now speak how that the sacrament in the mass, used to another purpose and end than Christ ordained it, yea,

[[1] "Gomer," or "omer," Exod. xvi. 16—36: Hebr. עֹמֶר.]

to an end clean contrary, as already I have showed, is no more Christ's sacrament but a devilish idol; even as if a man should carry about with him, or before him, the water of baptism, as though the Holy Ghost were there enclosed, and so now were[2] men to worship the water. This which hitherto I have spoken shall serve to give men occasion to weigh with themselves, how great and detestable an evil the mass is.

The sacrament in the mass is an idol.

We see plainly that it is against Christ himself, against his priesthood and so his kingdom, against his death and sacrifice, and so against our redemption, against his worship and true service, against faith, against prayer, repentance and the ministry of God's word, against his ordinance, institution, commandment and gospel. I pray you, what can be worse than such an one? If ever there was idol, who seeth not this to be Beelzebub, the chief of all idols? If ever antichrist had child or daughter, this mass is the most pestilent and pernicious: under the name of Christ it destroyeth Christ; under the title of God's service it destroyeth God's service; under the colour of the church it destroyeth the church.

If Christ be dear, if his death be dear, if his kingdom and priesthood be dear, if his service be dear, if faith be dear, if his word, commandment and ministry be dear, in that this, the mass I mean, is against them all horribly, it cannot be dear or tolerable in any wise, but detestable and monstrous unto us all that love Christ and be Christians indeed; and that so much more horrible, execrable monstrously and utter detestably, by how much it, under the colour of a friend to Christ and his church, is a most rank and cruel enemy; and therefore of none should be allowed, no of none should be, but detested not only in spirit (for that is well known) but also in body, as now I will prove by God's grace.

That it is unlawful to be present at mass.

First, out of the second commandment, "Thou shalt not make to thee," &c. This precept forbiddeth all kind of outward idolatry, as the first doth all kind of inward idolatry[3], to this end that God's true worship inwardly and outwardly might be observed. But now the mass is an outward idol, and the service of God there used is idolatry. Therefore they which are present at the mass, honesting it with their corporal pre-

It is idolatry.

[[2] "new," Copland's edition, evidently a misprint for "were."]

[[3] The last nine words now are first printed from the Lansdown MS.]

sence (as all they do which being there do not in open and exterior fact publicly disallow the same), they, I say, are open and manifest idolaters, and incur the danger of idolatry, that is, God's heavy wrath and eternal damnation: which thing I trow be no trifle, but to fools which make sin a thing of nothing. Howbeit I think best to make this more plain.

That the second commandment, "Thou shalt not make to thyself any graven image," &c., speaketh of outward idolatry, as the first, "Thou shalt have none other gods," &c., speaketh of inward and spiritual idolatry, I trust all men of any knowledge easily perceive. For, when God in the first commandment hath told us what he is unto us, even our Lord and our God, with all that ever he is and hath (for he that giveth himself to be ours giveth all that ever he hath to be ours also), then of equity he requireth that we should be content with him, and give ourselves to him to be his with all that ever we have: and therefore, first, we should "have none other gods but he;" that is, we should trust in none, love none, fear none, call upon none, worship none, but only him which [is] *El schaddai*[1], "an omnisufficient God" and Jehovah unto us.

What it is to have none other gods.

El schaddai.

Now, because man consisteth of two parts, the soul and the body, in that the Lord doth give himself wholly to us to be our Lord and God, he will that we give ourselves wholly unto him, to be his people. And therefore, as in the first commandment he wholly demandeth the soul, will, understanding and heart, that is, our faith, fear, love, thankfulness, invocation and inward adoration or worshipping, to be given to him only, and for his sake, as he shall appoint; so in the second commandment, "Thou shalt not make to thyself," &c., he generally requireth for the outward service of him, that we should follow his word in serving of him, and take it no less than idolatry or image-service, whatsoever thing is indented[2] by man, saint or angel, and not by him, concerning his worship and service. And to say the truth it is no marvel, for we see that there is no acceptable service done to man except it be according to the will of him to whom it is to be done, and not simply according to the will of him that doth it.

No service pleaseth God, but such as he teacheth.

[1 "El schaddai:" God Almighty, Exod. vi. 3, and elsewhere, authorised version. Hebr. אֵל שַׁדַּי. See Bullinger's Decades, Vol. I. p. 215, Park. Soc.]

[2 "Indented:" bargained, agreed for.—Nares' Glossary.]

Now, inasmuch as "none knoweth the will of man but the spirit of man," and he to whom by his word or signification he revealeth it, shall not we, yea, must not we of necessity, give so much to God? Then it is requisite that in God's service, which is acceptable to God, we must have for it the word of God, and not simply our good intents, the wisdom of man, general councils, custom, doctors, acts of parliament, or goodly outward shows and appearances: for, as Christ saith, "that which is in great estimation before men is abomination before God," if it be not according to his word. But of and for the mass where have we God's word? Nay, alas! as I have already shewed, it is a pitchy, patched poke[3], made of many a man, and that at divers times, and is clean contrary to God and his word. Therefore, it being done to the service of God, as it is done, it is abomination and a great idol in God's sight. So that the conclusion of my reason is strong, that such as dishonest it not by their absence, or by their word and fact publicly when they be present at it, but being there only in heart disallow it, the same, whosoever they be, are grievous sinners, and breakers of the second commandment, and so guilty of the threat following, namely of God's "visitation upon their children for their sins, unto the third and fourth generation:" for, in that they disallow and disworship it not with their bodies, they do worship it, although they bow not down to it as most men do. For in God's service there is no mean: he that loveth not hateth, he that worshippeth not disworshippeth, and so contrariwise.

1 Cor. ii.

Luke xvi.

Exod. xx.

But, to make all "as plain as a pack-staff[4]," let us note that there are two kinds of idolaters, one known to God only, the other to man also. To God only are they idolaters which serve God in the sight of man, according to his word, but their hearts are halting, deceivable, guileful, and hypocritical in God's sight. To man also are they idolaters which exteriorly[5] worship contrary to God's word: of this latter sort of idolaters there are three diverse kinds.

Two kinds of idolaters, spiritual and corporal.

Corporal idolaters are of three sorts.

One [is] of them which be obstinate defenders of their

[3 "Poke:" a bag.]

[4 "As plain as a pack-staff:" this proverbial expression occurs in Bp Hall's Satires, see Nares' Glossary.]

[5 "exteriorly," Lansd. MS.: not in Copland's edition.]

idolatry against God's word and manifest written verities, which they seeing will not see, &c., and therefore justly of God are blinded, as the wicked bishops and prelates of the papistical church be, with their champions and parasites. These had need to take heed that they sin not "against the Holy Ghost."

Winchester, Bonner, Weston, &c.

Another sort is of them which are simple and ignorant, who through common error are seduced, being persuaded that the thing they do pleaseth God, and is God's true service. Such are the simple souls of the country, whose eyes God I trust will open in his time, that they may see his truth: as, if they would be so diligent to inquire thereabouts, as they are in going any journey, which to them is unknown, of such as they meet withal, they could not but easily and soon perceive; and therefore ignorance cannot excuse their wilful negligence: howbeit it is not to be doubted but that God in his time, if they reject not his grace, will open to them his truth. Let us, as be careful we confirm them not in their error, by halting and bearing with them in this their evil, so privately after our vocation, and as we would be done by, admonish them of this error, above all things praying unto God for them, that "with their blind guides they fall not" into the pit of perdition. This kind[1] of idolaters is nothing so evil as the other; for the other do sin against the Holy Ghost, it is to be feared, but the error of these is savable.

Matt. xv.

The third and last sort is of them which indeed know the thing they use is not allowed of God, and therefore in heart they consent not unto it, although outwardly they seem not to disallow it. These are unlike to the second, for they fall of simplicity and a zeal, but not according to knowledge; but these do it wittingly and for lack of zeal, and yet of knowledge, and therefore surely are much more to be blamed than the other, to whom they are a grievous offence, confirming them in their error, that therein they should continue without conscience. And such be our mass-gospellers and popish protestants, which can "serve both God and mammon," take Elias' part and Baal priests' part, carry water in the one hand and fire in the other.

Matt. vi.

1 Kings xviii.

I would wish that such as these be would mark with themselves the causes wherefor they go to the mass, which they

[[1] "kind," Lansd. and Harl. MSS.: not in Copland's printed edition.]

know is evil. If they do it of obstinacy and malice, then are they to be reckoned amongst the number of the foremost sort, which are to be suspected of the sin "against the Holy Ghost." If they do it to get any worldly estimation or promotion thereby, or to keep still that which they have gotten (as I fear me many do), let them dread that they doing as Judas did drink not with him at the length. If they do it for company's sake or neighbourhood, let them consider the thing better, and mark into whose company they are called (1 Cor. i.); and so set before them[2] the example of Josaphat companying with Ahab to his great peril, and divers other more examples, whereof the scripture is not barren. If they do it for fear of the loss of goods, name, friends, liberty, life, &c., let them consider that Jesus Christ affirmeth such as be not ready so to do, in no point the same to be worthy of him. Read the places. And hereunto let them consider what estate they be in, as whether [they] be public or private persons, learned or unlearned, rich or poor, young or old, master or servant, householder, &c. These all considered, and the horrible greatness of the evil they allow and confirm by their not disallowing in deed, with examples of God's plagues upon such as have dissembled so with God and man, will help to make away them out of their security, to repent if they be fallen, and to take more heed if they be not fallen. The which thing God grant. Amen.

1 Cor. i.

1 Kings xxii.

Matt. x. xvi. Luke ix. xiv. and xvii.

But now, to bring more reasons to prove that to be at mass in body and not openly to disallow it is sin, although the spirit and heart consent not thereto—already out of the second commandment we see it is idolatry—now let us see how near it toucheth blasphemy out of the third commandment: "Thou shalt not take the name of the Lord thy God in vain." Hereout we may well gather that to be at mass in body[3], and not as in heart so in word openly to reprove it, is[4] a breach of this commandment, term the sin as we will. For the end of this commandment is not only to inform us, how with our tongues we[4] should abstain from taking God's name in vain, but much

To go to mass is a breach of the third commandment.

[[2] "before them," Lansd. MS.: not in printed editions.]

[[3] "in body," Lansd. MS.: not in Copland's printed edition.]

[[4] "is," "us, how with our tongues we," Lansd. MS.: "it is," "our tongue, how that we," Copland's edition.]

rather how we should use the name of God in prayer, confession of God's truth and religion, thanksgiving and preaching purely the gospel if we be ministers: if we be none, yet the other three, prayer, confession, and thanksgiving, pertain unto us, of what state soever we be.

Now, what using of the tongue in thanksgiving is in them which are present at that which overthroweth utterly the true worshipping of their Christ and God, without reproving it? What confessing of religion doth their tongue exercise, which hold their peace, and with their presence do honest that which setteth up another salvation than that which Christ brought, and bought dearly by the shedding and price of his precious blood? What use of their tongue in true prayer have they, which in holding their tongue say, "Amen," to all the blasphemous prayers of the mass? If indeed their Christ be between the priest's hands, if that which the priest doth be the self-same sacrifice which Christ did on the cross himself for our redemption, then let them hold their tongue a God's name, and do as they do. But if their Christ be "in heaven, on the right hand of the Father," concerning the corporal presence of his humanity, as he is everywhere by his virtue, grace, and Divinity; if Christ's sacrifice on the cross be but one and never more to be reiterate; in that God hath given them tongues, and now commandeth them not to use the same in vain, tying them in[1] their teeth, when he would have[2] them used and exercised in confessing him before men, I would they would tell me, why[3] they are mute and play mum at this horrible dishonour done to their sovereign lord, why take they his name being called on them as on his people in vain? The name of the Lord our God is called upon all that be his people, and that not in vain, but to be called upon, praised, and confessed of them all, when either his glory or their brother's necessity requireth it. But, to omit the necessity to our brethren in this case, which nippeth the conscience, I trow, where doth God's glory more require that we should confess his name and true service than in the mass? which of all things that ever was is most horrible adversary to it.

Acts i. Phil. iii. Mark xvi. Heb. vii. viii. ix. x.

[[1] "tying them in," Lansd. MS.: "lying, then to," Copland's printed edition.]
[[2] "have," Lansd. MS.: not in Copland's edition.]
[[3] "why," Lansd. and Harl. MSS.: "when," printed editions.]

Conclude therefore I well may, that it is a thorough out breach of this commandment, and a taking of God's name in vain, to be at mass and not reprove it. And what the punishment of this commandment is God sheweth, when he saith that he "will not hold him guiltless that taketh his name in vain." Look well hereon, guiltless though you be before the magistrates here, if in bodily presence you honest it, yet you are not guiltless before God. Choose now therefore whose hands you will fall into: if into God's hands, that is horrible, and none can deliver you: if into the hand of man, surely they cannot pull as much as one hair of your heads further than your good Father will, that is, than shall make to your eternal joy.

Heb. x.

Matt. x.

To go to mass breaketh the fourth commandment.

Let us now go to the fourth commandment, of the sanctifying of the sabbath-day; and we shall see no less occasion than we have done to gather going to the mass, and not disallowing it publicly in word and deed, to be sin and a breach of this commandment also. For in it the Lord requireth rest from bodily labour to the end of sanctification, except we should put no difference between the end of rest on the sabbath-day appointed to man, from that which is appointed to the beast. The end therefore, I say, of the rest in the sabbath to man is sanctification: that is, man is commanded to rest from bodily labour and other exercises, that he may with diligence and reverence hear God's word in his ministry, learn his law, use his sacraments and ceremonies as he hath ordained, convent[4] to common prayer in the place appointed and other holy exercises, helping to the conservation of the ministry, propagation of the gospel, and increase of love and charity one towards another: all which things still remain to us commanded in our resting times from our travails and labours for this life, although the Jews' seventh day be abrogated and taken away. This considered, who cannot but see the mass, which maketh to the profanation and unhallowing both of body and soul, to be forbidden? If the end of my rest should serve to sanctification, then can it not serve to the mass, which is abomination. If I may not use my rest simply for the pleasure of my body, which God alloweth, except I look to another end, namely, that I may be more able to endure the works of my vocation more to God's glory and my neighbour's commodity, much

[4 "Convent:" come together.]

more then I may not use my rest for the pleasure of another in that which God disalloweth.

But, to make this more evident, no man of any reading or godly consideration of the scriptures cannot but see, the principal thing God in this commandment did respect was the ministry of his word and sacraments, by the which God gathereth his church, increaseth it, and conserveth it: and therefore of all things he could worst away with[1] the breach of this commandment. Read how he commanded the man to be "stoned to death" for "gathering sticks on the sabbath-day;" and in the prophets, how he cried out all was marred when this commandment was broken. Now the mass (before I have shewed) is the only weeding worm and rooting sow of the gospel and sacraments for being truly preached and ministered, so that wheresoever the one is the other cannot be. True preaching and massing, true using Christ's supper and Sir John Masser's[2] dinner, be as contrary as light and darkness. Wherefore, as the mass is the end of Satan's commandment, and directly impugneth the end of God's commandment, here as the mass doers grievously offend, so the mass hearers and seers without disallowing it openly run into the same peril and vengeance of God, that is, to the gathering of stakes to be burned in hell-fire: look well therefore hereon. The pope and his prelates say, 'If thou come not to hear mass, but disallow it, thou shalt fry a faggot in Smithfield.' God almighty saith, 'If thou keep thee not from the mass, or if thou come to it and do not openly disallow it, thou shalt fry a faggot in hell-fire.'

Num. xv.

Jer. xvii. Ezek. xx.

Choose now whether thou wilt take heed, 'in flying from the smoke thou shalt into the fire[3].' Make not man thy god, but fear the Lord and "sanctify him in thine heart." Pray with David, "O Lord, knit and enforce my heart truly to fear thee." &c.

Psal. lxxxvi.

As now out of the first table I have shewed that every commandment therein is broken up by hearing and seeing mass (for there is no commandment broken but the first com-

[1 "Away with:" bear, endure.]

[2 "Sir John:" see Vol. I. p. 589, note E. "Masser:" the offerer of the mass.]

[3 ...τὸ πῦρ ἐκ τοῦ καπνοῦ...Lucian. Dial. Menipp. sive Necyomant. Tom. I. p. 459, ed. Hemsterhus., Amstel. 1743. Vide Erasmi et alior. Adagia, Proverb., Malum male vitiatum, p. 493, ed. 1629.]

mandment is broken tofore), so could I shew out of the second table, that it is a breach of all and every commandment there. It confirmeth the magistrate in his evil, when he seeth men without gainsaying obey his law as though it were good and godly: so that they which hear mass at the commandment of the magistrate are partakers also of the magistrate's evil, by their disobedience to God in this point confirming the law: for, if they would disallow it, and obey God more than man, giving their heads to the block, rather than to hear or see mass, it would not be but, as the wicked law would be infirmed, so the magistrate would call the matter into a further enquiry, and so the truth to take place. And hereof will I write an history.

To go to mass breaketh all the second table generally and particularly.

In the time of Valens the emperor, which favoured the opinion of Arius, and therefore laboured that the same might be received of the whole empire, there was at Edessa, a city of Mesopotamia, a church whereto the Christians of right judgment did resort. And therefore the emperor, being there, commanded the lieutenant of the city to put so many to death as did resort thither, being greatly displeased that he had used no greater tyranny against them. Now this lieutenant, rather favouring the Christians than otherwise, gave warning that they should not resort to the church the next day, because he was commanded to slay them. Howbeit they, not considering so much death as the confession of their faith, resorted more to the temple than ever they did: so that on the other day, when the lieutenant with a band of men went to the templeward to execute the emperor's commandment, he chanced to see a woman running with a child in her hand, which she haled to come apace in such sort, that the lieutenant, marvelling at her haste, commanded one to call her. And she being come, he demanded whither and wherefore she hasted so with the child: and, when he perceived by her answer, it was to the church whither he was going to execute the emperor's commandment, he demanded whether she had not had knowledge what he was commanded to do. She answered, 'Yes.'—'Then,' quoth he, 'art not thou afraid?'—'No,' said she, 'I pray God I may give my life in so good a cause.'—'Why,' quoth he, 'dost thou take thy child with thee?'—She answered, 'That he may die with me, for I had rather take him with me to God, than leave him behind me, for you to carry him to the devil; as by your false religion you will, if he should believe and do as you do.' The lieutenant hearing these words, as they amazed him to hear and see the constancy of the woman, so they caused him to return immediately, and to make relation hereof to the emperor, who hearing it ceased from his cruelty.

This history is written in the seventh book of the Tripartite History, the thirty-second chapter[1]: which I have rehearsed for this purpose, that men might see hereby, how that constancy to God's cause could not but cause the magistrate the more to consider what he commandeth.

But, to return to my former treatise, to go to mass, or to church where mass is, breaketh, you see, the first commandment of the second table[2]. Again it is a murdering of the soul, and the massmongers are procurers and abettors of others to fall into the destruction of their souls: for the obstinate papist triumpheth and is confirmed, the strong gospeller is weakened, the weaker gospeller is utterly overthrown by thy going to mass, which hast knowledge of the truth[3]. Moreover they are bawds, to bring the spouses of Christ to become Satan's whores. Besides this, they that are mass hunters are receivers and concealers of theft, and spoiling of Christ and his glory; yea, undoubtedly they are traitors, and guilty of high treason against God. Last of all, they are false witnesses against their neighbours, against God's church (as though the mass-church were the catholic church), yea, against Christ and his word by their going to mass, thereby witnessing the mass to be a true service of God, and a badge of his church, where their own consciences say they lie, and so condemneth them.

As for the last commandment of lusting, in that the same is an inward thing, as the first commandment is, and this which I spake of, namely going to the mass, is an outward act, I cannot therefore well apply it to them; albeit, to say the

[1 Vide Cassiod. Hist. Tripart. Lib. VII. cap. xxxii. foll. P. 3, 4, Paris. s. a. The original will be found in Socrat. Hist. Eccles. Lib. IV. cap. xviii. p. 228, ed. Vales. Mogunt. 1677.]

[2 The last forty-three lines, "And hereof will I write an history......the first commandment of the second table," are now printed for the first time, from the Lansdown MS.]

[3 The last thirty-two words, "for the obstinate......of the truth," are now printed for the first time, from the Lansdown MS.]

truth, there is no sin counted outwardly, but these two commandments, the first and the last, are broken before the sin come to the knowledge of any man.

And thus it is plain enough, I trow, that[4] the hearing or going to church where mass is[4], or seeing of mass, although in spirit it be abhorred, is no small sin, but such a sin as breaketh all God's law generally, and every commandment particularly. O then how grievous a sin is this! Look well on it, my dear brethren, to whom this my simple counsel shall come, "in the tender mercies of God I beseech you." If "he that continueth not in all things written in God's law be accursed," alas, how terribly is he accursed that continueth in nothing, but is a transgressor in all things! And such be popish protestants, mass-gospellers, or, as they would be called, bodily mass-mongers and spiritual gospellers. Deut. xxvii. Gal. iii.

Now, although this, which I have occasioned to be marked out of the decalogue or ten commandments, be enough for this matter, yet will I hereto add some more reasons, or at least occasion men so to do, by collecting and gathering divers sentences in such brevity as I can. More reasons to prove going to mass to be sin.

1. "He that is not with me is against me," saith our Saviour, "and he that gathereth not with me scattereth abroad." Now in that the mass is neither Christ nor in any point with him, but of all things on earth most against him (as before I have shewed), let them mark what they do by this sentence of Christ, that go to mass; and, if they be not wilful blind, they shall see that they are against Christ, that is, antichrist's, in this point, and gather with the devil. Matt. xii. Luke xi.

2. "Woe be to him," saith the Truth, "by whom an offence doth come," that is, which doth or saith anything whereby any are justly occasioned to evil, letted to do good, or confirmed in their naughty doctrine and customs. "It were better for such," if Christ say truly, "to have a millstone hanged about their neck, and to be cast into the bottom of the sea." And will you yet go to mass, then to occasion others to go with you, to let[5] the godly which would not go if you went not, to confirm the papists in their idolatry? Matt. xviii.

[4 "that," "or going to church where mass is," Lansd. MS.: not in Copland's printed edition.]

[5 "Let:" hinder.]

1 Cor. vi. 3. Paul willeth us to "glorify God in our souls and our bodies," as well requiring the body to be applied to the setting forth of God's glory as the soul; and no marvel, for God hath
1 Cor. iii. made it "his temple, that his holy Spirit should dwell therein," and gave his precious blood also therefor that it might be in eternal felicity with the soul. Yea, he hath coupled our flesh in himself unto his Godhead, to be one Person, one Christ, God and man, so great is the dignity thereof. And therefore full worthily warneth Paul, that we should keep ourselves clean
2 Cor. vii. from all that which would stain, not "the spirit" only, but "the flesh" and body also. So that a man with half an eye may see the mass-sayers and seers in body, though the spirit be absent, little to consider what they do.

4. Paul would not allow a Christian to come to the table in
1 Cor. viii. the idol's temple, lest thereby "the weak brother might perish." And would he allow coming to mass, trow you, which is another
1 Cor. x. [21.] manner of matter?

5. If that the thing were indifferent or lawful to be present at mass in body, in mind disallowing it, yet in that the end of our liberty is not what we may do, but what is best to be done, what most edifieth, seeing that going to mass is so far from edifying that it destroyeth, easily may we see that it is not to be used.

Hos. iv. [15.] 6. But, alas! this is far from lawful. It is a "Beth-aven,"
2 Tim. iii. "an house of iniquity;" and Paul willeth that they that "call on the name of the Lord should depart from iniquity:" and how then should they come to mass, if they should depart from it?

Gal. ii. 7. "If I should build up again that which I pulled down, I then should make myself an offender," saith the apostle: and what be they then that now by going to mass build it up again? which by going from it, and speaking against it, have holpen to pull it down.

2 Cor. vi. 8. "What agreement is there between light and darkness? what concord is with Christ and Belial," with the Christian and the pope's minion (the mass I mean), "with the temple of God and idols?" saith Paul. 'Wherefore come away from the mass,' saith the Lord, 'and separate yourselves from them that come to it,' "and I will receive you."

1 Cor. v. 9. Paul would have the Corinthians to shun the company

of whoremongers and idolatriers: and will he license now them to come and company with massers in their chiefest idolatry? This were to make Paul's preaching, not "yea, yea, and nay, nay," but "yea and nay."

10. "If any man come unto you," saith St John, "and bring not this doctrine with him," you shall not so much as greet him, lest you be partakers of his evil. And what doctrine is more contrary to God and his gospel than is the mass? The mass-sayers then and approvers should not we seek to, which may not receive them if they should seek unto us, except we would communicate with their evil. 2 John.

11. "No man that putteth his hand to the plough and looketh back is meet for God's kingdom:" much more then are we unmeet therefor if we, I say not, "look back," but run and go back to see and hear that which justly we have forsaken. Luke ix.

12. What happened to Core and his allowers, that he should take on him the priesthood without calling? And will nothing happen to our arrogant massers, that without calling take upon them Christ's priesthood, and to such as allow and seem to allow them? Read the history, Numbers xvi. Num. xvi.

13. John the evangelist durst not tarry in the house where Cerinthus the heretic was, which denied Christ's manhood; and indeed the house fell, and slew him and all that ever remained in the house with him. And shall not we fear God's vengeance, to be in company at mass with her minions? which deny Christ both God and man, making their own handywork as good as he, yea, he himself[1], say they. Eusebius in his ecclesiastical history, Lib. IV. cap. xiv.

14. O deaf ears, that will not hear the blast of the angel's trump, warning us to come from amongst these whorish Babylonians, belly-god massmongers, lest we perish with them! "Come out from her, my people," saith God. If thou be one of God's people, thou must come from her: but, if thou be not, tarry still. Rev. xviii.

15. Yea, he not only commandeth us to come out from her, but to declare ourselves to be open enemies against her. "Reward her," saith he, "as she hath rewarded you." Read the place, and mark it well.

16. O Lord God! that men think it be a trifle to make their bodies, [instead] of Christ and his church, the members of antichrist of Rome and his church. 1 Cor. vi.

[1 Compare p. 286, last paragraph, above.]

17. Will men never consider that they shall "receive according to that they do in their body, be it good or bad," and not simply according to their conscience?

[Deut. xii.] 18. Read how earnestly God commandeth the destruction even of the most dearest friend, that shall but devise or counsel thee to "go after a strange god," as the mass and the god therein is.

19. When thou goest to mass, see whither thou goest, forsooth even to the devil: for thou departest from verity, and so from God. Now there is no mean: if thou be not with God, thou art with the devil. But thou wilt say, in conscience thou departest not from the verity. Well but yet thou doest it in body: be sure, as before is said, thou shalt "receive according to that is done in the body[1]."

Gen. xix. 20. Lot's wife looked but back, and was "turned into a saltstone." And so are the hearts of our popish protestants, I fear me, hardened from fearing God, in that they look, yea, go back again to their sodomitical minion.

1 Macc. ii. 21. The good father Mattathias would in no point dissemble, as though he had worshipped; but our mass-gospellers are far unlike to him.

Matt. vi. 22. We pray to be "delivered from evil," *Libera nos a malo*, [Deliver us from evil;] and yet we, knowing the mass to be evil, resort unto it.

Rom. xiv. 23. "Whatsoever is not of faith is sin:" but to go see
Rom. x. or hear mass, though but in body, "is not of faith," for faith hangeth on God's word, and God's word is not herefor: therefore it is sin.

Rom. xiv. 24. "Happy is he that condemneth not himself in that thing which he alloweth:" mark by the contrary, whether our mass-gospellers are not unhappy and accursed by Paul's judgment.

Heb. xii. 25. "Halting," saith the apostle, "hindereth, yea, bringeth out of the way." And what other thing is it to go to mass
Matt. vi. in body, and to be away in spirit, but a plain "halting," a "serving of two masters?" which none can do, if Christ be true.

[[1] The last five paragraphs, and the two last sentences of paragr. No. 14, are now printed for the first time, from the Lansdown MS.

The numbers of the succeeding paragraphs are altered from those in Copland's printed edition, to correspond with the MS.]

26. If Jehu were judge, these bodily massers should drink with their brethren the Baalites. Read the history, and see whether he judged not, of their outward coming, whose servants they were. 2 Kings x.

27. "He that denieth Christ before men shall be of him denied before God:" but mass hearers "deny Christ before men" in fact and deed, although in tongue they profess otherwise. For there is three kinds of denial, in heart, in word, and in deed; in heart, as the wicked do, saying, "There is no God," Psal. xiv. and liii.; in word, Matt. x., Mark viii.; in deed, Titus i. Now, though the mass-gospellers do not, as they say, deny God's truth in heart and in word, yet, in that they by going to mass do it in deed, let them take better heed what they do, lest in deed Christ deny them at the last day[2]. Matt. x. 2 Tim. ii.

28. St Paul to "the belief of the heart" requireth "the confession of the mouth:" howbeit our popish protestants think this needs not. But yet Christ saith, "He that is ashamed of me," that is, of my true religion and gospel, "before this faithless generation, I will be ashamed of him before the angels of God in heaven." O heavy sentence! Rom. x. Mark viii.

29. "He that toucheth pitch shall be defiled therewith," saith Solomon. And shall not their bodies be something smutted with the filthiness of the mass, that honest it with their presence? [Ecclus. xiii. 1.]

30. If in the old law the touching of a carrion defiled him that touched it, at the least for a day's space, in that there is no carrion so stinking in God's sight as the mass, let him[3] that goeth to it, howsoever he be minded, or abideth in the church where it is—let them, I say[4], know that he is defiled so foul that all the holy water in Rome, Paris, and London, cannot purge him therefrom. Hag. ii. Levit. xi.

31. Unto these our popish protestants I cannot but say, as Elias said, "How long will you halt on both knees? If 1 Kings xviii. [Septuag.]

[[2] The last two sentences are now first published from the Lansdown MS. The printed edition of Copland has instead: "Therefore I advise them to take better heed. Read Titus i., and there shall you see that denying Christ is in fact as well as in words."]

[[3] "him," Lansd. MS.: "them," Copland's edition.]

[[4] The last twelve words are now printed for the first time, from the Lansdown MS.]

God be God, follow him:" if the mass be God and God's ordinance, follow it.

1 Kings xix. 32. When Elias lamented that all was gone astray but he, all were defiled with Baal, although in heart there were many hated Baal, as they thought, and would have confessed if Jezebel had not been, God said that he had "left seven thousand which had not bowed their knee to Baal." He saith not, "which in heart hate Baal," but, "which hath not bowed their knee to Baal;" of that outward sign demonstrating his servants. And so now let us not think, good brethren, any to be his true worshippers but such as not only in heart, but also in deed, detest the mass.

33. Therefore saith David, that God will not suffer "the sceptre of the ungodly" to lie long on the lot of his children, lest his people "should stretch forth their hands to iniquity." He saith not 'their hearts,' but "their hands," of the bodily fact noting his people[1].

Rom. xvi. 1 Tim. vi. 2 Tim. iii. 34. St Paul willeth us to "separate ourselves from such as teach other doctrine, and will not consent to the sound doctrine of our Saviour Jesus Christ." Wherefore, in that the massers teach another doctrine than Christ or his apostles ever taught, and by their massing depart from the sound doctrine of Jesus Christ, by God's commandment we must separate ourselves from them, as no part of Christ's catholic church, brag they thereof never so much.

1 Pet. i. ii. 2 Tim. i. 35. Peter would that we being "an holy people" should be pure, not in a piece but "in all our conversation;" and Paul would that we should abstain *ab omni specie mali*, "from all appearance of evil," "being as light (or lanterns) in the midst

Phil. ii. of a froward generation," and not darkness as that be. And how may this be? Forsooth by "holding fast the word of God," and following it, for so he teacheth there: read the place.

Dan. iii. 36. Azarias and his two companions knew they could not but displease God, if with any outward shew they would have seemed to allow the idol Nabugodonozer caused to be set up, and therefore hazarded the fire: which our mass-gospellers will not do, to alter and turn the queen's heart, as, by they three not obeying Nabugodonozer's precept, God turned his heart.

[[1] This paragraph is now first printed from the Lansdown MS.]

37. The body shall not be partaker of the sentence given to the soul in judgment of that whereof in this life it is not partaker with the spirit and soul. This is Tertullian's reason, *Liber de resurrectione carnis*[2].

38. "If thine eye be single," and true faith in thine heart, then all thy body and actions cannot but be pure: but, "if they be dark," it is a token thine eye and "light within thee to be darkness." This argueth faith to faint in them which [de]file their bodies in being present at the mass; for, as it is impossible light to be in an house, and not to show itself at the slifters[3], door, and windows of the same, so is it impossible, true faith of God's gospel to be in the heart of that man which coming to mass uttereth it not by something, whereby men may perceive the light of faith inwardly in the bosom. And therefore Christians are called "towns set upon hills," "candles upon bushel-tops," and commanded that "their light should shine tofore men:" which these massing-gospellers allow not, but think that a man can carry faith in the heart, and not utter it at the mass in word or deed; where it is no more possible, than a man to carry fire in his bosom, and not to burn his clothes.

39. "Our fellowship," saith St John, "is with the Fa- 1 John i.
ther, and with his Son Jesus Christ:" he saith not, "with the mass," which is mere darkness; and therefore, to signify the same, God hath suffered them to shew it by the candle-light[4] they must have at it, and further, that they that go to it wot not whither they go, nor what they do. "Our fellowship," I say, "is with God the Father, and with his Son Jesus Christ," but yet so that we must "walk in light," for else "we lie, and the truth is not in us." "If any man," saith he, "walk in darkness" (as, God knoweth, they do, which be at mass, and reprove it not openly), and "saith he hath fellowship with God, the same is a liar, and the truth is not in him[5]."

But, to make an end of collecting any more reasons to

[2 Et illi quidem delinquentias carnis enumerant: ergo peccatrix tenebitur supplicio. Nos vero etiam virtutes carnis opponimus: ergo et bene operata tenebitur præmio.—Tertull. Lib. de resurr. carn. cap. xv. Op. p. 320, Franeker. 1597.]

[3 "Slifter:" a cleft, a crevice.—Holloway's Prov. Dict. 1838.]

[4 "candle-light," Lansd. MS.: "light," Copland's edition.]

[5 This sentence is now printed for the first time, from the Lansdown MS.]

prove that which all wise men see plainly, namely, that they grievously do offend which honest with their presence God's greatest enemy upon earth, the mass, and do not disprove and disallow it, not only in heart, but also in deed and word openly —for else openly by their presence they honour it, the priest praying especially for all that be there present, and, as they affirm, receiving for all, and also turning himself divers times to the congregation with his *Dominus vobiscum*, the clerk answering in the name of all, *Et cum spiritu tuo*, and other responds: so that the standers by, if they openly disprove it not, are partakers with the priest of his idolatry and false serving of God: as Paul saith, "They which eat of the sacrifice are partakers of the altar;" they which are at the mass are partakers of the mass, that is, idolaters, false worshippers of God, blasphemers of Christ, destroyers of his death, merits, sacrifice, priesthood, and kingdom, destroyers of the ministers of his gospel and sacraments, destroyers of faith, repentance, and all godliness—*summa*, they are antichrist's—antichrist's, I say, in body though they feign their heart to [be] Christ's: but Christ and antichrist cannot dwell together; and therefore, if they be there and hold their tongue, they cannot but cry one day, *Væ mihi quia tacui*, "Woe is me because I held my tongue."

1 Cor. x.

Isai. vi. [Vulg.]

O that the latter end of the first Corinthians, tenth, were well weighed! namely, how that in worshipping God contrary to his word, as the massers do, we have fellowship with his devils. Then I trow his exhortation would take place, where he saith, "See that you give none occasion of evil to any man," but seek to please that way which may help to the salvation of others, and not to the destruction of others; as all they do, which being at mass and see[ing] their brethren take it for a God's service, it being a very devil's service, lay a pillow and a cushion under their knees and elbows, to hold on still, and so to increase God's further vengeance, as in England—in England—we do.

Ezek. xiii.

O Lord, be merciful unto us, and forgive us, open our eyes that we may see thy truth, and work in our wills that we may embrace, love, and have lust to it to live it, confess it, and suffer gladly loss of friends, name, goods, and life for it. Amen, Amen.

Now let us see how much the reasons of our popish protestants are of force.

First they say that "God is a spirit," and therefore "in spirit to be served;" so that it forceth not though the body be at mass, if the spirit serve God and be with him.

To this I answer that, though God be to be served "in spirit," yet not alone in spirit, but also in body; and therefore Paul willeth us to "glorify God" in both, and prayeth also that God would sanctify and make the body perfect as well as the spirit. When our Saviour saith, John fourth, that God is "to be served in the spirit," a man that marketh the text before and following, cannot but see how that our Saviour would have it opposed and set against the corporal and exterior service of God, which was used of both the Jews and Samaritans without "the spirit and verity."

The answer to the first reason made to prove coming to mass lawful.

John iv.
1 Cor. vi.
1 Thess. v.

The Jews' services instituted of God were void of the spirit and spiritual exercise of faith in the promises and Messias, so greatly was religion corrupted and gross ignorance increased. The Samaritans' services of God were not only void of "the spirit," but also of "verity," for they had no word of God for them. Therefore saith our Saviour, "that God must be worshipped in spirit and verity," that is to say, not in all external services, but in such as he hath appointed once, or rather then would appoint (for the verity of that figurative service was come), and not only in this externally, but also spiritually with the exercise of faith in his word and promises.

Now then, I pray you, what have they won of this sentence? Why do they not rather by "serving God in the spirit" understand the same to be required in his exterior service, which else were hypocrisy, than by it exclude that which God would not have excluded (I mean the exterior works and exercises he hath commanded), by this means take preaching away, vocal prayer, thanksgiving, obedience to the magistrates, &c., and all exterior things? And so they shall shew themselves libertines, as though whoredom, murder, and all exterior evils were no evils; for this can they do outwardly, and yet their spirit is still with God! What if any of their wives were taken in another man's bed? think you, they would be content with this excuse, that her heart was not there, though her body was in bed? Henceforwards therefore let them learn to put to the spirit this word "verity" also, as our Saviour doth: or else they must be as much blamed for taking up too soon as the papists

The papists begin too soon with, *Hoc est corpus*, mark well.

are for beginning too soon: for still they begin at, *Hoc est corpus meum*, where they should begin at, *Accipite, comedite*, "Take and eat," or else God is not bound to keep his promise, "This is my body," because it is conditional, requiring our obedience of taking and eating[1]: which thing maketh against the mart, if men should know that *Hoc est corpus meum* were not true to any others but to such as do indeed take and eat the sacrament as he commandeth, that is, in faithful remembrance how his body was broken for their sins, &c. So I say should they do to the "worshipping of God in spirit and verity:" and then would they use this sentence no more to cloak withal their dissimulation and hypocrisy, making men to believe they serve God, as they do, when in heart yet these men do say they detest that kind of serving God. Thus much for the first reason.

2. The second reason is, that it is no more sin for a man to be at mass in body, so that in spirit he allow it not, than it was for the prophets, Christ, and his apostles, to be at the idolatrous sacrifices in the temple of Jerusalem with the priests, bishops, scribes, and pharisees.

This is their second reason, which I will answer when that they shall prove either the prophets, either Christ and his apostles, at any time to have been present and communicate with the priests in any sacrifice or ceremony which was not according to God's word and commandment. Howbeit, to say the truth, there was never amongst the Jews in the temple of Jerusalem any such idolatry as the mass. The prophets, Christ, and the apostles, came to the temple at Jerusalem, and there used such sacraments, sacrifices and ceremonies, as God

Nothing in the mass after God's word.

had institute: but where did God institute the mass? where alloweth he any service to be done in an unknown tongue? where taught he adoration, elevation, reservation, and such horrible profanation, and gazing on his sacraments? where taught he praying for the dead or to the dead? where ordained [he] this sacrament to be eaten up of one alone? where is their sacrifice of the mass, the principalest thing in the mass—where, I say, is it founded in God's word?

But what go I about to reckon the things in the mass be-

[[1] Compare Vol. I. Last Examination, p. 489.]

sides God's word? in that there is nothing in it, being placed and used as it is, but the same is contrary to God's word, even as the holy prayers in exorcisms and conjurings are there placed and used, not holy prayers, but horrible blasphemies. So that the sacrifices and ceremonies used in the temple at Jerusalem were nothing like to our mass—nor our mass like to them, but rather like to those sacrifices which were at Bethel and Dan, and in their orchards, groves, woods, hills, &c. These sacrifices had a show of God's word; and in fact and appearance they were the self-same which were in the temple at Jerusalem. As in the temple they slew and offered rams, lambs, goats, oxen, &c., so did they in Dan, in Bethel, in their groves, hills, &c. But yet the one had God's word, and therefore they were of themselves God's servants[2], notwithstanding the error of the bishops and[3] priests concerning them: but the other had none of God's word, and therefore were idolatry, and the people idolaters. Wherefore all good people in the tribes of Israel came up to Jerusalem to the sacrifices there, and left Bethel and Dan, to their great perils, as we read of Tobias.

The mass and the groves in the old law were like.

Tobit i.

And so I pray God that many may hear of our English gospellers, that they will adventure their lives and goods, rather than to come to mass; wherein though there be the epistle, gospel, sacrament, some good prayers, giving of thanks, &c., yet in that the same be not after God's word, but after the imagination of man, all and every part thereof is leavened and sowered with the little lump, nay, massy piece of leaven papistical or antichristian; that is, is idolatry, to speak plain English, and whoso cometh to it be idolaters, howsoever their hearts seem, if outwardly they make it not known. And thus, because this reason is sufficiently answered, I will go to the third.

[3.] Naaman, say they, was bidden of the prophet to go home "in peace;" all should be well although he went into the temple of Rimmon to worship in body, his spirit and heart being all set on the God of Israel: whereupon they gather that, 2 Kings v.

[2 "servants," Harl. MS.: "service," Lansd. MS., and printed editions.]

[3 "the error of the bishops and," Lansd. and Harl. MSS.: not in the printed editions.]

although the mass be evil, yet it is no offence to be at it in body, the spirit being absent with God.

For answer to this reason let this suffice, that this Naaman was but an youngling in God's religion, a three hours' bird, and therefore not to be conferred with unto us Englishmen in this case, which should be past milk, I trow, now, if a man have respect either to the time of our baptism, [or] of the pure preaching of the gospel which we have had six or seven years. Again the Syrians to Naaman now were not so near as we be one to another, "being baptized into one body." Besides this Naaman acknowledged his fact to be sin, and therefore desireth the prophet to pray to God for the pardon of it, when he should commit it; but our men excuse their going to mass, as a thing not faulty. Last of all the prophet doth not excuse the fact, nor saith not that it is no sin, but, *Vade in pace*, "Go in peace;" as though he might say, 'Go thy ways, trust in God, he will teach thee what to do, and guide thee with his grace otherwise than thou art aware of.' And surely it is not to be doubted but God did so: he knoweth full well how to pull out his people from the peril of temptation. We read not that he went into the temple of Rimmon. As soon shall we find that God turned the heart of his master the king, either from his idolatry, or from fantasying Naaman as he was wont, as soon shall we find that Naaman was strengthened to "obey God more than man," as we shall find that Naaman went into Rimmon's temple with the king, the prophet bidding him "go in peace" down some way that God would preserve his servant from evil. So that we may perceive this example of Naaman little shadoweth the fact of the popish protestants.
[Gen. ii.] Surely this is but one of Adam's aprons.

In those days the knowledge of God was nothing so much and manifest as it hath been sithen Christ's coming, especially amongst the heathen: for the good men amongst the Israelites
Gal. iv. were but as "children" (so Paul calleth them) in comparison
1 Cor. xiii. to that we Christians in time of the New Testament should be. Child's age is past, and man's state is now come. Therefore God suffered many things with them, which he will not suffer with us; even as the father will bear many more things at the hands of his son being a child, than being at full growth and
Dan. iii. man's state. Why rather do not we set before our eyes Aza-

rias and his fellows, which would not bow their knees to Nabugodonozer's image? Why set not we for our example, to follow the "seven thousand Israelites which would not bow their knees to Baal?" Why doth not the fact of Mattathias move us? Why forget we to look on the example of the woman and her seven sons? Read the story: shall the examples of one heathen prevail against so many examples of others, and that in the Old Testament? What a shame is this for us that be in the New Testament, and in the last days of it: for surely the coming of our Saviour will shortly appear in glory with innumerable martyrs, which courageously adventured not goods but life, rather than they would be stained in soul or body, to our shame and confusion if we play the Laodiceans, become mere maids, and "seek to please men."

1 Kings xix. 1 Macc. ii. 2 Macc. vii. Rev. iii. Gal. i.

4. Their fourth reason is, that they will pray to God at mass for those that are deceived therewith; and besides this they will not knock nor hold up their hands at the elevation time, as commonly men do, whereby men may be something moved the less to set by the mass. And here they bring in the example of one Astyrius which was at the idolatrous sacrifice the Cæsareans made, and by his prayer there and then obtained their conversion[1].

I answer hereunto, that their prayer here is nothing as available; it wanteth these wings, faith and love to God, and love to our neighbours. For where is his faith or love to God, that seeth his own God horribly dishonoured, his good Christ robbed and spoiled, and yet dissembleth as though he were honoured, Christ were magnified? Where is his love to his brethren, that seeth their souls murdered, and they ready to drink poison as a preservative, and yet he dissembleth as though there were no peril? yea, he will drink with them of the same cup. &c. Should a man think this man's prayer is heard of God?

If God thy Master and Lord be dishonoured, Christ thy Saviour and Redeemer be robbed, the simple people thy brethren be murdered (as indeed spiritually all these be done in and by the mass), why dost thou dissemble as though Christ were honoured, God were served, thy brethren were edified? Is not this deep dissimulation, is not this lack of love to

[[1] See p. 341, note 3.]

God and his glory, is not this lack of love to thy brethren and to their salvation, and is not this iniquity? for every sin is iniquity. But, where iniquity hath ease and rest in the heart, there God will not receive the prayer. How will he hear thy prayer then, thou hypocrite, dissembler with God and man, mass-gospeller?

But thou keepest still thy pew, and holdest not up thy hands. As though none were papists but such as knock and hold up their hands; as though all men at the sacring-time[1] look on thee what thou only doest; as though he did eat no part of a pudding which eateth of both the ends of it but tasteth not of the midst of it. Is the holding up of the hands so great a matter with you now? What! I had thought this external work or behaviour had been nothing, if that the spirit had been right! Is the holding up of the hand at the sacring-time[1] more than the presence of thy body at all the whole mass? Is there nothing else amiss in the mass but the adoration of the sacrament? If thou wouldest men should know that thou dost disallow it, why comest thou to it? What doest thou there? Dost not thou go to the mass, that the magistrate might know that thou art of his religion, a good obedient subject to the devilish laws? Thus playest thou wily-beguile[2] thyself. Tell me, if thy servant should go with thieves to rob thy house, without gainsaying or doing to them, wouldst thou have him excused? And dost thou think that God will not be angry with thee, that goest with thieves to rob him of his true service and honour by the mass? Thy servant might have an excuse to say, if he should have reproved them for their fact and denied to have gone with them, it could not have holpen, but cast him away, for he had no help. But such excuse hast thou none, for God can deliver and help thee out
1 Kings xiii. of the hands of all thy adversaries. Read the story of Jeroboam, whether he was able to hurt the man of God, reproving his fact: and God is the same God now. The standing of the three young men overthrew the purposed idolatry of Nabugodonozer: and surely so would it do the wicked mass with us, if as obedient subjects we would obey God more than man.

As for the example of Astyrius being at sacrifice with idol-

[1 See Vol. I. p. 160, note 1.]
[2 "Playest wily-beguile:" deceivest. See Vol. I. p. 375, note 4.]

aters, and praying there, helpeth them nothing; for, as he openly declared himself to disallow their idolatry, which our mass-gospellers do not, so did not he accustom to resort thither as they do to the mass, but only by the way happened to be there at that time. And, [that] the thing may be more apparent, I will here write the story as I find it in Eusebius:

At Cæsarea Philippi which the Phenicians call Paneas, at the foot of an hill named Paneas, which is the head of the river of Jordan, there was a common custom amongst the people of that place, yearly upon a certain solemn day to offer and slay a sacrifice: the which sacrifice, by the sleight of Satan, suddenly after the slaughter of it vanished away, so that the people were persuaded it went up into heaven: and therefore this was no small miracle nor service of God, thought they and all the whole country. Now it came to pass that this Astyrius came by them in their sacrifice time, who perceiving that all this was done by the illusion of the devil in bewitching of the people's eyes, he in his heart lamenting the error and misery forthwith fell down on his knees, and lift up his eyes and hands to heavenward, and with heart and voice called upon the blessed name of the Lord Jesus Christ, the tears trickling down by his cheeks apace, and besought Christ to have mercy upon the poor people, and to deliver them from this their error. As soon as he prayed thus openly before all the people, behold, the Lord opened their eyes, and so they saw their sacrifice which they thought had been in heaven haled over the water there in all their sight manifestly: whereupon they amended their fault, and never used this superstition any more[3].

This God wrought by the prayer of this one Astyrius, which you see serveth nothing to this purpose. I purpose by God's grace shortly to put something forth of this Astyrius and other martyrs and confessors of Christ's faith, to comfort and confirm my afflicted brethren and sufferers. Now will I go to their fifth reason.

5. It is enough, say they, to "believe in the heart, and with our mouths to confess" it to God; and therefore, except a man were a preacher, he may not reprove or disannul the Rom. x.

[[3] Vide Euseb. Hist. Eccl. Lib. VII. cap. xvii. p. 264, ed. Vales. Mogunt. 1672.]

mass; yea[1] it is but a needless tempting of God to lose all we have. Thus reason they, but I will briefly answer them.

First, you make no difference between "believing with the heart," and "confessing with the mouth," where the one, that is, belief, is spoken in respect of God, which "searcheth the heart," and "looketh for faith;" and the other is spoken in respect of the church or men, as Christ saith, "He that confesseth me before men," &c. And this confession Paul putteth as a plain demonstration of faith in the heart, so that, wheresoever it be not, faith is not. Therefore this place utterly maketh against you; for, by your silence at that horrible idol and enemy unto Christ and his church, you utterly holding your tongues declare your faithless hearts, or else confession with the mouth could not but burst out, as light in an house cannot but burst out, at the door and windows of the same, to the sight of such as be without.

Jer. v. [3, Septuag. and Vulg.]

We have all care one over another.

Secondly, though we be not all public ministers and preachers of the gospel, yet we are all bishops one over another, and called to preach out and "shew the virtues of him that hath called us into his light:" so that our duty is to see, as much as we can, "that no man fall from the grace of God," (except we will follow Cain, and say, "Who made me keeper of my brother?") and, whensoever occasion is offered, to set forth and "shew the praises of the Lord," and reprove that which is evil, as Paul saith, *Arguite potius*, ["Rather reprove them,"] but after our vocation. Indeed, if the preachers did their duty to disallow and reprove this mass, we should have less cause so to do, it were enough to declare that we allow their doctrine. But, seeing that the preachers are lying praters, and the true speakers are put up to preach to posts, being companyless, bookless, paperless, and without pen and ink (so straitly are they looked unto), it is the duty of every Christian, after their vocation, to disallow all that he cannot obey and do with good conscience.

Heb. xii. vi.

Gen. iv.

1 Pet. ii. Eph. v.

Last of all, as concerning the loss of life, &c., I can none otherwise answer than with Christ's own words, "He that loveth father and mother better than me is not worthy of me. Yea, he that forsaketh not father and mother, wife and children,

Matt. x. xvi. Mark viii. Luke ix. xiv. xvii.

[[1] "yea," Lansd. and Harl. MSS.: "yet," printed editions.]

goods, and his own self also, cannot be my disciple; for he that will go about to save his life shall lose it, but he that adventureth, yea, loseth his life for my sake, the same shall find it eternally." One day, will we nill we, we must forsake all, and perchance go to the devil: now if willingly, for God's sake, we will do that which of necessity we must do, we cannot but be most certain to go to God, not for the suffering's sake, but for his mercy and promise sake.

6. Their sixth reason is of charity and offence: "knowledge maketh proud, but charity edifieth:" for else, if we should not go to mass, we should offend the simple. 1 Cor. viii.

I answer, that knowledge without charity is evil; and such had the Corinthians which abused their knowledge in the liberty of the gospel, to the sore wounding of many a poor conscience for whom Christ was crucified; as our mass-gospellers, puft up with knowledge of the liberty of the gospel in exterior things, do, thinking that they may go to mass, and so lacking whereof they brag are taken tardy with their own reason: for what charity call you that which not only suffereth, but also helpeth to hurl his blind brother headlong into the pit of perdition?

But surely their reasoning, as their doing, sheweth them to want knowledge also; for that which is spoken of indifferent things they apply to things utterly unlawful; for the mass is not to be placed among things indifferent, but amongst the greatest evils, for one most horrible. God send them more knowledge and charity; and then I doubt not but they will keep them at home rather than go to mass.

For offending our brethren in not coming to mass, a man must put a difference between offences: some are taken, some are given. The preacher that preacheth God's word truly offends the wicked, or rather the wicked taketh thereby offence: so doth the father offend the child if he be covetous, in giving liberally to the poor. But this offence cometh of the wickedness [of] the evil, and is taken and not given. The man that goeth to the mass giveth an offence, occasioning others to do the like: and woe be unto such! The man that goeth not to mass, or if he go thither doth reprove it publicly, this man, I say, giveth no offence, but the offence is taken; for he that followeth God's word, to do his will, can never give offence. But he that followeth his own will or reason, or the will and

Offences are either given or taken.

reason of any man, in religion or God's service, the same man giveth an offence, and sinneth damnably. Go to therefore, and see with thyself in going to mass, whether thou doest it to do God's will or thine own. If thou look well on it, thou shalt see it is not God's will, but thine own, or the will of others whom thou wouldest not displease. But now see what Paul
Gal. i. saith, "If I should please men, I were not the servant of Christ," and what saith thy conscience when thou prayest,
[Rom. xv.] 1 Cor. x. "Thy will be done," and doest the contrary. "Every man must study to please his brother, but yet to edification."

But of these offences much were to be spoken against our gospellers, which have given great offences in not resorting to the communion, to receive it when they might, also in contemning common prayer, in neglecting preaching and sermons, in abusing their liberty in meats, in church, goods. &c.

7. Their seventh reason they gather out of Christ's words,
Mark vii. that "not it which goeth into the mouth defileth man, but that which cometh forth of the heart;" and therefore going to mass being but an external thing, if so be the heart allow it not, "cannot defile a man."

Our Saviour's words do not exclude outward words and works contrary to his laws, but that they defile man, as murder, theft, whoredom, &c., albeit these indeed spring out of the heart. Howbeit, to make the matter manifest, a difference, as before I have spoken, there should be put always between things indifferent and things unlawful. The mass and going to it to serve God thereby is no indifferent thing. We should discern God's creatures from man's ignorance in the abuse of them. Wine is God's creature: drunkenness is man's error and the abusing of God's creature. The epistle, gospel, supper, good prayers, &c., are God's ordinances: but the mass is man's ignorance and horrible abusing of those holy things. To sacrifice calves, sheep, &c., was God's institution: but to sacrifice in the groves, woods, at Bethel, Dan, &c., was man's error and plain idolatry, as our mass is, and they that use it horrible idolaters. So that this their reason upon this text gathered is reasonless. If they used it against man's prescription of meats, as though some were more holy than some, some defiled upon Friday more than upon Thursday, &c., then used they it rightly.

[8.] Now let us see their eighth reason. 'It is anabaptistical,' say they, 'to abstain from the ministry and temple, because of other men's faults; rather men should prove and try themselves than others. The priest's illness[1], or the papists' error cannot hurt us if we in heart consent nòt to their evil or allow it.'

This reason is like the rest; for the ministry of God's word and the mass are two things, the one mere repugnant to the other, and destroyers the one of the other. He doth wickedly which with the anabaptists or Donatists[2] think the fault of the minister or people should impair Christ's ministry or sacraments, and the virtue and efficacy thereof is himwards. In using God's ordinances let us try ourselves and not others. But, sir, what ordinance of God call you the mass? who taught to pray publicly in an unknown tongue? who taught Christ's supper to be a private supper? but of this look more before.—Now will I dispatch their ninth and tenth reasons.

9, 10. Because "God beholdeth the heart, and not the outward appearance," because "the eyes of God look for faith," because the beauty of God's church is "within," therefore the outward deed of going to mass forceth not, if so be inwardly it be not approved. 1 Sam. xvi. Jer. v. [3, Septuag. and Vulg.] Ps. xlv.

To this I answer, that indeed it is true that "God looketh on the heart," but yet so that he beholdeth the words and works also. "His eyes look on faith," but so that he casteth his eyes on men's facts also, Psalm [xxxiii. 15]; and therefore the scripture saith that "God will judge after our works" and sayings. Read Matt. xxv. and xii: "Of thy words thou shalt be justified," &c. This therefore conclude not as they gather, but rather teach us God's privilege, which we must not meddle withal: only "we must know the tree by the fruits," the which fruits if at any time they deceive us, yet God can they never deceive, for he knoweth the heart, he knoweth the faith, and whether the fruits spring thereof or no. Yea, this sentence, well weighed, doth give us occasion to set the popish church to be no church in God's sight, as doth the sentence they allege for their tenth reason, of the beauty of "the king's daughter," that is, the church, "within:" for—if we behold the face of the Mal. [iii. 16.] [Jer. v. 3, Septuag. and Vulg.] [Rev. xx. 13.]

[1 "Illness:" ill or evil conduct or character.]
[2 See p. 179, note 3, above.]

popish church in respect of Christ's true church whose beauty indeed is all inward, being replenished with the Spirit of Christ and the fruits of the same, outwardly being but simple, for she will add nothing to Christ's commandments in God's service and religion, otherwise than for order's sake—if, I say, we behold the face of the popish church, Lord, how it glistereth, and gorgeous it is in comparison of Christ's true church! which is discerned[1] in these days but by the word of God truly preached, the sacraments purely ministered, and some discipline nothing so much as hath been, might be, and should be. Whereas the popish church wants nothing to set herself forth to the show—as he that considereth the persons (pope, cardinals, legates, archbishops, bishops, suffragans, abbots, priors, deans, prebendaries, archdeacons, canons, monks, friars, parsons, vicars, parish-priests, mass-priests, nuns, sisters, novices, deacons, subdeacons, &c., and a thousand more), the power[1], riches, honours, promotions, lands, houses, fair services[2] (as singing, saying, ringing, playing, censing, &c.), implements (crosses, chalices, relics, jewels, basins, copes, cruets, vestments, books, bells, candles, &c.)—he, I say, that considereth these things, he cannot but with Samuel, thinking Eliab had been he whom God had chosen, think this to be the catholic church and spouse of Christ.

But this sentence saith, the beauty of God's paramour is "within:" and therefore this may be suspected to be the rose-coloured whore St John speaketh of in the Apocalypse, for whom her ministers watch night and day, how to maintain their mistress and whore-madam, with endowing her with the riches, power, and pleasures of the earth. Whereas the ministers of Christ's true church watch and labour how to enrich and beautify God's people with heavenly riches, even with the knowledge of God and his Christ; and therefore they use daily preaching and public praying, and using the sacrament so as may edify; they urge men to repentance, and to begin a new life; they would have men to hoard up their treasures in heaven, &c. And this gear the world liketh not, but murmureth at the ministers, contemneth them, pilleth[3] them, that for poverty and

[[1] "discerned," "power," Lansd. and Harl. MSS.: "deformed," "poor" (clearly errors of the press), the printed editions.]

[[2] "fair services," Harl. MS.: "fare, service," Copland's edition.]

[[3] "Pill:" plunder, rob. See Vol. I. p. 44.]

living's sake they might speak to please, as experience hath taught here in England.

But, to make an end of this matter, I would wish that they which use such sentences as these be, to hide their manifest idolatry and fornication at the mass, would know that their spouse is jealous, and will as well be angry with them whoring so in their bodies, as they would be, if their wives were taken in bodily act with others. Would they take this excuse if the wife should say, 'Forsooth, husband, this is no matter, for I promise you nobody but you alone hath mine heart,' &c.?—God for his mercy's sake in Christ open our eyes and hearts to see, know, and love his will, that we may serve him thereafter. God pour into our hearts the sense of Christ's sweet sacrifice, made for our sins in his own person and by his own self.

Then surely we cannot but earnestly detest this mass, which is most enemy thereagainst, and that not only in spirit inwardly, but also in body outwardly, even as all honest women cannot but be sore grieved, in heart or bodily act to depart from their husbands. The greater love in heart the wife hath to her husband, the more pure will her body be kept from the fellowship of others; and so it goeth with us. Herein let us therefore pray God to engraft his love in our hearts, and then undoubtedly we will neither do nor say anything that shall displease him. Let his word be the "lantern unto our feet," none other Psal. cxix. way to go than we shall see it give light before us. Let his Matt. xiii. word so lie and remain in our hearts, that we sin not. Let us "keep our feet from all evil ways," that we may "keep God's Psal. cxix. laws and testimonies." And here I will write an history not unfit for this purpose as I think.

There was in the time of Sapores, king of Persia, which cruelly persecuted the Christians, a certain archbishop of Seleuchia and Ctesiphon, called Simeon, which was called before the king divers times, but at the last bound like a thief for Christ's gospel's sake. Howbeit all prevailed nothing. Constant he was in word and countenance to the comfort of all the Christians. On a day, coming from the king, of whom he was examined and threatened if he would not worship the sun and make a knee to it as god (but in vain as I said), it fortuned that one Ustazardes, an ancient officer in the king's court, I trow great master of his household, sat in the court-gates as Simeon came by, which Simeon so soon as this Ustazardes did see coming, forthwith he arose and did reverence: but Simeon, knowing that he had worshipped the sun for fear of the king, would not look at him, but seemed to contemn and despise him. This gear when Ustazardes perceived so pierced his heart, that he began to pull asunder his clothes, and to rend his garments, with weeping eyes crying out, and, alas, that ever he had so offended God as in body to bow to the sun! for, saith he, herein I have denied God, although I did it against my will: and how sore is God displeased with me, when mine old father and friend Simeon, his dear servant, will not speak, or look towards me! I may by the servant's countenance perceive the master's mind. &c. On this sort this Ustazardes lamented.

Now, sir, it came shortly to the king's ear; and therefore was he sent for, and demanded the cause of his mourning, and he out of hand told him the cause to be his unwilling bowing to the sun. 'By it, O king,' saith he, 'I have denied God, and therefore, because "he will deny them that deny him," I have no little cause to complain and mourn. Woe unto me!' quoth he, 'for I have played the traitor to Christ, and have dissembled with thee, my liege lord. No death therefore is sufficient for the least of my faults.' &c.

When the king heard this it went to his stomach, for he loved Ustazardes, who had been to him and his father a faithful servant and officer: howbeit the malice of Satan moved him to cause this man to be put to death, when he saw that by no means he would alter his mind to worship with the body the sun. Yet in this point he seemed to gratify him, for Ustazardes desired that the cause of his death might be published to be as it was: 'This I ask,' saith he, 'for guerdon and recompense of my true service to thee and thy father.' 'Marry,' quoth the king, 'thou shalt have it,' thinking thereby that, when the Christians should know how he would not spare his chiefest servants for religion, it would make them[1] more afraid, and sooner to consent unto him. But, so soon as it was published, and Ustazardes put to death, Lord, how it comforted

[[1] The Harleian MS. ends with the words "would make them," being imperfect.]

not only Simeon then being in prison, but also all the Christians[2]!

This history I wish were marked, as well of us as of[3] our popish gospellers, which have no more to say for them than Ustazardes had; for his heart was with God howsoever he framed his body, and therefore saith he, that unwillingly he bowed to the sun. We should behave ourselves strongly against such brethren, as Simeon did, and then they the sooner would play Ustazardes' part: which thing no marvel though they do not, so long as we rock them asleep by regarding them and their companies as daily we do, and so are partakers of their evil, and at the length shall feel of their smart.—God guide us all with his holy Spirit as his children for evermore. Amen[4].

[11.] As for the example of the three children, which, eleventhly, [they] bring in, that, because they, being with the others that worshipped the golden image, were therefore not blamed, so may they be at mass with the mass-worshippers, and that harmless or blameless, except they worship the idol there as the papists do—as for this example, I say, how little it maketh for their purpose we should easily perceive, if men would consider that the three children going thither was not so much to obey the king's precept in coming to the place appointed, as to declare their faith in public, condemning the false religion there by the king published whilst they were there present. There is no man that will find fault with thee if thou go to the church, for obedience to the magistrate, there publicly to declare thy faith, and to disallow, not only in heart but also in fact, the false religion there set forth. The three children, not only in heart, but also in outward gesture, condemned this religion. And wilt thou, by thy outward presence allowing antichristian religion, use their example to excuse thee?

'Yea, but their being there was not condemned: and therefore, if I go to mass,' saith one, 'so that I worship not the idol there, I am not blameworthy.' Ah! good brother, deceive not thyself; there was no religion, as far as we read, in any other thing than in falling down to worship the golden image:

[[2] The narrative will be found in Sozom. Hist. Eccles. Lib. II. cap. ix. p. 545, ed. Vales. Mogunt. 1677.]

[[3] "of," Lansd. MS.: not in printed editions.]

[[4] The printed editions end with the words, "for evermore. Amen."]

but here it is otherwise: it is not counted for a piece of religion to be at matins, at evensong, and at the prayers of the mass, as well as to knock and kneel, and lift up our hands to the sacrament. Again, this property hath public prayers, that all that be there present, and do not publicly disallow them, the same doth shew himself to consent to them. Now what idolatry is even in their matins and evensong (let the mass-prayers alone) by invocation to saints and such baggage! So that it is too evident, I hope, that the example of the three children will not serve for their purpose.

And truly no more will the testimony of Baruch: for, although he willeth the Jews in their captivity to honour God in their hearts, when they should see other men worship stocks and stones, yet meaneth he not that men should assemble to the places where their temples and places appointed for their false religion was; but—because they being captives could not but, going abroad [in] the streets and other places, see their enemies the Babylonians, Chaldees, &c., to fall down and worship their idols, standing in their open places, and being carried about with them—should by their example not be offended, but "sanctify the Lord in their hearts." As, for example's sake, if a man going by the street or way meet Sir John with his god about his neck, and see folks kneel down as many do, or if a man going through Cheapside and see folks worship the cross there, or Thomas Becket his image standing by his church[1], this going and seeing others committing idolatry is not defiled for passing by the way, so that he commit not idolatry with them, or in his heart consent not to their iniquity. Indeed, if a man should resort to the temples and places appointed for religion and worship of idols, and not to reprove the idolatry there committed, it were a matter. But to go by the way where a cross standeth, or men carry idols (as the priest in visitation of the sick, and the bishops in their processions, their cake-god), and to see others do thereto worship, doth not defile any that doth not in deed or heart consent to their iniquity.

Howbeit, if this were not which I have spoken, this saying

[[1] The chapel of St Thomas of Acre, Cheapside, London, occupied at that time the site of the house, in which Becket, Abp of Canterbury, was born.—Stow's London, Vol. I. book iii. p. 37, ed. Strype, Lond. 1720.]

of Baruch can little help our mass-gospellers, which, resorting to the church to the service, are defiled by communicating with the common prayers, whereto he consenteth that publicly doth not disallow them. I need not to recite the authority of Baruch as not canonical, which I well might if I saw any such cause or matter to make for a mass-gospeller's purpose in his testimony.

But—to make an end of all this matter—let every man be sure of his own meaning; let every one remember what he learned afore he began with A, B, C, that is, Christ's cross[2]; let every one remember what he hath professed, to "deny himself, to take up his cross, and to follow Christ;" let every one beware that in nothing he seek himself; but, in all things he goeth about, let him see that he seek God's glory and his neighbour's commodity. And then doubtless in this matter, and in many others, as there will be less reasoning, so there will be more edifying. [Conclusion.]

Now every man almost seeketh to avoid the cross: and, because they love themselves, they preferreth this before God's glory or good example. And therefore they seek out all shifts that can be, for a time, to shadow their self-love and their own selves: as indeed the man that had "bought the farm and the yoke of oxen," &c., which God admitted not, but "sware in his wrath," "they should not taste of his supper," "nor enter into his rest."

Into which rest God the eternal Father of mercy bring us, for his Christ's sake, our only Mediator. Amen[3].

[[2] See Vol. I. p. 264, note 1.]

[[3] The last seven paragraphs are now printed for the first time, from the Lansdown MS.]

[The following is the colophon of Copland's printed edition.]

¶ Imprinted by Wyllyam Copland,
for Wyllyam Martyne, and ar to be solde
at his shope ioininge to the myddle North
dore of Paules, at the sygne of the
blacke boye.

(XIV.) BRADFORDUS MARTINO BUCERO[1].

[Londini, forsan ineunte anno, 1550.]

Addit. MSS., No. 19, 400, (formerly belonging to D. Turner, Esq.) Original, Holograph. British Museum.

Dominus noster Jesus Christus te servet et regat in omnibus quæcunque conaris, ad sui nominis gloriam et ecclesiæ ejus ædificationem.

Pudet me scribere, quia tuæ expectationi minime satisfeci. Agnosco me in tuam dominationem, longe ultra quam veniam deprecari audeam, peccasse. Literæ quas misisti ad D. Utenhoffium (cum quo conveni, et a quo rursum referam) et ad D. Birkmannum, quo autem modo ignoro, perditæ sunt. Ea qua venerim Londinum nocte, cum irem cubitum, in cubiculo una cum reliquis tuis literis me habuisse memini. Postridie tamen summo mane, cum ad domum D. Bernardini Ochini, quo convenirem D. P. Perusinum, accesserim, et e sinu meo, satis fibulis connexo ut putavi, fasciculum tuarum literarum exerui, eæ duæ non apparebant.

Ad diversorium itaque statim reversus non potui nec adhuc possum eas invenire. Unde dolor ingens et pudor assiduus me extunc occupavit et occupat. Sed quorsum hæc, dices, ad extenuandum peccatum tuum? Domine Bucere, Deum omnipotentem, qui indicabit occulta hominum, testem invoco, me nec affectata nec spontanea negligentia (negligentia tamen) eas perdidisse. Hæc itaque ad accusationem et non ad excusationem mei scribo, non recusans quamcunque velis imponere mihi ultionem, modo non me prorsus a te abalienes. Nulla possum fronte petere, ut in posterum aliquid mihi mandes. Occasionem tamen percupio, ut inde, quod in hac parte peccatum est a me, diligentia, quam doctus sum meo et tuo damno implorare ac mendicare a Deo, si sarciendum sit resarciam.

Recordare obsecro, cum veneris ad, "Remitte nobis debita nostra sicut et nos, &c.," ut hanc mihi injuriam et negligentiam remittas, simulque orare ut Deus remittat propter suam misericordiam. Nam persuasum habeo, Deum hac pœna te punivisse propter meam impietatem, quæ quotidie in immensum crescit, quo me et meam horridam hypocrisim deinceps devites.

Jam quod ad reliqua tua attinet negotiola, ego ipse cum venero, quod Deo volente erit in die Lunæ proximæ ad extre-

[[1] This letter is now printed for the first time.]

mum, si mihi permiseris, referam. Interim et semper obsecro æternum Patrem Liberatoris nostri Christi, ut te Spiritu suo gubernet, ad tuam et multorum salutem, per eundem Christum Dominum nostrum. Amen.

Londini.

Tuæ dominationi deditissimus,

JOANNES BRADFORDUS.

Clarissimo viro, Domino Bucero, patri ac domino suo observandissimo, Cantabrigiæ.

Translation.

BRADFORD TO BUCER.

[London, perhaps early in 1550.]

OUR Lord Jesus Christ preserve and direct you in all your undertakings, to the glory of his own name and the edification of his church.

I am ashamed to write, because I have by no means satisfied your expectation. I acknowledge that I have, much further than I can venture to solicit forgiveness, sinned against your mastership. The letters you sent to Master Utenhovius (with whom I have met, and from whom I shall in turn report to you) and to Master Birkman have, by what means however I know not, been lost. The night that I came to London, when I was going to bed, I remember that I had them in my chamber, together with the rest of your letters. The following day however, very early in the morning, when I went to the house of Bernardine Ochinus, to meet Master P. Perusinus, and drew from my bosom (which was well fastened with clasps, as I supposed) the bundle of your letters, those two did not appear.

Having on that account returned straightway to the inn, I was and am still unable to discover them. For this reason very great sorrow and unceasing shame have, from that time, possessed and still possess me. But to what purpose is all this, you will say, for the extenuation of your fault?—Master Bucer, I appeal to almighty God, who shall reveal the secrets of men, as my witness, that I did not lose those letters either by intentional or voluntary negligence, and yet by negligence. To accuse and not to excuse myself therefore I write these things, nor do I refuse any retribution whatever, which you may choose to inflict upon me, provided you do not estrange me from yourself utterly. I cannot with any face ask you to trust me with anything in future. I earnestly desire the opportunity however of hereafter repairing (if it is to be repaired) the fault which I have committed in this matter, by the diligence which I have been taught by my own and your loss to implore and beg from God.

Remember, I entreat you, when you shall come to "Forgive us our debts, even as we," &c., to pardon me this wrong and negligence, and at the same time to pray God to forgive it for his mercy sake. For I am persuaded that God has visited you with this punishment for my ungodliness, which every day doth immensely increase, in order that you may henceforth strenuously avoid me, and my horrid hypocrisy.

Now, as far as pertaineth to the rest of your small matters, I will myself, if you shall allow me, report them to you, when I come, which will, God willing, be next Monday at the latest. In the meanwhile and alway I beseech the eternal Father of our Deliverer Christ to direct you by his Spirit, to your salvation and that of many, through the same Christ our Lord. Amen.

London.

Your mastership's most devoted,

JOHN BRADFORD.

To that most distinguished person, Master Bucer, his own most worshipful father and master, at Cambridge.

(XCVI.) CARELESS TO BRADFORD[1].

JESUS HELP.

Addit. MSS. No. 19, 400. (formerly belonging to D. Turner, Esq.) Original, Holograph. British Museum.

"THE heart is sorrowful even in laughter, and the end of mirth is heaviness."—*Proverbia* xiv.

As I do most heartily praise our God, most dearly beloved in the Lord, good Master Bradford, for that you received so great com-

[[1] This letter is now printed for the first time.]

fort by my last letter (the which, though it were simple, yet without doubt was most true in all points), even so do I greatly fear me now, that you will be as much discomforted at the reading of this letter, most lamentable to a Christian heart; the which without fail is as true in every part as the other was. O how full of wretchedness and corruption is our poisoned nature, that we can tarry no while in any good state! They that will not believe the scripture, that plainly reporteth the same, God send them such experience as I have now, that they may the better prove their own strength and what their free-will can do.

Peradventure you will marvel at this my sudden change: but the cause thereof was by you well foreseen, whereof you gave me warning, if I had been so happy to have taken it in time. The cause of this my misery is mine own great unthankfulness unto God for his benefits, and for not my regarding them whilst that I had them. Therefore am I now worthily deprived of them, and left unto myself most miserably. I pray God, that I be not made a fearful example to all unthankful persons that be yet for to come.

You complained, dear heart, of your unthankfulness, in your most loving letter: but, alas, alas! it is I, it is I indeed, that am the most unthankful wretch in the world; it is I, it is I, that hath just cause indeed day and night to lament and deplore my great ingratitude towards God and man. O, what hearty lauds, praises, and continual thanks ought I, most ungrateful wretch, to have given unto my good God and most dear loving Father, for all his great mercies and heavenly benefits that he hath poured upon me through Jesus Christ! Yea, what humble and hearty thanks ought I to have given to that Lord, for the godly acquaintance and faithful love and favour that he hath caused me to find, in the sight of you, my dear approved friend and most faithful loving brother, Master Bradford! whose faithful comfortable counsel the Lord hath not only made a strong fortress to defend me in all dangers and distress, but also whose godly example and life the Lord hath used for a line to lead me by, to keep me from falling into many perilous pits, that my frail flesh is apt to fall into. O, what due and convenient thanks ought I to have rendered unto our good God, for the gracious preservation of you thus long, contrary to all man's expectation, to my great joy and comfort, and most singular commodity both of body and soul; as for the manifold corporal benefits that the Lord hath and daily doth minister unto me by you—I will now speak nothing at all—only it is my mind herein, my dear heart in the Lord, right heartily to desire you and most humbly to require you to go unto our good God with me, by faithful and fervent prayer to help me to beg of him a more pure and thankful heart than hitherto I have had, or yet have at this present; that the Lord may take from me this crooked, crabbed, corrupt, hard, stony, and unthankful heart, and to create in the stead thereof "a pure heart, and to renew an upright spirit within me."

O, with what face shall I appear before the righteous judgment-seat of God? seeing that I have so beastly abused his gracious benefits, not only by mine great ingratitude and unthankfulness, but also in most unkindly recompensing the same with my grievous sins and manifold wickednesses from time to time. O how true have I proved, by too much experience, your sayings concerning the malice and envy of Satan against us! and yet could I not beware enough of him. He hath bitten me by the heel, alas! and hath given me a great fall, whereby I am all-to bruised and broken, so that there is no whole part in me. God, for his Son Christ's sake, help me up again and heal my soul, which at this present is full [of] woe, that it hath offended him so sore. Ah, dear heart! seeing that I would not be taught, by your godly example and friendly admonition, to beware of unthankfulness, I fear me that I shall feel, to my further peril, God's fearful judgments for mine ingratitude and folly. You gave me good warning to take heed and beware, lest after a lightening I catch a foil. But, alas! I took no heed, but went on presumptuously, saying in my prosperity, "Tush, I shall never more fall, because the Lord of his goodness had made my hill so strong!" But welaway[1] for mine unthankfulness and folly! the Lord hath now turned his face from me, and I am brought in great fear, trouble and misery: my foot is taken in the snare that Satan hath laid for me, the ropes of hell hath gotten hold upon me, I am fallen into the bottomless pit of mire; the floods of evil hath overwhelmed me, the deep hath well most swallowed me up, the pit is ready to shut her mouth upon me. O that the Lord would not cast me forth of his presence for ever, nor utterly "take his holy Spirit from me;" O that he would not correct me in his fearful anger, nor yet "chasten me in his heavy displeasure," but that he would in his mercy punish me well, to the example of all other unthankful persons; but yet never to take his lovingkindness from me, nor to suffer the truth of his merciful promises to fail me at my need! O that I might believe that it is of very love that God hath at this time hid a cheerful countenance from me! then should I yet live in some hope and comfort, and learn more expertly to use his godly gifts, better, against another time. Whereas now, by my great

[[1] See Vol. I. p. 39, note 5.]

ingratitude, ignorance, and corruption, I have indeed received great hurt thereby; even according as you, dear friend, did very well forewarn me. But, alas! I had no grace to be guided by your godly counsel: and therefore is this misery justly fallen upon me; and now I know no way how to escape. I was once rapt up with good Paul "unto the third heaven:" but now with proud Lucifer I am "cast down to the hell." O that the Lord would once more tread down Satan under my feet; O that he would break my bands, and deliver my soul out of his snare; O that I might once more taste and feel the gracious goodness and lovingkindness of the Lord, that I might obtain the blessing by faithful trust in him! Then would I walk more warily than ever I did before, and apply myself unto prayer that God might preserve me. Yea, then would I follow your friendly counsel, and beware of unthankfulness, and lovingly admonish all other to do the same.

Thus, my dear friend and most faithful loving brother, good Master Bradford, forasmuch as it hath pleased you so largely to reveal your great love and tender heart towards me, most unthankful and unhappy wretch, as well by your manifold deeds, as also by your loving godly and pithy letters, I am bold to make my woeful moan unto you, being also well assured that I shall not be destitute of your godly, faithful, and daily prayer; desiring you also, for Christ's sake, to let me hear from you what the Lord my God will say unto me by your mouth; whether that I shall die of this my sore and grievous disease, or else whether that I shall recover of the same: which God grant me for his own great mercy's sake. Amen, Amen.

Dear heart and most faithful brother, as you love me let me hear from you, in your good time, when the Lord shall open his good pleasure to you concerning this my misery. And in the mean space, as a weanling from the mother, I will bewail my woeful state. The Lord give true repentant tears unto my weeping eyes, that with the prophet David I may water my couch. Amen.

I have done your loving commendations to all my prison-fellows, who giveth you right hearty thanks for your manifold kindness. They praise God for you, and pray for you; and I trust they will observe your godly counsel better than I have done. But yet God hath hid my sin and hypocrisy forth of their sight, that they are not hurt by my wicked example, lest my damnation should be double to me. They much marvel to see me mourn: but the cause they do not know, nor no creature living besides myself but you only, to whom I am bold always to make my moan, by whom unto me hath come much comfort from the Lord: at the remembrance whereof I begin to weep afresh in consideration of my great sin and unthankfulness.—O good Lord, let never my sin separate me from the fellowship of such sweet members of thy mystical body, lest Satan swallow me up in perpetual sorrow.

Your most godly and comfortable work I have once perused over; and, when I had so done, I delivered it unto Trew and his company to read with your loving salutations, the which, as to me seemed, was very well accepted of them. I have it now again, and will write it by God's grace. I pray God work in the hearts of Trew and his company, as he hath done in the rest of them that were with them, as my hope and trust is that he will in his good time: and by God's grace I will be very circumspect that in no point they be not hindered by me. O that my heart were half so pure before God, as my hypocritical life seemeth before men! then should not my cursed conscience have so just cause to accuse me, neither my grievous sins so heavily oppress me down to hell. The Lord for his great mercy's sake give me some little spark and feeling of the comforts of his Spirit, and strengthen me with the same, that my faith never fail. Amen.

Thus, my most dearest beloved heart in the Lord, as I began with heaviness so I end with mourning, being right sorry (if I might otherwise do) to trouble you with this terrible tragedy of my woeful state. But, alas! to whom should I shew my wound, but to him that can apply a right plaster to the same? to whom should I make my moan, but to such a faithful friend as would gladly mourn with me? and not to the proud Pharisees that will laugh me to scorn. O that the Lord, our good God, who hath linked our love and unit[ed] and knit our hearts and minds together in the unity of his Spirit—O, I say, that the same Lord would communicate and participate to me some of your heavenly gifts and virtues, whereof he hath given you such store! that, as we have loved here heartily together in Christ, so we may joyfully live together with him, by the same Christ: to whom with the Father and the Holy Ghost be all honour, glory, power, praise, thanks, rule and dominion, for ever and ever. Amen.

Pray, pray, pray, for God's sake pray.

Your daily orator, but yet a most
unthankful wretch,
JOHN CARELESS.

"Lighten mine eyes, O Lord, that I sleep not in death, lest at any time mine enemies say, I have prevailed against him." Psalm xiii.

To my faithful friend, Master
John Bradford.

MEDITATION ON THE KINGDOM OF CHRIST.

[The following short meditation is now reprinted for the first time since the sixteenth century, from an exceedingly scarce little book printed by William Powell without date, which formerly belonged to the typographical antiquary Herbert[1], and is now in the library of the late W. H. Miller, Esq., of Britwell, near Burnham, Bucks. That book might possibly have been printed about 1561 or early in 1562: see Vol. I. p. 220, and List of editions, entry VIII., pp. xxxv, vi, above. Its title is as follows:

"A frutefull treatise and full of heauenly consolation against the feare of death. Whereunto are annexed certaine sweete meditations of the kingdom of Christ. of life euerlasting, and of the blessed state and felicitie of the same. Gathered by that holy marter of God, John Bradford. Perused corrected & augmented according to the originall, & Imprinted in Fletestrete nere to saint Dunstons Churche by William Powell."]

A meditation concerning the kingdom of Christ, and that it is no corporal thing, as the Jews and anabaptists do feign; to whom the papists in manner assent, making the church so glorious and gay a dame, far unlike to be Christ's spouse, who was here on earth in no such felicity and worldly glory as their church is. They make more of the good wife than of the good man, and therefore set forth to us a strumpet for Christ's spouse.

Open mine eyes, dear Lord, to see thy kingdom, for it is spiritual, and of carnal eyes simply cannot be considered: and therefore less ought we to marvel to see it contemned, and the children thereof persecuted, the most part of men, and specially the great men of the world, being carnal and not spiritual, although by title many be called so. Give me thy light to see that thy kingdom, O Christ, is thy sitting on the right hand of thy Father and ours, and thy interpellation and mediation for us, and also thy giving of pardon and forgiveness of sins and the Holy Spirit to thy church (that is, such as believe in thee, and call upon God the Father through confidence in thee), and hereto thy sanctifying of them, that thou mayst raise them up

[1 Herbert's book mark, "W. H.," is on the title. Both the title of the volume and long heading of this Meditation were transcribed by Herbert, among his MS. additions, written in the interleaved copy of his own work, now in the British Museum. The title and the heading were printed from thence by Dibdin, in his incomplete edition of Herbert, Vol. IV. pp. 287, 8, London, 1810—19.]

in the last day to life and glory everlasting. Grant me to know that for the attaining of all these benefits, which be the liberties and privileges of thy kingdom, thou hast ordained the ministry of thy gospel and sacraments, thereby to call and bring men to the knowledge of thy Father and thee, which "is eternal life." Grant that I may feel in myself lively and comfortably the efficacy and virtue of thy Holy Ghost, which is effectual by the ministry and word. And, lest afflictions should dismay me, and the company of evil men mingled with the godly overthrow me or offend me, grant that I may not only know how that thy church and the true children thereof shall in this world until the last day suffer persecution, and that goats will be amongst the sheep until the day of judgment; but also that I may in affliction rejoice and glorify thy holy name, being preserved always "from the counsel of the ungodly, from the way of the wicked, and from the seat of the scornful, to delight in thy law night and day," to be made spiritual, and to have the benefit of thy kingdom and priesthood; which be both spiritual, preserving thy people from the tyranny of sin and Satan; although in this life thou permit their enemies to vex them, to thy further glory and their increase in repentance and godliness. Which give unto me and increase in me for thy holy name's sake.

Scriptures proving Christ's kingdom to be spiritual.

John xviii. John xvii.

"My kingdom is not of this world." "Thou hast given him power over all flesh, that, how many soever thou hast given unto him, he might give to the same everlasting life." What is it, any worldly policy? No. Therefore it followeth: "And this is everlasting life, that they may know thee to be the only

Rom. viii.

true God, and whom thou didst send Jesus Christ," "which

Isai. xi. Isai. xlii. [Matt. xii. 21.]

sitteth on the right hand of God and prayeth for us." "The root of Jesse shall stand up," "and the Gentiles shall make their prayers unto him." &c. By these two sentences we may see Christ's kingdom and priesthood to be spiritual, and no politic regiment. He "prayeth for us" to his Father, and so reigneth that he will be called upon, will hear us, satisfy us, and keep us with his holy Spirit as God's children; for they "are led by the Spirit of God," "in their hearts he will write his law," &c.: which benefits let us look for, and no corporal kingdom.

"We are fellow-heirs with Christ." "If so be we do suffer with him, we shall be glorified with him." "We are saved by hope." "For thy sake we are killed all the day long." Psal. xliv.
"In this world you shall have affliction." "All that will live John xvi.
godly in Christ must suffer persecution." And many places 2 Tim. iii.
there be which teach us that the glory of Christ's kingdom is no worldly dominion or power, but a spiritual thing, that we should be resuscitated and have a new and an eternal life, righteousness and glory, even such as Christ hath. Besides this Paul telleth, that Antichrist shall bear rule in the church 2 Thess. ii.
until Christ come to judgment: then shall he destroy his kingdom. So that the true church of Christ shall not have worldly dominion and kingdom, but rather be persecuted, and especially towards the end of the world: as Peter telleth, that, as there was before Christ's coming in the church "false prophets," 2 Pet. ii.
and the regiment was with the adversaries, which bare the name of the church, under the which they destroyed the church, so shall it be in the church after Christ's time: "There will be," saith he, "many false teachers," which will deceive not a few or the fewer part, but many and the greater part[1], as now the papists have done almost all Christendom. Again he saith, that "there will come mockers," which will make a mock of religion; so that the church cannot but be persecuted. Daniel plainly sheweth that the "beasts," that is, the empires Dan. vii.
of the world, shall be cast into the fire when Christ shall come to judgment: so that some wicked empires shall continue until the last day.

The true church of Christ is careful for inward beauty, as it is written of "the king's daughter:" whereas the papistical Psal xlv.
church nothing passeth thereof, but altogether careth for external gear. So saith our papists in England: 'Come to the church, and do as other men do outwardly, and keep your conscience to yourselves.'

Scriptures proving that in Christ's church upon earth there shall be good and bad mingled until the day of judgment.

"As it was in the days of Lot, so shall it be in the coming" Luke xvii.
&c. "In that night there shall be two in one bed, one shall be taken" &c. "Let them"—the tares amongst the corn he

[1 Compare Vol. I. Conference with Harpsfield, p. 509.]

Matt. xvii. meaneth—"grow together until the harvest." "The harvest is the end of the world: then the Son of man shall send forth his angels, and they shall gather all offence-givers out of his kingdom, and those which work wickedness. So shall it go in the end of the world." The angels shall go forth and separate the evil from the righteous, "and cast them into the furnace of fire." By these sentences we may see that hypocrites shall be mingled with the godly until the day of judgment.

Whereas the anabaptists do cite the prophets, who speaking of Christ's kingdom use often figures and similitudes of worldly empires, that by temporal and visible things we may arise to a deep consideration of spiritual and eternal things in Christ's kingdom, let us learn so to do. And again let us know that the gospel is the exposition of the prophets: and therefore these corporal metaphors in the prophets, painting forth the kingdom of Christ, must be interpreted according to the gospel, which teacheth clearly Christ's kingdom to be a spiritual and no temporal thing, as before is shewed.

Moreover the prophets even themselves do plainly shew Christ's kingdom to be a spiritual thing. Doth not Daniel say
Dan. ix. that "Christ shall be killed?" And Esay also, doth not he
Isai. liii. say that Christ shall give "his life for sin?" So that we may see no affirmation of corporal dominion here on earth in this life. Besides this the prophets do affirm also Christ's kingdom to be eternal, and therefore cannot be temporal. Figures and metaphors can be no otherwise than allegorically understanded. I need not tell how that the prophets use to speak of Christ's kingdom, that they do not discern the times of this life and of the life to come, because Christ's eternal kingdom is begun in spirit and faith in this life, and afterward endureth for ever. Howbeit sometimes and often they do otherwise, and plainly shew that Christ's kingdom and church shall suffer persecution in this life, as in the second Psalm, and Psalm cxvi., "Precious in the sight of the Lord is the death of his saints;" and Psalm lxxii., Esay xxx., Daniel xii.[1]

[[1] With this Meditation compare the treatise on the "Restoration of all things," Vol. I. pp. 351—64.]

[COMPLAINT OF VERITY.]

[THIS metrical piece forms part of a book published the second year of Elizabeth, 1559 [2], but without the name of the printer, and now of most exceeding scarcity. It is republished here for the first time since the sixteenth century, from a copy, possibly unique[3], belonging to the Rev. Thomas Corser, F.S.A., Rector of Stand, Manchester. The entire volume consists of sixteen leaves, four of which contain the title and "Complaint of verity." Its possessor conjectures, it might have been issued by William Copland, who was fined for printing Bradford's Sermon on repentance, 1558 [4], and who published Bradford's Private prayers and meditations, March 15, 1559 [5], and also the "Hurt of hearing mass [6]." Its title [7] is as follows:

"The complaynt of Veritie, made by John Bradford. An exhortacion of Mathewe Rogers unto his children, The complaynt of Raufe Allerton and others, being prisoners in Lolers tower, & wrytten with their bloud, how god was their comforte. ¶ A songe of Caine and Abell. The saieng of maister Houper, that he wrote the night before he suffered, vppon a wall with a cole, in the newe In, at Gloceter [8], and his saiyng at his deathe. Anno Domini. 1559."

The short metrical piece "on affliction," p. 368, is certainly genuine, as it is published from Bradford's own autograph. The "Complaint of verity" having been attributed to Bradford within about four years after his death, it has been considered right to publish it in this volume. This piece might have been written by Bradford with a view to usefulness among the poor and illiterate.]

[[2] Bp Tanner gives the date incorrectly, in the Biblioth. Britann.—Hibern. 1748, article, Bradford, as 1539, for which the bishop refers to "A. Wood. MS. Cat. vi." That reference is to a manuscript catalogue of "Printed books and pamphlets," now bound in seven volumes in the Ashmolean Museum, Oxford, Vol. E, 4, div. 73, p. 56, where the following memorandum occurs: "Joh. Bradford, martyr. The Complaint of verite.—printed 1539."]

[[3] It was purchased from the Library of the late B. H. Bright, Esq. Catal. No. 649, Sotheby, A.D. 1845, through the late Mr Rodd.]

[[4] Herbert, Typogr. Antiq. Vol. I. p. 358.]

[[5] See Bradf. Vol. I. pp. 221, 2, 247.]

[[6] P. 354, above.]

[[7] The title in substance occurs in Maunsell's Catal. of Engl. printed books, p. 36, London, Windet, 1595, and is given more accurately in Herbert's Typograph. Antiq., Vol. III. p. 1600, Lond. 1785—90. Herbert's inference, that as Maunsell gives the title "with some variation there seem to have been two editions" in 1559, is invalid, as all Maunsell's entries of Bradford's writings are abridged from the actual titles.]

[[8] These metrical lines by bishop Hooper have been printed among his Works, Vol. II. p. xxx. Park. Soc.]

THE COMPLAINT OF VERITY.

O HEAVEN, O earth! to thee I call,
To witness what I say,
Which am causeless in England thrall,
And put to great decay.

Verity, of all things the light,
I am that thus do mourn,
Sent from God to teach them right,
Which in this world be born.

And, that of me none might it doubt,
Whereon-so-ever I preach,
I have for me the word throughout,
As Christ's gospel doth teach.

This truth to England have I taught,
With travail and with pain;
And for my hire now am I sought
Cruelly to be slain.

I that from bondage did thee shield,
Which was before opprest,
Am now by thee as captive held,
For preaching to the best.

From death to life I did thee bring,
That thou might live for aye:
And now my life for well doing
To death thou seekst a prey.

Was there ever age so cruel,
That thus could me reward,
So soon to cast into exile,
Whom they did once regard?

What unrighteousness have ye found
On me whom thus ye spite?
Let them speak, that would me confound
By reason and by right.

I seek, without unfeigned cloaks,
 To maintain that is right:
But falsity with her painted looks
 Will not abide that sight.

O false time of iniquity,
 O season most unjust,
Where exiled is Verity,
 And cast down to the dust!

What though false judges do me damn
 As Susan was most chaste,
Yet by a Daniel sure I am
 To be absolved at the last.

The Lord send me a judge upright,
 To listen to my cause:
Then doubt I not to put to flight
 Those that now lie and gloze.

Now whither shall I for remedy
 Seek that I may it find?
Thou, Lord, direct my steps ready
 To some that will me friend.

The clergy say, I am heresy,
 With me they fight apace:
For fashion[1] blinds them so wilfully,
 They have no better grace.

Learned men, which did me defend,
 Do now their judgment turn;
For living's sake they do intend
 Like wandering stars to run.

The lawyers say, they could not thrive
 Since scripture came in place;
Their vantage is when men do strive,
 And not by truth and peace.

The gentlemen, which once me had
 In praise and eke in price,
Now say, for them I am too sad,
 And would have them be wise.

[[1] "For fashed," orig. edit.]

The merchant-man saith, he must live,
And cannot with me gain;
But all to riches his mind doth give
With much danger and pain.

Women say, they must needs obey
Their husbands when they list:
Therefore in them I may not say
To have any great trust.

The common sort unlearned be,
To them I may not lean:
They know not by divinity
My cause for to maintain.

Thus have all persons some pretence
From me quite to decline;
And am put to my own defence,
To keep myself from ruin.

Yet in this may I glory plain,
That, though with few I stand,
I am of power and strength certain
More than all my foes' band.

For God so hath endued my tongue
With wisdom and with grace,
That I can shew their doings wrong,
Which dare stand face to face.

Therefore mine enemies villainously
Put me from men's hearings,
Lest I should most manifestly
Tell them of their leasings.

For this they would out of men's eyes
God's word to keep so high;
That where they preach boldly lies
None might against them reply.

All to maintain their pomp and pride,
Their belly, sloth and ease,
They force me in thraldom to hide,
For that I them displease.

Ah, England! what is the trespass,
That against God thou hast done?
That thou wouldst love darkness, alas,
More than light of the sun!

Ah, isle of most nobility!
Why art thou become band
To that proud harlot's falsity,
The ruin of all the land?

Woe that I must that day behold,
Which came to make thee free!
I would I had thee never told
The truth in each degree.

Then were thy sin much more less,
Which knowledge maketh great,
And of the same mightst seek redress,
To turn away the threat.

This damnation God doth say,
The Father of all right,
"That light is come now of the day,
Yet in darkness men more delight."

Thus do I weep with abundant tears,
With sighs and eke with groans.
Ah, that men will not give their ears
Unto my lawful moans!

Finis quod[1] JOHN BRADFORD.

[[1] "Quod:" quoth, saith, or said.]

ON AFFLICTION[1].

MS. on fly-leaf of copy of Tyndale's New Testament, Jugge, 1548, Holograph 1.

In the midst of my misery
To God will I make my moan,
And patiently abide
Till he shall hear my groan.

And therefore thou enemy
Rejoice not at my fall:
For, through the goodness of my God,
Get up again I shall.

Though now for God's good time
In darkness I do sit,
Yet doubtless will his mercy great
Restore me to his light.

In the meanwhile will I
Myself patiently sustain,
His anger and displeasure eke,
Though it be to my pain:

For I have sinned sore
Against his goodness oft.
Howbeit I know he will eftsoons
Set my poor soul aloft,

To see his light to my comfort
And gladding of my heart,
When without means shall fall
Death his grievous dart.

J. B.

[[1] The following twenty-four lines are now printed for the first time. See Vol. I. p. 253, and p. 248, editorial preface to "Meditations from the autograph of John Bradford," there printed for the first time, where see account of the New Testament, upon a fly-leaf of which these lines were written.]

REMAINS,

FOR THE MOST PART HITHERTO UNPUBLISHED,

OF BISHOPS RIDLEY, HOOPER, AND OTHERS.

THE VISITORS TO PROTECTOR SOMERSET[2].

[CAMBRIDGE, *May* 18, 1549.]

IT may please your grace to be advertised, that, according as it was committed unto us, we have diligently travailed in this present visitation of the university; and, proceeding in the same, from college to college, are now passed Clare Hall, the state whereof these two days we have throughbly pervised, and communed with the company. And, because the same house doth contain one of the chief points that we have in commandment, we have thought it good to certify your grace of our proceeding therein, what we have done, what answer we have received of the master and fellows there, and what stay we have taken hitherto amongst them. State Paper Office.

At our coming thither, calling the master and fellows severally before us, we declared unto them, as we had in instructions, that it was the king's majesty's pleasure to alter their house, to unite it and Trinity Hall together, and of them to make one college of civil law; and that we would, according to his highness' will and commandment, provide for the master and every fellow and scholar of the house, so as he should be well contented, desiring their conformity and consent that they would be ready with their good-will to accomplish the king's majesty's foresaid pleasure. Whereunto their answer was, that they were well contented that the king's majesty's pleasure for the alteration of their house should take effect, and that they would be ready to depart and give place. Marry, they would not themselves by their consent surrender or give up their house: "because," say they, "we be sworn to the maintenance of the corporation of our college, so much as shall lie in us." In this answer

[[2] This letter is now published for the first time.
It is printed here, to accompany the letter of bishop Ridley, which next follows. The ensuing pieces of bishops Ridley and Hooper are included in this volume, as it affords the opportunity of giving them to the members of the Parker Society. With regard to the subject of this letter, see Bp Ridley's Works, Letter I. pp. 327—30, Park. Soc.; and Life of Bp Ridley by Ridley, pp. 263—75, Lond. 1763.]

they all agree, and cannot by any persuasions be brought to give their consents to the alteration of their college.

Wherefore, having set a stay in all things there, so that they cannot alter, alienate or dispose anything otherwise than it is at this present, leaving them in expectation of a further order to be taken by us, before our departing, touching the said alteration, we go forward with other colleges, most humbly desiring your grace to know your grace's further pleasure in the point. For the which cause we have sent up the bearer, who can declare further unto your grace concerning our proceedings. And thus we desire almighty God to prosper all your grace's affairs with the increase of honour.

From Canterbury, the 18th of May, 1549.

Your grace's ever at commandment,

THOMAS ELIEN., NICHOLAS ROFFEN., JOANN. CHEKE, WILLIAM MAY, THOMAS WENDY.

To my lord protector's grace.

BP RIDLEY TO PROTECTOR SOMERSET[1].

[CAMBRIDGE, *May* 18, 1549.]

MS. Original, Holograph. And MS. transcript. State Paper Office.

It may please your grace to be advised concerning our proceeding in the visitation of the university of Cambridge, specially in that point of our instructions pretending to the uniting of Clare Hall to Trinity Hall for the study of the law: wherein I thought it my bound duty to signify unto your grace, besides our common letters, also with these my private letters the privities of my heart and conscience in that matter, nothing doubting but, as I shall disclose my mind unto your grace with your grace's leave frankly and plainly, and that moved upon[2] conscience and for fear of the offence of God, so likewise your grace, having before your grace's eyes the fear of God, will take in good worth the uttering of the same. For, as I do knowledge my bound duty to be no less than to be ready to serve the king's highness and your grace in God to the uttermost of my small power, wit, or learning, so I am assuredly persuaded, that it [is] neither the king's majesty's nor your

[1 This letter is now printed for the first time.]

[2 "upon," "and endued," "to whom," supplied from transcript, the autograph MS. being injured.]

grace's pleasure that in the execution of any such service I should do anything wherein I should judge myself to offend almighty God, or not to have in the doing of the same a clear quiet conscience.

It may please therefore your grace to wit that, when I consider this kind of uniting of these two colleges (the matter standing as by our common letters is signified unto your grace), I cannot but think it to be a very sore thing, a great slander to them that shall presently hear of the matter, and a dangerous example to the world to come, to take a college founded for the study of God's word, and to apply it to the use of students in man's laws—to take it, I mean, without the consent of the present possessioners of the same. For the history of Naboth['s][3] vineyard, taken away without the possessioner['s] good-will, which I have heard at divers times gravely preached in the court, doth terribly sound in mine ears, and maketh me to tremble when I hear of anything sounding to the like. I consider also, and it like your grace, that the fundatrix' purpose was wondrous godly, her fact was godly: so that in my judgment no fault can be found either in her intent, or in the mean ways whereby she wrought to accomplish the same, which were the glory of God and the setting forth of his word: and, if we do allow thus both her intent and the circumstances of the same, seeing that her fact is ratified by her death and thus approved of the living, methink St Paul's words doth much confirm it when he saith: *Hominis licet testamentum,* Gal. iii. *tamen sit comprobatum, nemo re*[*scindit*], *aut addit aliquid:* ["Though it be but a man's covenant, yet, if it be confirmed, no man disannulleth or addeth thereto."]

I consider also, not only what learned men may be brought up there in time to come, but also how many hath been already, some such as I think it is hard for the whole university to match them with the like. I will speak now but of one—I mean Master Latimer[4], which is, as I do think, a man appointed of God, and endued[2] with excellent gifts of grace to set forth God's word, to whom[2] in my judgment not only the king's majesty and his honourable council, but also the whole

[[3] The MSS. read, "Nabal."]

[[4] Latimer "was chosen fellow of Clare Hall, in the autumn of 1509, while yet an undergraduate."—Memoir of Bp Latimer by Corrie, in Works of L., Vol. I. p. ii. Park. Soc.]

realm is much bound, not only for his constant maintenance and defence of God's truth when papists and persecution did assault the godly, but also for that now he preacheth the gospel so purely, and so earnestly and freely rebuketh the world of his wickedness. Alexander, if I do right remember the history, in the victorious course of his conquest did spare a city for the memory of the famous poet Homer['s] sake[1]. Latimer far passeth that poet: and the king's highness, by your grace's advice, shall also excel that gentile prince in all kind of mercy and clemency.

Thus I am moved to make my most humble petition unto[2] your grace, not so much for the students of that college now being—of the which, if the report which is made of some of them be found true, I think no less but that some of them are worthy to be expulsed both thence and out of[2] the university, and some other grievously to be punished, to the[2] example of others—as for the study of God's word, that it may, according to the godly will of the fundatrix, continue there.

Finally, if it shall be otherwise seen unto your grace's wisdom, then I beseech your grace to give me leave with your grace's favour so to order myself, or by mine absence thence for the time, or by my silence, that I shall need to do no fact therein contrary to the judgment or peace of my conscience.

These things thus moved I have also the more boldly written unto your grace, because your grace, as methought most godly moved, willed and commanded once me in your grace's gallery at London so to do by my private letters whensoever I should think me[2] to have just occasion. Thus I wish most entirely your grace evermore to increase in all godliness, to the setting forth of God's glory, and to the attaining of your grace's own endless honour and salvation.

Your grace's humble and daily orator of his bound duty,

NICHOLAS ROFFENSIS.

To my lord protector's grace
be this delivered.

[[1] The house of the poet Pindar was spared by Alexander the Great, when the other buildings in the city of Thebes were destroyed, B.C. 335.]

[[2] "to," "of," "to the," "me," supplied from early transcript, the autograph MS. being injured.]

[REPLY OF BP RIDLEY TO BP HOOPER ON THE VESTMENT CONTROVERSY, 1550.

This treatise has never before been published. The original MS. is the property of Sir Thomas Phillipps, Bart., of Middlehill, near Worcester, to whose kindness in permitting a transcript to be executed the members of the Parker Society are greatly indebted. The respected proprietor however of that MS. having for some months mislaid it in his very extensive collection, it has not been possible for the editor to collate the transcript with the original. Various blanks having been left in the transcript, where the copyist had failed to decypher the original, every such blank is indicated by the usual mark ....

A fragment of the treatise or letter of bishop Hooper, to which the present treatise of bishop Ridley is a reply, and which is the only portion of it known to exist, is given by Glocester Ridley, in his Life of bishop Ridley, p. 316, London, 1763. It is as follows:

"Pauli doctrina hæc est (Gal. iii), quod quicunque revocat res abrogatas in Christo transgreditur voluntatem Domini. Atque idem manifeste docet Aaronis sacerdotium in Christi sacerdotio esse abolitum (Heb. vii, viii, ix, x), cum omnibus suis ritibus, vestibus, unctionibus, consecrationibus, et similibus. Si igitur istæ Aaronici sacerdotii umbræ cum Christi sacerdotio consistere non possunt, multo minus papisticum illud sacerdotium, quod vel suorum librorum testimonio aut ab Aarone aut ab ethnicis desumptum est. Neque vero mysterio suo caret, quod Servator noster Jesus Christus nudus in cruce pendebat. Nam Aaronici sacerdotes in suo ministerio vestimentis utebantur, quia sacerdotii ipsorum veritas, Christus ipse, nondum venerat: Christus vero, quando ipse esset sacrificandus, omnibus vestibus exutus, suum ex eo sacerdotium ostendens, quod, cum ipsa esset veritas, nullis jam amplius opus haberet velaminibus aut umbris.—Ex libro MS. D. Hoperi reg. consiliariis ab ipso exhibito, 3 Oct. 1550."

"The doctrine of Paul is this (Gal. iii), that whosoever recalls things abrogated in Christ transgresses the will of the Lord. And the same Paul openly teaches that the priesthood of Aaron has been abolished in the priesthood of Christ (Heb. vii, viii, ix, x), with all its rites, vestments, unctions, consecrations, and the like. If therefore those shadows of the Aaronic priesthood cannot consist with the priesthood of Christ, much less that popish priesthood, which even by the testimony of their own books has been derived either from Aaron or from the Gentiles. Neither does it indeed want its own mystery, that our Saviour Jesus Christ did hang naked on the cross. For the Aaronic priests used vestments in their ministry, because the truth of their priesthood, Christ himself, had not come: but Christ, when himself was to be sacrificed, was divested of all his vestments, showing his priesthood by this, that, because he was the truth itself, he now no longer had need of any veils or shadows.—From the MS. book of Master Hooper, exhibited by him to the king's counsellors, October 3, 1550."

The following extracts from the MS. Privy Council Books of Edward VI. refer to the case of bishop Hooper, and are of historical interest:

"At Greenwich, the 15th of May, 1550. ... Master Hoper was constituted bishop of Gloucester."

"At Richmond, the 6th of October, 1550.... A letter to the bishop of London, that whereas there hath been some difference betwixt him and the elect bishop of Gloucester, upon certain ceremonies belonging to the making of a bishop, wherein their lordships' desire is, because they would in no wise the stirring up of controversies betwixt men of one profession, did send for him, willing him to cease the occasions hereof; who humbly required, that he might for declaration of his doings put in writing such arguments as moved him to be of the opinion he held.

Which thing was granted, and [he] was by their lordships commanded to be at the court on Sunday next, bringing with him that he shall for answer have thought convenient."

"At Greenwich, the thirteenth of January, 1551.... This day Master Hoper, bishop of Gloucester, appeared before the Council touching his old matter of denial to wear such apparel as other bishops wear; and, having been before commanded to keep his house unless it were to go to the bishop of Canterbury, Ely, London, or Lincoln, for counsel or satisfaction of his conscience in that matter, and further, neither to preach nor read till he had further licence from the Council, it appeared both that he had not kept his house, and that he had also written and printed a book, wherein was contained matter that he should not have written. For the which, and for that also he persevered in his former opinion of not wearing the bishops' apparel, he was now committed to the bishop of Canterbury's custody, either there to be reformed, or further to be punished as the obstinacy of his case requireth."

"At Greenwich the 27th of January, 1551....Upon a letter from the archbishop of Canterbury, that Master Hoper cannot be brought to any conformity, but rather persevering in his obstinacy coveteth to prescribe orders and necessary laws of his head, it was agreed he should be committed to the Fleet.—A letter to the archbishop of Canterbury, to send Master Hoper to the Fleet upon the occasion aforesaid.—A letter to the warden of the Fleet, to receive the said Master Hoper, and to keep him from conference of any person, saving the ministers of that house[1]."

It is satisfactory to know that bishop Hooper's Christian candour induced him explicitly to acknowledge his error, and unreservedly to yield the matter which had been in debate between himself and bishop Ridley and archbishop Cranmer.

See letters of Hooper in Works of H., Vol. II. pp. xiv—xvi, Park. Soc.; also letters of Hooper, Micronius, Burcher, Martyr, Uthenhovius, nos. XXXIX., XL., CCLXIII., CCLXIV., CCCXVIII., CCXXX., CCLXX., in "Original Letters," or "Epistolæ Tigurinæ," Park. Soc.; letters of Bucer in Bucer. Script. Angl. pp. 681—84, 705—10, Basil. 1577, and in Strype, Ecc. Mem. Edward, Originals, Book I. LL and NN, Vol. II. part ii. pp. 444—65, Oxf. 1822; letter of a Lasco in Gerdes. Scrin. Antiq., Tom. II. pars II. pp. 656—70, Groning. et Brem. 1750—60; letter of Abp Cranmer, no. CCXCII. in Works of C., Vol. II. p. 428, Park. Soc.; letter of Martyr, no. IV. ad calc. Martyr. Loc. Comm., pp. 859—61, Amst. et Franc. 1656, and translated, no. 37, appended to Martyr's Common Places, pp. 116—20, London, 1583; and Bp Ridley's letter, no. IX., Works of R. pp. 355—58, Park. Soc.

The reader can also consult bishop Burnet's History of the Reformation, Part II. book I. Vol. II. pp. 242—46, and Part III. book IV. Vol. III. pp. 299—306, ed. Nares; Strype, Ecc. Mem., Edward VI. Book I. ch. xxviii. Vol. II. part I. pp. 350—55, Oxf. 1822; and Strype, Life of Cranmer, Book II. ch. xvii. Vol. I. pp. 302—9, Oxf. 1812; Foxe, Acts, &c. ed. 1583, pp. 1503—5, or ed. 1843—9, Vol. VI. pp. 640—43. Gerdes. Hist. Reform. Tom. IV. p. 374, Groning. et Brem. 1744—52; Ridley's Life of bishop Ridley, pp. 309—24, Lond. 1763; Soames, Hist. of Reformation, Vol. III. pp. 561—67, Lond. 1826—28; Preface by Cardwell to Two Books of Common Prayer of Edw. VI., pp. xxi—xxiv, Oxf. 1841; and Life of bishop Hooper, prefixed to his Works, Vol. II. pp. xii—xvi, Park. Soc.]

[[1] From the original MSS. in the Privy Council Office. Manuscript copies of the Council Books of Edward VI. exist in the British Museum, Addit. MSS. 14,026. These extracts are printed in Henry Wharton's (under the name, Anthony Harmer) Specimen of Errors in Bp Burnet's History of the Reformation, pp. 93–95, London, 1693.]

REPLY OF BISHOP RIDLEY TO BISHOP HOOPER ON THE VESTMENT CONTROVERSY, 1550[2].

MS. in possession of Sir T. Phillipps, Bart.

......[3]all the world should know I do grant......the appointed vestments be neither things to be re[garded]...of necessity to our health and salvation, or yet...as [if] without them the ministry might not...be done; nor that this use of them is...in scripture, nor that the same doth justify the doer and user by God's holy word. For so to say were indeed to defend the papistical and Aaronical priesthood both, against Christ's gospel. But all our controversy is in this, whether the vestments as they be now appointed by the authority of the church of England be things lawful to be used, or may be used without the breach of God's law: that is, whether they be things as of themselves indifferent, and not forbidden as sin against God's holy word or no.

Status Controversiæ.

My brother elect saith, 'They be things unlawful to be used.' He saith, that 'they may not be used without the breach of God's law.' He saith that 'they be not things indifferent, but very sin, for they be things forbidden by the word of God.' And I say plainly, in few words, that herein my brother elect doth err, and condemneth that to be sin of itself, that God never forbade, ungodly adding his own fantasy unto God's word. And herein standeth the whole state or point of this present controversy.

An ans[wer delivere]d unto the king hi[s most honorab]le council at their [meeting by] Nicholas bishop of London [to John] Hooper elect bishop of Glouce[ster on the use] of the appointed vestmen[ts in the] church of England.

"Nothing should be," &c.

In the first argument, which [is the] principal of all his whole treatise, I do note four fa[ults,] two in the major, and as many in the minor. In the major the first, that it is an insufficient division, for it lacketh one necessary member: for there

[[2] This treatise is now printed for the first time.]
[[3] The first page of the original MS. is wanting.]

be many things to be used in the church, which be neither expressed in the word of God, nor yet be things indifferent; as all such as, although they have not the express word, yet be employed in scripture, and may be by collation and conference of scripture truly deduced of the same, which in his second note hereafter he calleth God's commandments, although the examples there set forth for the same in every point I cannot allow.

Secondly, the said proposition in his second member of his division declareth the nature of a thing indifferent amiss, and contrary unto his own doctrine in his third note: for it is not necessary to that, that a thing be of itself indifferent, that the use thereof be not profitable, or the non use be not harmful. For many things of themselves be indifferent, whereof the use is profitable, and the non use harmful; as the due observation of all good ecclesiastical discipline in things which of their own nature be indifferent; as the times appointed for common prayer, preaching of God's word and receiving of the sacraments. The due use of these and such like do profit, for they do edify, and the wilful breaker of such is counted of St Paul contentious and [an] adversary to godly order in the church. Of the which he saith, *Si quis videtur esse contentiosus, nos ejusmodi consuetudinem non habemus, neque ecclesia Dei:* ["If any man seem to be contentious, we have not any custom of that sort, nor the church of God."]

In the minor neither is it true that he saith, 'The vestments be not things indifferent,' nor the proof that he bringeth thereof, by his four notes devised of himself without any ground; as shall by God's grace appear hereafter evidently in my answer following.

The first note or condition: 'Things indifferent should have their original.'

It is not necessary that all things necessary have their original and ground, as this note teacheth, of the word of God: for, although such ground, I grant, is always indeed to be required in things to be believed and done of necessity unto salvation, yet that is not required in all things that be of themselves indifferent. The proof that the writer hath here is not good, but is a sophistical fallacy, called, I ween, *fallacia amphibologiæ.* For 'not to be of faith' hath diverse significations.

St Paul, Rom. xiv., taketh it, for to be contrary to the persuasion of the faith and judgment of conscience: so St Paul is there to be understanded. But so it is not true, that what cannot be proved by the word of God is not of faith so taken—that is to say, is contrary to the persuasion of my faith. For then to take up a straw were a deadly sin; for, that thou shouldest so do, it is not found in the word of God. But if thou understand 'not to be of faith,' for not to be taken as an article of faith, then it is true, that what cannot be proved by the word of God is not of faith. But then it maketh nothing for the matter to be proved: for to have vestments is not an article of the faith, but a thing indifferent.

The second note or condition: 'Though the thing have her original,' &c.

This second note presupposeth the first for a sure ground, which was set upon the sand, and is ambiguous, obscure, and doubtful how the parties can stand together. For if they have their original in scripture, and can be proved of God's word, and be of faith as is said in the first note, how can they be such as neither be commanded nor forbidden in scripture, but must be left free to be done or undone, at the judgment of every man's conscience?

And whereas it is said, that the thing indifferent is to be left free to use it or not use it, as it shall seem profitable or disprofitable unto the conscience of the user, this is true in things indifferent not commanded thus, or so to be used, by an order: but in public ordinance it is not lawful, except in a lawful urgent cause, or in a case of necessity, to break the same; for then thou showest thyself a disordered person, disobedient, as [a] contemner of lawful authority, and a wounder of thy weak brother his conscience.

Then peradventure thou wilt say, 'Ye bring us again in bondage of the law, and do deprive us of our liberty.' I answer, No, for I make it not a matter of justification, but of order; and to be under the law is another thing. For the Christian liberty is not a licence to do what thou list, but to serve God in newness of thy mind, and for love, and not for servile fear.

And whereas it is said, 'If it be agreeable,' &c., the condition is superfluous, for it cannot be but if it have the express word of God, or may thereupon necessarily be deduced, but it must needs be agreeable unto faith, for God's word is the rule of faith.

The third note or condition: 'They must have a manifest and open utility, known in the church,' &c.—They should indeed edify, *juxta illud, Omnia ad ædificationem fiant,* [according to that, "Let all things be done to edifying,"] &c. And if they edify indeed, whether the profit be manifest and openly known, or but of a few privately known, they are not to be rejected. But how agreeable this note with his saying in the first, 'That a thing indifferently used profiteth not.' *Conveniet nulli, qui secum dissidet ipse:* 'How shall he agree with another, that cannot agree with himself?'

The fourth note or condition: 'Things indifferent should be instituted in the church,' &c.—Lenity indeed is required in the law-maker, and all tyranny to be eschewed. Nevertheless to teach that Christian liberty is free to use and not use, even as every man list, ordinances well made by lawful authority, is a seditious doctrine and liable to confound a good order. And where he saith, 'that things indifferent, degenerated, and abused, are no more indifferent,' this is true *ex accidente*, and not otherwise. For in such if the right use be profitable, and may be restored, and the abuse more easily taken away than the thing itself, then such are not, because they have been abused, to be taken away, but to be reformed and amended, and so kept still.

After these four notes now devised, are moved three things unto the magistrates. The first, 'that the matter pertaineth nothing unto them:' the second, 'to warn them of their foes:' and the third, 'a promise of maintenance unto death.'

The first is unreasonable, to say that the civil state hath not to meddle with this matter; for they have to meddle and maintain their own acts: but this matter is already defined both by the civil and ecclesiastical states. Therefore it must needs follow, that, before it be proved to be against God's law, they are bound both to model and maintain it, as their own fact. Yea, though there were no such act, yet, like as the spiritual minister ought by God's word to maintain the lawful authority of the civil magistrate, and to teach the people due obedience unto the same, according unto God's ordinance, so the civil magistrates must maintain, against the evil and disobedient, in all godliness, both the ecclesiastical minister in his ministry, and all godly ecclesiastical policy, as all godly Christian magistrates have heretofore done. But this is an old complaint of the Donatists and such like heretics, in St Augustine's days, which, being disobedient unto the ecclesiastical ministers, for their errors were duly punished of the civil powers[1]. And this to be a princely office only appertaining unto kings, princes, and unto the chief magistrates, is learnedly and substantially proved by the said writer, both by holy scripture, and also by many divers examples of most godly princes[2]. Wherefore neither the spiritual minister hath to be ashamed of this kind of begging of the civil assistance, nor the civil powers ought to deny it, seeing it is their office appointed them of God.

In the second thing this is uncharitable, to labour to bring all spiritual ministers that do allow and approve the order of the Book of Common Prayer into the hatred of the magistrates, by such odious terms, 'their foes, masking, dreaming, children of this world, superstitious and blind, and such like.'—This saying savoureth either of so great a presumption and confidence, as if a man should think that he is able to prove by his eloquence whatsoever he list (which is a perilous and a dangerous vice of a haughty stomach), or else of a too vile and too base an estimation of the magistrates, as though, otherwise than thus monished, they were not able to discern who are their friends, and who are their foes, who do maintain their estate by God's word in truth and in deed, and who can coll[3]

[1 De persecutionibus etiam quas perpeti se queruntur [Donatistæ], multa in suis literis posuerunt.—August. Brevic. collat. cum Donatist. tert. diei, cap. viii. Op. Tom. IX. col. 561, ed. Bened. Par. 1679—1700. Vide Contr. epist. Parmen. Lib. I. cap. viii. col. 19; Contr. Gaudent. Lib. I. cap. xviii.—xxviii. cols. 642—52; Contr. Lit. Petil. Lib. I. cap. xviii.—xxiii. Lib. II. cap. x.—xxiii. lxvi. lxvii. lxxi. lxxix.—c. cols. 213, 5, 223—35, 260, 1, 2, 266—88. See also Neander, Church History, Vol. III. pp. 258—308, Lond. 1850—52.]

[2 Nam et temporibus prophetarum omnes reges, qui in populo Dei non prohibuerunt nec everterunt quæ contra Dei præcepta fuerant instituta, culpantur; et quæ prohibuerunt et everterunt super aliorum merita laudantur. Et rex Nabuchodonosor...divino correctus miraculo piam et laudabilem legem pro veritate constituit, ut quicumque diceret blasphemiam in Deum verum Sidræ, Misæ, et Abdenago, cum domo sua penitus interiret.—Id. Lib. de correct. Donatist. seu Ad Bonifac. Epist. CLXXXV. cap. ii. Op. Tom. II. col. 646. See also cap. ii.—xi. cols. 645—63, and references in last note.]

[3 See p. 87, note 7, above.]

them and flatter them with glorious terms under the pretence of God's word, to maintain their own bold rashness, and to the subversion of all good and godly order.

The third thing (which is 'a promise of maintenance unto death') is a magnifical promise set forth with a stout style. But we have seen oftentimes great clouds and small rain, and heard great cracks of thunder, and (thanks be unto God) small harm done. I would wish us all well to remember St Paul's good lessons, 1 Cor. viii., *Si quis sibi videtur aliquid scire, nondum aliquid novit ut oportet:* ["If any man seemeth to himself to know anything, he knoweth not anything yet as he
1 Cor. iii. ought."] And again, *Si quis videtur sibi esse sapiens in hoc mundo, stultus fiat, ut reddatur sapiens:* ["If any man seemeth to himself to be wise in this world, let him become a fool, that he may be rendered wise."] And to make up the third place,
1 Cor. viii. *Scientia inflat, caritas ædificat:* ["Knowledge puffeth up, charity edifieth."] Which charity I beseech God send us each one toward another in our hearts, with an earnest carefulness to "keep the unity of the Spirit in the bond of peace." Amen.

OF VESTMENTS.

Now unto his first argument grounded upon the first note may be said, *Debile fundamentum fallit opus:* 'Where the foundation is not surely laid, how can the building abide?' But the foundation hereof, which was the first note of things indifferent, was framed together amiss, of scriptures wrong understanded, as is touched before in the annotation made upon the first note. Wherefore the lack of that property doth not exclude the vestments appointed to be things indifferent. And, where it is said that 'they show the pharisaical superstition and priesthood of Aaron,' first, if it be meant that Aaron's priesthood was pharisaical superstition, it is blasphemously spoken against God's holy ordinance: and, secondly, it is to be denied that they represent either the pharisaical superstition or Aaron's priesthood; as it may appear unto them that have read the form, fashion, and number of Aaron's mystical
Exod xxviii. garments in holy scripture, or St Hierom's description of the
Hieronymus ad Fabiolam. same in his epistles[1].

[[1] Vide Hieron. Epist. LXIV. (al. CXXXVII.) 19. Ad Fabiolam, De veste sacerdotali. Op. Tom. I. cols. 364—6, stud. Vallars. Veron. 1734—42.]

Now to the places of Polydore and Celestine. Admit this saying of Polydore: *Undecunque manarint, magis omnino Hebraica quam apostolica referunt instituta*[2]: [From whence soever these things may have flowed down, they altogether rather rehearse Hebrew than apostolic institutions.] I pray you, what reason is this, *ergo* they be not things indifferent? And, if this reason be not meant, to what purpose is this saying of Polydore here brought? And to that he saith, *In exordio surgentis ecclesiæ sacerdotes nihil [super]induere consuevisse, rem divinam facturos*[3], &c. [At the beginning of the rising church the priests, when about to conduct divine worship, were not accustomed to put on any additional garment]—although in some things instance may be given by more ancient and authentic than Polydore is of, as *de petalo pontificali*, [concerning the sacerdotal plate,] whereof Eusebius in *Ecclesiastica Historia* maketh mention in two diverse places[4]—yet admit Polydore's saying true, as surely I think it is after his meaning true, what followeth thereof? 'It is not lawful, for because they did it not.' This is a deceitful argument, and the very mother and well-spring of many both old and new schisms. Of old as of them that called themselves *Apostolicos* or *Apotacticas*[5], and

[2 Polyd. Vergil. De inventoribus rerum, Lib. IV. cap. vii., De primo ritu sacrorum, quibus initiantur ii qui sacerdotes fiunt, et amiciendi usu, ac ibidem de sacerdotis officii initio, p. 257, Amstel. 1671.]

[3 ...ab Hebræis sumptum est, ut...vestimenta ipsa sacerdotibus aliisque initiatis assignarentur...Quod Stephanus pontifex primus apud nostros primo faciendum statuit: nam in exordio surgentis religionis sacerdotes rem divinam facturi nihil superinduere consueverunt, cum potius sese intrinsecus animi virtutibus vestire, ac vitiis corporis exuere studerent, quam novos sumere apparatus... — Id. ibid. Lib. VI. cap. xii. pp. 415, 16.]

[4 Eusebius, on the authority of Polycrates, bishop of Ephesus, states concerning the apostle John, that he "bore the sacerdotal plate." *Ἔτι δὲ καὶ Ἰωάννης ὁ ἐπὶ τὸ στῆθος τοῦ Κυρίου ἀναπεσὼν, ὃς ἐγένηθη ἱερεὺς τὸ πέταλον πεφορεκὼς, καὶ μάρτυς καὶ διδάσκαλος. οὗτος ἐν Ἐφέσῳ κεκοίμηται.*—Polycr. Episc. Ephes. Epist. ad Vict. Episc. Rom. in Euseb. Hist. Eccl. Lib. III. cap. xxxi. pp. 102, 3, ed. Vales. Mogunt. 1672. The same words occur also, Lib. V. cap. xxiv. p. 191, on which place Valesius (annot. p. 104) observes: "De pontificatu Judæorum hæc non esse accipienda satis apparet...Quod autem de lamina dicit Polycrates, credibile est primos illos Christianorum pontifices exemplo Judaicorum pontificum hoc honoris insigne gestasse."]

[5 Apostolici, qui se isto nomine arrogantissime vocaverunt, eo quod in suam communionem non reciperent utentes conjugibus et res proprias possidentes: quales habet catholica et monachos et clericos plurimos. Sed ideo isti hæretici sunt, quoniam se ab ecclesia separantes nullam spem putant eos habere, qui utuntur his rebus, quibus ipsi carent. Encraticis isti similes sunt: nam et Apotacticæ [id est, Renuntiatores, *annot. ed. Bened.*] appellantur. Sed et alia nescio

of the Aerians[1]: of new in our days of the Anabaptists, who, considering neither the diversity of times concerning the external ecclesiastical polity, nor the true liberty of the Christian religion in extern rites and ceremonies, in matters neither commanded nor forbidden in God's law, nor the power of magistrates in the Christian congregation concerning the same, have boldly enterprised to stir up many heinous errors; as to make that necessary, and of necessity unto salvation, which though the apostles did it, yet they thought it to be left free to be done or not done, as the Holy Ghost should teach Christ's congregation from time to time what should be best; or to forbid and to make that sin which God never forbade, wickedly thus bringing in bondage the Christian liberty, and ungodly adding unto God's word.

And here is to be noted, that to make of things indifferent by lawful authority wholesome ordinances is not to add unto God's word, as the unlearned weeneth: but to command that as a thing of necessity, which God's word doth not require, or to forbid that for a thing of itself unlawful which God's word doth not forbid, this is to add unto God's word.

If this reason should take place, 'The apostles used it not, *ergo* it is not lawful for us to use it'—or this either, 'They did it, *ergo* we must needs do it'—then all Christians may have no place abiding, all must, under pain of damnation, depart with their possessions, as Peter said they did, *Ecce nos reliquimus omnia*, ["Behold, we have left all things,"] &c.; we may have no ministration of Christ's sacraments in churches, for they had no churches, but were fain to do all in their own houses; we must baptize abroad in the fields as the apostles did; we may not receive the holy communion but at supper, and with

quæ propria hæretica docere perhibentur.—August. Lib. de Hæres. XL. Op. Tom. VIII. col. 11, ed. Bened. Par. 1679—1700.]

[[1] Aëriani ab Aerio quodam sunt, qui cum esset presbyter, doluisse fertur quod episcopus non potuit ordinari, et in Arianorum hæresim lapsus propria quæque dogmata addidisse nonnulla, dicens, offerri pro dormientibus non oportere, nec statuta solemniter celebranda esse jejunia, sed cum quisque voluerit jejunandum, ne videatur esse sub lege. Dicebat etiam presbyterum ab episcopo nulla differentia debere discerni. Quidam perhibent istos, sicut Encraticas vel Apotacticas, non admittere ad communionem suam nisi continentes, et eos qui sæculo ita renuntiaverint, ut propria nulla possideant. Ab esca tamen carnium non eos abstinere dicit Epiphanius: Philaster vero et hanc eis tribuit abstinentiam.—Id. ibid. LIII. col. 18. See also Mosheim, Hist. Eccl., cent. IV. part II. ch. iii. 21; and Neander, Church History, Vol. III. pp. 486, 7, Lond. 1850—52.]

the table furnished with other meats, as the Anabaptists do now stiffly and obstinately affirm that it should be; our naming of the child in baptism, our prayer upon him, our crossing, and our threefold abrenunciation[2], and our white chrisom[3], all must be left, for these we cannot prove by God's word, that the apostles did use them. And, if to do anything which we cannot prove that they did be sin, then a greatest part is sin that we do daily in baptism. What followeth then other things, than to receive the Anabaptists' opinion, and to be baptized anew? O wicked folly and blind ignorancy!

The third place of Polydore, where he saith, "The use of linen vestments in holy rites descended from the Egyptians by the Hebrews unto us[4]," maketh no more against vestments now appointed in the church than the saying of the same Polydore, *Libro* IV. *capite* iv., of the baptism of Moses[5], maketh against the baptism which is by God's word now used in the church.

Unto Celestine's saying, "that the priests should be known from the people by their doctrine, not by their apparel[6]," I say, I wish the writer to have read and remembered here the learned answer that my lord of Canterbury maketh unto the

[2 Namely, of "the devil and all his works," of "the vain pomp and glory of the world, with all the covetous desires of the same," and of "the carnal desires of the flesh."—See Liturgies of Edward VI., Book of Common Prayer, 1549, Public Baptism, p. 111, Park. Soc.]

[3 "Then the godfathers and godmothers shall take and lay their hands upon the child; and the minister shall put upon him his white vesture, commonly called 'the chrisom,' and say: Take this white vesture for a token of the innocency, which by God's grace in this holy sacrament of baptism is given unto thee; and for a sign whereby thou art admonished, so long as thou livest, to give thyself to innocency of living, that, after this transitory life, thou mayest be partaker of the life everlasting. Amen."—Id. ibid. p. 112.]

[4 ...nostri sacerdotes, linteis vestimentis amicti, templum et altare adeunt, in sacrorumque pompa incedunt, ritu dubio procul ab Ægyptiis per manus Hebræorum usque ad nos translato.—Polyd. Vergil. De inventoribus rerum, Lib. IV. cap. vii. p. 256, Amstel. 1671.]

[5 Ego vero dixerim, Mosen primitus baptizandi rationem ostendisse, quippe qui baptizavit, sed in aqua solum, id est, in nube et mari: quod, teste Gregorio Nazianzeno, et baptismi Joannis et Christi exemplar fuisse constat, quando ista omnia a Deo proficiscebantur.—Id. ibid. cap. iv. p. 236.]

[6 Didicimus...quosdam Domini sacerdotes superstitioso potius cultui inservire, quam mentis vel fidei puritati....Amicti pallio, et lumbos præcincti, credunt se scripturæ fidem, non per spiritum, sed per literam completuros...Discernendi a plebe vel cæteris sumus doctrina non veste, conversatione non habitu, mentis puritate non cultu.—Cœlestin. Papæ I. Epist. II. Ad episc. provinc. Vienn. et Narbon. I. in Concil. stud. Labb. et Cossart. Tom. II. col. 1619, Lut. Par. 1671—2.]

Lib. II. cap. xii. papists, alleging such like places of Chrysostom for their monstrous transubstantiation, which is, that negatives by comparison are not simply to be understand, but by the way of comparison[1], as is declared there full diligently by many godly examples. So here, when Celestine saith, "Priests are to be known from the people by their doctrine, not by apparel," this is not meant that he damneth here all difference of honest apparel, but that that apparel is not the thing to be esteemed to be a note of difference in comparison unto learning; by the which if the priest cannot be known, the apparel is not to be regarded. And this my lord of Canterbury his answer well marked might have made the writer to have blotted out all his notes, that he maketh upon this place in the margent.

The argument drawn out of the second note of things indifferent.

In this reason the first proposition is very true, that is, the thing cannot be indifferent that God forbiddeth. Now that is said to be St Paul's doctrine, if it be rightly understanded, it is also true indeed: but the deduction of the sequel maketh me much to suspect that the writer doth here understand St Paul amiss. For Paul's doctrine of this place, *Nam si quo destruxi*, &c. (I suppose this place is meant, although obscurely set forth), that, if a man will "set up again those things which are" fulfilled in Christ, and so (as he calleth them) "destroyed, he is a trangressor"—if so be that he do the same, either that he believeth that the thing is necessary to be retained, and to be a figure still, as though the thing were not... or else that thereby he shall obtain justification, or that without that he cannot be justified. All such setting up of figures, ceremonies, rites and signs, fulfilled and abolished now in Christ, is plain

Gal. ii.

[[1] "St John Chrysostom meant not absolutely to deny that there is bread and wine, or to deny utterly the priest and the body of Christ to be there; but he useth a speech, which is no pure negative, but a negative by comparison: which fashion of speech is commonly used, not only in the scripture and among all good authors, but also in all manner of languages...As by example,...when the prophet David said in the person of Christ, 'I am a worm and not a man.'...'Christ sent me not to baptize, but to preach the gospel.'...'We do not wrestle against flesh and blood, but against the spirits of darkness.'"—Abp Cranmer, Defence of doctrine of the sacrament, Book II. Works, Vol. I. p. 313, or Latin version, Lib. II. cap. xii. p. 39, Park. Soc. Compare Abp Whitgift's reference to this passage of Abp Cranmer, Defence of the Answer to the Admonition, Works, Vol. I. p. 66, Park. Soc.]

transgression against Christ, setting forth of Aaron's priesthood and derogation of Christ's. Otherwise, if any of the said ceremonies, that be thought at any time for other laudable causes, as of health, or decent order, or for necessary instruction profitable, they may be used without the offence of God: as the unction in baptism and of the sick, though it be not a thing of necessity by God's word, yet, to teach the inward unction of the Holy Ghost, it may be used without the offence of God. And, to shave a man's head for his better health, he is worse than mad that dare deny it to be lawful: and so of other things, which thus be not Aaron's shadows, but as instruments of greater things to a godly purpose.

Where it is said, 'The naked hanging of Christ upon the cross lacketh not his mystery,' surely no more lacketh the purple wherein he was clad, nor the white garment wherewith Herod mocked him, in the time of his passion. Oh! this were a jolly argument for the sect of the Adamians, of the which Epiphanius saith that they assembled themselves, both men and women, naked, in the time of their divine service, to resemble the innocency of Adam and Eve in paradise[2]. And—where it is answered unto the usage of vestments in the church, before the pope was taken for head, we contend *de jure, et non de facto*—this argument, framed in his true kind, cannot be shaken off before learned men with so slight an answer: for to [condemn] the things used continually in the church, having the examples of the church before the corruption of the see of Rome, as things unlawful and against God's word, I fear me, will seem to come of a spirit that doth not proceed from the Head by the which Spirit ... [in the] bond of peace all the lively members of Christ be knit together.

To the entreating of the third note.

First, the writer here perceiving what may justly be said, for lack of authority or reason wherewith he should have confuted the same, he doth slide from his place, and requireth of

[[2] Ἐν δὲ τῷ εἰσιέναι, ἱματιοφύλακές εἰσί τινες πρὸς ταῖς θύραις,...καὶ ἕκαστος εἰσιὼν ἤτοι ἀνὴρ, ἤτοι γυνὴ, ἐκδυόμενος ἔξω εἴσεισι γυμνὸς, ὡς ἀπὸ μητρὸς, ὅλῳ τῷ σώματι,...ἡγοῦνται γὰρ τὴν ἑαυτῶν ἐκκλησίαν εἶναι τὸν παράδεισον, καὶ αὐτοὺς εἶναι τοὺς περὶ Ἀδὰμ καὶ Εὔαν.—Epiphan. Adv. Hær. Lib. II. Tom. i. Hær. lii. Op. Tom. I. p. 459, Par. 1622. Conf. August. Lib. de Hæres. xxxi. Tom. VIII. col. 11, ed. Bened. Par. 1679—1700.]

his adversary a further labour. Sir, a short proof is this, not framed after your appointment, for the nature of the cause needeth it not. The church hath received these vestments by lawful authority, and with an agreeable consent, for causes to them seen good and godly: and, until it shall be otherwise dispossessed by order ... and authority, we will plead a possession, and, ... if every subject shall be a judge, what profiteth or not profiteth, what order shall then follow? Wise men can judge, though you and I should both hold our peace.—As for the rest in the same note, because I perceive no strength in it that hurteth the cause of the vestments appointed, it shall not need, as methinks, to spend many words upon it. For unto a simple assertion set forth with great words, without authority or reason, what needeth a better answer, if a man will be short, than one of these two monosyllables, 'Yea,' or 'Nay,' as the matter shall require? I marvel what inconvenience is this, if minister may be known to be of that vocation by his outward garment. Nor I do ... [count it] no more an inconvenience that some be called, men of the clergy, and some, men of the laity, than in the university, that some be called 'scholars,' and some, 'men of the town,' although indeed they both dwell within one town.—But St Peter calleth all men "priests." What then, I pray you, will you thereof gather, that all men must have priests' apparel, or one kind of apparel? Then what shall we answer unto the Apoca[lypse] that calleth all men "kings"? Will you say therefore that all men must wear a princely apparel, or that the kings must wear like with all other? Truly so it is, for lack of true understanding of the scriptures all this business doth chance. And where it is said, that David and other good princes did rule the church after the perpetual and appointed laws thereunto, but the civil polity after the state and variety of causes, the further sentence is plain false; for David did set
1 Chron. xxv. an order in the temple, as it is written in the twenty-fifth of
Kings xviii. Paralipomenon, that was not before. And Hezekias the good
king, when he saw the case and state of necessity so required,
Numb. xxi. he brake asunder the brasen serpent that was set up before by
an appointed law of God's commandment.

To the entreating of the fourth note of things indifferent.

The entreating of this fourth note made me at the first not

a little to muse what the writer meant, when I saw the fourth note, and the argument that should be drawn thereof, so little to agree together. For the fourth note is, that things must be instituted with apostolical lenity, and not established by tyranny. Now who would look for other of him, that by this supposition would disapprove the vestments appointed, but that this minor or such a like should have here followed—that is to say: 'But the appointed vestments now in the church of England are not instituted by an apostolical lenity, but stablished by tyranny; wherefore they be not things indifferent.' To what purpose doth else the fourth note serve? But there was a cause why he would not thus reason, but pretendeth a society to be had with the papists, nothing remembering how both the excess and multitude, and the superstitious opinion in the Book of Common Prayer is taken away. The which thing done, the rest argueth no more a society and fellowship, than to wear short apparel, when a man doth journey, proveth a fellowship between a true man and a thief, because both do use the like form of garments. This reason moved the Aerians[1] to forsake the order of the church, and commanded their disciples that they should do the contrary of that the church did, that so they might be singular and live as they lusted, at their own liberty. Such a *Johannes ad oppositum* was one Cinesias, that would do the contrary, were it good or evil, whatsoever the Athenians did. And it is written that *Asiatici* would therefore make sacrifice of swine, and change the beginning of the year, because they would do the contrary in all things of the religion of the Jews.

But peradventure you will ask, what was the cause why the reason varieth from the fourth note? Surely, if the writer did think that the cause could not be espied, in my mind he may be compared unto him that thinketh himself well covered and invisible, when he is clad with a net.

I pray you, who hath appointed now and instituted our vestments in the church of England; and who hath established them? Hath not the archbishop with his company of learned men thereunto appointed by the king his highness and his majesty's council appointed them? Hath not the king his majesty and the whole parliament established them? If then

[[1] See p. 382, note 1, above.]

this fourth note had been followed as it was proponed, what would have followed after the wise may perceive. And, though it follow not in words, yet it is evident what followeth in meaning. Wherefore I cannot but wish the writer a better mind, both towards the composers, which was the company appointed of learned men, and also towards the parliament, which was the stablishers of the Book of Common Prayer in the church of England.

In the apostrophe unto the magistrates, the writer saith, "I dare as well defend the altar-stone, holy-bread, and holy-water, yea, and images too, with as good authority as they defend the vestments." This man putteth no difference between *adiaphora vera*, and *pseudodiaphora*, as all other men do, that write upon this matter. Now let the things he speaketh of be things of themselves indifferent, yet shall not men be able to do that he saith he dare take in him to do, that is, to defend them with as good authority as the appointed vestments may be, except either he do procure them to be authorized with like lawful authority of the magistrates, as the appointed vestments be. Or else he must confess that he counteth the magistrate's authority, in the constitution of things indifferent, to be of no force nor strength to be esteemed.

Hitherto unto certain points particularly is answered generally the whole form and manner of his reasoning. And [his] proof is *petitio principii*, or *ignotum per ignotum*, which is called in the schools *vitiosissimum genus argumentandi;* for he that frameth unto himself principles of his own device, grounded neither upon authority nor yet upon substantial reason, and thereupon the same will conclude his purpose, what is that else to say than, 'Let me first bind thee fast, both hand and foot, and I will beat thee both back and side, even at mine own pleasure'? But what folly were it to give thine adversary such an advantage upon thee! No less folly it is to grant such feeble principles without any better ground.

To the objections and answers made unto the same.

Generally neither the objections are fully made with their due form and strength, neither yet the answers do put away that poor pith that is left in them. In the answer unto the first objection the writer is deceived, thinking that God hath so straitly appointed unto man the ends of apparel only unto this or to that, and not use it as he list, so that it be without the breach of God's commandment unto his own or unto his brother's commodity, by any manner of means.

To that that is there of the decentness of the primitive church, I would wish the writer had learned one good pretty saying of St Augustine, *ad Marcellinum: Cum ipsi dicant, recte non fieri si mutetur, contra veritas clamet, recte non fieri nisi mutetur, quia utrumque tunc erit rectum, si erit pro temporum varietate diversum*[1]: [When they themselves say that a thing is not done rightly if it be changed, let truth on the other hand exclaim, that it is not done rightly if it be not changed, because both will then be right, if the diversity shall be in proportion to the change of times.] And I do not a little marvel that he will allow no respect or regard to be had either unto the diversity of times, places, or conditions of the people: whereas ancient authors do agree and say that these be reasonable causes, why ceremonies may vary, and that the variety thereof ought not to break the unity of faith; as by many examples and ancient histories is declared in *Tripartita Historia*, Lib. IX. cap. xxxviii.[2] Did not Irenæus, that excellent clerk and well learned bishop, reprove openly Victor, then the bishop of Rome, because he excommunicated those that varied from him in the observation of the feast of Easter[3]?

Afterward, where it is said, "And beareth us in hand yet to be decent, yea, and so necessary that in case it be not so accepted, if a man could use the talent," &c., I note here two things. The one is a slanderous lie, whereby the unlearned might think that the archbishop and the company of learned

[1 August. Ad Marcellin. Epist. cxxxviii. 4. Op. Tom. II. col. 411, ed. Bened. Par. 1679—1700, where, Non itaque verum est quod dicitur, semel recte factum nullatenus esse mutandum. Mutata quippe temporis causa, quod recte ante factum fuerat, ita mutari vera ratio plerumque flagitat, ut cum &c.]

[2 Vide Cassiod. Hist. Tripart. Lib. IX. cap. xxxviii. foll. T. 6, 7, Paris. s. a. The original will be found in Socrat. Hist. Eccles. Lib. v. cap. xxii. pp. 282—91, ed. Vales. Mogunt. 1677: as for instance, pp. 283, 4, 6, *οὐδαμοῦ τοίνυν ὁ ἀπόστολος οὐδὲ τὰ εὐαγγέλια, ζυγὸν δουλείας τοῖς τῷ κηρύγματι προσελθοῦσιν ἐπέθηκαν· ἀλλὰ τὴν ἑορτὴν τοῦ πάσχα καὶ τὰς ἄλλας ἑορτὰς τιμᾷν, τῇ εὐγνωμοσύνῃ τῶν εὐεργετηθέντων κατέλιπον· ... σκοπὸς μὴν οὖν γέγονε τοῖς ἀποστόλοις, οὐ περὶ ἡμερῶν ἑορταστικῶν νομοθετεῖν, ἀλλὰ βίον ὀρθὸν καὶ τὴν θεοσέβειαν εἰσηγήσασθαι·...καὶ ἐπειδὴ οὐδεὶς περὶ τούτου ἔγγραφον ἔχει δεῖξαι παράγγελμα, δῆλον ὡς καὶ περὶ τούτου τῇ ἑκάστου γνώμῃ καὶ προαιρέσει ἐπέτρεψαν οἱ ἀπόστολοι, ἵνα ἕκαστος μὴ φόβῳ, μηδὲ ἐξ ἀνάγκης τὸ ἀγαθὸν κατεργάζοιτο.*—Conf. Sozom. in eod. Lib. VII. cap. xix. pp. 734—7.]

[3 See Vol. I. p. 525, note 9; and Iren. in Euseb. Hist. Eccles. Lib. v. cap. xxiv.]

men with him that appointed the apparel judged the same to be a thing of necessity, and not a thing indifferent, to be done for order's sake, without any opinion of necessity, or of superstition in the same. And this my good lords, my lord of Somerset his grace, and my lord of Warwick his lordship, can bear me record, if my letters came into their hands, which I wrote unto their honors, that I then offered, and yet will offer the same. Let him revoke his errors, and agree and subscribe to the doctrine, and not to condemn that for sin, that God never forbade, ungodly adding unto God's word, and I shall not, for any necessity that I put in these vestments, let to lay my hands upon him and to admit him bishop, although he come as he useth to ride in a merchant's cloak, having the king's dispensation for the act, and my lord archbishop's commission orderly to do the thing.

The other thing I note is in the case which is covered with the colour of, "If," &c., wherein what is meant it is unto them plain that do know the circumstances of the matter. Surely a privy crack of coming, which I would wish to be rebated[1], and therefore I will knock it upon the pate with St Paul's sword:
1 Cor. viii. *Si quis videtur sibi aliquid scire, nondum aliquid novit ut oportet:* [" If any man think that he knoweth anything, he knoweth nothing yet as he ought to know."]

In the answer unto the second objection, "There is nothing to be done in the church, but is commanded or forbidden by the word of God, though not expressly, yet by necessary collection," &c.[2], this sentence is so far out of the way, and so erroneous, that it is intolerable; for it taketh away the most part of all due ceremonial circumstances, without the which, either after one manner or other, the very institutions of Christ cannot be observed. For how is it possible [to] receive the holy communion, but thou must either sit, stand, kneel, or lay?

[[1] See Vol. I. p. 199, note 4.]

[[2] The next eleven lines, "this sentence is......commanded in scripture," are embodied by Abp Whitgift in his "Defence of the Answer to the Admonition, against the Reply of Thomas Cartwright," Works, Vol. I. p. 62, Park. Soc.: where in reference to the words, "clothed or naked," Abp Whitgift observes, p. 64, "If this example so trouble you, I will tell you plainly from whom I had it, even from that famous martyr and notable learned man Doctor Ridley, sometime bishop of London, who used the same example to the same purpose in his conference by writing with Master Hooper, exhibited up to the Council in the time of king Edward the Sixth, the true copy whereof I have. Surely he was no Adamite, but a man of singular judgment and learning."]

Thou must either take it at one time or another, fasting or after meat, clothed or naked, in this place or in another. Without the sum of these circumstances it is impossible to do that that the Lord biddeth thee. But none of all these circumstances are commanded in scripture. Therefore, if the said sentence were true, none of them may be done; and so it must follow, that if we believe this doctrine, then can we not execute Christ's institutions. For those circumstances are left unto us uncommanded in the scripture; and therefore, if this doctrine be true, they may not be done. The same is to be said of baptism, of the observation of times of common prayer, of common fasting, and festival days.

And here I must monish the writer of one of his rash assertions, where he saith, that the precise day of Sunday is appointed by the law of the gospel, and not by order of Christ's congregation, to be solemnized holy-day, which he cannot approve by scripture, truly understanded; and it is manifestly against St Augustine[3], St Hierom[4], and other ancient writers[5].

[[3] Dominicum ergo diem apostoli et apostolici viri ideo religiosa solemnitate habendum sanxerunt, quia in eodem Redemptor noster a mortuis resurrexit... Apparet autem hunc diem etiam in scripturis sanctis esse solemnem...Ac ideo sancti doctores ecclesiæ decreverunt omnem gloriam Judaici sabbatismi in illam transferre; ut quod ipsi in figura nos celebraremus in veritate: quia tunc erit requies nostra vera, quando resurrectio fuerit perpetrata, et remuneratio in anima et corpore simul perfecta.—Serm. CCLXXX. supposit. in August. Op. Tom. V. Append. col. 467, ed. Bened. Par. 1679—1700.]

[[4] Qui...acutius respondere conatur illud affirmat, omnes dies æquales esse, nec per Parasceven tantum Christum crucifigi, et die Dominica resurgere, sed semper sanctum resurrectionis esse diem, et semper eum carne vesci Dominica. Jejunia autem et congregationes inter dies propter eos a viris prudentibus constitutos, qui magis sæculo vacant quam Deo...nobis licet vel jejunare semper, vel semper orare, et diem Dominicam accepto Domini corpore indesinenter celebrare gaudentibus...—Hieron. Comm. in Ep. ad Gal. Lib. II. cap. iv. Op. Tom. VII. col. 457, stud. Vallars. Veron. 1734—42. See also Comm. in Isai. Lib. XVI. cap. lix. Op. Tom. IV. col. 700.]

[[5] Among the schoolmen Aquinas writes:...observantia diei dominicæ in nova lege succedit observantiæ sabbathi, non ex vi præcepti legis, sed ex constitutione ecclesiæ et consuetudine populi Christiani. Nec enim hujusmodi observatio est figuralis, sicut fuit observatio sabbathi in veteri lege. Et ideo non est ita arcta prohibitio operandi in die dominica, sicut in die sabbathi: sed quædam opera conceduntur in die dominica, quæ in die sabbathi prohibebantur, sicut decoctio ciborum et alia hujusmodi. Et etiam in quibusdam operibus prohibitis facilius, propter necessitatem, dispensatur in nova quam in veteri lege, quia figura pertinet ad protestationem veritatis, quam nec in modico præterire oportet: opera autem secundum se considerata immutari possunt pro loco et tempore.—Thom. Aquin. Summ. Theol. Partis II. pars II. Quæst. cxxii. Artic. iv. 4, p. 251, Lut. Par. 1631.]

And I pray you tell me, if this be received, who shall in the order of the church regard either commandment of the king or of his council, either parliament, prelate or any other ordinary power, whatsoever they commanded, not commanded in scripture, though else it be never so good? And the aforesaid sentence—as a thing which is the subversion of good order, wholesome discipline and obedience, and of other many godly ordinances made for the amendment of people's manners, as the case diversely doth require—and as also the very root and well-spring of much stubborn obstinacy, sedition and disobedience of the younger sort against their elders, contrary unto St Paul's doctrine—I suppose no good man that is wise will or can allow.

In the answer unto the third objection here is declared openly the whole state of the controversy: that is, he deemeth the vestments appointed to be things indifferent, which he thinketh he hath...sufficiently proved. And why? Because αὐτὸς ἔφη: as now who that hath read the scriptures and the antiquities of the church, if he will judge by knowledge, can require any more?

In the answer unto the fourth objection, sir, the cause why St Paul did use certain Jewish ceremonies, was not therefore because they had their beginning of God's word. For, as they had thereof their beginning, even so had they by the same their appointed end, which was Christ. But the cause was, to bear with their weakness, and so to win them unto Christ. So that this answer is as good as none. This fallacy the writer useth so oft, *a causa ad causam.* And also it is not true that the manners that St Paul submitted himself unto among the gentiles had their original in the word of God. And, thirdly, here methinketh that the writer hath forgotten what he said before, that the vestments were Aaronical, which if they be granted to be, then this answer maketh all against himself. And therefore I say once again, *Conveniet nulli, qui secum dissidet ipse:* [He will agree with no man, who himself differs with himself.]

In the answer unto the fifth objection, "Our men," saith the writer, "be papists, with papists, to keep them still in their papistry." &c. This saying is an heinous slander against the archbishop and all the whole company of the appointed learned men—yea, against the whole parliament that hath allowed and approved the order set forth in the Book of Common Prayer.

He complaineth of persecution. I pray you, who is to be called worthily a persecutor. He that defendeth the truth with God's word with patience and all godly sobriety, or else he that furiously impugneth the same with daily railing and backbiting of the defenders of the truth? What is this else than to play the part of him that is mentioned in Erasmus his Colloquies, that did steal and ran away with the priest's purse, and yet cried always as he ran, "Stay the thief, stay the thief!" and thus crying escaped; and yet he was the thief himself[1].

In the answer to the sixth objection the objection is unsoluted, for he never proved that he saith, he hath always showed the vestments do pass the limits that God hath appointed. For this appointing he speaketh of is not prescribed by God's word, but left to be ordered to the discretion of the governors of Christ's congregation. He saith, they were brought into the church by them that abused both God and man: and yet he doth not deny but they were before the usurpation of the pope. Then let him show the first author of them, and then men shall judge the better, whether they were such that did abuse both God and man, or no.

In the answer to the seventh objection if St Paul's saying, "all things be clean unto the clean," be meant only of things accounted unclean to the Jews, then the estimation of the Gentiles' observation remaineth yet still. For, as they had *dies fastos et nefastos*, so had they in their superstition things counted for hallowed, and some things profane. But what will not boldness bid a man say, when he hath made an argument against himself, which he cannot solute?

In the answer unto the eighth objection, this argument is moved of Luther in a place, but far otherwise answered unto of him, and after another manner. For Luther alloweth ceremonies, though they be not in scripture, so that they be not

[[1] Sacrificus deponit crumenam: denuo contemplantur. Ibi impostor averso sacrifico crumenam arripit, ac semet in pedes conjicit. Sacerdos cursu insequitur, ut erat palliatus, et sacrificum venditor. Sacrificus clamat, 'Tenete furem:' venditor clamat, 'Tenete sacrificum:' impostor clamat, 'Cohibete sacrificum furentem:' et creditum est cum viderent illum sic ornatum in publico currere. Itaque dum alter alteri in mora est, impostor effugit.—Erasm. Colloq., Convivium fabulosum, p. 421, Norimb. 1774.]

taken from the principal points themselves, and in *predicamento substantiæ*, as he speaketh, but *in predicamento accidentis;* that is to say, not things of necessity, but that they may be done or undone, as the order requireth, without any opinion of justification in the same[1]. And surely I suppose, if this writer did understand the matter of justification truly, that therefore such things as they be, which all learned men do confess to be of themselves indifferent, and wherein no man ought to put trust or confidence, he would never have made so much ado, nor have been so serious in so small a matter.

"And in case the king his majesty," saith the writer, "would take many besides the scripture," &c.

Here it may seem that my brother elect would give the king his majesty leave to take in some ceremonies besides the scriptures, so that they were not things (as he calleth them) of papistry. But . . . [let] his highness take good heed with his doings. For if his majesty so do, and the thing cannot be proved by God's word, either expressly or by necessary collection, this writer will not let to condemn it for a transgression, though else the thing be both profitable and good. And that he doth both in this treatise, and in his book of the ten commandments[2]. For in this treatise he saith in his answer unto

[[1] Servare legalia non est malum, sed servire legalibus malum est. Servit autem qui timore (ut jam sæpe dictum) minarum eadem fecit coactus, velut necessaria quibus mereatur justificari. Libere autem facta nihil obsunt. Sic prophetæ ea observaverunt, non pro justitia obtinenda, sed pro caritate Dei et proximi exercenda, ipsi ex fide justificati.—Luther. Comm. in Epist. ad Galat. cap. iv. Op. Tom. V. fol. 244, Witt. 1558, &c.]

[[2] "Such as preach man's laws, and works not commanded in the scripture, robbeth the scripture of her riches."—Bp Hooper, Decl. of ten command., in Early Writings, p. 399, Park. Soc.

Bp Hooper writes more explicitly in his "Brief and clear confession of the Christian Faith," 1550, 58th Article, "...the Christian liberty of the gospel...doth deliver our consciences from all outward beggarly ceremonies by man ordained and devised without the word of God."—Later Writings of Bp H., p. 46, Park. Soc. And in the 83rd Article, "I believe also that the forbidding of marriage for certain persons, likewise the forbidding of certain meats, the difference of days, garments, and such-like, is the devilish doctrine of Antichrist, and wholly against the Christian liberty of the gospel taught by Jesus Christ, the which delivereth us from all outward ceremonies of the law, and setteth us at liberty to use all things with giving God thanks, so that it be not done to the hurt of our neighbour. For all things are made holy by the word of God and prayer to him that knoweth and receiveth the truth. Therefore to compel the Christian to these things is but to take from them and to rob them of their Christian liberty, and by tyranny to set them under the curse of the law, from the which Christ by his death and passion

the second objection, "There is nothing to be done in the church, but it is commanded or forbidden by the word of God, either expressly or by necessary collection[3]."

BP HOOPER TO SIR WILLIAM CECIL.

[*April* 17, 1551.]

After my very hearty commendations, although I have no great matter to write unto your mastership of, yet duty and bondage requireth me to show myself mindful of your old and accustomed friendship towards me, and to thank you for the same, with hearty desire you so always continue towards me.

MS. Original, Holograph. State Paper Office.

Tytler's England, reigns Edw. VI., Mary, Vol. I. p. 364, Lond. 1839.

As for the success and going forthward of God's word, praised be his holy name, every day the number doth increase, and would so do more and more, in case there were good teachers amongst them for the furtherance and help thereof. I pray you and in God's name require you, that ye stay what ye may, that no man obtain licence to have two benefices, which is a great destruction to this country, dangerous before God, as well to the king's majesty that giveth it, as to the person that receiveth.

For the love and tender mercy of God persuade and cause some order to be taken upon the price of things, or else the ire of God will shortly punish. All things be here so dear, that the most part of people lacketh, and yet more will lack, necessary food. The body of a calf in the market at fourteen shillings, the carcase of a sheep at ten shillings, white meat so dear as a groat, is nothing to a poor man to bestow in any kind of victuals. All pastures and breeding of cattle is turned into sheep's-meat; and they be not kept to be brought to the market, but to bear wool, and profit only to their master[4].

Master Secretary, for the passion of Christ take the fear of God and a bold stomach to speak herein for a redress, and that the goods of every shire be not thus wrested and taken

hath delivered them: and it is one true mark and note to know Antichrist by."—Id. ibid. pp. 55, 6.]

[3 Here the MS. ends, being imperfect, and apparently wanting the last leaf.]

[4 Compare Works of Bp Latimer, Vol. I. pp. 99, 527, Park. Soc.]

into few men's hands. If it continue, the wealth and strength of the realm must needs perish. What availeth great riches in a realm, and neither the head nor the greatest part of the members be the better for it, you best know[1]. *Apud Justinianum monopolia non essent [licita], quoniam non ad commodum reipublicæ, sed ad labem detrimentumque pertineant, inquit*[2]: [In Justinian monopolies would not be allowed, because they pertain, he affirms, not to the advantage but to the overthrow and destruction of the state.] Such as have more than enough buyeth when things be good cheap, to sell afterward dear: God amend it.

It is my bounden duty, and all other true men's, to persuade and teach obedience unto the people: and, thanks be unto the Lord, I can perceive none other here but love and reverence among the people to the king's majesty, and to the laws. But, Master Secretary, it is the magistrates' faults: and their own doings, that shall most commend them, and win love of the people. Ye know what a perilous and extreme, yea, in manner unruly evil hunger is. The prices of things be here as I tell ye: the number of people be great: their little cottages and poor livings decay daily. Except God by sickness take them out of the world, they must needs lack. God's mercy give you and the rest of my lords wisdom and good hearts to redress it: wherein I pray God ye may see the occasion of the evil, and so destroy it.

May it please you to be so good as to desire a licence of the king's majesty for me to eat flesh upon the fish-days. Doubtless my stomach is not as it hath been. In case it were, I could better eat fish than flesh: but I think it past for this life. There is also here a wise and sober man, one of the aldermen of the town, a good and necessary subject for this little commonwealth here, called John Samford, that is a weak and sickly man, desired me to be also a suitor to you for him in this case. And doubtless we will so use the king's authority, as none, I trust, shall take occasion for liberty and contempt of laws by us.

Thus praying you to commend me to Mistress Cecil, and

[[1] A line in the original in this place has perished, the ink having faded away.]

[[2] Vide Corp. Jur. Civil. Cod. Lib. IV. Tit. lix. Tom. II. pp. 139, 40, Amst 1663.]

to good Master Cecil your father, my singular good friends, I commend ye with all my heart and whole spirit to God: who keep you always in his fear, and give you wisdom and strength to do all things in your high business, troublous and perilous, to his glory. Amen.

17th April, 1551.

Your bounden for ever to his little power,

JOHN HOPER, GLOUCESTR. EPISC.

Sir, I dare be so bold of your gentleness, as to commend me to all my very friends that be of the robes, who have used towards me always, from my first coming to the court, a singular and painful friendship in all my business I have had to do.

To the right honorable Master William Cecil, one of the chief secretaries to the king's majesty.

BP HOOPER TO SIR WILLIAM CECIL[3].

[GLOUCESTER, *May* 25, 1551.]

RIGHT worshipful my singular friend, my duty remembered, I have here sent you a copy of such articles as be subscribed by a froward man, one Thomas Penn[4] (that hath defended with unquietness and danger of many in these parts, openly in his church, the body of Christ concerning his humanity to be everywhere), to this end, that it may please you to help, that such benefices as happen to fall in this country may be assigned to meet and convenient men: and then I doubt not but both God shall have his honour, and the king's majesty due obedi-

MS. Original, Holograph. State Paper Office.

[[3] This letter is now for the first time printed.]

[[4] The articles of Thomas Penn do not accompany this letter: but in place of them six articles occur, subscribed by John Gloucestr., John Rastell, John Samford, John Parkhurst, Guy Stow, Henry Willis, Nicolas Clotworthy, John Jewel, John Williams, Roger Tyler, without title, date, or endorsement: the signatures in that transcript are not autographs. The articles occupy three pages of foolscap folio, somewhat closely written, and refer to the being of God, the holy Trinity, the incarnation and two natures of Christ, and other topics. Probably, from their contents and the signature of Rastell, they may have been opposed to the opinions of Penn.]

ence; as it shall be better known unto your worship if it may please you to talk with this wise and learned bearer, Master Rastell, alderman of this town, whom you will not mislike, neither in the knowledge of civil matters nor in causes of religion. In the which the Lord grant we may godly continue to the end.

Gloucester, 25 [May,][1] 1551.

Your worship's with my poor prayers,

JOHN HOPER, GLOUCESTER EPISC.

To the right worshipful my very singular friend, Master William Cecil, one of the king's majesty's chief secretaries.

BP RIDLEY TO MASTER D.[2]

EMMANUEL.

MS. 2. 2. 15. No. 63. Emman. Coll. Cambridge.

THE almighty God, with his most gracious Spirit, illumine your heart, and teach you to walk in his ways; so that you may do at all times those things which may be acceptable and pleasant to his divine majesty, and at the end attain to that felicity and joy which he hath prepared for all them that from the bottom of their hearts embrace his gospel and love his Son Christ Jesus, who gave himself to be a ransom for the sins of all mankind, to cleanse and purify all such which unfeignedly believe in Christ.

The cause of my writing unto you at this present is such that I think neither you nor any that sincerely love God will be offended with it: for in this my writing I seek not mine own commodity but rather yours and the comfort of those which be afflicted for Christ's sake. And this you shall perceive by that I have opened the matter unto you, the which is this.

[[1] The date, "May," not being in Hooper's autograph, is supplied from a memorandum endorsed upon it in another hand.]

[[2] This letter is now printed for the first time.

It is assigned to Ridley upon internal evidence. Compare the style of Ridley's letter to Cecil, Works, Suppl. p. 535, Park. Soc. The original has not any heading, and is written in the autograph of Bernhere, by whom various transcripts from Ridley and Bradford, among the Emmanuel MSS., were executed.]

It is not unknown unto you, good Master D.[3], how the people of God is most grievously and tyrannically oppressed, and by the cruelty of the wicked papists cast into prisons everywhere, especially in and about London, where there be a great number at this present in hold, which have nothing at all to succour themselves withal, and to provide things necessary for the sustentation of this life. The which thing, as it is much to be lamented of all them that love God and his word, so is it also their duties to help and comfort such with their goods and substance, so far as they be able: for undoubtedly whosoever neglecteth or despiseth them that are in prison for the gospel's sake despiseth Christ himself as much as in him lieth, utterly contemneth the most precious "gospel which is the power of God to salvation of all them that believe" the same. For if "he that hath the substance of this world, and seeth his brother lack, and yet will not show pity upon him, is without the love of God," as St James saith, how much more then are they without the fear and love of God, which will not bestow some part of their goods upon Christ himself? which now at the present lieth in the foul and stinking prisons, destitute of all worldly comfort and help, full of misery and sorrow: for we may not consider them that be in prison now simply, but we must consider with ourselves the cause wherefor they be in prison.

The cause of their imprisonment is, because they cannot abide the glory of God to be blasphemed, his word to be falsified and corrupt with the poison of man's doctrine, the dignity, honour and majesty of Christ to be diminished or obscured. The love of God is so grafted in their hearts, that they be content rather to lose all they have in this world, yea, their own lives, rather than to see God's name blasphemed. What man or woman, what Christian heart, considering with himself this thing, and beareth a love towards God, will not be content to minister unto such things necessary for the sustentation of this bodily and sorrowful life? Truly they that have things received of God, and will not be content to spend some part in his cause, be not worthy to be named Christians, yea, they be worse than the very Turks and heathen: for there was never

[[3] The name for which this initial stands has in the original been crossed out and rendered illegible. The initial letter is clearly given near the end of this epistle.]

no kind of people under the sun but they had ever a singular care to their religions, which they took for God. And shall we Christians, which know the true word of God, the right way to everlasting life, store more the pelf of the world than the religion of Jesus Christ, his precious gospel, and suffer them that be in prison for it to be famished [and][1] to perish for [lack][1] of necessaries?—God forbid that we should do so: for then the very Jews, Turks and infidels, should give sentence against us at the dreadful day of judgment.

Therefore, good Master D., I require you in God's behalf to consider the great need the prisoners of God are in the prisons at London, and make some ingatherings amongst your neighbours for the relief of them. The which if you do you shall please God wholly, and partly discharge your conscience to the gospel of Jesus Christ.

MARTYR AD BULLINGERUM.

[Oxonii, 14 *Junii*, 1552.]

Ex Archiv. Eccles. Zuric. Repos. VI., Vol. VIII., pp. 2892 et 2893.

S. V. Scio quidem, vir clarissime, atque mihi pluribus nominibus observande, Johannem, cum ad vos pervenerit, plane ac fuse nuntiaturum esse, quid hic apud nos agatur. Quia tamen sunt nonnulla, quæ minus habet cognita, communibus et vulgaribus posthabitis, ea solummodo scribam. Cum Froschoverus junior hac hyeme hinc discederet, ad te scripsi, quidnam Londini eo tempore agerem: quid postea successerit sic habeto.

Negotium illud quod bonis omnibus optatum erat, neque parum cordi regiæ majestati, non potuit ad umbilicum perduci. Quare manent adhuc res magna ex parte ut antea erant, nisi quod Liber seu Ratio Rituum Ecclesiasticorum atque Administrationis Sacramentorum est emendatus, nam inde omnia sublata sunt quæ superstitionem fovere poterant. Cur autem cætera, quæ instituebantur, non obtinuerint, res præsertim sacramentaria obstitit, non sane quoad transubstantiationem, seu realem præsentiam (ut ita loquar), vel in pane vel in vino, cum, Deo gratia, jam de his, quoad eos qui profitentur evan-

[1 MS. torn.]

gelium, non videtur esse controversia: sed an gratia conferatur per sacramenta hæsitatum est a multis. Et fuerunt nonnulli qui omnino id affirmarunt, et in hanc partem voluissent decerni. Quod cum alii non obscure viderent, quantum secum ea sententia importaret superstitionum, principio quidem conati sunt omnibus modis ostendere, nihilo plus concedendum esse sacramentis quam verbo Dei externo, nam utroque verbi genere significatur et ostenditur salus nobis parta per Christum, quam percipiunt quotquot his verbis et signis credunt, non quidem vi verborum aut sacramentorum, sed efficacia fidei. Quin addebatur, fieri non posse, ut sacramenta digne perciperentur, nisi sumentes prius habeant quod per illa significatur; nam absque fide semper usurpantur indigne: at, si fide sint præditi qui ad sacramenta accedunt, jam per fidem apprehenderunt gratiam quæ nobis in sacramentis prædicatur, quorum deinde sumptio et usus perceptæ jam promissionis est σφραγὶς et obsignatio. Utque valent externa Dei verba ad fidem sæpe in nobis torpentem et quodammodo consopitam suscitandam et excitandam, hoc quoque idem sacramenta vi Spiritus Sancti facere possunt, neque parum est utilis eorum usus ad nostras mentes alioquin imbecillas de promissionibus et gratia Dei confirmandas.

In pueris vero, dum baptizantur, quia per ætatem habere non possunt assensum promissionibus divinis quæ fides est, hoc in eis efficit sacramentum, ut condonatio labis originis, reconciliatio cum Deo, et Spiritus Sancti gratia, qua per Christum donati sunt, in eis obsignetur, utque pertinentes jam ad ecclesiam visibiliter quoque illi inserantur. Quamvis et his qui tinguntur, sive parvulis, sive adultis, multum boni atque commodi accedere non sit negandum ex invocatione Patris, Filii atque Spiritus Sancti quæ fit super eos: nunquam enim Deus non audit fideles ecclesiæ suæ preces.

Hæc de sacramentis constitui atque decerni voluissemus, ut purus atque simplex illorum usus tandem restitueretur. Sed reclamatum est; et volunt multi, atque hi alias non indocti neque mali, per sacramenta ut aiunt conferri gratiam. Neque volunt concedere parvulos justificatos aut regeneratos ante baptismum. Sed, cum ad rationes illorum venitur, nullæ sunt quæ non solutæ sint et quidem facillime. Ex eo tamen haud parva nobis movetur invidia, quod ab Augustino prorsus dissentiamus. Et si authoritate publica fuisset probata nostra sententia, tunc inquiunt manifestissime damnatus esset Augustinus. Quid plura? Non possunt homines ab operum merito avelli; et, quod magis dolendum est, id fateri nolunt; suntque infinita semper impedimenta, eaque mutuo sibi succedunt, ut remorentur indies divini cultus restitutionem. Tantæ molis est puram veritatem in ecclesiam revocare. At propterea non est desperandum: immo non parum confidimus, alias fieri posse quod nunc minus feliciter successit.

Habes de negotiis ecclesiæ nostræ, quæ te non latere volui. Cetera, uti dixi, Johannes referet, quem tibi commendo plurimum: est enim modestus et pius, apud nos bene se gessit, neque parum profecit in bonis litteris. Rediit Londinum Byrchmannus, neque cum eo de libris adhuc transegi. Spero me post autumnum, si non fuero impeditus, ad vos missurum librum meum de cælibatu et votis monasticis imprimendum, quo calumniis respondeo Smythei. Doleo quod abs te diu litteras non acceperim: sed, cum res turbulentæ sunt per Germaniam, ad me [non] perferri non miror. At cum licuerit, non intermittas, oro, aliquid scribere.

Vale, atque pro regno Christi hic ampliando et propagando enixe Deum immortalem preceris, et omnibus tuis symmistis nomine meo salutem dicas, præcipue Gualtero, Bibliandro, et ante omnes D. Pellicano.

14 Junii, 1552. Oxonii.

Tuus in Christo,

PETRUS MARTYR.

Reverendo atque clarissimo viro, D. Heynrico Bullingero ecclesiæ Tigurinæ ministro fidelissimo, Tiguri.

[*Translation.*]

MARTYR TO BULLINGER[1].

[OXFORD, *June* 14, 1552.]

HEALTH to you. I know, most illustrious sir, and to me on many accounts worthy of regard, that John[2], when he shall have reached you, will clearly and fully inform you what is here taking place among us. Yet, since there are some things with which he is not well acquainted, I will postpone common and every-day topics, and write of these things alone. When Froschover junior departed hence this winter, I wrote to you what I was doing at that time at London: what happened afterward receive as follows.

That matter which was desired by all good men, and which the king's majesty had not a little at heart, could not be concluded. Wherefore as yet things remain to a great extent as they were before, except that the Book or Order of Ecclesiastical Rites and the Administration of the Sacraments has been reformed, for all things have been removed from it which could nourish superstition. But the chief reason, that prevented the other things which were purposed from being effected, was the matter of the sacraments: not truly as far as regards transubstantiation, or the real presence (so to speak), either in the bread or in the wine; since, thanks be to God, concerning these things there seems to be now no controversy as it regards those who profess the gospel: but, whether grace is conferred by virtue of the sacraments, is a point about which many have hesitated. And there have been some who have altogether affirmed that doctrine, and were desirous that a decision should be given to that effect. Concerning which,

[1 This letter, from the time at which it was written, is of historical interest. It was penned by Martyr (who was at the time regius professor of divinity at Oxford), between the completion of the second Book of Common Prayer of Edward VI., and the setting forth of the XLII. Articles, which last were published, May, 1553. It properly belongs to the series of "Original Letters," among Peter Martyr's letters, after letter CCXXXVI., Vol. II. p. 505, Park. Soc.: but, at the date of that publication, it had been overlooked. It was published for the first time, with Remarks, by the Rev. William Goode, London, 1850.]

[2 Possibly John ab Ulmis, who about this time was in England.]

because others clearly saw how many superstitions that sentence would bring with it, they endeavoured at first in all ways to show, that nothing more is to be granted to the sacraments than to the external word of God: for by both these kinds of word is signified and shown the salvation obtained for us through Christ, of which as many are made partakers as believe these words and signs, not indeed by the power of the words or sacraments, but by the efficacy of faith. Moreover it was added, that it was impossible that the sacraments should be worthily received, unless the recipients have beforehand that which is signified by them; for without faith they are always taken unworthily: but, if they who come to the sacraments are endued with faith, they have already through faith laid hold upon the grace which is proclaimed to us in the sacraments, the after reception and use of which is the seal and obsignation of the promise already received[1]. And, as the external words of God avail to the awakening and arousing faith, often torpid, and in a manner laid asleep in us, this same thing also the sacraments can effect by the power of the Holy Spirit; and their use is not of little benefit to confirm our minds, otherwise weak, concerning the promises and grace of God[2].

But in respect of children, while they are baptized, since on account of their age they cannot have that assent to the divine promises which is faith, in them the sacrament effects this, that pardon of original sin, reconciliation with God, and the grace of the Holy Spirit, bestowed on them through Christ, is sealed in them, and that those belonging already to the church are also visibly ingrafted into it[3]. Although even to

[[1] "In such only as worthily receive the same [the sacraments], they have a wholesome effect or operation."—Article XXV., Ch. of England. See also Article XXVI. of Edward VI., in Liturgies of Edw. VI. pp. 533, 78, Park. Soc.]

[[2] "Sacraments ordained of Christ be not only badges or tokens of Christian men's profession, but rather they be certain sure witnesses and effectual signs of grace and God's good-will towards us; by the which he doth work invisibly in us, and doth not only quicken, but also strengthen and confirm our faith in him."—The same. Compare also as in last note.]

[[3] "Baptism is not only a sign of profession, and mark of difference, whereby Christian men are discerned from others that be not christened; but is also a sign of regeneration or new birth, whereby as by an instrument they that receive baptism rightly are grafted into the church, the promises of forgiveness of sin and of our adoption to be the sons of God by the Holy Ghost are visibly signed and sealed, faith is confirmed and grace increased by virtue of prayer unto God. The

those that are baptized, whether little children or adults, it is not to be denied that much advantage and profit come to them from the invocation of the Father, the Son, and the Holy Spirit, which takes place over them: for God never fails to hear the faithful prayers of his church.

We should have wished that these things had been determined and decreed concerning the sacraments, in order that their pure and simple use might at length be restored. But it was exclaimed against: and many will have it, and those otherwise not unlearned nor evil, that grace is conferred, as they say, by the sacraments. Nor are they willing to grant that little children are justified or regenerated before baptism. But, when we come to their reasons, there are none which have not been answered, and that indeed most easily. Nevertheless, no little displeasure is stirred up against us on this account, that we altogether dissent from Augustine. And, if our doctrine had been approved by public authority, then, say they, Augustine would most manifestly have been condemned. Why should I say more? Men cannot be torn away from the merit of works: and, what is more to be lamented, they are unwilling to confess it: and there are always endless impediments, and they mutually succeed one another, so as to retard day after day the restoration of divine worship. A work of so great labor is it to bring back into the church pure truth. But we must not on that account despair: nay, we are not a little confident, that that may be done at another time, which now has not so happily prospered.

You have concerning the affairs of our church what I wished you not to be ignorant of. The rest, as I have said, John will report, whom I commend much to you: for he is modest and pious, has conducted himself well among us, and has made no slight advance in polite literature. Byrchman[4] has returned to London, and I have not yet arranged with him concerning the books. I hope to send you after the autumn, if I shall not have been hindered, my book on celibacy and monastic vows to be printed, in which I reply to the calumnies

baptism of young children is in any wise to be retained in the church, as most agreeable with the institution of Christ."—Article XXVII., Ch. of England. See also Article XXVIII. of Edward VI., ibid.]

[4 See p. xxi, note 4, above.]

of Smyth. I lament not to have received letters from you for a long time: but, as long as affairs are turbulent throughout Germany, I do not wonder that they do not reach me. But, when you have the opportunity, do not, I intreat you, omit to write something.

Farewell, and earnestly intreat the immortal God for the enlargement and extension here of the kingdom of Christ; and salute in my name all your fellow-laborers, especially Gualter, Bibliander, and, above all, Master Pellican.

14 June, 1552. Oxford.

Yours in Christ,

PETER MARTYR.

To that reverend and most illustrious person, Master Henry Bullinger, most faithful minister of the church of Zurich, Zurich.

CARELESS TO BP LATIMER[1].

MS. 1. 2. 8. No. 27. Transcript. Emman. Coll. Cambridge.

O my dear father, Master L[atimer], that I could do anything whereby I might effectuously utter my poor heart towards you! But for want of power my prayer unto God for you shall supply some little part of my duty. God increase faith in me, that the same may be effectual.

And, dear father, I beseech you to remember me when you talk with your good God, that he may give me the strength of his Spirit, that I manfully yielding my life for his truth may do you some honesty, who have put me into his service, to be a soldier in his camp: whereas, if I run away like a coward, I shall shame you and all other that have holpen me into his service; and yet at length I shall be hanged in hell like a traitor to God and man: from the which God defend me and all his children. Amen.

O that you knew how good your faithful servant Austin is to me for your sake. The Lord keep and preserve you now and ever. Amen.

Yours,

JOHN CARELESS.

[[1] This letter is now printed for the first time.]

BP RIDLEY ON THE VESTMENT CONTROVERSY.

It is a pleasure to the editor to state that the important MS. of bishop Ridley's Reply to bishop Hooper on the vestment controversy has, since the date of the statement, p. 373, above, been found; and that, through the kind courtesy of its possessor, Sir Thomas Phillipps, Bart., of Middle Hill, Worcestershire, he has been enabled carefully to collate the transcript with the original, and in consequence to supply the following:

P. 375, l. 3, *read* nor yet
l. 5, *read* is com[manded]in
377, l. 2, *read* conscience: and so
l. 18, *read* proved by God's
l. 29, 30, *read* disobedient, a contemner
378, l. 10, *read* how agreeth this
last l. but 6, *read* and also ecclesiastical
last l. but 4, *read* both to meddle and maintain
379, l. 4, *read* have ever heretofore
last l. but 7, *read* of too great
380, last l. but 13, *read* which is the
383, l. 4, *read* white cude[3], all
and prefix to note [[3] "Cude:" the linen cloth, or chrysom, formerly used in the baptism of infants.—Jamieson, Scotch Etymol. Dict.; Bailey, Dict.: and see Nares' Gloss., and Todd's Johnson's Dict., each, v. chrysom.
384, l. 17, *read* cannot to be
last l. but 3, *read* not yet complished[2], or
and add footnote, [[2] See Todd's Johnson's Dict. The MS. has "comed."]
385, l. 3, *read* ceremonies shall be
l. 4, *read* or of decent
l. 24, 25, *read* so light an answer: for to condemn the
l. 29, *read* Spirit in an unity and bond
386, l. 6, 7, *read* order and authority, we will plead in possession; and, blow ye at the coal, if
l. 17, *read* a minister
l. 18, *read* do account [it] no
l. 21, *read* dwell all within
l. 26, *read* princely apparel, or one apparel, or that
last l. but 5, *read* before him. And
387, l. 5, *read* who could look
l. 12, *read* why thus he would not reason
l. 15, *read* Prayer from all such things is
388, l. 15, *read* shall never men
l. 16, *read* take in hand to
l. 21, 22, *read* things being indifferent,
l. 25, read *per ignotius*, which
389, l. 1, *read* not to use
last l. but 3, *read* yea, and necessary in the church of Christ, and so necessary that in case
390, l. 13, *read* king's majesty's dispensation
391, l. 1, *read* or at another
l. 5, *read* scripture. Wherefore, if

P. 392, l. 2, *read* either the commandment
l. 4, *read* they command, not commanded
l. 10, *read* much stubbornness and obstinacy
392, l. 12, *read* St Peter's doctrine
l. 17, *read* hath sufficiently
l. 28, read *a non causa*
l. 29, *read* that Paul
394, l. 7, *read* that then for such
l. 16, *read* But [let] his
395, l. 3. *read* collection." &c.

The MS. is apparently a contemporary transcript. It has at the end the words in a different though early writing, "Contentio inter Hoperum et Ridleium." It was, at the beginning of the last century, in the possession of the Rev. George Harbin. Its number in the very extensive collection of Sir Thomas Phillipps is 4,901.

The MS. referred to in Vol. I. p. 193, note 1, which had once belonged to Foxe, and from which Strype printed the meditations "on the providence and presence of God," pp. 191—3, is now in the British Museum, Lansdown, no. 389. (See Vol. I. p. 399, Vol. II. p. 297.) Those meditations are on reverse of fol. 289—reverse of fol. 290. There is an early transcript of the treatise "Against the fear of death" (see Vol. I. p. 331, editorial preface) in that MS. fol. 206, seven leaves.

Letter XCV. pp. 238—42 of this volume, Careless to Bradford, exists also in a MS., which presents several variations, in the British Museum, Addit. MSS. no. 19,400, the collection which had formerly belonged to Dawson Turner, Esq.—A letter hitherto unpublished, addressed by Mistress Joyce Hales (see p. 108 above) to Careless, exists in that collection. Another unpublished letter, addressed by that lady to Mistress Hall (see pp. 247, 8, note 1, above), is to be found among the reformation MSS. in Emmanuel College Cambridge, Vol. 1. 2. 8. no. 74.

P. xlv, in the List of editions, between entries III. and IV. *insert:*

(III.) Exhortation of the carrying of Christ's cross, with confutation of papistical doctrine, n. d. See black-letter title, and editorial preface, pp. 267, 8. Copy, G. Offor, Esq., exceedingly scarce.

The first four chapters and part of the fourteenth were reprinted by bishop Coverdale, with Bradford's signature, in the "Letters of the Martyrs," 1564, pp. 427—46.

P. viii, transfer asterisk from last line but 6 to last line but 1.

ix, lines 15, 16, *instead of* two of Hooper *read* one of Hooper.

xlvi, entry XI., line 4, *instead of* and sixty-five *read* one was reprinted from the "Exhortation to the carrying of Christ's cross," see entry (III.), and sixty-four.

INDEX.

B.

C.

[1] The names of those councils which are denominated general are printed in Italic capitals.

D.

G.

H.

I.

J.

K.

L.

M.

N.

O.

P.

Q.

R.

T.

U.

V.

THE PRINCIPAL TEXTS ILLUSTRATED.

For others see the Index under their subjects or leading words.

Vol. II. p. 161, in date of letter, *instead of* 1555, read 1554.
p. 334, l. 16, *instead of* ministers, *read* ministry.
p. 415, l. 9, *insert* formerly earl of Warwick, ii. 390, *and cancel* lines 13, 14.